Graphics
Programming
Solutions

Graphics
Programming
Solutions

Julio Sanchez
Northern Montana College

Maria P. Canton
Skipanon Software Co.

McGraw-Hill, Inc.

New York   San Francisco Washington, D.C. Auckland   Bogotá
Caracas   Lisbon   London   Madrid   Mexico City   Milan
Montreal   New Delhi   San Juan   Singapore
Sydney   Tokyo   Toronto

Library of Congress Cataloging-in-Publication Data

Sanchez, Julio, date.
    Graphics programming solutions / Julio Sanchez, Maria P. Canton.
        p.   cm. — (J. Ranade workstation series)
    Includes index.
    ISBN 0-07-911464-4 (hc) — ISBN 0-07-911465-2 (sc)
    1. IBM Personal Computer—Programming   2. Computer graphics.
I. Canton, Maria P.   II. Title.   III. Series.
QA76.8.I2594S237   1993
006.6´765—dc20

92-47134
CIP

1 2 3 4 5 6 7 8 9 0   DOC/DOC   9 9 8 7 6 5 4 3

P/N 054616-9
PART OF
ISBN 0-07-911465-2 (SC)

*The sponsoring editor for this book was Jerry Papke, the editing super-
visor was David E. Fogarty, and the production supervisor was Donald
Schmidt.*

Printed and bound by R. R. Donnelley & Sons Company.

Contents

Preface

This book is intended as a general-purpose programmer's reference for IBM microcomputer graphics. It also serves as a *cookbook* since the text includes numerous programming examples as well as libraries on disk with over 100 graphics procedures. The book includes examples on using the furnished software from Assembly Language, C, Quickbasic, and Turbo Pascal. The topics and devices discussed in the text include VGA, XGA, 8514/A, and SuperVGA video systems, bit-mapped graphics, animation, as well as mouse, pen plotter, and laser printer programming.

To obtain maximum benefit, the reader should have programming skills in C, Basic, Pascal, or 80x86 Assembler languages. In any case, a working knowledge of 80x86 Assembly Language, sufficient to follow the logic of the code samples, will greatly enhance the reader's comprehension of the material presented.

A thorough discussion of graphics methods, devices, systems, and programming, even when limited to IBM microcomputers, would be an enterprise of encyclopedic proportions. In order to reduce this project to a manageable size, the authors have made decisions about the topics discussed and about the manner and extent to which these topics are treated. Our first decision was to minimize the repetition of material in the book and the furnished diskette. Usually the main purpose of diskettes or microdisks that accompany computer books is to save the reader the effort of typing the listed programs and exercises. In the present book we have used the enclosed microdisk to expand the material covered in the text. Specifically, the source and executable files for the graphics programming libraries are contained on the furnished microdisk. Only those points in these libraries which are useful in illustrating programming techniques are repeated in the text.

A reader unaware of this unusual design could easily under-estimate the total material available on a particular topic. For example, the book devotes three chapters to VGA systems, however, if you were to print all the disk source files related to VGA topics, the sum of material on VGA programming would be approximately equivalent to six book chapters. Similar proportions between the material supplied on the text and the disk apply to most other topics.

In selecting the material for this book we have tried to comply with the following common-sense guidelines:

1. We have avoided the fields of graphics programming that constitute a specialty or that are often associated with other spheres of computer science. In this manner, fractal graphics (generally judged to be a part of computer mathematics) and pattern recognition problems (often considered a topic in artificial intelligence) are not discussed.

2. The book does not discuss programming in high-level graphics environments such as Windows, or Operating System/2. Graphics programming in the environment of an operating system interface is a distinct subject which would, by itself, require one or more volumes.

3. We have also avoided specialty topics and those that would be of interest but to a small segment of the programming establishment. Therefore, we have not considered programming using the Postscript language, GKS, or PHIGS. This decision was forced by subject-matter economics and does not imply a judgment on the importance or usefulness of these standards.

4. For similar reasons we have not discussed the programming of devices that are no longer manufactured or that have been largely replaced in the marketplace. Therefore, the book does not discuss programming the Color Graphics Adapter, the Enhanced Graphics Adapter, the Hercules Graphics Cards, the IBM Professional Graphics System, and the IBM PCjr, among others.

In selecting the standards and devices to be considered in the book we have preferred those that combine popular acceptance and high graphics quality. For example, dot matrix printers are quite common and popular in microcomputers but the quality of their graphics output is usually not very high. On the other extreme, imagesetters and film recorders undoubtedly produce high quality graphics output, but their price tags and applicability places them out of practical range for most microcomputer users. Regarding other graphics devices, the decision has not been as simple. For example, color laser printers and scanners were excluded from the book only after considerable hesitation. Our final decision not to include these devices was based on the belief these technologies are still in the development stage, and that no pertinent standards or models has been generally accepted by the industry. Much of the material used in this book was not published at the time of the writing. We would like to thank the individuals and companies that provided us with information and artwork for this project. Very particularly, we thank James Wilkinson of IBM, who furnished very useful information on the XGA programming. Daryll Lively, of the IBM regional office in Helena, Montana, was also very kind and helpful every time we called on him. Other individuals and companies to which we are grateful for support are Carol Parcells of Hewlett-Packard Company, Laura of Aldus Corporation, Deborah B. Caldwell of Logitech, Jenifer Cohan of Adobe Systems Inc., Video Electronics Standards Association (VESA), Headland Technology Inc., and Robert Pressman of Unisys Corporation. The color artwork for the book was produced by McLain Images of San Jose, California. We thank them for the extra effort and for their patience.

The authors would also like to thank the friends, students, and associates who provided advice, support, and assistance. Jay Ranade, the series editor, was very helpful at every stage of this book. At McGraw-Hill, Gerald T. Papke, Gerry Fahey, David Fogarty, Rachel Hirschfield, and Eileen Kramer were always available when we needed help. Wes Tucker, Assistant Vice-President for Academic Affairs in Great Falls, and Kevin Carlson have made us feel their enthusiasm and support. Our thanks also go to Virgil Hawkinson, Roger Stone, and Sharon Lowman, also from Northern, for moral support and technical help. Several Northern Montana College students assisted in developing and testing the book's software; Frank Peirce, Brian Court, and Terry Coons deserve special thanks.

Great Falls, Montana   Julio Sanchez
                                                                                          Maria P. Canton

Abbreviations and Conventions

µs	microsecond	APA	all-points addressable
CDA	Color Display Adapter	CGA	Color Graphics Adapter
DOS	Disk Operating System	EGA	Enhanced Graphics Adapter
EIA	Electronic Industries Associationin	I/O	input/output
K	kilobyte	kHz	kilohertz
LSB	least significant bit	Mbytes	megabytes
MCGA	Multicolor Graphics Array	MDA	Monochrome Display Adapter
MHz	megahertz	MSB	most significant bit
NDP	Numeric Data Processor	NMI	nonmaskable interrupt
NPX	Numeric Processor Extension	ns	nanosecond
PCjr	PC Junior	PGS	Professional Graphics System
POST	Power-On Self-Test	PS/2	Personal System/2
RAM	random-access memory	ROM	read-only memory
s	second	TSR	terminate-and-stay resident
VGA	Video Graphics Array	W	watt
XGA	Extended Graphics Array		

Typographical symbols in tables and figures:

->   Pointer, as in ES:BX -> video buffer

Number Systems:

Hexadecimal numbers are postfixed with the uppercase letter H, for example, 7E23H. Binary numbers are postfixed with the uppercase letter B, for example, 00011001B. Numbers written without the H or B postifix are in decimal notation.

Abbreviations and Conventions

Several trademarks appear in this book. The companies listed here are the owners of the trademarks following thier names: Adobe Systems Incroporated (Postscript); Agfa Corporation (Font Access and Interchange Format, FAIS); Aldus Corportation (Pagemaker, TIFF); Autodesk Incorporated (AutoCAD); Borland International, Inc. (Turbo Pascal); Compuserve Incorporated (Compuserve, GIF); Corel Systems Corporation (CorelDraw); Hewlett-Packard Corporation (Hewlett-Packard, LaserJet, ColorPro, PCL, HP-GL); Intel Corporation (Intel); International Business Machines Corporation (IBM, Personal Computer, PC, PS/2, CGA, MDA, EGA, XGA, AT, PGC, PCjr, VGA, Video Gate Array, MCGA, Display Adapter 8514/A, 8515, IBM Systems Journal); Microsoft Corporation (Microsoft, Windows, MS-DOS, QuickBASIC, LIM, Microsoft Press, MASM, QuickC, Microsoft Pascal); Unisys Corporation (LZW, Welch Patent); Video Electronics Standards Association (VESA); Xerox Corporation (Ventura Publisher).

1

Introduction to Microcomputer Graphics

Chapter Summary

This chapter discusses the possibilities and limitations of computer graphics technology, microcomputer graphics in general, and the graphics standards and devices used in IBM microcomputers. Chapter 1 concludes with alphanumeric graphics programming and explains the use of the routines in the ALFAGRAF libraries contained in the furnished microdisk.

1.0 The Computer Graphics Predicament

The term computer graphics refers to the input, manipulation, analysis, and output of the pictorial representation of objects by means of digital devices. In addition to interactive graphics, the term includes digital image processing, pattern recognition, simulation, and animation. Scores of devices have been created to perform these functions, including several types of video display terminals, keyboards, lightpens, mice, digitizers, scanners, plotters, laser printers, imagesetters, and film recorders. Graphics fields have evolved into independent disciplines and even migrated to other spheres of computer science. For example, pattern recognition, originally a graphics issue, is today more closely associated with artificial intelligence. At the same time, the development of graphics software suggested the creation of device independent standards and programming languages, such as the Graphical Kernel System (GKS), Postscript, and PHIGS.

Nonartistic graphic images are usually judged by their level of realism. A specific computer graphics product is often compared to a known standard. For example, we refer to the quality of a high-class computer video display terminal by saying that it is of photographic grade or to a computer animated image by stating that the movements are as smooth as in a motion picture. But the digital storage, generation, and animation of lifelike images consumes considerable computer resources.

For example, assume a realistic image that takes up a 1-inch square surface. If this image is displayed at a resolution of 1200 dots per inch, it would have a total of 1,440,000 dots (1200 x 1200 = 1,440,000). In order to encode this image into three colors, each one represented in 256 shades, the color map would require 24 bits (3 bytes) per dot. Therefore, the total storage requirements in computer memory for a 1-inch, three-color image, at 1200 dots resolution, is 4,320,000 bytes. To store a 4-by-5 color snapshot (20 square inches of image surface) we will need more disk space than is available in an 80Mb hard drive.

Furthermore, displaying an image encoded in more than 80 million bytes demands considerable processing power. For example, to display the 4-by-5 snapshot mentioned above, the software would have to change the state of each of the 28.8 million screen dots that compose the image. If we optimistically assume that each dot can be addressed and modified by means of four machine instructions, a computer processing unit running at 10 million instructions per second would take approximately 12 seconds to display the 4-by-5 picture. This display speed excludes the possibility of any form of realistic animation, and could even prove unsatisfactory for many unanimated graphics applications.

It can be argued that the above calculations represent a worse-case scenario for computer graphics; in fact, many schemes and shortcuts have been devised to make the graphics task much more feasible. For example, graphics images can be encoded using lower resolutions than 1200 dots per inch and still produce satisfactory visual results. Also, image data can be compressed in order to reduce storage requirements, color maps scaled to less than 256 shades, and data stored in devices more efficient than a hard disk drive. In addition, some geometrical forms can be described mathematically (using vector graphics) further reducing the storage requirements, and screen animation can often be limited to portions of the image. But, even when using all conceivable simplifications and stratagems, it is commonly accepted that graphics systems that aim at a lifelike representation consume a considerable amount of data storage and processing capabilities.

This scarcity of storage and processing resources is a predicament often confronted by the developers of computer graphics hardware and software. This situation has led to the design of dedicated systems in which all available power and storage is devoted to the graphics job. Furthermore, graphics systems are often tailored to specific applications. Dedicated machines can be found in digital typesetting and image recording, computer assisted design and manufacturing, medical imaging, weather mapping, aircraft simulators and trainers, and many other fields.

1.1 IBM Microcomputer Graphics Hardware

In the original microcomputers, storage and processing resources were in such short supply that the machines were considered unsuited for memory- and power-hungry applications, such as computer graphics. However, even at the early stages, several microcomputer designers and entrepreneurs recognized the potential of computer graphics. In the early 1980's, Apple, NEC, and Atari began emphasizing the graphics capabilities of their systems. For Apple these efforts culminated in 1984 with the introduction of the Macintosh computer, operated by means of a graphical user interface called the desktop. The Macintosh desktop, originally developed by Xerox Corporation, consisted of a series of icons and pull-down menus selected and activated by a mouse. Soon thereafter (1985) Aldus Corporation released a digital composition program for the Macintosh. This application, named Pagemaker, allowed the user to compose and typeset documents as if working on a digital typesetting station. Pagemaker on the Macintosh was the first high-quality graphics application for microcomputers, and originated a new line of software products usually called *desktop publishing* programs.

1.1.1 Video Systems

The original IBM microcomputers, introduced in 1981, were offered with a Monochrome Video Adapter (which had no graphics capabilities) and with an optional graphics system named the Color/Graphics Monitor Adapter. The CGA card provided only simple and unsophisticated display functions and was plagued with interference problems. However, it signaled IBM's intention to support graphics in their microcomputer line. Starting with the CGA card, IBM and other companies have developed a long list of microcomputer graphics video devices, namely:

1. The IBM Color Graphics Adapter, previously mentioned, is the first color-graphics card for the IBM Personal Computer.

2. The IBM Enhanced Graphics Adapter. The EGA is a color-graphics card designed to overcome some of the problems and limitations of the Color Graphics Adapter. EGA was introduced in 1985 with the IBM Personal Computer AT.

3. The Professional Graphics Controller by IBM. The PGC is a high-end graphics card intended for applications requiring high-resolution and three-dimensional color graphics.

4. The Hercules Graphics Card, designed and manufactured by Hercules Computer Technology, features an 80-by-25 monochrome text mode, similar to that of the IBM Monochrome Display Adapter and an additional 720-by-348 bit monochrome graphics mode. A new version of this card, called the Graphics Card Plus, was released in 1986.

5. The Hercules Incolor Card. This card, which was released by Hercules Computer Technology in 1987, adds color capabilities to the 720-by-348 pixel modes of the Graphics Card.

6. The IBM PCjr Video Gate Array. The IBM PCjr was furnished with a color-graphics system on the motherboard. Its best graphics mode is 640-by-200 pixels resolution in four colors.

7. The Video Graphics Array or VGA. The VGA standard was released in 1987 with the introduction of the IBM PS/2 line. Its best graphics modes are 640-by-480 pixels resolution in 16 colors and 320-by-200 pixels in 256 colors. VGA cards and systems are also manufactured by other companies for use in IBM-compatible microcomputers.

8. The IBM Multi-Color Graphics Array or MCGA. This is the on-board graphics system developed by IBM for the original IBM PS/2 Model 25 and 30 microcomputers. The system's best graphics mode has 640-by-480 pixel graphics in two colors. MCGA has been replaced by VGA systems in the more recent versions of the Model 25 and the Model 30 microcomputers.

9. The IBM 8514/A Display Adapter. This is a refined color graphics system for the PS/2 microcomputers. It is sometimes considered the PS/2 version of the Professional Graphics Controller mentioned above. The 8514/A has a resolution of 1,024-by-768 pixels in 256 colors. The color can be selected from a palette of 262,144. The 8514/A system contains a dedicated graphic processor chip and includes a programming interface that uses a set of internal, hardware-assisted drawing functions.

10. The IBM Extended Graphics Array or XGA. XGA was released by IBM in 1990 with the PS/2 Model 90 and Model 95, and is also furnished as an add-on card for the 386 and 386SX based PS/2 machines. The system incorporates the features of both the VGA and the 8514/A and adds some new ones. Its best graphics resolution is 1024-by-768 pixels in 256 colors (the same as that of the 8514/A). There is also a 65,536 color mode at the VGA's 640-by-480 pixel resolution.

11. SuperVGA, sometimes called SVGA, is a popular name applied to several VGA clones that improve on the performance, resolution, and color range of the VGA standard. The most used high-resolution graphics mode offered by SuperVGA systems is of 1024-by-768 pixels in 256 colors, matcheing the one best modes of 8514/A and XGA systems.

1.1.2 Input and Output Devices

If the list of video systems for IBM microcomputers is impressive, more so is the list of graphics devices. These devices can be coarsely classified into two groups: those intended to input graphic data into the computer system and those intended for graphics output. The following are the better-known output devices used in computer graphics:

1. Monitors. In IBM microcomputers, a monitor, or CRT, is a raster-scan device that uses a technology similar to that of a television receiver. The various graphics standards, such as CGA, VGA, and XGA, are designed to operate with specific types of monitors. For this reason video display equipment is often not interchangeable. Figure 1.1 is a photograph of the IBM 8515 monitor used with the XGA display system.

Figure 1.1 *IBM Model 8515 Monitor*

2. Printers. Graphics printers produce hardcopy of the graphics data stored and manipulated in the computer system. Many types of printers, including those using dot-matrix technology, have graphics capabilities. However, it is the laser and the ink jet printers that currently dominate the microcomputer market. Laser printers are based on electro-photographic technology by which a digital image is first transferred to a charged metal drum, from which it is heat-fused onto a sheet of paper. Laser printer programming is discussed in Chapter 11. Ink jet printers generate the image by spraying ink droplets onto the paper. Figure 1.2 is a photograph of a Hewlett-Packard LaserJet 4 printer.

Figure 1.2 *Hewlett-Packard LaserJet 4 Laser Printer*

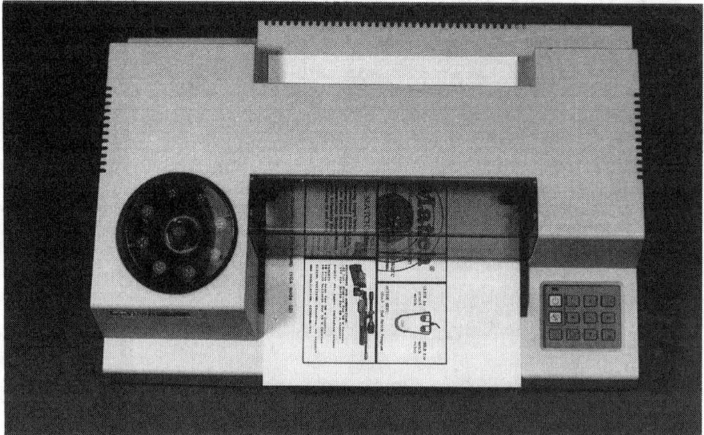

Figure 1.3 *Hewlett-Packard ColorPro Plotter*

3. Pen Plotters. Plotters are devices that produce graphics drawings by means of ink pens. Small pen plotters usually draw on a flat surface while larger one uses a drum. The drawing is done by a combination of movements along the paper's x and y axes. In some flatbed plotters the paper remains stationary while the pens perform all the necessary movements. In another flatbed plotter design, and in drum plotters, the paper moves along one of the drawing axes. Plotter programming is discussed in Chapter 11. Figure 1.3 is a photograph of a Hewlett-Packard ColorPro plotter.

4. Imagesetters. These are devices used to generate a printed image of text and graphics on paper or film. The output of the imagesetter is used to compose the camera-ready masters required for printing. The present gen-

Figure 1.4 *Linotronic 330 Imagesetter*
(Photo courtesy of Linotype-Hell Company

Figure 1.5 *Mouse Systems Electro-Optical Mouse*

eration of imagesetters use laser technology. Imagesetters, which are costly machines usually driven by dedicated mini or mainframe computers, are outside the scope of this book. Figure 1.4 shows a Linotronic imagesetter manufactured by Linotype Corporation.

The list of common graphics input devices includes the following:

1. Keyboard. This device is used to input text data into applications. For example, in a desktop publishing program the keyboard is used to enter or edit text data while a mouse or a digitizer tablet is used to draw the graphics images.

2. Mouse. The mouse is a small mechanical or electro-optical device that is rolled on a desktop, or on a special pad, to change the position of a screen cursor or a graphics object. The mouse, which was popularized in microcomputers by the Macintosh desktop, has become a standard input device for many graphics applications. Mouse programming is discussed in Chapter 9. Figure 1.5 shows an electro-optical mouse on its special pad.

3. Digitizer. This device, also called a digitizer tablet, is used in technical-graphics applications, such as computer assisted design (CAD), for input of drawings and for menu selection. The digitizer consists of a tablet and a connected pointing device in the form of a pen, puck, or mouse. The tablet is sometimes equipped with printed overlays of option menus and commands.

4. Scanners. The scanner is an electro-optical input device that directly reads printed matter into a computer system. The printed data, consisting of text, bar code, or graphics images, is digitalized and transferred to the machine's memory where it can be further processed by the software. Scanners are supplied in the form of box-like devices, usually called flatbed scanners, or as portable, hand-held units. Figure 1.6 shows a hand scanner.

Figure 1.6 *Logitech Model 256 Hand Scanner*

1.2 IBM Microcomputer Graphics Software

The general term *graphics software* applies to an extensive range of system, applications, and utility programs that can be divided into the following categories:

1. System programs with graphical interfaces, such as Microsoft Windows and IBM Operating System/2. Some operating systems include graphics programming services designed to facilitate applications development.

2. Graphical applications, such as computer assisted design, desktop publishing, image processing, drawing and painting, animated games, and font editor programs. These software products perform specific functions for the user. Some graphical applications are designed to operate in a particular graphics environment. For example, the CorelDraw drawing program requires the Windows operating system's graphical environment.

3. Graphical programming languages or graphical libraries for use with a specific, general-purpose, programming language. Postscript, for example, is a printer programming language developed by Aldus Corporation. Graphical Kernel System (GKS) is an international graphics standard intended as an interface between the application program and the graphics hardware. In addition, many versions of high-level languages, such as C, Pascal, and BASIC, have graphics functions or libraries designed to aid in the development of graphics applications.

4. Graphics utilities for the operation of specific hardware devices. This type of software, sometimes called a *device driver*, consists of one or more low-level routines required to control a particular hardware device. For example, MS DOS computers require a device driver for processing the signal data generated by a mouse input device. The mouse device driver software makes this information available to system and application software.

5. Graphics routines for performing a particular operation on a specific device. These software elements, sometimes called graphics primitives, are the building blocks of device drivers, graphical languages, libraries, and operating environments. An example of a graphics primitive is a routine to draw a circle on a VGA display.

1.2.1 The User's Perspective

From a user's point of view the graphics potential of an IBM microcomputer has evolved, in the span of a few years, from a coarse toy to a fully developed system of professional quality. The following graphics application fields are represented in IBM microcomputers:

1. Computer Assisted Design. CAD programs are mostly used in producing line-drawings for drafting, engineering, architecture, and graphics design. The AutoCAD program, developed and sold by Autodesk Incorporated, represents a high-end product in the CAD line for IBM microcomputers. In a professional environment CAD programs usually output to pen and laser plotters. Printers, usually of laser and ink-dot technology, are used mostly to obtain drafts. In most CAD programs the user can direct printer or plotter output to a disk file, which, in turn, can be loaded into other applications.

2. Drawing, painting, and graphics design programs have some of the basic drafting features of CAD programs plus a few more that add decorative, artistic, or special technical effects. CorelDraw, developed by Corel Systems, is one of the better-known drawing programs. Because CorelDraw runs under Windows, program output can be directed to any Windows device, including laser printers, plotters, and imagesetters. CorelDraw stores complete image data for drawings, however, the quality of the printed output depends on the device to which it is directed. In this manner, a drawing output to a black-and-white laser printer of 300 dpi resolution produces a coarse rendering of the image, while output to a film recorder, operating at 4,000 dpi, gives a full color, almost grainless image. For the same reason, the resolution of the video system determines the quality of the image displayed. For example, a VGA graphics image in 640-by-480 pixels in 16 colors has less quality than one on an XGA, 8514/A, or SuperVGA system with 1024-by-768 pixels in 256 colors. Color plate number 1 is a reproduction of one of the draft drawings developed for the book's cover using the CorelDraw program. The disk file was output to a high-resolution film recorder which generated a color transparency. The transparency was then printed for the illustration using conventional photographic methods.

3. Desktop publishing programs allow the creation of originals for publication. This line of microcomputer software products emulates the functions of more costly digital typesetting machines usually driven by mini- or mainframe computers. Two well-known desktop publishing programs for IBM microcomputers are Pagemaker, by Aldus Corporation, and Ventura Publisher, by Xerox Corporation. Here again, the quality of the printed output depends

on the output device. A Ventura Publisher document printed on a high-resolution imagesetter is virtually undistinguishable from one generated by a dedicated digital typesetting system. On the other hand, output to a 300 dpi laser printer produces much coarser results. This book was composed and typeset by the authors using the Ventura Publisher program.

In addition to these three general categories, we find many IBM microcomputer applications that offer graphics functions. For example, some word-processing programs, such as Wordperfect, provide desktop publishing facilities. Other graphics applications are designed to expand or enhance the operation of a graphics software product. For example, the Letterease program, by CAD Lettering Systems Incorporated, adds custom lettering to AutoCAD drawings. Another popular graphics support product is the Softkicker program, developed by Aristocad Incorporated, which provides automatic screen scrolling and other convenient display operations to some versions of Ventura Publisher.

The authors and publisher have used in the production of this book several hardware and software products available for IBM microcomputers. Our purpose has been to illustrate the capabilities, and perhaps the limitations, of these graphics devices and programs. Specifically:

1. The original manuscript, as well as the draft for tables and illustrations, were composed using the Wordperfect word processing program on an IBM Model 70 microcomputer.

2. The illustrations were produced in CorelDraw version 3.0.

3. The halftone monochrome images and color separation prints were scanned using a Logitech Scanman Model 256 gray scale scanner and the Ansel version 1.0 image editing software. Both of these products are by Logitech, Incorporated. Most scanned images were later imported into CorelDraw for additional manipulations.

4. Ventura Publisher, version 3.0 and 4.0, was used in composing and typesetting the original manuscript. AutoCAD and CorelDraw drawing files were imported into Ventura for the more elaborate illustrations, while the simpler ones were produced using the Ventura graphics commands.

5. The art for the book's cover was generated in AutoCAD and CorelDraw by the authors. The image of the space shuttle which appears on the cover, was made by reducing and cropping a drawing named COLUMBIA, which is furnished as a sample file with the AutoCAD program. While in the design stage, the CorelDraw files for the cover were transmitted through our modem to a bulletin board service operated by McLain Imaging Services of San Jose, California. We then printed these slides on Cibachrome photographic paper for detailed observation and editing by the authors and the publisher.

The previous list of programs and resources is not meant as an endorsement of these products and services or as a statement of preference over other ones. The fact that these, and not other, means were used in the production of this book was often a matter of availability and convenience.

1.2.2 The Programmer's Perspective

From a programmer's viewpoint, IBM microcomputer graphics have also suffered substantial transformations in recent years. Today the cutting-edge of graphics technology includes high-resolution displays with high pixel densities and palettes containing millions of colors, as well as high-quality scanners, printers, and plotters. The graphics possibilities of the IBM microcomputers and associated gadgetry has grown geometrically in recent years. However, note that some graphics devices have been designed to optimize image quality and performance, even at the expense of compatibility, programmability, and simplicity of construction.

The SuperVGA cards are an example of the multiplicity of technologies and programming methods used in similar devices. The developer of a stand-alone application that is to execute with optimum performance in the SuperVGA enhanced modes, must code a program version or provide a software driver for almost every make and model of SuperVGA card. The same applies to an image processing program that attempts to be compatible with scanners by different manufacturers, or to CAD programs that attempt to drive several brands and models of pen plotters. Regarding some specific devices the situation is slightly better, for example, most laser printers use either PostScript or the Hewlett-Packard PCL language. However, even when working within a particular standard, such as PCL, the graphics programmer encounters versions and updates that are not totally compatible.

One side-effect of today's profusion of graphics hardware technology for the IBM microcomputer field is the difficulty in obtaining clear and reliable programming information. Much of this information is available only from the manufacturer or distributor of the particular device, and even when the manufacturer or distributor is willing to provide data and manuals, the material is often insufficient.

The speed at which the graphics technology for microcomputers is developing determines that not many standards have had time to gain general acceptance. Nowhere has this fast development rate been more evident than in microcomputer video systems. The list of IBM microcomputer video systems developed in recent years includes the Monochrome Display Adapter, the Color Graphics Adapter, the Enhanced Graphics Adapter, the Professional Graphics Controller, the Hercules Graphics Card and Graphics Card Plus, the Hercules Incolor Card, the PCjr Video Gate Array, the Video Graphics Array, the Multi Color Graphics Array, the 8514/A Display Adapter, the Extended Graphics Array, and the SuperVGA cards. If we admit that today's state-of-the-art video graphics systems still leave much to be desired regarding image quality and performance, we can anticipate that the years to come will see other video display technologies and standards. This observation can be extended to other popular graphics devices used in IBM microcomputers, such as laser printers and scanners for monochrome and color images.

In order to avoid dealing with these variations and inconsistencies, the graphics programmer for IBM microcomputers can adopt a development environment in which this great variety of standards and devices is handled transparently by the system software. Such is the case when programming in the Windows or Operating System 2 graphics environments. However, this convenience comes at a substantial performance price. A second option is to deal with variations in graphics hardware and standards either by writing device-specific programs or by providing versions of software drivers that are capable of operating with more than one device. This is the alternative often used by programs that aim at the highest possible quality and performance.

1.3 Video Hardware

Before 1970, computer graphics workstations were expensive and complex devices that used elaborate video display technologies based on storage tube and vector-refresh CRTs. The graphics systems, driven by mini or mainframe computers, were usually dedicated to specific applications, for example, digital typesetting or computer assisted design. The high cost of these machines limited their economic feasibility to research, industrial, and commercial applications. Advances in the methods of image-refreshing, which originated in commercial television technology in the late sixties, have made possible the use of mass-produced components in computer displays. The pioneer research along these lines was done by Conrac Corporation. The result is a computer image processing technology known as raster-scan graphics.

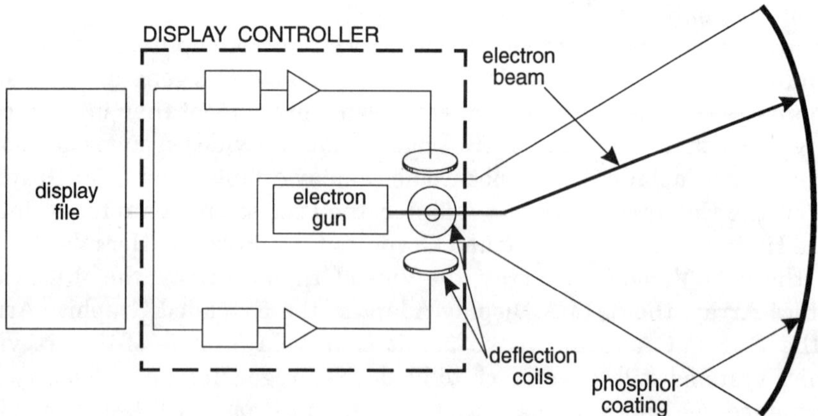

Figure 1.7 *Vector-Refresh Display*

Storage tube display technology is based on coating the inside surface of the cathode-ray tube with a special type of phosphor that when struck by an electron beam remains fluorescent for up to one hour. This mechanism makes the CRT screen serve both as a display and as a storage device. The major disadvantages of storage tube technology are that the entire screen must be drawn and erased, that the contrast is low, and that it has no capability for displaying colors. The vector-refresh display, on the other hand, uses a short-persistence phosphor coating that must be re-activated (refreshed) by the electron beam at an approximate rate of 30 times per second. The vector-refresh system includes a display file in which the image is stored as a set of straight line segments, called vectors. The display controller of a vector-refresh CRT uses magnetic coils to deflect the electron beam while drawing each individual vector. Figure 1.7 shows the operation of vector-refresh CRT.

The display surface of a raster-scan CRT is physically divided into a pattern of individual dots, called pixels. The term pixel was derived from the words "picture" and "element." A video system can reserve an area of RAM to record the state of each individual screen pixel. Using this storage scheme a black-and-white display system encodes each pixel in a single memory bit: if the bit is set the pixel is usually represented as white and if the bit is reset the pixel is left black. This area of memory reserved for storing the state of the video display is called the video buffer, and a system designed in this fashion is said to be memory mapped. Figure 1.8 represents a memory-mapped video display system such as the ones in most IBM microcomputers.

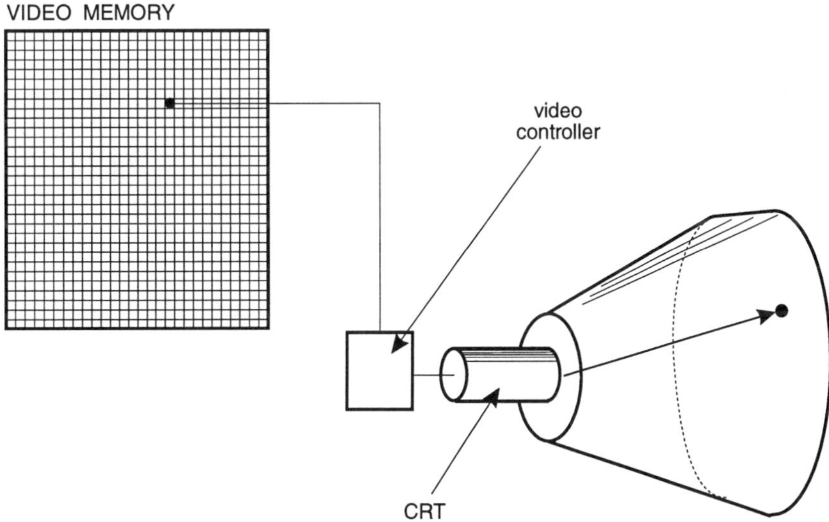

Figure 1.8 *Memory-Mapped Video System*

Table 1.1 *BIOS Video Modes in MDA. CGA, EGA, PCjr, and VGA Systems*

MODE	TYPE	DEFINITION	MONO OR COLOR	BUFFER ADDRESS	BUFFER SIZE	CHARACTER BOX SIZE	PC LINE				PS/2 LINE	
							MDA	CGA	EGA	PCjr	VGA	MCGA
0	Text	40 x 25	B & W	B8000H	2K	8 x 8		X	X	X	X	X
1	Text	40 x 25	Color	B8000H	2K	8 x 8		X	X	X	X	X
2	Text	80 x 25	B & W	B8000H	2K	8 x 8		X	X	X	X	X
3	Text	80 x 25	Color	B8000H	4K	8 x 8		X	X	X	X	X
4	APA	320 x 200	Color	A0000H	8K	8 x 8		X	X	X	X	X
5	APA	320 x 200	B & W	A0000H	8K	8 x 8		X	X	X	X	X
6	APA	640 x 200	B & W	A0000H	16K	8 x 8		X	X	X	X	X
7	Text	80 x 25	B & W	B0000H	4K	9 x 14	X		X		X	
8	APA	160 x 200	Color	B8000H	16K	8 x 8				X		
9	APA	320 x 200	Color	B8000H	32K	8 x 8				X		
10	APA	640 x 200	Color	B8000H	32K	8 x 8				X		
13	APA	320 x 200	Color	A0000H	8K	8 x 8			X		X	
14	APA	640 x 200	Color	A0000H	16K	8 x 8			X		X	
15	APA	640 x 350	B & W	A0000H	28K	8 x 14			X		X	
16	APA	640 x 350	Color	A0000H	28K	8 x 14			X		X	
17	APA	640 x 480	Color	A0000H	38K	8 x 16					X	X
18	APA	640 x 480	Color	A0000H	38K	8 x 16					X	
19	APA	640 x 480	Color	A0000H	38K	8 x 8					X	X

Abbreviations: **MDA** = Monochrome Display Adapter   **CGA** = Color Graphics Adapter
EGA = Enhanced Graphics Adapter   **VGA** = PS/2 Video Graphics Array   **MCGA** = PS/2 Multicolor Graphics Array

Table 1.2 *IBM Character Set*

Characters ØH to 7FH								
Hex	Ø	1	2	3	4	5	6	7
Ø		►		Ø	@	P	`	p
1	☺	◄	!	1	A	Q	a	q
2	☻	↕	"	2	B	R	b	r
3	♥	‼	#	3	C	S	c	s
4	♦	¶	$	4	D	T	d	t
5	♣	§	%	5	E	U	e	u
6	♠	▬	&	6	F	V	f	v
7	•	↨	'	7	G	W	g	w
8	◘	↑	(	8	H	X	h	x
9	○	↓	)	9	I	Y	i	y
A	◎	→	*	:	J	Z	j	z
B	♂	←	+	;	K	[	k	{
C	♀	∟	,	<	L	\	l	¦
D	♪	↔	-	=	M	]	m	}
E	♫	▲	.	>	N	^	n	~
F	☼	▼	/	?	O	_	o	Δ

Table 1.2 *IBM Character Set* (continued)

Characters 7FH to FFH							
Hex	**8**	**9**	**A**	**B**	**C**	**D**	**E**	**F**
Ø	Ç	É	á	░	└	╨	α	$\equiv$
1	ü	æ	í	▒	┴	╤	β	$\pm$
2	é	Æ	ó	▓	┬	╥	Γ	$\geq$
3	â	ô	ú	│	├	╙	π	$\leq$
4	ä	ö	ñ	┤	─	╘	Σ	$\lceil$
5	à	ò	Ñ	╡	┼	╒	σ	$\rfloor$
6	å	û	ª	╢	╞	╓	μ	$\div$
7	ç	ù	º	╖	╟	╫	τ	$\approx$
8	ê	ÿ	¿	╕	╚	╪	Φ	○
9	ë	Ö	⌐	╣	╔	┘	Θ	•
A	è	Ü	¬	║	╩	┌	Ω	·
B	ï	¢	½	╗	╦	█	δ	√
C	î	£	¼	╝	╠	▄	∞	**n**
D	ì	¥	¡	╜	═	▌	ϕ	²
E	Ä	₧	«	╛	╬	▐	$\in$	■
F	Å	ƒ	»	┐	┴	▀	∩	

1.3.1 IBM Microcomputer Video Technology

Video display hardware has undergone many changes with the different models of the IBM PC, the IBM PS/2, and the IBM compatible microcomputers. In the original systems the buyer would select between a monochrome display with no graphics capabilities or a graphics color system. Later machines contain a built-in video system and the user's options are limited to adding features to this basic hardware. For example, in the Personal Computer, the PC XT, and the AT the buyer configures the video system according to need. The original options were a monochrome display (MDA) and a color graphics display (CGA). In 1985 the Enhanced Graphics Adapter was added to the list of graphics options. On the other hand, the PCjr, the Portable PC, and the models of the PS/2 line come equipped with a video system that is an integral part of the system board. However, in some models, the user has certain configuration and upgrade options.

Most IBM microcomputer video display systems are *memory mapped*. (See Figure 1.8.) The exception is the 8514/A display adapter while operating in an advanced function mode; in this mode video buffer addressing has not been documented by IBM. A video display system is described as memory mapped when a part of the machine's memory space is dedicated to video functions. This video display area can be reached both by the microprocessor and by the electronic components that handle screen display operations. The configuration is sometimes called a dual-ported system.

Video Modes

The IBM BIOS classifies the possible settings of the video controller into display modes. These modes are numbered consecutively starting with mode 0. The alphanumerical modes, also called text or alpha modes, are capable of displaying the symbols in the IBM character set. The graphics modes, also known as all-points addressable or APA modes, allow the control of the individual screen dots that constitute the display surface. Table 1.1 shows the alphanumeric or text modes and the APA or graphic modes in IBM video systems.

Regarding text modes, the definition of the video system is usually expressed in the number of characters per screen row and total number of rows on screen. For example, text mode number 7 consists of 80 characters per row in 25 screen rows. (See Table 1.1.) It is referred to as a 80-by-25 text mode. In the APA modes the video system definition is the number of pixels in each row by the total number of pixel rows. For example, APA video modes number 17, 18, and 19 (see Table 1.1) consist of 640 pixels per row and 480 pixel rows. Therefore we refer to these graphics modes as consisting of 640-by-480 pixels.

The concept of video modes is associated with BIOS and MS DOS. Other operating systems, such as Operating System/2, do not use the BIOS number codes for the video display modes. Under OS/2, the display characteristics are defined by the number of colors, number of text columns, number of text rows, number of pixels per row, and number of pixel rows. In the OS/2 scheme the mode number is meaningless.

IBM Character Set

In IBM microcomputers the alphanumeric or text modes consist of the conventional ASCII codes used to represent the letters, numbers, and other symbols used in the English language as well as a collection of special symbols. Table 1.2 shows the character set available in all IBM video adapters and systems. The special characters in the IBM set include the following:

1. Four playing card suits (3H to 6H)
2. Male and female genetic symbols (BH and CH)
3. Two proofreader's marks (14H and 15H)
4. Two musical notes (DH and EH)
5. Several arrows, circles, triangles, happy, and sad faces
6. Letters and diacritic symbols used in the Spanish, French, and German alphabets
7. Graphics symbols for drawing boxes (B3H to DFH)
8. Graphics shading symbols (B0H to B2H)
9. Mathematical and engineering symbols (F0H to FDH)
10. Selected letters of the Greek alphabet (E1H to EDH)
11. Monetary symbols for yen, pound, dollar, and cents
12. Fractions (ABH and ACH)

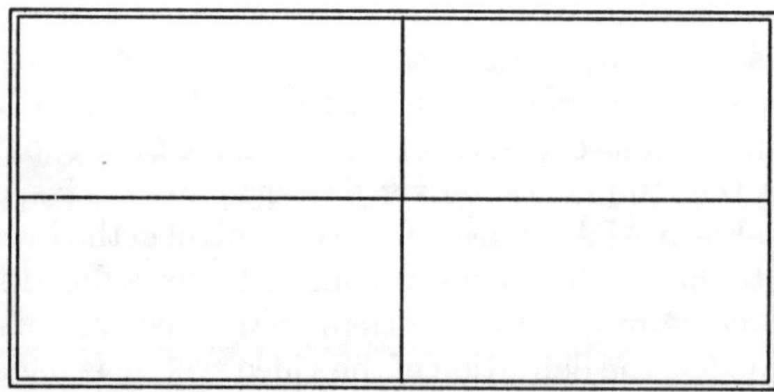

Characters used in box:

‖ = BAH	│ = B3H	⊣ = B6H
═ = CDH	─ = C4H	╧ = CFH
╗ = CBH	┼ = C5H	╤ = D1H
╔ = C9H	╝ = BCH	╚ = C8H
	╟ = C7H	

Figure 1.9   *Boxes Using Characters of the Extended Set*

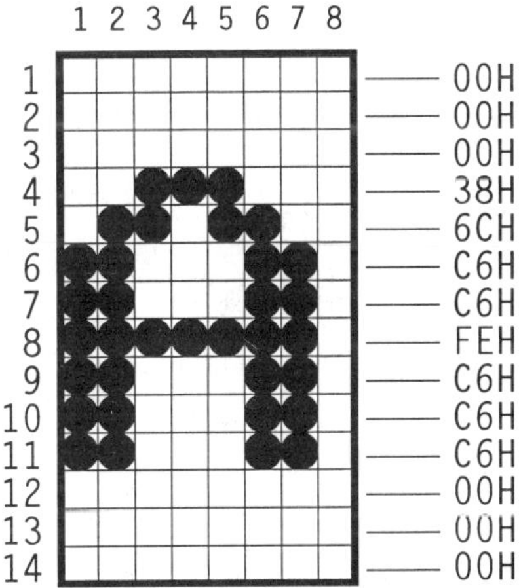

Figure 1.10 *Bitmap of the Letter "A"*

Notice, in Table 1.2, that the ASCII characters are in the range 20H to 7FH. The remaining symbols, those below 20H and above 7FH, can be used for simple graphics effects that are quite easy to generate. Many alphanumeric programs use these convenient graphics to their advantage. For example, the symbols in the range B3H to DAH can be combined to draw screen rectangles and boxes of various shapes and designs. Figure 1.9 shows one possible box variation using these symbols.

In alphanumeric modes characters are generated by setting and resetting pixels in a rectangular grid. In color systems each bright pixel can take two or more intensities of red, green, and blue colored light. In monochrome systems each bright pixel can take two or more shades of gray. The pixel patterns for each character are stored in the video adapter's ROM. Figure 1.10 shows the bit map for the letter "A" in an 8-by-14 pixel matrix.

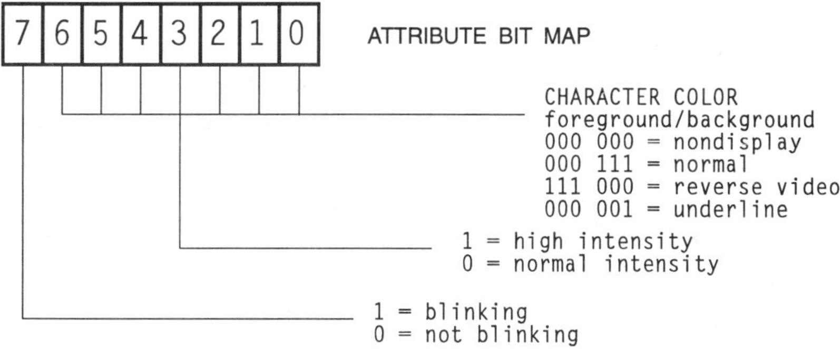

Figure 1.11 *Attribute Bitmap for Monochrome Alphanumeric Modes*

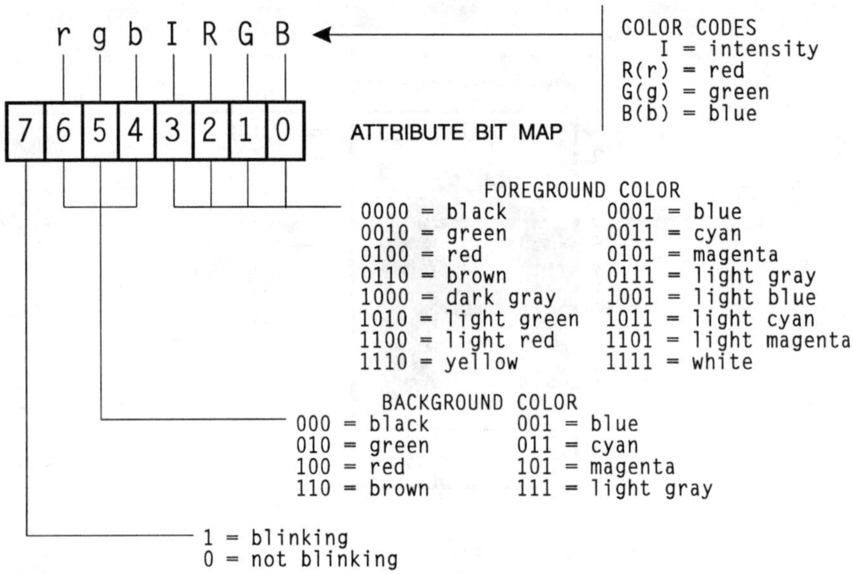

Figure 1.12 *Attribute Bitmap for Color Alphanumeric Modes*

The Character Attribute

Video memory in the alphanumeric modes is structured in two consecutive bytes. The first byte, called the *character byte*, encodes the character code in the IBM set. (See Table 1.2.) The memory byte following the character byte, called the *attribute byte*, encodes the manner in which the character is displayed. The bitmap for the attribute byte differs in monochrome and in color systems. Figure 1.11 shows the attribute byte bitmap for monochrome alphanumeric modes.

Notice that in the black-and-white (monochrome) modes the bit field comprised by bits 0, 1, 2, 4, 5, and 6, is used to determine the fundamental display characteristics. Also that the bit combination 000 001 in this field, which underlines the displayed characters, is available only in video mode number 7. The attribute bit map for the color alphanumeric modes is as shown in Figure 1.12.

Notice in Figure 1.12 that one 4-bit field controls the character's foreground color while a 3-bit field controls its background color. Since there is no intensity bit in the background field, the character background colors do not have a light color option.

Video Buffer Organization

The area of RAM dedicated to video functions is known by the names video memory, video buffer, display memory, display buffer, regen buffer, refresh buffer, and screen buffer. Video memory can be physically located in the video card, be a part of the display hardware, or (as is the case in the PCjr) be a part of main user memory. The address of the video buffer in system memory has been maintained by IBM and other manufacturers since the original release of the MDA and CGA cards 1981. For the MDA card, and for video mode number 7 in all systems that support this mode, the physical address of the video buffer is at B0000H. For all other alphanumeric modes the video buffer is located at physical address B8000H. These physical addresses translate to segment base B000H and B800H respectively.

In the alphanumeric modes, display data within the video buffer is stored as a series of alternative character and attributes codes. The character codes are placed at the even-numbered bytes and the attribute codes at the odd-numbered bytes. Figure 1.13 is a diagram of the video buffer organization in IBM microcomputers.

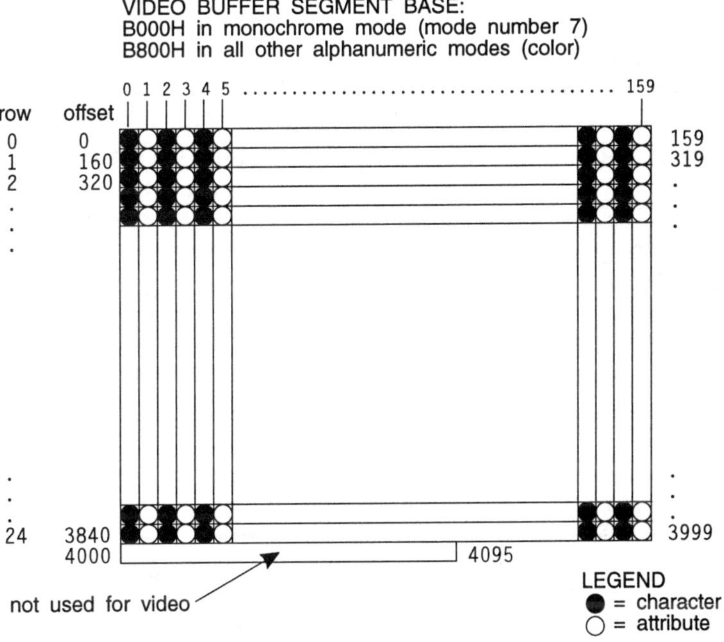

Figure 1.13 *Video Buffer Structure in Alphanumeric Modes*

In Figure 1.13 each screen row (assuming an 80 characters-per-row video mode) is represented by 160 buffer bytes. Eighty of these bytes are dedicated to storing the character codes and eighty bytes in each row store the attribute codes. In Figure 1.13 the character codes are represented by a black circle and the attribute codes by a white circle. Also, observe that buffer bytes from offset 4000 to 4095 are not mapped to the video screen. This 96-byte area at the end of the video buffer has sometimes been used by programmers to hide the system cursor and to store passwords and other secret codes.

1.4 The ALFAGRAF Library Modules

The programmer working in an alphanumeric mode does not deal with individual screen pixels, but rather with bitmaps that encode complete characters. Displaying these ASCII and graphics characters in an IBM microcomputer consist of selecting the corresponding character codes and placing them in the memory area mapped to the video display. This operation can be performed by accessing the video buffer directly, by means of a BIOS or MS DOS system service, or by using a high-level language function. Each method has its advantages and drawbacks.

Some high-level language implementations for IBM microcomputers provide a more or less extensive range of alphanumeric display functions. These functions are either part of the language itself or furnished as support libraries. On the other hand, other high-level language implementations are limited to row-by-row display at the current cursor position, resulting in a display style that is reminiscent of an adding machine tape. This means that the degree of display control available to a programmer working in a high-level language depends on the language itself and on the particular implementation.

Assembly language programmers, on the other hand, except for a few rudimentary system services, are left to their own resources regarding alphanumeric display. For this reason, we have included several elementary alphanumeric display functions in the ALFAGRAF module of the GRAPHSOL that are specifically designed for use from assembly language. Since these simpler display controls are available in most high-level languages, we have not anticipated their use from high-level language code. The assembly language specific routines have the corresponding notice in the descriptions of Section 1.6.1.

Table 1.3 *Data Types Used by Library Modules*

NAME	MACHINE STORAGE UNIT	HIGH-LEVEL EQUIVALENT
Byte integer	BYTE REGISTER (AH-AL,BH-BL, CH-CL,DH-DL)	unsigned integer in an 8-bit variable
Word integer	WORD REGISTER (AX,BX,CX,DX)	unsigned integer in a 16-bit variable
Dword integer	386/486 EXTENDED REGISTER	unsigned integer in a 32-bit variable
Segment	SEGMENT REGISTER (CS,DS,ES,SS)	segment of address in a 16-bit variable
Offset	POINTER REGISTER (SI,DI,BP)	offset of address in a 16-bit variable
Logical address	SEGMENT:POINTER REGISTER PAIR	32-bit logical address in SSSS:OOOO format

Most alphanumeric display routines in the ALFAGRAF module can also be used from high-level languages. In order to access and use the files in the accompanying microdisk the reader must follow the installation and unpacking instructions in Appendix A. The library's interface examples and descriptions are found in Appendix B.

1.4.1 ALFAGRAF Library Functions

The following are generic descriptions of the public functions contained in the ALFAGRAF module of the GRAPHSOL library. The values passed and returned by the individual functions are listed in the order in which they are recovered in the code. The data types used by all library modules can be seen in Table 1.3.

SET_CURSOR

Sets the system cursor to the row and column coordinates requested by the caller. Does not test for a valid range.
>Receives:
>>1. Byte integer of screen row. Valid range according to mode
>>2. Byte integer of screen column. Valid range according to mode
>Returns:
>>Nothing
>Action:
>>System cursor is repositioned

GET_CURSOR

Obtains the screen location of the system cursor in row and column coordinates. Also the cursor start and end lines.
>Receives:
>>1. Byte integer of active display page
>Returns:
>>1. Byte integer of start cursor line (cursor size)
>>2. Byte integer of end cursor line (cursor size)
>>3. Byte integer of present cursor row
>>4. Byte integer of present cursor column

CURSOR_OFF

Disables the system cursor by placing it in the buffer's undisplayed area.
>Receives:
>>Nothing
>Returns:
>>Nothing
>Action:
>>System cursor disappears from the screen

CLEAR_SCREEN

Clears the video display using direct access to the video buffer. Also sets the
attribute byte for the entire buffer.
>Receives:
>>1. Byte integer of attribute
>Returns:
>>Nothing
>Action:
>>Screen is cleared. Attribute is set

CLEAR_AREA

Clears a rectangular screen area defined by its row and column coordinates.
Also sets the attribute for all characters in the area. Optionally fills the area
with a character.
>Receives:
>>1. Byte integer of character code to be used in filling the screen rectangle.
>>A zero value serves to preserve displayed characters. A space charac-
>>ter (20H) must be used to blank the area
>>2. Byte integer of attribute
>>3. Byte integer of row number of top-left corner of rectangle (range 0 to
>>24)
>>4. Byte integer of column number of top-left corner of rectangle (range
>>0 to 79)
>>5. Byte integer of row number of bottom-right corner of rectangle (range
>>0 to 24)
>>6. Byte integer of column number of bottom-right corner of rectangle
>>(range 0 to 79)
>Returns:
>>Nothing
>Action:
>>Rectangular area is initialized to the first value passed by the caller. A
>>space character (20H) blanks the screen. A value of zero is used to (see
>>Table 1.1) preserve the displayed characters. The area's attribute is set
>>to the second parameter passed by the caller.

SHOW_BLOCK (Assembly Language Only)

Displays a formatted text message at the screen location specified by row and
column parameters embedded in the message block. The message attribute is
also embedded in the block. The message text can contain control codes for
end-of-line and end-of-row. To use this function from Assembly Language
programs see the SHOW_BLOCK procedure in the file ALFAGRAF.ASM.

REPEAT_HOR (Assembly Language Only)

Displays a number of horizontal characters using the current attribute. To use this function from Assembly Language programs see the REPEAT_HOR procedure in the file ALFAGRAF.ASM.

REPEAT_VER (Assembly Language Only)

Displays a number of vertical characters using the current attribute. To use this function from Assembly Language programs see the REPEAT_VER procedure in the file ALFAGRAF.ASM.

DRAW_BOX

Displays a box drawn using either the single or the double line box characters in the IBM extended set. (See Table 1.2.) The routine checks for valid box parameters; the column and row parameters for the bottom-right corner of the box must be at least one unit (row and column) greater than the parameters for the top-left corner. Also that the row and column values must be within the legal range for an 80-by-25 text mode. If the routine encounters invalid data the carry flag is set and execution is aborted.

 Receives:
  1. Byte integer of line type code. A value of 2 indicates a double-line box. Any other value produces a single-line box
  2. Byte integer of row number of top-left corner of box (range 0 to 24)
  3. Byte integer of column number of top-left corner of box (range 0 to 79)
  4. Byte integer of row number of bottom-right corner of box (range 0 to 24)
  5. Byte integer of column number of bottom-right corner of box (range 0 to 79)
 Returns:
  Nothing
 Action:
  Screen box is drawn if passed values are in the valid range. Current attribute is preserved

SHADE_BOX

Displays a shaded rectangular box using the shading characters in the range B0H to B2H in the IBM extended set. (See Table 1.2.) The routine checks for valid box parameters; the column and row parameters for the bottom-right corner of the box must be at least one unit (row and column) greater than the parameters for the top-left corner. The row and column values must also be within the legal range for an 80-by-25 text mode. If the routine encounters invalid data execution is aborted.

Receives:
   1. Byte integer of shade type code. A value of 1 indicates a lighter box
      (character B0H). A value of 2 is used for a medium shade box
      (character B1H). A value of 3 is passed for a darker box (character
      B2H)
   2. Byte integer of row number of top-left corner of box (range 0 to 24)
   3. Byte integer of column number of top-left corner of box (range 0 to 79)
   4. Byte integer of row number of bottom-right corner of box (range 0 to
      24)
   5. Byte integer of column number of bottom-right corner of box (range
      0 to 79)
Returns:
   Nothing
Action:
   Shaded screen box is drawn if passed values are in the valid range
   Current attribute is preserved

BOX_LINE_HOR

Draws a horizontal line dividing an existing screen box. The dividing line, which
extends from the left box edge to the right one, can be single or double width.
The routine checks the existing screen box to pick the best character with which
to link the line and the box's edge. If no valid graphics character is found at the
line's start point execution is aborted. The line is drawn left-to-right and ends
in the first box-drawing character encountered. The single-width horizontal
dividing line in Figure 1.9 can be drawn using the BOX LINE HOR function.
In this case, if the vertical dividing line was drawn first, then BOX_LINE_HOR
must be called twice; the first line would extend from the left box edge to the
central divider. The second line from the central divider to the right edge of the
box.
   Receives:
      1. Byte integer of line type code. A value of 2 indicates a double-width
         line. Any other value produces a single-width line
      2. Byte integer of row number of top-left corner of line start point (range
         0 to 24)
      3. Byte integer of column number of top-left corner of line start point
         (range 0 to 79)
      Note: The line's start point must coincide at the left edge of an existing
      screen box
   Returns:
      Nothing
   Action:
      Horizontal screen line is drawn if passed values are in the valid range
      Current attribute is preserved

BOX_LINE_VER

Draws a vertical line dividing an existing screen box. The dividing line, which extends from the top box edge to the bottom one, can be single or double width. The routine checks the existing screen box to pick the best character with which to link the line and the box's edge. If no valid graphics character is found at the line's start point execution is aborted. The line is drawn top-to-bottom and ends in the first box-drawing character encountered. The single-width vertical dividing line in Figure 1.9 be drawn using the BOX LINE VER function. In this case, if the horizontal dividing line was drawn first, then BOX_LINE_VER must be called twice; the first line would extend from the top edge to the central divider. The second line from the central divider to the bottom edge of the box.

Receives:

1. Byte integer of line type code. A value of 2 indicates a double-width line. Any other value produces a single-width line
2. Byte integer of row number of top-left corner of line start point (range 0 to 24)
3. Byte integer of column number of top-left corner of line start point (range 0 to 79)

Note: The line's start point must coincide with the top edge of an existing screen box

Returns:

Nothing

Action:

A vertical screen line is drawn if passed values are in the valid range
Current attribute is preserved

2

VGA Architecture

Chapter Summary

This chapter describes the VGA video standard and its programmable elements: the CRT Controller, the Graphics Controller, the Sequencer, the Attribute Controller, and the Digital-to-Analog converter (DAC). It also describes the VGA memory structure. VGA programming is discussed in Chapter 3.

2.0 The VGA Standard

In 1987 IBM introduced two video systems to be furnished as standard components for their PS/2 line. These video systems were named the MCGA (Multicolor Graphics Array) and VGA (Video Graphics Array). MCGA, an under-featured version of VGA, was furnished with the lower-end PS/2 machines Models 25 and 30. VGA was the standard video system for all other PS/2 microcomputers. At a later date IBM extended VGA to its low-end models of the PS/2 line. In fact, in August 1990 IBM announced a line of inexpensive home computers (designated as the PS/1 line) equipped with VGA graphics. Since the MCGA standard was short lived and not very popular it will not be specifically considered in this book. However, because MCGA is a subversion of VGA, its programming is identical to VGA in those video modes that are common to both systems. (See Table 1.1.)

The VGA standard introduced a change from digital to analog video display driver technology. The reason for this change is that analog monitors can produce a much larger color selection than digital ones. This switch in display technology explains why the monitors of the PC line are incompatible with the VGA standard and vice versa. VGA graphics also include a Digital-to-Analog converter, usually called the DAC, and 256K of video memory. The DAC outputs the red, green, and blue signals to the analog display. Video memory is divided into four 64K video maps, called the *bit planes*. VGA supports all the display modes in MDA, CGA, and EGA. (See Table 1.1.) In addition, VGA implements several new alphanumeric and graphics modes, the most notable of which are graphics mode number 18, with 640-by-480-pixel resolution in 16 colors, and graphics mode number 19, with 320-by-200 pixel resolution in 256 colors. The effective resolution of the VGA text modes is of 720-by-400 pixels. These text modes can execute in 16 colors or in monochrome. Three different fonts can be selected in the alphanumeric modes.

Access to the VGA registers and to video memory is through the system microprocessor. The microprocessor read and write operations to the video buffer are automatically synchronized by the VGA with the cathode-ray tube (CRT) controller so as to eliminate interference. This explains why VGA programs, unlike those written for the CGA, can access video memory at any time without fear of introducing screen snow or other unsightly effects.

2.0.1 Advantages and Limitations

The resolution of a graphics system is often measured in the total number of separately addressable elements per unit area. In video display systems the individually addressable elements are the screen pixels; the resolution is measured in pixels per inch. For example, the maximum resolution of a VGA system is of approximately 80 pixels per inch, both vertically and horizontally. In VGA this density is determined by a screen structure of 640 pixels per each 8-inch screen row and 480 vertical pixels per each 6-inch screen column. But not all video systems output a symmetrical pixel density. For example, the

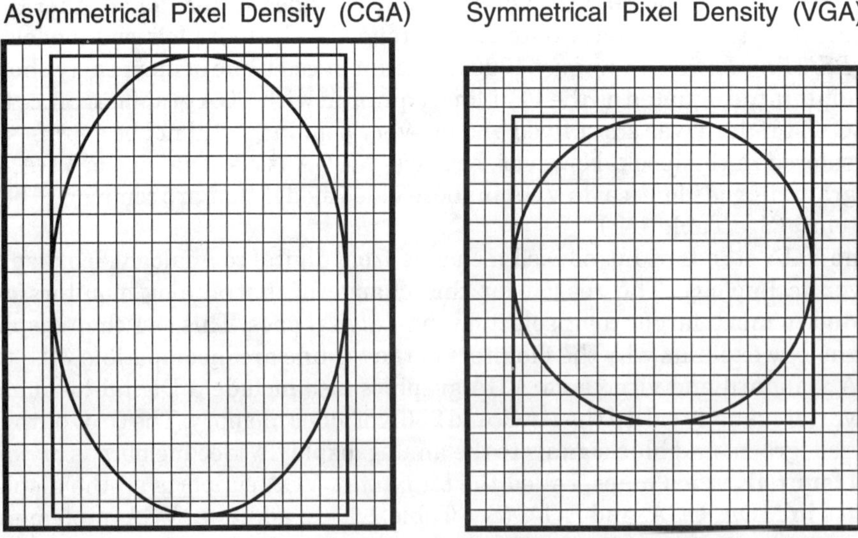

Figure 2.1   *Square and Circle on CGA and VGA Screens*

maximum resolution of the EGA standard is the same as that of the VGA on the horizontal axis (80 pixels per inch) but only of 58 pixels per inch on the vertical axis.

The asymmetrical pixel grid of the EGA and of other less refined video standards introduces programming complications. For example, in a symmetrical VGA screen a square figure can be drawn using lines of the same pixel length, but these lines would produce a rectangle in an asymmetrical system. By the same token, the pixel pattern of a circle in a symmetrical system will appear as an ellipse in an asymmetrical one. (See Figure 2.1.)

The major limitations of the VGA system are resolution, color range, and performance. VGA density of 80 pixels per inch is a substantial improvement in relation to its predecessors the CGA and the EGA, but still not very high when compared to the 300 dots per inch of a typical laser printer, or the 1200 and 2400 dots per inch of an imagesetter. The low resolution is one reason why VGA screen images are often not lifelike; bit maps appear grainy and we can often detect that geometrical figures consist of straight-line segments, as is the case in the conic curves shown in color plate number 2. In regards to color range VGA can display up to 256 simultaneous colors; however, this color range is not available in the mode with the best resolution. (See Table 1.1.) In other words, the VGA programmer must chose between an 80 pixels per inch resolution in 16 colors (mode number 18) or 40 pixels per inch resolution in 256 colors (mode number 19).

But perhaps the greatest limitation of the VGA standard is its performance. The video display update operations in VGA detract from general system efficiency, since it is the microprocessor that must execute all video read and write operations. In the second place, the video functions execute slowly when compared to dedicated graphics work stations. This slowness is particularly noticeable in the graphics modes, in which a full screen redraw can take several seconds. Most animated programs, which must update portions of the screen at a rapid rate, execute in VGA with a jolting effect that is unnatural and visually disturbing.

2.0.2 VGA Modes

The original video systems used in IBM microcomputers, such as CGA, MDA, and EGA, had monitor-specific modes. For example, the CGA turns the color burst off in modes 0, 2, and 4 and on in modes 1, 3, and 5. Mode number 7 is available in the Monochrome Display Adapter (MDA) and in an Enhanced Graphics Adapter (EGA) equipped with a monochrome display, but not in the CGA or EGA systems equipped with color monitors. In the VGA standard, on the other hand, the video modes are independent of the monitor. For example, a VGA equipped with any one of the standard direct drive color monitors can execute in monochrome mode number 7. Table 2.1 lists the properties of the VGA video modes.

Table 2.1 *VGA Video Modes*

mode	number of colors	type	text columns/rows	text pixel box	screen pages	buffer address	screen pixels
0,1	16	Alpha	40 by 25	8 x 8 8 x 14 * 9 x 16 +	8	B8000H	320 by 200 320 by 350 360 by 400
2,3	16	Alpha	80 by 25	8 x 8 8 x 14 * 9 x 16 +	8	B8000H	320 by 200 320 by 350 360 by 400
4,5	4	GRA	40 by 25	8 x 8	1	A0000H	320 by 200
6	2	GRA	80 by 25	8 x 8	1	A0000H	640 by 200
7	-	Alpha	80 by 28	9 x 14 9 x 16 +	8	B0000H	720 by 350 720 by 400
13	16	GRA	40 by 25	8 x 8	8	A0000H	320 by 200
14	16	GRA	80 by 25	8 x 8	4	A0000H	640 by 200
15	-	GRA	80 by 25	8 x 14	2	A0000H	640 by 350
16	16	GRA	80 by 25	8 x 14	2	A0000H	640 by 350
17	2	GRA	80 by 30	8 x 16	1	A0000H	640 by 480
18	16	GRA	80 by 30	8 x 16	1	A0000H	640 by 480
19	256	GRA	40 by 25	8 x 8	1	A0000H	320 by 200

Legend:
Alpha = alphanumeric modes (text)
GRA = graphics modes
  * = EGA enhanced modes
  + = VGA enhanced modes

In Table 2.1 we have used decimal numbers for the video modes. Our rationale is that video modes are a conventional ordering scheme used in organizing common hardware and software characteristics of a video system, therefore we can see no reason for using hexadecimal notation in numbering these modes. Consequently, throughout the book, we have used decimal numbers for video modes, offset values, and other forms of sequential orders that do not require binary or hexadecimal notation.

Observe in Table 2.1 that the VGA buffer can start in any one of three possible addresses: B0000H, B8000H, and A0000H. Address B000H is used only when mode 7 is enabled, in this case VGA is emulating the Monochrome Display Adapter. In enhanced mode number 7 the VGA displays its highest horizontal resolution (720 pixels) and uses a 9 by 16 dots text font. However, in this mode the VGA is capable of text display only. Buffer address A000H is active while VGA is in a graphics modes. Also note that the video modes number 17 and 18, with 480 pixel rows, were introduced with the VGA and MCGA standards. Therefore they are not available in CGA and EGA systems. Modes 17 and 18 offer a symmetrical pixel density of 640-by-480 screen dots. (See Figure 2.1.) Mode number 19 has 256 simultaneous colors, the most extensive one in the VGA standard, however, its linnear resolution is half of the one in mode number 18.

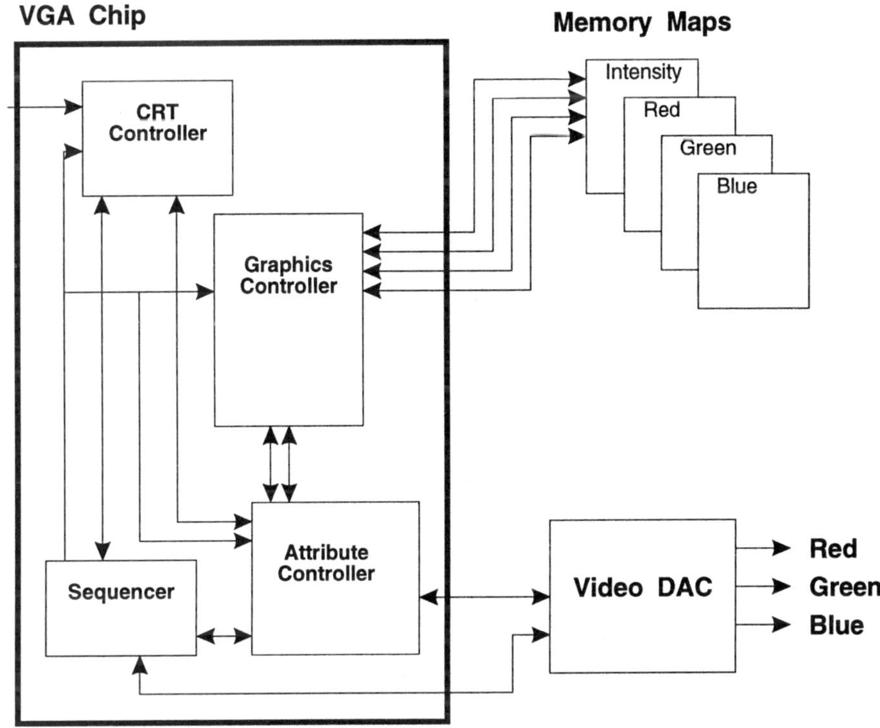

Figure 2.2   *Elements of the VGA System*

2.1 VGA Components

The VGA system is divided into three identifiable components: the VGA chip, video memory, and a Digital-to-Analog Converter (DAC). Figure 2.2 shows the interconnections between the elements of the VGA system.

2.1.1 Video Memory

All VGA systems contain the 256K of video memory that is part of the hardware. This memory is logically arranged in four 64K blocks that form the video maps (labeled blue, green, red, and intensity in Figure 2.2). The four maps are sometimes referred to as bit planes 0 to 3.

In EGA systems the display buffer consists of a 64K RAM chip installed in the card itself. Up to three more 64K blocks of video memory can be optionally added on the piggyback memory expansion card. The maximum memory supported by EGA is 256K divided into four 64K blocks.

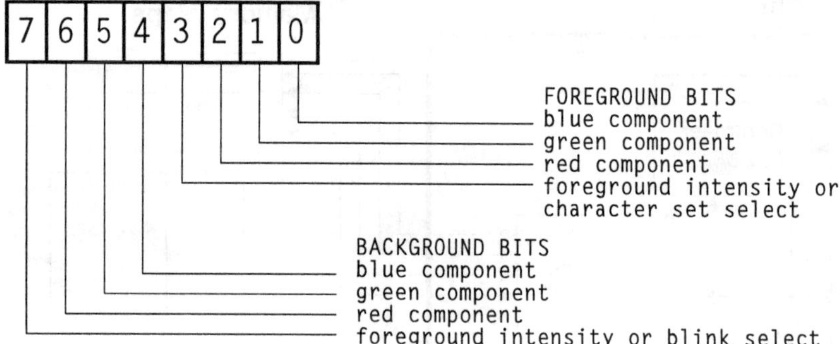

Figure 2.3 *Functions of the Attribute Byte in VGA Systems*

Alphanumeric Modes

In the alphanumeric modes 0, 1, 2, 3, and 7 the VGA video buffer is structured to hold character codes and attribute bytes. (See Table 2.1.) The organization of the video buffer in the alphanumeric modes was discussed in Chapter 1 (see Section 1.3.1). The default functions of the bits in the attribute byte can be seen in Figures 1.11 and 1.12. However, the VGA standard allows redefining two of the attribute bits in the color alphanumeric modes: bit 7 can be redefined to control the background intensity and bit 3 can be redefined to perform a character-set select operation. Figure 2.3 shows the VGA attribute byte, including the two re-definable bits.

The programmer can toggle the functions assigned to bits 3 and 7 of the attribute byte by means of BIOS service calls or by programming the VGA registers. These operations are performed by the VGA graphics library on the furnished microdisk. The VGA library is described in Chapter 3.

Graphics Modes

One of the problems confronted by the designers of the VGA system was the limited memory space of an IBM microcomputers under MS DOS. Recall that in VGA mode number 18 the video screen is composed of 480 rows of 640 pixels per row, for a total of 307,200 screen pixels. (See Table 2.1.) If eight pixels are encoded per memory byte, each color map would take up approximately 38K, and the four maps required to encode 16 colors available in this mode would need approximately 154K. The VGA designers were able to reduce this memory space by using a latching mechanism that maps all four color maps to the same memory area. Figure 2.4 is a diagram of the video memory structure in VGA mode number 18.

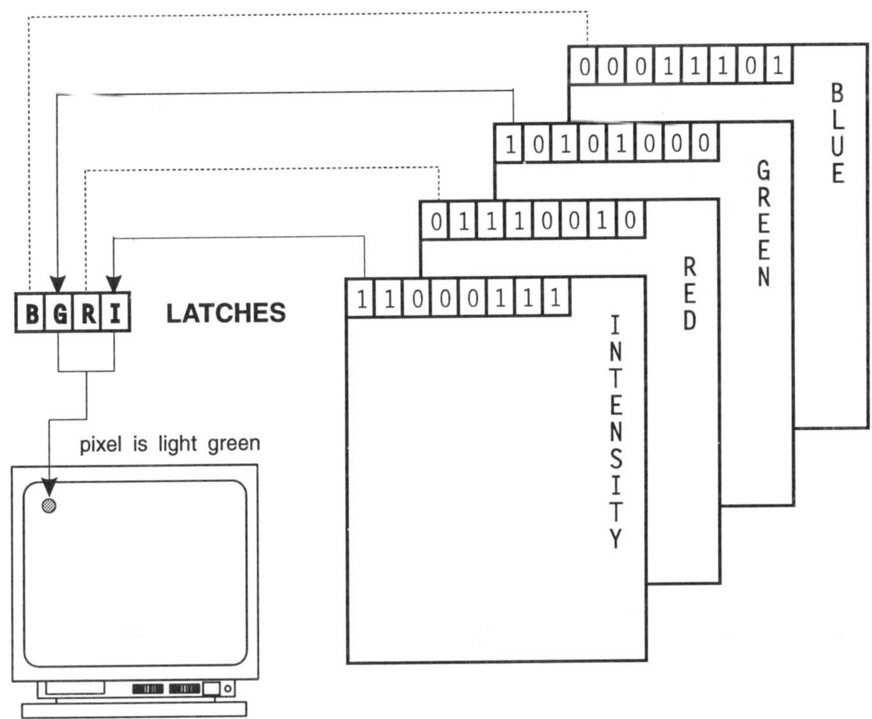

Figure 2.4 *VGA Video Memory Mapping in Mode Number 18*

Figure 2.4 shows how the color of a single screen pixel is stored in four memory maps, located at the same physical address. Note that the color codes for the first eight screen pixels are stored in the four maps labeled Intensity, Red, Green, and Blue. In VGA mode number 18 all four maps are located at address A0000H. The first screen pixel has the intensity bit and the green bit set, therefore it appears light green. For the same reason, the second pixel, mapped to the subsequent bits in the video buffer, will be displayed as light red, since it has the red and the intensity bits set.

VGA memory mapping changes in the different alphanumeric and graphics modes. In Figure 2.4 we see that in mode number 18 the color of each screen pixel is determined by the bit settings in four memory maps. However, in mode number 19, in which VGA can display 256 colors, each screen pixel is determined by one video buffer byte. Figure 2.5 shows the memory mapping in VGA mode number 19. In reality VGA uses all four bit planes to store video data in mode number 19, but, to the programmer, the buffer appears as a linear space starting at address A000H. The color value assigned to each pixel in the 256-color modes is explained in Chapter 3.

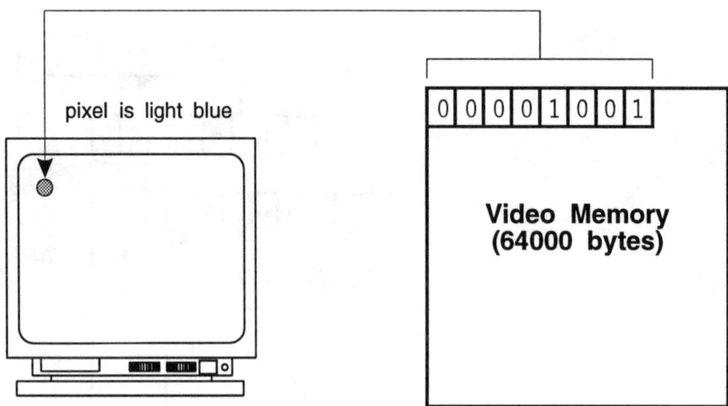

Figure 2.5 *VGA Video Memory Mapping in Mode Number 19*

Many VGA graphics modes were created to insure compatibility with previous video systems. Specifically: VGA graphics modes number 4, 5, and 6 are compatible with modes in the CGA, EGA, and PCjr; modes number 13, 14, 15, and 16 are compatible with EGA, and graphics mode number 17 (a two-color version of mode number 18) was created for compatibility with the MCGA standard. This leaves two proprietary VGA modes: mode numbers 18 with 640-by-480 pixels in 16 colors, and mode number 19, with 320-by-200 pixels in 256 colors. It is in these two most powerful VGA modes that we will concentrate our attention.

2.2 VGA Registers

We have seen that the VGA system includes a chip containing several registers, a memory space dedicated to video functions, and a digital-to-analog converter (see Figure 2.2). The VGA registers are mapped to the system's address space and accessed by means of the central processor. The VGA programmable registers (excluding the DAC) belong to five groups:

1. The General registers. This group is sometimes called the *external registers* due to the fact that, on the EGA, they were located outside the VLSI chip. The general registers provide miscellaneous and control functions.

2. The CRT Controller registers. This group of registers control the timing and synchronization of the video signal. Also the cursor size and position.

3. The Sequencer registers. This group of registers control data flow into the Attribute Controller, generate the timing pulses for the dynamic RAMs, and arbitrate memory accesses between the CPU and the video system. The Map Mask registers in the Sequencer allow the protection of entire memory maps.

Table 2.2 *VGA Register Groups*

| | | | EMULATING | |
REGISTER	READ/ WRITE	MDA	CGA	EITHER
GENERAL REGISTERS				
1. Miscellaneous output	Write Read			03C2H 03CCH
2. Input status 0	Read			03C2H
3. Input status 1	Read	03BAH	03DAH	
4. Feature control	Write Read	03BAH	03DAH	 03CAH
5. Video Subsystem enable	R/W			03C3H
6. DAC state	Read			03C7H
CRT CONTROLLER REGISTERS				
1. Index	R/W	03B4H	03D4H	
2. Other CRT Controller	R/W	03B5H	03D5H	
SEQUENCER REGISTERS				
1. Address	R/W			03C4H
2. Other	R/W			03C5H
GRAPHICS CONTROLLER REGISTERS				
1. Address	R/W			03CEH
2. Other	R/W			03CFH
ATTRIBUTE CONTROLLER REGISTERS				
1. Address	R/W			03C0H
2. Other	Write Read			03C0H 03C1H

4. The Graphics Controller registers. This group of registers provide an interface between the system microprocessor, the Attribute Controller, and video memory, while VGA is in a graphics mode.

5. The Attribute Controller registers. This group of registers determines the characteristics of the character display in the alphanumeric modes and the pixel color in the graphics modes.

Table 2.2 shows the VGA register groups and their respective port mapping.

2.2.1 The General Registers

The General registers, called the External registers in EGA, are used primarily in initialization of the video system and in mode setting. Most applications let the system software handle the initialization of the video functions controlled by the General registers. For example, the easiest and most reliable way for setting a video mode is BIOS service number 0, of interrupt 10H. Figure 2.6 and Figure 2.7 show some programmable elements in the VGA General Register group.

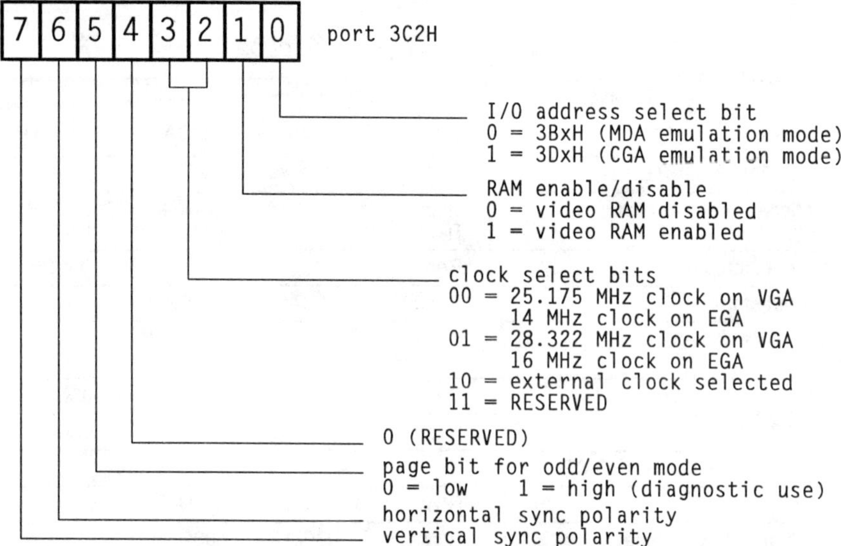

Figure 2.6 *EGA/VGA Miscellaneous Output Register*

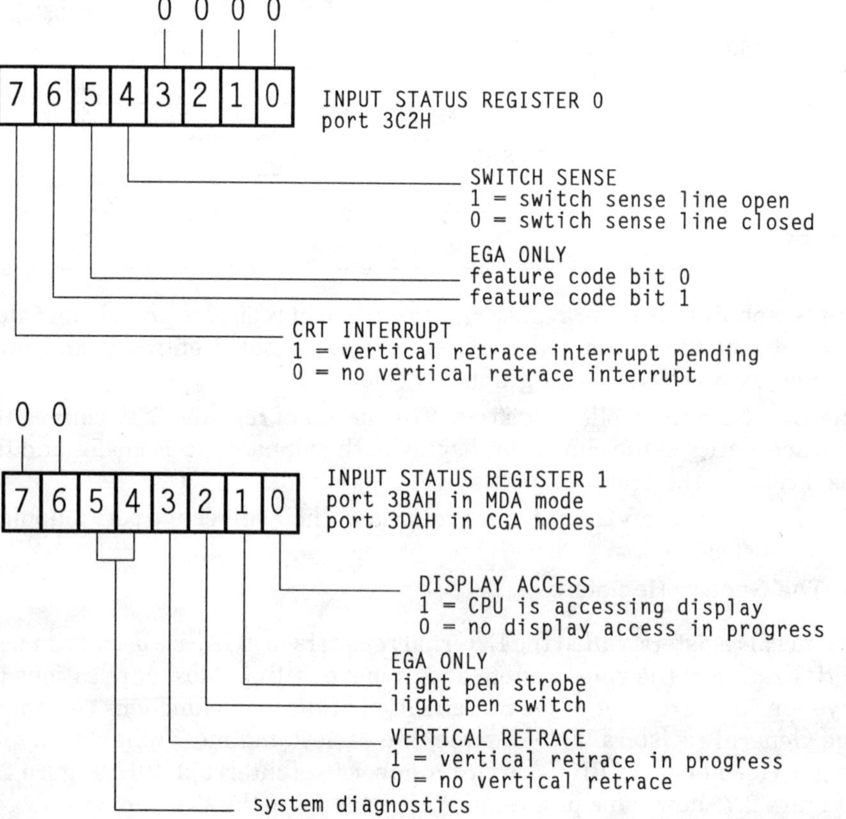

Figure 2.7 *VGA Input Status Registers*

Table 2.3 *VGA CRT Controller Register*

PORT	OFFSET	DESCRIPTION
03X4H		Address register
03x5H	0	Total horizontal characters minus 2 (EGA)
		Total horizontal characters minus 5 (VGA)
	1	Horizontal display end characters minus 1
	2	Start horizontal blanking
	3	End horizontal blanking
	4	Start horizontal retrace pulse
	5	End horizontal retrace pulse
	6	Total vertical scan lines
	7	CRTC overflow
	8 *	Preset row scan
	9	Maximum scan line
	10 *	Scan line for cursor start
	11 *	Scan line for cursor end
	12 *	Video buffer start address, high byte
	13 *	Video buffer start address, low byte
	14 *	Cursor location, high byte
	15 *	Cursor location, low byte
	16	Vertical retrace start
	17	Vertical retrace end
	18	Last scan line of vertical display
	19	Additional word offset to next logical line
	20	Scan line for underline character
	21	Scan line to start vertical blanking
	22	Scan line to end vertical blanking
	23	CRTC mode control
	24	Line compare register

Notes: Registers signaled with (*) are described separately
3x4H/3x5H = 3B4H/3B5H when emulating the MDA
3x4H/3x5H = 3D4H/3D5H when emulating the CGA

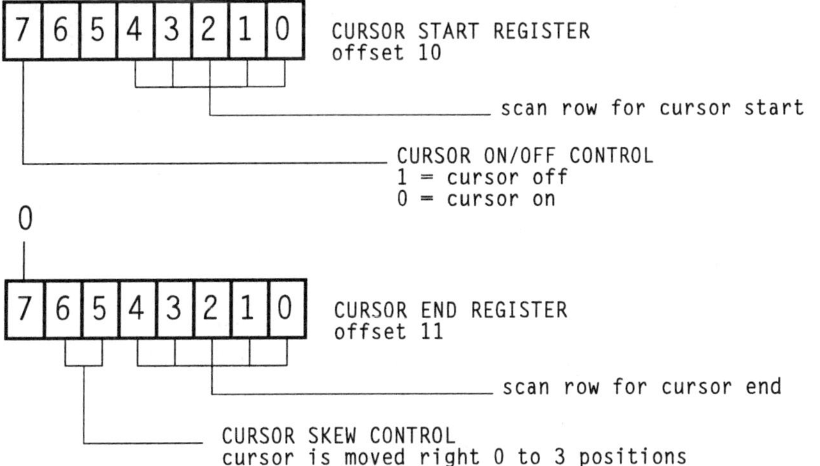

Figure 2.8 *VGA Cursor Size Register of the CRT Controller*

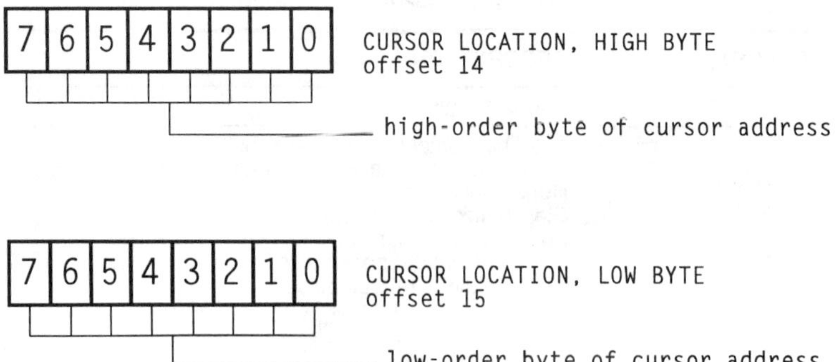

Figure 2.9 *VGA Cursor Location Registers of the CRT Controller*

Note that bit number 7 of Input Status Register 0, at port 3C2H is used in determining the start of the vertical retrace cycle of the CRT controller. (See Figure 2.7.) This operation is sometimes necessary to avoid interference when updating the video buffer. The procedure named TIME_VRC, in the VGA module of the GRAPHSOL library, described in Chapter 3, performs this timing operation.

2.2.2 The CRT Controller

The VGA CRT Controller register group is the equivalent of the Motorola 6845 CRT Controller chip of the PC line. When VGA is emulating the MDA, the port address of the CRT Controller is 3B4H, when it is emulating the CGA then the port address is 3D4H. These ports are the same as those used by the MDA and the CGA cards. Table 2.3 lists the registers in the CRT Controller group.
Most registers in the CRT Controller are modified only during mode changes. Since this operation is frequently performed by means of a BIOS service, most programs will not access the CRT Controller registers directly. The exception are the CRT Controller registers related to cursor size and position, which are occasionally programmed directly. The Cursor Size register is shown in Figure 2.8. and the Cursor Location register in Figure 2.9.
Figure 2.10 graphically shows the cursor scan lines and the default setting in a 8-by-14 pixel text mode. (See Table 2.1.)
A program can change the cursor size in alphanumeric modes using service number 1 of BIOS interrupt 10H or by programming the CRT Controller cursor register directly. The use of BIOS service number 10, interrupt 10H, is discussed in Appendix C. The following code fragment shows a sequence of instructions for programming the CRT Controller cursor size registers. The action performed by the code is to change the VGA default cursor in a 8-by-14 text mode from scan lines 12 and 13 to scan lines 1 to 7.

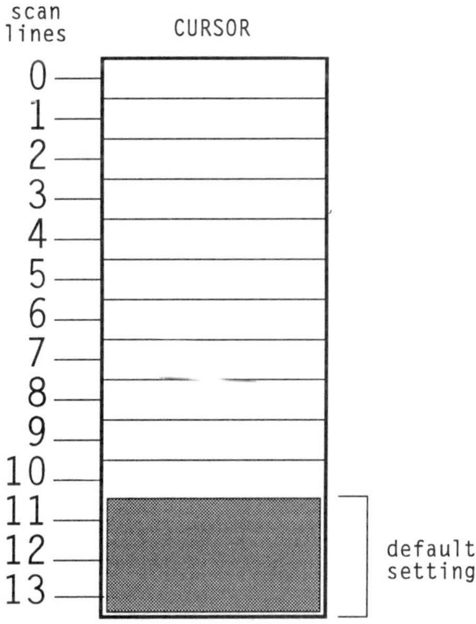

Figure 2.10 *Cursor Scan Lines in VGA Systems*

```
MOV     DX,3B4H          ; VGA CRTC address register
                         ; in the MDA emulation modes
MOV     AL,10            ; Cursor start register number
OUT     DX,AL            ; Select this register
MOV     DX,3B5H          ; CRTC registers
MOV     AL,1             ; Start scan line for new cursor
OUT     DX,AL            ; Set in 6845 register
MOV     DX,3B4H          ; Address register again
MOV     AL,11            ; Cursor end register number
OUT     DX,AL            ; Select this register
MOV     DX,3B5H          ; CRTC registers
MOV     AL,7             ; End scan line for new cursor
OUT     DX,AL            ; Set in 6845 register
```

The cursor location on an alphanumeric mode can also be set using a BIOS service or programming the CRT Controller registers directly. BIOS service number 0, interrupt 10H, allows setting the cursor to any desired column and row address. Alternatively the cursor can be repositioned by setting the contents of the cursor address registers on the VGA CRT Controller. The cursor address registers are located at offset 14 and 15 respectively. The following code fragment will position the cursor at the start of the third screen row. The code assumes an 80-by-25 alphanumeric mode in the Monochrome Display Adapter.

The offset of the second row is calculated as 80 x 2 = 160 bytes from the start of the adapter RAM. Consequently, the Cursor Address High register must be zeroed and the Cursor Address Low register set to 160.

```
        MOV     DX,3B4H         ; VGA CRTC address register
                                ; in the MDA emulation mode
        MOV     AL,14           ; Cursor Address High register
        OUT     DX,AL           ; Select this register
        MOV     DX,3B5H         ; CRTC registers
        MOV     AL,0            ; Zero high bit of address
        OUT     DX,AL           ; Set in CRTC register
        MOV     DX,3B4H         ; Address register again
        MOV     AL,15           ; Cursor Address Low register
        OUT     DX,AL           ; Select this register
        MOV     DX,3B5H         ; CRTC programmable registers
        MOV     AL,160          ; 160 bytes from adapter start
        OUT     DX,AL           ; Set in 6845 register
; Cursor now set at the start of the third screen row
```

Another group of registers within the CRT Controller that are occasionally programmed directly are those that determine the start address of the screen window in the video buffer. This manipulation is sometimes used in scrolling and panning text and graphics screens. In VGA systems the CRT Controller Start Address High and Start Address Low registers (offset 0CH and 0DH) locate the screen window within a byte offset, while the Preset Row Scan register (offset 08H) locates the window at the closest pixel row. Therefore the Preset Row Scan register is used to determine the vertical pixel offset of the screen window. The horizontal pixel offset of the screen window is programmed by changing the value stored in the Horizontal Pixel Pan register of the Attribute Controller, described later in this chapter. Figure 2.11 shows the Start Address registers of the CRT Controller. Figure 2.12 is a bitmap of the Preset Row Scan register.

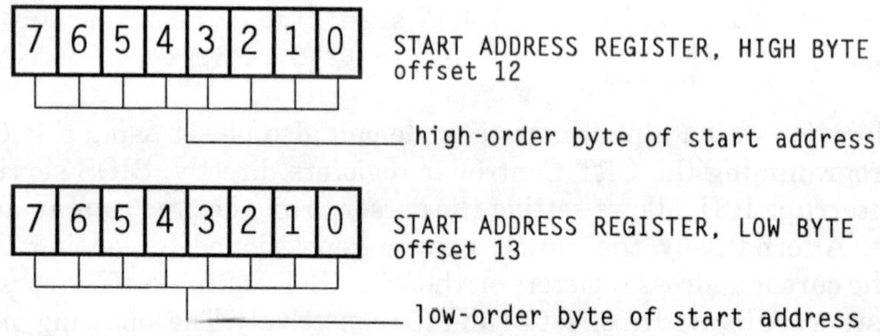

Figure 2.11 *VGA Video Start Address Register of the CRT Controller*

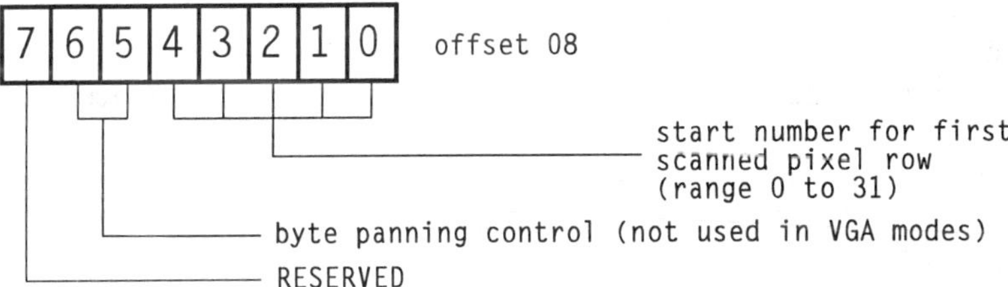

Figure 2.12 *VGA Preset Row Scan Register of the CRT Controller*

2.2.3 The Sequencer

The VGA Sequencer register group controls memory fetch operations and provides timing signals for the dynamic RAMs. This allows the microprocessor to access video memory in cycles inserted between the display memory cycles. Table 2.4 shows the registers in the VGA Sequencer.

Table 2.4 *The VGA Sequencer Registers*

PORT	OFFSET	DESCRIPTION
03C4H		Address register
03C5H	0	Synchronous or Asynchronous reset
	1	Clocking Mode
	2 *	Map Mask
	3 *	Character Map Select
	4 *	Memory Mode

Note: Registers signaled with an (*) are described separately

The Map Mask register in the Sequencer group allow the protection of any specific memory map by masking it from the microprocessor and from the Character Map select register. Figure 2.13 is a bitmap of the Map Mask register.

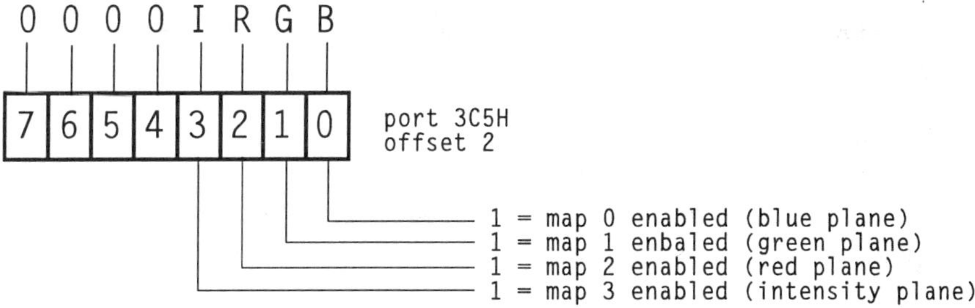

Figure 2.13 *VGA Map Mask Register of the Sequencer*

If VGA is in a color graphic mode, the Map Mask register can be used to select the color at which one or more pixels are displayed. The color is encoded in the IRGB format, as shown in Figure 2.13. To program the Map Mask register we must first load the value 2 into the address register of the Sequencer, at port 3C4H. This value corresponds to the offset of the Map Mask register (see Table 2.4). After the pixel or pixels have been set, the Map Mask register should be restored to its default value (0FH). The following code fragment shows the usual program operations:

```
; Setting 8 bright-red pixels in VGA mode number 18
; The code assumes that video mode number 18 is selected,
; that ES is set to the video segment base, and that BX points
; to the offset of the first pixel to be set
;
;**********************|
;    select register   |
;**********************|
        MOV     DX,3C4H          ; Address register of Sequencer
        MOV     AL,2             ; Offset of the Map Mask
        OUT     DX,AL            ; Map Mask selected
        MOV     DX,3C5H          ; Data to Map Mask
        MOV     AL,00001100B     ; Intensity and red bits set
                                 ; in IRGB encoding
        OUT     DX,AL            ; Map Mask = 0000 IR00
;**********************|
;        set pixels    |
;**********************|
; Setting the pixels consists of writing a 1 bit in the
; corresponding buffer address.
        MOV     AL,ES:[BX]       ; Dummy read operation
        MOV     AL,11111111B     ; Set all bits
        MOV     ES:[BX],AL       ; Write to video buffer
;**********************|
;    restore Map Mask  |
;**********************|
; Restore the Map Mask to the default state
        MOV     DX,3C4H          ; Address register of Sequencer
        MOV     AL,02H           ; Offset of the Map Mask
        OUT     DX,AL            ; Map Mask selected
        MOV     DX,3C5H          ; Data to Map Mask
        MOV     AL,00001111B     ; Default IRGB code for Map Mask
        OUT     DX,AL            ; Map mask = 0000 IRGB
```

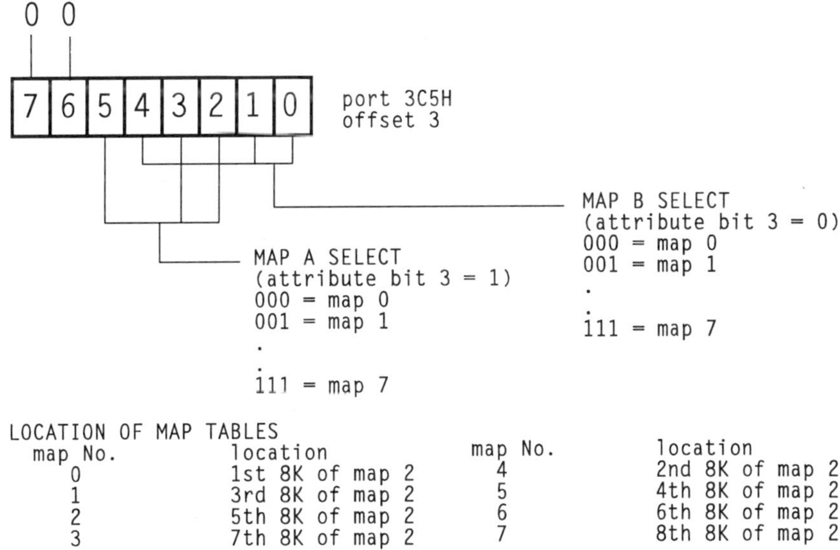

Figure 2.14 *VGA Character Map Select Register of the Sequencer*

The use of the Character Map Select register of the Sequencer is related to reprogramming of bit 3 of the attribute byte so that it will serve to select one of two character sets. (See Figure 2.3.) Normally the character maps, named A and B, have the same value and bit 3 of the attribute byte is used to control the bright or normal display of the character foreground. In this case only one set of 256 characters is available. However, when the Character Map Select register is programmed so that character maps A and B have different values, then bit 3 of the attribute byte is used to toggle between two sets of 256

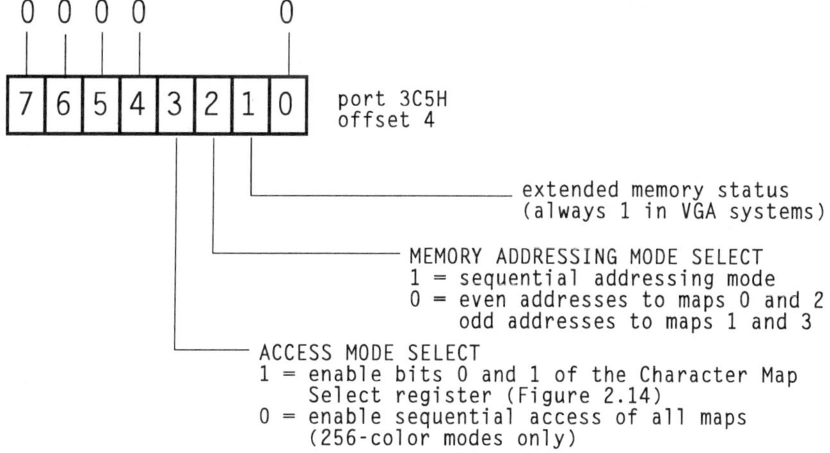

Figure 2.15   *VGA Memory Mode Register of the Sequencer*

characters each. The programming operations necessary for using multiple VGA character sets is described in Chapter 3. Figure 2.14 is a bitmap of the Character Map Select register.

The Memory Mode register of the sequencer is related to the display modes. Most programs will leave the setting of this register to the BIOS mode select services. Figure 2.15 shows a bitmap of the Memory Mode register.

2.2.4 The Graphics Controller

The registers in the Graphics Controller group serve to interface video memory with the Attribute Controller and with the system microprocessor. The Graphic Controller is bypassed in the alphanumeric modes. Table 2.5 lists the registers in the VGA Graphics Controller group. All the registers in the Graphics Controller are of interest to the graphics applications programmer.

Table 2.5   *The VGA Graphics Controller Registers*

PORT	OFFSET	DESCRIPTION
03CEH		Address register
03CFH	0	Set/Reset
	1	Enable Set/Reset
	2	Color compare for read mode 1 operation
	3	Data rotate
	4	Read operation map select
	5	Select graphics mode
	6	Miscellaneous operations
	7	Read mode 1 color don't care
	8	Bit mask

The Set/Reset register of the Graphics Controller may be used to permanently set or clear a specific bit plane. This operation can be useful if the programmer desires to write a specific color to the entire screen or to disable a color map. The Set/Reset register, shown in Figure 2.16, affects only write mode 0 operations. The use of the Set/Reset register requires the use of the Enable Set/Reset register. Enable Set/Reset determines which of the maps is accessed by the Set/Reset register. This mechanism provides a double-level control over the four maps. The Enable Set/Reset register is shown in Figure 2.17.

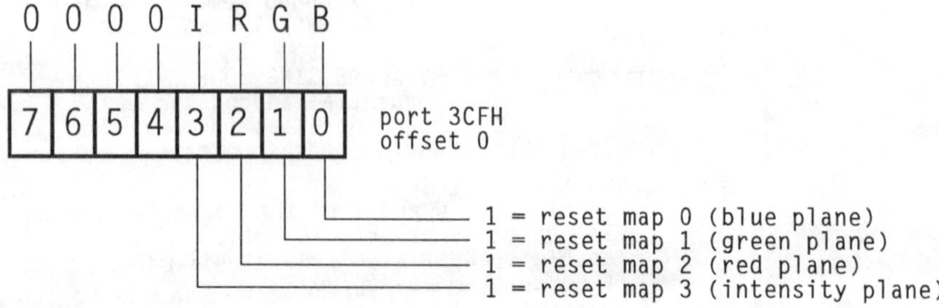

Figure 2.16 *VGA Write Mode 0 Set/Reset Register of the Graphics Controller*

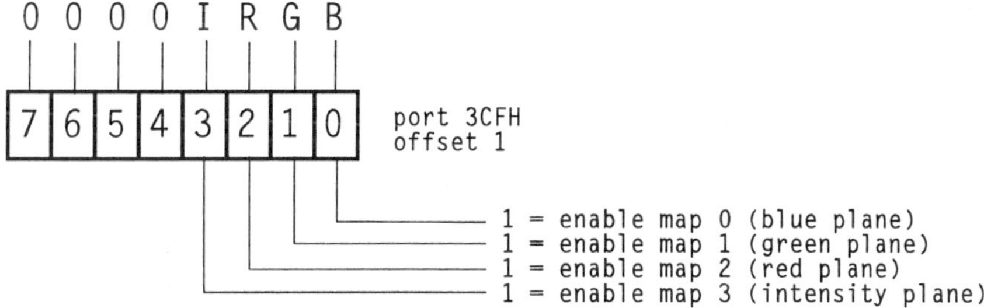

Figure 2.17 *VGA Enable Set/Reset Register of the Graphics Controller*

The Color Compare register of the Graphics Controller group, shown in Figure 2.18, is used during read mode 1 operations to test for the presence of memory bits that match one or more color maps. For example, if a program sets bit 0 (blue) and bit 3 (intensity) of the Color Compare register, a subsequent memory read operation will show a 1-value for those pixels whose intensity and blue maps are set, while all other combinations will be reported with a zero value. One or more bit planes can be excluded from the compare by clearing (value equal zero) the corresponding bit in the Color Don't Care register. For example, if the intensity bit is zero in the Color Don't Care register, a color compare operation for the blue bit map will be positive for all pixels in blue or bright blue color. The Color Don't Care register is shown in Figure 2.19.

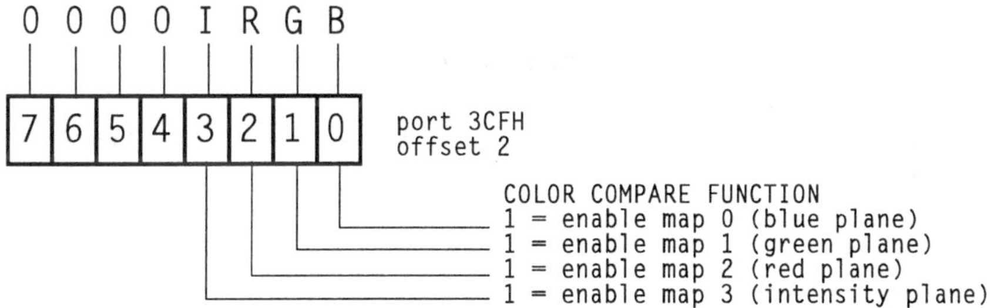

Figure 2.18 *VGA Color Compare Register of the Graphics Controller*

The Data Rotate register of the Graphics Controller determines how data is combined with data latched in the system microprocessor registers. The possible logical operations are AND, OR, and XOR. If bits 3 and 4 are reset, data is unmodified. A second function of this register is to right-rotate data from 0 to 7 places. This function is controlled by bits 0 to 2. The Data Rotate register is shown in Figure 2.20.

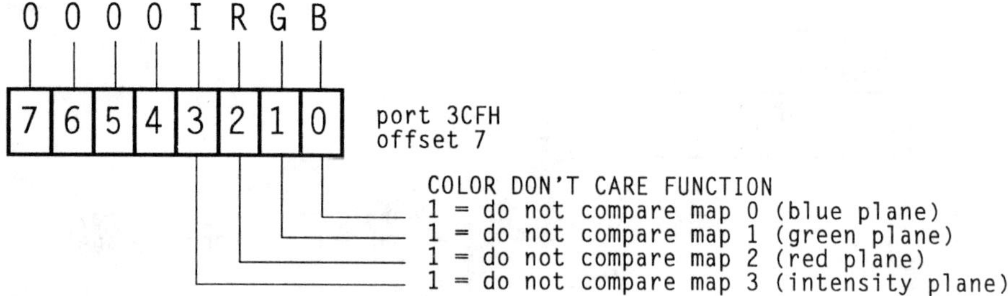

Figure 2.19 *VGA Color Don't Care Register of the Graphics Controller*

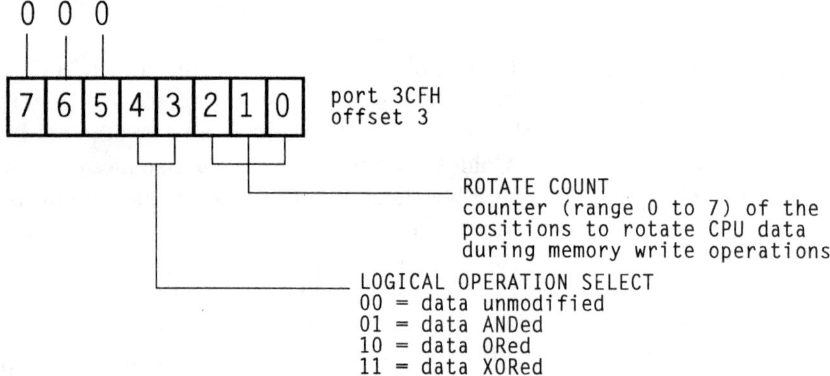

Figure 2.20 *VGA Data Rotate Register of the Graphics Controller*

We have seen that VGA video memory in the graphics modes is based on encoding the color of a single pixel into several memory maps. The Read Map Select register, in Figure 2.21, is used to determine which map is read by the system microprocessor.

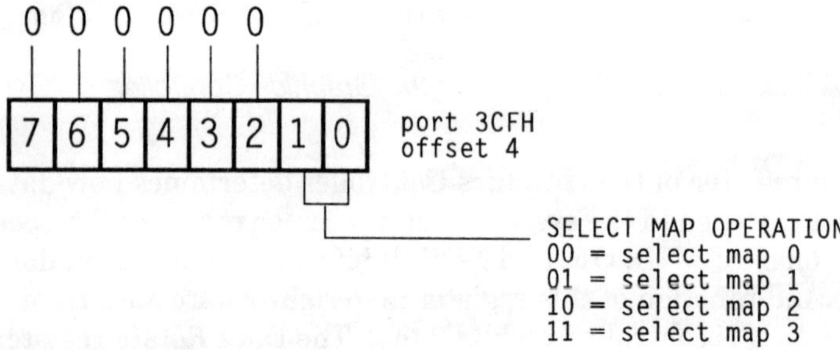

Figure 2.21 *VGA Read Map Select Register of the Graphics Controller*

The following code fragment shows the use of the Read Operation Map Select register:

```
; Code to read the contents of the 4 color maps in VGA mode 18
; Code assumes that read mode 0 has been previously set
; On entry:
;                     ES = A000H
;                     BX = byte offset into video map
; On exit:
;                     CL = byte stored in intensity map
;                     CH = byte stored in red map
;                     DL = byte stored in green map
;                     DH = byte stored in blue map
;
; Set counter and map selector
        MOV     CX,4         ; Counter for 4 maps to read
        MOV     DI,0         ; Map selector code
READ_IRGB:
; Select map from which to read
        MOV     DX,3CEH      ; Graphic Controller Address
                             ; register
        MOV     AL,4         ; Read Operation Map Select
        OUT     DX,AL        ; register
;
        INC     DX           ; Graphic controller at 3CFH
        MOV     AX,DI        ; AL = map selector code (in DI)
        OUT     DX,AL        ; IRGB color map selected
; Read 8 bits from selected map
        MOV     AL,ES:[BX]   ; Get byte from bit plane
        PUSH    AX           ; Store it in the stack
        INC     DI           ; Bump selector to next map
        LOOP    READ_IRGB    ; Execute loop 4 times
; 4 maps are stored in stack
; Retrieve maps into exit registers
        POP     AX           ; B map byte in AL
        MOV     DH,AL        ; Move B map byte to DH
        POP     AX           ; G map byte in AL
        MOV     DL,AL        ; Move G map byte to DL
        POP     AX           ; R map byte in AL
        MOV     CH,AL        ; Move R map byte to CH
        POP     AX           ; I map byte in AL
        MOV     CL,AL        ; Move I map byte to CL

                .
                .

                .
```

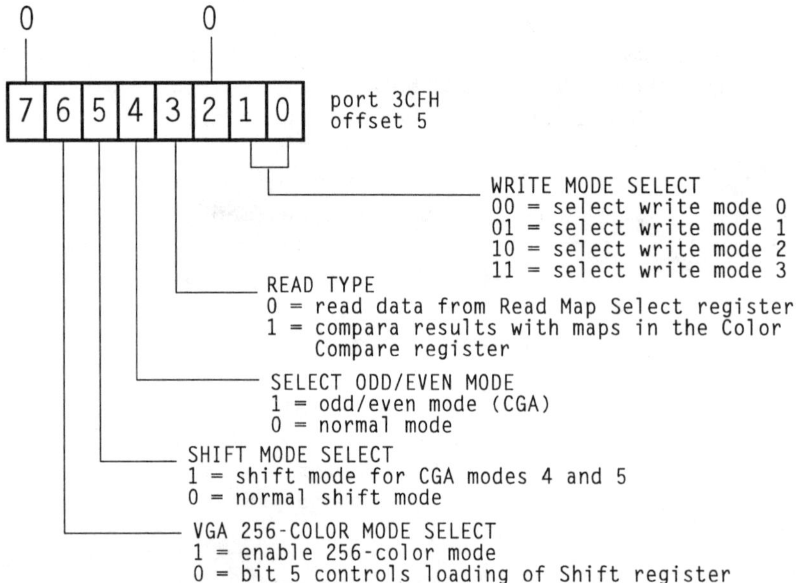

Figure 2.22 *VGA Select Graphics Mode Register of the Graphics Controller*

VGA systems allow several ways for performing memory read and write operations, usually known as the read and write modes. The Select Graphics Mode register of the Graphics Controller group allows the programmer to select which of two read and four write modes is presently active. The Select Graphics Mode register is shown in Figure 2.22.

The four VGA write modes can be described as follows:

Write mode 0 is the default write mode. In this write mode, the Map Mask register of the Sequencer group, the Bit Mask register of the Graphics Controller group, and the CPU, are used to set the screen pixel to a desired color.

In *write mode 1* the contents of the latch registers are first loaded by performing a read operation, then copied directly onto the color maps by performing a write operation. This mode is often used in moving areas of memory.

Write mode 2, a simplified version of write mode 0, also allows setting an individual pixel to any desired color. However, in write mode 2 the color code is contained in the CPU byte.

In *write mode 3* the byte in the CPU is ANDed with the contents of the Bit Mask register of the Graphic Controller.

The write mode is selected by setting bits 0 and 1 of the Graphic Controller's Graphic Mode register. It is a good programming practice to preserve the remaining bits in this register when modifying bits 0 and 1. This is performed by reading the Graphic Mode register, altering the write mode bits, and then resetting the register without changing the remaining bits. The following code fragment sets a write mode in a VGA system. The remaining bits in the Select Graphics Mode register are preserved.

```
; Set the Graphics Controller's Select Graphic Mode register
; to the write mode in the AH register
        MOV     DX,3CEH         ; Graphic Controller Address
                                ; register
        MOV     AL,5            ; Offset of the Mode register
        OUT     DX,AL           ; Select this register
        INC     DX              ; Point to Data register
        TN      AL,DX           ; Read register contents
        AND     AL,11111100B    ; Clear bits 0 and 1
        OR      AL,AH           ; Set mode in AL low bits
        MOV     DX,3CEH         ; Address register
        MOV     AL,5            ; Offset of the Mode Register
        OUT     DX,AL           ; Select again
        INC     DX              ; Point to Data register
        OUT     DX,AL           ; Output to Mode Register
; Note: the Select Mode register is read-only in EGA systems
;       therefore this code will not work correctly
```

Note that bit 6 of the Graphics Mode Register must be set for 256-color modes and cleared for the remaining ones. The SET_WRITE_256 procedure in the VGA module of the VGA graphics library sets write mode 0 and the 256-color bit so that VGA mode number 19, in 256 colors, operates correctly. (See Chapter 3.) Once a write mode is selected the program can access video memory to set the desired screen pixels, as in the following code fragment:

```
; Write mode 2 pixel setting routine
; On entry:
;                   ES = A000H
;                   BX = byte offset into the video buffer
;                   AL = pixel color in IRGB format
;                   AH = bit pattern to set (mask)
;
; Note: this procedure does not reset the default read or write
; modes or the contents of the Bit Mask register.
; The code assumes that write mode 2 has been set previously
        PUSH    AX          ; Color byte
        PUSH    AX          ; Twice
;*********************|
;      set bit mask   |
;*********************|
; Set Bit Mask register according to value in AH
```

```
        MOV      DX,3CEH      ; Graphic controller address
        MOV      AL,8         ; Offset = 8
        OUT      DX,AL        ; Select Bit Mask register
        INC      DX           ; To 3CFH
        POP      AX           ; Color code once from stack
        MOV      AL,AH        ; Bit pattern
        OUT      DX,AL        ; Load bit mask
;********************|
;    write color     |
;********************|
        MOV      AL,ES:[BX]   ; Dummy read to load latch
                              ; registers
        POP      AX           ; Restore color code
        MOV      ES:[BX],AL   ; Write the pixel with the
                              ; color code in AL
        .
        .
        .
```

The VGA also provides two read modes. In read mode 0, which is the default read mode, the CPU is loaded with the contents of one of the color maps. In read mode 1, the contents of the maps are compared with a predetermined value before being loaded into the CPU. The active read mode depends on the setting of bit 3 of the Graphic Mode Select register, in the Graphics Controller. (See Figure 2.22.) The SET_READ_MODE procedure in the VGA1 module of the graphics library performs this operation (see Chapter 3).

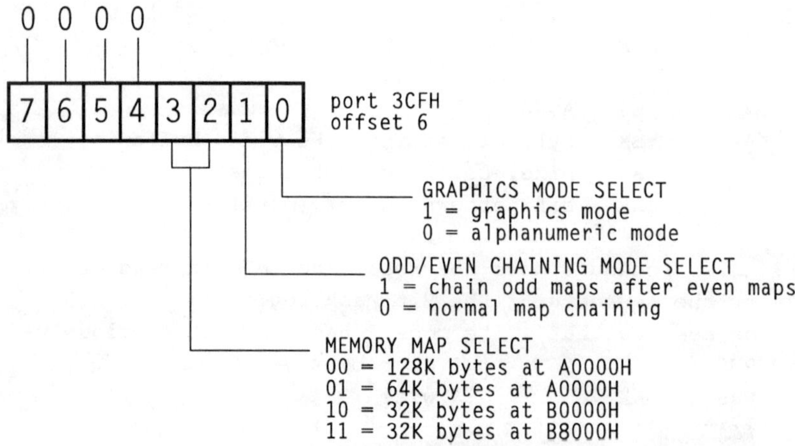

Figure 2.23   *VGA Miscellaneous Register of the Graphics Controller*

The Miscellaneous register of the Graphics Controller, in Figure 2.23, is used in conjunction with the Select Graphics Modes register to enable specific graphics function. Bits 2 and 3 of the Miscellaneous register control the mapping of the video buffer in the system's memory space. The normal mapping of each mode con be seen in the buffer address column of Table 1.1. The manipulation of the Miscellaneous register is usually left to the BIOS mode change service.

All read and write operations performed by the VGA take place at a byte level. However, in certain graphics modes, such as mode number 18, video data is stored at a bit level in four color maps. In this case, the code must mask out the undesired color maps in order to determine the state of an individual screen pixel or to set a pixel to a certain color. In 80x86 Assembly Language the TEST instruction provides a convenient way for determining an individual screen pixel following a read operation. The Bit Mask register of the Graphics Controller, in Figure 2.24, permits setting individual pixels while in write modes 0 and 2.

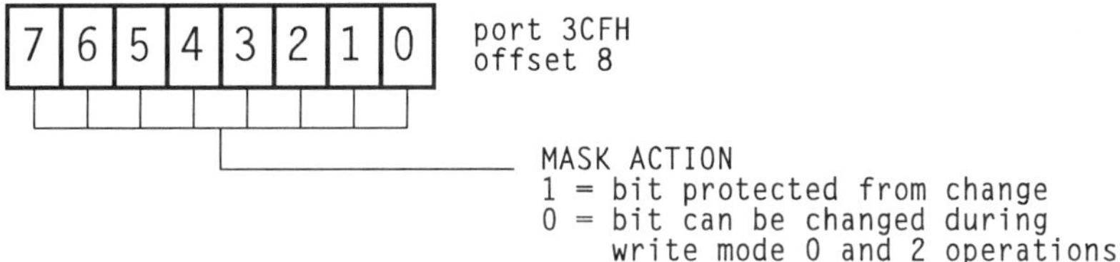

Figure 2.24   *VGA Bit Mask Register of the Graphics Controller*

In the execution of write operations while in VGA mode number 18, the bit mask for setting and individual screen pixel can be found from a look-up table or by right-shifting a unitary bit pattern (10000000B). The following code fragment calculates the offset into the video buffer and the bit mask required for writing an individual pixel using VGA write modes 0 or 2:

```
; Mask and offset computation from x and y pixel coordinates
; Code is for VGA mode number 18 (640 by 480 pixels)
; On entry:
;                CX = x coordinate of pixel (range 0 to 639)
;                DX = y coordinate of pixel (range 0 to 479)
; On exit:
;                BX = byte offset into video buffer
;                AH = bit mask for the write operation using
;                     write modes 0 or 2
;*********************|
;   calculate address |
;*********************|
        PUSH    AX              ; Save accumulator
```

```
        PUSH    CX              ; Save x coordinate
        MOV     AX,DX           ; y coordinate to AX
        MOV     CX,80           ; Multiplier (80 bytes per row)
        MUL     CX              ; AX = y times 80
        MOV     BX,AX           ; Free AX and hold in BX
        POP     AX              ; x coordinate from stack
; Prepare for division
        MOV     CL,8            ; Load divisor
        DIV     CL              ; AX / CL = quotient in AL and
                                ; remainder in AH
; Add in quotient
        MOV     CL,AH           ; Save remainder in CL
        MOV     AH,0            ; Clear high byte
        ADD     BX,AX           ; Offset into buffer to BX
        POP     AX              ; Restore AX
; Compute bit mask from remainder
        MOV     AH,10000000B    ; Unitary mask for 0 remainder
        SHR     AH,CL           ; Shift right CL times
; The byte offset (in BX) and the pixel mask (in AH) can now
; be used to set the individual screen pixel
        .
        .
        .
```

2.2.5 The Attribute Controller

The Attribute Controller receives color data from the Graphics Controller and
formats it for the video display hardware. Input to the Attribute Controller,
which is in the form of attribute data in the alphanumeric modes and in the
form of serialized bit plane data in the graphics modes, is converted into 8-bit
digital color output to the DAC. Blinking, underlining, and cursor display logic
are also controlled by this register. In VGA systems the output of the Attribute
Controller goes directly to the video DAC and the CRT. Table 2.6 shows the
registers in the Attribute Controller group.

Table 2.6 *The VGA Attribute Controller Registers*

PORT	OFFSET	DESCRIPTION
03C0H		Attribute Address and Palette Address register
03C1H		Read operations
03C0H	0 to 15	Palette registers
	16	Attribute mode control
	17	Screen border color control (overscan)
	18	Color plane enable
	19	Horizontal pixel panning
	20	Color select

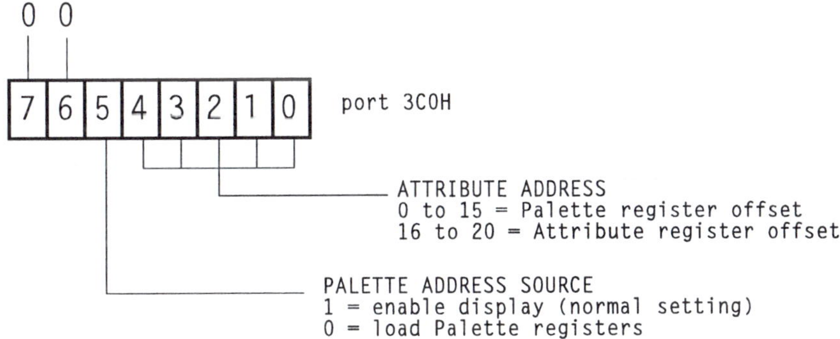

Figure 2.25 *VGA Attribute Address and Palette Address Registers of the Attribute Controller*

Register addressing in the Attribute Controller group is performed differently than with the other VGA registers. This is due to the fact that the Attribute Controller does not have a dedicated bit to control the selection of its internal address and data registers, but uses an internal flip-flop to toggle the address and data functions. This explains why the Index and the Data registers of the Attribute Controller are both mapped to port 3C0H. (See Table 2.6.) Figure 2.25 shows the Attribute and Palette Address registers in the VGA Attribute Controller.

Programming the Attribute Controller requires accessing Input Status Register 1 of the General Register (see Figure 2.7) in order to clear the flip-flop. The address of the Status Register 1 is 3BAH in monochrome modes and 3DAH in color modes. The complete sequence of operations for writing data to the Attribute Controller is as follows:

1. Issue an IN instruction to address 3BAH (in color modes) or to address 3DAH (in monochrome modes) to clear the flip-flop and select the address function of the Attribute Controller.

2. Disable interrupts.

3. Issue an OUT instruction to the address register, at port 3C0H, with the number of the desired data register.

4. Issue another OUT instruction to this same port to load a value into the Data register.

5. Enable interrupts.

The 16 Palette registers of the Attribute Controller, at offsets 0 to 15, determine how the 16 color values in the IRGB bit planes are displayed. The default values for the Palette registers is shown in Table 2.7. The colors of the default palette can be seen in color plate 3 or by running the program named PALETTE furnished as software in the book's microdisk.

Table 2.7 *Default Setting of VGA Palette Registers*

REGISTER OFFSET	VALUE	BITS 0-5 r g b R G B	COLOR
0	0	0 0 0 0 0 0	Black
1	1	0 0 0 0 0 1	Blue
2	2	0 0 0 0 1 0	Green
3	3	0 0 0 0 1 1	Cyan
4	4	0 0 0 1 0 0	Red
5	5	0 0 0 1 0 1	Magenta
6	20	0 1 0 1 0 0	Brown
7	7	0 0 0 1 1 1	White
8	56	1 1 1 0 0 0	Dark grey
9	57	1 1 1 0 0 1	Light blue
10	58	1 1 1 0 1 0	Light green
11	59	1 1 1 0 1 1	Light cyan
12	60	1 1 1 1 0 0	Light red
13	61	1 1 1 1 0 1	Light magenta
14	62	1 1 1 1 1 0	Yellow
15	63	1 1 1 1 1 1	Intensified white

In VGA systems each Palette register consists of 6 bits, which allow 64 color combinations in each register. The bits labeled "RGB" in Table 2.7 correspond to the primary values for red, green, and blue colors and the bits labeled "rgb" correspond to the secondary values. Since each color is represented by two bits, each one can have four possible levels of saturation, for example, the levels of saturation for the color red are:

SATURATION	rgbRGB	INTERPRETATION
0	000000	no red
1	100000	low red
2	000100	red
3	100100	high red

The Palette registers can be changed by means of BIOS service number 16, interrupt 10H or by programming the Attribute Controller registers directly. (See Appendix C.) Note that the setting of the Palette registers does not affect the color output in 256-color mode number 19, in which case the 8-bit color values in video memory are transmitted directly to the DAC. Figure 2.26 is a bit map of the Palette register of the Attribute Controller.

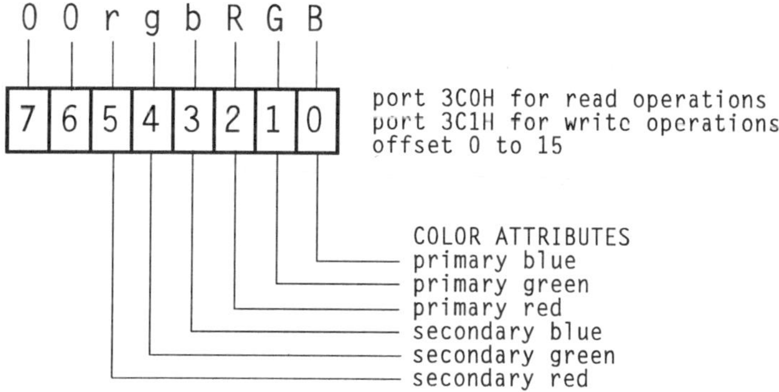

Figure 2.26 *VGA Palette Register of the Attribute Controller*

The Attribute Mode Control register of the Attribute Controller serves to select the characteristics associated with the video mode. Bit 0 selects whether the display is in an alphanumeric or in a graphics mode. Bit 1 determines if VGA operates in a monochrome or color emulation. Bit 2 is related to the handling of the ninth screen dot while displaying the graphics characters in the range C0H to DFH. (See Table 1.2.) If this bit is set, the graphics characters in this range generate unbroken horizontal lines. This feature refers to the MDA emulation mode only, since other character fonts do not have the ninth dot. BIOS sets this bit automatically in the modes that require it. The function of the bit fields of the Attribute Mode Control register can be seen in Figure 2.27.

Bit 5 of the Attribute Mode Control register in the Attribute Controller group relates to independently panning the screen sections during split-screen operation. Split screen programming is discussed in Chapter 3. Bit 6 of the Attribute Mode Control register is set to 1 during operation in mode number 19 (256-colors) and cleared for all other modes. Finally, bit 7 of the Attribute Mode Control register determines the source for the bits labeled r and g (numbers 4 and 5) in the Palette register. If bit 7 is set the r and g bits in the Palette register are replaced by bits 0 and 1 of the Color Select register. If bit 7 is reset then all Palette register bits are sent to the DAC.

In some alphanumeric and graphics modes the VGA display area is surrounded by a colored band. The width of this band is the same as the width of a single character (8 pixels) in the 80-column modes. The color of this border area is determined by the Overscan Color register of the Attribute Controller. Normally the screen border is not noticeable, due to the fact that the default border color is black. The border color is not available in the 40-columns alphanumeric modes or in the graphics modes with 320 pixel rows, except for VGA graphics mode number 19. The bit map of the Overscan register is shown in Figure 2.28.

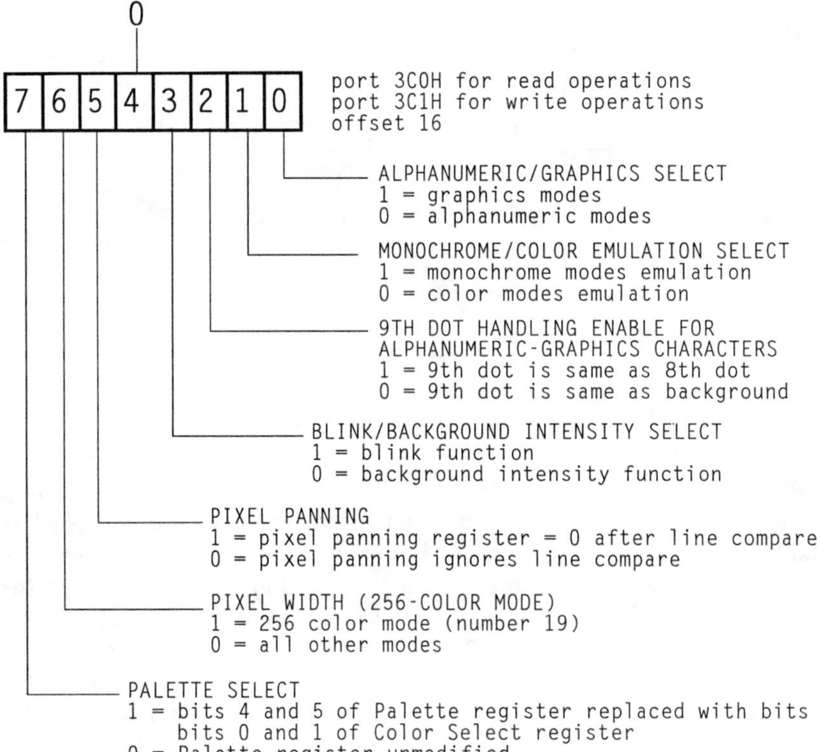

Figure 2.27 *VGA Attribute Mode Control Register of the Attribute Controller*

The Color Plane Enable register allows excluding one or more bit planes from the color generation process. The main purpose of this function is to provide compatibility with EGA systems equipped with less than 256K of memory. Bits 4 and 5 of this register are used in system diagnostics. The bitmap of the Color Plane Enable register of the Attribute Controller group is shown in Figure 2.29.

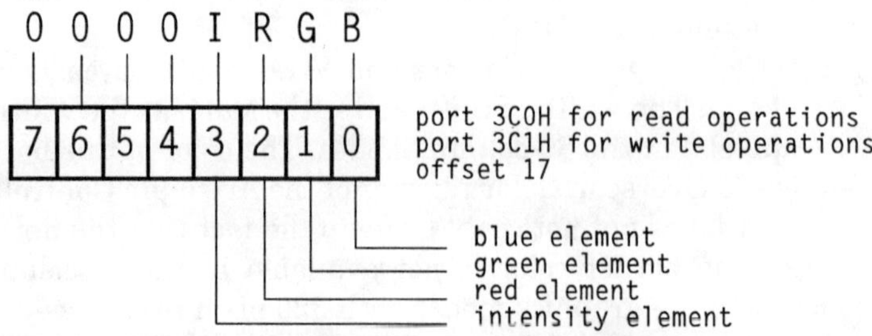

Figure 2.28 *VGA Overscan Color Register of the Attribute Controller*

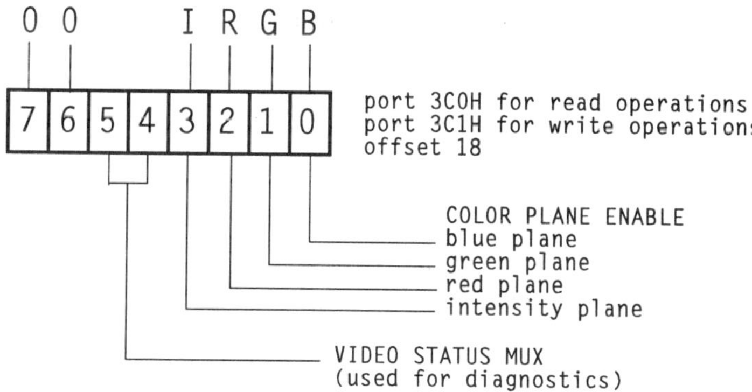

Figure 2.29 *VGA Color Plane Enable Register of the Attribute Controller*

The Horizontal Pixel Panning register of the Attribute Controller is used to shift video data horizontally to the left, pixel by pixel. This register is shown in Figure 2.30. This feature is available in the alphanumeric and graphics modes. The number of pixels that can be shifted is determined by the display mode. In the VGA 256-color graphics mode the maximum number of allowed pixels is three. In alphanumeric modes 0, 1, 2, 3, and 7, the maximum is eight pixels. In all other modes the maximum is seven pixels. The Horizontal Pixel Panning register can be programmed in conjunction with the Video Buffer Start Address registers of the CRT Controller to implement smooth horizontal screen scrolling in alphanumeric and in graphics modes. (See Figure 2.11.) These manipulations are described in Chapter 3.

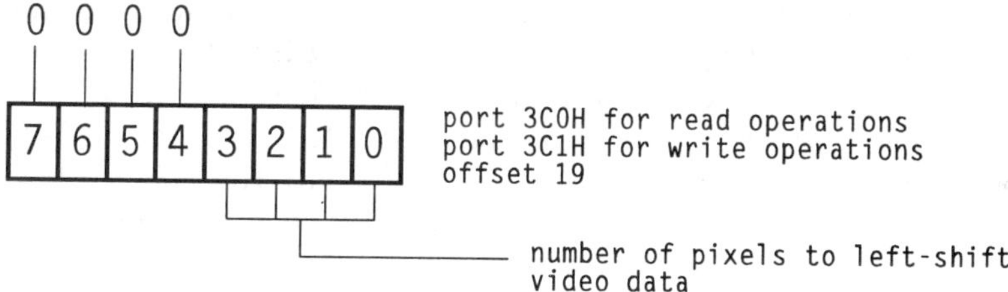

Figure 2.30 *VGA Horizontal Pixel Panning Register of the Attribute Controller*

The Color Select register of the Attribute Controller provides additional color selection flexibility to the VGA system, as well as a way for rapidly switching between sets of displayed colors. When bit 7 of the Attribute Mode Control register is clear (see Figure 2.27) the 8-bit color value sent to the DAC is formed by the 6 bits from the Palette registers and bits 2 and 3 of the Color Select register. (See Figure 2.27.) If bit 7 of the Attribute Mode Control register is set, then the 8-bit color value is formed with the lower four bits of the Palette register and the four bits of the Color Select register. Since these bits affect all

Palette registers simultaneously, the program can rapidly change all colors displayed by changing the value in the Color Select register. The Color Select register is not used in the 256-color graphics mode number 19. The Color Select Register bitmap is shown in Figure 2.31.

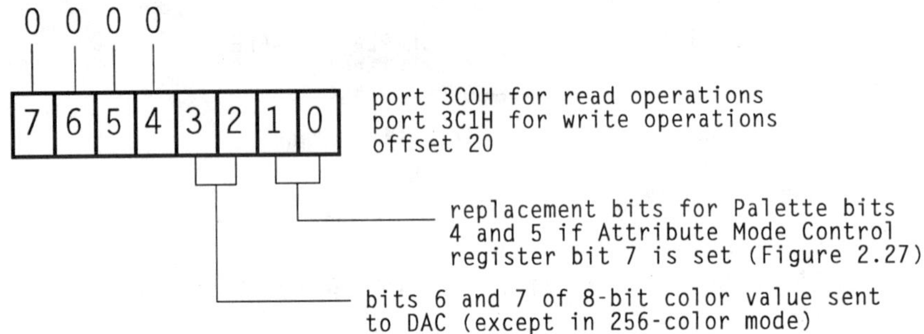

Figure 2.31 *VGA Color Select Register of the Attribute Controller*

2.3 The Digital-to-Analog Converter (DAC)

The Digital-to-Analog Converter, or DAC, provides a set of 256 color registers, sometimes called the color look-up table, as well as three color drivers for an analog display. The DAC register set permits displaying 256 color combinations from a total of 262,144 possible colors. Table 2.8 shows the DAC registers.

Each of the DAC's 256 registers use 6 data bits to encode the value of the primary colors red, green, and blue. The use of 6-bits per color make each DAC register 18 bits wide. It is the possible combinations of 18 bits that allow 262,144 DAC colors. Note that the VGA color registers in the DAC duplicate the color control offered by the Palette registers of the Attribute Controller. In fact, the VGA Palette registers are provided for compatibility with the EGA card, which does not contain DAC registers. When compatibility with the EGA is not an

Table 2.8 *VGA Video Digital-to-Analog Converter Addresses*

REGISTER	OPERATIONS	ADDRESS
Pixel address (read mode)	WRITE ONLY	03C7H
Pixel address (write mode)	READ/WRITE	03C8H
DAC State	READ ONLY	03C7H
Pixel Data	READ/WRITE	03C9H
Pixel Mask	READ/WRITE	03C6H

Note: applications must not write to the Pixel Mask register to avoid destroying the color look-up table

issue, VGA programming can be simplified by ignoring the Palette registers and making all color manipulations in the DAC. Furthermore, the Palette registers are disabled when VGA is in the 256-color mode number 19, since mode number 19 has no EGA equivalent.

The DAC Pixel Address Register

The DAC Pixel Address register holds the number (often called the address) of one of the 256 DAC registers. Read operations to the Pixel Address register are performed to port 3C7H and write operations to port 3C8H (see Table 2.8). A write operation changes the 18-bit color stored in the register (in Red/Green/Blue format). A read operation is used to obtain the RGB value currently stored in the DAC register. Figure 2.32 is a bitmap of the DAC Pixel Address register.

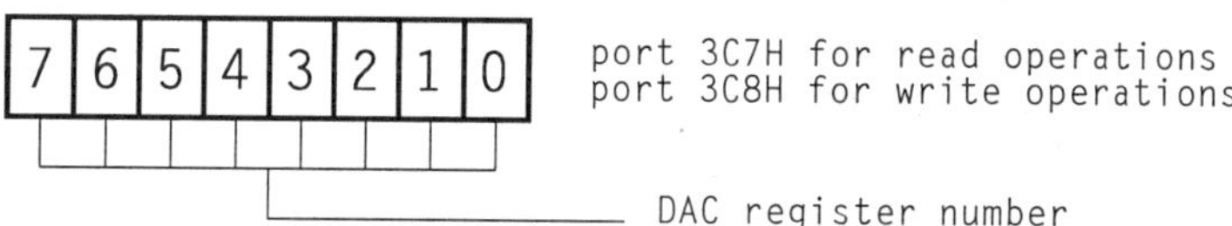

Figure 2.32 *VGA Pixel Address Register of the DAC*

The DAC State Register

The DAC State register encodes whether the DAC is in read or write mode. A mode change takes place when the Pixel Address register is accessed: if the Pixel Address register is set at port 3C7H then the DAC goes into a read mode, if it is set at port 3C8H then the DAC goes into a write mode. (See Figure 2.32.) The DAC State register is shown in Figure 2.33. Notice that although the Pixel Address register for read operations and the DAC State register are both mapped to port 3C7H there is no occasion for conflict, since the DAC State register is read only and the Pixel Address register for read operations is write only. (See Table 2.8.)

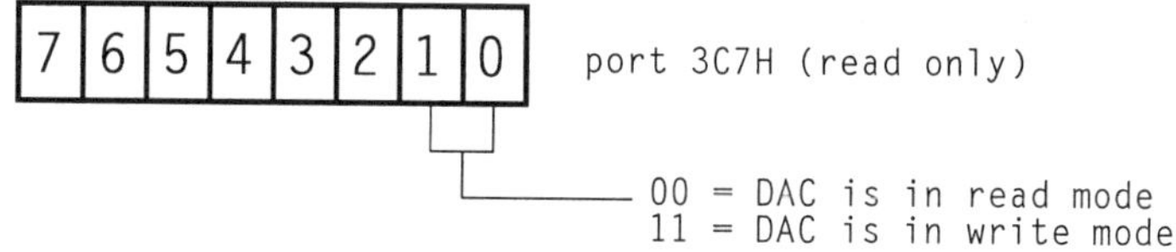

Figure 2.33 *VGA DAC State Register of the DAC*

The DAC Pixel Data Register

The Pixel Data register in the DAC is used to hold three six-bit data items representing a color value in RGB format. The Pixel Data register can be read after the program has selected the corresponding DAC register at the Pixel Address read operation port 3C7H. The Pixel Data register can be written after the program has selected the corresponding DAC register at the Pixel Address write operation port 3C8H. (See Table 2.8.) The current read or write state of the DAC can be determined by examining the DAC State register.

Once the DAC is an a particular mode (read or write), an application can continue accessing the color registers by performing a sequence of three operations, one for each RGB value. The read sequence consists of selecting the desired DAC register in the Pixel Address register at the read operations port (3C7H) then performing three consecutive IN instructions. The first one will load the 6-bit red value stored in the DAC register, the second one will load the green value, and the third one the blue value. The write sequence takes place in a similar fashion. This mode of operation allows rapid access to the three data items stored in each DAC register as well as to consecutive DAC registers. Because each entry in the DAC registers is 6 bits wide, the write operation is performed using the least significant 6 bits of each byte. The order of operations for the WRITE function are as follows:

1. Select the starting DAC color register number by means of a write operation to the Pixel Address write mode register at port 3C8H.

2. Disable interrupts.

3. Write the 18-bit color code in RGB encoding. The write sequence consists of three bytes consecutively output to the pixel data register. Only the six low-order bits in each byte are meaningful.

4. The DAC transfers the contents of the Pixel Data register to the DAC register number stored at the Pixel Address register.

5. The Pixel Address register increments automatically to point to the subsequent DAC register. Therefore, if more than one color is to be changed, the sequence of operations can be repeated from step number 3.

6. Re-enable interrupts.

Read or write operations to the video DAC must be spaced 240 nanoseconds apart. Assembly language code can meet this timing requirement by inserting a short JMP instruction between successive IN or OUT opcodes. The instruction can be conveniently coded in this manner:

```
JMP        SHORT $ + 2      ; I/O delay
```

Programming of the DAC color registers is discussed in Chapter 3.

3

VGA Device Drivers

Chapter Summary

This chapter describes the various levels at which the VGA system can be programmed and establishes the difference between device driver and graphics primitive routines. Section 3.1 studies the design and coding of device drivers for calculating pixel address at the fine- and course-grain levels and for reading and writing pixels and pixel tiles. Section 3.2 discusses color operations in 16- and 256-color modes. Chapter 3 concludes with an explanation of the operation and use of the device driver routines included in the VGA1 libraries furnished as software.

3.0 Levels of VGA Programming

Because the VGA system provides all the video functions in an IBM microcomputer, any display programming operations on these machines must inevitably access the VGA hardware or its memory space. However, at the higher levels of VGA programming many of the programming details are hidden by the interface software. For example, a programmer working in Microsoft QuickBASIC has available a collection of program functions that allow drawing lines, boxes, circles, and ellipses, changing palette colors, performing fill operations, and even executing some primitive animation. Therefore, the QuickBASIC programmer can perform all of the above mentioned graphics functions while ignoring the complications of VGA registers, video memory mapping, and DAC output.

The programming levels in an IBM microcomputer equipped with VGA video are as follows:

1. VGA services provided by the operating system. This includes the video services in BIOS, MS DOS, OS/2, WINDOWS, or other operating system programs or graphical environments.

2. VGA services provided by high-level languages and by programming libraries that extend the functions of high-level languages.

3. General purpose VGA libraries that can be used directly or interfaced with one or more high-level languages. The VGA graphics library furnished with this book belongs to this category.

4. Low-level routines, usually coded in 80x86 assembly language, that access the VGA or DAC registers or the memory space reserved for video functions.

Observe that this list refers exclusively to the VGA system. Other graphics standards, such as 8514A, XGA, and SuperVGA, include high-level functions that are furnished as a programming interface with the hardware. However, the VGA standard does not furnish higher level programming facilities. In this chapter we discuss the lowest level of VGA programming, principally at the adapter hardware level (number 4 in the previous list). These lowest level services are often called *device driver* routines. The VGA services in the BIOS are also mentioned occasionally. The reader wishing a greater detail in the programming descriptions should refer to the code listings (files with the extension .ASM) that are contained in the book's libraries and to Appendix C, which describes the VGA services in the BIOS. In Chapter 4, we extend the discussion of VGA programming to higher level routines, usually called *graphics primitives*. The VGA services in high-level languages, in operating systems, or in graphical environments, such as WINDOWS and OS/2, are not discussed in the book.

3.0.1 Device Drivers and Primitive Routines

The term device driver is often used to denote the most elementary software elements that serve to isolate the operating system, or the high- and low-level programs, from the peculiarities of hardware devices and peripherals. It was the UNIX operating system that introduced the concept of an installable device driver. In UNIX a device driver is described as a software element that can be attached to the UNIX kernel at any time. The concept of a device driver was perpetuated by MS DOS (starting with version 2.0) and by OS/2.

A second level of graphics routines, usually more elaborate than the device drivers, are called the graphics primitives. For example, to draw a circular arc on the graphics screen of a VGA system we need to perform programming operations at two different levels. The higher level operation consists of calculating the x and y coordinates of the points that lay along the arc to be drawn. The second, and more elementary operation, is to set to a desired color the screen pixels that lay along this arc. In this case we can say that the coordinate calculations for the arc are performed in a routine called a graphics primitive, while the setting of the individual screen pixels is left to a VGA device driver.

Strictly speaking it is possible to reduce the device driver for a VGA graphic system to two routines: one to set to a predetermined color the screen pixel located at certain coordinates, and another one to read the color of a screen pixel. With the support of this simple, two-function driver, it is possible to develop VGA primitives to perform all the graphic functions of which the device is capable. Nevertheless, a system based on minimal drivers performs very poorly. For instance, a routine to fill a screen area with a certain color would have to make as many calls to the driver as there are pixels in the area to be filled. In practice, it is better to develop device drivers that perform more than minimum functions. Therefore, in addition to the pixel read and write services, it is convenient to include in the device driver category other elementary routines such as those that perform address calculations, read and write data in multi-pixel units, and manipulate the color settings at the system level.

In IBM microcomputers, under MS DOS, the VGA graphics hardware is accessed by device drivers that are not installed as part of the operating system. Several interface mechanisms are possible for these drivers. One option is to link the graphics device driver to a software interrupt. Once this driver is loaded and its vector initialized, applications can access its services by means of the INT instruction. But this type of operation, while very convenient and efficient, requires that the driver be installed as a terminate-and-stay-resident program (TSR), therefore reducing the memory available to applications. An alternative way of making the services of graphics device drivers accessible to applications is to include the drivers in one or more graphics libraries. The library routines requested in the code, which are accessed by high- and low-level programs at link time, are incorporated into the program's run file. Because of its simplicity this is the approach selected for the graphics routines provided with this book. Chapter 4 is devoted to developing the primitive routines necessary in VGA programming.

3.1 Developing the VGA Device Drivers

The VGA system can be considered as a different device in each operational mode. In fact, as we mentioned in Chapter 2, many VGA modes exist for no other reason than to provide compatibility with other devices. Therefore, the device drivers for VGA mode number 18, with 640-by-480 pixels in 16 colors, are unrelated and incompatible with VGA mode number 19, with 320-by-200 pixels in 256 colors. Since these two modes (numbers 18 and 19) provide the most powerful graphics functions in the VGA standard, and considering that compatibility with previous adapters is no longer a major consideration, the VGA drivers developed for this book refer exclusively to VGA modes number 18 and 19.

3.1.1 VGA Mode Number 18 Write Pixel Routine

In VGA mode number 18 each screen pixel is mapped to four memory maps, each map encoding the colors red, green, and blue, as well as the intensity component. (See Figure 3.1.)

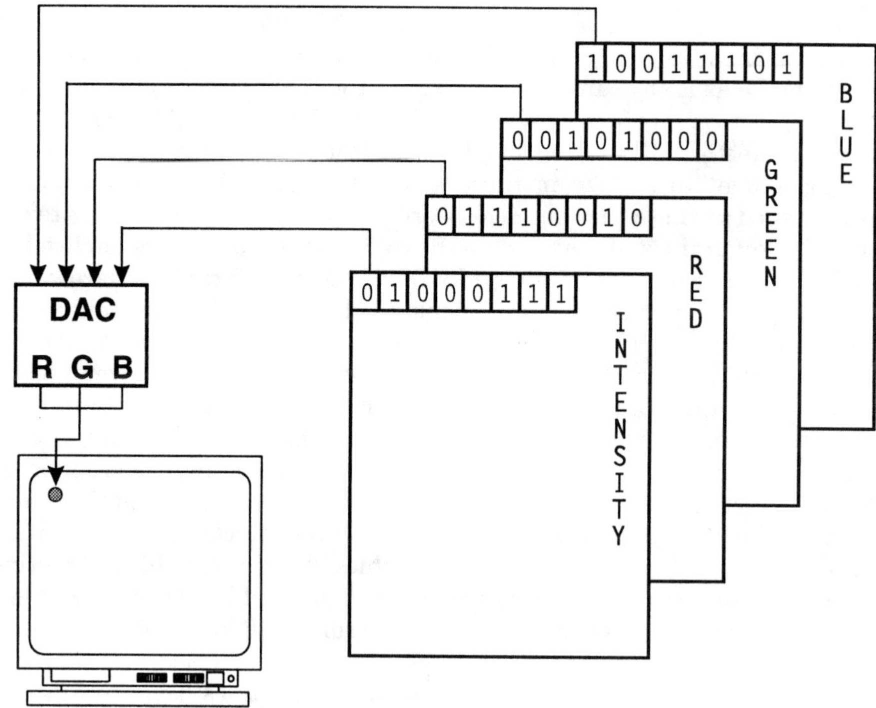

Figure 3.1 *Color Maps in VGA Mode Number 18*

To set a screen pixel in VGA mode number 18 the program must access individual bits located in four color maps. In Figure 3.1 the screen pixel displayed corresponds to the first bit in each of the four maps. But, due to the fact that the 80x86 instruction set does not contain operations for accessing individual bits, read and write operations in 80x86 Assembly Language must take place at the byte level. Consequently, to access the individual screen pixels while in VGA mode number 18 the program has to resort to bit masking. Figure 3.2 illustrates bit-to-pixel mapping in VGA mode number 18.

Notice in Figure 3.2 that the eleventh screen pixel (pointed at by the arrow) corresponds to the eleventh bit in the memory map. This eleventh bit is located in the second byte.

We saw in Chapter 2 that VGA write operations can take place in four different write modes, labeled 0 to 3. Also that the write mode is selected by means of bits 0 and 1 of the Select Graphics Mode register of the Graphics Controller group. (See Figure 2.22.) The VGA behaves as a different device in each write mode. Therefore, the device driver for a pixel write operation in mode number 18 must be write-mode specific.

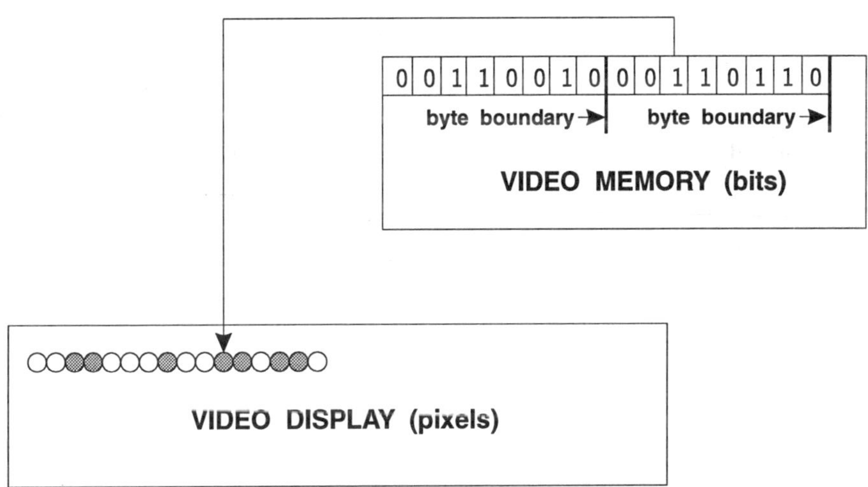

Figure 3.2 *Example of Bit-to-Pixel Mapping in VGA Mode Number 18*

Each VGA write mode has its strong points but, perhaps, write mode 2 is the most direct and useful one. In write mode 2 the individual pixel within a video buffer byte is selected by entering an appropriate mask in the Bit Mask register of the Graphics Controller group. This bit mask must contain a 1 bit for the pixel or pixels to be accessed and a zero bit for those to be ignored. For example, the bit mask 00100000B can be used to select the pixel shown in Figure 3.2.

Fine Grain Address Calculations

In the case of Figure 3.2 the code must take into account that the eleventh pixel is located in the second buffer byte. In VGA mode number 18 programming this is usually accomplished by using a word-size variable, or an 80x86 machine register, as an offset pointer. Since the VGA video buffer in a graphics mode always starts at physical address A0000H, the ES register can be set to the corresponding segment base. The Assembly Language code to set the ES:BX register pair as a pointer to the second screen byte would be as follows:

```
; Code fragment to set the 11th screen pixel while in VGA mode
; number 18, write mode 2
    MOV    AX,0A000H     ; Segment base for video buffer
    MOV    ES,AX         ; To ES register
; ES -> base of VGA video buffer
    MOV    BX,1          ; Offset of byte 2 to BX
; At this point ES:BX can be used to access the second byte in
; the video buffer
        .
        .
        .
```

In practice a VGA mode number 18 device driver should include a routine to calculate the pixel's byte offset and bit mask from its screen coordinates. The actual calculations are based on the geometry of the video buffer in this mode, which corresponds to 80 bytes per screen row (640 pixels) and a total of 480 rows. The following code fragment shows the necessary calculations:

```
; Address computation from x and y pixel coordinates
; On entry:
;          CX = x coordinate of pixel (range 0 to 639)
;          DX = y coordinate of pixel (range 0 to 479)
; On exit:
;          BX = byte offset into video buffer
;          AH = bit mask for the write VGA write modes 0 or 2
;          AL is preserved
; Save all entry registers
      PUSH   CX
      PUSH   DX
;
;*********************|
;    calculate address   |
;*********************|
            PUSH   AX           ; Save accumulator
            PUSH   CX           ; Save x coordinate
            MOV    AX,DX        ; y coordinate to AX
            MOV    CX,80        ; Multiplier (80 bytes per row)
            MUL    CX           ; AX = y times 80
            MOV    BX,AX        ; Free AX and hold in BX
            POP    AX           ; x coordinate from stack
; Prepare for division
            MOV    CL,8         ; Divisor
            DIV    CL           ; AX / CL = quotient in AL and
                               ; remainder in AH
; Add in quotient
            MOV    CL,AH        ; Save remainder in CL
            MOV    AH,0         ; Clear high byte
            ADD    BX,AX        ; Offset into buffer to BX
            POP    AX           ; Restore AX
;
;*********************|
;    calculate bit mask   |
;*********************|
; The remainder (in CL) is used to shift a unitary mask
            MOV    AH,10000000B    ; Unit mask for 0 remainder
            SHR    AH,CL        ; Shift right CL times
; Restore registers
            POP    DX
```

```
        POP     CX
          .

          .

          .
```

This address calculation routine is similar to the PIXEL_ADD_18 device driver in the VGA1 module of the graphics library furnished with this book. This library service is discussed in Section 3.3.

Setting the Pixel

Once the bit mask and byte offset into the buffer have been determined, the individual screen pixel can be set in VGA mode number 18, write mode 2. This is accomplished in two steps: first the program sets the mask in the Bit Mask register of the Graphics Controller group, then it performs a memory write operation to the address in ES:BX. The following code fragment shows both operations:

```
; VGA mode number 18 device driver for writing an individual
; pixel to the graphics screen
;
; On entry:
;               ES:BX = byte offset into the video buffer
;                  AL = pixel color in IRGB format
;                  AH = bit pattern to set (mask)
; This routine assumes VGA mode 18 and write mode 2
        PUSH    DX              ; Save outer loop counter
        PUSH    AX              ; Color byte
        PUSH    AX              ; Twice
;*********************|
;     first step      |
;    set bit mask     |
;*********************|
; Set Bit Mask Register according to mask in AH
        MOV     DX,3CEH         ; Graphic controller latch
        MOV     AL,8
        OUT     DX,AL           ; Select data register 8
        INC     DX              ; To 3CFH
        POP     AX              ; AX once from stack
        MOV     AL,AH           ; Bit pattern
        OUT     DX,AL           ; Load bit mask
;*********************|
;     second step:    |
;   write IRGB color  |
;*********************|
; Write color code to memory maps
```

```
        MOV       AL,ES:[BX]    ; Dummy read to load latch
                                ; registers
        POP       AX            ; Restore color code
        MOV       ES:[BX],AL    ; Write the pixel with the
                                ; color code in AL
        POP       DX            ; Restore outer loop counter
          .
          .
          .
```

The above code is similar to the one in the WRITE_PIX_18 device driver listed in the VGA1 module of the graphics library furnished with this book. The WRITE_PIX_18 routine is discussed in Section 3.3.

Coarse Grain Address Calculations

The finest possible degree of control over a video display device is obtained at the screen pixel level. However, it is often convenient to access video display device in units of several pixels. For example, when VGA mode number 18 text display operations are performed by means of the BIOS character display services, these take place on a screen divided into 80 character columns and 30 character rows. (See Table 2.2.) This means that each character column is 8 pixels wide (640/80 = 8) and each row is 16 pixels high (480/30 = 16). In addition, graphics software can often benefit from operations that take place at coarser-than-pixel levels. For instance, to draw a horizontal line from screen border to screen border, in mode number 18, requires 640 bit-level operations, but only 80 byte-level operations. Consequently, routines that read or write pixels in groups achieve substantially better performance than those that read or write the pixels individually.

In this book, while describing VGA mode 18 routines that write to the video display at a byte level we have used the term *coarse grain*, while those that output at the pixel we have labeled *fine grain*. In order to give the coarse grain routine a symmetrical pixel pattern, we have used 8-bit pixel groups both on the horizontal and on the vertical scale. For lack of a better word we refer to these 8-by-8 pixel units as *screen tiles*, or simply tiles. Coarse-grain operations, in mode number 18, see the video display as 80 columns and 60 rows of screen tiles, for a total of 4800 tiles. In this manner the programmer can envision the VGA screen in mode number 18 as consisting of 640-by-480 pixels (fine grain visualization) or as consisting of 80-by-60 screen tiles of 8-by-8 pixels (coarse grain visualization). Furthermore, the coarse grain visualization can easily be adapted to text display operations on an 80-by-30 screen by grouping the 60 tile rows into pairs. The following code fragment calculates the coarse-grain offset into the video buffer from the vertical and horizontal tile count:

```
; On entry:
;     CH = horizontal tile number (range 0 to 79) = x coordinate
;     CL = vertical tile number (range 0 to 59) = y coordinate
;
; Compute coarse-grain address (in BX) as follows:
;     BX = (CL * 640) + CH
;
; On exit:
;           BX = tile offset into video buffer
;           CX is destroyed
;
        PUSH    AX              ; Save accumulator
        PUSH    DX              ; For word multiply
        PUSH    CX              ; To save CH for addition
        MOV     AX,CX           ; Copy CX in AX
; AL = CL
        MOV     AH,0            ; Clear high byte
        MOV     CX,640          ; Multiplier
        MUL     CX              ; AX * CX results in AX
; The multiplier (640) is the product of 80 tiles columns
; times 8 vertical pixels in each tile row
        POP     CX              ; Restore CH
        POP     DX              ; and DX
        MOV     CL,CH           ; Prepare to add in CH
        MOV     CH,0
        ADD     AX,CX           ; Add
        MOV     BX,AX           ; Move sum to BX
        POP     AX              ; Restore accumulator
        .
        .
        .
```

The above code is similar to the one in the TILE_ADD_18 device driver listed in the VGA1 module of the graphics library furnished with this book. The TILE_ADD_18 routine is discussed in Section 3.3.

Setting the Tile

Once the tile address has been determined, the individual tile (8-by-8 pixel groups) can be set by placing an all-ones mask in the Bit Mask register of the Graphics Controller group, and then performing write operations to 8 successive pixel rows. The following code fragment shows the setting of a screen tile:

```
; Set Bit Mask Register to all one bits
        MOV     DX,3CEH         ; Graphic controller latch
        MOV     AL,8
```

```
        OUT     DX,AL           ; Select data register 8
        INC     DX              ; To 3CFH
        MOV     AL,0FFH         ; Bit pattern of all ones
        OUT     DX,AL           ; Load bit mask
; Set counter for 8 pixel rows
        MOV     CX,8            ; Counter initialized
        POP     AX              ; Restore color code
;*********************|
;     set 8 pixels    |
;*********************|
SET_EIGHT:
        MOV     AH,ES:[BX]      ; Dummy read to load latch
                                ; registers
        MOV     ES:[BX],AL      ; Write the pixel with the
                                ; color code in AL
        ADD     BX,80           ; Index to next row
        LOOP    SET_EIGHT
; Tile is set
```

The above code is similar to the one in the WRITE_TILE_18 device driver
listed in the VGA1 module of the graphics library furnished with this book. The
WRITE_TILE_18 routine is discussed in Section 3.3.

3.1.2 VGA Mode Number 18 Read Pixel Routine

A program attempting to determine the state of the eleventh pixel in Figure
3.2 would read the second memory byte and mask-out all other bits. The mask,
in this case, would have the value 00100000B. We have seen that video memory
in VGA mode number 18 is divided into four memory maps, labeled I, R, G, and
B for the intensity, red, green, and blue components respectively. Also that all
four maps are located at the same address. For this reason, in order to read the
color code for an individual pixel, the program must successively select each of
the four memory maps. This is done through the Read Operation Map Select
register of the Graphics Controller. (See Figure 2.21.) In other words, to
determine the color of a single pixel in VGA mode number 18 it is necessary to
perform four separate read operations, one for each of the IRGB maps.

  As in the write operation, the code to read a screen pixel must calculate the
address of the video buffer byte in which the bit is located and the bit mask for
isolating it. This can be done by means of the code listed in Section 3.1.1 or by
using the PIXEL_ADD_18 device driver in the VGA1 module of the graphics
library furnished with the book. (See Section 3.3.) The following code fragment
reads a screen pixel and returns the IRGB color value in the CL register:

```
; On entry:
;               ES:BX = byte offset into the video buffer
;               AH = bit pattern for mask
```

```
;
; On exit:
;              CL = 4 low bits hold pixel color in IRGB format
;              CH = 0
;
; The code assumes that read mode 0 is set
;
; Move bit mask to CH
         MOV     CH,AH          ; CH = bit mask for pixel
;***********************|
;   set-up read loop    |
;***********************|
         MOV     AH,3           ; Counter for 4 color maps
         MOV     CL,0           ; Clear register for pixel color
                                ; return
;***********************|
; execute 4 read cycles |
;***********************|
; AH has number for current IRGB map (range 0 to 3)
READ_MAPS:
; Select map from which to read
         MOV     DX,3CEH        ; Graphic Controller Address
                                ; register
         MOV     AL,4           ; Read Map Select register
         OUT     DX,AL          ; Activate
         INC     DX             ; Graphic Controller = 3CFH
         MOV     AL,AH          ; AL = color map number
         OUT     DX,AL          ; IRGB color map selected
;***********************|
;      read one byte    |
;***********************|
; Read 8 bits from selected map
         MOV     AL,ES:[BX]     ; Get byte from bit plane
;***********************|
; shift return register |
;***********************|
; Previous color code is in bit 0. The shift operation will free
; the low order bit and move previous bit codes to higher
; positions
         SHL     CL,1
;***********************|
;   mask out pixels     |
;***********************|
         AND     AL,CH          ; Pixel mask in CH
         JZ      NO_PIX_SET     ; Jump if no pixel in map
; Pixel was set in bitmap
```

```
        OR       CL,00000001B    ; Set bit 0 in pixel color
                                 ; return register
NO_PIX_SET:
        DEC      AH              ; Bump counter to next map
        JNZ      READ_MAPS       ; Continue if not last map
; 4 low bits in CL hold pixel color in IRGB format
        MOV      CH,0            ; Clear CH
        .
        .
        .
```

The above code is similar to the one in the READ_PIX_18 device driver listed
in the VGA1 module of the graphics library furnished with this book. (See
Section 3.3.)

3.1.3 VGA Mode Number 19 Write Pixel Routine

VGA programmers use mode number 19 when screen color range is more
important than definition. In mode number 19 the VGA video display consists
of 200 pixel rows of 320 pixels each. Each pixel, which can be in one of 256
colors, is determined by one byte in the video buffer. This scheme can be seen
in Figure 3.3.

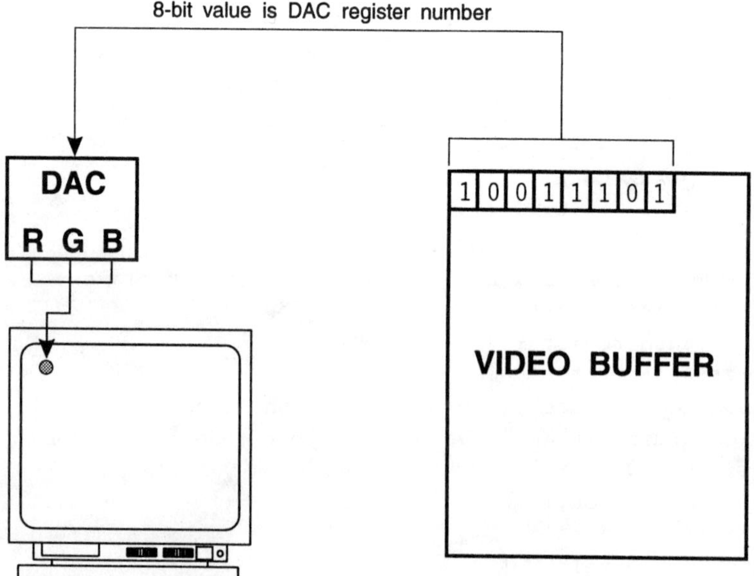

Figure 3.3 *Color Mapping in VGA Mode Number 19*

The fact that each screen pixel in mode number 19 is mapped to a video buffer byte simplifies programming by eliminating the need for a bit mask. The VGA video buffer in mode number 19 consists of 64,000 bytes. This number is the total pixel count obtained by multiplying the number of pixels per row by the number of screen rows (320 x 200 = 64,000). Although the 64,000 buffer bytes are distributed in the four bit planes, the VGA hardware makes it appear to the programmer as if they resided in a continuous memory area. In this manner, the top-left screen pixel is mapped to the byte at physical address A0000H, the next pixel on the top screen row is mapped to buffer address A0001H, and so forth. This byte-to-pixel mapping scheme can be seen in Figure 3.4.

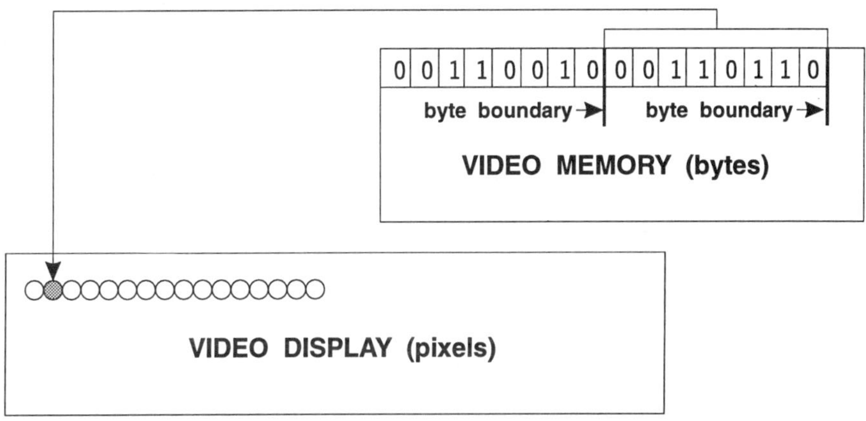

Figure 3.4 *Example of Byte-to-Pixel Mapping in VGA Mode Number 19*

Address Calculations

Address calculations in mode number 19 are simpler than those in mode number 18. All that is necessary to obtain the offset of a pixel into the video buffer is to multiply its row address by the number of buffer bytes per pixel row (320) and then add the pixel column. The processing is shown in the following code fragment:

```
; Address computation for VGA mode number 19
; On entry:
;               CX = x coordinate of pixel (range 0 to 319)
;               DX = y coordinate of pixel (range 0 to 199)
; On exit:
;               BX = offset into video buffer
;
        PUSH    CX              ; Save x coordinate
        MOV     AX,DX           ; y coordinate to AX
```

```
        MOV     CX,320          ; Multiplier is 320 bytes per row
        MUL     CX              ; AX = y times 320
        MOV     BX,AX           ; Free AX and hold in BX
        POP     AX              ; x coordinate from stack
        ADD     BX,AX           ; Add in column value
```

The above code is similar to the one in the WRITE_PIX_19 device driver listed in the VGA1 module of the graphics library furnished with this book. (See Section 3.3.)

Setting the Pixel

Once the segment and the offset registers are loaded, the program can set an individual screen pixel by means of a simple MOV instruction, as in the following code fragment:

```
; Write one pixel in VGA mode number 19 (256 colors)
; Code assumes that write mode 0 for 256 colors is selected
; Register setup:
;       ES = A000H (video buffer segment base)
;       BX = offset into the video buffer (range 0 to 64000)
;       AL = 8-bit color code
;
        MOV     ES:[BX],AL      ; Write pixel
```


3.1.4 VGA Mode Number 19 Read Pixel Routine

We have seen that in VGA mode number 19 each screen pixel is mapped to a single video buffer byte. There are 64,000 bytes in the video buffer, which is the same as the total number of screen pixels obtained by multiplying the number of pixels per row by the number of screen rows (320 x 200 = 64,000). The mapping scheme in VGA mode number 19 can be seen in Figure 3.4. The address calculations for mode number 19 were shown in Section 3.1.3. The actual read operation is performed by means of a MOV instruction, as in the following code fragment:

```
; Read one pixel in VGA mode number 19 (256 colors)
; Code assumes that read mode 0 is selected
; Register setup:
;       ES = A000H (video buffer segment base)
;       BX = offset into the video buffer (range 0 to 64000)
;
        MOV     AL,BYTE PTR ES:[BX]     ; Read pixel
; AL now holds the 8-bit color code
```

3.2 Color Manipulations

The theory of additive color reproduction is based on the fact that light in the primary colors (red, green, and blue) can be used to generate all the colors of the spectrum. Red, green, and blue are called the *primary colors*. Technically, it is possible to create white light by blending just two colors. The color that must be blended with a primary color to form white is called the complement of the primary color, or the *complementary color*. Color plate number 3 shows the primary and the complementary colors. The complementary colors can also be described as white light minus a primary color. For example, white light without red, not-red, gives a shade of blue-green known as cyan; not-green gives a mixture of red and blue called magenta; and not-blue gives yellow, which is a mixture of red and green light. Video display technology is usually designed on additive color blending. Subtractive methods are based on dyes that absorb the undesirable, complementary colors. A cyan-colored filter, for example, absorbs the green and blue components of white light. Subtractive mixing is used in color photography and color printing.

In describing a color we use three characteristics that can be precisely determined: its *hue*, its *intensity*, and its *saturation*. A method of color measurement based on hue, intensity, and saturations (sometimes called the *HIS*) was developed for color television. The hue can be defined as the color of a color. Physically the hue can be measured by the color's dominant wavelength. The intensity of a color is its brightness. This brightness is measured in units of luminance or *nits*. The saturation of a color is its purity. If the color contains no white diluent it is said to be fully saturated.

3.2.1 256-Color Mode

While address mapping in VGA mode number 19 is simpler than in mode number 18, the pixel color encoding is considerably more complicated. This is so not only because there is a more extensive color range in mode number 19 than in mode number 18 (16 versus 256 colors) but also because the default encoding scheme is not very straightforward. This default scheme is determined by the setting of the 256 color registers in the DAC. (See Section 2.3.) The start-up value stored in these registers by the BIOS initialization code is designed to provide compatibility with the CGA and EGA systems. Figure 3.5 shows the default setting of the DAC Color registers in VGA mode number 19. The demonstration program named MODE19, furnished in the book's microdisk, is an on screen display of the default setting of the DAC registers in the VGA mode number 19. Color plate number 4 is a screen print of the MODE19 program.

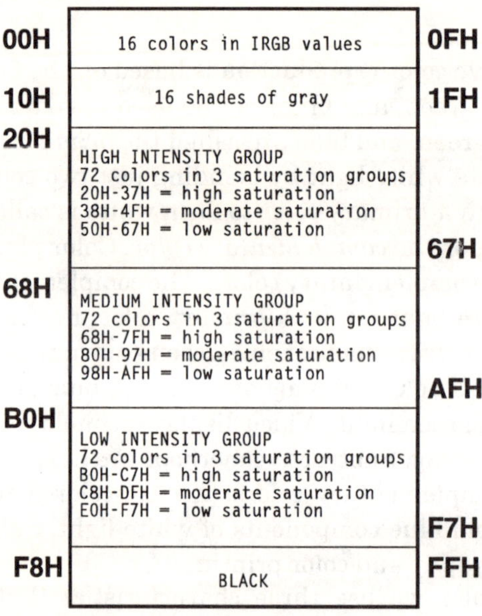

Figure 3.5 *VGA Mode Number 19 Default Color Register Settings*

In Figure 3.5 the first group of default colors (range 00H to 0FH) corresponds to those in the 16-color modes. In other words, if only the four low-order bits of the 8-bit color code are programmed, the resulting colors in the 256-color mode are the same as those in the 16-color modes. The second group of default colors (range 10H to 1FH) corresponds to 16 shades of gray. The following group of colors (range 20H to 67H) consists of 72 colors divided into 3 sub-groups, each one representing a different level of color saturation. Each of the saturation sub-groups consists of 24 colors in a circular pattern of blue-red-green hues, as shown in color plate number 4. Another 72-color group is used for medium intensity colors and a third one for low intensity colors.

But the programmer of VGA in 256-color mode is by no means restricted to the default values installed by the BIOS in the DAC Color registers. In fact, we can readily see that this default grouping is not convenient for many applications. Because, as we can see in color plate number 4, the default tones of red, green, or blue are not mapped to adjacent bits or to manageable fields. For example, using the default setting of the DAC Color registers, the various shades of the color green are obtained with the values shown in Table 3.1.

A more rational 256-color scheme can be based on assigning 2 bits to each of the components of the familiar IRGB encoding. Figure 3.6 shows the bit mapping for this IRGB double-bit encoding.

Table 3.1 *Shades of Green in VGA 256-Color Mode (Default Values)*

VALUE/RANGE		INTENSITY	SATURATION
02H	00000010B	medium	high
0AH	00001010B	high	high
2EH to 34H	00101110B to 00110100B	high	high
46H to 4CH	01000110B to 01001100B	high	moderate
5EH to 64H	01011110B to 01100100B	high	low
76H to 7CH	01110110B to 01111100B	medium	high
8EH to 94H	10001110B to 10010100B	medium	moderate
A6H to ACH	10100110B to 10101100B	medium	low
BEH to C4H	10111110B to 11000100B	low	high
D6H to DCH	11010110B to 11011100B	low	moderate
EEH to F4H	11101110B to 11110100B	low	low

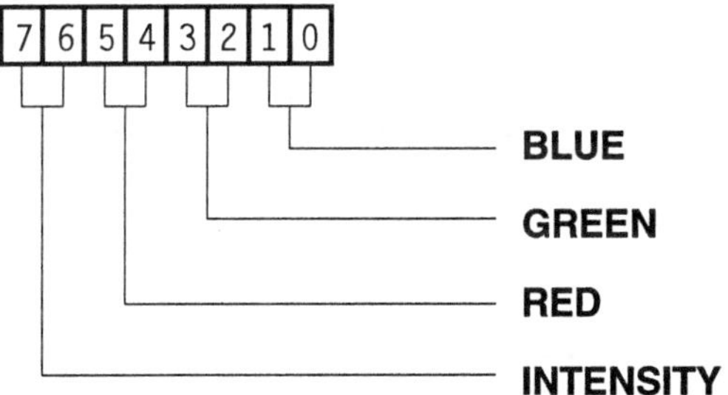

Figure 3.6 *Double-Bit Mapping for 256-Color Mode*

To enable the double-bit encoding in Figure 3.6 it is necessary to change the default setting of the DAC Color registers. In Chapter 2 we saw that the DAC Color registers consist of 18 bits, 6 bits for each color (red, green, and blue). The bit map of the DAC Color registers is shown in Figure 3.7.

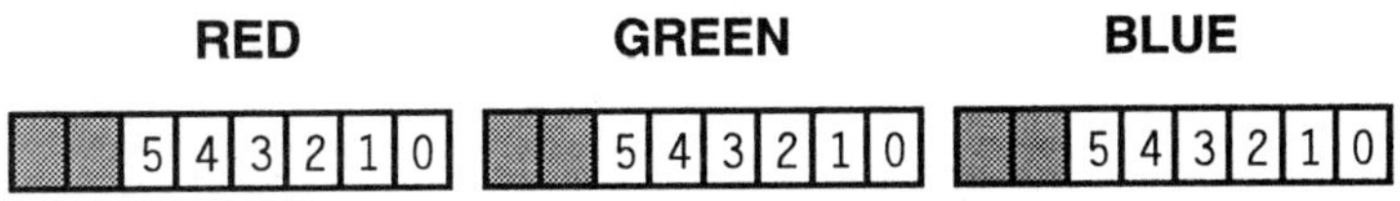

Figure 3.7 *Bitmap of the DAC Color Registers*

Table 3.2 *DAC Register Setting for Double-Bit IRGB Encoding*

NUMBER	6-BIT VALUE	INTENSITY	COLOR
0	9	OFF	dark
1	18	OFF	.
2	27	OFF	.
3	36	OFF	.
4	45	ON	.
5	54	ON	.
6	63	ON	bright

To design an 8-bit encoding in a 4-element (IRGB) format we have assigned 2 bits to each color and to the intensity component. (See Figure 3.6.) In this manner, the 2-bit values for red, green, and blue, allow four tones. Since each tone can be in four brightness level, one for each intensity bit setting, each pure hue would have 16 saturations. In order to achieve a double-bit IRGB encoding by reprogramming the DAC Color registers, as shown in Figure 3.7, we assign eight values to each DAC Color register, as shown in Table 3.2.

The first four bit settings in Table 3.2 correspond to the color tones controlled by the red, green, and blue bits when the intensity bits have a value of 00B. The last three 6-bit values correspond to the three additional levels of intensity. This means that, excluding the intensity bit, the three DAC Color registers will have 64 possible combinations. Table 3.3 shows the pattern of register settings for the double-bit IRGB format.

Table 3.3 *Pattern for DAC Register Settings in Double-Bit IRGB Encoding*

I = 00			I = 01			I = 10			I = 11		
No.	R G B		No.	R G B		No.	R G B		No.	R G B	
0	9 9 9		64	9 9 18		128	9 9 27		192	9 9 36	
1	9 9 18		65	9 9 27		129	9 9 36		193	9 9 45	
2	9 9 27		66	9 9 36		130	9 9 45		194	9 9 54	
3	9 9 36		67	9 9 45		131	9 9 54		195	9 9 63	
4	9 9 9		68	9 18 18		132	9 27 18		196	9 36 18	
5	9 18 9		69	9 27 18		133	9 36 27		197	9 45 36	
.	.		.			.			.		
.	.		.			.			.		
63	36 36 36		127	45 45 45		191	54 54 54		255	63 63 63	

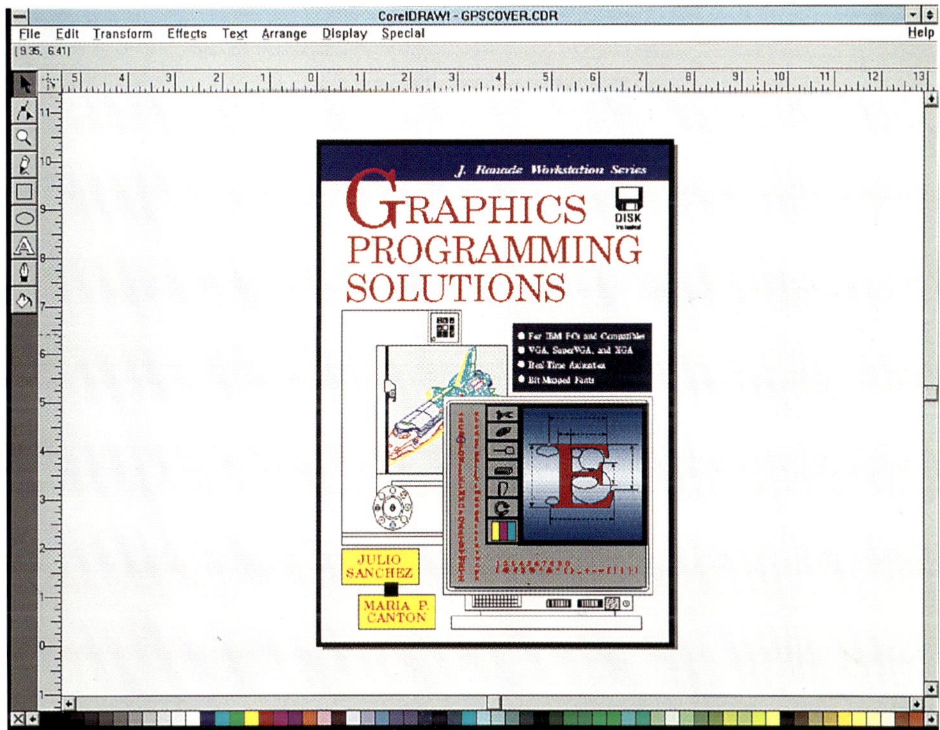

Plate 1. *Draft Image for the Book's Cover in Coreldraw 3.0*

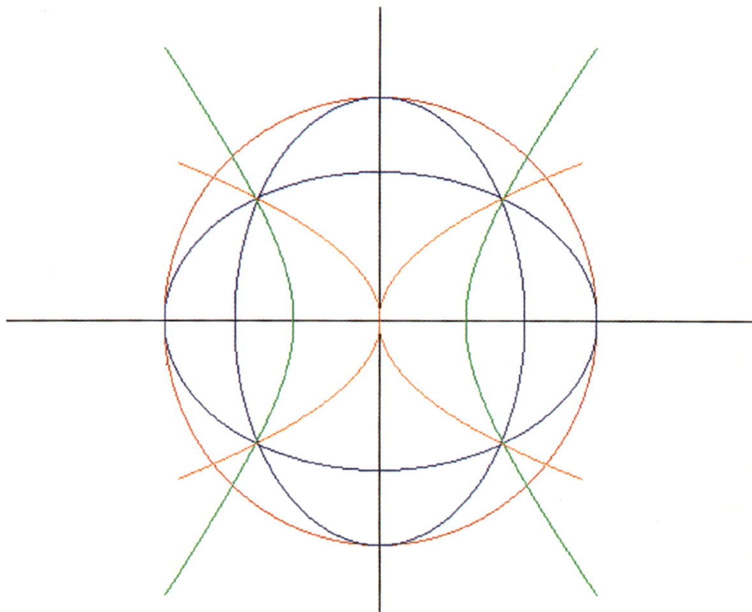

Plate 2. *VGA Conic Curves Using the Library Primitives*

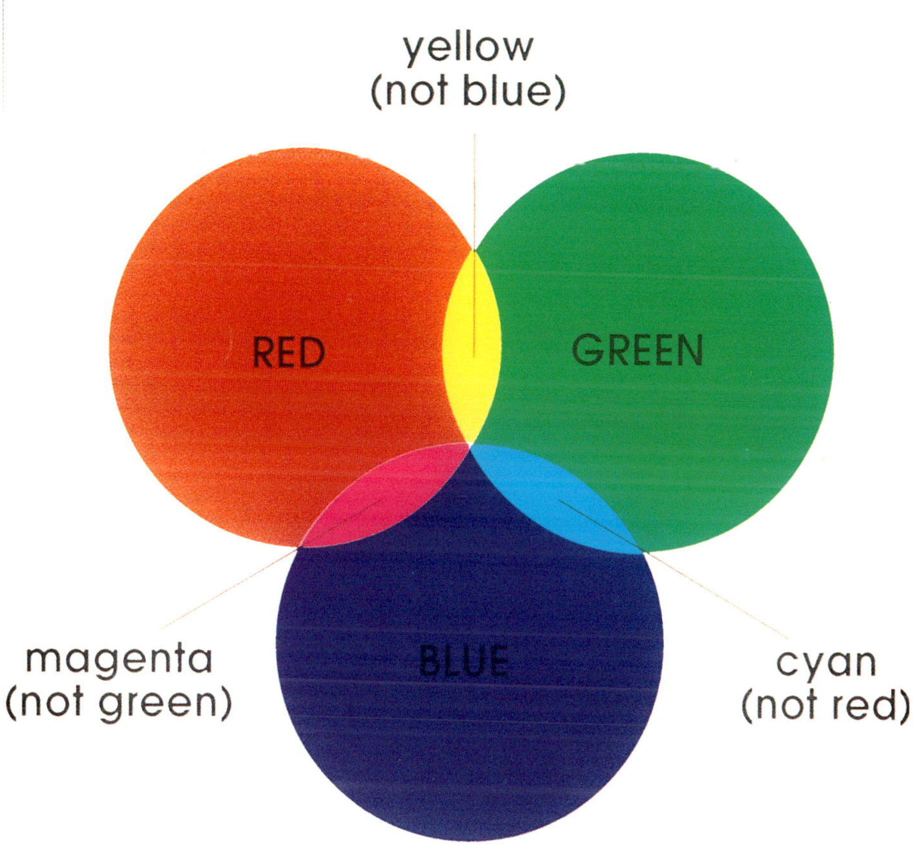

Plate 3. *Additive Primary Colors*

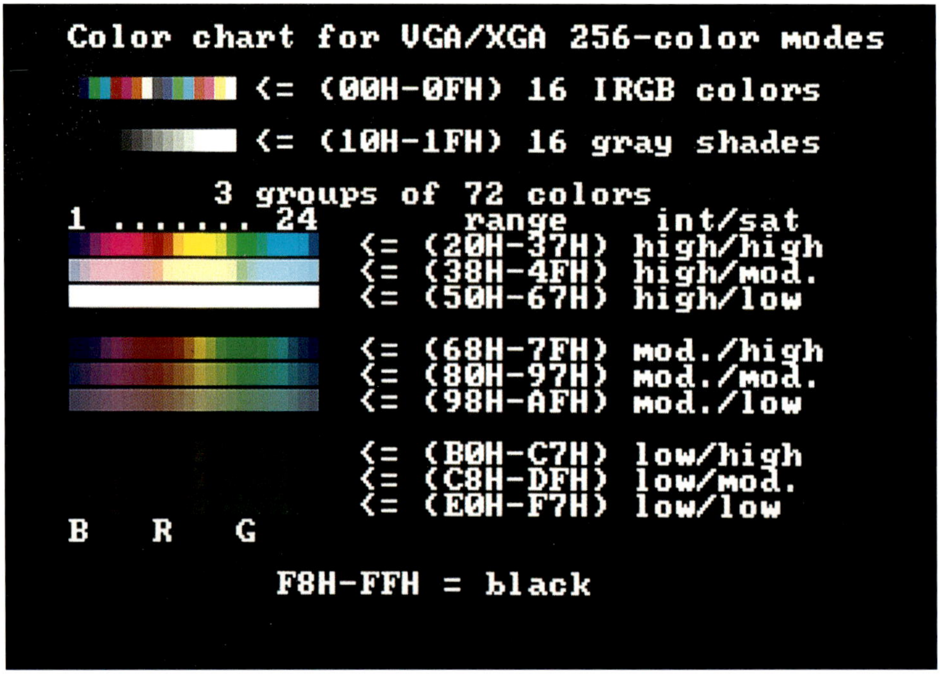

Plate 4. *VGA Mode 19 Default Palette in 256 Colors (MODE19.EXE Program)*

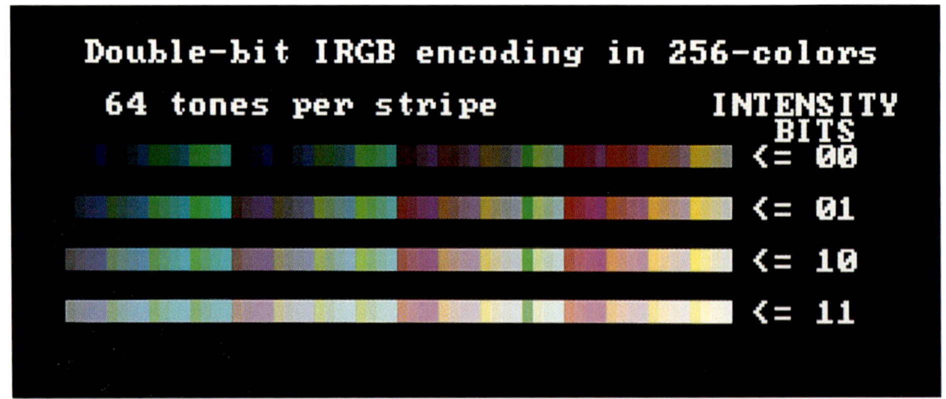

Plate 5. *VGA Mode 19 Double-bit IRGB Palette (IRGB256.EXE Program)*

Plate 6. *MATCH Program First Screen*

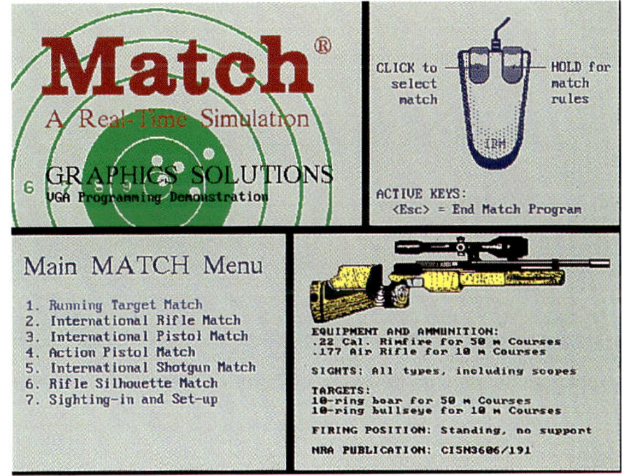

Plate 7. *MATCH Program Main Menu*

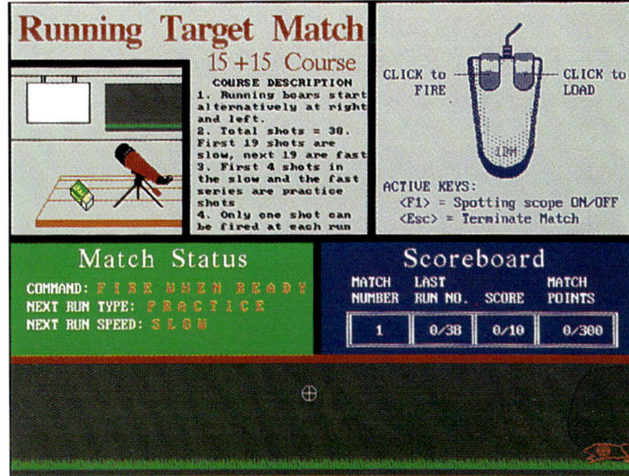

Plate 8. *MATCH Program Running Target Match*

Default Palette

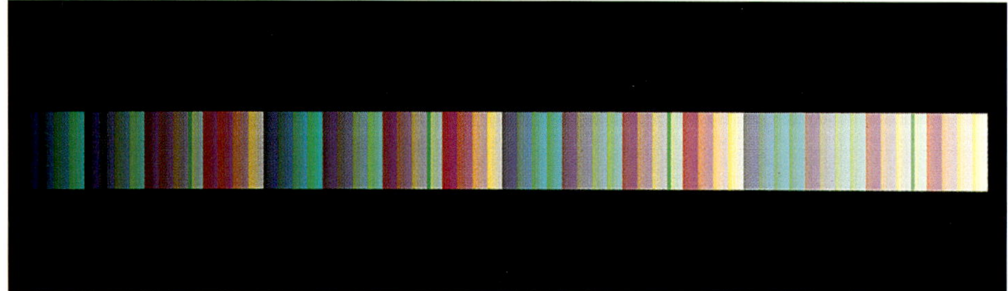

IIRRGGBB Palette

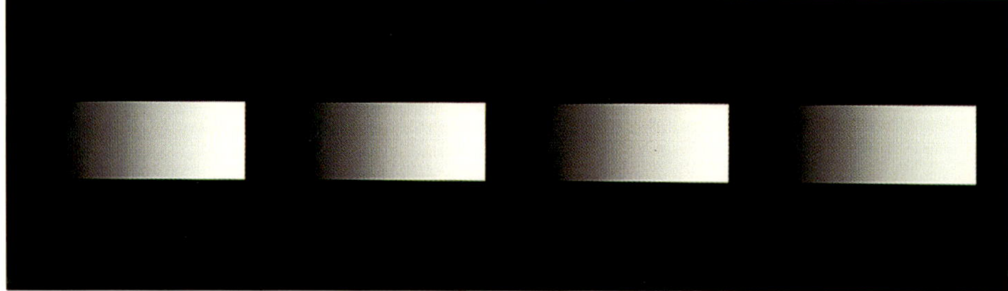

Gray Scale Palette

Plate 9. *XGA and 8514/A Palettes*

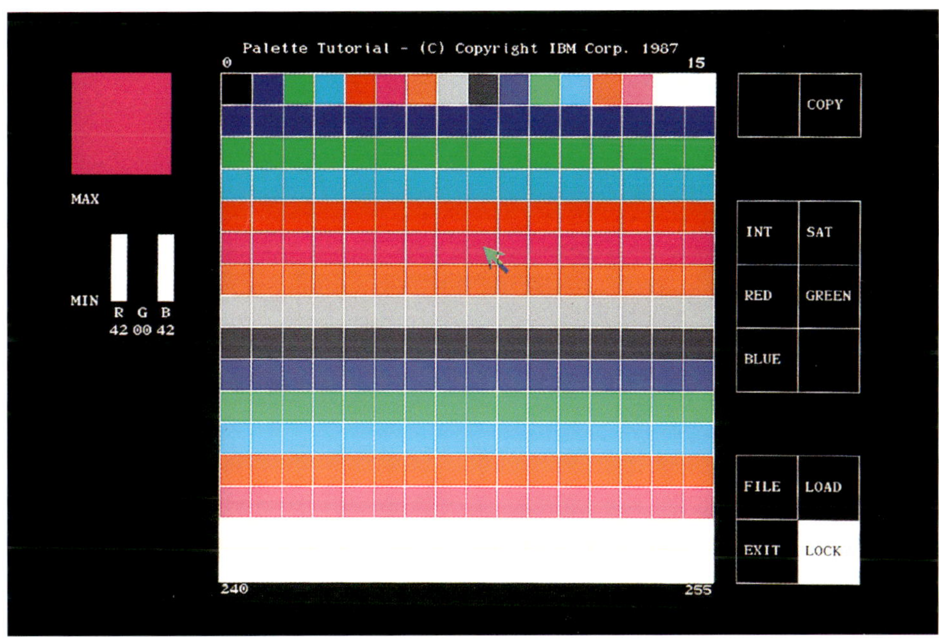

Plate 10. *Screen from the Palette Tutorial Utility furnished with the IBM Display Adapter 8514/A Adapter Interface Programmer's Guide*

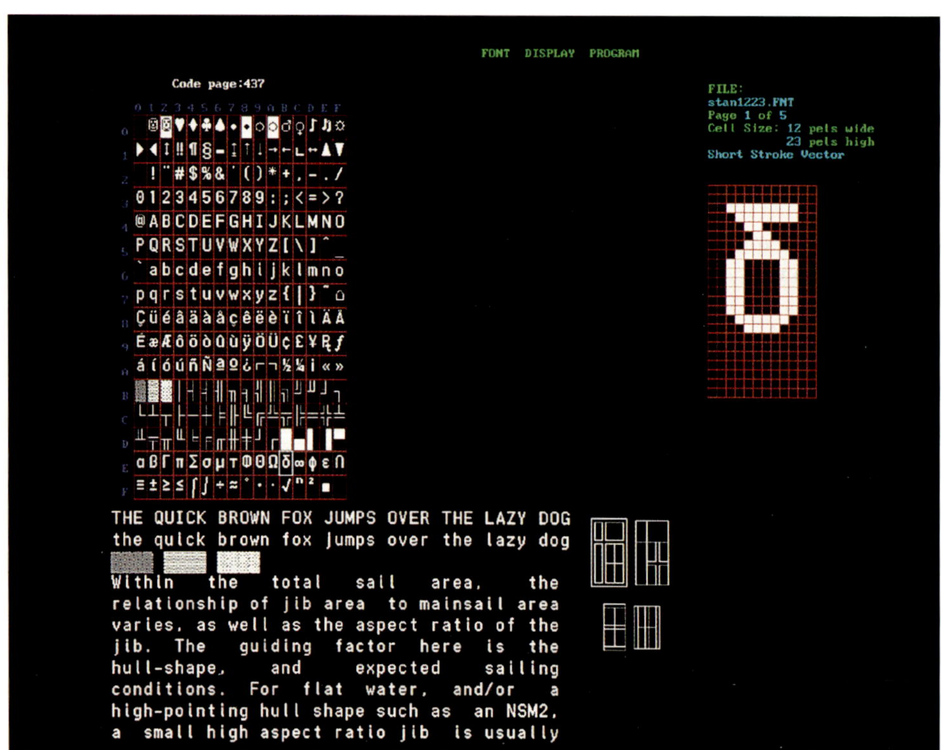

Plate 11. *Screen from the Font Display Program furnished with the IBM Display Adapter 8514/A Adapter Interface Programmer's Guide*

Notice in Table 3.3 that a value of 9 in the red, green, and blue color registers corresponds with the color black. It has been found that the colors generated by the low range of the DAC scale are less noticeable than those on the high range. By equating the value 9 to the color black we enhance the visible color range on a standard VGA. Although, in some CRTs, this setting could appear as a very dark gray. The procedure named TWO_BIT_IRGB in the VGA1 module of the graphics library changes the default setting of the DAC Color registers to the values in Table 3.3. The procedure is described in Section 3.3. The program named IRGB256 furnished in the book's microdisk shows the double-bit IRGB colors. Color plate number 5 is a screen print of the IRGB256 program.

We have seen that a double-bit IRGB setting for the DAC registers simplifies programming in the VGA 256-color mode when compared to the default setting shown in Figure 3.5. Once the DAC registers are set for the double-bit IRGB encoding the programmer can choose any one color by setting the corresponding bits in the video buffer byte mapped to the pixel. For example, the bit combinations in Table 3.4 can be used to display 16 pure tones of the complementary color named magenta (not green). Notice that the purity of the hue is insured by the zero value in the green DAC register.

Table 3.4 *16 Shades of the Color Magenta Using Double-Bit IRGB Code*

NUMBER	I	R	G	B	TONE
0	00	01	00	01	darkest magenta
1	00	10	00	10	.
2	00	01	00	01	.
3	00	11	00	11	.
4	01	01	00	01	.
.		.			.
15	11	11	00	+11	brightest magenta

But no single color encoding is ideal for all purposes. Often the programmer prefers to enhance certain portions of the color range at the expense of other portions. For example, in displaying a mountain landscape it might be preferable to extend shades of blue and green at the expense of the red. On the other hand, a volcanic explosion may require more shades of red than of green and blue. The programmer can manipulate the displayed range by choosing which set of 256 colors, from a possible total of 262,143, are installed in the DAC Color registers.

Shades of Gray

The color gray is defined as equal intensities of the primary colors, red, green, and blue. In the DAC Color registers any setting in which the three values are equal generates a shade of gray. For example, the value 20, 20, 20 for red, green, and blue respectively, produce a 31 percent gray shade, while a value of 32, 32, 32 produce a 50 percent gray shade. Since the gray shades require that all three colors have the same value, and considering that each color register can hold

64 values, there are 64 possible shades of gray in the VGA 256-color modes. The actual setting of the VGA registers will go from 0, 0, 0, to 63, 63, 63, for red, green, and blue.

A graphics program operating in VGA 256-color mode can simultaneously use the full range of 64 gray shades, as well as 192 additional colors. This requires reprogramming the DAC Color registers. If a program were to execute in shades of gray only, then the low order 6-bits of the color encoding can be used to select the gray shades. The range would extend from a value of 0, for black, to a value of 63 for the brightest white. The setting of the DAC Color registers for a 64-step gray scale is shown in Table 3.5.

Table 3.5 *Pattern for DAC Register Setting for 64 Shades of Gray*

No.	R	G	B	No.	R	G	B	No.	R	G	B	No.	R	G	B
0	0	0	0	64	0	0	0	128	0	0	0	192	0	0	0
1	1	1	1	65	1	1	1	129	1	1	1	193	1	1	1
2	2	2	2	66	2	2	2	130	2	2	2	194	2	2	2
3	3	3	3	67	3	3	3	131	3	3	3	195	3	3	3
.	.			.				.				.			
.	.			.				.				.			
63	63	63	63	127	63	63	63	191	54	54	54	255	63	63	63

Notice in Table 3.5 that the gray settings are repeated 4 times. The effect of this repeated pattern is that the high-order bits of the color code are ignored. In other words, all possible color values will generate a gray shade, and the excess of 63 (00111111B) has no visible effect. The device driver named GRAY_256 in the VGA1 module of the graphics library changes the default setting of the DAC Color registers to the values in Table 3.5. The GRAY_256 procedure is described in detail in the discussion of the VGA1 module later in the chapter. The program named GRAY256 furnished in the book's microdisk shows the setting of the DAC registers for 64 gray shades, repeated four times.

Summing to Gray Shades

A program can read the red, green, and blue values installed in a DAC Color register and find an equivalent gray shade with which to replace it. If this action is performed simultaneously on all 256 DAC Color registers the result will be to convert a displayed color image to monochrome. Considering that the human eye is more sensitive to certain regions of the spectrum, this conversion is usually based on assigning different weighs to the red, green, and blue components. In any case, this relative color weight is used to determine the gray shade, on a scale of 0 to 63. However, as mentioned in the previous paragraph, the resulting gray scale setting must have equal proportions of the red, green, and blue elements.

BIOS Service number 16, of interrupt 10H, contains sub-service number 27, which sums all color values in the DAC registers to gray shades. The BIOS code uses a weighted sum based on the following values:

```
  red = 30%
green = 59%
 blue = 11%
-------------
total = 100%
```

The BIOS service does not preserve the original values found in the DAC registers. The primitive routine named SUM_TO_GRAY in the VGA1 module of the graphics library can be used to perform a gray scale sum based on the action of the above mentioned BIOS service. (See Section 3.3.)

The IBM BIOS performs several automatic operations on the VGA DAC Color registers. For example, during a mode change call (BIOS service number 0, interrupt 10H) the BIOS loads all 256 DAC Color registers with the default values. If the mode change is to a monochrome mode then a sum-to-gray operation is performed. The programmer can prevent this automatic loading of the DAC registers. BIOS service number 18, sub-service number 49, of interrupt 10H, enables and disables the default pallet loading during mode changes. Sub-service number 51 of service number 18 enables and disables the sum-to-gray function. These services are described in Appendix C. The FREEZE_DAC and THAW_DAC device drivers in the VGA1 module of the graphics library provide a means for preventing and enabling default palette loading during BIOS mode changes. These procedures are described in Section 3.3.

3.2.2 16-Color Modes

In Table 2.2 we saw that VGA color modes can be in 2, 4, 16, and 256 colors. Since the 2 and 4 color modes are provided for compatibility with now mostly obsolete standards, they are of little interest to today's VGA programmer. The same can be said of the lower-resolution graphics modes. This elimination leaves us with the 16-color text modes number 0 to 4 and graphics mode number 18. In the following discussion we will refer exclusively to the 16-color range in VGA graphics mode number 18.

Video memory mapping in mode number 18 can be seen in Figure 3.2, however, this illustration does not show how the color is obtained. Refer to Figure 2.4 to visualize how the pixel color in mode number 18 is determined by the values stored in four maps, usually named intensity, red, green, and blue. But this four-bit IRGB encoding is, in reality, the number of one of sixteen palette registers located in the Attribute Controller group. (See Section 2.2.5.) Furthermore, the value stored in the Palette register is also an address into the corresponding DAC Color register. This dual-level color indirect addressing scheme was developed in order to provide VGA compatibility with the CGA and the EGA cards. The matter is further complicated by the fact that the DAC

Color register number (an 8-bit value in the range 0 to 255) can be stored differently. If the Palette Select bit of the Attribute Mode Control register is clear, then the DAC Color register number is stored in the six bits of the Palette register and in bits 2 and 3 of the Color Select register. While if the Palette Select bit is set, then the DAC Color register number is stored in the four low-order bits of the Palette register and in the four low-order bits of the Color Select register. The two addressing modes are shown in Figure 3.8.

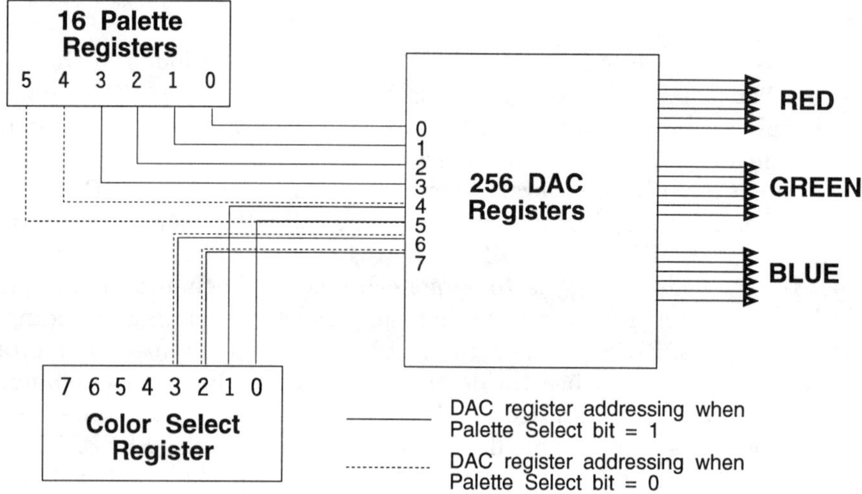

Figure 3.8 *DAC Register Selection Modes*

Notice in Figure 3.8 that when the Palette Select bit is set, bits 4 and 5 of the DAC register address are determined by bits 0 and 1 of the Color Select register, and not by bits 4 and 5 of the Palette register. This means that a program operating in this addressing mode will have to manipulate bits 4 and 5 of the desired DAC register number so that they are determined by bits 0 and 1 of the Color Select register, while bits 6 and 7 of the address are determined by bits 3 and 2 of the Color Select register.

Perhaps the simplest and most straightforward color option for VGA mode number 18 would be to set the Palette Select bit and to clear bits 0 to 3 of the Color Select register. In this manner the Palette and Color Select registers become transparent to the software, since the DAC register number is now determined by the four low bits of the Palette register, which, in turn, match the IRGB value in the bit planes. Nevertheless, this color setup would be incompatible with the one in the CGA and EGA standards, which are based on the value stored in the 16 Palette registers. The method followed by the BIOS, which is designed to achieved compatibility with the Palette registers of the CGA and EGA cards, is based on a customized set of values for the DAC Color registers which are loaded during mode 18 initialization. This set, which includes values for the first 64 DAC Color registers, can be seen in Table 3.6.

Table 3.6 *BIOS Settings for DAC Registers in Mode Number 18*

No.	R	G	B	No.	R	G	B	No.	R	G	B	No.	R	G	B
0	0	0	0	16	0	21	0	32	21	0	0	48	21	21	0
1	0	0	42	17	0	21	42	33	21	0	42	49	21	21	42
2	0	42	0	18	0	63	0	34	21	42	0	50	21	63	0
3	0	42	42	19	0	63	42	35	21	42	42	51	21	63	42
4	42	0	0	20	42	21	0	36	63	0	0	52	63	21	0
5	42	0	42	21	42	21	42	37	63	0	42	53	63	21	42
6	42	42	0	22	42	63	0	38	63	42	0	54	63	63	0
7	42	42	42	23	42	63	42	39	63	42	42	55	63	63	42
8	0	0	21	24	0	21	21	40	21	0	21	56	21	21	21
9	0	0	63	25	0	21	63	41	21	0	63	57	21	21	63
10	0	42	21	26	0	63	21	42	21	42	21	58	21	63	21
11	0	42	63	27	0	63	63	43	21	42	63	59	21	63	63
12	42	0	21	28	42	21	21	44	63	0	21	60	63	21	21
13	42	0	63	29	42	21	63	45	63	0	63	61	63	21	63
14	42	42	21	30	42	63	21	46	63	42	21	62	63	63	21
15	42	42	63	31	42	63	63	47	63	42	63	63	63	63	63

We can corroborate the mapping of Palette and DAC registers in VGA mode number 18 by referring to Table 2.8 and Table 3.6. For example, the encoding for light red in Palette Register number 16 is 00111100B, which is 60 decimal. Recalling that the value in the VGA Palette register is interpreted as an index into the DAC Color register table, we can refer to Table 3.6 and observe that the setting of DAC register number 60 is 63, 21, 21 for the red, green, and blue elements respectively. This setting corresponds to the color light red. In summary: the Palette register (in this case number 12) holds an encoding in rgbRGB format, that is also an index to the DAC Color table (in this case the rgbRGB value is equal to 60). It is the DAC Color register that holds the 18-bit RGB encoding that drives the analog color display.

Color Animation

An interesting programming technique for VGA systems is to use the bits in the Color Select register to change some or all of the displayed colors. For example, if the Palette Select bit of the Attribute Mode Control register is clear, then bits 2 and 3 of the Color Select register provide two high-order bits of the DAC register number. (See Figure 3.8.) Since two bits can encode 4 combinations (00, 01, 10, and 11), a program can change the value of bits 2 and 3 of the Color Select register to index into four separate areas of the DAC, each one containing 64 different color registers. By the same token, if the Palette Select bit is set, then the four low-order bits in the Color Select register can be used to choose one of 16 DAC areas, each one containing 16 color registers. The areas of the DAC determined through the Color Select register are sometimes referred to as *color pages*. Some interesting animation effects can be achieved by rapidly shifting these color pages. For example, a program can simulate an explosion by shifting the pixel colors to tints of red, orange, and yellow.

BIOS service number 16, subservice number 19, provides a means for setting the paging mode to 4 color pages of 64 registers or to 16 color pages of 16 registers each. Also for selecting an individual color page within the DAC. The use of this BIOS service is described in Appendix C. In this kind of programming it is important to remember that the BIOS initialization routines for mode number 18 set color values for the first 64 DAC registers only. It is up to the software to initialize the color values in the DAC registers as necessary.

3.3 Device Drivers in the VGA1 Libraries

The VGA device driver routines are contained in the module named VGA1 of the GRAPHSOL library that is furnished with this book. Other library modules that start with the letters VGA also contain VGA primitive routines. The other VGA libraries are described in forthcoming chapters. In order to access and use the files in the accompanying microdisk the reader must follow the installation and unpacking instructions in Appendix A. Interfacing the library procedures with the various high-level languages supported by this book is described in Appendix B.

3.3.1 VGA1 Library Functions

The following are generic descriptions of the device driver routines contained in the VGA1 module of the GRAPHSOL library. The values passed and returned by the individual functions are listed in the order in which they are referenced in the code. The data types used by all library modules can be seen in Table 1.3. The following listing is in the order in which the routines appear in the library source files.

ES_TO_VIDEO (Assembly Language Only)

Set the ES segment register to the base address of the video buffer while in an alphanumeric mode.

    Receives:
        Nothing
    Returns:
        ES set to video buffer segment for alpha mode
    Action:
        Video buffer can now be addressed in the form: ES:xx

ES_TO_APA (Assembly Language Only)

Set the ES segment register to the base address of the video buffer while in a graphics mode. VGA graphics buffer is at A000H.
    Receives:
        Nothing
    Returns:
        ES set to video buffer segment for graphics mode
    Action:
        Video buffer can now be addressed in the form: ES:xx

PIXEL_ADD_18 (Assembly Language Only)

Calculate buffer offset from pixel coordinates while in VGA mode number 18.
    Receives:
        1. Word integer of x-axis pixel coordinate. Range is 0 to 639
        2. Word integer of y-axis pixel coordinate. Range is 0 to 479
    Returns:
        1. Word integer of offset into video buffer
        2. Byte integer of pixel mask for write mode 0 or 2
    Action:
        Prepare for pixel read and write operations in VGA mode number 18.

WRITE_PIX_18 (Assembly Language Only)

Set (write) an individual screen pixel while in VGA mode number 18, write mode 2.
    Receives:
        1. Logical address of pixel in video buffer
        2. Byte integer of pixel color in IRGB form
        3. Pixel mask for write mode 2
    Returns:
        Nothing
    Action:
        Pixel is set to one of 16 colors

TILE_ADD_18 (Assembly Language Only)

Calculate the coarse-grain address of an 8-by-8 pixel block (tile) while in VGA mode number 18.
    Receives:
        1. Byte integer of x-axis tile coordinate. Range is 0 to 79
        2. Byte integer of y-axis tile coordinate. Range is 0 to 59
    Returns:
        1. Word integer of offset into video buffer
    Action:
        Prepare for tile write operation

WRITE_TILE_18 (Assembly Language Only)

Set (write) a screen tile (8-by-8 pixel block) while in VGA mode number 18, write mode 2.
>   Receives:
>>   1. Logical address of tile in video buffer
>>   2. Byte integer of tile color in IRGB form
>   Returns:
>>   Nothing
>   Action:
>>   Tile is set to one of 16 colors

READ_PIX_18 (Assembly Language Only)

Read the color code of a screen pixel in VGA mode number 18, read mode 0.
>   Receives:
>>   1. Logical address of pixel in video buffer
>>   2. Pixel mask for write mode 2
>   Returns:
>>   1. Byte integer of pixel's IRGB color code
>   Action:
>>   Pixel is read in read mode 0

TWO_BIT_IRGB

Initialize DAC registers for VGA mode number 19 (256 colors) for the double bit IRGB format shown in Figure 3.6.
>   Receives:
>>   Nothing
>   Returns:
>>   Nothing
>   Action:
>>   DAC registers in the pattern shown in Table 3.3

GRAY_256

Initialize DAC registers for VGA mode number 19 in 64 shades of gray, repeated 4 times.
>   Receives:
>>   Nothing
>   Returns:
>>   Nothing
>   Action:
>>   DAC registers in the pattern shown in Table 3.5

SUM_TO_GRAY

Perform sum-to-gray function by means of BIOS service number 16, sub-service number 27, of interrupt 10H. Previous contents of DAC registers are not preserved.

    Receives:
        Nothing
    Returns:
        Nothing
    Action:
        All DAC registers are converted to equivalent gray shades

SAVE_DAC

Save current color codes in all DAC registers. Values are stored in RAM.

    Receives:
        Nothing
    Returns:
        Nothing
    Action:
        The color codes in all DAC registers are stored in RAM

RESTORE_DAC

The DAC registers are restored to the color values saved by the SAVE_DAC procedure.

    Receives:
        Nothing
    Returns:
        Nothing
    Action:
        The color codes in all DAC registers are restored from the values saved in RAM by SAVE_DAC

PIXEL_ADD_19 (Assembly Language Only)

Calculate buffer offset from pixel coordinates while in VGA mode number 19.

    Receives:
        1. Word integer of x-axis pixel coordinate. Range is 0 to 319
        2. Word integer of y-axis pixel coordinate. Range is 0 to 199
    Returns:
        1. Word integer of offset into video buffer
    Action:
        Prepare for pixel read and write operations in mode number 19

TILE_ADD_19 (Assembly Language Only)

Calculate the coarse-grain address of an 8-by-8 pixel block (tile) while in VGA mode number 19.

Receives:
1. Byte integer of x-axis tile coordinate. Range is 0 to 39
2. Byte integer of y-axis tile coordinate. Range is 0 to 25
Returns:
1. Word integer of offset into video buffer
Action:
Prepare for tile write operation

FREEZE_DAC

Disable changes to the Palette and DAC registers during BIOS mode changes.
Receives:
Nothing
Returns:
Nothing
Action:
The color codes in the Palette and DAC registers are preserved during BIOS mode changes

THAW_DAC

Enable changes to the Palette and DAC registers during BIOS mode changes.
Receives:
Nothing
Returns:
Nothing
Action:
The color codes in the Palette and DAC registers are replaced by the default values during BIOS mode changes

VGA Setup, Text, and Bitmap Primitives

Chapter Summary

This chapter describes three groups of VGA primitive routines:
1. primitives for video system setup, inquiry, and control
2. primitives for text display operations
3. primitives for displaying images encoded in bit-blocks and for filling rectangular screen areas at the coarse level

4.0 Classification of VGA Primitives

In Chapter 3 we discussed the development of the most elementary and fundamental routines used in graphics programming called the device drivers. A second level of graphics routines, usually providing higher-level functions than device drivers, are the graphics primitives. VGA primitive routines can be arbitrarily classified into the following fields:

1. Set-up, inquiry, and control primitives. This group of functions include video mode-setting, read and write mode selection, initialization of palette and border color, inquiry of active video parameters, and other preparatory and initialization functions.

2. Text primitive routines. This group includes the selection of fonts and character attributes and the display of text characters in graphics modes.

3. Bit-block and area fill primitive routines. This group includes routines to manipulate bit-mapped images in video or RAM memory.

4. Raster graphics primitive routines. This group includes object-oriented routines to draw the most common geometrical figures, to fill screen areas with colors or attributes, and to transform figures stored in the video buffer or in data files.

The primitive routines in the GRAPHSOL VGA library furnished with this book are organized in the listed fields. In the present chapter we will discuss the primitive routines in the first three groups. Because of their complexity, all of Chapter 5 is devoted to object-oriented VGA primitives.

4.1 VGA Primitives for Set-up, Control, and Query

The VGA graphics programmer must perform operations that are preparatory, controlling, or inquisitory. For example, an application using VGA graphics could start its execution by setting the desired video mode and the read and write modes, initializing a segment register to the base address of the video buffer, and installing a set of color values in the pallet and border color registers. These preparations could also require investigating the present state of the video system in order to restore it at the conclusion of the application.

Many VGA preparatory and initialization operations can be performed by means of services in the BIOS interrupt 10H. (See Appendix C.) For example, a graphics program that uses a standard video mode will usually let the BIOS handle the complications of initializing the VGA registers that control display characteristics. Since mode setting usually takes place once or twice during the execution of an application, the slowness usually associated with BIOS services can be disregarded for this purpose. The same applies to many other initialization and set-up operations, which can be conveniently executed through the BIOS, and which seldom appear in the code. Such is the case with operations to set and read the Palette, Overscan, and DAC Color registers, to select the color paging mode, to sum DAC output to gray shades, and to obtain VGA system data.

On the other hand, some initialization operations are conspicuously missing from the services offered by BIOS interrupt 10H. For example, there are no BIOS services to set the VGA read and write modes. This is particularly noticeable when operating in mode number 19 (256 colors) which requires setting bit 6 of the Graphics Controller Graphics Mode Register. (See Figure 2.22.) Furthermore, other BIOS graphics services, such as those to set and read an individual screen pixel, perform so poorly that they are practically useless.

In summary: while most applications can benefit from BIOS VGA initialization and setup services, very few graphics programs could execute satisfactorily if they were limited to these BIOS services.

4.1.1 Selecting the VGA Write Mode

To make the VGA more useful and flexible its designers implemented several ways in which to write data to the video display. These are known as the *write modes*. VGA allows four different write modes, which are selected by means of bits 0 and 1 of the Graphics Mode register of the Graphics Controller. (See Figure 2.22.) The fundamental functions of the various write modes are as follows:

Write mode 0 is the default mode. In write mode 0 the CPU, Map Mask register of the Sequencer (Figure 2.13), and the Bit Mask register of the Graphics Controller (Figure 2.24), are used to set a screen pixel to any desired color. Other VGA registers are also used for specific effects. For example, the Data Rotate register of the Graphics Controller (Figure 2.20) has two fields which are significant during write mode 0 operations. The data rotate field (bits 0 to 3) determines how many positions to rotate the CPU data to the right before performing the write operation. The logical operation select field (bits 3 and 4) determines how the data stored in video memory is logically combined with the CPU data. The options are to write the CPU data unmodified or to AND, OR, or XOR it with the latched data.

In *write mode 1* the contents of the latch registers, previously loaded by a read operation, are copied directly onto the color maps. Write mode 1, which is perhaps the simplest one, is often used in moving one area of video memory into another one. This write mode is particularly useful when the software takes advantage of the unused portions of video RAM. The location and amount of this unused memory varies in the different video modes. For example, in VGA graphics mode 18 the total pixel count is 38,400 pixels (640 pixels per row in 480 rows). Since the video buffer maps are 64K bytes, in each map there are 27,135 unused buffer bytes available to the programmer. This space can be used for storing images or data. On the other hand, video mode number 19 consists of one byte per pixel and there are 320-by-200 screen pixels, totaling 64,000 bytes. Since the readily addressable area of the video buffer is limited to 65,536 bytes, the programmer has available only 1,536 bytes for image manipulations.

Write mode 2 is a simplified version of write mode 0. Like mode 0, it allows setting an individual pixel to any desired color. However, in write mode 2 the data rotate function (Data Rotate register) and the set-reset function (Set/Reset register) are not available. One advantage of write mode 2 over write mode 0 is its higher execution speed. Another difference between these write modes is that in write mode 2 the pixel color is determined by the contents of the CPU, and not by the setting of the Map Mask register or the Enable Set-Reset and Set-Reset registers. This characteristic simplifies coding and is one of the factors that determines the better performance of write mode 2. The WRITE_PIX_18 device driver routine developed in Chapter 3 uses write mode 2.

In *Write mode 3* the Data Rotate register of the Graphics Controller (Figure 2.20) operates in the same manner as in write mode 0. The CPU data is ANDed with the Bit Mask register. The resulting bit pattern performs the same function as the Bit Mask register in write modes 0 and 2. The Set/Reset register also performs the same function as in write mode 0. However, the Enable Set/Reset register is not used. Therefore, the pixel color can be determined by programming either the Set/Reset register or the Map Mask register. The Map Mask register can also be programmed to selectively enable or disable the individual maps.

An application can use several read and write modes without fear of interference or conflict, since a change in the read or write mode does not affect the displayed image. On the other hand, a change in the video mode will normally clear the screen and reset all VGA registers. The code for changing the write mode, which is quite simple and straightforward, is shown in the following fragment:

```
; Set the Graphics Controller's Graphic Mode Register to the
; write mode in the AL register
        PUSH    AX              ; Save mode
        MOV     DX,3CEH         ; Graphic Controller Address
                                ; register
        MOV     AL,5            ; Offset of the Mode register
        OUT     DX,AL           ; Select this register
        INC     DX              ; Point to Data register
        POP     AX              ; Recover mode in AL
        OUT     DX,AL           ; Selected
```

The VGA graphics programmer must be aware that certain BIOS services reset the write mode. For example, BIOS service number 9, of interrupt 10H, often used to display text messages in an APA mode, sets write mode number 0 every time it executes. For this reason graphics software must often reset the write mode after executing a BIOS service. The procedure named SET_WRITE_MODE in the VGA1 module of the GRAPHSOL library sets the video mode in a similar manner as the previous fragment. In addition, SET_WRITE_MODE resets the Bit Mask register to its default value.

Writing Data in the 256-color Modes

Writing a pixel in VGA mode number 19 (256 colors) requires that bit 6 of the Graphics Controller Graphics Mode register be set. Therefore a set write mode routine for VGA 256-color mode operation takes this into account. The following code fragment shows the required processing:

```
; Set the Graphics Controller's Graphic Mode Register to the
; write mode in the AL register, for 256 colors
        PUSH    AX              ; Save mode
        MOV     DX,3CEH         ; Graphic Controller Address
                                ; register
        MOV     AL,5            ; Offset of the Mode register
        OUT     DX,AL           ; Select this register
        INC     DX              ; Point to Data register
        POP     AX              ; Recover mode in AL
; Set bit 6 to enable 256 colors
        OR      AL,01000000B    ; Mask for bit 6
        OUT     DX,AL           ; Selected
```

The procedure named SET_WRITE_256 in the VGA1 module of the GRAPHSOL library sets the video mode in a similar manner as the previous fragment. In addition, SET_WRITE_256 resets the Bit Mask register to its default value.

4.1.2 Selecting the Read Mode

The VGA standard provides two different read modes. Read Mode 0, which is the default, loads the CPU with the contents of one of the bitmaps. In mode number 18 we conventionally designate the color maps with the letters I, R, G, and B, to represent the intensity, red, green, and blue elements. In this mode, which map is read into the CPU depends on the current setting of bits 0 and 1 of the Read Operation Map Select register of the Graphics Controller. (See Figure 2.21.) Sometimes we say that the selected read map is *latched* onto the CPU. In order to read the contents of all four maps, the program must execute four read operations to the same video buffer address; this latching is usually preceded by code to set the Read Operations Map Select register.

Read Mode 0 is useful in obtaining the contents of one or more video maps, while Read Mode 1 is more convenient when the programmer wishes to test for the presence of pixels that are set to a specific color or color pattern. In Read Mode 1 the contents of all four maps are compared with a predetermined mask. This mask must have been stored beforehand in the Color Compare register of the Graphics Controller. (See Figure 2.18.) For example, to test for the presence of bright blue pixels, the IRGB bit pattern 1001B is stored in the Color Compare register. Thereafter, a read operation appears to execute four successive logical ANDs with this mask. If a bit in any of the four maps matches the bit mask in the Color Compare register, it will be set in the CPU; otherwise it will be clear.

The read mode is determined by bit 3 of the Select Graphics Mode register of the Graphics Controller. (See Figure 2.22.) The code to set the read mode is shown in the following fragment:

```
; Set the Graphics Controller Graphic Mode Select register to
; read mode 0 or 1, according to the value in AL
          CMP     AL,1              ; If entry value is not 1
          JNE     OK_BIT3           ; read mode 0 is forced
          MOV     AL,08H            ; 00001000B to set bit 3
OK_BIT3:
          PUSH    AX                ; Save mode
          MOV     DX,3CEH           ; Graphic controller address
                                    ; register
          MOV     AL,5              ; Offset of the mode register
          OUT     DX,AL             ; Select this register
          INC     DX                ; Point to data register
          POP     AX                ; Recover mode in AL
          OUT     DX,AL             ; Selected
```

The procedure named SET_READ_MODE in the VGA1 module of the GRAPHSOL library sets the read mode in a similar manner as the previous fragment. The procedure named READ_MAPS_18, also in the VGA1 module, reads the contents of all four maps while in mode number 18 and returns the result in machine registers. This operation is performed by successively selecting the I, R, G, and B maps by means of the Read Map Select register of the Graphics Controller.

4.1.3 Selecting Logical Operation Modes

We have seen in Chapter 2 (Section 2.2.4) that the Data Rotate register of the Graphics Controller determines how data is combined with data latched in the system microprocessor registers. The programmer can select the AND, OR, and XOR logical operations by changing the value of bits 3 and 4. (See Figure 2.20.)

Although all three logical operation modes find occasional use in VGA graphics programming, the XOR mode is particularly useful. In animation routines the XOR mode provides a convenient way of drawing and erasing a screen object. The advantages of the XOR method are simpler and faster execution, and an easier way for restoring the original screen image. This is a convenient programming technique when more than one moving object can coincide on the same screen position.

One disadvantage of the XOR method is that the object's color depends on the color of the background over which it is displayed. If a graphics object is moved over different backgrounds, its color will change. The reader can observe that the cross-hair symbol of the MATCH program appears in different colors when overlaid over the running boar than when over the gray background. In this case the effect is not objectionable, but in other applications it could make the XOR technique unsuitable.

The programmer should note that some BIOS services set the Data Rotate register of the Graphics Controller to the normal mode. For example, if BIOS service number 9 of interrupt 10H is used to display text messages in a graphics application, when execution returns the logical mode is set to normal operation. Therefore, a program that uses the XOR, AND, or OR logical modes must reset the Data Rotate register after using this BIOS service.

XOR Operations in Animation Routines

The illusion of movement of a screen object is often produced by means of geometrical transformations. The simple transformations are named *translation*, *rotation*, and *scaling*. Complex transformations consist of combining two or more of simple transformations; for instance, a screen object moves across the screen while becoming progressively larger. The combined transformations generate the feeling that a three-dimensional object is diagonally approximating the viewer.

Geometrical transformations are usually performed by replacing the previous image of the object with a new image. In *lateral translation* an object appears to move across the screen by progressively redrawing it at closely different horizontal coordinates. The boar symbol in the MATCH program is translated in this manner. Note that the graphics software must not only draw a series of consecutive images, but also erase the previous images from the screen. Otherwise, the animated object leaves a visible track of illuminated screen pixels. This effect could be occasionally desirable, frequently this is not the case. Also note that erasing the screen object is at least as time consuming as drawing it, since each pixel in the object must be changed to its previous state.

Erasing and redrawing of the screen object can be performed in several ways. One method is to save that portion of the screen image that is to be replaced by the object. The object can then be erased by redisplaying the original image. This method adds an additional burden to the graphics routine, which must also read and store every screen pixel that will be occupied by the object, but in many situations it is the only satisfactory solution. We have mentioned that another method of erasing the screen image is based on performing a logical XOR operation. The effect of the XOR is that a bit in the result is set if both operands contain opposite values. Consequently, XORing the same value twice restores the original contents, as in the following example:

```
            10000001B
   XOR      10110011B
            ----------
            00110010B


   XOR      10110011B
            ----------
            10000001B
```

An application that has set the Data Rotate register to the XOR mode can successively display and erase a screen object by XORing its bitmap. The effect can be used to animate the screen object by progressively changing its screen coordinates. The MATCH program, which is furnished on the book's microdisk as an illustration of VGA programming techniques, uses the XOR mode to display and erase two animated objects; one represents the outline of a running boar target and the other one the cross-hair of a rifle scope. The procedure named XOR_XHAIR in the MATCHD.ASM source file and the procedures XOR_RBOAR and XOR_LBOAR in the MATCHC.ASM source file, perform the draw/erase operations. Both procedures assume that the logical mode for the XOR operation has been previously set.

4.1.4 Investigating and Saving the System Status

In contrast with its predecessors (EGA and CGA) all VGA registers that hold relevant system data can be read by the processor. This allows a program to investigate the video status by performing a read operation to the relevant register. In addition, BIOS service number 27 and number 28 provide means for obtaining VGA data and for saving and restoring the video state. (See Appendix C.)

A function that is conspicuously missing in the BIOS is one to save the setting in the 256 VGA DAC color registers. For this reason, a program that uses BIOS sum-to-gray-shades function (service number 16, sub-service 27, of interrupt 10H) has no way of restoring the original DAC colors. The procedure named SAVE_DAC in the VGA1 module of the GRAPHSOL library, provides a way for saving the state of the DAC registers. The procedure RESTORE_DAC can be used to restore the DAC register setting saved with SAVE_DAC.

4.1.5 Vertical Retrace Timing

In Chapter 1 we saw that raster scan displays operate by projecting an electron beam on each horizontal row of screen pixels. Pixel scanning proceeds, row by row, from the top left screen corner to the bottom right. To avoid visible interference, the electron beam is turned off during the period in which the gun is re-aimed back to the start of the next pixel row (horizontal retrace). The beam is also turned off while it is re-aimed from the last pixel on the bottom right corner of the screen to the first pixel at the top left corner (vertical retrace). Because of the distance and directions involved, the vertical retrace period takes much longer than the horizontal retrace one.

In the CGA card it was the programmer's responsibility to time each access to the video buffer with the vertical retrace cycle of the CRT controller. Otherwise the result would be a visible interference, usually called snow. The VGA was designed to avoid this form of interference when using conventional display programming methods. However, animation techniques, which must flash consecutive screen images at a rapid rate are not free from interference. Therefore, in this case the program must time the buffer accesses with the vertical retrace cycle of the CRT controller.

This timing requirement introduces an additional burden on animated graphics software. For example, the screen refresh periods in VGA graphics modes take place at an approximate rate of 70 times per second. An animated program that flashes images on the screen at a minimum rate of 20 per second must take into account that each display operation has to be timed with a vertical retrace cycle that takes place 70 times per second. This synchronization delay must be added to the processing time in order to maintain an interference-free image-flashing rate.

The start of the vertical retrace cycle can be determined by reading bit 7 of the VGA Input Status register 0 in the General register group. (See Figure 2.7.) This bit is set if a vertical retrace is in progress. But in order to maximize the interference-free time available during a vertical retrace, the code must wait for the start of a vertical retrace cycle. This requires first waiting for a vertical retrace cycle to end, if one is in progress, and then detecting the start of a new cycle. The programming is shown in the following code fragment:

```
; Test for start of the vertical retrace cycle
; Bit 7 of the Input Status register 0 is set if a vertical
; cycle is in progress
        MOV     DX,3C2H                 ; Input status register 0
                                        ; In VGA color modes
VRC_CLEAR:
        IN      AL,DX                   ; Read byte at port
        JMP     SHORT $+2               ; I/O delay
        TEST    AL,10000000B            ; Is bit 7 set?
        JNZ     VRC_CLEAR               ; Wait until bit clear
; At this point the vertical retrace ended. Wait for it to
; restart
VRC_START:
        IN      AL,DX                   ; Read byte at port
        JMP     SHORT $+2               ; I/O delay
        TEST    AL,10000000B            ; Is bit 7 set?
        JZ      VRC_START               ; Wait until bit set
; Vertical retrace has now started
```

The procedure named TIME_VRC, in the VGA1 module of the GRAPHLIB library, detects the start of the CRT vertical retrace cycle so that video access operations can be synchronized.

4.2 VGA Text Display Primitives

Very few graphics applications execute without some form of text display. If the text display functions in an application take place in separate screens from the graphics operations, the programmer has the convenient option of selecting a text mode and either using text output keywords in a high-level language or one of the text display functions available in the BIOS. However, if a graphics program must combine text and graphics on the same screen, the text display functions available to the programmer are more limited.

4.2.1 BIOS Text Display Functions

In any mode, alphanumeric or graphics, BIOS service number 9, INT 10H, can be used to display a character at the current cursor position. Note that this is the only BIOS character display service that can be used in a graphics mode, but that several other services can be used in alphanumeric modes. (See Appendix C.) Service number 2, INT 10H, to set the cursor position, can also be used in conjunction with service number 9. Note that there is no physical cursor in VGA graphics modes, and that the action of service number 2, interrupt 10H, is simply to fix a position for the text display operation that will follow. This invisible cursor is sometimes called a *virtual cursor*. The procedure named SET_CURSOR, in the ALFA modules of the GRAPHSOL library, uses service number 2, interrupt 10H, to set the cursor. Once the virtual cursor is positioned at the desired screen location, the program can display characters on the graphics screen by means of service number 9, interrupt 10H.

Text Block Display

But VGA programs that have frequent need to display text while in a graphics mode often need a more convenient method than setting a virtual cursor and calling BIOS service number 9. One option is a routine capable of displaying any number of text lines, starting at any screen position, and using any desired color available in the active mode. A convenient way of storing the display parameters for the text message is in a header block preceding the message itself. The GRAPHIC_TEXT procedure in the VGA2 module of the GRAPHSOL library displays a text message with embedded parameters. In this case the first byte in the header encodes the screen row at which the message is to be displayed, the second byte encodes the screen column, and the third one the color code. Since the procedure operates in any text of graphics mode, the range and encoding for these parameters depend on the active mode.

BIOS Character Sets

The BIOS stores several sets of text characters encoded in bitmap form. (See Figure 1.10.) VGA systems contain three complete character fonts and two supplemental fonts. The characteristics of these fonts are shown in Table 4.1.

   The supplemental character sets (Table 4.1) do not contain all of the 256 character maps of the full sets, but only those character maps that are different in the 9-bit wide fonts. In the process of loading a 9-bit character set the BIOS first loads the corresponding set of 8-bit character maps and then overwrites the ones that need correction and that appear in the supplemental set. This mechanism is usually transparent to the programmer, who sees a full set of 9- by-14 or 9-by-16 characters.

Table 4.1 *VGA BIOS Character Sets*

CHARACTER BOX SIZE	MODE
8 by 8	0, 1, 2, 3, 4, 5, 13,14, and 19
8 by 14	0, 1, 2, 3, 15, and 16
8 by 16	17, and 18
9 by 14 *	7
9 by 16 *	0, 1, and 7
* = supplemental sets	

4.2.2 Character Generators

VGA graphics programs can perform simple character display operations by means of the BIOS functions, but for many purposes these functions are too limiting. (See Appendix C.) Perhaps the most obvious limitation of character display by means of BIOS services is that the text characters must conform to a grid of columns and rows determined by the active character font and video mode. For example, a graphics program executing in mode number 18 uses BIOS service number 9, interrupt 10H, to display screen text using the 8 by 16 character font. This program will be constrained to a text screen composed of 80 character columns by 30 rows and will not be able to locate text outside this imaginary grid.

Moving a BIOS Font to RAM

A program can obtain considerable control in text display functions by operating its own character generator, in other words, by manipulating the text character maps as if they were a regular bitmap. The process can often be simplified by using existing character maps. In VGA systems the most easily available character maps are the BIOS character sets. (See Table 4.1). The software can gain the necessary information regarding the location of any one of the BIOS character maps by means of service number 17, sub-service number 48, of interrupt 10H. (See Appendix C). Once the address of the character table is known, the code can move all or part of this table to its own address space, where it becomes readily accessible. The procedure named FONT_TO_RAM in the VGA2 module of the GRAPHSOL library can be used to load any one of the three full VGA character sets into a buffer furnished by the caller.

In loading a BIOS character font to RAM memory so that the font can be used with the display procedures in the GRAPHSOL library the caller must precede the font storage area with two data bytes that encode the font's dimensions. For example, the storage area for the BIOS 8-by-8 font can be formatted as follows:

```
;********************|
;    storage for BIOS  |
;    symmetrical font  |
;********************|
; RAM storage for symmetrical font table from BIOS character
; maps; Each font table is preceded by two bytes that determine
; its dimensions, as follows:
;    Byte at font table minus 1 = number of pixel rows
;    Byte at font table minus 2 = number of horizontal bytes
;
; 1 x 8 built in ROM font
                DB      1         ; Bitmap x dimension, in bytes
                DB      8         ; Bitmap y dimension, in bytes
FONT_1X8        DB      2048 DUP (00H)
```

Note that 2048 bytes are reserved for the 8-by-8 BIOS font, which contains 256 character maps of 8 bytes each (256 x 8 = 2048). By the same token, the 1 by 16 character font would require 4096 bytes of storage.

Once the BIOS font table is resident in the caller's memory space it can be treated as a collection of bitmaps, one for each character in the set. In this manner the programmer is able to control, at the pixel level, the screen position of each character. Consequently, the spacing between characters, which is necessary in line justification, also comes under software control. Also the spacing between text lines, and even the display of text messages at screen angles becomes possible.

The VGA2 module of the GRAPHSOL library contains three display procedures for displaying text messages using a BIOS character set resident in the program's memory space. The procedure named COARSE_TEXT provides a control similar to the one that can be obtained using BIOS service number 9, interrupt 10H, that is, text is displayed at column and row locations. Its operation is also similar to the GRAPHIC_TEXT procedure previously described. The procedure named FINE_TEXT allows the display of a single text line starting at any desired pixel location and using any desired spacing between characters on the horizontal and the vertical axes. This means that if the vertical spacing byte is set to zero in the text header block all the characters will be displayed on a straight line in the horizontal plane. However, by assigning a positive or negative value to this parameter, the programmer using this procedure can display a text message skewed at any screen angle. Finally, the procedure named MULTI_TEXT in the VGA2 module of the GRAPHSOL library makes possible the display of a text message consisting of multiple lines, starting at any desired pixel location. When using the MULTI_TEXT procedure the programmer has two header parameters to control character and row spacing, but the skewing option is not available.

The program named TEXTDEMO furnished in the book's microdisk contains a demonstration of the use of the text display procedures contained in the VGA2 library.

Display Type

The use of character generator software and BIOS character tables, as described in the previous paragraphs, considerably expands the programmer's control over text display on the VGA graphics modes. However, the BIOS character sets consist of relatively small symbols. Many graphics application require larger characters (sometimes called display type) for use in logos, titles, headings, or other special effects. Since the largest character sets available in BIOS are the 8-by-16 and 9-by-16 fonts, the programmer is left to his or her own resources in this matter.

The programmer has many ways of creating, or obtaining, display type screen fonts. These include the use of scalable character sets, the design of customized screen font tables, the adaptation of printer fonts to screen display, the enlargement of existing screen fonts, and even the artistic design of special letters and logos. Which method is suitable depends on programming needs and availability of resources. Ideally, the display programmer would have available scalable text fonts in many different typefaces and styles. In fact, some sophisticated graphics programs and programming environments furnish screen version of the Postscript language, which comes close to achieving this optimum level of text display control.

In the development of text intensive applications, such as desktop publishing and graphics design software, the programmer should aim at the most sophisticated levels of text display technology. On the other hand, this absolute control over text display operations is often not necessary. In the MATCH program, which is provided in the book's microdisk as a demonstration of VGA programming techniques, we can see the use of two methods for creating display type. The first method was used for the program logo; in this case a large rendering of the word "Match" was created in the AutoCAD program, then output to a pen plotter, scanned, edited, and saved as a disk file image in TIFF format. This rendering of the word "Match," scaled to two sizes, can be seen in color plates number 6 and 7. The second method was to use a Hewlett-Packard style printer font (also called a PCL format) as a screen display type. The text in the first MATCH screen: "GRAPHICS SOLUTIONS – VGA Demo Press any Key to Start Match" is displayed using a PCL printer font. (See color plate 6.) We have used a PCL font in the programming demonstrations because they provide acceptable display quality and are often available to the programmer.

Using a PCL Font

One noticeable difference between the BIOS screen fonts and the printer fonts in PCL format is that the former have a symmetrical pattern for all the text characters, that is, all character maps occupy the same memory space. For example, in a BIOS 8-by-16 font each character map takes up 16 bytes of storage. In this case the software can reach any character map by adding a multiple of 16 to the address that marks the start of the font table. In other words, the offset of any desired character map is the product of its ASCII code by the number of bytes in each character map.

However, the optimization methods followed in the creation of PCL printer fonts determine that all character maps are not of identical size. Therefore, in a typical PCL font the character map for the letter "M" is larger than the character map for the letter "i." This characteristic complicates the problem of finding the start of a desired character map in the font table and in obtaining its specific horizontal and vertical dimensions. The procedure named INDEX_HP in the VGA2 module of the GRAPHSOL library is an auxiliary routine to find the offset and the character dimensions of any character in a PCL font. The details of the PCL encoding can be found in Chapter 10 and in the source code of the INDEX_HP procedure. (See the file VGA2.ASM in the book's microdisk.)

The use of a PCL font in screen display operation requires loading the font's character maps into the program's address space. This operation is similar to loading a BIOS font as performed by the FONT_TO_RAM procedure. One difference is that the BIOS font resides in system memory while the PCL font is stored in a disk file. The procedure READ_HPFONT in the VGA2 module loads a printer font in PCL format into a RAM buffer provided by the caller. In this case the caller must provide a pointer to a buffer that holds an ASCIIZ string with the filename of the PCL disk file as well as a pointer to another buffer that will hold the loaded character set. Note that an ASCIIZ string is an MS DOS structure that holds a pathname followed by a zero byte. An example of the necessary structures and operations for loading a PCL font can be found in the TEXTDEMO program contained in the book's microdisk.

Once the PCL font is resident in the program's memory space, its characters can be conveniently displayed on the screen by means of a character generator routine. The FINE_TEXTHP procedure in the VGA2 module of the GRAPHSOL library is a character generator routine for use with PCL format character maps. This routine provides, for PCL fonts, the text control features provided by the FINE_TEXT procedure for BIOS character maps.

Note that PCL font sizes are scaled to the standard density of a Hewlett-Packard laser printer, which is of 300 dots per inch. Since the pixel density in mode number 18 is of 75 pixels per inch, the displayed characters appear four times larger than printed ones. In other words, an 8 point PCL font will be displayed as 32-point characters.

4.3 Bit-Block and Fill Primitives

Computer graphics images are roughly classified into two types: bit-mapped and object-oriented. A bitmap is a data structure that serves to encode image elements into memory units. The character maps discussed in the previous section are bitmaps. In VGA systems the structure of a bitmap depends on the video mode. For example, in mode number 18, in with each screen pixel can be in one of sixteen colors (IRGB format) a full bitmap requires four bits per pixel. Figure 3.1 shows how the screen pixels (in mode number 18) are mapped to the VGA memory planes. However, a RAM bitmap for a mode 18 graphics image does not necessarily have to encode data in all four color planes. For example, a monochrome image can be encoded in a single map, while its color code is stored in a separate variable.

Mode 18 Bit Map Primitives

The most convenient bitmap format depends on the characteristic of the image, the video hardware, and the computer system. Chapter 10 is devoted to the most used bitmap formats in IBM microcomputers. In the present section we discuss the VGA primitive routines to display the images encoded in bitmaps that have been customized for a specific VGA mode. In Chapter 10 we discuss TIFF, GIF, and other formats used in a hardware-independent encoding of color images.

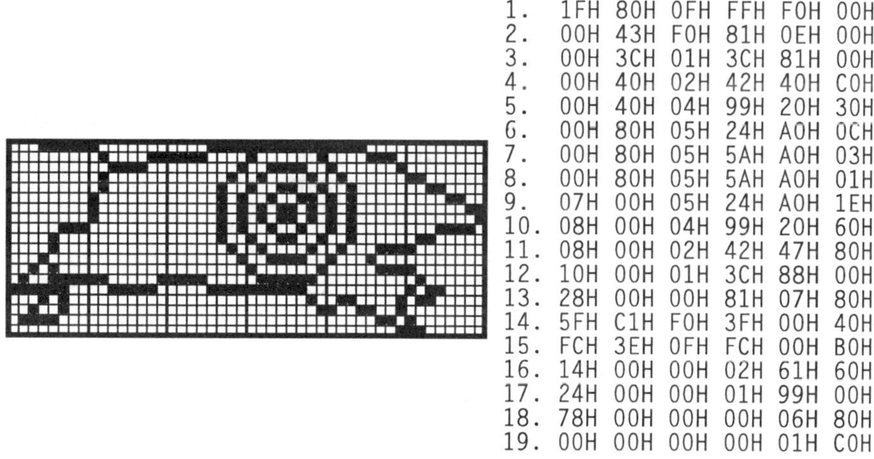

```
 1.   1FH  80H  0FH  FFH  F0H  00H
 2.   00H  43H  F0H  81H  0EH  00H
 3.   00H  3CH  01H  3CH  81H  00H
 4.   00H  40H  02H  42H  40H  C0H
 5.   00H  40H  04H  99H  20H  30H
 6.   00H  80H  05H  24H  A0H  0CH
 7.   00H  80H  05H  5AH  A0H  03H
 8.   00H  80H  05H  5AH  A0H  01H
 9.   07H  00H  05H  24H  A0H  1EH
10.   08H  00H  04H  99H  20H  60H
11.   08H  00H  02H  42H  47H  80H
12.   10H  00H  01H  3CH  88H  00H
13.   28H  00H  00H  81H  07H  80H
14.   5FH  C1H  F0H  3FH  00H  40H
15.   FCH  3EH  0FH  FCH  00H  B0H
16.   14H  00H  00H  02H  61H  60H
17.   24H  00H  00H  01H  99H  00H
18.   78H  00H  00H  00H  06H  80H
19.   00H  00H  00H  00H  01H  C0H
```

Figure 4.1 *Pixel Image and Bitmap of a Running Boar Target*

Figure 4.1 is a bitmap of the running boar target used in the MATCH demonstration program furnished in the book's microdisk. (See color plate number 8.) Also in Figure 4.1 is the bitmap that encodes in one-bits the screen pixels that are set in the running boar image. Because the bitmap is on a bit-to-pixel ratio it is quite suited to VGA mode number 18. (See Figure 3.2.)

A VGA mode number 18 graphics routine to display a bit-mapped image as the one shown in Figure 4.1 will need to know the screen coordinates at which the image is to be displayed, the dimensions of the bitmap, and the color code for the total image, or for each pixel or group of pixels. Two procedures in the VGA2 library can be used to display a bitmap in mode number 18. The procedure MONO_MAP_18 displays an image in single color while the procedure COLOR_MAP_18 can be used to display an image in which each pixel is encoded in a different color. In the MONO_MAP_18 procedure the color is stored in a single IRGB byte that is used to display all pixels in the map.

In the COLOR_MAP_18 procedure the color is passed as a pointer to an array of color codes stored in a byte-per-pixel table. This scheme, although simple and fast, is not the most memory efficient one, since in mode number 18 the 4-bit color code can be represented in one nibble (4 bits). However, the masking and indexing operations required in a nibble-per-pixel encoding would considerably slow down execution. An alternative and quite feasible bitmap scheme for VGA mode number 18 can be based on the video system's color map structure. (See Figure 3.1.) In this design the image is stored in four RAM bitmaps, each map representing an element in the IRGB format. While this encoding requires less than half the storage than the one used by the COLOR_MAP_18 procedure, it requires almost 4 times more space than a single monochrome code, as the one in the MONO_MAP_18 procedure. Another advantage of the design adopted in the bitmap display procedures in the VGA2 module is that either routine (MONO_MAP_18 and COLOR_MAP_18) can be used with the same image map by changing the color table pointer.

Mode 19 Bit Map Primitive

We have seen that in mode number 19 each screen pixel is mapped to a memory byte which encodes its color. The procedure named COLOR_MAP_19, in the VGA2 module of the GRAPHSOL library, displays a bitmap in VGA mode number 19. The code assumes that the bitmap is preceded by a header that holds the screen coordinates for the graphics image and the dimensions of the pixel map. Following this header is the byte-to-pixel map of the graphics image.

Fill Primitives

Primitives to perform fill operations are used to clear or initialize the screen, to set a geometrical area to a color or pattern, or to fill a closed boundary figure. The VGA2 module of the GRAPHSOL library contains fill routines to clear the video screen and to initialize a rectangular pixel area. Geometrical fill routines are developed in Chapter 5.

4.4 Primitive Routines in the VGA1 and VGA2 Modules

The library module named VGA1 of the GRAPHSOL library contains the VGA device drivers routines, discussed in Chapter 3, as well as the setup, inquiry, and control primitives mentioned in the present chapter. The VGA2 module contains the text display primitives and the bitmap display and rectangular fill primitives. In order to use the files in the accompanying microdisk the reader must follow the installation and unpacking instructions in Appendix A. Using the library routines from high-level languages is described in Appendix B.

4.4.1 Primitive Routines in the VGA1 Module

The following are generic descriptions of the setup, inquiry, and control primitive routines contained in the VGA1 libraries. The values passed and returned by the individual functions are listed in the order in which they are referenced in the code. The data types used by all library modules can be seen in Table 1.3. The following listing is in the order in which the routines appear in the library source files.

SET MODE

Sets the BIOS video display mode using service number 0 of interrupt 10H.
　　Receives:
　　　　1. Byte integer of desired video mode
　　Returns:
　　　　Nothing
　　Action:

New video mode is enabled. Screen is cleared

GET MODE

Obtains the current BIOS video mode using service number 15 of interrupt 10H.
>   Receives:
>>   Nothing
>   Returns:
>>   1. Byte integer of number of character columns. Valid values are 40 and 80
>>   2. Byte integer of active video mode
>>   3. Byte integer of active display page

TIME_VRC

Test for start of the vertical retrace cycle of the VGA CRT controller.
>   Receives:
>>   Nothing
>   Returns:
>>   Nothing
>   Action:
>>   Execution returns to caller at start of vertical retrace cycle

SET_WRITE_MODE

Set the Graphics Controller Write Mode register in VGA less-than-256-color modes.
>   Receives:
>>   1. Byte integer of desired write mode
>   Returns:
>>   Nothing

SET_WRITE_256

Set the Graphics Controller Write Mode register in VGA 256-color mode.
>   Receives:
>>   1. Byte integer of desired write mode
>   Returns:
>>   Nothing

SET_READ_MODE

Set the Graphics Controller Mode Select register to read mode 0 or 1.
>   Receives:
>>   1. Byte integer of desired read mode
>   Returns:
>>   Nothing

LOGICAL_MODE

Set the Graphics Controller Data Rotate register to XOR, OR, AND, or NOR-
MAL mode.
    Receives:
        1. Byte integer encoding desired logical mode
    Returns:
        Nothing

READ_MAPS_18

Read contents of four color maps in VGA mode number 18.
    Receives:
        1. Logical address of video buffer byte to read
    Returns:
        1. Byte integer of intensity map
        2. Byte integer of red map
        3. Byte integer of green map
        4. Byte integer of blue map
    Action:
        Routine assumes that read mode 0 is active
    Assumes:
        ES —> video buffer base address

4.4.2 Primitive Routines in the VGA2 Module

The following are generic descriptions of the text display, bitmap display and
rectangular fill primitives contained in the VGA2 libraries. The values passed
and returned by the individual functions are listed in the order in which they
are referenced in the code. The data types used by all library modules can be
seen in Table 1.3. The following listing is in the order in which the routines
appear in the library source files.

GRAPHIC_TEXT

Display a formatted text message using BIOS service number 9, interrupt 10H.
This procedure can be used in VGA modes number 18 and 19.
    Receives:
        1. Offset pointer to message text (DS assumed)
    Returns:
        Nothing
    Message format:

OFFSET	STORAGE UNIT	CONTENTS
0	Byte integer	Screen row for start of display
1	Byte integer	Screen column for start of display
2	Byte integer	Color code

Control codes:

CODE	ACTION
00H	End of message
FFH	End of text line

FINE_TEXT

Display a single-line text message using a RAM font table in which all bitmaps have the same dimensions (symmetrical font). Display position is defined at a pixel boundary. Mode number 18 only.

Receives:
1. Offset pointer to message text (DS assumed)
2. Offset pointer to RAM font table (DS assumed)

Returns:

Nothing

Message format:

OFFSET	STORAGE UNIT	CONTENTS
0	Word integer	Pixel row for start of display
2	Word integer	Pixel column for start of display
4	Word integer	Character spacing on x axis
6	Word integer	Character spacing on y axis
8	Byte integer	Color code in IRGB format

Control codes:

CODE	ACTION
00H	End of message

Assumes:

ES —> video buffer base address

MULTI_TEXT

Display a multiple-line text message using a RAM font table in which all bitmaps have the same dimensions (symmetrical font). Display position is defined at a pixel boundary. Mode number 18 only.

Receives:
1. Offset pointer to message text (DS assumed)
2. Offset pointer to RAM font table (DS assumed)

Returns:

Nothing

Message format:

OFFSET	STORAGE UNIT	CONTENTS
0	Word integer	Pixel row for start of display
2	Word integer	Pixel column for start of display
4	Word integer	Character spacing (x axis)
6	Word integer	Line spacing (y axis)
8	Byte integer	Color code in IRGB format

Control codes:
    CODE   ACTION
    00H   End of message
    FFH   End of text line
Assumes:
    ES —> video buffer base address

FINE_TEXTHP

Display a single-line text message using a RAM font table in PCL format
(asymmetrical font). Display position is defined at a pixel boundary. Mode
number 18 only.
    Receives:
        1. Offset pointer to message text (DS assumed)
        2. Offset pointer to RAM font table (DS assumed)
    Returns:
        Nothing
    Message format:
        OFFSET   STORAGE UNIT   CONTENTS
        0   Word integer   Pixel row for start of display
        2   Word integer   Pixel column for start of display
        4   Word integer   Character spacing on x axis
        6   Word integer   Character spacing on y axis
        8   Byte integer   Color code in IRGB format
    Control codes:
        CODE   ACTION
        00H   End of message
    Assumes:
        ES —> video buffer base address

READ_HPFONT

Read into RAM a PCL format printer font stored in a disk file
    Receives:
        1. Offset pointer to ASCIIZ filename for PCL soft font located in current
           path (DS assumed)
        2. Offset pointer to RAM storage area (DS assumed)
    Returns:
        Carry clear if no error
        Carry set if file not found or disk error

FONT_TO_RAM

Read a BIOS character map into RAM
    Receives:
        1. Byte integer encoding BIOS font desired
            8 = 8-by-8 font
            14 = 8-by-14 font

    16 = 8-by-16 font
  2. Offset pointer to RAM storage area (DS assumed)
Returns:
  Nothing

MONO_MAP_18

Display a single-color, bit-mapped image stored in the caller's memory space, while in VGA mode 18.

  Receives:
    1. Offset pointer to bitmap (DS assumed)
    2. Offset pointer to color code (DS assumed)
  Returns:
    Nothing
  Bitmap format:

OFFSET	STORAGE UNIT	CONTENTS
0	Word integer	Pixel row for start of display
2	Word integer	Pixel column for start of display
4	Byte integer	Number of rows in bitmap
5	Byte integer	Bytes per row in bitmap
6		Start of bit-mapped image

  Assumes:
    ES —> video buffer base address

COLOR_MAP_18

Display a multicolored, bit-mapped image stored in the caller's memory space, while in VGA mode 18.

  Receives:
    1. Offset pointer to bitmap (DS assumed)
    2. Offset pointer to color table (DS assumed)
  Returns:
    Nothing
  Bitmap format:

OFFSET	STORAGE UNIT	CONTENTS
0	Word integer	Pixel row for start of display
2	Word integer	Pixel column for start of display
4	Byte integer	Number of rows in bitmap
5	Byte integer	Bytes per row in bitmap
6		Start of bit-mapped image

  Color table format:
    One color byte per image pixel
  Assumes:
    ES —> video buffer base address

COLOR_MAP_19

Display a multicolored, byte-mapped image stored in the caller's memory space, while in VGA mode 19. One byte encodes each image pixel for display in 256 color mode.

    Receives:
        1. Offset pointer to header data of color byte map (DS assumed)
    Returns:
        Nothing
    Bitmap format:

OFFSET	STORAGE UNIT	CONTENTS
0	Word integer	Pixel row for start of display
2	Word integer	Pixel column for start of display
4	Byte integer	Number of rows in bitmap
5	Byte integer	Bytes per row in bitmap
6		Start of color byte-mapped image

    Color table format:
        One color byte per image pixel
    Assumes:
        ES — video buffer base address

CLS_18

Clear screen using IRGB color code while in VGA mode number 18.
    Receives:
        1. Byte integer of IRGB color code
    Returns:
        Nothing
    Action:
        Entire 640-by-480 pixel screen area is initialized to the color passed by the caller.

CLS_19

Clear screen using IRGB color code while in VGA mode number 19. Encoding depends on setting of DAC registers.
    Receives:
        1. Byte integer of IRGB color code
    Returns:
        Nothing
    Action:
        Entire 320-by-200 pixel screen area is initialized to the color passed by the caller

TILE_FILL_18

Initialize a rectangular screen area, at the tile level, to a passed color code while in mode 18.

Receives:
    1. Byte integer of x axis start tile
    2. Byte integer of y axis start tile
    3. Byte integer of horizontal tiles in rectangle
    4. Byte integer of vertical tiles in rectangle
    5. Byte integer of color code in IRGB format
Returns:
    Nothing
Assumes:
    ES —> video buffer base address

TILE_FILL_19

Initialize a rectangular screen area, at the tile level, to a passed color code while in mode 19.
    Receives:
        1. Byte integer of x axis start tile
        2. Byte integer of y axis start tile
        3. Byte integer of horizontal tiles in rectangle
        4. Byte integer of vertical tiles in rectangle
        5. Byte integer of color code (format depends on DAC color register settings)
    Returns:
        Nothing
    Assumes:
        ES —> video buffer base address

5

VGA Geometrical Primitives

Chapter Summary

This chapter describes vector graphics in relation to the calculation and display of geometrical figures that can be expressed in a mathematical formula. Geometrical primitives are developed for calculating and displaying straight lines, circles, ellipses, parabolas, and hyperbolas, as well as for performing rotation and clipping transformations and for filling the inside of a geometrical figure.

5.0 Geometrical Graphics Objects

Bit-mapped graphics are used to encode and display pictorial objects, such as the running boar target in Figure 4.1. However, graphics applications often also deal with geometrical objects, that is, graphical objects that can be represented by means of algebraic equations; such is the case with straight lines, parallelograms, circles, ellipses, and other geometrical figures. The terms *vector graphics*, *raster graphics*, and *object-oriented graphics* are often used, somewhat imprecisely, when referring to computer graphics operations on geometrical objects.

In VGA graphics, any image, including geometrical objects, can be encoded in a bitmap and displayed using the bitmap routines developed in Chapter 3. However, objects that can be represented mathematically can be treated by the graphics software in mathematical form. For example, it is often more compact and convenient to encode a screen circle by means of the coordinates of its origin and the magnitude of its radius than by representing all its adjacent points in a bitmap. The same applies to other geometrical figures; even to complex figures if they can be broken down into individual geometric elements.

5.0.1 Pixel-Path Calculations

In previous chapters we saw that the VGA graphics screen appears to the programmer as a two-dimensional pixel grid. Geometrical images on VGA can be visualized as points in this two-axes coordinate system, equated to x and y axes of the Cartesian plane. In dealing with geometrical figures the graphics programmer can use the equation of the particular curve to determine the pixel path that will represent it on the video screen or other device. In the VGA video display this process involves the calculation of the pixel addresses that lie along the path of the desired curve.

In high-level language graphics the software can use the language's mathematical functions. However, mathematical operations in high-level languages are generally considered too slow for screen graphics processing. Since performance is so important in video graphics programming, the preferred method of geometrical pixel plotting is usually the fastest one. In IBM microcomputers this often means low-level mathematics.

5.0.2 Graphical Coprocessors

One approach to performing the required pixel path calculations in the manipulation of geometrical images is the use of graphical coprocessor hardware. Several such chips have been implemented in silicon. For example, the XGA video graphics system, discussed in Chapter 6, contains a graphical coprocessor chip that assists in performing block fills, line drawings, logical mixing, masking, scissoring, and other graphics functions. Unfortunately, the VGA system does not contain a graphical coprocessor chip.

The 80x87 as a Graphical Coprocessor

Since no graphical coprocessor is included in VGA systems the programmer is often forced to use the central processor to perform geometrical and other calculations necessary in graphics software. But 80x86 mathematics are slow, cumbersome, and limited. However, most IBM microcomputers can be equipped with an optional mathematical coprocessor chip of the Intel 80x87 family. The power of the math coprocessor can be a valuable asset in performing the pixel path calculation required in the drawing of geometrical figures. For example, suppose that a graphics program that must plot a circular arc with a radius of z pixels, start coordinates at x1, y1 and end coordinates at x2, y2. One approach to this pixel-plotting problem is to calculate the set of x and y coordinates, starting at point x1, y1, and ending at x2, y2. The computations can be based on the Pythagorean expression

$$y = \sqrt{r^2 + x^2}$$

where x and y are the Cartesian coordinates of the point and r is the radius of the circle. The software can assign consecutive values to the x variable, starting at x1, and calculate the corresponding values of the y variable that lie along the arc's path. The pixels can be immediately plotted on the video display or the coordinates can be stored in a memory table and displayed later.

It is in performing such calculations that the mathematical coprocessor can be of considerable assistance. One advantage is that many mathematical operations are directly available, for example, the FSQRT instruction can be used to calculate the square root of a number. On the other hand, the main processor is capable only of integer arithmetic. Therefore, the calculation of powers, roots, exponential, and trigonometric functions on the 80x86 must be implemented in software. A second, and perhaps more important factor, is the speed at which the calculations are performed with the coprocessor, estimated at 30 to 50 times faster than with the CPU. Convenience and speed make the 80x87 a powerful programming tool for VGA geometrical graphics.

By limiting the calculations to integer values, the VGA programmer can simplify pixel plotting using the 80x87. We have seen that in VGA mode number 18 the y coordinate of a screen point can be represented by an integer in the range 0 to 479, and the x coordinate, an integer in the range 0 to 639. Since the 80x87 word integer format is a 16-bit value, with an identical numerical range as a main processor register, a graphical program can transfer integer data from processor to coprocessor, and vice-versa. These manipulations are illustrated in the examples contained in the VGA3 module of the GRAPHSOL library. The details of programming the 80x87 coprocessor, which is beyond the scope of this book, can be found in several titles listed in the Bibliography.

Emulating the 80x87

One practical consideration is that the 80x87 mathematical coprocessor is an optional device in IBM microcomputers; the exceptions are the machines equipped with the 486 chip, in which coprocessor functions are built-in. This optional nature of the coprocessor determines that applications that assume the presence of this chip will not execute in machines not equipped with an 80x87. This could create a serious problem for graphics code that rely on the coprocessor for performing pixel plotting calculations. Fortunately there is a solution to this problem: a software emulation of the coprocessor.

An 80x87 emulator is a program that simulates, in software, the operations performed by the 80x87 chip. Once the emulator software is installed, machines not equipped with an 80x87 are able to execute 80x87 instructions, although at a substantial performance penalty. Ideally, a program that uses 80x87 code could test for the presence of an 80x87 hardware component; if one is found, the chip is used in the calculations, if not, its operation is simulated by an emulator program. In reality, this ideal solution is possible only in machines that are equipped with the 80286 or 80386 CPU. The reason is that in 8086 and 8088 machines not equipped with an 8087 chip the presence of a coprocessor instruction hangs up the system in a wait-forever loop.

This problem was solved in the design of the 80286 CPU by means of two bits in the Machine Status Word register. These bits, named Math Present (MP) and Emulate (EM), allow encoding the presence, absence, or availability of the 80287 component. If the EM bit is set, then the execution of a coprocessor opcode will automatically generate an interrupt 7 exception. In this case a handler vectored at this interrupt can select an emulated version of the opcode, and the machine will not hang-up. A similar mechanism is used in the 80386 CPU, but not in the 8086 or the 8088 processors.

Therefore, 8086/8088 software that alternatively uses the real 8087 if one is present or the emulator if no chip is installed in the system, must contain both real and emulated code. In this case a routine can be devised to test for the presence of the hardware component. If one is found, execution is directed to routines that use real 8087 code. If no 8087 is detected, the emulator software is initialized and execution is directed to routines that contain calls to the emulator package. Since this method works in any IBM microcomputer, it is the one adopted in the GRAPHSOL graphics library furnished with this book. The test for the presence of the 80x87 chip, the installation of the emulator software, and the setting of the code selection switch is performed in the INIT_X87 procedure in the VGA3 module of the GRAPHSOL library, which also contains the routines that use 80x87 hardware instructions.

Emulated instructions for the geometrical calculation routines can be installed as a TSR program or incorporated in the code. TSR emulator programs are available from Intel, Ingenierburo Franke, and other vendors. The microdisk furnished with this book contains a Shareware 80x87 emulator program by Ron Kimball, RR01 Box 15Y, Brookfield, MA, 01506. The reader wishing to use this software should read the file EM87.DOC furnished in the microdisk. The Intel 80387 emulator program is part of the 80386 Numerics Support Library (part number D86-NUM-NL). This product is available from Intel Corporation.

5.1 Plotting a Straight Line

Geometrical figures can be drawn on the video display by mathematical pixel plotting when the pattern of screen pixels lies along a path that can be expressed in a mathematical equation. In this case, the graphical software calculates successive coordinate pairs and sets the pixels that lie along the curve's path. We have mentioned that the 80x87 mathematical coprocessor is a valuable tool for performing these calculations rapidly and precisely. Figure 5.1 shows a pixel representation of three straight lines.

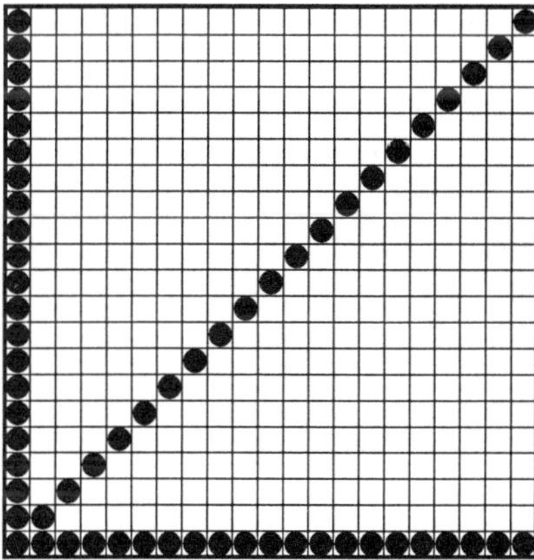

Figure 5.1   *Pixel Plots for Straight Lines*

In Figure 5.1 we see that horizontal and vertical lines are displayed on the screen by setting adjacent pixels. A line at a 45-degree angle can also be rendered accurately by diagonally adjacent pixels, although pixel to pixel distance will be greater in a diagonal line than in a horizontal or vertical one. But the pixel plot of a straight line that is not in one of these three cases cannot be exactly represented on a symmetrical grid, whether it be a pixel grid, or a quadrille drawing paper. Figure 5.2 shows the staircase effect that results from displaying an angled straight line on a symmetrical grid.

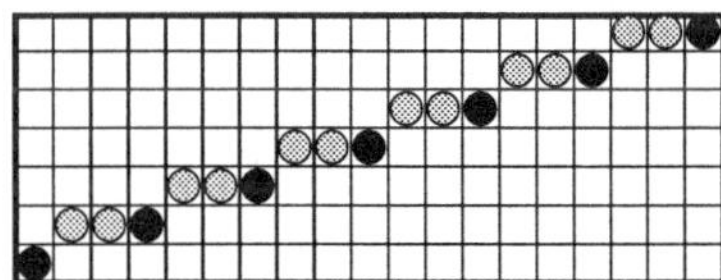

Figure 5.2   *Nonadjacent Pixel Plot of a Straight Line*

Notice that the black-colored pixels in Figure 5.2 represent the coordinates that result from calculating successive unit increments along the vertical axis. If only the black colored dots were used to represent the straight line in Figure 5.2, the graph would be discontinuous and the representation not very accurate. An extreme case of this discontinuity would be a straight line at such a small angle that it would be defined by two isolated pixels, one at each screen border. In conclusion, if no corrective measures are used, the screen drawing of a line or curve by simple computation of pixel coordinates can produce unsatisfactory results. The nonadjacency problem can be corrected by filling in the intermediate pixels. This correction is shown in gray-colored pixels in Figure 5.2.

5.1.1 Insuring Pixel Adjacency

Notice that the pixel plotting routines in the VGA3 module of the GRAPHSOL library store in memory the coordinate pairs found during the calculations phase, rather than immediately setting the screen pixels. Due to this mode of operation, the program must establish the necessary structures for holding the data. The following code fragment shows several storage assignations used in the routines contained in the VGA3 module.

```
; Scratch-pad for temporary data
THIS_X   DW       0            ; Normalized coordinate of x
THIS_Y   DW       0            ; Normalized coordinate of y
LAST_Y   DW       0            ; Internal control for
                               ; noncontinuous y-axis points
; Buffers for storing 1K of x and y coordinates of the first
; quadrant and a counter for the number of points computed
Y_BUFFER         DB       2048 DUP (00H)
X_BUFFER         DB       2048 DUP (00H)
POINTS_CNT       DW       0          ; Number of entries in buffers
```

Programmers have devised many computational strategies for generating the coordinate pairs to plot geometrical curves. Consider, at this point, that the straight line is geometrically defined as a curve. One of the processing operations performed by pixel-plotting routines is to fill in the spaces left empty by the mathematical computations (see Figure 5.1), thus insuring that the screen pixels representing the curve are adjacent to each other. The following code fragment corrects nonadjacent plots generated by any pixel-plotting primitive that calculates y as a function of x. The routine also assumes that x is assigned consecutive values by decrementing or incrementing the previous x value by one.

```
;**********************|
;    Test for adjacent |
;       y coordinates  |
;**********************|
; On entry:
;          CS:SI — buffer holding x coordinates of curve
;          CS:DI — buffer holding y coordinates of curve
; Adjacency correction is required if the previous y coordinate
; is not adjacent (one less) to the present y coordinate. Code
; assumes that the data variables are located in the code
; segment
         MOV      DX,CS:THIS_Y
         MOV      CX,CS:THIS_X
TEST_ADJACENT:
; Is this y  last y minus 1
         MOV      BX,CS:LAST_Y
```

```
        DEC     BX                      ; Last y minus 1
        CMP     DX,BX                   ; Compare to this y
        JL      FILL_IN_PIXEL
; Is this y  last y plus 1
        MOV     BX,CS:LAST_Y
        INC     BX                      ; Last y plus 1
        CMP     DX,BX                   ; Compare to this y
        JG      FILL_IN_PIXEL
        JMP     STORE_PIX_XYS
;*********************|
; correct nonadjacency  |
;*********************|
; BX = last y coordinate minus 1
FILL_IN_PIXEL:
        MOV     CS:[SI],BX              ; Store y coordinate
                                        ; adjacent to previous
                                        ; point
        MOV     CS:[DI],CX              ; Store this x coordinate
        ADD     SI,2                    ; Bump pointers
        ADD     DI,2
        INC     CS:POINTS_CNT           ; Bump points counter
        MOV     CS:LAST_Y,BX            ; Update to this point
        JMP     TEST_ADJACENT
;*********************|
;    store coordinates   |
;*********************|
STORE_PIX_XYS:
        MOV     CS:[SI],DX              ; Store normalized
                                        ; y coordinate
        MOV     CS:[DI],CX              ; Store normalized x
                                        ; coordinate
; Bump both buffer pointers
        ADD     SI,2
        ADD     DI,2
        INC     CS:POINTS_CNT           ; Bump points counter
        MOV     CS:LAST_Y,DX            ; Update LAST_Y variable
        .
        .
        .
```

The auxiliary procedure named ADJACENT in the VGA3 module of the
GRAPHSOL library uses similar logic as the above fragment.

5.1.2 Calculating Straight Lines Coordinates

A straight line in the Cartesian plane can be defined in several ways. One common mathematical expression consists of defining the line by means of the coordinates of its two end points. In this manner, we can refer to a line with start coordinates at $x1, y1$ and end coordinates at $x2, y2$. An alternative way of defining a straight line is by means of the coordinates of its start point, its angle, and one of its end point coordinates. In this manner, we can refer to a straight line from $x1, y1$, with a slope of 60 degrees, to a point at $x2$. Both expressions are useful to the graphics programmer.

Bresenham's Algorithm

One of the original algorithms for plotting a straight line between two points was developed by J. E. Bresenham and first published in the *IBM Systems Journal* in 1965. Bresenham's method consists of obtaining two pixel coordinates for the next y value and then selecting the one that lies closer to the path of an ideal straight line. The following code fragment shows the plotting of a straight line in VGA mode number 18 using Bresenham's method.

```
; Routine to draw a straight line with starting coordinates
; stored at CS:ORIGIN_X and CS:ORIGIN_Y and end coordinates at
; CS:END_X   and CS:END_Y
;
; Set unit increments for pixel-to-pixel operation
        MOV     CX,1
        MOV     DX,1
; Determine negative or positive slope from difference between
; the y and x coordinates of the start and end points of the
; line. This difference is also the length of the line
        MOV     DI,CS:END_Y
        SUB     DI,CS:ORIGIN_Y   ; Length
        JGE     POS_VERTICAL     ; Vertical length is positive
        NEG     DX               ; DX = -1 in 2's complement form
        NEG     DI               ; Make distance positive
POS_VERTICAL:
        MOV     CS:INCR_FOR_Y,DX ; Increments on the y axis will
                                 ; be positive or negative
; Calculate horizontal distance
        MOV     SI,CS:END_X
        SUB     SI,CS:ORIGIN_X
        JGE     POS_HORZ         ; Horizontal length is positive
        NEG     CX               ; CX = -1 in 2's complement form
        NEG     SI               ; Distance has to be positive
POS_HORZ:
        MOV     CS:INCR_FOR_X,CX ; Increments on the x axis can
                                 ; also be positive or negative
```

```
        ; Compare the horizontal and vertical lengths of the line to
        ; determine if the straight segments will be horizontal (if
        ; this length is greater) or vertical (otherwise)
                CMP     SI,DI             ; SI = horizontal length
                                          ; DI - vertical length
                JGE     HORZ_SEGMENTS
        ; Vertical length is greater, straight segments are vertical
                MOV     CX,0              ; No horizontal segments
                XCHG    SI,DI             ; Invert lengths
                JMP     SET_CONTROLS
        HORZ_SEGMENTS:
                MOV     DX,0              ; No vertical segments
        SET_CONTROLS:
                MOV     CS:STRT_HSEGS,CX ; Will be 1 or 0
                MOV     CS:STRT_VSEGS,DX ; Also 1 or 0
        ; Calculate adjustment factor
                MOV     AX,DI             ; Smaller direction component
                ADD     AX,AX             ; Double the shorter distance
                MOV     CS:STRT_TOTAL,AX ; Straight component total
                                          ; pixels
                SUB     AX,SI             ; Subtract larger direction
                                          ; component
                MOV     BX,AX             ; General component counter
                SUB     AX,SI             ; Calculate
                MOV     CS:DIAG_TOTAL,AX ; Diagonal component total
                                          ; pixels
        ; Prepare to draw line
                MOV     CX,CS:ORIGIN_X
                MOV     DX,CS:ORIGIN_Y
        ; SI = the length of the line along the longer axis
                INC     SI
                MOV     AL,CS:LINE_COLOR ; Color code for line
        ;********************|
        ;   draw line points  |
        ;********************|
        LINE_POINTS:
                DEC     SI                ; Counter for total pixels
                JNZ     PIX_DRAW
                JMP     END_OF_LINE       ; Line is finished
        ;********************|
        ;   display pixel     |
        ;********************|
        PIX_DRAW:
                CALL    PIXEL_WRITE_18   ; Routine to set pixel
                CMP     X,0               ; If BX  0 then straight segment
                                          ; diagonal segment otherwise
```

```
        JGE           DIAGONAL
; Draw straight line segments
        ADD           CX,CS:STRT_HSEGS ; Increment CX if horizontal
        ADD           DX,CS:STRT_VSEGS ; Increment DX if vertical
        ADD           BX,CS:STRT_TOTAL ; Counter plus adjustment
        JMP           LINE_POINTS
; Draw diagonal segment
DIAGONAL:
        ADD           CX,CS:INCR_FOR_X        ; X direction
        ADD           DX,CS:INCR_FOR_Y        ; Y direction
        ADD           BX,CS:DIAG_TOTAL        ; Adjust counter
        JMP           LINE_POINTS
END_OF_LINE:

                .

                .

                .
```

The procedure named BRESENHAM in the VGA3 module of the GRAPHSOL library is based on this algorithm.

An Alternative to Bresenham's Method

A program can use the 80x87 code to calculate the coordinates of a line defined by means of its end points. In an machine equipped with the coprocessor hardware this method performs better than the Bresenham routine listed above. On the other hand, if the 80x87 code is to be emulated in software, then Bresenham's algorithm executes faster. The 80x87 calculations can be based on the differential equation for the slope of a straight line:

```
if
Dy/Dx = constant
then
Dy/Dx = (y2 - y1) / (x2 - x1)
therefore, the slope of the line is expressed:
m = Dy/Dx
```

The actual calculations are as follows:

```
; Memory variables stored in the code segment:
;        CS:X1 = x coordinate of leftmost point
;        CS:Y1 = y coordinate of leftmost point
;        CS:X2 = x coordinate of second point
;        CS:Y2 = y coordinate of second point
; During computations:
;        x coordinate .......... CS:THIS_X ......... Word
;        y coordinate .......... CS:THIS_Y ......... Word
```

```
; On exit:
;          CS:BUFFER_X holds the set of x coordinates for the line
;          CS:BUFFER_Y holds the set of y coordinates
;          CS:POINTS_CNT is a counter for the number of x,y pairs
;                         stored in BUFFER_X and BUFFER Y
;*********************|
;      preparations   |
;*********************|
; Set registers and variables to coordinates
        LEA     SI,CS:Y_BUFFER              ; y buffer pointer
        LEA     DI,CS:X_BUFFER              ; x buffer pointer
        MOV     CS:LAST_Y,0                 ; First iteration
        MOV     CS:POINTS_CNT,0             ; Reset points counter
;
; Calculate Dy/Dx (slope m)
;                                  |  ST(0)  |   ST(1)   |   ST(2)   |
        FILD    CS:X1            ;    x1     |
        FILD    CS:X2            ;    x2     |     x1    |
        FSUB    ST,ST(1)         ;  x2 - x1  |     x1    |
        FSTP    ST(1)            ;  x2 - x1  |   empty   |
; Store in variable for the normalized x coordinate of
; start point
        FIST    CS:THIS_X
        FILD    CS:Y1            ;    y1     | x2 - x1 |
        FILD    CS:Y2            ;    y2     |     y1    | x2 - x1  |
        FSUB    ST,ST(1)         ;  y2 - y1  |     y1    | x2 - x1  |
        FSTP    ST(1)            ;  y2 - y1  |  x2 - x1  |   empty   |
        FDIV    ST,ST(1)         ;  Dy/Dx    |  x2 - x1  |
        FSTP    ST(1)            ;  Dy/Dx    |   empty   |
;*********************|
;     y coordinate    |
;     calculations    |
;*********************|
Y_POINT:
        FILD    CS:THIS_X    ;     x     |   Dy/Dx   |           |
; Solve y = x * Dy/Dx
        FMUL    ST,ST(1)     ;  x*Dy/Dx  |   Dy/Dx   |
; Store in variable for normalized y coordinate of this point
        FISTP   CS:THIS_Y    ;  Dy/Dx    |   empty   |
;*********************|
;   test for adjacent |
;       y values      |
;*********************|
        CALL    ADJACENT        ; Adjacency procedure
;*********************|
; test for last pixel |
```

```
;********************|
        CMP      CS:THIS_X,0    ; x = 0 must be calculated
        JE       EXIT_POINTS
        DEC      CS:THIS_X
        JMP      Y_POINT
; Adjust 80x87 stack pointer
EXIT_POINTS:
        FSTP     ST(0)

        .

        .

        .
```

A Line by its Slope

We saw, in the previous example, that a straight line can be defined by its slope. The mathematical expression for this line, called the point-slope form, in which the y coordinate is a function of the x coordinate can be expressed in the following equation:

$$y = mx$$

where x and y are the coordinate pairs and m is the slope. The slope is the difference between the y coordinates divided by the difference between the x coordinates of any two points in the line, expressed as follows:

$$m = \frac{(y2 - y1)}{(x2 - x1)}$$

Notice that $y2 - y1$ can have a positive or negative value, therefore m can be positive or negative. The following code fragment calculates the y coordinates for successive x coordinates using the point-slope equation for a straight line. The calculations, which use 80x87 code, assume that a real or emulated 80x87 coprocessor is available.

```
; Routine to plot and store the pixel coordinates of a straight
; line of slope s, located in the fourth quadrant
; The slope is in degrees and must be in the range 0   s   90
;
; On entry:
;               CS:X1    = x coordinate of origin
;               CS:Y1    = y coordinate of origin
;               CS:X2    = x coordinate of end point
;               CS:SLOPE = slope in degrees
;
; During computations:
```

```
;             X coordinate .......... CS:THIS_X ......... word
;             Y coordinate .......... CS:THIS_Y ......... word
;
; Formula:
;           y = x tan s
;********************|
;      preparations  |
;********************|
; Set registers and variables to coordinates
        LEA     SI,CS:Y_BUFFER  ; y buffer pointer
        LEA     DI,CS:X_BUFFER  ; x buffer pointer
        MOV     CS:LAST_Y,0     ; First iteration
        MOV     CS:POINTS_CNT,0 ; Reset points counter
; Calculate the normalized x coordinate for the rightmost point
;                                 |  ST(0)   |   ST(1)   |   ST(2)
|
        FILD    CS:X1           ;    x1      |
        FILD    CS:X2           ;    x2      |     x1    |
        FSUB    ST,ST(1)        ; x2 - x1    |     x1    |
        FSTP    ST(1)           ; x2 - x1    |   empty   |
; Store in variable for the normalized x coordinate of
; rightmost point
        FIST    THIS_X
        FSTP    ST(0)           ; empty      |
; Obtain and store tangent of slope
;                                 |  ST(0)   |   ST(1)   |   ST(2)  |
        FILD    CS:SLOPE        ; s(deg)     |
        CALL    DEG_2_RADS      ; s(rads)    |
        CALL    TANGENT         ; tan s      |
Y_BY_SLOPE:
;                                 |  tan s   |
        FILD    CS:THIS_X       ;    x       |   tan s   |
        FMUL    ST,ST(1)        ;    y       |   tan s   |
; Store in variable for normalized y coordinate of this point
        FISTP   CS:THIS_Y       ;  tan s     |
;********************|
;  test for adjacent |
;      y values      |
;********************|
        CALL    ADJACENT             ; Adjacency test procedure
;********************|
; test for last pixel |
;********************|
        CMP     CS:THIS_X,0     ; x = 0 must be calculated
        JE      EXIT_SLOPE
        DEC     CS:THIS_X
```

```
        JMP       Y_BY_SLOPE
; Adjust 8087 stack registers
EXIT_SLOPE:
        FSTP      ST(0)
          .

          .

          .
```

Notice that the graphic primitives named BRESENHAM and LINE_BY_SLOPE, in the VGA3 module of the GRAPHSOL library, share several code segment variables. Also notice that the procedure named ADJACENT is called by the LINE_BY_SLOPE primitive to correct nonadjacent pixel conditions that can arise during the plotting calculations. The VGA3 module includes a local procedure, named TANGENT, that performs the calculations for the tangent function required in the line-by-slope formula. Since the calculations performed by the TANGENT procedure use the radian measure of the angle, the auxiliary procedure named DEG_2_RADS in the VGA3 module is used to convert from degrees to radian.

Displaying the Straight Line

The LINE_BY_SLOPE procedure in the VGA3 module of the GRAPHSOL library is limited to calculating and storing the pixel coordinates of the straight line defined by the caller. This mode of operation makes the routine more device-independent and also makes possible certain manipulations of the stored data. However, most applications will, sooner or later, need to draw the line on the screen. The following code fragment shows the necessary operations.

```
; Display coordinates stored in CS:X_BUFFER and CS:Y_BUFFER
while
; in VGA mode number 18
; Total number of coordinates is stored in CS:POINTS_CNT
; Setup pointers and counter
        LEA       SI,CS:Y_BUFFER          ; y coordinates
        LEA       DI,CS:X_BUFFER          ; x coordinates
        MOV       CX,CS:POINTS_CNT
        MOV       CS:OPS_CNT,CX           ; Operational counter
DISP_1:
        MOV       CX,CS:X1                ; x coordinate of origin
        MOV       DX,CS:Y1                ; y coordinate of origin
; Add stored values to origin
        ADD       CX,WORD PTR CS:[DI]
        SUB       DX,WORD PTR CS:[SI]
; CS:CX = x coordinate
; CS:DX = y coordinate of point
        PUSH      AX                      ; Save color code
```

```
        CALL    PIXEL_ADD_18        ; Procedures in VGA1 module
        CALL    WRITE_PIX_18
        POP     AX                  ; Restore color code
        ADD     CS:SI,2             ; Bump coordinates pointers
        ADD     CS:DI,2
        DEC     CS:OPS_CNT          ; Operation points counter
        JNZ     DISP_1

          .
          .
          .
```

The procedure named DISPLAY_LINE in the VGA3 module of the GRAPHSOL library can be used to display a straight line plotted by means of the LINE_BY_POINTS procedure. Notice that the procedure named BRESENHAM displays the pixels as the coordinates are calculated.

5.2 Plotting Conic Curves

By intersecting a right circular cone at different planes it is possible to generate several geometrical curves. These curves, or conic sections, are the circle, the ellipse, the parabola, and the hyperbola. A VGA graphics program can plot the coordinates of the conic curves employing similar methods as the ones developed for plotting straight lines. (See Section 5.1.)

5.2.1 The Circle

A circle in the Cartesian plane can be described by the coordinates of its origin, and by its radius. As far as the calculation of the coordinate points only the radius parameter is necessary, although the origin coordinates is required to position the circle in the viewport. To calculate the pixel coordinates of a circle described by its radius we can use the Pythagorean formula, which allows us

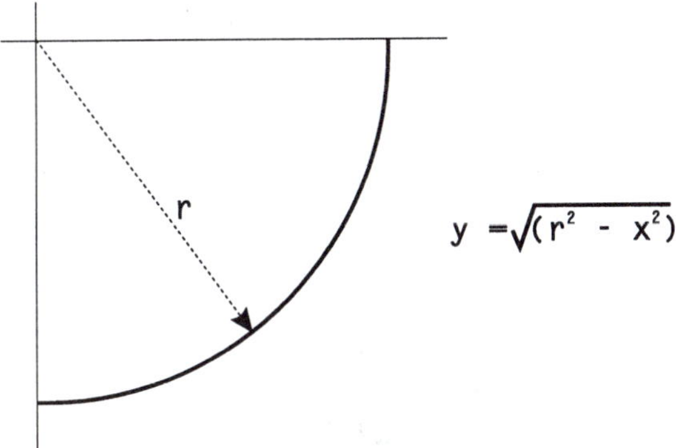

Figure 5.3 *Plot and Formula for Circle*

to obtain the corresponding values of y for each x. The curve and formula can be seen in Figure 5.3.

The following code fragment shows the calculations necessary for plotting the coordinates of a circular arc in the fourth quadrant. The calculations are performed by means of the 80x87 mathematical coprocessor.

```
; Routine to plot and store the pixel coordinates of a circular
; arc in the fourth quadrant
;
; On entry:
;           Radius: ........... CS:R ........ word
; During computations:
;           x coordinate ... CS:THIS_X ........ word
;           y coordinate ... CS:THIS_Y ........ word
;
;********************|
;     preparations   |
;********************|
; Reset counters and controls
        MOV      CS:THIS_X,0            ; Start values for x
        MOV      CS:LAST_Y,0            ; and LAST_Y
; Buffer pointers:
;       SI — Y values buffer
;       DI — X values buffer
        LEA      SI,CS:Y_BUFFER
        LEA      DI,CS:X_BUFFER
        MOV      CS:POINTS_CNT,0        ; Reset counter
;
;********************|
; calculate y values |
;********************|
CIRCLE_Y:
;                                   | ST(0)    |   ST(1)  |
        FILD     CS:THIS_X         ;    x      |
        FMUL     ST,ST(0)          ;    x^2    |
        FILD     CS:R              ;    r      |     x^2
        FMUL     ST,ST(0)          ;    r^2    |     x^2
        FSUB     ST,ST(1)          ; r^2 - x^2 |     x^2
        FSQRT                      ;Rt(r^2-x^2)|     x^2
        FISTP    CS:THIS_Y         ;    x^2    |
        FSTP     ST(0)             ;  EMPTY    |
; Test adjacency condition
        CALL     ADJACENT              ; Library procedure
        INC      CS:THIS_X             ; x increments in a circle's
                                       ; fourth quadrant
```

```
        CMP     CS:THIS_Y,0      ; Test for end of execution
        JNE     CIRCLE_Y
; At this point all coordinates have been plotted
        .

        .

        .
```

The procedure named CIRCLE in the VGA3 module of the GRAPHSOL library can be used to plot the coordinates of a circular arc in the fourth quadrant. The code used by this procedure is similar to the one in the preceding listing.

5.2.2 The Ellipse

An ellipse in the Cartesian plane can be described by the coordinates of its origin, and by its major and minor semi-axes. As far as the calculation of the coordinate points only the axes parameters are necessary, although the origin coordinates will be required to position the ellipse in the viewport. The curve and formula can be seen in Figure 5.4.

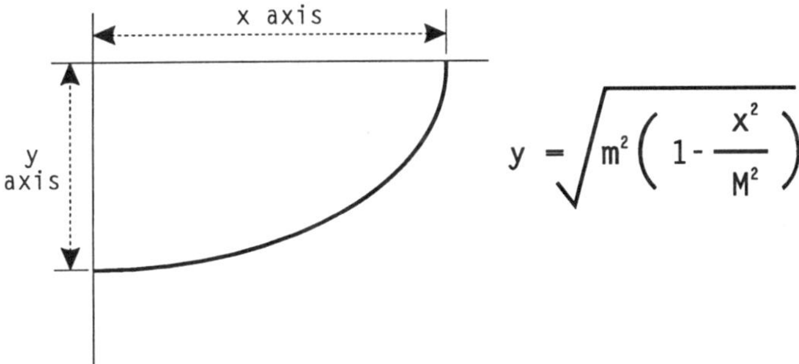

$$y = \sqrt{m^2 \left(1 - \frac{x^2}{M^2} \right)}$$

Figure 5.4 *Plot and Formula for Ellipse*

In Figure 5.4, the variable M represents the major semi-axis of the ellipse and the variable m, the minor semi-axis. The following code fragment shows the calculations necessary for plotting the coordinates of an elliptical curve in the fourth quadrant.

```
; Routine to plot and store the pixel coordinates of an
; elliptical curve in the fourth quadrant
;
; On entry:
;       x semi-axis (M) .... CS:X_AXIS ........ word
;       y semi-axis (m) .... CS:Y_AXIS ........ word
;
; During computations:
;       x coordinate ... CS:THIS_X ........ word
```

```
;              y coordinate ... CS:THIS_Y ........ word
; Variables:
;       CS:m = minor axis (X_AXIS or Y_AXIS variables)
;       CS:M = major axis (X_AXIS or Y_AXIS variables)
;
;*******************|
;     preparations  |
;*******************|
; Reset counters and controls
        MOV     CS:THIS_X,0          ; Start value for x
        MOV     CS:LAST_Y,0          ; and for LAST_Y
;
; Buffer pointers:
;       SI — Y values buffer
;       DI — X values buffer
        LEA     SI,CS:Y_BUFFER
        LEA     DI,CS:X_BUFFER
        MOV     CS:POINTS_CNT,0   ; Reset counter
;
ELLIPSE_Y:
; Calculate primitive coordinate of y
; First solve x^2 / M^2
;                               | ST(0)     |   ST(1)   |
        FILD    CS:X_AXIS       ;   M       |
        FMUL    ST,ST(0)        ;   M^2     |
        FILD    CS:THIS_X       ;   x       |    M^2    |
        FMUL    ST,ST(0)        ;   x^2     |    M^2    |
        FDIV    ST,ST(1)        ; x^2/M^2   |    M^2    |
; Solve 1 - (x^2 / M^2)
        FLD1                    ;   1       | x^2/M^2   | ? |
        FSUB    ST,ST(1)        ;1-(x^2/M^2)| x^2/M^2   | ? |
; Solve  m^2 * [1-(x^2/M^2)]
        FILD    CS:Y_AXIS       ;   m       |1-(x^2/M^2)| ? | ? |
        FMUL    ST,ST(0)        ;   m^2     |1-(x^2/M^2)| ? | ? |
        FMUL    ST,ST(1)        ;m^2 * [1-(x^2/M^2)]| ? | ? | ? |
; Find square root
        FSQRT                   ;   y       | ? | ? | ? |
        FISTP   CS:THIS_Y       ; Store y in memory
;
; Adjust stack
        FSTP    ST(0)           ; ? | ? |
        FSTP    ST(0)           ; ? |
        FSTP    ST(0)           ; Stack is empty
; Insure pixel adjacency condition
        CALL    ADJACENT        ; Library procedure
        INC     CS:THIS_X       ; x increments in clockwise plot
```

```
                                        ; of the first quadrant
        CMP       CS:THIS_Y,0      ; Test for end of processing
        JNE       ELLIPSE_Y
; At this point all coordinates have been plotted
        .
        .
        .
```

The procedure named ELLIPSE in the VGA3 module of the GRAPHSOL library can be used to plot the coordinates of an elliptical curve in the fourth quadrant. The code used by this procedure is similar to the one in the preceding listings.

5.2.3 The Parabola

A parabola in the Cartesian plane can be described by the coordinates of its origin and by its focus. The curve and formula can be seen in Figure 5.5.

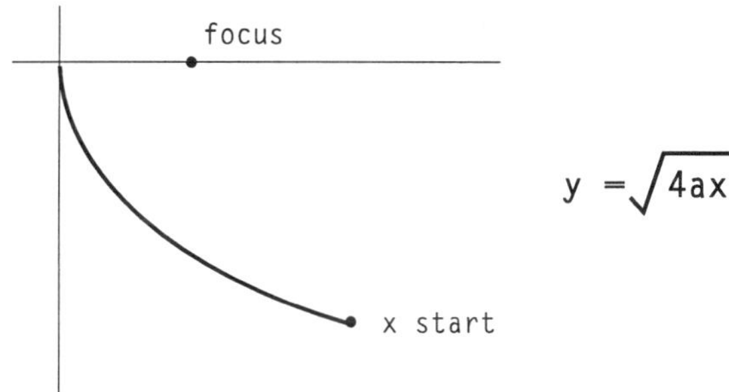

Figure 5.5 *Plot and Formula for Parabola*

In order to plot and store the coordinates of a parabolic curve two input parameters are required: the focus of the parabola and the start value for the x coordinate. Notice that no initial x value is required in the circle and the ellipse plotting routines, while the routines for plotting a parabola and a hyperbola both require an initial value for the x coordinate. The reason for this difference is that the circle and the ellipse are closed curves, therefore their fourth quadrant plot extends from axis to axis. On the other hand, the parabola and the hyperbola are open curves, therefore a start value for the x coordinate is required to define the curve. The following code fragment shows the calculations necessary for plotting the coordinates of a parabolic curve in the fourth quadrant.

```
; Routine to plot and store the pixel coordinates of a parabolic
; curve in the fourth quadrant
; On entry:
```

```
;       focus of parabola  ......... CS:FOCUS   ........ word
;       start x coordinate ......... CS:X_START ....... word
;
; During computations:
;             x coordinate ......... CS:THIS_X ........ word
;             y coordinate ......... CS:THIS_Y ........ word
; Formula:
;         y = SQR. ROOT (4ax)
;         Y_ABS = SQR. ROOT (4 * FOCUS * X_ABS)
;
;********************|
;      preparations  |
;********************|
; Reset counters and controls
        MOV      AX,CS:X_START          ; Start value for X
        MOV      CS:THIS_X,AX
        MOV      CS:LAST_Y,0            ; Reset LAST_Y
; Buffer pointers:
;       SI — Y values buffer
;       DI — X values buffer
        LEA      SI,CS:Y_BUFFER
        LEA      DI,CS:X_BUFFER
        MOV      CS:POINTS_CNT,0       ; Reset counter
;
PARA_Y:
; Calculate primitive coordinate of y
;         y = SQR. ROOT (4ax)
;         THIS_Y = SQR. ROOT (4 * FOCUS * THIS_X)
;                                 |  ST(0)   |   ST(1)  |  |
        FILD     CS:THIS_X       ;   x     |
        FILD     CS:FOCUS        ;   a     |     x    |
        FMUL     ST,ST(1)        ;   ax    | ? |
        FLD1                     ;   1     |    ax    | ? |
        FADD     ST,ST(0)        ;   2     |    ax    | ? |
        FADD     ST,ST(0)        ;   4     |    ax    | ? |
        FMUL     ST,ST(1)        ;  4ax    | ? | ? |
        FSQRT                    ;   y     | ? | ? |
        FISTP    CS:THIS_Y       ; Store y in memory
; Adjust stack
        FSTP     ST(0)           ; ? |
        FSTP     ST(0)           ; Stack is empty
; Insure pixel adjacency conditions
        CALL     ADJACENT        ; Library procedure
        DEC      CS:THIS_X
        CMP      CS:THIS_Y,0     ; Test for end of processing
        JNE      PARA_Y
```

```
; At this point all coordinates have been plotted

        .

        .

        .
```

The procedure named PARABOLA in the VGA3 module of the GRAPHSOL library can be used to plot the coordinates of a parabolic curve in the fourth quadrant. The code used by this procedure is similar to the one in the preceding listings.

5.2.4 The Hyperbola

A hyperbola in the Cartesian plane can be described by its focus, vertex, and by the coordinates of its start point. The curve and formula can be seen in Figure 5.6.

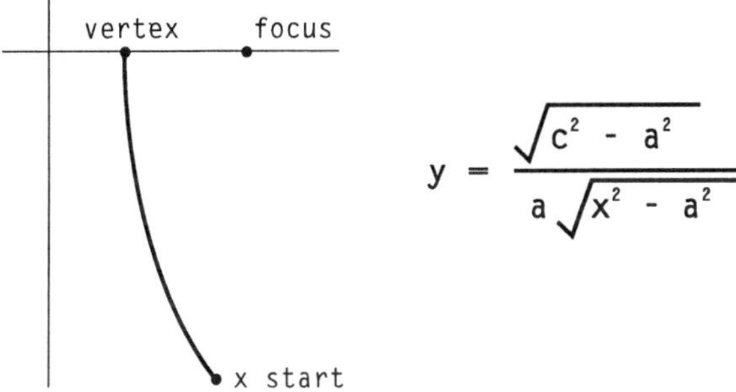

$$y = \frac{\sqrt{c^2 - a^2}}{a\sqrt{x^2 - a^2}}$$

Figure 5.6 *Plot and Formula for Hyperbola*

In order to plot and store the coordinates of a hyperbolic curve the routine requires the focus and vertex parameters, as well as the start value for the x coordinate. The following code fragment shows the calculations necessary for plotting the coordinates of a hyperbolic curve in the fourth quadrant.

```
; Routine to plot and store the pixel coordinates of a
; hyperbolic curve in the fourth quadrant
;
; On entry:
;     focus of hyperbola .......... CS:FOCUS   ......... word
;     vertex of hyperbola ......... CS:VERTEX ......... word
;     start x coordinate .......... CS:X_START ........ word
;
; During computations:
;            X coordinate .......... CS:THIS_X ......... word
;            Y coordinate .......... CS:THIS_Y ........ word
; Scratch-pad variables:
```

```
;               Numerator radix ..... CS:B_PARAM .......... word
;               Vertex squared ...... CS:VERTEX2 .......... word
;
;********************|
;     preparations   |
;********************|
; Reset counters and controls
        MOV     AX,CS:X_START           ; Start value for X
        MOV     CS:THIS_X,AX
        MOV     CS:LAST_Y,0             ; Reset LAST_Y
;
; Buffer pointers:
;       SI — Y values buffer
;       DI — X values buffer
        LEA     SI,CS:Y_BUFFER
        LEA     DI,CS:X_BUFFER
        MOV     CS:POINTS_CNT,0         ; Reset counter
; Compute numerator radical from VERTEX and FOCUS
; Solve: B_PARAM = SQR. ROOT (FOCUS^2 - VERTEX^2)
;                              |  ST(0)   |   ST(1)  |   |   |
        FILD    CS:VERTEX      ;    a     |
        FMUL    ST,ST(0)       ;   a^2    |
        FILD    CS:FOCUS       ;    c     |    a^2   |
        FMUL    ST,ST(0)       ;   c^2    |    a^2   |
        FSUB    ST,ST(1)       ; c^2 - a^2|    a^2   |
        FSQRT                  ;    b     |    a^2   |
; Store b
        FISTP   CS:B_PARAM     ;   a^2    |
; Store VERTEX^2 for calculations
        FISTP   CS:VERTEX2     ; Stack is empty
;
HYPER_Y:
; Calculate primitive coordinate of y
;  y = b / a * SQR ROOT (x^2 - a^2)
;  or:
;  Y_ABS = B_PARAM / VERTEX * SQR ROOT (X_ABS^2 - VERTEX2)
;                              |  ST(0)   |   ST(1)  |   |   |
        FILD    CS:VERTEX2     ;   a^2    |
        FILD    CS:THIS_X      ;    x     |    a^2   |
        FMUL    ST,ST(0)       ;   x^2    |    a^2   |
        FSUB    ST,ST(1)       ; x^2-a^2  | ? |
        FSQRT                  ; SR(x^2-a^2)| ? |
        FILD    CS:B_PARAM     ;    b     | # | ? |
        FILD    CS:VERTEX      ;    a     |    b     | # | ? |
        FDIV    ST(1),ST       ;    b     |    b/a   | # | ? |
        FSTP    ST(0)          ;   b/a    | # | ? |
```

```
        FMUL    ST,ST(1)        ;    y        | ? | ? |
        FISTP   CS:THIS_Y       ; Store y in memory
; Adjust stack
        FSTP    ST(0)           ; ? |
        FSTP    ST(0)           ; Stack is empty
; Insure pixel adjacency condition
        CALL    ADJACENT        ; Library procedure
        DEC     CS:THIS_X
        CMP     CS:LAST_Y,0     ; Test for end of processing
        JNE     HYPER_Y
; At this point all coordinates have been plotted
        .
        .
        .
```

The procedure named HYPERBOLA in the VGA3 module of the GRAPHSOL library can be used to plot the coordinates of a hyperbolic curve in the fourth quadrant. The code used by this procedure is similar to the one in the preceding listings.

5.2.5 Displaying the Conic Curve

In Section 9.3.6, we developed the procedure named DISPLAY_LINE to output to the CRT display in VGA mode number 18, the pixel patterns stored by the line plotting routine. The DISPLAY_LINE procedure assigns a positive value to all the coordinates stored in X_BUFFER and Y_BUFFER. This determines that the displayed curve is always located in the fourth quadrant.

Notice that the routines for plotting and storing the coordinates of the four conic curves (circle, ellipse, parabola, and hyperbola), described in the previous sections, assume that the curve is located in the fourth Cartesian quadrant. In other words, the plotted curves are normalized to the signs of x and y in this quadrant. However, at display time, it is possible to change the sign of the coordinates so that the curve can be located in any one of the four quadrants.

The VGA3 module of the GRAPHSOL library includes four procedures to display the conic curves in any one of the four quadrants. These primitives are named QUAD_I, QUAD_II, QUAD_III, and QUAD_IV. The procedure named DO_4_QUADS can be used to display the curve in all four Cartesian quadrants.

5.3 Geometrical Operations

The design of program structures to be used in storing graphics image data is one of the most challenging tasks of designing a graphic system or application. The details of the storage format depends on several factors:

1. The programming language or languages that manipulate the stored data.

2. The available storage resources.

3. The transformations applied to the stored images.

In the manipulation of graphical data it is usually preferable to design independent procedures to interface with the data structures. An advantage of this approach is that the routines that perform the graphics transformations are isolated from the complexities of the storage scheme. Principles of memory economy usually advise that each data item be encoded in the most compact format that allows representing the full range of allowed values. Also, a data structure should not be of a predetermined size, but that its size should be dynamically determined according to the number of parameters to be stored.

In implementing these rules, the more elaborate graphics systems or applications create a hierarchy of image files, display files, and image segments of varying degrees of complexity. The entire structure is designed to facilitate image transformation by manipulating the stored data. For example:

1 An image can be mirrored to the other Cartesian quadrants by changing the sign of its coordinates.

2. An image can be translated (moved) by performing signed addition on its coordinates.

3. An image can be rotated by moving its coordinates along a circular arc. The rotation formulas are obtained from elementary trigonometry.

4. An image can be scaled by multiplying its coordinates by a scaling factor.

5. An image can be clipped by eliminating all the points that fall outside a certain boundary.

At the lowest level, the ideal storage structure for image coordinates is in a *matrix form*. A *matrix* is a mathematical concept in which a set of values is arranged in a rectangular array. Each value in the array is called an *element* of the matrix. In the context of graphics programming, matrices are used to hold the coordinate points of graphical figures. This form of storing graphical data allows the use of the laws of linear algebra to perform geometrical transformations by performing mathematical operations on the matrix.

In the VGA3 module we have used a very simple storage scheme in which the image coordinate points are placed in two rectangular matrices: X_BUFFER holds the x coordinates and Y_BUFFER the y coordinates. Although each matrix is stored linearly, the programmer can visualize it as a two-dimensional array by screen columns and rows. The geometrical routines operate on normalized coordinates. In other words, the code calculates the pixel pattern for a line or a conic curve independently of the screen position at which the curve is displayed. In this manner, once the basic coordinates for a given curve have been calculated and stored, the software can display as many curves as necessary in any screen position. Furthermore, since the conic curves are symmetrical in all four quadrants, only the coordinates of one quadrant need to be calculated. The images in the other quadrants are obtained by operating on the stored data.

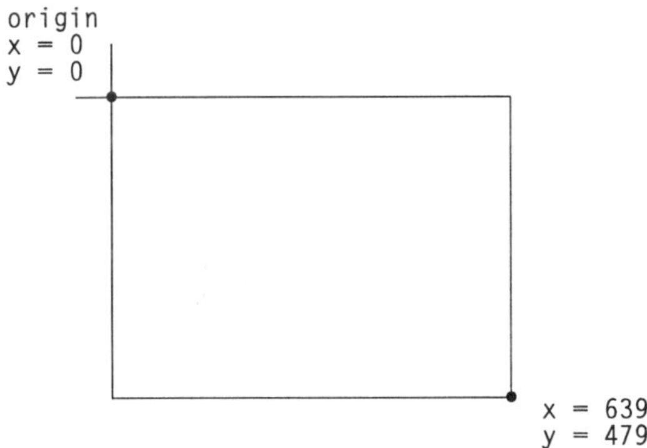

Figure 5.7 *Normalization of Coordinates for VGA Mode Number 18*

5.3.1 Screen Normalization of Coordinates

To further simplify calculations for VGA mode number 18, the origin of the coordinate system is relocated on the Cartesian plane so that the screen map of 640-by-480 pixels lies entirely in one quadrant. Also, the values of the y coordinate are made to grow downward, as in the conventional representation of the video screen. This concept is shown in Figure 5.7.

The use of only positive values for representing the x and y coordinate points simplifies image calculations and manipulations.

5.3.2 Performing the Transformations

The routines named QUAD_I, QUAD_II, QUAD_III, and QUAD_IV, in the VGA3 module of the GRAPHSOL library, display at any desired screen position, the pixel coordinate pairs stored in X_BUFFER and Y_BUFFER. Since the coordinates are stored in screen-normalized form (see Section 5.3.1), the display routines must make the corresponding sign correction at the time of translating the image map to the specific screen position. For example, to display an image in the first quadrant the QUAD_I routine adds the pixel column at which the image is to be displayed to each of the coordinates in the matrix named X_BUFFER, and subtracts the pixel row from each coordinate in Y_BUFFER. Table 5.1 shows the operations performed on the screen-normalized coordinate pairs according to the quadrant.

Table 5.1 *Transformation of Normalized Coordinates According to Quadrant (VGA Convention)*

QUADRANT I		QUADRANT II		QUADRANT III		QUADRANT IV	
x	y	x	y	x	y	x	y
+	-	-	-	-	+	+	+

Translation

Translation is the movement of a graphical object to a new location by adding a constant value to each coordinate point. The operation requires that a constant be added to all the coordinates, but the constants can be different for each plane. In other words, a two-dimensional graphical object can be translated to any desired screen position by adding or subtracting values from the set of x and y coordinates that define the object. Notice that display routines QUAD_I, QUAD_II, QUAD_III, and QUAD_IV in fact perform an image translation from the screen top left corner to the screen position requested by the caller. The VGA3 module also contains a routine named DO_4_QUADS that displays an image in all four Cartesian quadrants.

Scaling

In graphical terms, to scale an image is to apply a multiplying factor to its linear dimensions. Thus, a scaling transformation is the conversion of a graphical object into another one by multiplying each coordinate point that defines the object. The operation requires that all the coordinates in each plane be multiplied by the same scaling factor, although the scaling factors can be different for each plane. For example, a three-to-four scaling transformation takes place when the x coordinates of a two-dimensional object are multiplied by a factor of two and the y coordinates are multiplied by a factor of three.

The fundamental problem of scaling a pixel map is that the resulting image can be discontinuous. This determines that it is often easier for the software to calculate the parameters that define the image, rather than to scale those of an existing one. For this reason we have not provided a scaling routine in the VGA3 library.

Rotation

Rotation is the conversion of a graphical object into another one by moving, by the same angular value, all coordinate points that define the original object along circular arcs with a common center. The angular value is called the *angle of rotation*, and the fixed point common to all the arcs is called the *center of rotation*. Some geometrical figures are unchanged by some rotations. For example, a circle is unchanged by a rotation about its center, and a square is unchanged if it is rotated by an angle that is a multiple of 90 degrees and using the intersection point of both diagonals as a center of rotation.

To perform a rotation transformation each coordinate that defines the object is moved along a circular arc. The effect of a 30-degree counterclockwise rotation of a polygon can be seen in Figure 5.8.

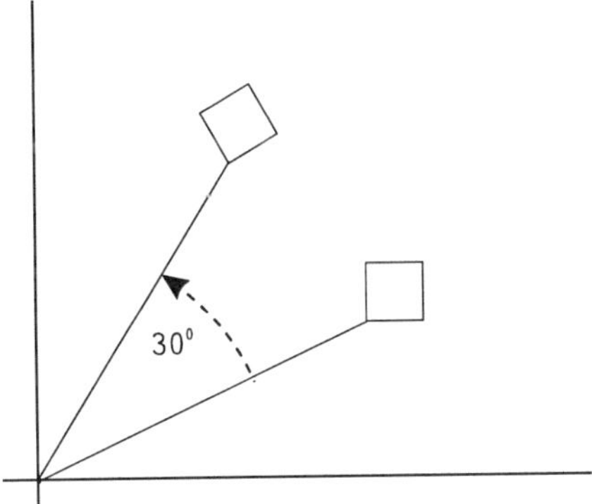

Figure 5.8   *Rotation Transformation of a Polygon*

The rotation formulas, which can be derived using elementary trigonometry, are:

```
x' = x cos @ - y sin @
y' = y cos @ + x sin @
```

where *x',y'* are the rotated coordinates of the point *x,y* and @ is the angle of rotation in clockwise direction. Since the rotation calculations require the sine and cosine functions, the VGA3 module includes the procedures SINE and COSINE that calculate these trigonometric functions. Notice that the calculations performed by the SINE and COSINE procedures use the radian measure of the angle. The auxiliary procedure named DEG_2_RADS, in the VGA3 module, perform the conversion from degrees to radians. Rotation is performed by the procedures named ROTATE_ON and ROTATE_OFF. The actual rotation calculations are performed by the local procedure named ROTATE.

Clipping

The graphical concept of clipping is related to that of a *clipping window*. in general, a graphics window can be defined as a rectangular area that delimits the computer screen, also called the *viewport*. Clipping a graphical object is excluding the parts of this object that lie outside a defined clipping window. Figure 5.9 shows the clipping transformation of an ellipse.

In Figure 5.9, the dotted portion of the ellipse, which lies outside of the clipping window, is eliminated from the final image, while the part shown in a continuous line is preserved. In the VGA3 library, clipping is performed by the procedures named CLIP_ON and CLIP_OFF. The actual clipping calculations are done by the local procedure named CLIP.

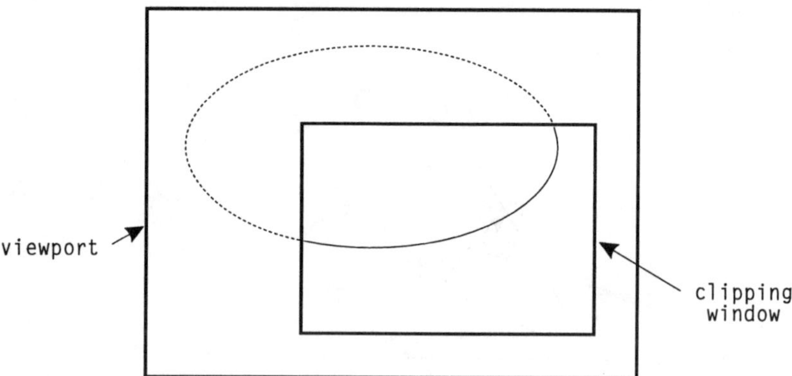

Figure 5.9   *Clipping Transformation of an Ellipse*

Notice that in the VGA3 module the actual translation, rotation, and clipping transformations are done at display time, with no change to the stored image. In this manner, a program to display the clipped ellipse in Figure 5.9 would first call the ELLIPSE procedure, which calculates and stores the coordinates of the curve to screen-normalized parameters. Then the program calls the CLIP_ON procedure and defines the clipping window. Finally, the DO_4_QUADS routine can be used to translate the ellipse to the actual screen position and display those portions of the curve that lie inside the clipping rectangle. If a rotation transformation is to be used, it must be executed before the clipping takes place.

Clipping transformations can also be used to make sure that the coordinate points of a geometrical image are within the physical limits of the graphics device. For example, an application working in VGA mode number 18, with a screen definition of 640-pixel columns by 480-pixel rows, can set the clipping rectangle to the dimensions of this viewport to make sure that the display routines do not exceed the physical screen area. In this manner the clipping routine serves as an error trap for the display function.

5.4 Region Fills

The graphics routines described in the previous sections of this chapter were designed to display the outline of a geometrical figure in the form of a continuous pixel line. But often a graphics application needs to display geometrical images filled with a uniform color or with a monochrome pattern. If the geometrical figure delimits a closed screen area, it is possible to use a fill operation to set all the pixels within the enclosed area to a specific color or pattern. This enclosed area is sometimes called a *region*.

5.4.1 Screen Painting

The name *screen painting* is usually given to routines that perform a general region fill in which all closed screen areas are colored with the value of its border pixels. The border pixels serve as a boundary for the fill operation. The logic of many screen painting routines is based on alternating between a searching and a coloring mode. One variation is to define a background color and then to scan the entire screen, pixel by pixel, searching for pixels that do not match the background. These nonmatching pixels are said to define a boundary. When a boundary pixel is encountered, the searching mode is changed to the coloring mode, and each successive pixel is changed to the color of the boundary pixel. When another boundary pixel is encountered, the mode is toggled back to searching.

In screen painting algorithms the scanning usually starts at the top-left screen corner. The mode is changed to searching at the start of each new pixel row. The algorithms must take into account conditions that require special handling, for example, how to proceed if there is a single boundary pixel on a scan line, several adjoining boundary pixels, an odd number of boundaries, or if a vertex is encountered.

5.4.2 Geometrical Fills

The geometrical fill is a special case of the fill algorithms that is suited to filling closed geometrical figures with a given color or pattern. The geometrical fill is different from a general painting case in that in the geometrical fill the caller must define a pixel location inside the figure. The simplest case is based on the following assumptions:

1. That the starting location, sometimes called the seed point, is inside a closed-boundary figure within the viewport.

2. That there are no other figures or lines within the boundary of the figure to be filled.

3. That all consecutive points within the same horizontal line are adjacent.

Figure 5.10 shows two classes of geometrical shapes in regards to a region fill operation.

The geometrical shapes in Figure 5.10*a* meet the constraints defined above, while the polygon in Figure 5.10*b* does not. In Figure 5.10*b*, consecutive points p1 and p2, located on the same horizontal line, are not adjacent. The simplest fill algorithm, based on a line-by-line scan for a single boundary pixel, works only with geometric figures similar to those in Figure 5.10*a*. The logic requires a preliminary search for the figure's low and high points. This precursory operation simplifies the actual fill by insuring that the scan does not exceed the figure's boundaries at any time, therefore avoiding the tests for vertices and for external boundaries. Figure 5.11 is a flowchart of a region fill algorithm for a figure that meets the three constraints mentioned above.

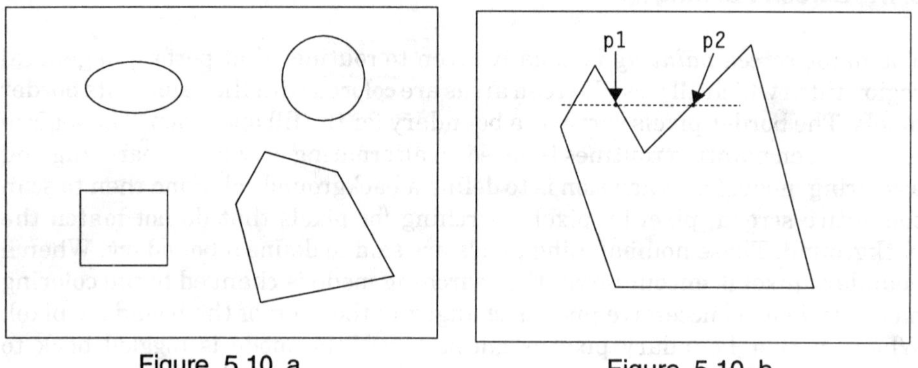

Figure 5.10 a   Figure 5.10 b

Figure 5.10 *Geometrical Figure for a Region Fill*

The procedure named REGION_FILL in the VGA3 module of the GRAPHSOL library furnished with this book performs a region fill operation on geometrical shapes of the type shown in Figure 5.10*a*. The logic of this routine is based on the flowchart in Figure 5.11.

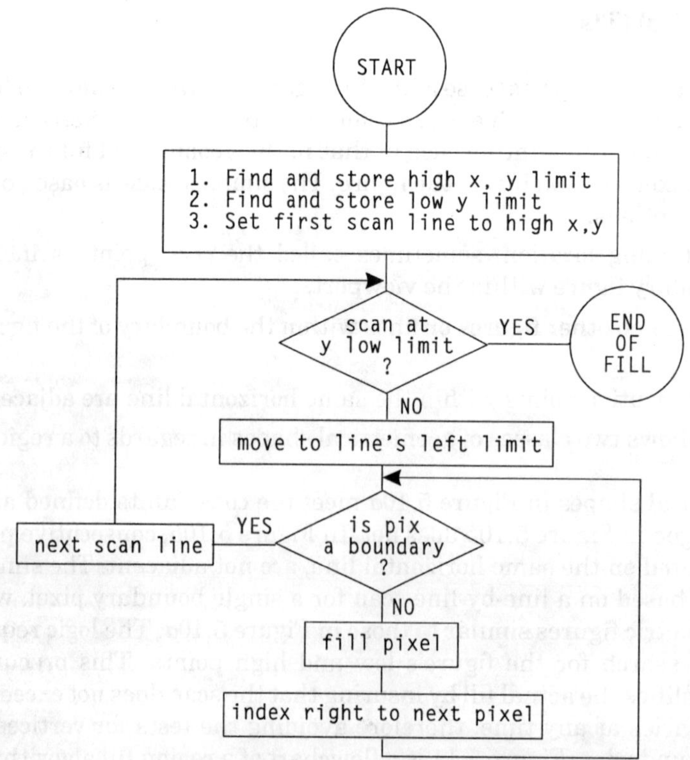

Figure 5.11 *Region Fill Flowchart*

An algorithm like the one illustrated in the flowchart of Figure 5.11 is sometimes classified as a line-adjacency iteration. In VGA mode number 18 the performance of the line-adjacency method can be considerably improved by prescanning a group of 8 horizontal pixels for a boundary. If no boundary is found, all 8 pixels are set at once. Pixel-by-pixel scanning takes place only if the pre-scan detects a boundary pixel.

An alternative algorithm for a region fill operation consists of scanning the pixels that form the outside border of the figure and storing their x, y coordinates in a data structure. After the border of the figure is defined, the code scans the interior of the figure for holes. Once the exterior boundary and the holes are known, the fill operation can be reduced to displaying line segments that go from one exterior boundary to another, or from an exterior boundary to a hole boundary. This algorithm, sometimes called a border fill method, is relatively efficient and can be used to fill more complex shapes than those in Figure 5.10a.

5.5 Primitive Routines in the VGA3 Module

The library module named VGA3 of the GRAPHSOL library contains several VGA mode number 18 geometric primitives. In order to access and use the files in the accompanying microdisk the reader must follow the installation and unpacking instructions in Appendix A. The library's interface with the various languages supported by this book are described in Appendix B.

The following are generic descriptions of the geometrical primitive routines contained in the VGA3 libraries. The values passed and returned by the individual functions are listed in the order in which they are referenced in the code. The data types used by all library modules can be seen in Table 1.3. The following listing is in the order in which the routines appear in the library source files.

BRESENHAM

Draw a straight line using Bresenham's algorithm
>   Receives:
>> 1. Byte integer of color of line
>> 2. Word integer of start point of x coordinate
>> 3. Word integer of start point of y coordinate
>> 4. Word integer of end point of x coordinate
>> 5. Word integer of end point of y coordinate
>   Returns:
>> Nothing
>   Action:
>> Straight line is displayed

LINE BY SLOPE

Plot and store the pixel coordinates of a straight line of slope s, located in the fourth quadrant. The slope must be in the range 0 s 90 degrees.

Receives:

1. Word integer of start point of x coordinate
2. Word integer of start point of y coordinate
3. Word integer of end point of x coordinate
4. Word integer of slope

Returns:

Nothing

Action:

Straight line is calculated and stored

CIRCLE

Plot and store the pixel coordinates of a circular arc in the fourth quadrant.

Receives:

1. Word integer of radius of circle

Returns:

Nothing

Action:

Circular arc is calculated and stored

ELLIPSE

Plot and store the pixel coordinates of an ellipse in the fourth quadrant.

Receives:

1. Word integer of x semi-axis of ellipse
2. Word integer of y semi-axis of ellipse

Returns:

Nothing

Action:

Elliptical arc is calculated and stored

PARABOLA

Plot and store the pixel coordinates of a parabola in the fourth quadrant.

Receives:

1. Word integer of x focus of parabola
2. Word integer of start x coordinate

Returns:

Nothing

Action:

Parabolic arc is calculated and stored

HYPERBOLA

Plot and store the pixel coordinates of a hyperbola in the fourth quadrant.
Receives:
1. Word integer of x focus of hyperbola
2. Word integer of vertex of hyperbola
3. Word integer of start x coordinate

Returns:
Nothing

Action:
Hyperbolic arc is calculated and stored

QUAD_I

Display a geometrical curve in the first quadrant, while in VGA mode number 18, using its stored coordinates.
Receives:
1. Byte integer of IRGB color code
2. Word integer of x coordinate of origin
3. Word integer of y coordinate of origin

Returns:
Nothing

Action:
Curve is displayed

QUAD_II

Display a geometrical curve in the second quadrant, while in VGA mode number 18, using its stored coordinates.
Receives:
1. Byte integer of IRGB color code
2. Word integer of x coordinate of origin
3. Word integer of y coordinate of origin

Returns:
Nothing

Action:
Curve is displayed

QUAD_III

Display a geometrical curve in the third quadrant, while in VGA mode number 18, using its stored coordinates.
Receives:
1. Byte integer of IRGB color code
2. Word integer of x coordinate of origin
3. Word integer of y coordinate of origin

Returns:
Nothing

Action:
   Curve is displayed

QUAD_IV

Display a geometrical curve in the fourth quadrant, while in VGA mode number 18, using its stored coordinates.
   Receives:
      1. Byte integer of IRGB color code
      2. Word integer of x coordinate of origin
      3. Word integer of y coordinate of origin
   Returns:
   Nothing
   Action:
   Curve is displayed

DO_4_QUADS

Display all four quadrants by calling the procedures QUAD_I, QUAD_II, QUAD_III, and QUAD_IV.
   Receives:
   Nothing
   Returns:
   Nothing
   Action:
   Curve is displayed in all four quadrants

ROTATE_ON

Activate the rotate operation during display.
   Receives:
      1. Word integer of clockwise angle of rotation in the range 0 to 90 degrees
   Returns:
   Nothing
   Action:
   Rotation angle is stored and rotation is enabled during display operations

ROTATE_OFF

De-activate the rotate operation during display.
   Receives:
   Nothing
   Returns:
   Nothing
   Action:
   Rotation is disabled during display operations

CLIP_ON

Activate clipping operation during display.

Receives:

1. Word integer of left corner of clipping window
2. Word integer of top corner of clipping window
3. Word integer of right corner of clipping window
4. Word integer of bottom corner of clipping window

Returns:

Nothing

Action:

Clipping values are stored and clipping is enabled during display operations

CLIP_OFF

De-activate clipping during display.

Receives:

Nothing

Returns:

Nothing

Action:

Clipping is disabled during display operations

INIT_X87

Initialize 80x87 hardware or emulator and set rounding control to even.

Receives:

Nothing

Returns:

Nothing

Action:

If 80x87 hardware is detected an internal switch is set so that the coprocessor will be used during geometrical calculations. Otherwise the switch will direct execution to emulated code. In both cases the control word is set to round to even numbers.

REGION_FILL

Fill a closed geometrical surface, with no internal holes, composed of un-broken horizontal lines. Uses VGA mode number 18.

Receives:

1. Byte integer of IRGB color code
2. Word integer of x coordinate of seed point
3. Word integer of y coordinate of seed point

Returns:

Nothing

Action:

Figure is filled

The XGA and 8514/A Adapter Interface

Chapter Summary

This chapter describes the XGA and 8514/A video systems and their architecture as well as programming XGA and 8514/A systems by means of the Adpter Interface (AI) software package that is furnished by IBM. The chapter includes programming examples in assembly language.

6.0 From 8514/A to XGA

In 1987, IBM introduced a high-end video graphics system intended for applications that demand high-quality graphics, such as CAD, desktop publishing, graphical user interfaces to operating systems, image editing, and graphics art software. The best graphics mode available in a fully-equipped 8514/A system is of 1,024-by-768 pixels in 256 colors. Compared to VGA mode number 18 (640-by-480 pixels in 16 colors) this 8514/A graphics mode offers 2.5 times the number of screen pixels and 16 times as many colors. The major features of the 8514/A standard are the following:

1. 8514/A is furnished as an add-on card for PS/2 Micro Channel microcomputers with VGA systems on the motherboard. The 8514/A board is installed in a slot with a special connector that allows a VGA signal to pass through.

2. Memory architecture follows a planar scheme similar to the one used by the CGA, EGA, and VGA systems. The card is furnished in two versions, one with 512K of on-board VRAM and another one with 1,024K. The maximum resolution of 1,024-by-768 pixels in 256 colors is available only in the board equipped with 1,024K of video RAM.

3. 8514/A is furnished with three character fonts. The character sizes are of 12-by-20, 8-by-14, and 7-by-15 pixels for the 1,024-by-768 resolution mode.

The 8-by-14 pixel character size is the only one available in the 640-by-480 pixel mode. (See Table 6.11 later in this chapter.) The character fonts are stored as disk files in the diskette supplied with the adapter.

4. The adapter contains ROM code that is used by the BIOS Power-On Self Test (POST) to initialize the hardware, but no BIOS programmer services are included.

5. Programming the 8514/A adapter is by means of an Adapter Interface (AI) software. The software is in the form of a TSR program. The TSR installation routine is an executable program named HDILOAD.EXE.

6. The 8514/A AI contains services to control the adapter hardware, to draw lines, rectangles, and small bitmaps (markers), to fill enclosed figures, to manipulate the color palette, to perform bit block transfers (bitBLTs), to change the current drawing position, line type, width, and display color, to select among 16 logical and 14 arithmetic mix modes, and to display text strings and individual characters.

7. The color palette consists of 262,144 possible colors of which 256 can be displayed simultaneously. The gray scale is of 64 shades.

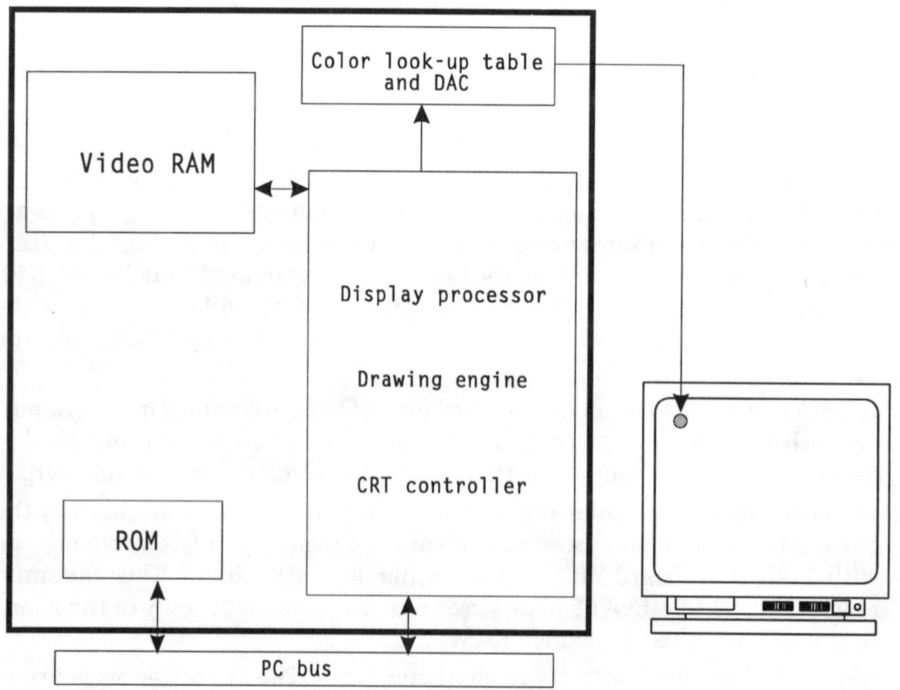

Figure 6.1 *Component Diagram of 8514/A*

The internal architecture of the 8514/A consists of three central components: a drawing engine, a display processor, and the on-board video RAM. In addition, the board contains a color look-up table (LUT), a digital-to-analog converter (DAC), and associated registers, as well as a small amount of initialization code in ROM. Figure 6.1 is a diagram of the components in the 8514/A system.

The 8514/A adapter, in spite of the substantial improvements that it brought to PC video graphics, enjoyed only limited success. The following limitations of the 8514/A adapter have been noted:

1. 8514/A requires a Micro Channel bus. This makes the card unusable in many IBM-compatible computers.

2. The AI interface offers limited graphics services, for example, no curve drawing functions are available, nor are there direct services for reading or setting an individual screen pixel.

3. Video memory operations must take place through a single transfer register. The absence of DMA slows down image transfer procedures.

4. 8514/A requires the presence of a VGA system on the motherboard. This duplication of video systems often constitutes an unnecessary expense.

5. Register information regarding the 8514/A was published by IBM only after considerable pressure from software developers. For several years there was no other way for programming the system than using the AI services.

6. 8514/A support only interlaced displays. This determines that applications that generate single-pixel horizontal lines (such as CAD programs) are afflicted with flicker. Notice that some clone 8514/A cards offer non-interlaced display.

7. IBM documentation for programming 8514/A refers almost exclusively to C language. Programmers working in assembler or in high-level languages other than C were left to their own resources.

In September 1990, IBM disclosed preliminary information on a new graphics standard designated as the Extended Graphics Array, or XGA. Two configurations of the XGA standard have since been implemented: as an adapter card and as part of the motherboard. The XGA adapter is compatible with PS/2 Micro Channel machines equipped with the 80386 or 486 CPU. The XGA system is integrated in the motherboard of the IBM Model 95 XP 486. Figure 6.2 is a diagram of the XGA system.

Several features of the XGA system are similar to those of the 8514/A:

1. The maximum resolution is of 1,024-by-768 pixels in 256 colors.

2. The XGA system is compatible with the 8514/A Adapter Interface software.

3. The display driver is interlaced at 1,024-by-768 pixel resolution.

4. The XGA digital-to-analog converter (DAC) and color look-up table (LUT) operate identically to those in the 8414/A. This means that palette operations are compatible in both systems.

5. The adapter version of XGA is furnished with either 512K or 1,204K of on-board video RAM.

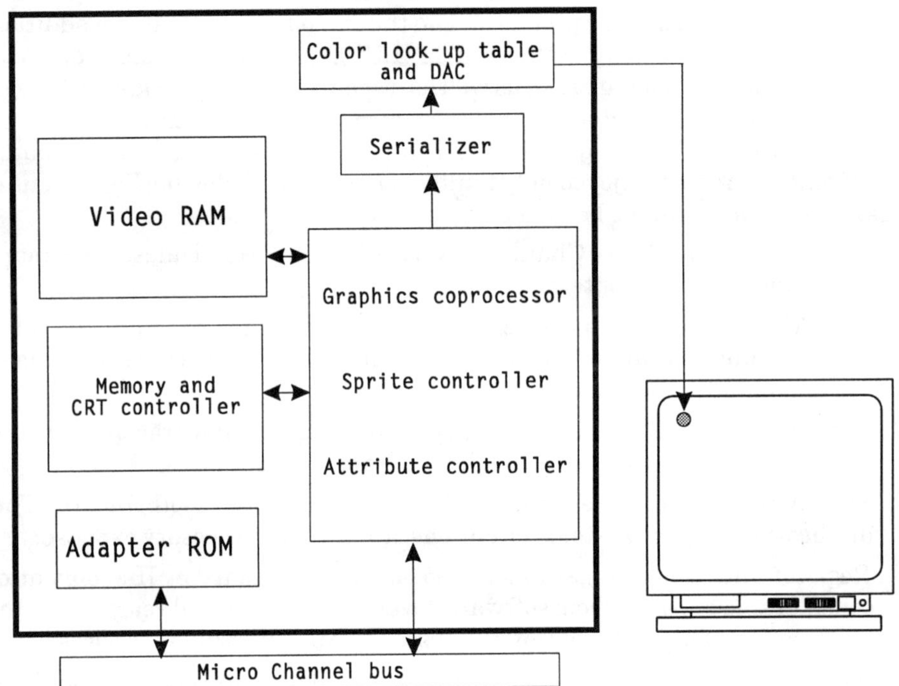

Figure 6.2 *XGA Component Diagram*

However, there are several differences between the two systems, such as:

1. The XGA is compatible with the VGA standard at the register level. This makes possible the use of XGA in the motherboard while still maintaining VGA compatibility. This is the way in which it is implemented in the IBM Model 95 XP 486 microcomputer.

2. XGA includes two display modes that do not exist in 8514/A: a 132-column text mode, and a direct color graphics mode with 640-by-480 pixel resolution in 64K colors. Notice that this graphics mode is available only in cards with 1,024K video RAM installed.

3. XGA requires a machine equipped with a 80386 or 486 CPU while 8514/A can run in machines with the 80286 chip.

4. XGA implements a three-dimension, user-definable drawing space, called a bitmap. XGA bitmaps can reside anywhere in the system's memory space. The application can define a bitmap in the program's data space and the XGA uses this area directly for drawing, reading, and writing operations.

5. XGA is equipped with a hardware controlled cursor, called the sprite. It maximum size is of 64-by-64 pixels and it can be positioned anywhere on the screen without affecting the image stored in video memory.

6. The XGA Adapter Interface is implemented as a .SYS device driver while the driver for the 8514/A is in the form of a TSR program. The module name for the XGA driver is XGAAIDOS.SYS. The XGA AI adds 17 new services to those available in 8514/A.

7. The XGA was designed taking into consideration the problems of managing the video image in a multitasking environment. Therefore, it contains facilities for saving and restoring the state of the video hardware at any time.

8. The XGA hardware can act as a bus master and access system memory directly. This bus-mastering capability frees the CPU for other tasks while the XGA processor is manipulating memory.

9. IBM has provided register-level documentation for the XGA system. This will facilitate cloning and development of high-performance software.

Some of the objections raised for the 8514/A still apply to the XGA, for instance, the Micro Channel requirement, the limitations of the AI services, and the interlaced display technology. On the other hand, the XGA offers several major improvements in relation to the 8514/A.

6.1 The Adapter Interface

The Adapter Interface (AI) is a software package furnished with 8514/A and XGA systems that provides a series of low-level services to the graphics programmer. In the 8514/A the AI software is in the form of a Terminate and Stay Resident (TSR) program while in the XGA the AI is a .SYS driver. The respective module and directory names are shown in Table 6.1.

Table 6.1 *Module and Directory Names for the Adapter Interface Software*

8514/A		XGA	
FORM	PATHNAME	FORM	PATHNAME
TSR	HDIPCDOS\HDILOAD.EXE	.SYS	XGAPCDOS\XGAAIDOS.SYS

The AI was originally documented by IBM in the *IBM Personal System/2 Display Adapter 8514/A Technical Reference* (document number S68X-2248-0) published in April, 1987. IBM has also published a document named the *IBM Personal System/2 Display Adapter 8514/A Adapter Interface Programmer's Guide* (document number 00F8952). This product includes a diskette containing a demo program, a collection of font files, and several programmer utilities. The corresponding IBM document for XGA AI is called the *IBM Personal System/2 XGA Adapter Interface Technical Reference* (document number S-15F-2154-0). All of the above documents are available from IBM Technical Directory (1-800-426-7282). Other IBM documents regarding XGA hardware are mentioned in Chapter 7.

6.1.1 Software Installation

The AI driver software must be installed in the machine before its services
become available to the system. In the case of the 8514/A, the AI driver is in
the form of a TSR program, while in the XGA it is furnished as a .SYS file.
Installation instructions for the AI software are part of the adapter package.
In the case of the XGA AI several versions of the AI are furnished by IBM: one
for MS-DOS, another one for Windows, and a third one for the OS/2 operating
system.

In the MS-DOS environment the installation routine, for either the 8514/A
or XGA, creates a dedicated directory selects the appropriate driver software,
and optionally includes an automatic setup line. (See Table 6.1.) In the 8514/A
the automatic setup line is added to the user's AUTOEXEC.BAT file and in the
XGA to the CONFIG.SYS file. This insures that the driver software is made
resident every time the system is booted.

The 8514/A installation process makes the AI functions available, but does
not automatically switch video functions to the 8514/A display system. Notice
that, since 8514/A does not include VGA, a typical 8514/A configuration is a
machine with two display adapters, one attached to the motherboard VGA and
the other one to the 8514/A card. With XGA, which includes VGA functions, it
is possible to configure a machine with a single display attached either to a
motherboard XGA or to an adapter version of the XGA. Alternatively, the
adapter version of the XGA can be configured with two or more displays. For
example, a machine with VGA on the motherboard can be furnished with an
XGA card and monitor. In this case, the XGA resembles the typical 8514/A
arrangement described above.

6.1.2 XGA Multidisplay Systems

If and when XGA becomes the video standard for IBM microcomputers, a
typical machine will probably be equipped with a single display attached to
XGA hardware on the motherboard. This is already the case in the IBM Model
95 XP 486 microcomputer. However, most present day implementations of XGA
consist of PS/2 machines, originally equipped with VGA on the motherboard,
and which have been supplemented with an XGA adapter card. Since XGA
includes VGA, this upgrade version can be configured with a single monitor
attached to the XGA video output connector. An alternative setup uses two
monitors: one attached to the VGA connector on the motherboard and one to
the XGA card.

A multidisplay XGA system setup offers some interesting possibilities. For
example, in graphics applications in which the XGA system displays the
graphics image while the VGA on the motherboard is used in interactive
debugging operations. XGA systems can have up to six adapters operating
simultaneously, although in most machines the number of possible XGA
adapters is limited by the number of available slots. This is not the case with
8514/A, which cannot have more than two displays per system.

The possibility of multidisplay XGA systems creates new potentials in applications and systems programming. For example, by manipulating the XGA address decoding mechanism an application can display different data on multiple XGA screens. In this manner it is possible to conceive an XGA multitasking program with several display systems. One feasible setup is to use the first monitor to show output of a word processing program, the second monitor a database, and the third one a spreadsheet. The user could switch rapidly between applications while the data displayed remains on each screen. Another sample use of a multi-display system is an airport software package that would show arrival schedules on one screen, and departures on another one, while a third monitor is attached to the reservations desk. Finally, in a graphics applications environment, we can envision a desktop publishing system in which the central monitor would display the typesetting software, the monitor on one side would be attached to a graphics illustration program, and the one on the other side to a text editor.

6.1.3 Operating Modes

Both 8514/A and XGA systems can operate in one of two modes: the VGA mode or the advanced functions mode. The operating mode is selected by the software. In the VGA mode the graphics system is a full featured VGA. (See Table 2.2.) The advanced function mode refers to the Adapter Interface software. Table 6.2 shows the characteristics of the display modes available in the AI.

Table 6.2 *XGA and 8514/A Advanced Function Modes*

	LOW RESOLUTION MODE	HIGH RESOLUTION MODE
RAM installed	512K	1,024K
Interlaced	NO	YES
pixel columns	640	1,024
pixel rows	480	768
number of colors	16	256
palette	256K	256K

6.1.4 The XGA and 8514/A Palette

8514/A and XGA video memory is organized in bit planes. Each bit plane encodes the color for a rectangular array of 1,024-by-1,024 pixels. In practice, since the highest available resolution is of 1,024-by-768 pixels, there are 256 unused bits in each plane. This unassigned area is used by AI software as a scratchpad during area fills and in marker manipulations, as well as for storing bitmaps for the character sets. When the graphics system is in the low resolution mode video memory consists of eight 1,024-by-512 bit planes. However, the eight bit planes are divided into two separate groups of four bit planes each. These two-bit planes can be simultaneously addressed. In low-resolution mode, the color range is limited to 16 simultaneous colors. In the high-resolution mode video memory consists of eight bit planes of 1,024 by 1,024 pixels. (See Table 6.2.) In this mode the number of simultaneous colors is 256. Figure 6.3 shows the bit-plane mapping in XGA and 8514/A high-resolution modes.

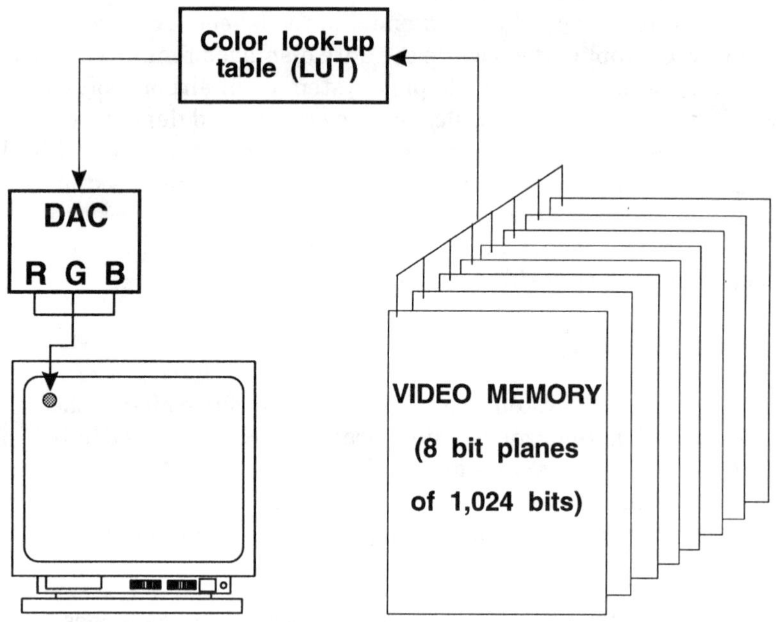

Figure 6.3 *Bit Plane Mapping in XGA/8514/A High Resolution Modes*

Color selection is performed by means of a color look-up table (LUT) associated with the DAC. The selection mechanism is similar to the one used in VGA mode number 19, described in Section 3.2.1. This means that the eight-bit color code stored in XGA and 8514/A video memory serves as an index into the color look-up table. (See Figure 6.3.) For example, the color value 12 in video memory selects LUT register number 12, which in the default setting stores the encoding for bright red. The default setting of the LUT registers can be seen in Table 6.3.

Color plate number 9 is a print of the first screen of the XGALUT program provided in the book's microdisk. The colors in plate number 9 match those in Table 6.3. Notice that the default setting for the XGA and 8514/A LUT registers represent only 16 color values, which correspond to registers 0 to 15 in Table 6.3. The default colors encoded in LUT registers 16 to 255 are but a repetition, in groups of 15 registers, of the encodings in the first 16 LUT registers. Consequently, software products that intend to use the full color range of XGA and 8514/A systems must reset the LUT registers.

Table 6.3 *Default Setting of LUT Registers in XGA and 8514/A*

REGISTER NUMBER	6-BIT COLOR (HEX VALUE) R	G	B	COLOR
0	00	00	00	Black
1	00	00	2A	Dark blue
2	00	2A	00	Dark green
3	00	2A	2A	Dark cyan
4	2A	00	00	Dark red
5	2A	00	2A	Dark magenta
6	2A	15	00	Brown
7	2A	2A	2A	Gray
8	15	15	15	Dark gray
9	15	15	3F	Light blue
10	15	3F	15	Light green
11	15	3F	3F	Light cyan
12	3F	15	15	Light red
13	3F	15	3F	Light magenta
14	3F	3F	15	Yellow
15	3F	3F	3F	Bright white
16 to 31	00	00	2A	Dark blue
32 to 47	00	2A	00	Dark green
48 to 63	00	2A	2A	Dark cyan
64 to 79	2A	00	00	Dark red
80 to 95	2A	00	2A	Dark magenta
96 to 111	2A	15	00	Brown
112 to 127	2A	2A	2A	Gray
128 to 143	15	15	15	Dark gray
144 to 159	15	15	3F	Light blue
160 to 175	15	3F	15	Light green
176 to 191	15	3F	3F	Light cyan
192 to 207	3F	15	15	Light red
208 to 223	3F	15	3F	Light magenta
224 to 239	3F	3F	15	Yellow
240 to 255	3F	3F	3F	Bright white

In the documentation for Display Adapter 8514/A, IBM recommends an 8-bit color coding scheme in which 4 bits are assigned to the green color and 2 bits to the red and blue colors respectively. This scheme is related to the physiology of the human eye, which is more sensitive to the green area of the spectrum than to the red or blue areas. One possible mapping, which conforms with the XGA direct color mode, is to devote bits 0 and 1 to the blue range, bits 2 to 5 to the green range, and bits 6 and 7 to the red range. This bit-mapping is shown in Figure 6.4.

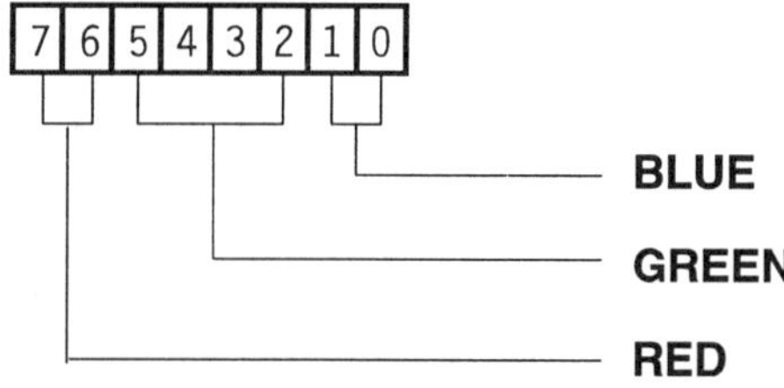

Figure 6.4 *Red, Green, and Blue Bit Mapping for 8-Bit Color*

An alternative mapping scheme can be based on assigning two bits to the intensity, red, green, and blue elements respectively. A similar double-bit IRGB encoding was developed in Section 3.2.1 and in Table 3.3 for VGA 256-color mode number 19. The XGA and 8514/A color registers (color look-up table) consist of 18 bits, 6 bits for each color (red, green, and blue). The bitmap of the LUT registers is shown in Figure 6.5.

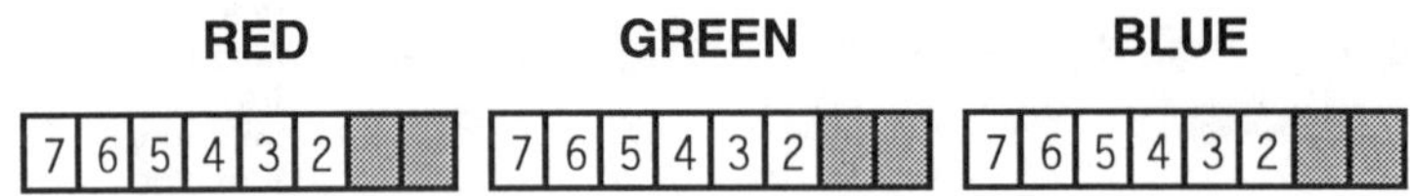

Figure 6.5 *Bitmap of the XGA and 8514/A LUT Registers in the DAC*

Notice that the XGA bitmap for the LUT register uses the six high-order bits while the VGA bitmap uses the 6 low-order bits. (See Figure 3.7.) As a result of this difference, the values for a VGA palette must be shifted left two bits (multiplied by 4) in order to convert them to the XGA bit range.

6.1.5 Alphanumeric Support

The XGA and 8514/A Adapter Interface provides services for the display of text strings and of individual characters. The string oriented services are designated as *text functions* in the AI documentation while the character oriented services are called *alphanumeric functions*. The AI text and character display services are necessary since BIOS and DOS functions for displaying text do not operate on the XGA and the 8514/A video systems.

Both text and alphanumeric functions in the AI require the use of character fonts, several of which are part of the XGA and 8514/A software package. These character fonts are stored in disk files located in the adapter's support diskette. During installation the font files are moved to a special directory in the user's hard disk drive. The 8514/A adapter is furnished with three standard fonts while there are four standard fonts in the XGA diskette. In addition, the XGA diskette contains four supplementary fonts that have been optimized for XGA hardware. Finally, the diskette furnished with the IBM Personal System/2 Display Adapter 8514/A Adapter Interface Programmer's Guide contains 22 additional fonts, which are also compatible with the XGA system. (See Section 6.1.)

Fonts for the AI software can be in three different formats: short stroke vector, single-plane bitmaps, and multiplane bitmaps. The fonts furnished with 8514/A are of short stroke vector type. The supplementary fonts furnished with the XGA diskette are in single-plane bitmap format. The fonts furnished with the 8514/A Programmer's Guide diskette are also in the single-plane bitmap format. Multiplane bit-mapped fonts, although documented in the Display Adapter 8514/A Technical Reference, have not been furnished by IBM for either

8514/A or XGA systems. In the XGA diskette it is possible to identify the fonts in short stroke vector format by the extension .SSV, while the single-plane bitmap fonts have the extension .IMG. However, the 8514/A short stroke vector fonts have the extension .FNT. An additional complication is that the XGA installation routine changes the extension .SSV for .FNT. For these reasons it is not always possible to identify the font format by means of the extension to the filename.

Font File Structure

All font files compatible with the AI software must conform to a specific format and structure. Each of the standard fonts supplied in the Adapter Interface diskette contains five different character sets, named *code pages* in the IBM documentation. The code page codes and corresponding alphabets can be seen in Table 6.4.

Table 6.4 *IBM Code Pages*

CODE	DESIGNATION
437	US/English alphabet
850	Multilingual alphabet
860	Portuguese alphabet
863	Canadian/French alphabet
865	Nordic alphabet

At the start of each font file is a font file header that contains general information about the number of code pages, the default code pages, and the offset of each character set within the disk file. The font file header can be seen in Table 6.5.

Table 6.5 *Adapter Interface Font File Header*

OFFSET	UNIT	CONTENTS
0	word	Number of code pages in the font file
2	word	Number of the default code page (range is 0 to 4)
4	word	Number of the alternate default codepage (range is 0 to 4)
6	doubleword	4-character id string for the first code page ('437'0)
10	word	Offset within the disk file of the first code page
12	doubleword	4-character id string for the second code page ('850'0)
16	word	Offset within the disk file of the second code page
18	doubleword	4-character id string for the third code page ('860'0)
22	word	Offset within the disk file of the third code page
24	doubleword	4-character id string for the fourth code page ('863'0)
28	word	Offset within the disk file of the fourth code page
30	doubleword	4-character id string for the fifth code page ('865'0)
34	word	Offset within the disk file of the fifth code page

Each code page (character set) in a font file is preceded by a header block that contains the necessary data for displaying the encoded characters. The *character set header* is called the *character set definition block* in IBM documentation. The offset of the character set headers can be obtained from the corresponding entry in the font file header. (See Table 6.5.) In this manner, a program can locate the header block for the first code page (US/English alphabet) by adding the word value at offset 10 of the font file header to the offset of the start of the disk file. (See Table 6.5.) Table 6.6 shows the data encoded in the character set header.

Table 6.6 Adapter Interface Character Set Header

OFFSET	UNIT	CONTENTS
0	byte	Reserved
1	byte	Image formatted as follows:
		0 = single or multiplane image
		3 = short stroke vector image
2-6	Reserved	
7	byte	Pixel width of character cell
8	byte	Pixel height of character cell
9	byte	Reserved
10-11	word	Cell size (in bytes per character)
12-13	word	Character image format:
		Bit 14:
		0 = single plane image
		1 = multiplane image
		Bit 13:
		0 = not proportionally spaced
		1 = proportionally spaced
		All other bits are reserved (0)
14-17	doubleword	Offset:segment of index table
18-21	doubleword	Offset:segment of porportional spacing table
22	byte	Code for first character
23	byte	Code for last character
24-27	doubleword	Offset:segment of first character definition table (all font types)
28-29	Reserved	
30-33	doubleword	Offset:segment of second character definition table (multiplane fonts)
34-35	Reserved	
36-39	doubleword	Offset:segment of third character definition table (multiplane fonts)

Notice in Table 6.6 that the byte at offset 1 of the character set header encodes the image format as bit-mapped (value 0) or as short stroke vector type (value 1). If the image is in bit-mapped format, then bit 14 of the word at offset 12 determines if the image is single or multiplane. The byte at offset 7 of the character set header measures the number of horizontal pixels in the character cell while the byte at offset 8 measures its vertical dimension. The cell size, which is stored at the word at offset 10, represents the number of bytes used in storing each character encoded in bitmap format. This value is obtained by multiplying the pixel width (offset 7) by the pixel height (offset 8) and dividing the product by 8.

The index table, which can be located by means of the address stored at offset 14 of the character set header, contains the offset of the character definitions for each individual character. For single-plane fonts, the start location of the character definition table can be found from the address stored at offset 24. Therefore, a program can locate the bitmap for a particular character by adding its offset in the table, obtained from the index table, to the offset of the start of the character definition table. The code for first and last characters, at offsets

22 and 23 of the character set header, serves to delimit the character range of the font. For example, if a font does not start with character code 1, the value at offset 22 in the character set header must be used to scale the character codes into the index table.

Multiplane fonts consist of three monochrome images whose bitmaps can be located by means of the addresses stored at offsets 24, 30, and 36 of the character set header. (See Table 6.6.) To the present date, multiplane image fonts have not been furnished by IBM. Single-plane image fonts are encoded in a single bitmap, which is located at the address stored at offset 24 of the character set header (see Table 6.6). The character's image is encoded in a bit-to-pixel scheme. The character's foreground and background colors are determined by means of foreground color and background color settings described later in this chapter.

The location of the character definition table for short stroke vector fonts is the same as for single stroke, bit-mapped fonts. However, short stroke vector characters are encoded in the form of drawing orders, each of which is represented in a one-byte command. The character drawings are made up of a series of straight lines (vectors) that can be no longer than 15 pixels. Each vector must be drawn at an angle that is a multiple of 45 degrees. Therefore, the lines must be either vertical, horizontal, or diagonal. Figure 6.6 shows the bitmap of the short stroke vector commands.

The vector direction field, marked with the letters d in Figure 6.6, determines the direction and angle of each vector. The reference point is at the origin of the Cartesian plane and the angle is measured in a counterclockwise direction. In this manner, the value 010 corresponds with a vector drawn in the vertical direction, downward from the start point. The field marked with the letter m

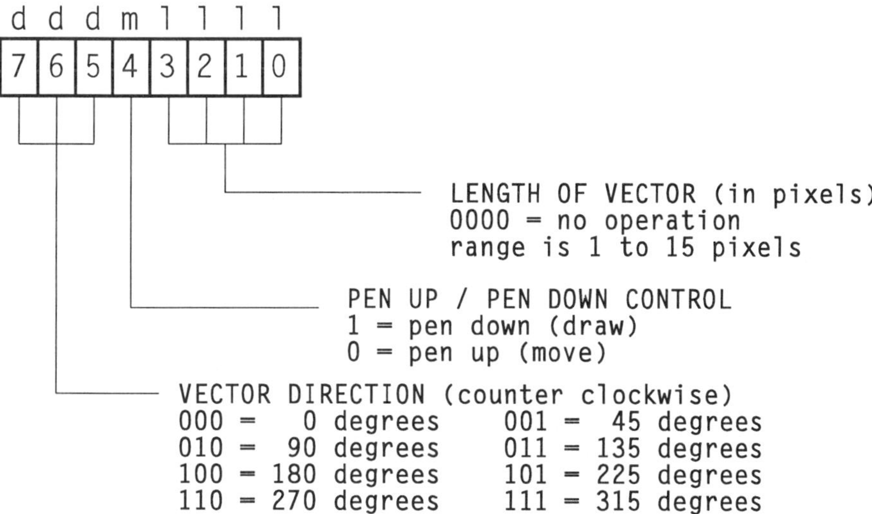

Figure 6.6 *Bitmap of Short Stroke Vector Command*

in Figure 6.6 determines if the vector is a draw or move operation. We have used the plotter terminology of pen-up and pen-down to illustrate this function. If a vector is defined as a pen-up vector, the current position is changed but no drawing takes place. If the m bit is set (pen-down), then the vector command draws a line on the video screen. The length of the vector is determined by the four bits in the field marked with the letters l in Figure 6.6. A 0000 value in this field is interpreted as no operation. The maximum length of a vector corresponds with the field value of 1111, which is equivalent to 15 pixels. The current drawing position is moved one pixel further than the value encoded in the l field.

6.2 Communicating with the AI

The Adapter Interface software was conceived as a layer of software services for initializing, configuring, and programming the 8514/A graphics system. XGA is furnished with a compatible set of services, which are a superset of those furnished for 8514/A. In both cases, 8514/A and XGA, the programming interface documentation assumes that programming is in C language. Access methods from other languages have not been described to this date. One difference between the AI software, as furnished for 8514/A and XGA, is that the former is a Terminate and Stay Resident (TSR) program while the latter is an MS-DOS device driver of the .SYS file type.

The AI installation selects one of two versions of the software according to the amount of memory in the graphics system. Once installed, the address of the AI handler is stored at interrupt vector 7FH. The AI services are accessed by means of an INT 7FH instruction or by a far call to the address of the service routine.

6.2.1 Interfacing with the AI

Before an application can start using the AI services it must first certify that the software is correctly installed and obtain the address of the service routine. Since interrupt 7FH has been documented as a reserved vector in IBM literature, the application can assume, with relative certainty, that the value stored at this vector is zero if no AI has been installed. However, this assumption risks that a non-conforming program has improperly used the vector for its own purposes. In which case the vector could store a non-zero value, while no AI is present.

The documented access mechanism for the AI services is by means of a far call. It appears that the AI is preceded by a jump table to each of its service routines and that each address in the jump table is a four-byte far pointer. Therefore, the calling program must multiply the AI service request by four to obtain the offset in the jump table. This jump table offset is placed in the SI register, the offset element of the address of the AI service routine is in BX, and its segment in ES. Once these registers are set up, the far call to a particular AI service can be performed by means of the instruction

```
CALL     DWORD PTR ES:[BX+SI]
```

Table 6.7 *8514/A and XGA Adapter Interface Services*

NAME	ENTRY POINT NUMBER	DESCRIPTION
HLINE	0	Draw line
HCLINE	1	Draw line at current point
HRLINE	2	Draw line from start point
HCRLINE	3	Draw line from start point
HSCP	4	Set current point
HBAR	5	Begin area for fill operation
HEAR	6	End area for fill operation
HSCOL	7	Set current color
HOPEN	8	Open adapter for AI operations
HSMX	9	Set mix
HSBCOL	10	Set background color
HSLT	11	Set line type
HSLW	12	Set line width
HEGS	13	Erase graphics screen
HSGQ	14	Set graphics quality
HSCMP	15	Set color compare register
HINT	16	Synchronize with vertical retrace
HSPATTO	17	Set pattern reference
HSPATT	18	Set pattern shape
HLDPAL	19	Load palette
HSHS	20	Set scissor
HBBW	21	Write bit-block image data
HCBBW	22	Write bit-block at current point
HBBR	23	Read bit block
HBBCHN	24	Chain bit block data
HBBC	25	Copy bit block
HSCOORD	26	Set coordinate type
HQCOORD	27	Query coordinate type
HSMODE	28	Set adapter mode
HQMODE	29	Query adapter mode
HQMODES	30	Query adapter modes
HQDPS	31	Query drawing process state
HRECT	32	Fill rectangle
HSBP	33	Set bit plane controls
HCLOSE	34	Close adapter
HESC	35	Escape (terminate processing)
HXLATE	36	Assign multiplane color tables
HSCS	37	Select character set
HCHST	38	Display character string
HCCHSET	39	Display string at current point
ABLOCKMFI	40	Display character block (MFI mode)
ABLOCKCGA	41	Display character block (CGA mode)
AERASE	42	Erase character rectangle
ASCROLL	43	Scroll character rectangle
ACURSOR	44	Set current cursor position
ASCUR	45	Set cursor shape
ASFONT	46	Select character set
AXLATE	47	Assign color index
HINIT	48	Initialize adapter state
HSYNC	49	Synchronize adapter with task
HMRK	50	Display marker
HCMRK	51	Display marker at current point
HSMARK	52	Set marker shape
HSLPC	53	Save line-pattern count
HRLPC	54	Restore saved line-pattern count
HQCP	55	Query current point
HQDFPAL	56	Query default palette
HSPAL	57	Save palette
HRPAL	58	Restore palette
HSAFP	59	Set area fill plane
ASCELL	60	Set cell size

Notice that the offset element of the address is determined by the sum of the pointer register (BX) and the offset of the service routine in the jump table (SI).

C Language Support

Two support files and a demonstration program for the AI are included in both the 8514/A and the XGA diskettes furnished with the adapters. The C language header files are named AFIDATA.H and IBMAFI.H. In addition, the assembly language source file named CALLAFI.ASM contains three public procedures for initializing and calling the AI. The object file CALLAFI.OBJ must be linked with the application's C language modules in order to access the AI. The header files and the object module CALLAFI.OBJ provide a convenient interface with the AI for C language applications.

AI Entry Points

We saw that an application accesses the AI services by means of a jump table of service numbers. The C language support software provided with XGA and 8514/A contains an ordered list of the code names of the services and their associated entry points. In this manner an application coded in C language need only reference the service name and the support software will calculate the routine's entry point from the furnished table. Table 6.7 lists the service routine code names and entry point numbers for the AI services available in both 8514/A and XGA systems.

The XGA adapter contains eighteen additional AI services that are not available in 8514/A. These XGA proprietary services are listed in Table 6.8.

Table 6.8 *XGA Adapter Interface Services*

NAME	ENTRY POINT NUMBER	DESCRIPTION
ASGO	61	Set alpha grid origin
HDLINE	62	Disjoint line at point
———	63	
HPEL	64	Write pixel string
HRPEL	65	Read pixel string
HPSTEP	66	Plot and step
HCPSTEP	67	Plot and step at current position
HRSTEP	68	Read and step
HSBMAP	69	Set bitmap attributes
HQBMAP	70	Query bitmap attributes
HBMC	71	Bitmap copy
HSDW	72	Set display window
HSPRITE	73	Sprite at given position
HSSPRITE	74	Set sprite shape
HRWVEC	75	Read/write vector
———	76	
———	77	
HSFPAL	78	Save full palette
HRFPAL	79	Restore full palette
HQDEVICE	80	Query device specific (no action)

Obtaining the AI Address

The following procedure can be used to test the AI initialization and, if the service software is installed, to acquire the address of the AI service routines.

```
AI_VECTOR        PROC    FAR
; Procedure to obtain the address of the XGA and 8514/A Adapter
; Interface. This procedure must be called before calls are made
; to the Adapter Interface services
;
; On entry:
;           nothing
; On exit:
;           carry set if no AI installed
;           carry clear if AI present
;               CX => segment of AI link table
;               DX => offset of AI link table
;
;*********************|
;     get vector 7FH  |
;*********************|
; Use MS DOS service number 53, interrupt 21H, to obtain the
; vector for the XGA and 8514-A AI interrupt (7FH)
        MOV     AH,53           ; MS DOS service number
        MOV     AL,7FH          ; AI interrupt
        INT     21H             ; MS DOS interrupt
; ES = segment of interrupt handler
; BX = offset of handler
;*********************|
;     test for no AI  |
;*********************|
; The code assumes that the vector at INT 7FH will be 0000:0000
; if the AI is not initialized
        MOV     AX,ES           ; Segment to AX
        OR      AX,BX           ; OR segment and offset
        JNZ     OK_AI           ; Go if address not 0000:0000
;*********************|
;     ERROR - no AI   |
;*********************|
NO_AI:
        STC                     ; Error return
        RET
;*********************|
;   get AI address    |
;*********************|
; Service number 0105H, interrupt 7FH, returns the address of
```

```
; the XGA/8514-A entry point
OK_AI:
          MOV       AX,0105H           ; Service request number
          INT       7FH                ; in XGA AI interrupt
          JNC       OK_AI              ; Go if no error code returned
          JMP       NO_AI              ; Take error exit
; At this point CX:DX holds the address of the XGA and 8514/A
; Adapter Interface handler (in segment:offset form)
          CLC                          ; No error
          RET
AI_VECTOR           ENDP
```

Typically, the application calling the AI_VECTOR procedure will store the
address of the service routine in its own data space. For example, a doubleword
storage can be reserved for the logical address of the service routine, in this
manner:

```
AI_ADD              DD        0        ; Doubleword storage for address
                                       ; of Adapter Interface services
```

After a call to the AI_VECTOR procedure the code can proceed as follows:

```
;*********************|
;    get AI address   |
;*********************|
; The procedure AI_VECTOR obtains the segment:offset address of
; the AI handler
          CALL      AI_VECTOR          ; Local procedure
          JNC       OK_VECTOR          ; Go if no carry
; If execution reaches this point there is no valid AI installed
; and an error exit should take place

          .

          .

          .

OK_VECTOR:
; Store segment and offset of AI handler
          MOV       WORD PTR AI_ADD,DX         ; Store offset of
address
          MOV       WORD PTR AI_ADD+2,CX       ; and segment
; AI entry point is now stored in a DS variable
```

Using the AI Call Mechanism

Once the application has stored the address of the AI service routine in a data
variable, it can access any of its services. The access mechanism requires the
entry point number for the desired service as well as a pointer to a parameter

block containing the data received and passed by the service routine. (See Table 6.7 and 6.8.) Notice that a few AI service do not require or return user data and, in these cases, the parameter block is a dummy value. The following procedure, named AI_SERVICE, performs the arithmetic operations required to obtain the offset of the desired routine in the AI jump table, sets up the registers for the far call to the service routine, and performs some housekeeping operations.

```
AI_SERVICE        PROC    NEAR
; Procedure to access the services in the XGA and 8514/A Adapter
; Interface software
;
; On entry:
;          AX = service number
;          DS:BX = address of parameter block
;
        PUSH    BP                    ; Save base pointer
        MOV     BP,SP                 ; Set BP to stack
; Push address of caller's parameter block
        PUSH    DS
        PUSH    BX                    ; the offset
;
; Multiply by 4 to form offset as required by AI
        SHL     AX,1                  ; AX times 2
        SHL     AX,1                  ; again
        MOV     SI,AX                 ; Offset to SI
        LES     BX,AI_ADD             ; Entry block address (ES:BX)
        CALL    DWORD PTR ES:[BX+SI]    ; Call AI service
        POP     BP                    ; Restore caller's BP
        RET
;
AI_SERVICE        ENDP
```

The parameter block passed by the caller to the AI service is a data structure whose size and contents vary in each service. One common element in all parameter blocks is that the first byte serves to determine the size of the block. In this manner, the word at offset 0 of the parameter block indicates the byte size of the remainder of the block. Table 6.9 shows the structure of the AI parameter block.

Table 6.9 *Structure of the Adapter Interface Parameter Block*

OFFSET	DATA SIZE	CONTENTS
0	word	Byte length of parameter block
2	byte, word,, doubleword, or string	First data item
.		
.		
length + 2		Last data item

AI Initialization Operations

Before the general AI services can be used by an application the adapter must be initialized by presetting it to a known state. Two AI services, named HOPEN and HINIT, are provided for this purpose. The HOPEN service (entry point number 8 in Table 6.7) presets the adapter's control flags and selects an extended function mode. If the adapter is successfully opened, the AI call clears a field in the parameter block. A non-zero value in this field indicates that a hardware mismatch is detected. The following code fragment shows the data segment setup of the parameter block of the HOPEN service as well as a call to this AI service.

```
DATA       SEGMENT
           .

           .

           .

HOPEN_DATA       DW        3          ; Length of data block
INIT_FLAGS       DB        0          ; 7 6 5 4 3 2 1 0 <= flags
                                      ; | |  ___________
                                      ; | |          |_______ Reserved
                                      ; | |_ Do not load default
                                      ;        palette
                                      ; |___ Do not clear bit planes
AF_MODE          DB        0          ; Advanced function mode
                                      ; No.    Pixels      Text
                                      ; 00     1024x768    85x38
                                      ; 01     640x480     80x34
                                      ; 02     1024x768    128x54
                                      ; 03     1024x768    146x51
RET_STATUS       DB        0          ; Status returned by AI call
                                      ; 0 if initialization successful
                                      ; Not 0 if initialization failed
           .

           .

DATA       ENDS
CODE       SEGMENT
           .

           .

;*********************|
;     initialize AI   |
;*********************|
; Call HOPEN service (enable adapter)
        MOV     INIT_FLAGS,0     ; Set initialization flags
                                 ; to clear memory and load
; default palette
        MOV     AF_MODE,0        ; Set 1024-by-768 mode number 0
```

```
        MOV     AX,8               ; Code number for this service
        LEA     BX,HOPEN_DATA      ; Pointer to parameter block
        CALL    AI_SERVICE         ; Procedure to perform AI call
; The RET_STATUS field is filled by the service call
; This field is not zero if an error was detected
        CMP     RET_STATUS,0       ; Not zero if open error
        JE      OK_OPEN            ; Go if no error
; At this point an error was detected during HOPEN function

        .

        .

; At this point adapter was successfully opened
OK_OPEN:

        .

        .

CODE    ENDS
```

Once the adapter has been successfully opened, the program must inform the
AI of the location (in the application's memory space) of a special task state
buffer. The main purpose of the task state buffer is to assist multitasking by
providing a record of the adapter's state for each concurrent task. When a task
is restored to the foreground, the task state buffer provides to the AI software
all the necessary information for restoring the adapter to its previous state.
Although DOS programs have absolute control of the machine's hardware, they
must also allocate a task state buffer before beginning AI operations. Table 6.10
lists the data items stored in the task state buffer as well as their initial
settings.

Table 6.10 Task State Buffer Data after Initialization

ITEM	VALUE
Current point	Coordinates 0,0
Foreground color	White (all bits are 1)
Background color	Black (all bits are 0)
Foreground mix	Destination = source (overpaint mode)
Background mix	Leave alone
Comparison color	Not initialized
Comparison logic	False
Line type	Solid
User line	Not initialized
Line width	1 pixel
Line pattern	Position not initialized
Saved line pattern	Position not initialized
Area pattern	Solid
Pattern origin	Coordinates 0,0
Text control	Block pointer not initialized
Marker shape	Not intialized
Scissors	Clipping to full screen
Graphics quality	High precision
Plane mask	All planes enabled
Color index table	8 entries set linearly (0 to 7)
Alphanumeric cursor	Top left of screen (0,0)
Cursor definition	Invisible
Translate table	16 values for foreground and background
Character set	Not selected

In order to allocate space for the task state buffer, an application must know its size, but the length of the task state buffer is not hard-coded in the adapter's software. However, an application can use the HQDPS function (listed in Table 6.7 and described later in the chapter) in order to determine the memory space required for this data structure. Once the size of the task state buffer is known, the code can dynamically allocate sufficient memory for it. An alternative, although not as elegant, method is to assume that the task state buffer for DOS is 360 bytes and allocate this amount of space. In fact, the task state buffer for XGA systems is 341 bytes, so assigning 360 bytes leaves a 19-byte safety margin.

Space for the task state buffer is allocated and its values initialized by means of the HINIT adapter function. The call requires the segment address of the task state buffer, while it assumes that the buffer is at offset 0000 in this segment. This characteristic of the HINIT service suggests that the task state buffer be placed in a separate segment. This assignation has the added advantage of not using the application's data space for this purpose. In DOS the assignment of buffer space and the HINIT call can be performed as in the following code fragment

```
;****************************************************************
;                    segment for task state data
;****************************************************************
TASK_STATE      SEGMENT
;********************|
;  AI state buffer   |
;********************|
STATE_BUF          DB        360 DUP (00H)
;
TASK_STATE      ENDS


;****************************************************************
;                         data segment
;****************************************************************
DATA        SEGMENT
               .
               .
               .

;
HINIT_DATA         DW        2        ; Length of data block
BUF_SEG            DW        0        ; Segment of task state buffer
               .
               .
               .
DATA        ENDS


;****************************************************************
```

```
;                                 code segment
;********************************************************************
CODE      SEGMENT
              .

              .


; Call HINIT (Initialize adapter state)
          MOV       AX,TASK_STATE      ; Segment for task state buffer
          MOV       BUF_SEG,AX         ; Store segment in parameter
                                       ; block
          MOV       AX,48              ; Code number for this service
          LEA       BX,HINIT_DATA      ; Pointer to data block
          CALL      AI_SERVICE         ; Procedure to perform AI call
; No information is returned by HINIT. Software must assume that
; task state buffer was successfully allocated and initialized

              .

              .

              .
```

The program named AI_DEMO.ASM, furnished in the book's microdisk, is a demonstration of some elementary AI functions. The code performs AI initialization and setup following a method similar to the one described in the present section. The source file named AI_INIT.ASM is an initialization template that performs the conventional AI operations usually required to start programming XGA or 8514/A systems. The programmer can use AI_INIT.ASM as a coding template for programs that use AI operations.

6.2.2 AI Data Conventions

Many Adapter Interface functions operate on data passed by the caller while some functions return information. In the previous section we discussed the structure of the parameter block whose address is passed to the AI by the calling program. (See Table 6.9.) The calling program uses this parameter block to transfer data to and from the AI. However, notice that not all AI functions operate on data items. Some functions (such as HEGS and HCLOSE) require no parameters and return no data to the calling program.

The data items operated on by the AI can be classified into three general groups: numeric data, screen data, and address data.

8514/A numeric data is defined in three integer formats: byte, word, and doubleword. The IBM XGA documentation adds quadword to this list. Byte ordering of numeric data is according to the Intel convention: that is, the least significant byte is located at the lowest numbered memory address. Usually, the programmer need not be concerned with this matter since the assembler or compiler will handle multi-byte ordering automatically. Bit numbering is also in the conventional format; that is, the least significant bit is assigned the number zero.

Screen data refers to coordinates and to dimensions. Absolute coordinates are stored in a word field, in 2's complement binary format. Relative coordinates are stored in byte fields, also in 2's complement binary form. Screen dimensions are defined in the Cartesian plane: the x coordinate represents the horizontal value and the y coordinate the vertical value. The origin is located at the top-left screen corner. In the 8514/A, the valid coordinate range is from -512 to +1535 in the x and y planes respectively, while in XGA it is from -2048 to +6143 for both Cartesian coordinates. The viewport (video buffer) is in one of two modes in both systems: in low resolution mode the x coordinate is in the range 0 to 639 and the y coordinate in the range 0 to 479. In high-resolution mode the x coordinate is in the range 0 to 1023 and the y coordinate in the range 0 to 767. The image buffer and viewports for XGA systems are shown in Figure 6.7.

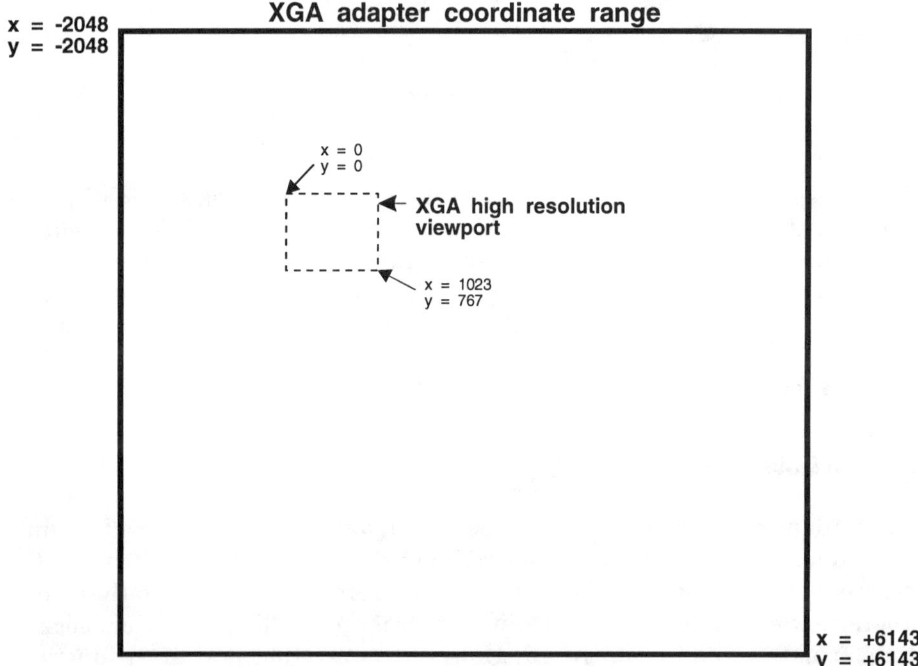

Figure 6.7 *Adapter Coordinate Range and Viewport in XGA Systems*

Address data is in conventional Intel logical address format, that is, in segment:offset form. If offset and segment are stored separately in word-size data items, the offset element precedes the segment element, as in the following parameter block for the HSCS (select character set) command:

```
HSCS_DATA          DW         4          ; Length of data block
FONT_OFF           DW         0          ; Offset of loaded font
FONT_SEG           DW         0          ; Segment of loaded font
```

Address data does not always require a logical address. For example, in the parameter block for the HINIT function call, only the segment element of the address is required, as shown in the following code fragment:

```
HINIT_DATA      DW      2       ; Length of data block
BUF_SEG         DW      0       ; Segment of task state buffer
```

6.3 AI Concepts

Before venturing into the details of AI programming, it is convenient to gain familiarity with some graphics concepts often mentioned in the adapter's literature. Most of these concepts are taken from the general terminology of computer graphics. Although, in a few cases, IBM documentation varies from the more generally accepted terms.

6.3.1 Pixel Attributes

A pixel's color is primarily determined by the value stored in the memory maps and by the setting of the LUT registers, as shown in Figure 6.3 and discussed in section 6.1.4. By means of the AI services an application can access the color value stored in the bit planes through the HSCOL (set current color) and HSBCOL (set background color) commands. Generally, a 1-bit in a draw order is displayed using the current foreground color while a 0-bit is displayed using the current background color. In text operations, the background color refers to the rectangular pixel block on which text characters are drawn, while the foreground color refers to the text characters themselves.

Mixes

XGA and 8514/A system provide a second level of control over pixel display by means of a mechanism called *mixes*. Mixes are logical or mathematical operations performed between a new color value and the one already stored in display memory. The mix mode is selected independently for the foreground and background colors.

Color Compares

The color compare mechanism in the XGA and 8514/A AI provides a means by which the programmer can exclude specific bit planes from graphics operations. Comparison logic allows operations of equal-to, less-than, greater-than, greater-than-or-equal-to, and less-than-or-equal-to. When the comparison evaluates to TRUE, the bit plane data is unmodified. When the comparison evaluates to FALSE, then the active mix operation is allowed to take place. The color compare function is selected by means of the HSCMP (set color compare register). Notice that the color compare function is not active during the AI alphanumeric services.

Bit-Plane Masking

In addition to the controls offered by foreground and background colors, mix mode and the color compare setting, an application can use masking to selectively enable and disable individual bit-planes. The bit-plane masking function allows separate control for graphics and alphanumeric operations. The masking function takes place before compares and mixes are applied, therefore the mask can be used to exclude compare and mix operations. Bit-plane masking is performed by means of the HSBP (set bit-plane control) function.

6.3.2 Scissoring

The AI software provides a function by which an application can limit graphics operations to a rectangular area within the viewport. This function, called *scissoring* in the IBM documentation, is useful in developing programs that use screen windows, since it inhibits operations outside a predefined screen rectangle. During adapter initializing the scissoring rectangle is set to the size of the viewport, but an application can redefine it by means of the HSHS (set scissor) function.

6.3.3 Absolute and Current Screen Positions

Several AI graphics and text functions are based on absolute screen locations. For example, the HLINE function (see Section 6.4.2) can be used to draw one or more straight lines starting at a given screen coordinate point. On the other hand, other AI graphics and text functions operate from a current screen position which is maintained by the adapter. For example, the HCLINE function can be used to draw one or more straight line segments starting at the current position. In this function the current screen position is automatically updated to the end point of the last line segment. The current screen position can be set by means of the HSCP (set current position) function, described in Section 6.4.2.

6.3.4 Polymarkers

A *marker*, in the context of the XGA and 8514/A AI programming, is a bit-mapped object that can be as large as 255 by 255 pixels. The AI software allows displaying one or more markers at the predefined absolute coordinates or at the current display position. Since more than one marker can be displayed by the same command, the AI function should be classified as a polymarker operation.

The marker image is a rectangular, unpadded bitmap. If defined as a monochrome marker it is displayed using the current foreground color and according to the selected mix. If the marker is defined as a multicolor one, it is displayed using a color table supplied by the caller.

In 8514/A the multicolor table consists of a one-byte color code for each bit in the marker bitmap. In XGA the program can select a color table in byte-per-pixel mode (compatible with 8514/A) or in packed format. In the packed format the mapping of the color table depends on the system's resolution. For example, if the pixel color is determined by four video memory bits, then the color table consists of a series of packed, four-bit color codes. Notice that the packed format is not supported in the 8514/A.

The current marker is defined by means of the HSMARK (set marker shape) function. One or more markers are displayed at absolute screen positions by means of the HMRK (display marker) function. The HCMRK (marker at current point) function is used to display one or more markers at the current position. These functions are described in Section 6.4.4.

6.3.5 Line Widths and Types

The XGA and 8514/A AI allow selecting the line width and type to be used in line drawing operations. Line width options are of one or three pixels. Three-pixel wide lines are drawn as three separate lines, one pixel apart. There are eight built-in line types in the AI software: dotted, short dashed, dash-dot, double dot, long dashed, dash-double-dot, solid, and invisible lines. In addition, the XGA AI offers a second doted line type not available in 8514/A. An application can also define its own customized line type.

Each line type consists of a repeating pattern of dots and dashes. While drawing a non-continuous line, the AI software keeps track of the current position in the line pattern. Although most line drawing functions reset the pattern counter at the start of a line, an application can override this mode of operation by saving and restoring the current position in the line pattern. The AI function named HSLPC (save line pattern count) and HRLPC (restore line pattern count) are used for this purpose. These functions are particularly useful when a noncontinuous line must straddle a scissor boundary.

The line type selection option in the AI simplifies considerably the development of drafting and computer assisted design software. On the other hand, the line width selection option is often considered too limited to be of practical use. Line width selection is performed by means of the HSLW (select line width) function while line type is chosen by the HSLT (select line type) function.

6.3.6 Bit Block Operations

Graphics programs often operate on rectangular blocks of bit-mapped data called bit blocks. The manipulation of these blocks are called bit block transfers; the expression is often shortened to bitBLTS (pronounced "bit blits"). BitBLT operations often refer to a *source block*, a *destination blocks*, and to the logical operation to be performed in combining them into a *result block*. In the AI the logical operation is selected by means of the mix. (See Section 6.3.1.)

BitBLTs are one of the most powerful graphics tools in the AI. The bit block transfer operations can take place from the application's memory space to video memory, from video memory to the application's memory space, and from video memory to video memory. When the bit-mapped image stored by the applications is transferred to the adapter's video memory we speak of a bitBLT write. When the data stored in the adapter's video RAM is moved to the application's memory we speak of a bitBLT read. Operations by which data is moved within the application's video space are called a bitBLT copy.

BitBLTs operate on a rectangular area. They proceed from the top-left corner of the rectangle, left-to-right and top-to-bottom. Due to this mode of operations they are sometimes called *raster functions*.

BitBLT Copy

An AI bitBLT copy operation produces a second screen image based on the pixel data stored in a screen rectangle defined by the caller. The second image is displayed according to the current mix and comparison and clipped according to the scissoring. If the two images overlap, the AI correctly places the new image overlapping the existing one. The copy operation can be performed in one of two modes. In the single-plane mode the application selects a single image plane which is copied by the AI service. In the multiplane mode the entire image is copied to the new position.

The AI function for performing a bitBLT copy operation is named HBBC (bitBLT copy). In this function the caller must provide a parameter block containing the desired mode (single-plane or multiplane), the dimensions of the bitBLT rectangle, the selected bit plane if the single-plane mode is active, and the coordinates of the source and destination areas.

BitBLT Write

An application can display a bit-mapped image stored in its own memory space by performing a bitBLT write operation. The screen image is displayed according to the current mix and comparison values and is clipped according to the scissoring. In XGA and 8514/A systems the write operation can take place in one of two modes. If the monochrome mode is selected, the image bitmap is displayed using the current foreground color for the 1-bits and the current background color for the 0 bits. In this case the bitmap is assumed to be encoded in a one-bit-per-pixel format.

If the color mode is selected then the AI assumes that the image is encoded in a byte-per-pixel format. In other words, the caller provides an image map in which each screen pixel is represented by the color code stored in one data byte. The actual color displayed depends on the present setting of the LUT registers and the number of active bit planes. In addition to the monochrome and color modes, the XGA AI offers an additional packed bits mode. In the packed mode the number of bits per pixel depends on the current display mode. For example, if the adapter is in a four bit plane display mode, then the AI assumes that the caller's image data is encoded in a one-nibble-per-pixel format. The packed mode is not available in 8514/A systems.

Three different AI functions are related to bitBLT write operations. The function named HBBW (bitBLT write) is used to transfer image data to a screen location specified by the caller. HCBBW (bitBLT write at current position) transfers the image data to the current position. Both of these functions are of preparatory nature. The actual display of the bit block requires the use of an AI service named HBBCHN (bitBLT chain). This command includes the address of the bitmap in the application's memory space as well as its dimensions. The use of HBBW, HCBBW, and HBBCHN commands is illustrated in Section 6.4.4.

BitBLT Read

An application can also use the AI bitBLT services to move a video image to its own memory space. In this type of operation, called a bitBLT read, the application defines the coordinates of a screen rectangle, as well as the location, in its application's memory space, of a buffer for storing the video data. The AI then makes a copy of the screen image in the application's RAM. The size of the image rectangle can be as small as a single pixel or as large as the entire screen.

As is the case in the bitBLT write operation, XGA and 8514/A systems allow bitBLT reads in one of two modes. If the monochrome mode is selected, the image is read from the bit-plane specified by the caller. In this case the application must provide a storage space of one bit per screen pixel. If the color mode is selected the AI will read all eight bit planes and store a byte-per-pixel color code in the buffer provided by the caller. In addition to the monochrome and color modes, the XGA AI offers an additional packed bits mode, similar to the one described for the bitBLT write operation. The packed mode is not available in 8514/A systems.

Two AI functions are related to bitBLT read operations. The function named HBBR (bitBLT read) is used to transfer video image data to a buffer supplied by the caller. This AI function is of preparatory nature. The actual storage of bit block data requires the use of the HBBCHN (bitBLT chain) AI service. The HBBCHN command provides the address of the storage buffer in the application's memory space as well as its dimensions.

6.4 Details of AI Programming

In the present section we offer examples of AI programming. The examples are presented in the form of assembly language code fragments with the corresponding comments and explanations. We have mentioned that the IBM AI documentation uses C language almost exclusively. In our examples we have selected assembly language instead in order to provide an alternative programming medium. Also, because we feel that examples in assembly language provide clearer illustration of data structure and of the machine hardware operations than do examples in high-level languages. Once a reader understands the fundamental programming elements in an AI function, this knowledge can be easily applied in using the function from any particular programming language.

We remind the reader that the documentation published by IBM for XGA and 8514/A (see Section 6.1) contains descriptions, examples, and utility programs that are practically indispensable to the AI programmer. The book by Ritcher and Smith, *Graphics Programming for the 8514/A* (see Bibliography) will also be useful. In addition, the programs named AI_DEMO and AI_LUT included in the microdisk furnished with this book include demonstration of AI programming examples.

6.4.1 Initialization and Control Functions

The fundamental initialization operations for the AI as well as the access mechanism for using the AI commands were described in Section 6.2. The following code fragment shows the typical sequence of AI commands that an application would execute in order to establish communications with the adapter software. In this example we assume that the access mechanism is by the procedure named AI_SERVICE described in Section 6.2.1. The code is virtually identical to the one in the AI_INIT.ASM template furnished in the book's microdisk.

```
;*****************************************************************
;                          stack segment
;*****************************************************************
STACK    SEGMENT stack
         DB       0400H DUP ('?')     ; Default stack is 1K
;
STACK    ENDS
;
;*****************************************************************
;               segment for task state data
;*****************************************************************
TASK     SEGMENT
;********************|
;  AI state buffer   |
;********************|
STATE_BUF       DB       360 DUP (00H)
;
TASK     ENDS
;
;*****************************************************************
;                          data segment
;*****************************************************************
DATA     SEGMENT
;********************|
;   AI list address  |
;********************|
AI_ADD          DD       0           ; Doubleword storage for address
```

```
                                        ; of Adapter Interface services
        ;
        HQDPS_DATA      DW      6       ; Length of data block
        BUF_SIZE        DW      0       ; Buffer size
        STK_SIZE        DW      0       ; Stack usage, in bytes
        PAL_SIZE        DW      0       ; Palette buffer size, in bytes
        ;
        HOPEN_DATA      DW      3       ; Length of data block
        INIT_FLAGS      DB      0       ; 7 6 5 4 3 2 1 0 <= flags
                                        ; | | ___________
                                        ; | |         |_______ Reserved
                                        ; | |_ Do not load palette
                                        ; |___ Do not clear bit planes
        AF_MODE         DB      0       ; Advanced function mode
                                        ; No.    Pixels      Text
                                        ; 00     1024x768    85x38
                                        ; 01     640x480     80x34
                                        ; 02     1024x768    128x54
                                        ; 03     1024x768    146x51
        RET_FLAGS       DB      0       ; Status
                                        ; 0 if initialization successful
                                        ; Not 0 if initialization failed
        ;
        HINIT_DATA      DW      2       ; Length of data block
        BUF_SEG         DW      0       ; Segment of AI buffer
        ;
        HCLOSE_DATA     DW      0       ; Length field is zero for
        HCLOSE
        HEGS_DATA       DW      0       ; Length field is zero for HEGS
        DUMMY           DW      0       ; Dummy data area
                        .
                        .
                        .
        DATA    ENDS


        ;********************************************************************
        ;                       code segment
        ;********************************************************************
        ;
        CODE    SEGMENT
                ASSUME  CS:CODE
        ;
        START:
        ; Establish data and extra segment addressability
                MOV     AX,DATA         ; Address of DATA to AX
```

```
            MOV     DS,AX               ; and to DS
            ASSUME  DS:DATA             ; Assume from here on
;********************|
;   get adapter address |
;********************|
; The local procedure AI_VECTOR obtains the segment:offset
; address of the adapter handler
            CALL    AI_VECTOR           ; Local procedure
            JNC     OK_VECTOR           ; Go if no carry
;********************|
;       error exit        |
;********************|
AI_ERROR:
; HEGS (erase graphics screen)
            MOV     AX,13               ; Code number for this service
            LEA     BX,HEGS_DATA        ; Pointer to dummy data block
            CALL    AI_SERVICE
;********************|
;       exit to DOS        |
;********************|
DOS_EXIT:
            MOV     AH,4CH              ; DOS service request code
            MOV     AL,0                ; No error code returned
            INT     21H                 ; TO DOS
;********************|
;     AI installed        |
;********************|
OK_VECTOR:
; Store segment and offset of AI handler
            MOV     WORD PTR AI_ADD,DX          ; Store offset of
address
            MOV     WORD PTR AI_ADD+2,CX        ; and segment
; Entry point for AI services is now stored in a DS variable
;********************|
;     initialize AI       |
;********************|
; Call HQDPS service (query drawing process state)
            MOV     AX,31               ; Code number for this service
            LEA     BX,HQDPS_DATA       ; Pointer to data block
            CALL    AI_SERVICE
; The following information is stored by the query drawing
; process command
; 1. size of task state buffer
; 2. stack usage, in bytes
; 3. size of palette buffer
; This information may later be required by the application
```

```
; Call HOPEN service (enable adapter)
        MOV     INIT_FLAGS,0     ; Set initialization flags
                                 ; to clear memory and load
                                 ; default palette
        MOV     AF_MODE,0        ; Set 1024-by-768 mode number 0
        MOV     AX,8             ; Code number for this service
        LEA     BX,HOPEN_DATA    ; Pointer to data block
        CALL    AI_SERVICE
; The HOPEN command returns system information in the RET_FLAGS
; field of the parameter block.
        MOV     AL,RET_FLAGS     ; Not zero if open error
        CMP     AL,0             ; Test for no error
        JZ      OK_OPEN          ; Go if no error
        JMP     AI_ERROR         ; Error exit
;
; Call HINIT (Initialize adapter state)
OK_OPEN:
        MOV     AX,TASK          ; Segment for task state
        MOV     BUF_SEG,AX       ; Store segment of adapter state
                                 ; buffer
        MOV     AX,48            ; Code number for this service
        LEA     BX,HINIT_DATA    ; Pointer to data block
        CALL    AI_SERVICE
; At this point the AI is initialized and ready for use
;**********************************************************************
;                       application's code
;**********************************************************************


             .
             .
             .

;**********************************************************************
;                           procedures
;**********************************************************************
AI_VECTOR       PROC    NEAR
; Procedure to obtain the address vector to the XGA/8514/A
; AI. This procedure must be called before calls are made
; to the Adapter Interface services (by means of the AI_SERVICE
; procedure)
; On entry:
;           nothing
; On exit:
;           carry set if no AI installed
;           carry clear if AI present
;              CX => segment of AI link table
;              DX => offset of AI link table
;**********************|
```

```
;      get vector 7FH     |
;*********************|
; Use MS DOS service number 53, interrupt 21H, to obtain the
; vector for the XGA/8514-A AI interrupt (7FH)
        MOV     AH,53           ; MS DOS service number
        MOV     AL,7FH          ; AI interrupt
        INT     21H             ; MS DOS interrupt
; ES => segment of interrupt handler
; BX => offset of handler
        MOV     AX,ES           ; Segment to AX
        OR      AX,BX           ; OR segment and offset
        JNZ     OK_AI           ; Go if address not 0000:0000
;*********************|
;   ERROR - no AI     |
;*********************|
NO_AI:
        STC                     ; Error return
        RET
;*********************|
;   get AI address    |
;*********************|
; Service number 0105H, interrupt 7FH, returns the address of
; the XGA and 8514/A jump table
OK_AI:
        MOV     AX,0105H        ; Service request number
        INT     7FH             ; in XGA AI interrupt
        JC      NO_AI           ; Go if error code returned
; At this point CX:DX holds the address of the XGA/8514-A entry
; point (in segment:offset form)
        CLC                     ; No error code
        RET
AI_VECTOR       ENDP
;****************************************************************
;
AI_SERVICE      PROC    NEAR
; Procedure to access the services in the XGA and 8514/A Adapter
; Interface
;
; On entry:
;       AX = service number
;       DS:BX = address of parameter block
;
        PUSH    BP              ; Save base pointer
        MOV     BP,SP           ; Set BP to stack
; Push address of caller's parameter block
        PUSH    DS
```

```
          PUSH     BX                  ; the offset
; Multiply by 4 to form offset as required by AI
          SHL      AX,1                ; AX time 2
          SHL      AX,1                ; again
          MOV      SI,AX               ; Offset to SI
          LES      BX,AI_ADD           ; Entry block address (ES:BX)
          CALL     DWORD PTR ES:[BX][SI]    ; Call AI service
          POP      BP                  ; Restore caller's BP
          RET
AI_SERVICE          ENDP
;*****************************************************************
;
CODE      ENDS
          END      START
```

6.4.2 Setting the Color Palette

The structure of the XGA and 8514/A color look-up table (LUT) and the
digital-to-analog converter is discussed in Section 6.1.4. The actual manipulation of the XGA and 8514/A DAC registers is by means of three palette
commands: HSPAL (save palette), HLDPAL (load palette registers), and
HRPAL (restore palette). The following code fragment shows the use of the AI
palette commands.

```
;*****************************************************************
;                         data segment
;*****************************************************************
DATA      SEGMENT
             .
             .
             .
;
;*********************|
;    palette data     |
;*********************|
; Data area for HLDPAL (load palette) function
HLDPAL_DATA      DW       10       ; Length of data block
LOAD_CODE        DB       0        ; Palette code
                                   ; 0 = load user pallete
                                   ; 1 = load default pallete
                 DB       0        ; Reserved
                 DW       0        ; Number of first entry
                 DW       256      ; Number of entries to load
PAL_OFF          DW       0        ; Offset of user palette
PAL_SEG          DW       0        ; Segment of user palette
```

```
; Data area for HSPAL (save palette data)
; and HRPAL (restore palette)
HSPAL_DATA        DW        769       ; Length of palette
                  DW        769 DUP (00H)    ; Storage for palette
;
; Double-bit IRGB palette in the following format
;           7 6 5 4 3 2 1 0  <= Bits
;           | | | | | | | |
;           | | | | | | | |_|_______ Blue
;           | | | | |_|___________ Green
;           | | |_|_______________ Red
;           |_|___________________ Intensity


;
; First group of 64 registers
; Notice that the DAC color registers are in the order
; Red-Blue-Green
;                        | R   B   G     R   B   G    |
IRGB_SHADES       DB     000,000,000,000,036,072,036,000 ; 1
                  DB     036,108,036,000,036,144,036,000 ; 3
                  DB     036,036,072,000,036,072,072,000 ; 5
                  DB     036,108,072,000,036,144,072,000 ; 7
                  DB     036,036,108,000,036,072,108,000 ; 9
                  DB     036,108,108,000,036,144,108,000 ; 11
                  DB     036,036,144,000,036,072,144,000 ; 13
                  DB     036,108,144,000,036,144,144,000 ; 15
                  DB     072,036,036,000,072,072,036,000 ; 17
                  DB     072,108,036,000,072,144,036,000 ; 19
                  DB     072,036,072,000,072,072,072,000 ; 21
                  DB     072,108,072,000,072,144,072,000 ; 23
                  DB     072,036,108,000,072,072,108,000 ; 25
                  DB     072,108,108,000,072,144,108,000 ; 27
                  DB     072,036,144,000,072,072,144,000 ; 29
                  DB     072,108,144,000,072,144,144,000 ; 31
                  DB     108,036,036,000,108,071,036,000 ; 33
                  DB     108,108,036,000,108,144,036,000 ; 35
                  DB     108,036,072,000,108,072,072,000 ; 37
                  DB     108,108,072,000,108,144,072,000 ; 39
                  DB     108,036,108,000,108,072,108,000 ; 41
                  DB     108,108,108,000,108,144,108,000 ; 43
                  DB     036,036,144,000,108,072,144,000 ; 45
                  DB     108,108,144,000,108,144,144,000 ; 47
                  DB     144,036,036,000,144,072,036,000 ; 49
                  DB     144,108,036,000,144,144,036,000 ; 51
                  DB     144,036,072,000,144,072,072,000 ; 53
                  DB     144,108,072,000,144,144,072,000 ; 55
```

```
            DB        144,036,108,000,144,072,108,000  ; 57
            DB        144,108,108,000,144,144,108,000  ; 59
            DB        144,036,144,000,144,072,144,000  ; 61
            DB        144,108,144,000,144,144,144,000  ; 63
; Second register group
            DB        072,072,072,000,072,108,072,000  ; 1
            DB        072,144,072,000,072,180,072,000  ; 3
            DB        072,072,108,000,072,108,108,000  ; 5
            DB        072,144,108,000,072,180,108,000  ; 7
            DB        072,072,144,000,072,108,144,000  ; 9
            DB        072,144,144,000,072,180,144,000  ; 11
            DB        072,072,180,000,072,108,180,000  ; 13
            DB        072,144,180,000,072,180,180,000  ; 15
            DB        108,072,072,000,108,108,072,000  ; 17
            DB        108,144,072,000,108,180,072,000  ; 19
            DB        108,072,108,000,108,108,108,000  ; 21
            DB        108,144,108,000,108,180,108,000  ; 23
            DB        108,072,144,000,108,108,144,000  ; 25
            DB        108,144,144,000,108,180,144,000  ; 27
            DB        108,072,180,000,108,108,180,000  ; 29
            DB        108,144,180,000,108,180,180,000  ; 31
            DB        144,072,072,000,144,108,072,000  ; 33
            DB        144,144,072,000,144,180,072,000  ; 35
            DB        144,072,108,000,144,108,108,000  ; 37
            DB        144,144,108,000,144,180,108,000  ; 39
            DB        144,072,144,000,144,108,144,000  ; 41
            DB        144,144,144,000,144,180,144,000  ; 43
            DB        072,072,180,000,144,108,180,000  ; 45
            DB        144,144,180,000,144,180,180,000  ; 47
            DB        180,072,072,000,180,108,072,000  ; 49
            DB        180,144,072,000,180,180,072,000  ; 51
            DB        180,072,108,000,180,108,108,000  ; 53
            DB        180,144,108,000,180,180,108,000  ; 55
            DB        180,072,144,000,180,108,144,000  ; 57
            DB        180,144,144,000,180,180,144,000  ; 59
            DB        180,072,180,000,180,108,180,000  ; 61
            DB        180,144,180,000,180,180,180,000  ; 63
; Third register group
            DB        108,108,108,000,108,144,108,000  ; 1
            DB        108,180,108,000,108,216,108,000  ; 3
            DB        108,108,144,000,108,144,144,000  ; 5
            DB        108,180,144,000,108,216,144,000  ; 7
            DB        108,108,180,000,108,144,180,000  ; 9
            DB        108,180,180,000,108,216,180,000  ; 11
            DB        108,108,216,000,108,144,216,000  ; 13
            DB        108,180,216,000,108,216,216,000  ; 15
```

```
        DB      144,108,108,000,144,144,108,000  ; 17
        DB      144,180,108,000,144,216,108,000  ; 19
        DB      144,108,144,000,144,144,144,000  ; 21
        DB      144,180,144,000,144,216,144,000  ; 23
        DB      144,108,180,000,144,144,180,000  ; 25
        DB      144,180,180,000,144,216,180,000  ; 27
        DB      144,108,216,000,144,144,216,000  ; 29
        DB      144,180,216,000,144,216,216,000  ; 31
        DB      180,108,108,000,180,144,108,000  ; 33
        DB      180,180,108,000,180,216,108,000  ; 35
        DB      180,108,144,000,180,144,144,000  ; 37
        DB      180,180,144,000,180,216,144,000  ; 39
        DB      180,108,180,000,180,144,180,000  ; 41
        DB      180,180,180,000,180,216,180,000  ; 43
        DB      108,108,216,000,180,144,216,000  ; 45
        DB      180,180,216,000,180,216,216,000  ; 47
        DB      216,108,108,000,216,144,108,000  ; 49
        DB      216,180,108,000,216,216,108,000  ; 51
        DB      216,108,144,000,216,144,144,000  ; 53
        DB      216,180,144,000,216,216,144,000  ; 55
        DB      216,108,180,000,216,144,180,000  ; 57
        DB      216,180,180,000,216,216,180,000  ; 59
        DB      216,108,216,000,216,144,216,000  ; 61
        DB      216,180,216,000,216,216,216,000  ; 63
; Fourth register group
        DB      144,144,144,000,144,180,144,000  ; 1
        DB      144,216,144,000,144,252,144,000  ; 3
        DB      144,144,180,000,144,180,180,000  ; 5
        DB      144,216,180,000,144,252,180,000  ; 7
        DB      144,144,216,000,144,180,216,000  ; 9
        DB      144,216,216,000,144,252,216,000  ; 11
        DB      144,144,252,000,144,180,252,000  ; 13
        DB      144,216,252,000,144,252,252,000  ; 15
        DB      180,144,144,000,180,180,144,000  ; 17
        DB      180,216,144,000,180,252,144,000  ; 19
        DB      180,144,180,000,180,180,180,000  ; 21
        DB      180,216,180,000,180,252,180,000  ; 23
        DB      180,144,216,000,180,180,216,000  ; 25
        DB      180,216,216,000,180,252,216,000  ; 27
        DB      180,144,252,000,180,180,252,000  ; 29
        DB      180,216,252,000,180,252,252,000  ; 31
        DB      216,144,144,000,216,180,144,000  ; 33
        DB      216,215,144,000,216,252,144,000  ; 35
        DB      216,144,180,000,216,180,180,000  ; 37
        DB      216,216,180,000,216,252,180,000  ; 39
        DB      216,144,216,000,216,180,216,000  ; 41
```

```
                DB        216,216,216,000,216,252,216,000 ; 43
                DB        144,144,252,000,216,180,252,000 ; 45
                DB        216,216,252,000,216,252,252,000 ; 47
                DB        252,144,144,000,252,180,144,000 ; 49
                DB        252,216,144,000,252,252,144,000 ; 51
                DB        252,144,180,000,252,180,180,000 ; 53
                DB        252,216,180,000,252,252,180,000 ; 55
                DB        252,144,216,000,252,180,216,000 ; 57
                DB        252,216,216,000,252,252,216,000 ; 59
                DB        252,144,252,000,252,180,252,000 ; 61
                DB        252,216,252,000,252,252,252,000 ; 63
;
; Gray shades palette. Notice that the pattern in the first 64
; registers is repeated 3 times
GRAY_SHADES     DB        000,000,000,000,004,004,004,000 ; 1
                DB        008,008,008,000,012,012,012,000 ; 3
                DB        016,016,016,000,020,020,020,000 ; 5
                DB        024,024,024,000,028,028,028,000 ; 7
                DB        032,032,032,000,036,036,036,000 ; 9
                DB        040,040,040,000,044,044,044,000 ; 11
                DB        048,048,048,000,052,052,052,000 ; 13
                DB        056,056,056,000,060,060,060,000 ; 15
                DB        064,064,064,000,068,068,068,000 ; 17
                DB        072,072,072,000,076,076,076,000 ; 19
                DB        080,080,080,000,084,084,084,000 ; 21
                DB        088,088,088,000,092,092,092,000 ; 23
                DB        096,096,096,000,100,100,100,000 ; 25
                DB        104,104,104,000,108,108,108,000 ; 27
                DB        112,112,112,000,116,116,116,000 ; 29
                DB        120,120,120,000,124,124,124,000 ; 31
                DB        128,128,128,000,132,132,132,000 ; 33
                DB        136,136,136,000,140,140,140,000 ; 35
                DB        144,144,144,000,148,148,148,000 ; 37
                DB        152,152,152,000,156,156,156,000 ; 39
                DB        160,160,160,000,164,164,164,000 ; 41
                DB        168,168,168,000,172,172,172,000 ; 43
                DB        176,176,176,000,180,180,180,000 ; 45
                DB        184,184,184,000,188,188,188,000 ; 47
                DB        192,192,192,000,196,196,196,000 ; 49
                DB        200,200,200,000,204,204,204,000 ; 51
                DB        208,208,208,000,212,212,212,000 ; 53
                DB        216,216,216,000,220,220,220,000 ; 55
                DB        224,224,224,000,228,228,228,000 ; 57
                DB        232,232,232,000,236,236,236,000 ; 59
                DB        240,240,240,000,244,244,244,000 ; 61
                DB        248,248,248,000,252,252,252,000 ; 63
```

```
;

        DB      000,000,000,000,004,004,004,000 ; 1
        DB      008,008,008,000,012,012,012,000 ; 3
        DB      016,016,016,000,020,020,020,000 ; 5
        DB      024,024,024,000,028,028,028,000 ; 7
        DB      032,032,032,000,036,036,036,000 ; 9
        DB      040,040,040,000,044,044,044,000 ; 11
        DB      048,048,048,000,052,052,052,000 ; 13
        DB      056,056,056,000,060,060,060,000 ; 15
        DB      064,064,064,000,068,068,068,000 ; 17
        DB      072,072,072,000,076,076,076,000 ; 19
        DB      080,080,080,000,084,084,084,000 ; 21
        DB      088,088,088,000,092,092,092,000 ; 23
        DB      096,096,096,000,100,100,100,000 ; 25
        DB      104,104,104,000,108,108,108,000 ; 27
        DB      112,112,112,000,116,116,116,000 ; 29
        DB      120,120,120,000,124,124,124,000 ; 31
        DB      128,128,128,000,132,132,132,000 ; 33
        DB      136,136,136,000,140,140,140,000 ; 35
        DB      144,144,144,000,148,148,148,000 ; 37
        DB      152,152,152,000,156,156,156,000 ; 39
        DB      160,160,160,000,164,164,164,000 ; 41
        DB      168,168,168,000,172,172,172,000 ; 43
        DB      176,176,176,000,180,180,180,000 ; 45
        DB      184,184,184,000,188,188,188,000 ; 47
        DB      192,192,192,000,196,196,196,000 ; 49
        DB      200,200,200,000,204,204,204,000 ; 51
        DB      208,208,208,000,212,212,212,000 ; 53
        DB      216,216,216,000,220,220,220,000 ; 55
        DB      224,224,224,000,228,228,228,000 ; 57
        DB      232,232,232,000,236,236,236,000 ; 59
        DB      240,240,240,000,244,244,244,000 ; 61
        DB      248,248,248,000,252,252,252,000 ; 63

;

        DB      000,000,000,000,004,004,004,000 ; 1
        DB      008,008,008,000,012,012,012,000 ; 3
        DB      016,016,016,000,020,020,020,000 ; 5
        DB      024,024,024,000,028,028,028,000 ; 7
        DB      032,032,032,000,036,036,036,000 ; 9
        DB      040,040,040,000,044,044,044,000 ; 11
        DB      048,048,048,000,052,052,052,000 ; 13
        DB      056,056,056,000,060,060,060,000 ; 15
        DB      064,064,064,000,068,068,068,000 ; 17
        DB      072,072,072,000,076,076,076,000 ; 19
        DB      080,080,080,000,084,084,084,000 ; 21
        DB      088,088,088,000,092,092,092,000 ; 23
```

```
        DB      096,096,096,000,100,100,100,000  ; 25
        DB      104,104,104,000,108,108,108,000  ; 27
        DB      112,112,112,000,116,116,116,000  ; 29
        DB      120,120,120,000,124,124,124,000  ; 31
        DB      128,128,128,000,132,132,132,000  ; 33
        DB      136,136,136,000,140,140,140,000  ; 35
        DB      144,144,144,000,148,148,148,000  ; 37
        DB      152,152,152,000,156,156,156,000  ; 39
        DB      160,160,160,000,164,164,164,000  ; 41
        DB      168,168,168,000,172,172,172,000  ; 43
        DB      176,176,176,000,180,180,180,000  ; 45
        DB      184,184,184,000,188,188,188,000  ; 47
        DB      192,192,192,000,196,196,196,000  ; 49
        DB      200,200,200,000,204,204,204,000  ; 51
        DB      208,208,208,000,212,212,212,000  ; 53
        DB      216,216,216,000,220,220,220,000  ; 55
        DB      224,224,224,000,228,228,228,000  ; 57
        DB      232,232,232,000,236,236,236,000  ; 59
        DB      240,240,240,000,244,244,244,000  ; 61
        DB      248,248,248,000,252,252,252,000  ; 63
;
        DB      000,000,000,000,004,004,004,000  ; 1
        DB      008,008,008,000,012,012,012,000  ; 3
        DB      016,016,016,000,020,020,020,000  ; 5
        DB      024,024,024,000,028,028,028,000  ; 7
        DB      032,032,032,000,036,036,036,000  ; 9
        DB      040,040,040,000,044,044,044,000  ; 11
        DB      048,048,048,000,052,052,052,000  ; 13
        DB      056,056,056,000,060,060,060,000  ; 15
        DB      064,064,064,000,068,068,068,000  ; 17
        DB      072,072,072,000,076,076,076,000  ; 19
        DB      080,080,080,000,084,084,084,000  ; 21
        DB      088,088,088,000,092,092,092,000  ; 23
        DB      096,096,096,000,100,100,100,000  ; 25
        DB      104,104,104,000,108,108,108,000  ; 27
        DB      112,112,112,000,116,116,116,000  ; 29
        DB      120,120,120,000,124,124,124,000  ; 31
        DB      128,128,128,000,132,132,132,000  ; 33
        DB      136,136,136,000,140,140,140,000  ; 35
        DB      144,144,144,000,148,148,148,000  ; 37
        DB      152,152,152,000,156,156,156,000  ; 39
        DB      160,160,160,000,164,164,164,000  ; 41
        DB      168,168,168,000,172,172,172,000  ; 43
        DB      176,176,176,000,180,180,180,000  ; 45
        DB      184,184,184,000,188,188,188,000  ; 47
        DB      192,192,192,000,196,196,196,000  ; 49
```

```
                DB      200,200,200,000,204,204,204,000  ; 51
                DB      208,208,208,000,212,212,212,000  ; 53
                DB      216,216,216,000,220,220,220,000  ; 55
                DB      224,224,224,000,228,228,228,000  ; 57
                DB      232,232,232,000,236,236,236,000  ; 59
                DB      240,240,240,000,244,244,244,000  ; 61
                DB      248,248,248,000,252,252,252,000  ; 63
;
DATA     ENDS


;***********************************************************************
;                          code segment
;***********************************************************************
;
CODE     SEGMENT
         ASSUME  CS:CODE
            .

            .

            .

; Call HSPAL to save current palette
         MOV    AX,57              ; Code number for this service
         LEA    BX,HSPAL_DATA      ; Pointer to data block
         CALL   AI_SERVICE
            .

            .

            .

; Initialize DAC registers for 256-color mode in the following
; format:
;                7 6 5 4 3 2 1 0   bits
;                |_| |_| |_| |_|
;                 I   R   G   B
;*********************|
;   set LUT registers |
;*********************|
; Set address of color table in HLDPAL data area
         PUSH   DS                 ; DS to stack
         POP    PAL_SEG            ; Store segment in variable
         LEA    SI,IRGB_SHADES     ; Pointer to offset of address
         MOV    PAL_OFF,SI         ; Store offset
; Call HLDPAL to set palette registers
         MOV    AX,19              ; Code number for this service
         LEA    BX,HLDPAL_DATA     ; Pointer to data block
         CALL   AI_SERVICE
            .

            .

            .
```

```
; Initialize DAC registers for 64 gray shades, repeated 4 times
;*********************|
;  set LUT registers  |
;*********************|
; Set address of color table in HLDPAL data area
        PUSH    DS                  ; DS to stack
        POP     PAL_SEG             ; Store segment in variable
        LEA     SI,GRAY_SHADES      ; Pointer to offset of address
        MOV     PAL_OFF,SI          ; Store offset
; Call HLDPAL to set palette registers
        MOV     AX,19               ; Code number for this service
        LEA     BX,HLDPAL_DATA      ; Pointer to data block
        CALL    AI_SERVICE

            .

            .

            .

; Call HRPAL to restore original palette
        MOV     AX,58               ; Code number for this service
        LEA     BX,HSPAL_DATA       ; Pointer to saved palette data
        CALL    AI_SERVICE
; Notice that the same data area in which the palette was saved
; is used during the restore operation

            .

            .

            .

CODE    ENDS
```

In addition to the three palette commands mentioned above, the AI contains a function named HQDFPAL (query default palette) that reports the default setting of the first 16 palette registers. HQDFPAL appears to be of little practical use, since the setting of all palette registers can be obtained by means of the HSPAL (save palette) function, and the default settings of the first 16 registers is usually known beforehand. (See Table 6.3.)

6.4.3 Geometrical Functions

Drawing operations on the XGA and 8514/A Adapter Interface are limited to straight line segments. The other geometrical functions are rectangular fill area fill operations.

Drawing Straight Lines

The AI documentation classifies the line drawing commands into three types: vertex, offset, and disjoint lines. All three line types are of the polyline category, since several line segments can be drawn with the same command. In all AI line drawing commands the characteristics of the line depend on the selected line type and width, as well as on the active color mix and comparison. The color of the line and its background is determined by the setting of the foreground and background colors.

HLINE (polyline at given position) and HCLINE (polyline at current position) are vertex-type commands. Both commands require a parameter block that encodes a set of coordinate points. The draw operation connects these coordinate points by means of straight line segments.

HRLINE (relative polyline at given position) and HCRLINE (relative polyline at current position) are offset-type commands. In HRLINE the start point of the polyline is the coordinate of a screen point. In the HCRLINE command the polyline starts at the current point. The remaining points in the polyline are described as offsets from the start point or the from the previous end point. The offsets are encoded as a one-byte signed integers for the x coordinate and another one for the y coordinate. Since each offset is encoded in one byte, its range is limited to -128 to +127 pixels.

The disjoint line command is named HDLINE. This function is part of the XGA extended set, therefore, it is not available in 8514/A systems. In HDLINE the polyline is described by two coordinate points for each line segment; one marks the start of the line and the next one its end point. Since each line is described independently, the line segments that form the polyline can be disconnected from each other.

The following code fragment shows drawing a four-segment polyline using the HLINE command.

```
;********************************************************************
;                          data segment
;********************************************************************
DATA       SEGMENT
                .
                .
                .
; HLINE (polyline at given position)
HLINE_DATA          DW        18         ; Length of data block
                    DW        500        ; x coordinate of first point
                    DW        300        ; y coordinate of first point
                    DW        600        ; next x coordinate
                    DW        300        ; next y coordinate
                    DW        600        ; x
                    DW        350        ; y
                    DW        700        ; x
                    DW        350        ; y
                    DW        700        ; x
                    DW        200        ; y
```

```
DATA      ENDS

;************************************************************
;                         code segment
;************************************************************
;
CODE      SEGMENT
          ASSUME  CS:CODE
            .

            .

            .
;********************|
;     draw polyline  |
;********************|
POLYGON:
; Call HSCOL (set color)
          MOV     FORE_COL,00001001B       ; Bright blue
          MOV     AX,7              ; Code number for this service
          LEA     BX,HSCOL_DATA    ; Pointer to data block
          CALL    AI_SERVICE
; Use the HLINE (polyline at given position) to draw a polyline
          MOV     AX,0             ; Code number for this service
          LEA     BX,HLINE_DATA    ; Pointer to data block
          CALL    AI_SERVICE
            .

            .

            .
CODE      ENDS
```

Rectangular Fill

The AI provides a service named HRECT (fill rectangle) which can be used to fill a rectangular area using the current foreground color and mix as well as an optional fill pattern defined by the caller. The optional pattern, which can be monochrome or color, is enabled by means of the HSPATT (set pattern shape) command. The rectangular fill operation can be conveniently used to clear a window within the viewport, or even the entire display. Notice that the HEGS (erase graphics screen) command can also be used to clear the entire display area. HEGS is independent of colors and mixes but is limited by the scissors and enabled planes.

The following code fragment shows the use of a rectangular fill operation in an XGA or 8514/A system.

```
;************************************************************
;                         data segment
;************************************************************
```

```
DATA       SEGMENT
           .
           .
           .

; Data block for rectangle draw
HRECT_DATA       DW       8         ; Length of data block
RECT_X           DW       0         ; x coordinate of top-left
corner
RECT_Y           DW       0         ; y coordinate of top-left
corner
RECT_WIDTH       DW       0         ; Width (1 to 1024)
RECT_HIGH        DW       0         ; Height (1 to 768)
           .
           .
           .

DATA       ENDS

;******************************************************************
;                          code segment
;******************************************************************
;
CODE       SEGMENT
           ASSUME   CS:CODE
           .
           .
           .

; Fill a rectangular area using HRECT
           MOV       RECT_X,100        ; x origin
           MOV       RECT_Y,50         ; y origin
           MOV       RECT_WIDTH,500    ; Width, in pixels
           MOV       RECT_HIGH,200     ; Height, in pixels
           MOV       AX,32             ; Code number for this service
           LEA       BX,HRECT_DATA     ; Pointer to data block
           CALL      AI_SERVICE
           .
           .
           .

CODE       ENDS
```

Area Fill

An application using the AI services can define a closed area before it is drawn
and then fill its enclosed boundary with a solid color or a pattern. The HBAR
(begin area definition) command is used to mark the start of the draw or move
commands that will delimit the area to be filled. If the figure defined after the
HBAR command is not properly closed, that is, if its start and end points do

not coincide, it is closed automatically by the AI software. The actual fill operation is performed by means of the HEAR (end area definition) command. A control byte in the HEAR parameter area allows selecting one of three operations mode: fill area, suspend area definition, or abort. The control setting to suspend the area definition has the effect of leaving the presently defined area in an internal AI buffer until another HBAR or HEAR command is executed. Area fill operations take place using the current foreground color, as well as the pattern and mix.

The following code fragment shows the definition, drawing, and filling of a polygon.

```
;********************************************************************
;                          data segment
;********************************************************************
DATA      SEGMENT
            .
            .
            .
; Data for connected straight line segments to form a 7-segment
; polygon
HCLINE_DATA      DW      26        ; Length of data block
                                   ; for 14 coordinate points
X1               DW      562       ; x coordinate of first end
point
Y1               DW      384       ; y coordinate of first end
point
X2               DW      700       ; Second pair of x,y coordinates
Y2               DW      500
X3               DW      520       ; Third pair of x,y coordinates
Y3               DW      550
X4               DW      400       ; Fourth pair of x,y coordinates
Y4               DW      500
X5               DW      450       ; Fifth pair of x,y coordinates
Y4               DW      384
X6               DW      530       ; Sixth pair of x,y coordinates
Y6               DW      450
X7               DW      512       ; Last pair of x,y coordinates
Y7               DW      384       ; are on screen center
            .
            .
            .
DATA      ENDS

;********************************************************************
;                          code segment
;********************************************************************
```

```
CODE      SEGMENT
          ASSUME   CS:CODE
               .

               .

               .

; Call HSCP (set current coordinate position)
; Coordinates are set at the center of the screen on 1024 by 768
; pixels modes
          MOV      NEW_X,512        ; Middle of screen column
          MOV      NEW_Y,384        ; Middle of screen row
          MOV      AX,4             ; Code number for this service
          LEA      BX,HSCP_DATA     ; Pointer to data block
          CALL     AI_SERVICE
; Call HBAR to begin fill area
          MOV      AX,5             ; Code number for this service
          LEA      BX,DUMMY         ; Pointer to data block
          CALL     AI_SERVICE
; Call HCLINE (draw line at current coordinate position)
; Coordinates of the line's start point were set by the HSCP
; service. Coordinates of polygon points already in data block
          MOV      AX,1             ; Code number for this service
          LEA      BX,HCLINE_DATA   ; Pointer to data block
          CALL     AI_SERVICE
; Call HEAR to fill area
          MOV      AX,6             ; Code number for this service
          LEA      BX,HEAR_DATA     ; Pointer to data block
          CALL     AI_SERVICE
               .

               .

               .

CODE      ENDS
```

6.4.4 Raster Operations

The XGA and 8514/A AI support two types of raster operations: polymarker
display and bitBLTs. These functions were described in Sections 6.3.4 and 6.3.6
respectively. In addition, the extended XGA AI services provide a means for
manipulating on and off screen bitmaps. The bitmap functions are not available
in 8514/A systems.

Polymarkers

Polymarkers are useful in displaying one or more copies of bit-mapped objects.
A typical use is in the animated display of one or more mouse-controlled screen
objects. The following code fragment shows the display of two copies of a marker
symbol.

```
;****************************************************************
;                          data segment
;****************************************************************
DATA      SEGMENT

          .
          .
          .

; Data area for HSMARK (define marker symbol)
HSMARK_DATA       DW        14        ; Length of data block
MARK_WIDE         DB        8         ; Pixel width of marker symbol
MARK_HIGH         DB        16        ; Pixel height of marker
MARK_TYPE         DB        0         ; 7 6 5 4 3 2 1 0 <= BITS
                                      ; | |_|_|_|_|_|_|_ reserved (0)
                                      ; |____________ 0 = monochrome
                                      ;                1 = multicolor
                  DB        0         ; Reserved
MARK_SIZE         DW        16        ; Number of bytes in marker
                                      ; image
                                      ; size = ((width * height)+7)/8
MARK_OFF          DW        0         ; Offset of marker image map
MARK_SEG          DW        0         ; Segment of marker image map
M_COLOR_OFF       DW        0         ; Offset of color image map
M_COLOR_SEG       DW        0         ; Segment of color image map
; Bit map for marker image
; Marker image is a vertical arrow symbol
MARK_MAP          DB        00100100B         ; 1
                  DB        00111100B         ; 2
                  DB        00111100B         ; 3
                  DB        00111100B         ; 4
                  DB        00011000B         ; 5
                  DB        00011000B         ; 6
                  DB        00011000B         ; 7
                  DB        00011000B         ; 8
                  DB        00011000B         ; 9
                  DB        00011000B         ; 10
                  DB        00011000B         ; 11
                  DB        11111111B         ; 12
                  DB        01111110B         ; 13
                  DB        00111100B         ; 14
                  DB        00011000B         ; 15
                  DB        00011000B         ; 16
;
; Marker display command
HMRK_DATA         DW        8         ; Length of data block
MARKER_X0         DW        40        ; x coordinate of first marker
MARKER_Y0         DW        500       ; y coordinate of first marker
```

```
MARKER_X1          DW       55       ; x coordinate of second marker
MARKER_Y1          DW       500      ; y coordinate of second marker
                     .
                     .
                     .
DATA     ENDS

;*****************************************************************
;                          code segment
;*****************************************************************
;
CODE     SEGMENT
         ASSUME   CS:CODE
                     .
                     .
                     .
;
;*********************|
;   marker display    |
;*********************|
; Display monochrome marker (down arrow) stored at MARK_MAP
; First use HSMARK to define the marker bitmap
; Set address marker bitmap in control block variables
         PUSH     DS               ; Data segment
         POP      MARK_SEG         ; Store in variable
         LEA      SI,MARK_MAP      ; Offset of marker bitmap
         MOV      MARK_OFF,SI      ; Store offset of bitmap
; Call HSMARK
         MOV      AX,52            ; Code number for this service
         LEA      BX,HSMARK_DATA   ; Pointer to data block
         CALL     AI_SERVICE
; Call HMRK (display markers)
         MOV      AX,50            ; Code number for this service
         LEA      BX,HMRK_DATA     ; Pointer to data block
         CALL     AI_SERVICE
                     .
                     .
                     .
CODE     ENDS
```

BitBLT

BitBLT operations in the AI allow read, write, and copy functions, as described
in Section 6.3.6. Except for the polymarker function, bitBLT provides the only
way in which an 8514/A application can read, write, or copy a bitmap. The

following code fragment shows two bitBLT operations: first, a bit-mapped image of a running boar target, resident in RAM, is displayed using a bitBLT write operation. Second, the displayed image is copied to another screen position.

```
;*****************************************************************
;                         data segment
;*****************************************************************
DATA       SEGMENT
             .

             .

             .

; Data for bitBLT write operation
HBBW_DATA         DW       10        ; Length of data block
WR_FORMAT         DW       0         ; Format
                                     ; 0000H = across the planes
                                     ; 0008H = through the planes
WR_WIDTH          DW       48        ; Block's pixel width
WR_HEIGHT         DW       19        ; Pixel rows in block
DEST_X            DW       100       ; x coordinate for display
DEST_Y            DW       500       ; y coordinate for display
;
; Data for bitBLT chain image operation
HBBCHN_DATA       DW       6         ; Length of data block
BBLOK_OFF         DW       0         ; Offset of image map
BBLOK_SEG         DW       0         ; Segment of image map
BBLOK_SIZE        DW       114       ; Byte size of image buffer
;
; Data block for bit block copy
HBBC_DATA         DW       16        ; Length of data block
BLT_FORMAT        DW       8         ; Format
                                     ; 0000H = across the planes
                                     ; 0008H = through the planes
BLT_WIDTH         DW       60        ; Block's pixel width
BLT_HEGHT         DW       20        ; Pixel rows in block
PLANE_NUM         DB       0         ; Bit plane for across plane
                                     ; mode
                  DB       0         ; Reserved value
SOURCE_X          DW       20        ; x coordinate of source image
SOURCE_Y          DW       490       ; y coordinate of source
DESTIN_X          DW       200       ; x coordinate of destination
DESTIN_Y          DW       500       ; y coordinate of destination
;
;**************************|
;  bit-mapped image in RAM |
;**************************|
```

```
; Bitmap for a running boar target
; Bitmap dimensions are 6 bytes (48 pixels) by 19 rows
BOAR_MAP             DB          01FH,080H,00FH,0FFH,0F0H,000H ; 1
                     DB          000H,043H,0F0H,081H,00EH,000H ; 2
                     DB          000H,03CH,001H,03CH,081H,000H ; 3
                     DB          000H,040H,002H,042H,040H,0C0H ; 4
                     DB          000H,040H,004H,099H,020H,030H ; 5
                     DB          000H,080H,005H,024H,0A0H,00CH ; 6
                     DB          000H,080H,005H,05AH,0A0H,003H ; 7
                     DB          000H,080H,005H,05AH,0A0H,001H ; 8
                     DB          007H,000H,005H,024H,0A0H,01EH ; 9
                     DB          008H,000H,004H,099H,020H,060H ; 10
                     DB          008H,000H,002H,042H,047H,080H ; 11
                     DB          010H,000H,001H,03CH,088H,000H ; 12
                     DB          028H,000H,000H,081H,007H,080H ; 13
                     DB          05FH,0C1H,0F0H,03FH,000H,040H ; 14
                     DB          0FCH,03EH,00FH,0FCH,000H,0B0H ; 15
                     DB          014H,000H,000H,002H,061H,060H ; 16
                     DB          024H,000H,000H,001H,099H,000H ; 17
                     DB          078H,000H,000H,000H,006H,080H ; 18
                     DB          000H,000H,000H,000H,001H,0C0H ; 19

            .

            .

            .

DATA        ENDS

;****************************************************************
;                            code segment
;****************************************************************
;
CODE        SEGMENT
            ASSUME   CS:CODE
            .

            .

            .

;*********************|
;   bitBLT operations |
;*********************|
; BitBLT bitmap of boar from memory to video
; Call HBBW (bit block write)
            MOV      AX,21              ; Code number for this service
            LEA      BX,HBBW_DATA       ; Pointer to data block
            CALL     AI_SERVICE
; Call HBBCHN to chain bit block
; Set address marker bitmap in control block variables
            PUSH     DS                 ; Data segment
```

```
              POP     BBLOK_SEG          ; Store in variable
              LEA     SI,BOAR_MAP        ; Offset of marker bitmap
              MOV     BBLOK_OFF,SI       ; Store offset of bitmap
; Call HBBCHN service
              MOV     AX,24              ; Code number for this service
              LEA     BX,HBBCHN_DATA     ; Pointer to data block
              CALL    AI_SERVICE
; Re-display boar image using a bit block copy
; Call HBBC (bit block copy)
              MOV     AX,25              ; Code number for this service
              LEA     BX,HBBC_DATA       ; Pointer to data block
              CALL    AI_SERVICE
                .
                .
                .

CODE      ENDS
```

6.4.5 Character Fonts

XGA and 8514/A systems are furnished with disk-based character fonts that can be used in text display operations. Since the BIOS text functions do not operate on the XGA and 8514/A, the use of disk-based fonts is the simplest option for text display in the advanced function modes. In the loading of a disk-based font file the application is left to its own resources, since the AI provides no command to perform this operation. In addition to loading the font file into RAM, the application must also inform the AI of the font's address and select the desired character set. The following code fragment shows the necessary operations for loading a disk-resident font file into RAM, for initializing the necessary AI parameter blocks, and for selecting a character set for text and alphanumeric operations.

```
;*********************************************************************
;                              data segment
;*********************************************************************
DATA      SEGMENT
                .

                .

                .

;*********************|
; text operations data |
;*********************|
; Parameter block for HSCS (text select character set)
HSCS_DATA        DW      4          ; Length of data block
FONT_OFF         DW      0          ; Offset of loaded font
FONT_SEG         DW      0          ; Segment of loaded font
;
```

```
; Parameter block for ASFONT (alpha select character set)
ASFONT_DATA     DW      6       ; Length of data block
                DB      0       ; Font number
                DB      0       ; Reserved
AFONT_OFF       DW      0       ; Offset of loaded font
AFONT_SEG       DW      0       ; Segment of loaded font
;
;*********************|
;       fonts         |
;*********************|
; ASCIIZ filename for XGA 85-by-38 font
F1220_NAME      DB      'STAN1220.FNT',00H
FONT_HANDLE     DW      0       ; Handle for font file
;
;*********************|
;    storage for font |
;*********************|
; Font header area
FONT_BUF        DW      0       ; Number of code pages
                DW      0       ; Default code page (0 to 4)
                DW      0       ; Alternate default (0 to 4)
                DD      0       ; 4-byte ID string ('437',0)
PAGE_1_OFFSET   DW      0       ; Offset of CSD within file
                DD      0       ; 4-byte ID string ('850',0)
                DW      0       ; Offset of CSD within file
                DD      0       ; 4-byte ID string ('860',0)
                DW      0       ; Offset of CSD within file
                DD      0       ; 4-byte ID string ('863',0)
                DW      0       ; Offset of CSD within file
                DD      0       ; 4-byte ID string ('865',0)
                DW      0       ; Offset of CSD within file
;
; Character set definition block for first code page
                DB      0       ; Reserved

                DB      0       ; Font type:
                                ; 0 = multiplane image
                                ; 3 = short vector font
                DB      0       ; Reserved
                DD      0       ; Reserved
CELL_WIDTH      DB      0       ; Pixel width of character cell
CELL_HEIGHT     DB      0       ; Pixel height of cell
                DB      0       ; Reserved
                DW      0       ; Cell size
CSD_FLAGS       DW      0       ; Flag bits:
                                ; Bit 14 ... 0 = single-plane
```

```
                                         ;                  1 = multiplane
                                         ;        13 ... 0 = not prop. space
                                         ;                  1 = prop. space
IDX_TABLE_O     DW       0               ; Offset of index table
IDX_TABLE_S     DW       0               ; Segment of index table
                DW       0               ; Offset of envelope table
                DW       0               ; Segment of envelope table
                DB       0               ; Initial code point
                DB       0               ; Final code point
CSD_TABLE_O     DW       0               ; Offset of character definition
CSD_TABLE_S     DW       0               ; Segment of character
definition
                DB       14250 DUP (00H)

                     .
                     .
                     .

DATA     ENDS
;*****************************************************************
;                       code segment
;*****************************************************************
CODE     SEGMENT
         ASSUME  CS:CODE

                 .
                 .
                 .

;*********************|
;    load font file   |
;*********************|
; Before using text display operations one of the four font
files
; provided with the adapter must be loaded into RAM
         LEA     DX,F1220_NAME   ; Filename for XGA 12x20 font
         LEA     DI,FONT_BUF     ; Buffer for storing font
         CALL    XGA_FONT        ; Local procedure to load font
; Carry set if error during font load
         JNC     OK_XGA_FONT     ; Go if no error
;*********************|
;    font load error  |
;*********************|
; At this point the application must provide a handler to take
; care of the error that occurred during the font load operation

                 .
                 .
                 .

;*********************|
; init parameter block |
```

```
;*********************|
; The AI is informed of the address of the loaded font by means
; of the HSCS (set character set) function
OK_XGA_FONT:
        PUSH    DS                  ; DS to stack
        PUSH    DS                  ; twice
        POP     FONT_SEG            ; Store in parameter block
; Alphanumeric display operations require a separate parameter
; block initialization
        POP     AFONT_SEG           ; For alphanumeric operations
; The offset of the font's character set definition block is
; located at byte 10 of the font header
        LEA     SI,FONT_BUF         ; Offset of font buffer
        MOV     BX,[SI+10]          ; Get offset of first code page
        ADD     BX,SI               ; Add offset to pointer
        MOV     FONT_OFF,BX         ; Store pointer in block
        MOV     AFONT_OFF,BX        ; For alphanumeric operations
;*********************|
; update font pointers |
;*********************|
; Update pointers in character set definition area by adding
; the load address of the font (in SI)
        ADD     IDX_TABLE_O,SI  ; Add to index table offset
        ADD     CSD_TABLE_O,SI  ; and to CSD table offset
; AX still holds the segment address. Store segment portion of
; address
        MOV     IDX_TABLE_S,AX  ; In index table
        MOV     CSD_TABLE_S,AX  ; In character set table
;*********************|
; select character set |
;*********************|
; Call HSCS (set character set) function
        MOV     AX,37               ; Code number for this service
        LEA     BX,HSCS_DATA        ; Pointer to data block
        CALL    AI_SERVICE
          .

          .

          .

;****************************************************************
;                            procedures
;****************************************************************
;
XGA_FONT        PROC    NEAR
; Read an XGA or 8514-a font file into RAM
; On entry:
;         DS:DX -> ASCIIZ filename for font file
;                   (must be in the current path)
```

```
;             DS:DI —> RAM buffer for font storage
;
; On exit:
;       Carry clear if font read and stored in buffer
;       Carry set if file not found or disk error
;
; Open font file using MS-DOS service
        PUSH    DI                      ; Save entry pointer
        MOV     AH,61                   ; DOS service request number
                                        ; to open file (handle mode)
        MOV     AL,2                    ; Read/write access
        INT     21H
        POP     DI                      ; Restore pointer
; File opened?
        JNC     OK_XOPEN                ; Go if no error code
;*********************|
;    disk open error  |
;*********************|
; Open operation failed. Set carry flag and return to caller
        STC                             ; Signal error
        RET
;*********************|
;    read font into RAM |
;*********************|
OK_XOPEN:
        MOV     FONT_HANDLE,AX          ; Store file handle
NEW_128:
        MOV     BX,FONT_HANDLE
        LEA     DX,DATA_BUF     ; Buffer for data storage
        PUSH    DI              ; Save buffer pointer
; Use MS-DOS service to read 128 bytes
        PUSH    CX              ; Save entry CX
        MOV     AH,63           ; MS-DOS service request
        MOV     CX,128          ; Bytes to read
        INT     21H
        POP     CX              ; Restore
; 128 bytes read into buffer
        POP     DI              ; Restore buffer pointer
        CMP     AX,0            ; Test for end of file
        JNE     MOVE_128        ; Go if not at end of file
;*********************|
;    end of file      |
;*********************|
        MOV     BX,FONT_HANDLE  ; Handle for font file
; Close file using MS-DOS service
        MOV     AH,62           ; DOS service request
```

```
        INT     21H
        JMP     END_OF_READ
;*********************|
;   move sector to    |
;     font buffer      |
;*********************|
; At this point DATA_BUF holds 128 bytes from disk file
; DI — storage position in the font's buffer
MOVE_128:
        MOV     CX,128          ; Byte counter
        LEA     SI,DATA_BUF     ; Pointer to data just read
PLACE_128:
        MOV     AL,[SI]         ; Byte from DATA_BUF
        MOV     [DI],AL         ; Into font's buffer
        INC     SI              ; Bump pointers
        INC     DI
        LOOP    PLACE_128       ; Continue until all sector read
; At this point the 128 bytes read from the disk file are stored
; in the font's buffer
        JMP     NEW_128
END_OF_READ:
        CLC
        RET
XGA_FONT        ENDP
        .
        .
        .
CODE    ENDS
```

6.4.6 Displaying Text

Once the preparatory operations described in Section 6.4.5 have been success-fully executed, the application is able to use AI commands to display text characters and strings. Two types of text display services are available in the AI: string and alphanumeric commands.

Character String Operations

The character string commands are HCHST (character string at given position) and HCCHST (character string at current position). AI string display opera-tions allow positioning the text characters at a screen pixel boundary. This offers a level of control that exceeds the one in BIOS text display services. The following code fragment shows the display of a character string using HCHST.

```
;*****************************************************************
;                              data segment
;*****************************************************************
DATA      SEGMENT
          .
          .
          .
HCHST_DATA_1      DW        59          ; Length of data block
PIXEL_COL         DW        150         ; Column address for start
PIXEL_ROW         DW        20          ; Row address for start
                  DB        'XGA and 8514/A Adapter Interface'
                  DB        ' bitBLT Operations Demo'
;*********************|
;     color data      |
;*********************|
; Parameter blocks for foreground and background colors
; Foreground color
HSCOL_DATA        DW        4           ; Length of data block
FORE_COL          DB        0F0H        ; 8-bit color code
                  DB        0           ; Padding for double word
                  DW        0
; Background color
HSBCOL_DATA       DW        4           ; Length of data block
BACK_COL          DB        11110000B        ; Bright red in 2-bit
                                             ; IRGB format
                  DB        0           ; Padding for double word
                  DW        0
          .
          .
          .
DATA      ENDS
;
;*****************************************************************
;                              code segment
;*****************************************************************
;
CODE      SEGMENT
          ASSUME    CS:CODE
          .
          .
          .
;*********************|
;    select colors    |
;*********************|
; AI string commands perform text display operations at the
```

```
; pixel level. First set foreground color to bright red
        MOV       FORE_COL,00001100B        ; Bright red
        MOV       AX,7                ; Code number for this service
        LEA       BX,HSCOL_DATA     ; Pointer to data block
        CALL      AI_SERVICE
; Now set the background color to dark blue
        MOV       BACK_COL,00000001B        ; Dark blue
        MOV       AX,10               ; Code number for this service
        LEA       BX,HSBCOL_DATA   ; Pointer to data block
        CALL      AI_SERVICE
;*********************|
;  display text string |
;*********************|
; Call HCHST (display character string at given position)
        MOV       AX,38               ; Code number for this service
        LEA       BX,HCHST_DATA_1          ; Pointer to data block
        CALL      AI_SERVICE
        .
        .
        .
CODE      ENDS
```

Alphanumeric Operations

Alphanumeric commands in the AI can be easily identified since their names start with the letter "A." In Section 6.4.5 we saw the use of the ASFONT (alpha select character set) to inform the adapter of the address of the character map resident in RAM and to select a character set. The other preparatory operations described in Section 6.4.5 must also be performed in order for an application to use the alphanumeric commands.

One difference between the string display commands and the alphanumeric commands is that the string commands allow positioning of the text characters at the screen pixel level while the alphanumeric commands use a screen grid of the size of the character cells. Table 6.11 shows the cell size of the different font files furnished with XGA and 8514/A systems.

Table 6.11 *XGA and 8514/A Font Files and Text Resolution*

FILE NAME	SCREEN SIZE	CHARACTER SIZE		ALPHA MODE GRID	
		WIDTH	HEIGHT	COLUMNS	ROWS
STAN1220.FNT	1024 by 768	12	20	85	38
STAN1223.FNT	1024 by 768	12	23	85	33
STAN0814.FNT	640 by 480	8	14	80	34
	1024 by 768	8	14	128	54
STAN0715.FNT	1024 by 768	7	15	146	52

On the other hand, the AI alphanumeric commands allow the attributes of each character to be individually controlled. In addition, alphanumeric commands provide the control and display of a cursor character. Since the blinking attribute is not available in XGA and 8514/A systems, this alphanumeric cursor is nothing more than a static graphics symbol which must be handled by the application. The grid for cursor operations is also determined by the character size.

There are two alphanumeric display commands in the AI. The command named ABLOCKMFI (write character block in mainframe interactive mode) is designed to simulate character display in a mainframe environment. The command ABLOCKCGF (write character block in CGA mode) is designed to simulate the display controls in the IBM Color Graphics Adapter. The following code fragment shows the use of alphanumeric commands in cursor and text display operations.

```
;***************************************************************
;                        data segment
;***************************************************************
DATA        SEGMENT

                  .

                  .

                  .

; ASCUR (set cursor shape)
ASCUR_DATA        DW        3         ; Length of data block
                  DB        16        ; Cursor start line
                  DB        19        ; Cursor stop line
CUR_SHAPE         DB        00        ; Cursor attribute:
                                      ; 00 = normal
                                      ; 01 = hidden
                                      ; 02 = left arrow
                                      ; 03 = right arrow
; ACURSOR (set cursor position)
ACURSOR_DATA      DW        2         ; Length of data block
CUR_COLUMN        DB        0         ; Cursor column
CUR_ROW           DB        0         ; Cursor row
;
; ASFONT (select character set)
ASFONT_DATA       DW        6         ; Length of data block
                  DB        0         ; Font number
                  DB        0         ; Reserved
AFONT_OFF         DW        0         ; Offset of loaded font
AFONT_SEG         DW        0         ; Segment of loaded font
;
; ABLOCKCGA (writes a block of characters in CGA emulation mode)
ABLOCKCGA_DATA    DW        10        ; Length of data block
COL_START         DB        0         ; Start column for display
```

```
ROW_START         DB        0            ; Start row for display
CHAR_WIDE         DB        0            ; Width of block (characters)
CHAR_HIGH         DB        0            ; Height of block (characters)
STRING_OFF        DW        0            ; Offset of string address
STRING_SEG        DW        0            ; Segment of string address
BUF_WIDE          DB        85           ; Characters per row displayed
ATTRIBUTE         DB        0            ; 7 6 5 4 3 2 1 0 <= BITS
                                         ; | | | | | | | |
                                         ; | | | | | | |_|_ font (0 to 3)
                                         ; | | | | | |_|______ reserved
                                         ; | | | | |________ 1 = transparent
                                         ; | | | |              0 = opaque
                                         ; | | |_________ overstrike
                                         ; | |___________ reverse video
                                         ; |_____________ underscore
;
;                                 ___________ background color
;                                 |    _____ foreground color
;                                 |    |
; String for ABLOCKCGA    C   |-||-|
STRING_1          DB        'T',00001001B
                  DB        'h',00001001B
                  DB        'i',00001001B
                  DB        's',00001001B
                  DB        ' ',00001001B
                  DB        'i',00001100B
                  DB        's',00001100B
                  DB        ' ',00001100B
                  DB        'a',00001010B
                  DB        ' ',00001010B
                  DB        't',00011100B
                  DB        'e',00011100B
                  DB        's',00011100B
                  DB        't',00011100B

                  .
                  .
                  .

DATA      ENDS
;*****************************************************************
;                         code segment
;*****************************************************************
;
CODE      SEGMENT
          ASSUME    CS:CODE
;
;********************|
```

```
;   alphanumeric text     |
;*********************|
; AI commands that start with the prefix letter A are used to
; perform alphanumeric operations at the character cell level.
; The alphanumeric commands allow controlling the attribute of
; each individual character displayed.
;*********************|
;   cursor operations    |
;*********************|
; Display cursor
        MOV     CUR_COLUMN,30    ; Column number
        MOV     CUR_ROW,4        ; Row number
; Call ASCUR (set cursor shape)
        MOV     AX,45            ; Code number for this service
        LEA     BX,ASCUR_DATA    ; Pointer to data block
        CALL    AI_SERVICE
; CAll ACURSOR (set cursor position)
        MOV     AX,44            ; Code number for this service
        LEA     BX,ACURSOR_DATA ; Pointer to data block
        CALL    AI_SERVICE
; Call ASFONT (select font)
; Code assumes that the address of the RAM-resident font has
; been previously set in the parameter block
        MOV     AX,46            ; Code number for this service
        LEA     BX,ASFONT_DATA   ; Pointer to data block
        CALL    AI_SERVICE
; Display text message using ABLOCKCGA function
; Set display parameters in control block variables
        MOV     COL_START,20     ; Start at column 20
        MOV     ROW_START,30     ; and at row number 30
        MOV     CHAR_WIDE,14     ; Characters wide
        MOV     CHAR_HIGH,1      ; Characters high
        PUSH    DS               ; Data segment
        POP     STRING_SEG       ; Store in variable
        LEA     SI,STRING_1      ; Offset of text string
        MOV     STRING_OFF,SI    ; Store offset of string
; Call ABLOCKCGA
        MOV     AX,41            ; Code number for this service
        LEA     BX,ABLOCKCGA_DATA        ; Pointer to data block
        CALL    AI_SERVICE
        .
        .
CODE    ENDS
```

XGA Architecture and Programming

Chapter Summary

This chapter describes the XGA architecture and its programmable hardware components. It also illustrates XGA programming by manipulating the video hardware directly and by accessing video memory, describes the XGA graphics coprocessor, its capabilities, initialization, and programming, as well as the XGA sprite, its hardware elements, and the programming of sprite operations. The chapter concludes with a listing of the procedures in the GRAPHSOL library furnished with the book.

7.0 XGA Hardware Programming

In Chapter 6 we saw how the Adapter Interface software can be used in graphics programming of 8514/A and XGA systems; at that time we also mentioned some of its limitations. For example, we noted that, at the system level, the use of AI services would almost certainly be discarded for reasons of code autonomy. On the other hand, the applications programmer can find objections to using the AI, particularly its limited services and its performance penalty. In summary, one or more of the following reasons will often determine that the programmer use direct access to the XGA hardware:

1. The process of loading and initializing the Adapter Interface cannot be conveniently performed at the program's level.

2. The services provided by the Adapter Interface are insufficient for the program's purpose.

3. The performance of the adapter interface services do not meet the requirements of the code.

In the case of system programs, device drivers, and other low-level graphics software the decision will often be to not use the AI at all; especially if objection number one, listed above, is applicable. Then the programmer would take control of the XGA hardware and proceed with the XGA device as described in Chapters 2 to 5 regarding the VGA system. Although, even when assuming control over the hardware, it is possible that the software developers could benefit from using the character fonts furnished with the AI.

On the other hand, most graphics applications could be developed either by using AI services exclusively or in a mixed environment in which the code complements the AI services with direct hardware programming. For example, an application could be designed to use the AI services when their control and performance is at an acceptable level. In this manner, the AI commands described in Chapter 6 can be useful and convenient in initializing the XGA, setting the color palette, loading font files into RAM, displaying text messages, clearing the screen, and closing the adapter. All of the above are functions in which performance is often not an important issue. At the same time, the application may assume direct control of the XGA hardware in setting individual pixels, drawing lines and geometrical figures, performing bitBlt operations to and from video memory, manipulating graphics markers, and other functions in which control or performance factors are important.

7.0.1 XGA Programming Levels

Regarding the XGA and system hardware, the graphics programmer can operate at four different levels. The first and highest level is the graphics function offered by operating systems and graphics environments. Such is the case in applications that execute under the Windows and OS/2 operating systems and use the graphics services provided by the system software. The second level of XGA programming is by means of the AI services discussed in Chapter 6. The third level is by programming the XGA registers and the graphics coprocessor. The fourth and lowest level of XGA graphics programming is by accessing video memory directly. Graphics programming in high-level environments such as the Windows and OS/2 operating systems are outside of the subject matter of this book. XGA programming by means of AI services was discussed in Chapter 6. The present chapter is devoted to programming the XGA graphics coprocessor and accessing XGA video memory directly.

These same four levels of programming are possible in 8514/A systems. Since the 8514/A is no longer state-of-the-art, we have not included its low-level programming. Readers interested in programming the 8514/A at the register level should consult *Graphics Programming for the 8514/A* by Jake Richter and Bud Smith (see Bibliography), as well as the 8514/A documentation available from IBM.

7.1 XGA Features and Architecture

Figure 6.2 shows the elements of the XGA system. The XGA is furnished as an optional adapter card for microchannel computers equipped with the 80386, 80386SX, or 486 processor. The XGA system is integrated in the motherboard of the Model 90 XP 486. Sections 6.0 and 6.1 (Chapter 6) describe the evolution of the XGA from the 8514/A adapter, its comparative features as well as its presentation. To the programmer the XGA system presents the following interesting features:

1. It includes all VGA modes and is compatible with VGA at the register level. That is, software developed for VGA can be expected to run satisfactorily in XGA. One exception is programs that make use of the VGA video space for other purposes. For example, a popular VGA enhancement for the Ventura Publisher typesetting program, called Soft Kicker, will not operate in the VGA modes of an XGA system.

2. XGA includes a 132-column text mode that represents a substantial enhancement to the 80-column text modes of the VGA. This mode requires an XGA system equipped with the appropriate video display. At this time no BIOS support is provided for the 132-column mode or for XGA graphics operations.

3. The XGA Extended Graphics modes, or enhanced modes, provide a maximum resolution of 1024-by-768 pixels in 256 colors, which can be selected from a palette of 256K colors. The enhanced modes also provide a 64-by-64 pixels hardware-controlled graphics object, whose shape is defined by the application. This graphics object, called the *sprite*, is usually animated by mouse movements and used to non-destructively overlay a displayed image. The XGA graphics modes support systems with multiple video displays.

4. The XGA direct color mode, also called the palette bypass mode, is capable of displaying 65,536 colors on a 640-by-480 pixel grid. In this mode the pixel color is encoded in a 16-bit value that is used to set the red, blue, and green electron guns without intervention of the LUT registers.

7.1.1 The XGA Graphics Coprocessor

One characteristic of XGA hardware that differentiates it from VGA and SuperVGA systems is the presence of a graphics coprocessor chip. Much of the enhanced performance of the XGA system is due to this device. The following are the most important features of the graphics coprocessor:

1. The coprocessor can obtain control of the system bus in order to access video and system memory independently of the central processor. This bus-mastering feature allows the coprocessor to perform graphics operations while the main processor is executing other functions.

2. The graphics coprocessor can directly perform drawing operations. These include straight lines, filled rectangles, and bit-block transfers.

3. The coprocessor provides support for saving its own register contents. This feature is useful in a multitasking environment.

4. The coprocessor supports several logical and arithmetic mixes including OR, AND, XOR, NOT, source, destination, add, subtract, average, maximum, and minimum operands.

5. The coprocessor can manipulate images encoded in 1, 2, 4, or 8 bits per pixel formats. Pixel maps can be defined as coded in Intel or Motorola data storage formats.

6. The coprocessor can be programmed to generate system interrupts. These interrupts can occur when the coprocessor operation has completed, an access to the coprocessor was rejected, a sprite operation completed, or at the end or start of the screen blanking cycle.

The coprocessor registers are memory-mapped. To an application, programming the coprocessor consists of reading and storing data into these reserved memory addresses. In contrast, the XGA main registers are port-mapped and programming consists of reading and writing to these dedicated ports.

The execution of a coprocessor operation consists of the following steps:

1. The system microprocessor reads and writes data to coprocessor registers that must be initialized for the operations.

2. The coprocessor operation starts when a command is written to its Pixel Operations register.

3. The coprocessor executes the programmed operation. During this time the system microprocessor can be performing other tasks. The only possible interference between processor and coprocessor is when both are accessing the bus simultaneously, In this case the access takes place according to the established priorities.

4. At the conclusion of the programmed operation the graphics coprocessor informs the system and becomes idle.

7.1.2 VRAM Memory

Since the XGA is a memory-mapped system the color code for each screen pixel is encoded in video RAM. How many units of memory are used to encoded the pixel's color depends on the adopted format. Possible values are of 1, 2, 4, 8, and 16 bits per pixel. The number of colors are respective powers of 2, as shown in Table 7.1.

Table 7.1 *Pixel to Memory Mapping in XGA Systems*

BITS PER PIXEL	POWER OF 2	NUMBER OF COLORS
1	2^1	2
2	2^2	4
4	2^4	16
8	2^8	256
16	2^{16}	65536

Notice that the 256 and 65536 color modes are available only in XGA systems with maximum on-board RAM (1Mb). The total amount of VRAM required depends on the number of screen pixels and the number of encoded colors. For example, to store the contents of the entire XGA screen at 1024-by-768 pixels resolution requires a total of 786,432 memory units. In the 8 bits per pixel format the number of memory units is of 786,432 bytes (8 bits per byte). However, this same screen can be stored in 98,304 bytes if each screen pixel is represented in a single memory bit (786,432 / 8 = 98,304).

Therefore, the video memory space of an XGA system in 1024-by-768 pixel mode, with each pixel encoded in 256 colors, exceeds by far the limit of an 80x86 segment register (65,536). Therefore an application accessing video memory directly while executing in 80x86 real mode requires some sort of memory banking mechanism by which to access a total of 768,432 bytes of VRAM memory. In fact, a minimum of 12 memory banks of 65,536 bytes are required to encode the 768,432 XGA pixels in 1024-by-768 pixel mode in 256 colors. This banking mechanism is discussed in detail later in Section 7.3

Video Memory Apertures

In general, an XGA system can access video memory by means of three different apertures, described as follows:

1. The largest memory aperture is of a 22-bit space. This range of 4Mb allows addressing 4 times the maximum VRAM that can be present in an XGA system. The 4Mb address space must be represented in an 80386 or 486 extended register. This is the aperture used by the XGA graphics coprocessor.

2. The second possible aperture into video memory is of 1Mb. Since this is also the maximum VRAM that can be present in an XGA system, the 1Mb aperture allows addressing all video memory consecutively by means of an 80386 or 486 extended register.

3. The third possible aperture is of 16 banks of 64K each. This aperture, which is the only one possible in the MS-DOS environment, requires bank switching to access the maximum VRAM.

Notice that in a particular display mode not all 16 banks are required to access the mapped video memory space.

Data Ordering Schemes

XGA memory mapping can be according to the Intel or the Motorola storage conventions. The XGA hardware allows selecting the Intel or Motorola formats for every operation that accesses a pixel map or image stored in system or video memory. In the Intel convention, also known as the *little-endian addressing* scheme, the smallest element (little end) of a number is stored at the lowest numbered memory location. In the Motorola convention, known as *big-endian addressing*, the largest element (big end) is stored at the lowest numbered memory location. Table 7.2 shows the results of storing bytes, words and doublewords according to the Intel and the Motorola conventions.

Table 7.2 *Data Storage According to the Intel and Motorola Conventions*

DATA	STORAGE UNIT	INTEL	MOTOROLA
00 11 AA FF	byte	00I11IAAIFF	00I11IAAIFF
00 11 AA FF	word	11 00IFF AA	00 11IAA FF
00 11 AA FF	doubleword	FF AA 11 00	00 11 AA FF
		low — high	low — high

Notice that since the unit of memory storage in IBM microcomputers is one byte, the Intel and Motorola storage schemes are identical in byte-ordered data. Also that the value of bits within the stored byte is in the conventional format, that is, the low order bit (bit number 0) is located at the rightmost position.

7.1.3 The XGA Display Controller

Another programmable device of the XGA system is the Display Controller chip. This IC contains the color look-up table, the CRT Controller, and the hardware registers for the operation of a special cursor, called the sprite. (See Section 7.5.) The XGA display controller registers are a superset of the VGA registers. As in the VGA, these registers are mapped into the systems I/O space. Therefore they appear to the programmer as input and output ports.

The base address of the XGA display controller is port 21x0H. The variable x in the port number depends on the *instance* of the XGA adapter. Recall that more than one XGA system can co-exist in a microcomputer. The instance is the number that corresponds to a particular XGA adapter or motherboard implementation. The user can change the instance number of an installed XGA adapter by means of the setup procedures provided by the reference diskette. The default instance value for a single XGA adapter card is 6, which determines a base address for the Display Controller of 2160H. Notice that the instance number replaces the variable x in the general formula.

The programmable registers in the XGA Display Controller are in the range 21x0H to 21xFH. Here again the variable x represents the instance number. Table 7.3 shows some of the Display Controller registers and the values to which they must be initialized during mode setting.

The Display Controller registers are divided into two groups: direct access and indexed access registers. The direct access registers are the ten registers in the range 21x0H to 21x9H. The indexed access registers are related to the Index register (port 21xAH) and the data registers (ports 21xBH to 21xFH). The index values are in the range 04H to 70H but not all values in this range are actually used in XGA. The direct access registers in the Display Controller are programmed by means of IN or OUT instructions to the corresponding port; for example, the Memory Access Mode register, at 21x9H can be programmed for 8 bits per pixel and Intel data format as follows:

```
; Programming a direct access register of the XGA Display
; Controller group
        MOV     DX,XGA_REG_BASE ; Register base
        ADD     DX,9            ; Add offset of Memory Access
                                ; Mode register
        MOV     AL,00000011B    ; Bitmap for Intel format
                                ; and 8 bits per pixel
        OUT     DX,AL
```

The above code fragment assumes that the base address of the Display
Controller register groups has been previously determined and is stored in the
variable XGA_REG_BASE. The operations necessary for determining this base
address are shown in Section 7.2.

Programming the indexed access registers takes place in two steps: first, the
desired register is selected by writing a value to the Index register at port
21xAH; second, data is read or written to the register by means of the data
registers in the range 21xBH to 21xFH. The following fragment shows writing
all one bits (FFH) to the Palette Mask register at offset 64H of the Index
register.

```
; Programming an indexed access register of the XGA Display
; Controller group
        MOV     DX,XGA_REG_BASE ; Register base
        ADD     DX,0AH          ; Add offset of Index register
        MOV     AL,64H          ; Select Palette Mask register
                                ; at offset 64H
        MOV     AH,0FFH         ; Data byte to write
        OUT     DX,AX           ; Select and write data
```

Notice that the 80x86 instruction OUT DX,AX writes the value in AL to the
port number in DX and the value in AH to the port number in DX + 1. The
result is that by using this form of the OUT instructions we can select and
access the register with a single operation.

The following Display Controller registers are particularly interesting to the
programmer:

1. The Interrupt Enable register (located at base address plus 4) is used to
   unmask the interrupt or interrupt sources that will be used by the software.

2. The Operating Mode register (located at the base address) is usually set to
   extended graphics mode.

3. The Aperture Control register (located at base address plus 1) allows
   enabling the 64K memory aperture mentioned in Section 7.1.2. as well as
   selecting the start address of video memory either at A0000H or at B0000H.
   Most applications executing under MS-DOS use A0000H, the VGA start
   address for dot addressable graphics.

4. The Memory Access Mode register (located at base address plus 9) allows selecting the number of bits per pixel and the Intel or Motorola data format.

7.2 Initializing the XGA System

The first XGA programming operation usually consists of initializing and enabling the video system. The simplest initialization method is by means of the AI services described in Chapter 6. An application that is to access the XGA exclusively by means of AI services need do nothing more than use the HOPEN and HINIT functions to initialize the system. However, programs that access the XGA directly must often perform additional initialization operations. Two possibilities can be considered:

1. Programs can use the AI HINIT and HOPEN services and, in addition, perform other initialization operations so as to enable the use of AI services and direct access to XGA hardware simultaneously.

2. A program can rely entirely on its own hardware initialization routines, and not use the AI HINIT and HOPEN functions.

Which method is adopted depends on the program's characteristics. If the software is to use both, AI services and direct access methods, then the HINIT and HOPEN functions are necessary. On the other hand, programs that do not use AI services can perform the necessary hardware initialization operations. Notice that the AI is a software black box which manipulates registers and video memory in ways that are not visible to the application. This creates additional problems for programs that mix AI services and direct access methods.

The following discussion relates to direct initialization of the XGA system. The use of the AI HINIT and HOPEN was explained in Chapter 6.

7.2.1 Locating the XGA Hardware

The first initialization task consists of locating the XGA components in the system's space. The necessary information is found in the PS/2 Programmable Option Select (POS) registers. Figure 7.1 shows important POS data related to the XGA hardware.

The first step in reading the POS registers is determining where these registers are located. BIOS service number 196, subservice number 0, of INT 15H, returns the POS registers base address in the DX register. The following code fragment shows the required processing.

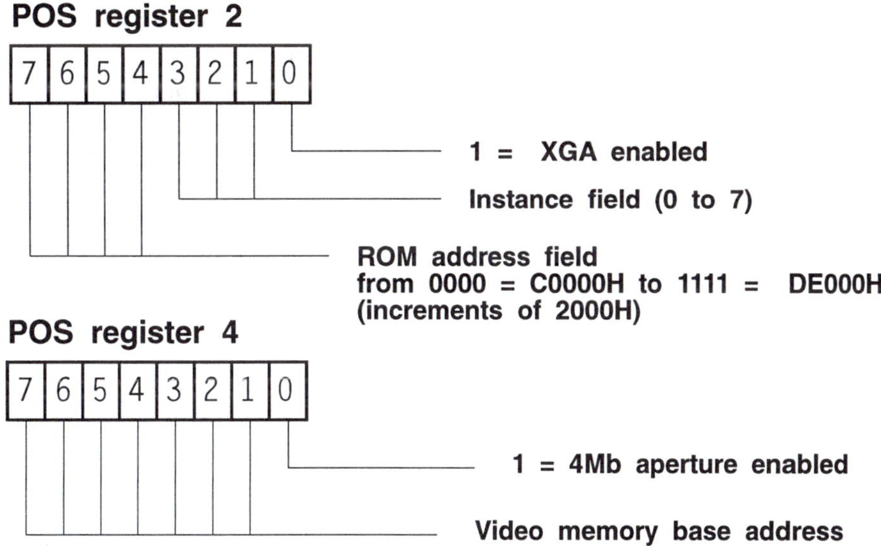

Figure 7.1 *XGA Data in POS Registers*

```
;*********************|
;   get POS address   |
;*********************|
; Use service number 196, INT 15H, with AL = 0 to determine base
; address of Programmable Option Select (POS) registers
        MOV     AX,0C400H       ; AH = C4H (service request)
                                ; AL = 0 (sub-service)
        INT     15H             ; BIOS interrupt
                                ; for microchannel machines only
        JNC     VALID_POS       ; Go if POS address returned
        JMP     NO_XGA          ; Error - not microchannel
VALID_POS:
        MOV     XGA_POS,DX   ; Save base address of POS
; An XGA system can be located on the motherboard or in one
; of 9 possible slots. Initialize CX = 0 for motherboard XGA
; CX = 1 to 9 for XGA in adapter card
        XOR     CX,CX           ; Start with motherboard
        CLI                     ; Interrupts off
        .
        .
        .
```

Not all POS values encode XGA data. The valid range for XGA systems is 8FD8H to 8FDBH. Service number 196, subservice number 1, of INT 15H can be used to enable each one of 9 possible slots for setup. Then the value stored at the POS register base is read and compared to the valid range. If the value is within the range an XGA adapter or motherboard implementation has been detected. In this case the POS registers contain data required for the initialization of the XGA system. The following code fragment illustrates the required processing.

```
; Use BIOS service 196, sub-service number 1, to enable slot
; for setup
GET_POS_0:
          MOV       AH,0C4H             ; BIOS service
          MOV       AL,01H              ; Subservice number
          MOV       BX,CX               ; Slot number to BX
          INT       15H
; Slot enabled for setup
          MOV       DX,XGA_POS          ; POS register 0 and 1
          IN        AX,DX               ; Read ID low and high bytes
; Valid range for XGA systems is 8FD8H to 8FDBH
          CMP       AX,08FD8H           ; Test low limit
          JAE       TEST_HIGH_LIM       ; Go if equal or greater
; At this point the POS reports that system is not an XGA
; adapter
NOT_XGA_POS:
          INC       CX                  ; CX is options counter
          CMP       CX,9                ; Done all slots?
          JB        GET_POS_0           ; Go if not at last slot
          JMP       NO_XGA              ; No XGA exit
TEST_HIGH_LIM:
          CMP       AX,08FDBH           ; Test high limit of range
          JA        NOT_XGA_POS         ; Go if out of range
;*********************|
;      XGA found      |
;*********************|
          CLI                           ; Disable interrupts
; Test if XGA is in motherboard
          CMP       CX,0                ; 0 is motherboard value
          JNE       XGA_CARD            ; Go if not on the motherboard
;*********************|
;   motherboard XGA   |
;*********************|
; Port 94H is used to enable and disable motherboard video
          MOV       AL,0DFH             ; Bit 5 = 0 for video setup
          MOV       DX,94H              ; 94H is system board enable
          OUT       DX,AL
```

```
        JMP     SHORT GET_POS       ; Skip slot setup
;*********************|
;       XGA card      |
;*********************|
XGA_CARD:
        MOV     AX,0C401H           ; Place adapter in setup mode
        MOV     BX,CX               ; Slot number to BL
        INT     15H
;*********************|
;  save POS registers |
;*********************|
GET_POS:
        MOV     DX,XGA_POS          ; Get POS record for the slot id
        ADD     DX,2                ; POS register at offset 2
        IN      AL,DX               ; Read data byte
        MOV     POS_2,AL            ; and store it
        INC     DX                  ; Next POS register
        INC     DX                  ; is number 4
        IN      AL,DX               ; Get contents
        MOV     POS_4,AL            ; Store it
; At this point POS registers 2 and 4 have been saved in
; variables
;*********************|
;   re-enable video   |
;*********************|
; Test for XGA in motherboard
        CMP     CX,0                ; Treat the motherboard
                                    ; differently
        JNE     XGA_ADAPTER         ; Go if not in motherboard
; XGA in motherboard. Set bit 5 in port 94H to re-enable video
        MOV     AL,0FFH             ; All bits set
        OUT     094H,AL
        JMP     SHORT REG_BASE
XGA_ADAPTER:
        MOV     AX,0C402H           ; Enable the slot for normal
        MOV     BX,CX               ; operation
        INT     15H
        .
        .
        .
```

The next step in the XGA initialization is calculating the XGA Display
Controller register base by adding the instance value to the template 21x0H
mentioned in Section 7.1.3. The following code fragment shows the necessary
manipulation of the instance bits.

```
;*********************|
; calculate and store |
; XGA register base   |
;*********************|
REG_BASE:
        STI                              ; Interrupts on again
        MOV     AL,POS_2                 ; Get value at POS register 2
        AND     AX,0EH                   ; Mask out all bits except
                                         ; instance
        SHL     AX,1                     ; Multiply instance by 8
        SHL     AX,1                     ; to move to second digit
        SHL     AX,1                     ; position
        ADD     AX,2100H                 ; Add instance to base address
        MOV     XGA_REG_BASE,AX          ; Store result in variable
```

7.2.2 Setting the XGA Mode

Once the XGA Display Controller register base has been established the
initialization usually proceeds to set the XGA hardware in a pre-established
display mode. Although the XGA display modes are un-official, Table 7.3 shows
the ones mentioned in IBM's documentation.

Table 7.3 XGA Modes

MODE NUMBER	TYPE	HORIZONTAL PIXELS	VERTICAL PIXELS	COLORS
1	132-column text			
2	graphics	1024	768	256
3	graphics	1024	768	16
4	graphics	640	480	256
5	direct color	640	480	65536

The fundamental mode setting operation consists of loading most of the
Display Controller registers with pre-established values. These values are
listed in the XGA Video Subsystem section of the IBM Technical Reference
Manual for Options and Adapters, document number 504G-3287-000. This
document can be obtained from IBM Literature Department. Table 7.4 lists the
Display Controller registers which must be initialized during mode setting.

The registers in Table 7.4 are listed in the order in which they must be set.
Notice that before the last group of registers are set, the initialization routine
must load the XGA palette and clear all video memory. Failure to do this last
operation could result in the display of random data at the conclusion of the
mode setting operation. The actual coding can be based on data stored in two
arrays: one holds the values for the first group of Display Controller registers
and the second one for the group of registers to be initialized after the palette
is loaded and the screen cleared. The following fragment demonstrates the
necessary manipulations.

Table 7.4 *XGA Display Controller Register Initialization Settings*

		2	3	4	5	<= MODE
		1024	1024	640	640	<= rows
ADDRESS/		768	768	480	480	<= columns
INDEX	REGISTER NAME	256	16	256	65536	<= colors
21x4	Interrupt Enable	00H	00H	00H	00H	All interrupts OFF
21x5	Interrupt Status	8FH	8FH	8FH	8FH	Reset interrupts
21x0	Operating Mode	04H	04H	04H	04H	Graphics modes
21xA	Index Register					
64	Palette mask	00H	00H	00H	00H	Blank display
21x1	Aperture Control	01H	01H	01H	01H	64K at A0000H
21x8	Aperture Index	00H	00H	00H	00H	
21x6	Video Memory Ctrl.	00H	00H	00H	00H	Initial values
21x9	Memory Access Mode	03H	02H	03H	04H	
21xA	Index Register					
50	Display mode 1	01H	01H	01H	01H	Prepare for reset
50	Display mode 1	00H	00H	00H	00H	Reset CRT
10	x total low	9DH	9DH	63H	63H	
11	x total high	00H	00H	00H	00H	
12	x display end low	7FH	7FH	4FH	4FH	
13	x display end high	00H	00H	00H	00H	
14	x blank start low	7FH	7FH	4FH	4FH	
15	x blank start high	00H	00H	00H	00H	
16	x blank start low	9DH	9DH	63H	63H	
17	x blank end high	00H	00H	00H	00H	
18	x sync start low	87H	87H	55H	55H	
19	x sync start high	00H	00H	00H	00H	
1A	x sync end low	9CH	9CH	61H	61H	
1B	x sync end high	00H	00H	00H	00H	
1C	x sync possition	40H	40H	00H	00H	
1E	x sync possition	04H	04H	00H	00H	
20	y total low	30H	30H	0CH	0CH	
21	y total high	03H	03H	02H	02H	
22	y display end low	FFH	FFH	DFH	DFH	Initial values
23	y display end high	02H	02H	01H	01H	
24	y blank start low	FFH	FFH	DFH	DFH	
25	y blank start high	02H	02H	01H	01H	
26	y blank start low	30H	30H	0CH	OCH	
27	y blank end high	03H	03H	02H	02H	
28	y sync start low	00H	00H	EAH	EAH	
29	y sync start high	03H	03H	01H	01H	
2A	y sync end	08H	08H	ECH	ECH	
2C	y line comp low	FFH	FFH	FFH	FFH	
2D	y line comp high	FFH	FFH	FFH	FFH	
36	Sprite control	00H	00H	00H	00H	
40	Start address low	00H	00H	00H	00H	
41	Start address med	00H	00H	00H	00H	
42	Start address high	00H	00H	00H	00H	
43	Buffer pitch low	80H	40H	50H	A0H	
44	Buffer pitch high	00H	00H	00H	00H	
54	Clock select 1	0DH	0DH	00H	00H	
51	Display mode 2	03H	02H	03H	04H	
70	Clock select 2	00H	00H	00H	00H	
50	Display mode 1	0FH	0FH	C7H	C7H	

At this point XGA palette registers must be loaded and memory must be cleared

		2	3	4	5	
55	Border color	00H	00H	00H	00H	
60	Sprite/Pal low	00H	00H	00H	00H	
61	Sprite/Pal high	00H	00H	00H	00H	Initial values
62	Sprite pre-low	00H	00H	00H	00H	
63	Sprite pre high	00H	00H	00H	00H	
64	Palette mask	FFH	FFH	FFH	FFH	Make visible

```
DATA          SEGMENT

; Mode number ----|
; 640x480x65536    5 --------------------|
; 640x480x256      4 --------------|     |
; 1024x768x16      3 ----------|    |     |
; 1024x768x256     2 -----|    |     |     |
; Index ------------|     |    |     |     |
; Register ----|    |     |    |     |     |
;              _|__ _|__ _|__ _|__ _|__ _|__
XGA_V1   DB     004H,000H,000H,000H,000H,000H ; Interrupt enable
         DB     005H,000H,08FH,08FH,08FH,08FH ; Interrupt status
         DB     000H,000H,004H,004H,004H,004H ; Operating mode
         .
         .     (missing values as in Table 7.4)
         .
         DB     00AH,050H,00FH,00FH,0C7H,0C7H ; Display mode 1
         DB     0FFH,0FFH,0FFH,0FFH,0FFH,0FFH ; End of the list
;
XGA_V2   DB     00AH,055H,000H,000H,000H,000H ; Border color
         .
         .     (missing values as in Table 7.4)
         .
         DB     00AH,064H,0FFH,0FFH,0FFH,0FFH ; Palette mask
         DB     0FFH,0FFH,0FFH,0FFH,0FFH,0FFH ; End of the list
;
Variables used by the XGA_MODE procedure
MODE          DW    0              ; Mode number
; Previously initialized base address of the XGA Display
; Controller (see Section 7.2.1)
XGA_REG_BASE  DW    0              ; Address variable
;
DATA     ENDS

CODE     SEGMENT
         .
         .
         .
XGA__MODE    PROC     NEAR
; Procedure to initialize an XGA graphics mode by setting the
; video system registers directly
; On entry:
;        AL = mode number (valid range is 2 to 5)
; On exit:
;        carry clear if no error
;
```

```
        MOV     AH,0            ; Clear high byte
        MOV     MODE,AX         ; Mode to variable
        CMP     MODE,6          ; Mode number out of range?
        JB      TEST_MODE1      ; Go if less than 9
        JMP     BAD_MODE        ; illegal entry value for mode
; Mode 0 = VGA BIOS mode number 3
; Mode 1 = 132 column VGA text mode
; These modes are not valid
TEST_MODE1:
        CMP     MODE,1          ; 80-column VGA text mode?
        JA      VALID_MODE      ; Go if range is > 1
        JMP     BAD_MODE        ; Error exit for invalid mode
;********************|
;  initialize first  |
;    register group  |
;********************|
VALID_MODE:
; The table at XGA_V1 contains the values to be sent to the
; XGA register in order to initialize the corresponding mode
        LEA     SI,XGA_V1       ; Point to start of values table
        MOV     BX,MODE         ; Use mode as an offset
        CALL    INIT_REG_BLK    ; Local init procedure
;********************|
;     init palette   |
;********************|
; Palette initialization at this point
; Notice that this routine must be mode-specific
        .
        .
        .
;********************|
; clear video memory |
;********************|
; Video memory cleared at this point
; Notice that this routine must be mode-specific
        .
        .
        .
;********************|
;  initialize second |
;    register group  |
;********************|
; The table at XGA_V2 contains the values to be sent to the
; XGA register in order to initialize the second group of XGA
; registers
        LEA     SI,XGA_V2       ; Point to start of values table
```

```
        MOV     BX,MODE             ; Use mode as an offset
        CALL    INIT_REG_BLK        ; Local init procedure
;
        MOV     XGA_CURBK,-1        ; Reset the bank counter
        MOV     AX,MODE             ; Remember the mode we're in
        MOV     XGA_CUR_MODE,AX
        MOV     AX,1                ; Return ok
        RET
BAD_MODE:
        MOV     AX,0                ; Return failure
        RET
XGA_MODE    ENDP
;
INIT_REG_BLK    PROC    NEAR
; Auxiliary procedure for XGA_SET_MODE
; Initialize block of XGA register until FFH is found
; On entry:
;           SI -> formatted register data
;           BX = display mode
; The value at offset 0 of XGA_V1 is the register number
; The value at offset 1 is the index register number if the
; register is 0AH. The remaining entries is register data for
; each mode
REG_DATA:
        MOV     DX,XGA_REG_BASE ; XGA register base
        MOV     AH,0                ; High byte of offset is 0
        MOV     AL,[SI]             ; Low byte of offset
; Register value 0FFH marks the end of the table
        CMP     AL,0FFH             ; End of the table?
        JE      END_OF_BLOCK        ; End of register setup
        ADD     DX,AX               ; Add register offset to base
        CMP     AL,0AH              ; Test for an index register
        JE      INDEXED             ; Go if index register
; At this point register is not at offset 0AH, therefore data
; is output directly
        MOV     AL,[SI+BX]          ; Get data value from table
        OUT     DX,AL               ; and send to port
        JMP     SHORT NEXT_REG      ; Continue
INDEXED:
        MOV     AL,[SI+1]           ; Get index register number
        MOV     AH,[SI+BX]          ; Get data byte from table
        OUT     DX,AX               ; Output data to index register
NEXT_REG:
        ADD     SI,6                ; Index to next register in
                                    ; table
        JMP     REG_DATA
```

```
END_OF_BLOCK:
        RET
INIT_REG_BLK     ENDP
```

An XGA initialization routine can be found in the procedure named
INIT_XGA contained in the XGA2 module of the GRAPHSOL library included
in the book's software. Because of the complexities in the design of mode-specific
palette initialization and screen clearing routines for all XGA modes, the
INIT_XGA procedure does not perform these operations.

7.2.3 Loading the XGA Palette

Color display in XGA systems is by means of a Color Look-up Table (LUT), a
Digital to Analog converter (DAC) and associated hardware. The actual structure is reminiscent, although not identical, of the one used in VGA systems.
The XGA palette was described in Section 6.1.4. Bit plane mapping for a 256
color mode can be seen in Figure 6.3. The XGA color palette registers can be
set by means of the HLDPAL AI service described in Section 6.4.2. In addition,
a program can assume control of the XGA palette hardware and set its values
directly.

We saw that XGA palette data consists of red, blue, and green values that are
stored in corresponding registers. The mechanism resembles the one used by
the VGA palette in the 256 color modes. However, the XGA palette is a simpler
device than the one in VGA since no Palette or Color Select registers are used.
(See Figure 3.8.) In other words, the XGA palette consists of 256 registers in
which the red, blue, and green DAC values are stored. A pixel color is nothing
more than a palette register number; the actual color in which the pixel is
displayed depends on the value stored in the corresponding Palette register.

The XGA palette consists of 256 locations; each location is divided into three
fields. The first field corresponds to the red DAC value, the second one to the
blue, and the third field to the green. The XGA allows two update modes. In
the 3-value update mode, data is written to the palette registers in groups of
three items representing the red, blue, and green colors. In the 4-value update
mode, data is written in groups of four items, the first three represent the red,
blue, and green values, and the fourth item is a padding byte which is ignored
by the hardware. The 3-value sequence is similar to the one used in VGA
systems. The 4-value sequence is the one used by the AI HLDPAL function.
The update mode is selected by means of bit 2 of the Palette Sequence register.
Notice that in the XGA palette the six high order bits are significant while in
VGA the significant bits are the 6 low ones. (See Figure 6.5.)

The following code fragment shows the necessary processing for setting the
256 XGA palette registers from an array in RAM.

```
DATA        SEGMENT
;
; Double-bit IRGB palette in the following format
;           7 6 5 4 3 2 1 0   <= Bits
;           I I R R G G B B   <= Color codes
;
;                           | R   B   G       R   B   G     | REG
IRGB_SHADES     DB          000,000,000,000,036,072,036,000 ; 1
                DB          036,108,036,000,036,144,036,000 ; 3
                .           (missing data as in the code fragment
                .            in Section 6.4.2)

                .
                DB          252,144,252,000,252,180,252,000 ; 254
                DB          252,216,252,000,252,252,252,000 ; 255
;
; Previously initialized base address of the XGA Display
; Controller (see Section 7.2.1)
XGA_REG_BASE DW    0                ; Address variable

DATA        ENDS
;
;
CODE        SEGMENT

                .

                .

                .
; Code to set 256 XGA Palette registers
; On entry:
;       SI --> 1024-byte color table in RGBx format
; Assumes that XGA system is set in a graphics mode
;
        LEA     SI,IRGB_SHADES    ; Pointer-to-data array
        MOV     DX,XGA_REG_BASE   ; Base address of XGA Display
                                  ; Controller register
; Select Index register at offset 0AH
        ADD     DX,0AH            ; To Index register
; Write 00H (in AH) to Palette Mask register (64H)
; This value is ANDed with display memory. Clearing all bits
; makes the palette invisible during setup
        MOV     AX,0064H          ; make invisible
        OUT     DX,AX
; Write 00H (in AH) to Border Color register (55H)
        MOV     AX,0055H          ; border color
        OUT     DX,AX
; Write 00000100B (in AH) to Palette Sequence register (66H) to
; select four-color write mode (RGBx) and to start with the
```

```
; Red color code
        MOV     AX,0466H                ; Palette Sequence register
        OUT     DX,AX
; Write 00H (in AH) to Palette Index register low (60H)
; and high (61H) to select first DAC register
        MOV     AX,0060H                ; Start at palette 0
        OUT     DX,AX
        MOV     AX,0061H                ; Sprite index high
        OUT     DX,AX
; SI -> table of palette colors
        MOV     CX,1024                 ; Counter for 256 * 4
        MOV     AX,065H                 ; Select Data register
        OUT     DX,AL
        INC     DX                      ; Point to first register
; Loop to send 4 blocks of 256 bytes each to port 065H
NEW_PALETTE:
        MOV     AL,[SI]                 ; Get byte from table
        OUT     DX,AL                   ; Send to port
        INC     SI                      ; Bump table pointer
        LOOP    NEW_PALETTE
;
        DEC     DX                      ; Back to Select register
; Write FFH (in AH) to Palette Mask register (64H)
; This value is ANDed with display memory. Setting all bits
; makes the palette visible again
        MOV     AX,0FF64H               ; All bits set
        OUT     DX,AX                   ; To make visible
; At this point all Palette registers have been loaded from
; the data array supplied on entry
            .
            .
            .
```

The procedure named XGA_PALETTE in the XGA2 module of the GRAPHS-OL library can be used to perform palette loading. The code in this procedure is similar to the one listed above.

7.3 Processor Access to XGA Video Memory

An application can access XGA video memory through the CPU or by means of the XGA graphics coprocessor. Coprocessor programming is discussed in Section 7.4. The present discussion relates to accessing the XGA video memory space by means of the 80386 or 486 Central Processing Unit.

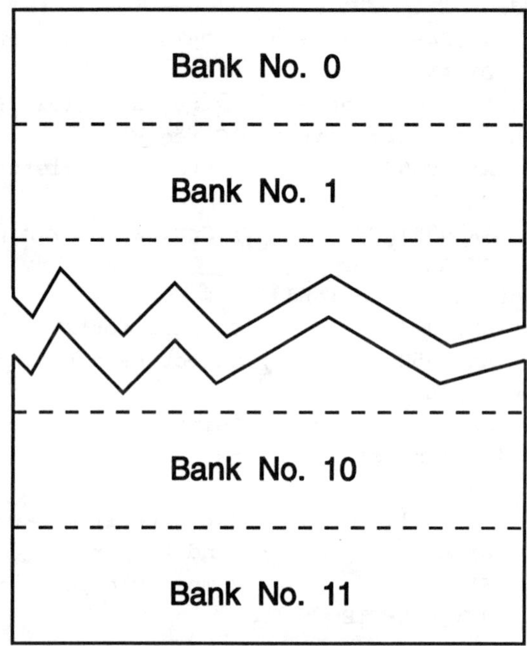

Figure 7.2 *Bank Structure in XGA 64K Aperture*

The system processor can access XGA memory to perform write and read operations. The write operation sets one or more screen pixels to the value stored in a processor register. The read operations transfers a pixel's value into a processor register. In Section 7.1.2 we saw that the XGA system can configure video memory by means of three possible apertures. The 4Mb aperture is the one used by the graphics coprocessor. The use of this memory aperture will be discussed later in this chapter. The 1Mb memory aperture is typically used in multitasking environments.

MS-DOS applications usually access XGA video memory by means of multiple memory banks of 64K each. This is called the 64K aperture. Before this aperture is used the program must make sure that the Aperture Control register (at base address plus 1) has been initialized to the value 01H. (See Table 7.4.) The banks' structure at this aperture depends on the display mode. At the 1024-by-768 modes the 64K aperture can be visualized as 12 memory blocks of 64K each. This visualization is shown in Figure 7.2.

Notice that, when using the 64K aperture, the start address for the video memory in each bank is selected by means of the Aperture Control register. The valid values are A0000H and B0000H. The first one coincides with the base address used in VGA graphics modes. If the start address of A0000H is selected, then each bank extends from A0000H to B0000H. Which bank is currently selected depends on the setting of the Aperture Index register, located at base address plus 8 of the XGA Display Controller group. If the base address of the

Display Controller group is stored in the variable XGA_REG_BASE and the bank number in the AL register, then enabling the bank can be coded as follows:

```
MOV     DX,XGA_REG_BASE     ; XGA base register address
ADD     DX,08H              ; Aperture Index register
OUT     DX,AL               ; Bank number is in AL
```

The total number of banks available depends on the display mode selected. We saw that 12 banks of 65536 memory units are needed to encode all the pixels in the 1024-by-768 modes. However, in the 640-by-480 pixel mode each full screen consists of 307,200 pixels, which require only 5 memory banks of 65536 units each.

7.3.1 Setting Screen Pixels

In order to set a screen pixel the display logic must take into account whether the base address of the video buffer for the 64K aperture is located at A000H or at B000H. In addition, the code must perform the necessary bank switching operation. Processing performance in this case can be improved by storing the value of the currently selected bank in a memory variable so that bank switching can be bypassed if the pixel is located in the currently selected bank. The following code fragment writes a data byte to a video memory address. This fragment does not take into account the currently selected bank.

```
; Write a screen pixel accessing XGA memory directly
; On entry:
;         CX = x coordinate of pixel
;         DX = y coordinate of pixel
;         BL = pixel color in 8-bit format
; Note: code assumes that XGA is in a 1024 by 768 pixel mode
;       in 256 colors and that A0000H is the start address for
;       the video buffer using the 64K aperture


;
; Set ES to video buffer base address
        MOV     AX,0A000H           ; Base for all graphics modes
        MOV     ES,AX               ; To ES segment
        MOV     AL,BL               ; Color to AL
; Get address in XGA system
        CLC                         ; Clear carry flag
        PUSH    AX                  ; Save color value
        MOV     AX,1024             ; 1024 dots per line
        MUL     DX                  ; DX holds line count of address
        ADD     AX,CX               ; Plus this many dots on the
                                    ; line
        ADC     DX,0                ; Answer in DX:AX
```

```
                                           ; DL = bank, AX = offset
         MOV      BX,AX                     ; Save offset in BX
         MOV      AX,DX                     ; Move bank number to AL
;********************|
;     change banks   |
;********************|
         MOV      DX,XGA_REG_BASE ; XGA base register address
         ADD      DX,08H                    ; Aperture index register
         OUT      DX,AL                     ; Bank number is in AL
         POP      AX                        ; Restore color value
;********************|
;   set the pixel    |
;********************|
         MOV      ES:[BX],AL                ; Write the dot
         .
         .
         .
```

The procedure named XGA_PIXEL in the XGA2 module of the GRAPHSOL
library sets a screen pixel using processing similar to that shown in the above
code sample. A routine to set the entire screen to a specific color value can be
simplified by using 80x86 string move instructions. The following code fragment shows the processing necessary to clear the entire video display in an
XGA 1024-by-768 pixel mode.

```
; Clear video memory using block move
         MOV      AX,0A000H           ; Video memory base address
         MOV      ES,AX               ; To the ES register
         MOV      BL,0                ; BL is bank counter
; Select bank
NEXT_BANK:
         MOV      DX,XGA_REG_BASE ; Select Page
         ADD      DX,08H              ; To Aperture Index register
         MOV      AL,BL               ; Bank number
         OUT      DX,AL               ; Select bank in AL
; Write 65536 bytes of 00H in current bank
         MOV      CX,0FFFFH           ; CX is byte counter
         MOV      AX,0                ; Attribute to place in VRAM
         CLD                          ; Forward direction
         MOV      DI,0                ; Start of block
         REP      STOSB               ; Store 65536 bytes
; Bump bank
         INC      BL
         CMP      BL,12               ; 12 is past last bank
         JNE      NEXT_BANK
```

.
.
.

The procedure named XGA_CLS in the XGA2 module of the GRAPHSOL library clears the screen using processing similar to the one listed above.

7.3.2 Reading Screen Pixels

A write routine that accesses the video memory space through the Central Processing Unit can be easily converted to read the value of screen pixels. The conversion consists mainly of changing the write operation for a read operation and in making other minor register adjustments. The following code fragment can be used to read the value of a screen pixel into a CPU register.

```
; Read a screen pixel accessing XGA memory directly
; On entry:
;       CX = x coordinate of pixel
;       DX = y coordinate of pixel
; On exit:
;       BL = pixel color
; Note: code assumes that XGA is in a 1024-by-768 pixel mode
;       in 256 colors and that A0000H is the start address for
;       the video buffer using the 64K aperture
;
; Set ES to video buffer base address
        MOV     AX,0A000H        ; Base for all graphics modes
        MOV     ES,AX            ; To ES segment
; Get address in XGA system
        CLC                      ; Clear carry flag
        PUSH    AX               ; Save color value
        MOV     AX,1024          ; 1024 dots per line
        MUL     DX               ; DX holds line count of address
        ADD     AX,CX            ; Plus this many dots on line
        ADC     DX,0             ; Answer in DX:AX
                                 ; DL = bank, AX = offset
        MOV     BX,AX            ; Save offset in BX
        MOV     AX,DX            ; Move bank number to AL
;********************|
;    change banks    |
;********************|
        MOV     DX,XGA_REG_BASE ; XGA base register address
        ADD     DX,08H           ; Aperture Index register
        OUT     DX,AL            ; Bank number is in AL
        POP     AX               ; Restore color value
;********************|
```

```
;    read the pixel       |
;*********************|
        MOV      BL,ES:[BX]        ; Read pixel in BL
        .
        .
        .
```

7.3.3 Programming the XGA Direct Color Mode

Mode number 4 in Table 7.3 is called the *direct color mode*. It consists of 640 by 480 pixels in 65,536 colors. Notice that this mode is available in XGA systems equipped with the full maximum VRAM of 1,024K. The XGA direct color mode presents some unique characteristics, among them the most extensive color range. In this mode the pixel color is determined by a 16-bit value, which encodes 65,536 colors that can be represented. The actual pixel color is generated independently of the setting of the DAC registers, for which reason the direct color mode has also been referred to as the *palette bypass mode*. The color encoding of the 16-bit value for the direct color mode is shown in Figure 7.3.

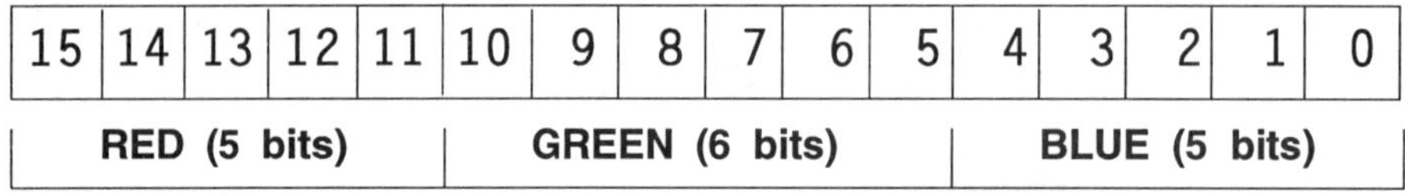

Figure 7.3 *Bit Mapping in the XGA Direct Color Mode*

Notice that the color bit map in Figure 7.3 contains 5 bits for the blue and red elements and 6 bits for the green element. This 5-6-5 configuration allows 64 shades of green and 32 shades of both blue and red colors. The argument in favor of having more shades of green than of red and blue is that the human eye is more sensitive to the green portion of the spectrum.

The Direct Color Palette

Although the DAC registers are bypassed during direct color mode operation, the IBM documentation states that the DAC registers must be loaded with specific data for operating in the Direct Color mode. Table 7.5 shows the values recommended by IBM.

Notice that bit 7 of the Border Color register (at offset 55H) is used to select between the first and second group of values to be entered in the direct color palette. Also that the red and blue components are always zero, while the green component is incremented by 8 for each successive register. The following code fragment allows setting the Palette registers for the direct color mode.

Table 7.5 *Palette Values for XGA Direct Color Mode*

LOCATION	BORDER COLOR BIT 7	RED	BLUE	GREEN
0	1	0	0	0
1	1	0	0	8
2	1	0	0	16
3	1	0	0	24
.	.	.	.	.
31	1	0	0	256
32	1	0	0	0
33	1	0	0	8
.	.	.	.	.
126	1	0	0	240
127	1	0	0	248
128	0	0	0	0
129	0	0	0	8
130	0	0	0	16
131	0	0	0	24
.	.	.	.	.
159	0	0	0	256
160	0	0	0	0
161	0	0	0	8
.	.	.	.	.
254	0	0	0	240
255	0	0	0	248

```
; Code to set 256 XGA Palette registers for the 65535 color mode
; Note: the values are those recommended by IBM
; Code assumes that XGA system is set in a graphics mode
;
        MOV     DX,XGA_REG_BASE  ; Wait for a retrace
        ADD     DX,0AH           ; To index register
; Write 00H (in AH) to Palette Mask register (64H)
; This value is ANDed with display memory. Clearing all bits
; makes the palette invisible during setup
        MOV     AX,0064H         ; Make invisible
        OUT     DX,AX
; Write 00H (in AH) to Palette Sequence register (66H) to enable
; three-color write mode (RGB) and to start with the
; R color code
        MOV     AX,0066H         ; Palette sequence register
        OUT     DX,AX
; Write 00H (in AH) to Palette Index register low (60H)
; and high (61H) to select first DAC register
        MOV     AX,0060H         ; Start at palette 0
        OUT     DX,AX
```

```
        MOV     AX,0061H           ; Also set the Sprite Index
        OUT     DX,AX              ; High register
;*********************|
; first 128 registers |
;*********************|
; Write 80H (in AH) to Border Color register (55H) to select
; first group of 128 registers
        MOV     AX,8055H           ; Border Color bit 7 set
        OUT     DX,AX
        CALL    LOAD_128           ; Local procedure
;*********************|
; second 128 registers |
;*********************|
; Write 00H (in AH) to Border Color register (55H) to select the
; second group of 128 registers
        MOV     AX,0055H           ; Border Color bit 7 clear
        OUT     DX,AX
        CALL    LOAD_128           ; Local procedure
; Write FFH (in AH) to Palette Mask register (64H)
; This value is ANDed with display memory. Setting all bits
; makes the palette visible again
        MOV     AX,0FF64H          ; All bits set
        OUT     DX,AX              ; To make visible

        .

        .

        .

;****************************************************************
LOAD_128        PROC    NEAR
; Auxiliary procedure for XGA_DC_PALETTE to load a group of 128
; DAC registers with the recommended values
;
        MOV     DX,XGA_REG_BASE ; Base address
        ADD     DX,0AH             ; Index register
        MOV     AX,0065H           ; Select data register
        OUT     DX,AL
        INC     DX                 ; To data register
        MOV     BX,0               ; BX is value for blue register
        MOV     CX,128             ; Counter for 128 registers
; Loop to send 3 bytes to 128 registers
DC_128:
        MOV     AL,0               ; Send red
        OUT     DX,AL              ; Send to port
        JMP     SHORT $ + 2        ; I/O delay
        OUT     DX,AL              ; Send blue
        MOV     AL,BL              ; Load green value
        OUT     DX,AL              ; Send green
```

```
            ADD       BL,8                  ; Bump green value in BL
                                            ; Wraps around automatically
            LOOP      DC_128
            DEC       DX                    ; Back to Index register
            RET
LOAD_128              ENDP
```

The procedure named DC_PALETTE in the XGA2 module of the GRAPHSOL library con be used to set the XGA Palette registers to the direct color mode.

Pixel Operations in Direct Color Mode

The programmer working in the direct color mode has fewer options than in other XGA modes. In the first place there is no AI support for direct color mode operations. Another limitation is that the XGA graphics coprocessor (discussed in Section 7.4) is not operational in the direct color mode. In the direct color mode the actual setting of screen pixels is performed with a word write operation, as shown in the following code fragment.

```
; Word write operation for 16-bit per pixel mode
; AX = 16-bit color code in 5-6-5 format
; BX = offset into video buffer
; ES = video memory segment (A000H or B000H)
;
            MOV       ES:[BX],AX            ; Writes the pixel
```

In the direct color mode the programmer must take into account that each screen pixel is mapped to two video buffer bytes. For example, the tenth pixel from the start of the first screen row is located 20 bytes from the start of the buffer. By the same token, each pixel is at a word boundary in the video buffer. The display routine must make the necessary adjustment, as in the following code fragment.

```
; Display 10 pixels in the brightest red color at the center
; of the first screen row while in XGA direct color mode
; Assumes:
;      1. ES = video buffer base address (A000H or B000H)
;      2. Direct color palette has been loaded
;      3. Mode number 6 (640 by 480 in 65,536 colors) has been
set
;      4. XGA_REG_BASE variable holds base address of XGA Display
;         Controller
;
; First select video bank number 0
            MOV       DX,XGA_REG_BASE ; Select Page
            ADD       DX,08H               ; To Aperture Index register
```

```
              MOV      AL,0              ; Bank number
              OUT      DX,AL            ; Select bank in AL
      ; Setup operational variables
              MOV      CX,10            ; Counter for 10 pixels
              MOV      AX,0F800H        ; All red bits set
              MOV      DI,640           ; Offset pointer to word number
                                        ; 320 on first screen row
      ; Write 10 bytes of AX into video memory
      SET_10_PIXS:
              MOV      ES:[DI],AX       ; Write to memory
              ADD      DI,2             ; Bump pointer to next word
              LOOP     SET_10_PIXS
              .
              .
              .
```

Notice in the above code fragment that the value initially loaded into the
buffer pointer register (DI) is the word offset of the first pixel to be set. Also
that the pointer is bumped to the next word (ADD DI,2) in each iteration of the
loop.

7.4 Programming the XGA Graphics Coprocessor

To a programmer the most important XGA hardware component is the graphics
coprocessor chip. The general features of the XGA graphics coprocessor were
discussed in Section 7.1.1. The present discussion relates to performing graphics operations by programming the XGA coprocessor. The reader should notice
that the XGA Graphics Coprocessor is a complex and sophisticated IC. In the
following sections we will cover only its programming at the elementary level.
A detailed technical description of this device, as well as of the XGA system in
general, can be found in the XGA Video Subsystem section of the IBM Technical
Reference Manual for Options and Adapters, document number 504G-3287-
000. This document can be obtained from the IBM Literature Department.

To the programmer the XGA graphics coprocessor appears as a set of memory-mapped registers. The area of memory devoted to these registers is called
the *coprocessor's address space*. Table 7.6 is a map of the coprocessor registers.

The coprocessor registers can be accessed using either the Intel or the
Motorola data formats. Table 7.6 represents the register structure in the Intel
format. Most coprocessor registers are write only. The second column in Table
7.6 shows which registers can be read by the CPU. Notice that the Current
Virtual Address, State A Length, and State B Length registers are read-only.
Software should not write to these registers. The Page Directory Base Address
and the Current Virtual Address registers (offset plus 0 and plus 4 respectively)
are used only in a virtual memory environment. Real mode programs, such as
those executing in MS-DOS, need not access these registers.

Table 7.6 *XGA Graphic Coprocessor Register Map*

OFFSET READ/ WRITE	+ 0	+1	+ 2	+ 3
0 W	Page Directory Base Address			
4 R	Current Virtual Address			
8				
C R	State A Length	State B Length		
10 R/W W		Coprocessor Control	Pixel Map Index	
14 W	Pixel Map n Base Pointer			
18 W	Pixel Map n Width		Pixel Map n Height	
1C W	Pixel Map format			
20 R/W	Bresenham Error Term			
24 W	Bresenham K1 Term			
28 W	Bresenham K2 Term			
2C W	Direction Steps			
. . 44				
48 W	Foreground Mix	Background Mix	Destination Color Compare Condition	
4C W	Destination Color Compare Value			
50 W	Pixel Bit Mask			
54 W	Carry Chain Mask			
58 W	Foreground Color			
5C W	Background Color			
60 W	Operations Dimension 1		Operations Dimension 2	
64				
68				
6C W	Map Mask Origin x Offset		Map Mask Origin y Offset	
70 R/W	Source Map x Coordinate		Source Map y Coordinate	
74 R/W	Pattern Map x Coordinate		Pattern Map y Coordinate	
78 R/W	Destination Map x Coordinate		Destination Map y Coordinate	
7C W	Pixel Operations			

The XGA coprocessor can access all memory in the system and treats video memory and system memory in the same fashion. Once the coprocessor is informed of the VRAM address it uses it to determine if the memory access is local or remote. In remote accesses the coprocessor obtains direct control of the bus. This capability of the coprocessor improves XGA performance by allowing the CPU to continue executing code while the coprocessor manipulates memory data.

The XGA Graphics Coprocessor is designed to take advantage of the 80386 instruction set. Since XGA requires an 80386 CPU, XGA programs can safely use 80386 instructions without fear of hardware incompatibility. Therefore, in the code samples that follow we have used 80386/486 instructions when programming coprocessor operations.

7.4.1 Initializing the Coprocessor

The initial action taken by a program that accesses the XGA coprocessor is its initialization. The first two steps in coprocessor initialization consist of calculating and storing two data items required in programming this device: the base address of the coprocessor register space and the physical address of the start of video memory. Notice that the video memory address used by the coprocessor corresponds with the 4Mb aperture mentioned in Section 7.1.2. The data for calculating these addresses is found in the XGA POS registers (Section 7.2.1 and Figure 7.1). In addition, the initialization routine should make certain that the appropriate value is stored at the Memory Access Mode Register of the XGA Display Controller group.

Obtain the Coprocessor Base Address

The coprocessor base address is calculated from the ROM address field in POS register 2 (see Figure 7.1) and from the instance field in this same POS register. The coprocessor address formula is:

coprocessor address = (((i * 128) +1C00H) + (R + 2000H) + C000H)

where i is the instance and R is the value in the ROM field of POS register 2. The code for calculating the coprocessor address is as follows:

```
DATA        SEGMENT


; The following variables are loaded from the XGA POS registers
; as shown in the code sample in Section 7.2.1
POS_2       DW          ????        ; POS register 2
POS_2       DW          ????        ; POS register 4


DATA        ENDS


CODE        SEGMENT
               .
               .
               .
; Calculate coprocessor base address
; Code assumes that the POS_2 and POS_4 variables have been
; initialized to the contents of the corresponding POS registers
; Coprocessor base address is calculated as follows:
```

```
; ROM address = (ROM field + 2000H) + C0000H
; COP address = (((Instance * 128) + 1C00H) + ROM address)
;
; First calculate ROM address from data in POS register 2
        MOV     EAX,0               ; Clear EAX
        MOV     AL,POS_2            ; Get POS register 2
        AND     EAX,0F0H            ; Preserve ROM bits
        SHR     EAX,4               ; Shift ROM to low nibble
        MOV     ECX,2000H           ; Multiplier
        MUL     ECX                 ; EAX * ECX in EAX
        ADD     EAX,0C0000H         ; Add constant
        MOV     EBX,EAX             ; Store ROM address in EBX
;
; EBX now holds ROM address
; Instance is stored in bits 1-3 of POS register 2
        MOV     EAX,0               ; Clear EAX
        MOV     AL,POS_2            ; Get POS register 2
        AND     EAX,0EH             ; Preserve Instance bits
        SHR     EAX,1               ; Shift right Instance bits
        MOV     ECX,128             ; Multiplier to ECX
        MUL     ECX
        ADD     EAX,1C00H           ; Add constant from formula
; Add ROM address
        ADD     EAX,EBX
        SHR     EAX,4               ; Shift right one nibble to
                                    ; to obtain segment value
; Store segment value in GS
        MOV     GS,AX               ; Move segment into GS
                .
                .
                .
;
```

Notice that the segment value of the coprocessor base address is stored in segment register GS. This is consistent with the notion of making full use of the 80386 architecture and instruction set.

Obtain the Video Memory Address

The physical address of video memory is a 32-bit value determined from the video memory base address field in POS register 4 and from the instance field in POS register 2. (See Figure 7.1.) The address is formed by relocating the POS data items as shown in Figure 7.4.

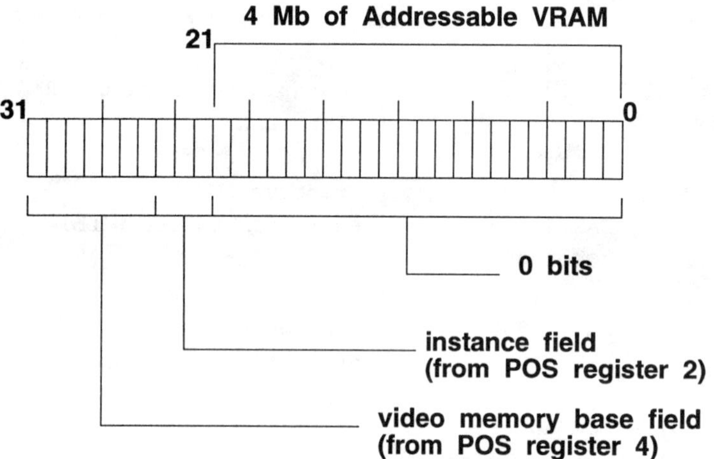

Figure 7.4   Physical Address of Video Memory Bitmap

The required processing for calculating the VRAM physical address is shown
in the following code fragment.

```
;********************|
;    get VRAM base    |
;********************|
; First get the video memory field in POS register 4
        MOV     AL,POS_4          ; VRAM field
        AND     AL,11111110B      ; Clear low bit
        SHL     AX,8              ; Shift to high position
; Now get instance bits in POS register 2
        MOV     BL,POS_2          ; Instance field
        AND     BL,00001110B      ; Mask out other bits
        MOV     BH,0              ; Clear high part of BX
        SHL     BX,5              ; Move instance bits to position
        OR      AX,BX             ; OR with B bits (in AX)
        MOV     FS,AX             ; Store in FS segment
```

Notice that the high-order part (16 bits) of the VRAM physical address is now
stored in the FS segment register. The 80386 FS segment is a convenient
storage for this value, which must later be used in coprocessor programming.

Select Access Mode

Coprocessor operation requires that the Memory Access Mode register of the
Display Controller be set to 1, 2, 4, or 8 bits per pixel and to the Intel or Motorola
data storage format. In the PC environment with a fully equipped XGA (1Mb
of VRAM) the coprocessor is typically set to 8 bits per pixel and to match the

Intel format of the CPU. The following code fragment shows selecting the access mode for coprocessor operation.

```
; Select Intel order and 8 bits per pixel in the Memory Access
; Mode register (offset + 9)
        MOV       DX,XGA_REG_BASE ; Register base
        ADD       DX,9            ; To Mode register
        MOV       AL,03H          ; 7 6 5 4 3 2 1 0   <= bit map
                                  ; | | | | | | | |    Bits/pixel
                                  ; | | | | | | |_|_|_ 000 = 1 bit
                                  ; | | | | | |        001 = 2 bits
                                  ; | | | | | |        010 = 4 bits
                                  ; | | | | | |       *011 = 8 bits
                                  ; | | | | | |        100 = 16 bits
                                  ; | | | | | |    FORMAT:
                                  ; | | | | | |___ *0 = Intel
                                  ; | | | | |        1 = Motorola
                                  ; |_|_|_|____ RESERVED
                                  ; 03H = 00000011B
        OUT       DX,AL
```

At this point the coprocessor is ready for use. The procedure INIT_COP in the XGA2 module of the GRAPHSOL library uses similar processing to initialize the coprocessor. The programmer must consider that if this initialization code is used, the software must make sure that the 80386 segment registers FS and GS are preserved, since their contents are repeatedly required in setting up the coprocessor operations.

7.4.2 Coprocessor Operations

The XGA graphics coprocessor can autonomously perform drawing operations in parallel with the CPU. The coprocessor can execute in 1, 2, 4, and 8 bits per pixel formats, but not in the direct color mode described in Section 7.3.3. The execution of a coprocessor operation requires the following steps:

1. The CPU initializes the coprocessor registers to be used in the operation.
2. Coprocessor operation starts when the CPU writes a command to the Pixel Operations register.
3. The coprocessor executes the programmed operation. During this time the system microprocessor can be performing other tasks.

The graphics functions that can be performed by the coprocessor are pixel block transfer (abbreviated pixBlt), line draw, and draw and step.

The programmer can set up the coprocessor so that it generates an interrupt at the conclusion of its operations. This mechanism can be used in optimizing parallel processing, in task switching in a multitasking environment, in error recovery, and in synchronizing coprocessor access. The coprocessor Operation

Complete interrupt is enabled by setting bit 7 of the Interrupt Enable register of the Display Controller group. The interrupt source is identified by testing the corresponding bit in the Interrupt Status register of the Display Controller group. (See Figure 9.4 and Figure 9.5 in Chapter 9.) Notice that this is set if an interrupt occurred, regardless of the setting of the Interrupt Enable register.

Synchronizing Coprocessor Access

Since the coprocessor operates asynchronously regarding the CPU, the central processor must wait until the coprocessor has concluded its previous operation before issuing a new command. This can be performed in two ways: by enabling the Coprocessor Operation Complete interrupt described in the previous paragraph or by polling the busy bit in the coprocessor Control register. Both methods are quite feasible, each having its advantages and disadvantages.

An XGA interrupt handler for testing the conclusion of coprocessor operation (or any other XGA interrupt for that matter) is designed to intercept vector 0AH, which corresponds with the IRQ2 line of the system's Interrupt Controller. Since this interrupt can be shared, the handler must first make sure that the interrupt was caused by the coprocessor. This requires testing bit 7 of the Interrupt Status register (at offset 05H). If the Coprocessor Operation Complete bit is set, then the code can proceed with the next coprocessor operation. At this time the code must write 1 to bit number 7 in order to clear the interrupt condition so that the next interrupt can take place.

Since polling the busy bit is easier to implement in software this is the method illustrated in the present section. The main objection to polling for hardware not busy is that it slows down operations since the coprocessor must pause execution to read its own Control register. This can be partially overcome by designing routines that includes a delay loop so that so that the coprocessor is not polled constantly. The following procedure from the XGA2 module of the GRAPHSOL library polls bit 7 of the coprocessor Control register to test for a not-busy condition. The COP_RDY procedure is called by the drawing routines in the XGA2 module before emitting a new coprocessor command. The delay period in the wait loop is an arbitrary value.

```
COP_RDY            PROC      NEAR
; Poll bit 7 of coprocessor Control register (offset 11H) to
; determine if coprocessor is busy, if so, wait until ready
; Code assumes that GS segment holds coprocessor base address

        PUSH      AX                      ; Save context
        PUSH      CX
TEST_COP:
        MOV       AL,GS:[+11H]            ; Read control register
        TEST      AL,10000000B            ; Test bit 7
        JZ        COP_READY               ; Go if bit is clear
        MOV       CX,100                  ; Counter for wait loop
```

```
; A 100 iteration wait loop is introduced so that the
coprocessor
; is not polled constantly, since constant polling would slow
; down execution
WAIT_100:
        NOP                        ; Delay
        NOP
        LOOP    WAIT_100           ; Wait
        JMP     TEST_COP           ; Test again after wait
COP_READY:
        POP     CX                 ; Restore context
        POP     AX
        RET
COP_RDY         ENDP
```

General Purpose Maps

The XGA graphics coprocessor can operate on three general purpose pixel maps, designated as Map A, Map B, and Map C in the IBM literature. The identification letters A, B, and C, are sometimes generically represented by the variable n, as is the case in the Pixel Map n Base Pointer designation used in Table 7.6. Notice that, in actual coding, Map n is either Map A, Map B, or Map C. Pixel maps can be located in system or in video memory. The maximum size of a map is of 4,096-by-4,096 pixels.

The following coprocessor registers are related to pixel maps:

1. The Pixel Map n Base Pointer register (at offset 14H) contains the map's start address.

2. The Pixel Map n Width register (at offset 18H) determines the horizontal dimension of the pixel map and the Pixel Map n Height register (at offset 1AH) determines its vertical dimension. The values loaded into these registers must be one less than the required size.

3. The Pixel Map Format register (at offset 1CH) determines if the map is in 1, 2, 4, or 8 bits per pixel and whether it is encoded in Intel or Motorola data format.

4. The Pixel Map Index register (at offset 12H) is used to determine if the mask map is of type A, B, C, or M. The different mask map types are explained in the following paragraphs.

The x and y coordinates of a pixel map are based on the same convention used for the video display, that is, the top-left corner of the pixel map has coordinates $x = 0$, $y = 0$. The value of x increases to the right and the value of y increases downward. The pixel map coordinate system conventions and dimensions are shown in Figure 7.5.

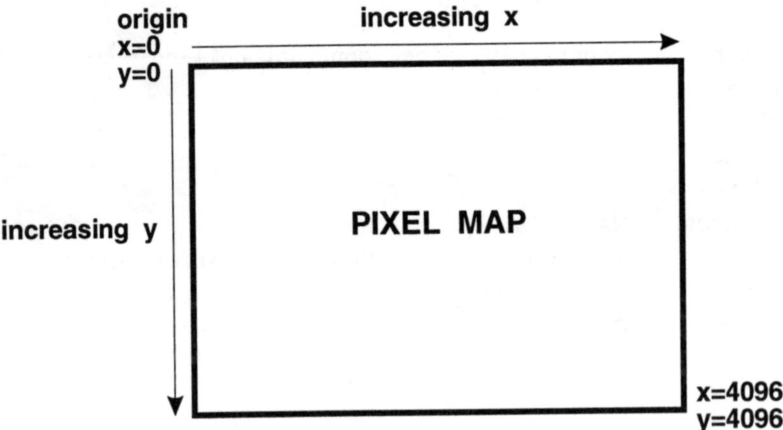

Figure 7.5 *Pixel Map Origin and Dimensions*

In relation to the coprocessor operation a pixel map can represent a source, a destination, or a pattern. The following cases represent common bitBlt operations:

1. In displaying a bit map stored in the applications address space the source map is the application's data, and the destination map is a location in video memory.

2. In an operation that consists of reading video data into system memory the source is a VRAM map and the destination a location in the application's memory space.

3. An operation that copies a video image into another screen area has both source and destination in video memory.

4. The coprocessor can also copy an area of user memory into another one. In this case both source and destination maps are located in the application's memory space.

The pattern map is used in determining if a pixel is considered a foreground or a background. A value of 1 indicates a foreground and a value of 0 a background. This action is shown later in this section.

The Mask Map

The mask map is an additional type of pixel map closely related to the destination map. The mask map, also called Map M, is used to protect the destination map on a pixel-by-pixel basis. In contrast with the other general purpose maps, the mask map is always fixed to a 1 bit per pixel ratio. A 0 bit in the Mask Map (inactive mask) protects the corresponding destination pixel from update, while a 1 bit allows the pixel's normal update.

The x and y dimensions of the mask map can be equal or less than the corresponding coordinates in the destination map. If the mask map and destination map have the same dimensions, then masking is a simple bit to pixel relation. If the mask map is smaller than the destination map then a scissoring operation is performed. In this respect the mask map action can be in one of three modes, as follows:

1. Mask Map Disabled. In this mode the Mask Map is ignored.

2. Mask Map Boundary Enabled. In this mode the Mask Map performs an outline scissoring action similar to a rectangular window. The contents of the Mask Map are ignored.

3. Mask Map Enabled. In this mode the mask map's border acts as a scissoring rectangle, at the same time its contents provide a pixel by pixel masking operation.

The masking mode is selected by a two-bit field in the Pixel Operations register. The difference between the Mask Map Enabled and the Boundary Enabled modes can be seen in Figure 7.6.

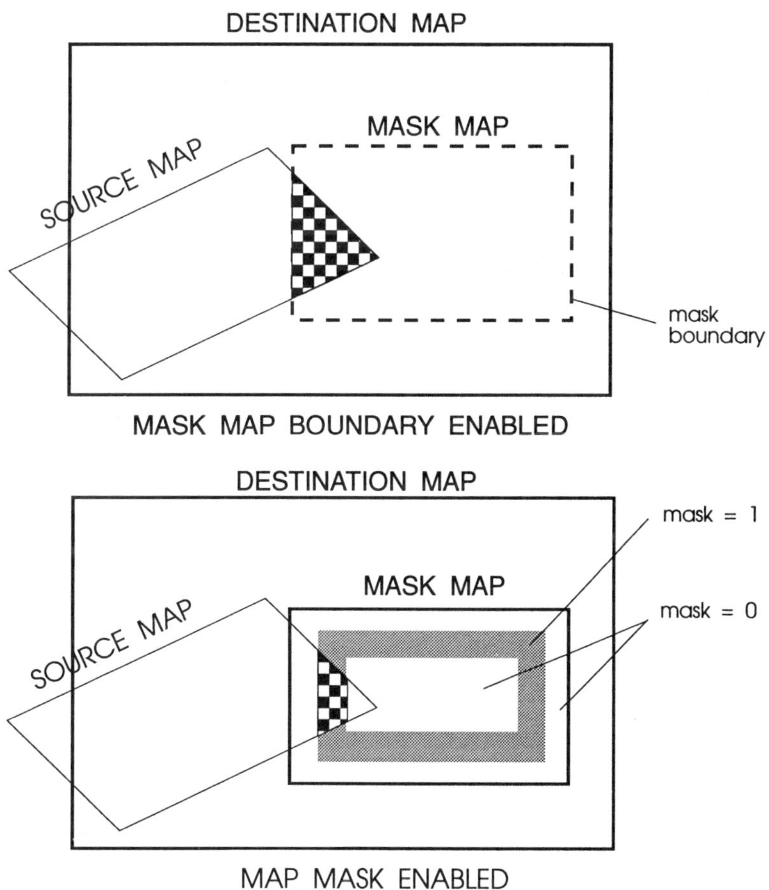

Figure 7.6 *Mask Map Scissoring Operations*

Notice that the action of a mask map in the Boundary Enabled mode is identical to that of a mask map of all one bits. The difference is that the Boundary Enabled mask map consumes no memory while a normal mask map can take up as much as 94Kb in 1024 by 768 pixels resolution.

In addition to the map address the program can define the pixel map's x and y coordinates. These value can be interpreted as offsets within the map. For example, if the destination pixel map is the video screen, the physical address of VRAM is entered in the Pixel Map n Base Pointer register and the actual position within the video display is determined by the x and y coordinates entered in the Destination Map x Coordinate and Destination Map y Coordinate registers. On the other hand, if the pixel map is within the application's address space, the offset is usually zero. This value signals the start of the pixel map as the reference position, however, the coordinates can be changed to indicate another position within the defined rectangle.

Coordinate registers for source and pattern pixel maps are available at offset 70H and 74H. (See Table 7.6.) However, there are no x and y coordinate registers for the mask map, because its origin is assumed to coincide with that of the destination map. Nevertheless, if the mask map is smaller than the destination map it becomes necessary to locate the mask map within the destination map. This is done by means of the Mask Map Origin x Offset and the Mask Map Origin y Offset registers at offset 6CH and 6EH respectively. The use of these mask map offset values is shown in Figure 7.7.

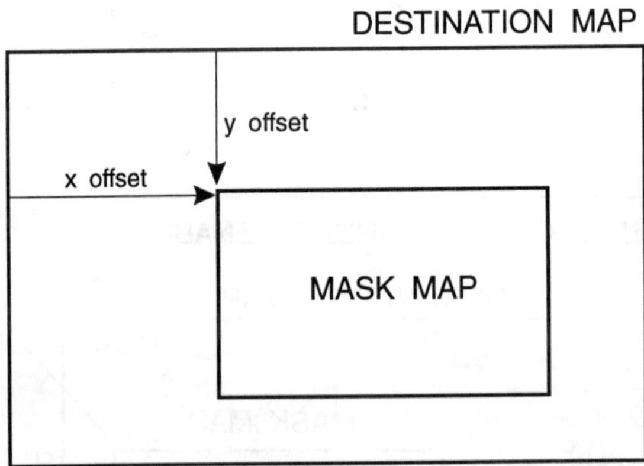

Figure 7.7   *Mask Map x and y Offset*

Pixel Attributes

The coprocessor generates a pixel with specific attributes by combining the source, pattern, and destination, according to a certain mix mode. The pattern pixel map, if used, serves as a filter to determine if a bit corresponds to a foreground or a background pixel. A value of 1 in the pattern pixel map determines that the bit is mapped to a foreground pixel, a value of 0 determines that the bit is mapped to a background pixel. If no pattern map is used then the foreground and background sources can be a specific color or determined by the color encoding stored in a source map. If the foreground source is a specific color, it is stored at the Foreground Color register at offset 58H. The background color is stored at the register at offset 5CH. The elements that take part in determining a pixel's attributes are shown in Figure 7.8.

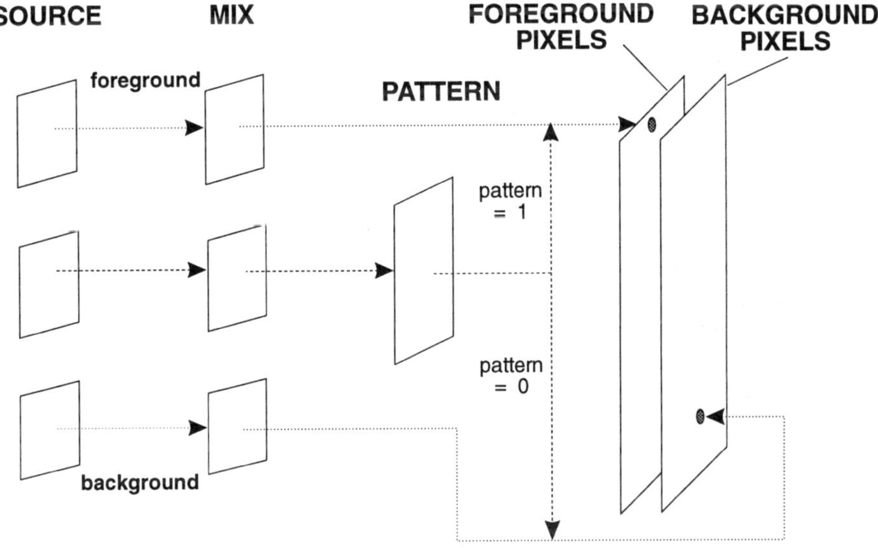

Figure 7.8 *Determining the Pixel Attribute*

Pixel Masking and Color Compare Operations

In addition, it is possible to protect individual pixels by masking. The Pixel Bit Mask register (offset 50H) is used for this purpose. A value of 1 in the Pixel Bit Mask register enables the corresponding pixel for update, while a value of 0 determines that the pixel is excluded from the update operation. Notice that the Pixel Bit Mask is related to the adopted format. In 8 bits per pixel mode, the Pixel Bit Mask has active the 8 low order bits of the register, while in a 2 bit per pixel mode only the lowest two bits are used.

The coprocessor also allows a color compare operation that further inhibits certain pixel patterns from upgrade. The Destination Color Compare Value register (offset 4CH) is used for storing the bitmap to be used in the comparison. As with the Pixel Bit Map register, the number of bits effectively used in the color compare operation depends on the number of bits per pixel in the adopted format. Several color compare conditions are allowed. The code for the selected condition is stored in the Destination Color Compare Condition register (offset 4AH). Table 7.7 lists the condition codes and their respective action.

Table 7.7 *Destination Color Compare Conditions*

CODE	BINARY	CONDITION
0	000	Always true (disable update)
1	001	Destination > color compare value
2	010	Destination = color compare value
3	011	Destination < color compare value
4	100	Always false (enable update)
5	101	Destination > = color compare value
6	110	Destination < > color compare value
7	111	Destination < = color compare value

Mixes

In Figure 7.8 we see that the attribute of the destination pixels depends upon a mix. The mix is a logical or arithmetic operation used in combining the source and the destination bitmaps. The mix is selected independently for the foreground and the background pixels (see Figure 7.8). The foreground mix is entered into the Foreground Mix register (offset 48H) and the background mix into the Background Mix register (offset 49H). The actual mix operation is determined by a mix code. The mix codes and action are shown in Table 7.8.

The word *saturate* in Table 7.8 means that if the result of an addition or subtraction operation is greater than 1, the final result is left at 1, while if it is smaller than 0 it is left at 0.

Table 7.8 *Logical and Arithmetic Mixes*

CODE	HEX	ACTION
0	00H	Zeros
1	01H	Source AND destination
2	02H	Source AND NOT destination
3	03H	Source
4	04H	NOT source AND destination
5	05H	Destination
6	06H	Source XOR destination
7	07H	Source OR destination
8	08H	NOT source AND NOT destination
9	09H	Source XOR NOT destination
10	0AH	NOT destination
11	0BH	Source OR NOT destination
12	0CH	Source NOT destination
13	0DH	NOT source OR destination
14	0EH	NOT source OR NOT destination
15	0FH	Ones
16	10H	Maximum
17	11H	Minimum
18	12H	Add with saturate
19	13H	Destination minus source (with saturate)
20	14H	Source minus destination (with saturate)
21	15H	Average
22	16H	
.	.	Reserved
255	FFH	

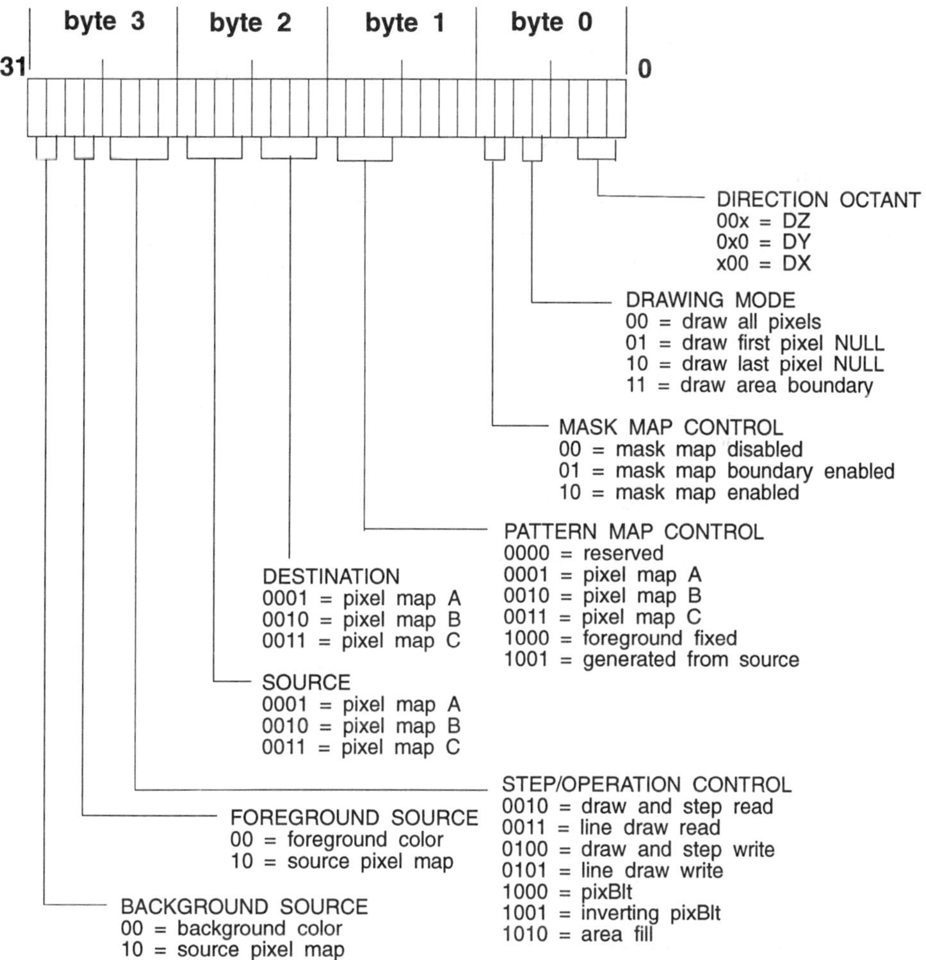

Figure 7.9 *Pixel Operations Register Bitmap*

Pixel Operations

The coprocessor starts executing the programmed operation when data is written to the Pixel Operations register (offset 7CH). The one exception to this statement is the draw and step command which is initiated by writing to the Direction Steps register (at offset 2CH). The Pixel Operations register also defines the flow of data during coprocessor operations. Figure 7.9 is a bitmap of the Pixel Operations register.

The action performed by each field of the Pixel Operations register is explained in the discussion of the various coprocessor commands contained in the sections that follow.

7.4.3 PixBlt Operations

A pixel block transfer operation (pixBlt) consists of moving rectangular memory block from a source area to a destination area. Both the source and the destination can be system or video memory. The dimensions of the pixel rectangles are entered into the Operations Dimension registers; the width into Operations Dimension 1 and the height into Operation Dimension 2. The pixBlt can be programmed to start at any one of the four corners of the rectangle. The operation always proceeds in the direction of the diagonally opposite corner. The direction is entered into the Pixel Operations register (at offset 7CH).

Rectangular Fill PixBlt

Perhaps the simplest pixBlt operations is filling a rectangular screen area using the Foreground Color register as source data. The following code fragment shows the coprocessor commands necessary to perform this form of pixBlt.

```
; Use graphics coprocessor to perform a pixBlt on a rectangular
; screen area
; Code assumes XGA 1024-by-768 mode in 256 colors (8 bits per
; pixel)
; At this point:
;             CX = x coordinate of top-left corner
;             DX = y coordinate of top-left corner
;             SI = width of rectangle, in pixels
;             DI = height of rectangle, in pixels
;             BL = 8-bit color code
;             segment register setting:
;             GS = Coprocessor base address (Section 7.4.1)
;             FS = VRAM base address (Section 7.4.2)
;
;*********************|
;    test for not busy  |
;*********************|
            CALL    COP_RDY          ; Routine developed in
                                     ; Section 7.4.2
; At this point the coprocessor is not busy
;*********************|
;    prepare to pixBlt  |
;*********************|
; Memo: GS holds the coprocessor base address (see Section
; 7.4.1)
            MOV     AL,01H           ; Data value for Map A
            MOV     GS:[+12H],AL     ; Write to Pixel Map Index
            MOV     AX,0H            ; Data value for VRAM low
            MOV     GS:[+14H],AX     ; Write to pix map base address
; Memo: FS register holds the high order word of VRAM address.
```

```
;   ( see Section 7.4.2)
        MOV     AX,FS               ; Data for VRAM high
        MOV     GS:[+16H],AX        ; Write to pix map segment
                                    ; address
; Code assumes 1024 by 768 pixel mode and Intel format
        MOV     AX,1023             ; Value for pix map width
        MOV     GS:[+18H],AX        ; Write to Width register
        MOV     AX,767              ; Value for pix map height
        MOV     GS:[+20H],AX        ; Write to Height register
        MOV     AL,3                ; Select Intel order and 8 bits
                                    ; per pixel
        MOV     GS:[+1CH],AL        ; Write to Format register
;********************|
;   enter pixBlt data    |
;********************|
        MOV     AL,03H              ; Select source mix mode
        MOV     GS:[+48H],AL        ; Write to Mix register
; Write color (in BL) to foreground register
        MOV     GS:[+58H],BL        ; Write to Foreground Color
                                    ; register
; Write coordinates of rectangle's start point to coprocessor
; registers
        MOV     GS:[+78H],CX        ; Write to Destination x Address
                                    ; register
        MOV     GS:[+7AH],DX        ; Write to Destination y Address
                                    ; register
; Store width in Operations Dimension 1 register
        MOV     GS:[+60H],SI        ; Write to Operation Dimension 1
; Store height in Operations Dimension 2 register
        MOV     GS:[+62H],DI        ; Write to Operation Dimension 2
;********************|
;   setup pix operation |
;        registers      |
;********************|
; Bit map of Pixel Operations register for pixBlt operation:
; byte 3 = bbss|pppp
;                       bb = background source
;                           00 = fixed register pixBlt
;                       ss = foreground source
;                           00 = fixed register pixBlt
;                       pppp = step/operation control
;                           1000 = pixBlt
;                       BYTE 3 = 00001000B = 08H
; byte 2 = SSSS|DDDD
;                       SSSS = source
;                           0001 = pixel map A
```

```
;                              DDDD = destination
;                                     0001 = pixel map A
;                              BYTE 2 = 00010001B = 11H
; byte 1 = PPPP|0000
;                              PPPP = pattern map control
;                                     1000 = foreground fixed
;                              BYTE 1 = 10000000B = 80H
; byte 0 = mm00|0oox
;                              mm = mask pixel map
;                                   00 = mask map disabled
;                              oox = octant bits (x = don't care)
;                                    00 = start at top left and move
;                                         right and down
;                              BYTE 0 = 00000000B = 00H
;*********************|
;     execute pixBlt  |
;*********************|
; Coprocessor operation commences when data is written to the
; Pixel Operations register
        MOV     EAX,08118000H    ; Value from bitmap
        MOV     GS:[+7CH],EAX    ; Write to Pixel Operations
                                 ; register
```

If XGA is initialized to 1024-by-768 pixels in 256 colors, and if on entry to the above code fragment the CX register holds 512, the DX register holds 384, the SI register holds 100, the DI register holds 80, and BL = 00001100B, then an 100-by-80 pixel rectangle is drawn with its left-top corner at the center of the screen. If the default palette is active, the color of the rectangle is bright red.

Notice, in the above example, that the direction octant bits in byte 0 of the Pixel Operations register determine the direction in which the pixBlt takes place. (See Figure 7.9.) For performing a nonoverlapping pixBlt the direction octant bits are normally set to zero. However, if the source and destination rectangles overlap, the direction octant bits must be used in order to avoid pixel corruption. Table 7.9 shows the action of the direction octant bits in pixBlt operations. Notice that these bits are interpreted differently during the coprocessor line draw functions.

Table 7.9 *Action of the Direction Octant Bits During PixBlt*

VALUE	ACTION
00x	From top-left to bottom-right
10x	From top-right to bottom-left
01x	From bottom-left to top-right
11x	From bottom-right to top-left

x = dont't care

The procedure named COP_RECT in the XGA2 module of the GRAPHSOL library can be used to perform a rectangular fill pixBlt operation. Processing and entry parameters are the same as in the above code fragment.

System Memory to VRAM PixBlt

Another frequent use of the pixBlt operation is to display an image stored in the application's memory space. The processing of a system-to-video-memory pixBlt is similar to the one used in the rectangular fill pixBlt discussed in the preceding paragraphs. The following code fragment is a memory-to-video pixBlt of an image encoded in 1 bit per pixel format.

```
; Use graphics coprocessor to perform a pixBlt operation
; from a source in system memory to a destination in video
; memory. Image map is encoded in 1 bit per pixel format
; Code assumes XGA 1024 by 768 mode in 256 colors (8 bits per
; pixel)
; At this point:
;           DS:SI = offset of source bitmap in RAM
;           CX = source map pixel width
;           DX = source map pixel height
;           SI = x coordinate of video image
;           DI = y coordinate of video image
;           BL = 8-bit color code to use in displaying image
;
; Segment register setting:
;           GS = Coprocessor base address (Section 7.4.1)
;           FS = VRAM base address (Section 7.4.2)
;
;*********************|
;    test for not busy |
;*********************|
        CALL    COP_RDY              ; Routine developed in
                                     ; Section 7.4.2
; At this point the coprocessor is not busy
;*********************|
; map A is destination |
;    (video memory)     |
;*********************|
        PUSH    AX                   ; Bitmap offset to stack
        MOV     AL,01H               ; Data value for Map A
        MOV     GS:[+12H],AL         ; Write to Pixel Map index
        MOV     AX,0H                ; Data value for VRAM low
        MOV     GS:[+14H],AX         ; Write to pix map base address
; FS register holds the high order word of VRAM address
        MOV     AX,FS                ; Data for VRAM high
```

```
        MOV       GS:[+16H],AX       ; Write to pix map segment
                                     ; address
; Destination map is 1024 by 768 pixel mode and Intel format
        MOV       AX,1023            ; Value for pix map width
        MOV       GS:[+18H],AX       ; Write to Width register
        MOV       AX,767             ; Value for pix map height
        MOV       GS:[+20H],AX       ; Write to Height register
; Bit map of Pixel Format register:
; 7 6 5 4 3 2 1 0 <= bits
; | | | | | | |_|_|______ pixel image size (* = selected value)
; | | | | | |             000 = 1 bit per pixel
; | | | | | |             001 = 2 bits per pixel
; | | | | | |             010 = 4 bits per pixel
; | | | | | |            *011 = 8 bits per pixel
; | | | | | |          format control
; | | | | |            1 = Motorola order
; | | | | |           *0 = Intel order
; |_|_|_|________________________________________ RESERVED
;
        MOV       AL,3               ; Select Intel order and 8 bit
                                     ; per pixel
        MOV       GS:[+1CH],AL       ; Write to Format register
;*********************|
;    map B is source  |
;    (system memory)  |
;*********************|
        MOV       AL,02              ; Data value for Map B
        MOV       GS:[+12H],AL       ; Write to Pixel Map index
; AX = offset of source bitmap (in stack)
; DS = segment of source bitmap
; To convert logical address to physical address the segment
; value is shifted left 4 bits and the offset added
        MOV       EAX,0              ; Clear 32 bits
        MOV       AX,DS              ; Segment to AX
        SHL       EAX,4              ; Shift segment 4 bits
        POP       BP                 ; Offset to BP
        ADD       AX,BP              ; Add offset to segment
        MOV       GS:[+14H],EAX      ; Write to pix map base address
; Dimensions of source map are in CX and DX registers
        DEC       CX
        DEC       DX
        MOV       GS:[+18H],CX       ; Write to Width register
        MOV       GS:[+20H],DX       ; Write to Height register
; Bit map of pixel format register:
; 7 6 5 4 3 2 1 0 <= bits
; | | | | | | |_|_|______ pixel image size (* = selected value)
```

```
;  |  |  |  |  |  |              *000 = 1 bit per pixel
;  |  |  |  |  |  |               001 = 2 bits per pixel
;  |  |  |  |  |  |               010 = 4 bits per pixel
;  |  |  |  |  |  |               011 = 8 bits per pixel
;  |  |  |  |  |  |________ format control
;  |  |  |  |  |             ^1 = Motorola order
;  |  |  |  |  |              0 = Intel order
;  |_|_|_|____________ RESERVED
        MOV     AL,08H              ; Select Motorola order and 1
                                    ; bit per pixel
        MOV     GS:[+1CH],AL        ; Write to Format register


;*********************|
;    select mix mode  |
;*********************|
        MOV     AL,03H              ; Select source mix mode
        MOV     GS:[+48H],AL        ; Write to Mix register
; Write color (in BL) to foreground register
        MOV     GS:[+58H],BL        ; Write to Foreground Color
                                    ; register
; Write coordinates of source and destination
; Source coordinates are 0,0, destination coordinates are in SI
; and DI
        MOV     AX,0                ; Source coordinates
        MOV     GS:[+70H],AX        ; Write to Source x Address
        MOV     GS:[+72H],AX        ; Write to Source y Address
        MOV     GS:[+78H],SI        ; Write to Destination x Address
        MOV     GS:[+7AH],DI        ; Write to Destination y Address
; Store width in Operations Dimension 1 register
        MOV     GS:[+60H],CX        ; Write to Operation Dimension 1
; Store height in Operations Dimension 2 register
        MOV     GS:[+62H],DX        ; Write to Operation Dimension 2
;*********************|
; set up Pix Operation |
;       registers      |
;*********************|
; Bit map of Pixel Operations register for pixBlt operation:
; byte 3 = bbss|pppp
;                       bb = background source
;                             00 = background color
;                       ss = foreground source
;                             00 = foreground color
;                       pppp = function
;                             1000 = pixBlt
;                       BYTE 3 = 00001000B = 08H
; byte 2 = SSSS|DDDD
```

```
;                            SSSS = source pixel map
;                                0010 = pixel map B
;                            DDDD = destination pixel map
;                                0001 = pixel map A
;                            BYTE 2 = 00100001B = 21H
; byte 1 = PPPP|0000
;                            PPPP = pattern pixel map
;                                0010 = pixel map B
;                            BYTE 1 = 00100000B = 20H
; byte 0 = mm00|0oox (* = values for this operation)
;                            mm = mask pixel map
;                                00 = mask map disabled
;                            oox = octant bits (x = don't care)
;                                00 = start at top left and move
;                                        right and down
;                            BYTE 0 = 00000000B = 00H
;*********************|
;     execute pixBlt  |
;*********************|
; Coprocessor operation commences when data is written to the
; Pixel Operations register
        MOV     EAX,008212000H  ; Value from bit map
        MOV     GS:[+7CH],EAX   ; Write to Pixel Operations
                                ; register
```

The procedure named COP_SYSVID_1 in the XGA2 module of the GRAPHSOL library can be used to perform a system memory to VRAM pixBlt operation. Processing and entry parameters are the same as in the above code fragment. The procedure named COP_SYSVID_8, also in the GRAPHSOL library, assumes an 8 bit per pixel encoding in the source bit map. This last procedure can be used to display a memory stored image in 1024-by-768 pixels in 256 colors.

7.4.4 Line Drawing Operations

The XGA draws a straight line following a method originally described by J.E. Bresenham (*IBM Systems Journal,* 1965) and since known as Bresenahm's algorithm. Bresenham's method is based on the differential equation for the slope of a straight line, which states that the difference between the y coordinates divided by the difference between the x coordinates is a constant. This constant, usually called the slope, is designated by the letter m. The formula is:

$$m = \frac{Dy}{Dx}$$

where Dy is the difference between the y values and Dx the difference between the x values. Therefore y can be expressed as a function of x, as follows:

$$y = mx$$

Bresenham's algorithm, as implemented on XGA, requires that all parameters be normalized to the first octant (octant number 0). Figure 7.10 shows the octant numbering in the Cartesian plane.

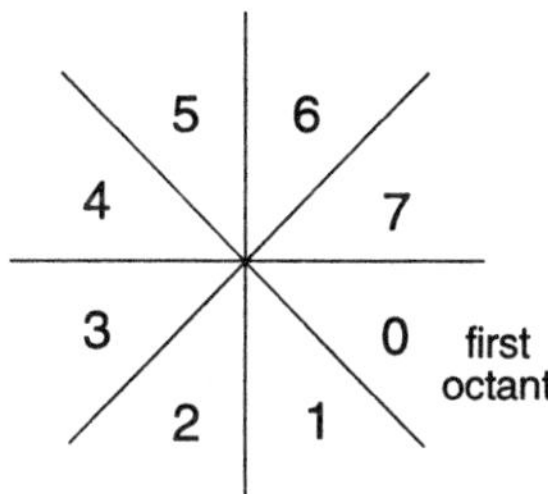

Figure 7.10 *Octant Numbering in the Cartesian Plane*

Reduction to the First Octant

The octant is selected by the octant field bits in the Pixel Operations register. (See Figure 7.9.) The one-bit values designated DX, DY, and DZ have the following meaning:

1. DX encodes the direction of the x values in reference to the line's start point. DX = 0 if x is in the positive direction and DX = 1 if it is in the negative direction.
2. DY encodes the direction of the y values in reference to the line's start point. DY = 0 if y is in the positive direction and DY = 1 if it is in the negative direction.
3. DZ encodes the relation between the absolute value of the x and y coordinates. DZ = 0 if $|x| > |y|$, and DZ = 1 otherwise.

The following rules allows normalizing any line defined by its start and end points to the first octant:

1. If the end x coordinate is smaller than the start x coordinate set the DX bit in the Pixel Operations register.
2. If the end y coordinate is smaller than the start y coordinate set the DY bit in the Pixel Operations register.
3. If the difference between the y coordinates is greater than or equal to the difference between the x coordinates set the DZ bit in the Pixel Operations register.

4. After the octant bits DX, DY, and DZ are set according to the above rules, the code can use the unsigned difference between y coordinates (delta y or Dy) and the unsigned difference between x coordinates (delta x or Dx) in the remaining calculations.

Calculating the Bresenham Terms

Three coprocessor registers are use to encode values that result from applying Bresenham's algorithm, these are the Bresenham Error Term register (offset 20H), the Bresenham K1 Term register (offset 24H), and the Bresenham K2 Term register (offset 28H).

The Bresenham K1 constant is calculated by the formula:

$$\text{Term K1} = 2 * \text{Dy}$$

Recall that Dy is the absolute difference between y coordinates, and Dx the absolute difference between x coordinates. The Bresenham K2 constant is calculated by the formula:

$$\text{Term K2} = 2 * (\text{Dy} - \text{Dx})$$

Finally, the Bresenham error term is calculated by the formula:

$$\text{Term E} = (2 * \text{Dy}) - \text{Dx}$$

The Bresenham terms are entered into the corresponding coprocessor registers. (See Table 7.6.) The Operation Dimension 1 register (at offset 60H) is loaded with the value of Dx. The following code fragment shows the necessary processing for drawing a straight line using the XGA coprocessor.

```
; Use graphics coprocessor to draw a straight line
; Code assumes XGA 1024-by-768 mode in 256 colors (8 bits per
; pixel)
;
; At this point:
;            CX = x pixel coordinate of line start
;            DX = y pixel coordinate of line start
;            SI = x pixel coordinate of line end
;            DI = y pixel coordinate of line end
;            BL = 8-bit color code
;            segment register setting:
;            GS = Coprocessor base address (Section 7.4.1)
;            FS = VRAM base address (Section 7.4.2)
;
;*********************|
;   test for not busy |
```

```
;********************|
        CALL    COP_RDY             ; Routine developed in
                                    ; Section 7.4.2
; At this point the coprocessor is not busy
;
;********************|
;   prepare to draw  |
;********************|
; Prime coprocessor registers
        MOV     AL,01H              ; Data value for Map A
        MOV     GS:[+12H],AL        ; Write to pixel map index
        MOV     AX,0H               ; Data value for VRAM low
        MOV     GS:[+14H],AX        ; Write to pix map base address
; FS register holds the high order word of VRAM address. This
; value is calculated by the INIT_COP routine in this module
        MOV     AX,FS               ; Data for VRAM high
        MOV     GS:[+16H],AX        ; Write to pix map segment
                                    ; address
; Code assumes 1024 by 768 pixel mode and Intel format
        MOV     AX,1023             ; Value for pix map width
        MOV     GS:[+18H],AX        ; Write to Width register
        MOV     AX,767              ; Value for pix map height
        MOV     GS:[+20H],AX        ; Write to Height register
        MOV     AL,3                ; Select Intel order and 8 bits
                                    ; per pixel
        MOV     GS:[+1CH],AL        ; Write to Format register
;
;********************|
;     mix, color and |
;       coordinates  |
;********************|
        MOV     AL,03H              ; Select source mix mode
        MOV     GS:[+48H],AL        ; Write to Mix register
; Write color (in BL) to Foreground register
        MOV     GS:[+58H],BL        ; Write to Foreground Color
                                    ; register
; Write coordinates of line start point to coprocessor registers
        MOV     GS:[+78H],CX        ; Write to Destination x Address
                                    ; register
        MOV     GS:[+7AH],DX        ; Write to Destination y Address
                                    ; register
;********************|
;  reduce to octant 0 |
;********************|
```

```
;               CX = x pixel coordinate of line start
;               DX = y pixel coordinate of line start
;               SI = x pixel coordinate of line end
;               DI = y pixel coordinate of line end
; Octant bits in Pixel Operations register as follows:
; xxxx x210
;               |||________ DZ bit = 0 if |x| > |y|
;               ||_________ DY bit = 0 if y is positive (DI >= DX)
;               |__________ DX bit = 0 if x is positive (SI >= CX)
; BL will hold octant bits
        MOV     BL,0                ; Clear Octant register
        CMP     SI,CX               ; Test for DX bit
        JGE     DX_ISOK             ; Go if horizontal line
; At this point SI < CX, therefore DX bit must be set
        OR      BL,00000100B        ; DX bit is now set in BL
        XCHG    SI,CX               ; Exchange so that CX > SI
DX_ISOK:
; Now test DX bit condition
        CMP     DI,DX               ; Test for DY bit
        JGE     DY_ISOK             ; Go if horizontal line
; At this point DI < DX, therefore DY bit must be set
        OR      BL,00000010B        ; DY bit is now set in BL
        XCHG    DI,DX               ; Exchange so that DX  DI
; Now test DX bit condition
DY_ISOK:
        SUB     DI,DX               ; Find |y|
        XCHG    DX,DI               ; |y| to DX
        SUB     SI,CX               ; and |x|
        XCHG    CX,SI               ; |x| to CX
        CMP     CX,DX               ; Is |x| > |y|
        JG      BRZ_TERMS           ; Go to leave DZ = 0
; At this point |x| <= |y|, therefore DZ bit must be set
; and |y| must be exchanged with |x|
        OR      BL,00000001B        ; Set DZ bit
        XCHG    CX,DX               ; Exchange
;********************|
;    Bresenham terms |
;      calculations  |
;********************|
BRZ_TERMS:
; Bresenham terms:
;       Term E (error) = (2 * |y|) - |x|
;       Term K1        = 2 * |y|
;       Term K2        = 2 * (|y| - |x|)
; AT this point CX = |x| and DX = |y|
; First store |x| in Operations Dimensions register
```

```
        MOV     GS:[+60H],CX        ; Write to Operation Dimension 1
                                    ; register
; Then calculate Term E
        PUSH    DX                  ; Save |y|
        ADD     DX,DX               ; 2 * |y|
        SUB     DX,CX               ; - |x|
        MOV     SI,DX               ; Store Term E in SI
        POP     DX                  ; Restore |y|
        PUSH    CX                  ; and save |x|
        MOV     CX,DX               ; |y| to CX
        ADD     CX,CX               ; Calculate 2 * |y|
        MOV     DI,CX               ; Store Term K1 in DI
        POP     CX                  ; Restore |x| from stack
        SUB     DX,CX               ; |y| - |x|
        ADD     DX,DX               ; times 2
; DX = Term K2
        MOV     GS:[+20H],SI        ; Write to Error Term register
        MOV     GS:[+24H],DI        ; Write to K1 register
        MOV     GS:[+28H],DX        ; Write to K2 register
; Bit map of Pixel Operations register:
; byte 3 = 0000|0101 = line draw write operation
; byte 2 = 0001      = source pixel map is map A
;            0001     = destination pixel map is map A
; byte 1 = 1000|rrrr = special code for foreground and all 1s
; byte 0 = 00    0   = Mask map disabled
;               00   = Drawing mode for all pixels drawn
;                    OCTANT DATA:
;             o   = DX = 0 for x in positive direction
;            o   = DY = 0 for y in positive direction
;           o = DZ = 0 for |x| > |y|
;********************|
;   execute operation  |
;********************|
        MOV     EAX,05118000H       ; All bits except octant
; BL holds octant bits
        OR      AL,BL               ; OR-in octant bits
        MOV     GS:[+7CH],EAX       ; Write to Pixel Operations
                                    ; register
```

7.5 The XGA Sprite

Many graphics programs, at both the system and the application level, must manipulate some sort of animated screen marker image. A typical example of screen marker is a mouse-controlled pointer or icon often used to facilitate selecting from option boxes or menus. Since the marker image overlays the screen, the software has to find some way of saving and restoring the screen contents as this image is translated over the pixel grid. In our discussion of animation techniques (see Chapter 9), we describe how the XOR operation is used in VGA graphics to display and erase an icon without affecting the screen contents. In XGA, the operation of a small screen pointer icon is considerably simplified thanks to a device called the *sprite*.

The XGA sprite mechanism consists of hardware elements designed to store and display a small graphics object. The sprite operation is independent of the video display function. The maximum size of the sprite image is of 64-by-64 pixels. This image is stored in a 32K static RAM chip (which is not part of video memory) called the sprite buffer. This buffer is used for storing alphanumeric characters when XGA is in a VGA mode or in its proprietary 132-column text mode. The main advantage of the XGA sprite is that it does not affect the image currently displayed, therefore the XGA programmer need not worry about preserving the video image as the sprite is moved on the screen. This action can be best visualized as a transparent overlay that is moved over the picture without changing it. Figure 7.11 shows the structure of the sprite buffer.

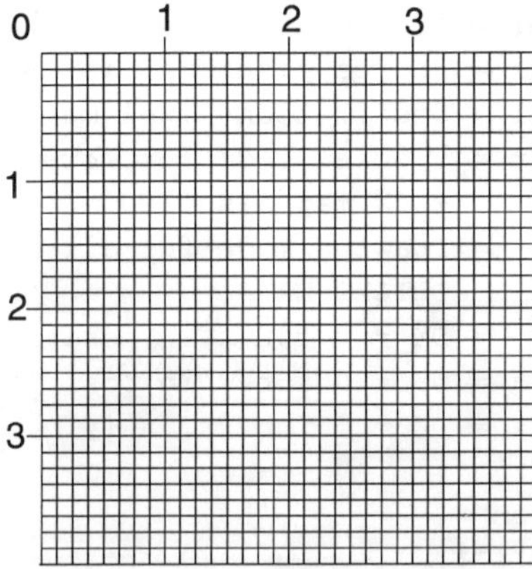

Figure 7.11 *The Sprite Buffer*

The XGA registers related to sprite image display and control are located in the indexed access registers of the Display Controller group. (See Section 7.1.3.) Table 7.10 lists the location and purpose of the sprite-related registers.

7.5.1 The Sprite Image

The sprite image consists of 64 by 64 pixels. Each sprite image pixel can have one of four attributes. The storage structure is in Intel data format and encoded in 2 bits per pixel. The bit codes for the sprite image is shown in Table 7.11.

Table 7.10 *Sprite-Related Registers in the Display Controller*

INDEX REGISTER OFFSET	REGISTER NAME
30H	Sprite horizontal start, low part
31H	Sprite horizontal start, high part
32H	Sprite horizontal preset
33H	Sprite vertical start, low part
34H	Sprite vertical start, high part
35H	Sprite vertical preset
36H	Sprite control register
38H	Sprite color 0, red component
39H	Sprite color 0, green component
3AH	Sprite color 0, blue component
3BH	Sprite color 1, red component
3CH	Sprite color 1, green component
3DH	Sprite color 1, blue component
60H	Sprite/palette index, low part
61H	Sprite/palette index, high part
62H	Sprite/palette prefetch, low part
63H	Sprite/palette prefetch, high part
6AH	Sprite data
6BH	Sprite prefetch save (RESERVED)

Table 7.11 *Sprite Image Bit Codes*

BIT CODE	ACTION
00	Pixel displayed in sprite color 0
01	Pixel displayed in sprite color 1
10	Transparent (image pixel is visible)
11	Complement (one's complement of image pixel is visible)

The displayed sprite can be smaller than 64-by-64 pixels. In this case, the software controls which part of the sprite image is displayed by means of the Sprite Horizontal Preset (offset 32H) and Sprite Vertical Preset registers (offset 35H) in the Display Controller. (See Table 7.10.) However, the sprite image always extends to the full 64-bit length and width of the sprite buffer. Nevertheless, transparent sprite codes can be used to locate the sprite image within the pixel rectangle defined by the 64-byte sprite buffer. The elements used in controlling the size of the sprite image are shown in Figure 7.12.

The location of the sprite image within the viewport is determined by the Sprite Horizontal Start and Sprite Vertical Start registers. (See Table 7.11.) Both of these registers are word-size, however, the valid range of values is limited to 0 to 2047. The low-order bit in the Sprite Control register (offset 36H) determines the sprite's visibility. The sprite is displayed when this bit is set and is invisible if the bit is cleared.

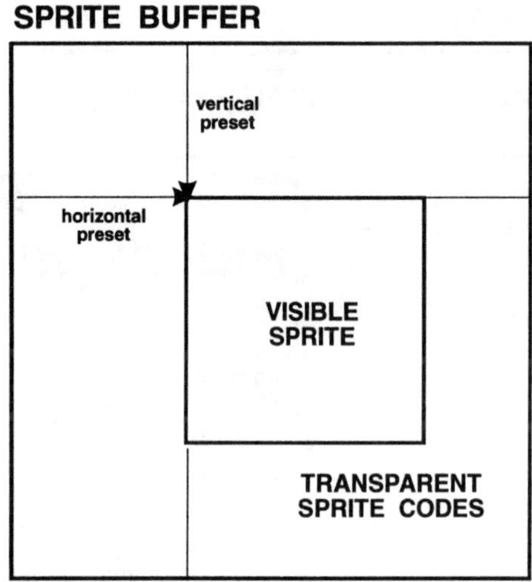

Figure 7.12 *Visible Sprite Image Control*

Encoding of Sprite Colors and Attributes

In Section 7.1 5 we mentioned that the sprite's attributes are coded into a 2-bit field. The first two codes refer to sprite color attributes, the third code defines a transparent attribute, and the last one a one's complement operation (see Table 7.10). The sprite colors 0 and 1 are determined by the setting in two sets of registers in the Display Controller group: registers 38H to 3AH select the red, green, and blue values of sprite color 0, while registers 3BH to 3DH select the same values in sprite color 1. In this manner, if the first byte in the sprite buffer is encoded with the value 01010101B, then the first four bits in the sprite are displayed using the color value for sprite color 1. Figure 7.13 shows how the sprite pixels are mapped to the binary values stored in the sprite buffer.

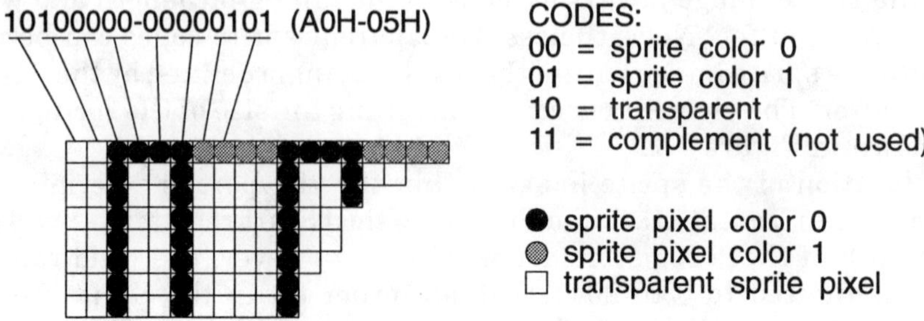

Figure 7.13 *Bit-to-Pixel Mapping of Sprite Image*

In summary, the attribute of each sprite pixel corresponds to the two-bit code stored in the sprite buffer. Therefore, designing a sprite image is a matter of installing the red, green, and blue values for each sprite color and then composing a pixel map using the two-bit values in Table 7.10. The Sprite Horizontal and Vertical Preset registers can be used to adjust a sprite image that does not coincide with the top-left corner of the map stored in the sprite buffer.

Loading the Sprite Image

Once the sprite map has been composed and stored in an application's memory variable, the software must proceed to set the sprite color registers and load the image into the sprite buffer. The following code fragment assumes that the sprite colors and bit map have been placed in a formatted parameter block. From this data the sprite color values and image are loaded into the corresponding Display Controller registers.

```
DATA       SEGMENT
             .
             .
             .

;*********************|
;     sprite data     |
;*********************|
; The 64 by 64 pixel sprite is defined at 64 lines of 4
; doublewords per line
;
; First 6 bits of the sprite color are significant
; In this example color number 0 is bright red and color number
1
; is bright white
SPRITE_MAP_0      DB        11111100B          ; Red for color 0
                  DB        0                  ; Green for color 0
                  DB        0                  ; Blue for color 0
                  DB        11111100B          ; Red for color 1
                  DB        11111100B          ; Green for color 1
                  DB        11111100B          ; Blue for color 1
; The 64 by 64 pixel sprite is defined as 64 lines of 4
; doublewords per line, encoded as follows:
; 00H = 00 00 00 00 B = 4 pixels in sprite color 0
; 55H = 01 01 01 01 B = 4 pixels in sprite color 1
; AAH = 10 10 10 10 B = 4 transparent pixels
; FFH = 11 11 11 11 B = 4 pixels in one's complement of image
;
                  DD        256 DUP (0055AAFFH)
DATA       ENDS
```

```
CODE        SEGMENT
                  .

                  .

                  .

; Load sprite image and select color registers
; On entry:
;            DS:SI —> caller's sprite image formatted as follows:
;
;    OFFSET     UNIT        CONTENTS
;       0       byte        6 low bits are RED for sprite color 0
;       1       byte        6 low bits are GREEN for sprite color 0
;       2       byte        6 low bits are BLUE for sprite color 0
;       3       byte        6 low bits are RED for sprite color 1
;       4       byte        6 low bits are GREEN for sprite color 1
;       5       byte        6 low bits are BLUE for sprite color 1
;       6       16 bytes per 64 rows (1024 bytes) encoding the
;               sprite image at 2 bits per pixel
;    1030       end of sprite image
;
; Code assumes that the variable XGA_REG_BASE holds the XGA
; register base address (see Section 7.2.1)
;
;*********************|
; set sprite color 0  |
;*********************|
; Load sprite color 0 registers using values in parameter block
; supplied by caller (DS:SI)
        MOV     DX,XGA_REG_BASE ; Register base
        ADD     DX,0AH          ; To Index register
; Index register 38H is Sprite Color 0, red value
        MOV     AL,38H          ; Sprite register
        MOV     AH,[SI]         ; Data from caller's buffer
        INC     SI              ; Bump pointer to next byte
        OUT     DX,AX           ; Write data
;
        MOV     DX,XGA_REG_BASE ; Register base
        ADD     DX,0AH          ; To Index register
; Index register 39H is Sprite Color 0, green value
        MOV     AL,39H          ; Sprite register
        MOV     AH,[SI]         ; Data from caller's buffer
        INC     SI              ; Bump pointer to next byte
        OUT     DX,AX           ; Write data
;
        MOV     DX,XGA_REG_BASE ; Register base
        ADD     DX,0AH          ; To Index register
```

```
; Index register 3AH is Sprite Color 0, blue value
        MOV     AL,3AH          ; Sprite register
        MOV     AH,[SI]         ; Data from caller's buffer
        INC     SI              ; Bump pointer to next byte
        OUT     DX,AX           ; Write data
;
;********************|
; set sprite color 1   |
;********************|
; Load sprite color 1 registers to GREEN
        MOV     DX,XGA_REG_BASE ; Register base
        ADD     DX,0AH          ; To Index register
; Index register 3BH is Sprite Color 1, red value
        MOV     AL,3BH          ; Sprite register
        MOV     AH,[SI]         ; Data from caller's buffer
        INC     SI              ; Bump pointer to next byte
        OUT     DX,AX           ; Write data
;
        MOV     DX,XGA_REG_BASE ; Register base
        ADD     DX,0AH          ; To index register
; Index register 3CH is Sprite Color 1, green value
        MOV     AL,3CH          ; Sprite register
        MOV     AH,[SI]         ; Data from caller's buffer
        INC     SI              ; Bump pointer to next byte
        OUT     DX,AX           ; Write data
;
        MOV     DX,XGA_REG_BASE ; Register base
        ADD     DX,0AH          ; To Index register
; Index register 3DH is Sprite Color 1, blue value
        MOV     AL,3DH          ; Sprite register
        MOV     AH,[SI]         ; Data from caller's buffer
        INC     SI              ; Bump pointer to next byte
        OUT     DX,AX           ; Write data

;********************|
;   prepare to load    |
;     sprite image     |
;********************|
; First set the Sprite Index registers to zero
        MOV     DX,XGA_REG_BASE ; Register base
        ADD     DX,0AH          ; To Index register
; Index register 60H is Sprite/Palette index Low
        MOV     AX,0060H        ; 00 to register at offset 60H
        OUT     DX,AX           ; Write data
; Reset to base
        MOV     DX,XGA_REG_BASE ; Register base
```

```
        ADD     DX,0AH              ; To index register
; Index register 61H is Sprite/Palette index High
        MOV     AX,0061H            ; 00 to register at offset 60H
        OUT     DX,AX               ; Write data
; Select the Sprite Data register at offset 6AH
        MOV     DX,XGA_REG_BASE ; Register base
        ADD     DX,0AH              ; To Index register
        MOV     AL,06AH             ; Offset of Data register
        OUT     DX,AL               ; Select Sprite Data register
;*********************|
;   load sprite image    |
;*********************|
; DS:SI -> buffer area containing the sprite bit-mapped image in
;          2 bits per pixel format, as follows:
;              00 = sprite color 0
;              01 = sprite color 1
;              10 = transparent pixel
;              11 = complement pixel
        MOV     CX,512              ; Word item counter
SPRITE_DATA:
        MOV     DX,XGA_REG_BASE ; Register base
        ADD     DX,0CH              ; To second Data register
        MOV     AX,[SI]             ; Get data from buffer
        OUT     DX,AX               ; Send to data port
        INC     SI                  ; Bump data pointer
        INC     SI                  ; to next word
        LOOP    SPRITE_DATA         ; Repeat 512 times
; At this point sprite color and image have been loaded
```

The procedure named **SPRITE_IMAGE** in the XGA2 module of the GRAPHSOL library loads the sprite image and colors using the same processing as in the above code fragment.

7.5.2 Displaying the Sprite

As mentioned in Section 7.5.1, if the low-order bit of the Sprite Control register is set, the sprite image is displayed on the video screen. The position at which it is displayed is determined by the setting of the Sprite Horizontal Start and Vertical Start registers. (See Table 7.11.) The following code fragment displays the sprite image at the screen coordinates supplied by the caller.

```
; Display sprite image at coordinates furnished by the caller
; as follows:
;           BX = x coordinate of sprite location (0 to 1023)
;           CX = y coordinate of sprite location (0 to 767)
; Code assumes that the variable XGA_REG_BASE holds the XGA
```

```
; register base address (see Section 7.2.1)
;
        MOV     DX,XGA_REG_BASE ; Register base
        ADD     DX,0AH          ; To Index register
; Index register 30H is Sprite x Start LOW register
        MOV     AH,BL           ; Value to Start register
        MOV     AL,30H          ; Address of Start x Low
        OUT     DX,AX           ; Write data
;
        MOV     DX,XGA_REG_BASE ; Register base
        ADD     DX,0AH          ; To Index register
; Index register 31H is Sprite x Start HIGH register
        MOV     AH,BH           ; Value to start register
        MOV     AL,31H          ; Address of Start register
        OUT     DX,AX           ; Write data
; Set Sprite x Preset register to 0
        MOV     DX,XGA_REG_BASE ; Register base
        ADD     DX,0AH          ; To Index register
; Index register 32H is Sprite x Preset register
        MOV     AH,00           ; Value to preset register
        MOV     AL,32H          ; Address of Start register
        OUT     DX,AX           ; Write data
; Select y coordinate registers
        MOV     DX,XGA_REG_BASE ; Register base
        ADD     DX,0AH          ; To Index register
; Index register 33H is Sprite y Start LOW register
        MOV     AH,CL           ; Value to start register
        MOV     AL,33H          ; Address of Start x Low
        OUT     DX,AX           ; Write data
;
        MOV     DX,XGA_REG_BASE ; Register base
        ADD     DX,0AH          ; To Index register
; Index register 34H is Sprite y Start HIGH register
        MOV     AH,CH           ; Value to Start register
        MOV     AL,34H          ; Address of Start register
        OUT     DX,AX           ; Write data
; Set Sprite y Preset register to 0
        MOV     DX,XGA_REG_BASE ; Register base
        ADD     DX,0AH          ; To Index register
; Index register 35H is Sprite x Preset register
        MOV     AH,00           ; Value to preset register
        MOV     AL,35H          ; Address of Start register
        OUT     DX,AX           ; Write data
;*********************|
;    display sprite   |
;*********************|
```

```
; Sprite is displayed by setting bit 0 of the Sprite Control
; register at offset 36H
        MOV       DX,XGA_REG_BASE ; Register base
        ADD       DX,0AH          ; To Index register
; Sprite control register offset is 36H
        MOV       AH,01           ; Value to start register
        MOV       AL,36H          ; Address of Start register
        OUT       DX,AX           ; Write data
; At this point the sprite has been displayed
```

The procedure named SPRITE_AT in the XGA2 module of the GRAPHSOL library displays the sprite using the same processing as in the above code fragment. To turn off the sprite the program need only clear the low-order bit in the Sprite Control Register. This operation is performed by the SPRITE_OFF procedure in the XGA2 module of the GRAPHSOL library.

7.6 Using the XGA Library

The GRAPHSOL library furnished in the book's microdisk includes two modules that contain XGA specific routines: XGA1.ASM and XGA2.ASM. XGA1.ASM contains procedures that use the AI services described in Chapter 6. The purpose of this module is to simplify initializing the XGA system and the AI software as well as to facilitate the use of AI text services. The module XGA2.ASM of the XGA library contains routines that access the XGA registers directly. These procedures serve to initialize the XGA system, to select the display mode, to set an individual screen pixel using the 1024-by-768 pixel definition in 256 colors, to perform the display of geometrical figures, and to load and manipulate the sprite.

In addition to the routines in the GRAPHSOL library, XGA programs can also use several procedures in the VGA modules of GRAPHSOL.LIB. The use of the VGA procedures by an XGA system requires a previous call to the SET_DEVICE routine in the VGA3 module. For XGA systems this call is made with the AL register holding the character "X." The call sets a device-specific display switch to the XGA display routine. This enables the use of several geometrical display routines in the VGA3 module, including the named BRESENHAM, LINE_BY_SLOPE, DISPLAY_LINE, CIRCLE, ELLIPSE, PARABOLA, and HYPERBOLA. Also the following procedures in the VGA2 module: FINE_TEXT, FINE_TEXTHP, and MULTITEXT, as well as the corresponding text display support routines, such as FONT_TO_RAM and READ_HPFONT. Information regarding the VGA text display and geometrical routines can be found in Chapters 4 and 5 as well as in the source files VGA2.ASM and VGA3.ASM contained in the book's software.

7.6.1 Procedures in the XGA1.ASM Module

OPEN_AI

Initialize Adapter Interface software
>   Receives:
>   Nothing
>   Returns:
>   Carry clear if AI initialized
>   Carry set if error

CLOSE_AI

Erase video and close Adapter Interface
>   Receives:
>   Nothing
>   Returns:
>   Nothing

AI_FONT

Read an XGA or 8514/A font file into RAM to enable text display using AI functions
>   Receives:
>   Far pointer to ASCIIZ filename for font file (must be in the current path)
>   Returns:
>   Carry clear if font read and stored in buffer
>   Carry set if file not found or disk error

AI_COLOR

Set foreground and background colors for AI services
>   Receives:
>   1. Byte integer of foreground color
>   2. Byte integer of background color
>   Returns:
Nothing
>   Action:
>   Foreground and background colors selected

AI_CLS

Clear screen using AI service
>   Receives:
>   Nothing
>   Returns:
>   Nothing
>   Action:
>   Video display is cleared

AI_TEXT

Display a text message on XGA screen using an AI service
>   Receives:
>>   1. word integer of x pixel coordinate for message
>>   2. word integer of y pixel coordinate for message
>>   3. byte integer of foreground color
>>   4. byte integer of background color
>>   5. far pointer to text message
>   Returns:
>>   Nothing
>   Action:
>>   Text message is displayed

AI_PALETTE

Initialize 256 DAC color registers from a 4-byte per color table using an AI service
>   Receives:
>>   1. far pointer to 1024 byte table of palette colors. (4 bytes per color encoding)
>   Returns:
>>   Nothing
>   Action:
>>   LUT registers are set according to value table furnished by the caller

AI_COMMAND

Access the services in the XGA/8514-A Adapter Interface
>   Receives:
>>   1. word integer of AI service number
>>   2. far pointer to parameter block
>   Returns:
>>   Nothing
>   Action:
>>   AI command is executed

7.6.2 Procedures in the XGA2.ASM Module

XGA_MODE

Initialize an XGA graphics mode by setting the video system registers directly.
>   Receives:
>>   1. byte integer of XGA mode number
>   Assumes:
>>   INIT_XGA has been previously called
>   Returns:
>>   1. carry clear if no error

2. carry set if invalid mode
Action:
XGA system is set to mode requested by the caller. Valid range is 2 to
5, as follows:

```
Mode number:            Resolution:                 Colors:
    2                   1024-by-756                 256
    3                   1024-by-768                 16
    4                   640-by-480                  256
    5                   640-by-48065                536
```

INIT_XGA

Initialize XGA registers and report machine setup
Receives:
Nothing
Returns:
1. byte integer of machine setup, as follows:

```
7 6 5 4 3 2 1 0
| | | | | | | | |___ 1 = XGA in system
| | | | | | | |      0 = no XGA found
| | | | | | | |_____ 1 = XGA color monitor
| | | | | | |        0 = XGA monochrome monitor
| | | | | | |_______ 1 = high resolution (1024-by-768)
| | | | | |          0 = no high resolution
| | | | | |_________ 1 = RAM = 1Mb
| | | | |            0 = RAM = 512Kb
| | | | |___________ 1 = dual monitor system
| | | |              0 = single monitor system
|_|_|_______________ UNUSED
```

Action:
XGA system is initialized and setup is tested. This initialization is
required by many other procedures in this module.

XGA_PIXEL_2

Write a screen pixel accessing XGA memory directly while in XGA mode
number 2.
Receives:
1. word integer of x coordinate of pixel
2. word integer of y coordinate of pixel
3. byte integer of pixel color in 8-bit format
Assumes:
INIT_XGA has been previously called
Returns:
Nothing

Action:

  Pixel is set

XGA_CLS_2

Clear video memory while in XGA mode number 2 using block move

  Receives:

  Nothing

  Assumes:

  INIT_XGA has been previously called

  Returns:

  Nothing

  Action:

  Direct access version of the AI_CLS procedure in the XGA1.ASM module

XGA_OFF

Turn off XGA video by clearing the Palette Mask register

  Receives:

  Nothing

  Assumes:

  INIT_XGA has been previously called

  Returns:

  Nothing

  Action:

  XGA display is disabled

XGA_ON

Turn on XGA video by setting the Palette Mask register

  Receives:

  Nothing

  Assumes:

  INIT_XGA has been previously called

  Returns:

  Nothing

  Action:

  XGA display is enabled

XGA_PALETTE

Load 256 XGA LUT color registers with data supplied by the caller

  Receives:

  1. Far pointer of 1024-byte color table in RGBx format

  Assumes:

  INIT_XGA has been previously called

Returns:
>Nothing

Action:
>LUT registers are initialed to supplied values. Caller's data to be formatted in red, blue, green, ignored, pattern.

DC_PALETTE

Set 256 XGA palette registers for the direct color mode using values recommended by IBM.

Receives:
>Nothing

Assumes:
>INIT_XGA has been previously called

Returns:
>Nothing

Action:
>XGA palette registers are initialized for mode number 5, in 65,536 colors

INIT_COP

Initialize XGA coprocessor. This procedure assumes that the procedure INIT_XGA (in this module) has been previously called and that the POS_x variables have been loaded.

Receives:
Nothing

Returns:
>1. GS = coprocessor base address
>2. FS = base address of video memory (VRAM)

Action:
>Coprocessor is initialized. The GS and FS segment registers are set for calling the coprocessor commands in this module.

COP_RECT_2

Graphics coprocessor pixBlt operation on a rectangular screen area.

Receives:
>1. word integer of x coordinate of top-left corner
>2. word integer of y coordinate of top-left corner
>3. word integer of rectangle's pixel width
>4. word integer of rectangle's pixel height
>5. byte integer of 8-bit color code

Assumes:
>1. Mode number 2 (1024-by-768 pixels in 256 colors)
>2. GS and FS segment set by INIT_COP procedure

Returns:
>Nothing

Action:
   Rectangular pixBlt is performed

COP_SYSVID_1

Graphics coprocessor pixBlt operation from a source in system memory to a
destination in video memory, using an image map encoded in 1 bit per pixel
format.
   Receives:
      1. far pointer to source bit map in RAM
      2. word integer of pixel map width
      3. word integer of pixel map height
      4. word integer of x coordinate for display
      5. word integer of y coordinate for display
      6. byte integer of 8-bit color value
   Assumes:
      1. Mode number 2 (1024-by-768 pixels in 256 colors)
      2. GS and FS segment set by INIT_COP procedure
   Returns:
      Nothing
   Action:
      PixBlt is performed

COP_SYSVID_8

Graphics coprocessor pixBlt operation from a source in system memory to a
destination in video memory, using an image map encoded in 8 bit per pixel
format.
   Receives:
      1. far pointer to source bit map in RAM
      2. word integer of pixel map width
      3. word integer of pixel map height
      4. word integer of x coordinate for display
      5. word integer of y coordinate for display
   Assumes:
      1. Mode number 2 (1024-by-768 pixels in 256 colors)
      2. GS and FS segment set by INIT_COP procedure
   Returns:
      Nothing
   Action:
      PixBlt is performed.

COP_LINE_2

Draw a line using XGA graphics coprocessor, while in mode number 2 (1024 by
768 pixels in 256 colors).
   Receives:
      1. word integer of x coordinate of line start

2. word integer of y coordinate of line start
3. word integer of x coordinate of line end
4. word integer of y coordinate of line end
5. byte integer of 8-bit color value

Assumes:

1. Mode number 2 (1024-by-768 pixels in 256 colors)
2. GS and FS segment set by INIT_COP procedure

Returns:

Nothing

Action:

Line is drawn

SPRITE_IMAGE

Load sprite image and install values in Sprite Color registers.

Receives:

1. far pointer to color code and image buffer, formatted
as follows:

```
OFFSET    UNIT        CONTENTS
  0       byte        6 low bits are RED for sprite color 0
  1       byte        6 low bits are GREEN for sprite color 0
  2       byte        6 low bits are BLUE for sprite color 0
  3       byte        6 low bits are RED for sprite color 1
  4       byte        6 low bits are GREEN for sprite color 1
  5       byte        6 low bits are BLUE for sprite color 1
  6                   16 bytes per 64 rows (1024 bytes) encoding the
                        sprite image at 2 bits per pixel
 1030     end of sprite image
```

Assumes:

INIT_XGA has been previously called

Returns:

Nothing

Action:

Sprite image and colors codes are stored in Display Controller registers

SPRITE_AT

Display sprite image at coordinates furnished by the caller.

Receives:

1. word integer of x coordinate of sprite location (range is 0 to 1023)
2. word integer of y coordinate of sprite location (range is 0 to 768)

Assumes:

INIT_XGA has been previously called

Returns:

Nothing

Action:

Sprite is displayed at entry coordinates

SPRITE_OFF

Sprite is turned off by clearing bit 0 of the Sprite Control register.

    Receives:

        Nothing

    Assumes:

        INIT_XGA has been previously called

    Returns:

        Nothing

    Action:

        Sprite image is no longer displayed

Chapter

8

SuperVGA Programming

Chapter Summary

This chapter describes the SuperVGA video hardware and its architecture, as well as the VESA SuperVGA standards and the use of the various VESA BIOS Services. It also covers programming the SuperVGA system by accessing the video hardware directly and by the use of the VESA BIOS services. The chapter concludes with a listing of the procedures in the SVGA library furnished with the book.

8.0 SuperVGA Chipsets

The term SuperVGA refers to enhancements to the standard VGA modes as furnished in some non-IBM adapters developed for PC compatible computers. The list of vendors of SuperVGA boards include the following companies:

> Appian Technology
> ATI Technologies, Inc.
> Chips and Technologies
> Cirrus Logic
> Everex Systems, Inc.
> Genoa Systems
> Oak Technology, Inc.
> Orchid Technology
> Paradise
> Sigma Designs
> SMOS Systems, Inc.
> STB Systems, Inc.
> Tecmar
> Tseng Labs
> Video Seven, and
> Western Digital

The common characteristic of all SuperVGA boards is the presence of graphics features that exceed the VGA standard in definition or color range. In other words, a SuperVGA graphics board is capable of executing not only the standard VGA modes, but also other modes that provide higher definition or greater color range than VGA. These are usually called the SuperVGA Enhanced Modes.

In the late eighties, the proliferation of SuperVGA hardware gave rise to many compatibility problems, due to the fact that the enhanced features of the SuperVGA cards were not standardized; therefore the SuperVGA enhancements in the card produced by one manufacturer were incompatible with the enhancements in a card made by another company. This situation often presented unsurmountable problems to the graphics application programmer, who would find that an application designed to take advantage of the graphics enhancements in a SuperVGA card would not execute correctly in another one.

At the operating system level these incompatibility problems are easier to correct than at the application level. For example, the manufacturers of SuperVGA boards often furnish software drivers for Windows and Operating System /2. Once the driver is installed, the graphics environment in the operating system will be able to use the enhancements provided by a particular SuperVGA board. By the same token, applications that perform graphics functions by means of operating system services will also take advantage of the SuperVGA enhancements.

On the other hand, graphics applications that control the hardware directly would not be able to take advantage of a system-level driver. Fortunately, some graphics programs are designed with a flexible video interface. In this case, the application software can be more easily adapted to the features of a particular SuperVGA. This is the case with AutoCad, Ventura Publisher, Wordperfect, Lotus 1-2-3, and other high-end graphics applications for the PC. But, for those applications in which the video functions are embedded in the code, the adaptation to a nonstandard video mode often implies a major program redesign.

In 1989, in an attempt to solve this lack of standardization, several manufacturers of SuperVGA boards formed the Video Electronics Standards Association (VESA). Most of the companies listed at the beginning of this section are now members of VESA. In October of 1989, VESA released its first SuperVGA standard. The VESA standard defined several enhanced video modes and implemented a BIOS extension designed to provide a few fundamental video services in a compatible fashion. Because of this advantage in compatibility and portability, our treatment of SuperVGA programming focuses on the use of the VESA BIOS functions.

8.0.1 SuperVGA Memory Architecture

In previous chapters we saw that the IBM microcomputer video systems are memory mapped. In VGA the video memory space extends from A0000H to BFFFFH. The 64K space starting at segment base A000H is devoted to graphics and the 64K space starting at segment base B000H is for alphanumeric modes. This means that the total space reserved for video operations is of 128K. But, since some systems are set up with two monitors, one operating in alphanumeric modes (base address B000H for monochrome systems and B800H for color systems), the actual video space for graphics operations is practically limited to 64K.

Not much video data can be stored in a 64K memory space. For example, if each screen pixel is encoded in one memory byte, then the maximum screen data that can be stored in 65,536 bytes is of 256 square pixels. In Chapter 2 we saw that the VGA screen in 640-by-480 pixels resolution requires 307,200 bytes. We also saw how the VGA designers were able to compress video data by implementing a latching scheme and a planar architecture. Consequently, in VGA mode number 18 a pixel is encoded into a single memory bit, although it can be displayed in 16 different colors. The latching mechanism (see Figure 2.4) is based on four memory maps of 38,400 bytes each. All four color maps (red, green, blue, and intensity) start at segment base A000H. The pixel displayed is determined by the value stored in the Bit Mask register of the VGA Graphics Controller group. (See Section 2.2.4.)

16 Color Extensions

Simple arithmetic shows a memory surplus in many VGA modes. For example, if the resolution is of 640-by-480 pixels, the video data stored in each map takes up 38,400 bytes of the available 65,536. Therefore, there are 27,136 unused bytes in each map. The original idea of enhancing the VGA system was based on using this surplus memory to store video data. It is clearly possible to have an 800-by-600 pixel display divided into four maps of 60,000 bytes each, and yet not exceed the 64K space allowed for each color map nor the total 265K furnished with the VGA system.

The 800-by-600 pixel resolution in 16 colors appears as a natural extension to VGA mode number 18. This mode, which was later designated as mode 6AH by the VESA standards, could be programmed in a similar manner as mode number 18. This extension, which could be achieved with minor changes in the VGA hardware, provided a 36 percent increase in the display area.

Another extension to the VGA system is a wider pixel mask register to make possible more than the 16 colors that can be encoded in a 4-bit field. However, this has never been implemented in a SuperVGA system due to performance factors and other hardware considerations.

Memory Banks

In Chapter 2 we saw that the memory structure for VGA 256-color mode number 19 is based, not on a multiplane scheme but on a much simpler format that maps a memory byte to each screen pixel. (See Figure 2.5.) In this manner, 256 color combinations can be directly encoded into a data byte, which correspond to the 256 DAC registers of the VGA hardware. The method is straightforward and uncomplicated. However, if the entire video space is to be contained in 64K of memory, the maximum resolution would be limited to the 256 square pixels previously mentioned. In other words, a rectangular screen of 320-by-200 pixels nearly fills the allotted 64K.

Therefore, if the resolution for a 256-color mode were to exceed 256 square pixels, it would be necessary to find other ways of mapping video memory into 64K of system RAM. The mechanism adopted by the SuperVGA designers was based on the well-known technique known as bank switching. In a bank switching scheme the video display hardware maps several 64K blocks of RAM to different locations in video memory. Addressing of the multisegment space is by means of a hardware mechanism that selects which video memory area is currently located at the system's aperture. In the SuperVGA implementation, the system aperture is usually located at segment base A000H. The entire process is reminiscent of memory page switching in the LIM (Lotus/Intel/Microsoft) Extended Memory environment. Figure 8.1 schematically shows mapping of several memory banks to the video space and the map selection mechanism for CPU addressing.

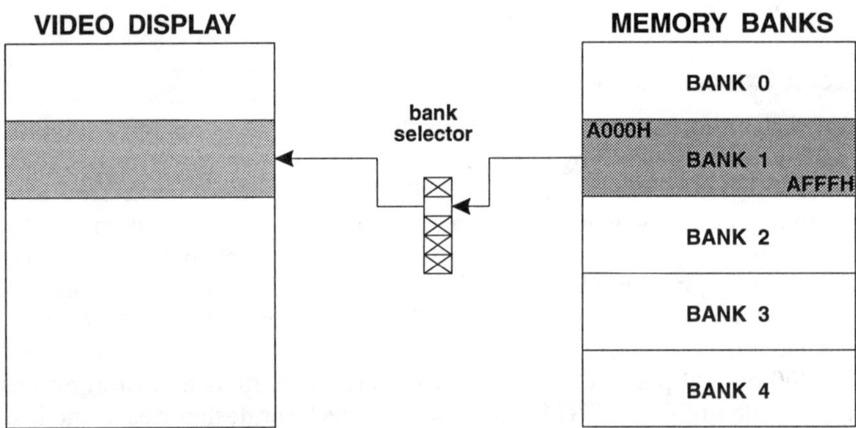

Figure 8.1 *Memory Maps to Video Memory Mapping*

In Chapter 7 we adopted the term aperture from the XGA terminology, which is used to denote the processor's window into video memory. For example, if the addressable area of video memory starts at physical address A0000H and extends to B0000H, we say that the CPU has a 64K aperture into video memory (10000H = 64K). In SuperVGA documentation the word "granularity" is often used in this context. In Figure 8.1 we can see that the bank selector determines which area of video memory is mapped to the processor's aperture. Therefore, the area of the video display can be updated by the processor. In other words, in the memory banking scheme the processor cannot access the entire video memory at once. In Figure 8.1 we can see that we would have to perform five bank switches in order to update the entire screen.

256 Color Extensions

The SuperVGA alternative for increasing definition beyond the VGA limit is a
banking mechanism similar to the one shown in Figure 8.1. This scheme, in
which a memory byte encodes the 256 color combinations for each screen pixel,
does away with the pixel masking complications of VGA mode number 18. On
the other hand, it introduces the complications of a bank selection device which
we already encountered in XGA programming. (See Section 7.1.2.) The Super-
VGA method has no precedent in CGA, EGA, or VGA systems since it is not
interleaved nor does it require memory planes or pixel masking. Although it is
similar to VGA mode number 19 regarding color encoding, mode number 19
does not require bank switching.

It should be noted that the neat, rectangular window design shown in Figure
8.1 does not always conform with reality. Several implementations of Super-
VGA multicolor modes use non-rectangular windows that start and end inside
a scan line. This complicates the use of optimizing routines since the software
cannot restrict its checking for a window boundary to the start and end of scan
lines.

Pixel Addressing

The calculations required for setting an individual pixel in the 256 color modes
depend upon the size of the memory banks, the number of pixels per row and
of screen rows, and the start address of video memory. Although it is quite
feasible to design a routine that performs in different SuperVGA chipsets, the
efficiency of such coding would be necessarily low. The VESA standardization
offers a solution to the programming complications brought on by different
architectures of the various SuperVGA chipsets. In reality, since most Super-
VGA systems use a 64K bank size and a processor's window into video memory
located at segment base A000H, the variations are reduced to the bank
switching operations.

8.1 The VESA SuperVGA Standard

The Video Electronics Standards Association was founded in 1989 with the
intention of providing a common programming interface for SuperVGA extended modes. In order to achieve this, each manufacturer furnishes a VESA
SuperVGA BIOS extension. The BIOS can be in the adapter ROM or in a TSR
routine. Today, most SuperVGA manufacturers are members of VESA and
provide a VESA BIOS with their products.

The first release of the VESA SuperVGA standard was published in October
1, 1989 (version 1.0). A second release was published in June 2, 1990 (version
1.1). The present release is dated October 22, 1991 (version 1.2).

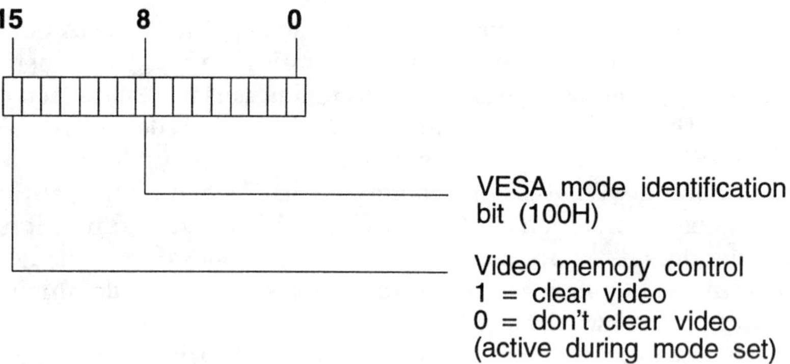

Figure 8.2 *VESA Mode Bitmap*

8.1.1 VESA SuperVGA Modes

The first element of VESA standardization is the definition of standard modes for the SuperVGA extensions. The VESA mode numbering scheme takes into account that the VGA modes are in the range 0 to 7FH. This range limitation is due to the fact that the VGA BIOS mode setting function (service number 0) uses the high-order bit to determine if video memory is to be cleared. To get around this restriction, the VESA mode number is a word-size value, which is passed to the VESA BIOS in the BX register. Figure 8.2 shows the bitmap of the VESA MODE numbers.

Notice that bit number 8 identifies a VESA mode. That is, all VESA modes start at number 100H. Also that bit number 15 is used during mode set operations to indicate if video memory is to be cleared. Table 8.1 lists the VESA extended modes.

8.1.2 Memory Windows

The VESA standard accommodates variations in the SuperVGA implementations by recognizing two different types of hardware windows into video memory. The first and simpler type consists of a single window which can be read and written by the CPU. The disadvantage of a read-write window becomes evident when a pixBlt operation crosses the limit of this window. Because, in this case, the software is forced to switch banks and the CPU to reset the segment register base during the transfer. This double burden can considerably degrade performance.

A partial solution is to provide separate windows for read and write operations. One possible option is to have two windows located at the same address: one for read and the other one for write operations. This scheme, sometimes called *dual overlapping windows*, allows selecting both windows simultaneously. Once the source and destination windows are selected, the data block can be rapidly moved by means of a REP MOVSB instruction.

Table 8.1 *VESA BIOS Modes*

| MODE NUMBER | | TEXT/ | RESOLUTION | | |
15 BITS	7 BITS	GRAPHICS	PIXELS	COLUMNS/ROWS	COLORS
100H		GRAPHICS	640 by 400		256
101H		GRAPHICS	640 by 480		256
102H	6AH	GRAPHICS	800 by 600		16
103H		GRAPHICS	800 by 600		256
104H		GRAPHICS	1024 by 768		16
105H		GRAPHICS	1024 by 768		256
106H		GRAPHICS	1280 by 1024		16
107H		GRAPHICS	1280 by 1024		256
108H		TEXT		80 by 60	
109H		TEXT		132 by 25	
10AH		TEXT		132 by 43	
10BH		TEXT		132 by 50	
10CH		TEXT		132 by 60	
* 10DH		GRAPHICS	300 by 200		32K
10EH		GRAPHICS	320 by 200		64K
10FH		GRAPHICS	320 by 200		16.8Mb
110H		GRAPHICS	640 by 480		32K
111H		GRAPHICS	640 by 480		64K
112H		GRAPHICS	640 by 480		16.8Mb
113H		GRAPHICS	800 by 600		32K
114H		GRAPHICS	800 by 600		64K
115H		GRAPHICS	800 by 600		16.8Mb
116H		GRAPHICS	1024 by 768		32K
117H		GRAPHICS	1024 by 768		64K
118H		GRAPHICS	1024 by 768		16.8Mb
119H		GRAPHICS	1280 by 1024		32K
11AH		GRAPHICS	1280 by 1024		64K
11BH		GRAPHICS	1280 by 1024		16.8Mb

* modes after 10DH were introduced in VESA BIOS version 1.2

A second alternative to the two windows option is to locate the read and write windows at separate addresses. For example, a SuperVGA chipset can locate the write window at base address A000H and the read window at base address B000H. This would extend addressable memory to 128K and considerably simplify pixBlt operations. The objection to this approach is that a two monitor system requires the B000H window for text operations, therefore this configuration would not be possible. Another solution is to cut the 64K window in half and provide separate 32K windows, one for read and the other one for write operations. The objection in this case is that normal display operation would require twice as many bank switches. Figure 8.3 is a schematic representation of the three possible windowing options.

8.2 The VESA BIOS

The VESA BIOS has been designed to perform only those operations that are strictly necessary to achieve portability and hardware transparency of the SuperVGA system. The fundamental functions of the VESA BIOS, as used in SuperVGA programming, are the following:

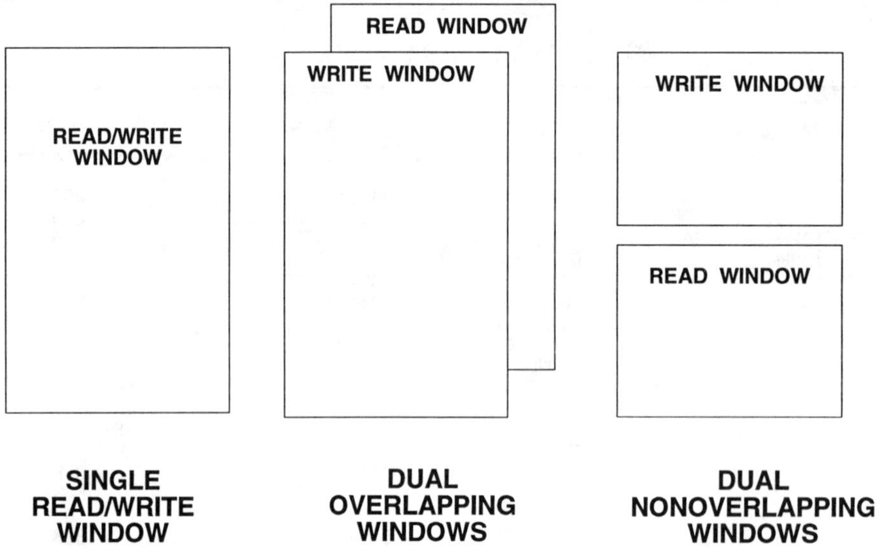

Figure 8.3 *VESA Window Types*

1. Obtaining SuperVGA and mode information

2. Setting a standard VESA extended mode

3. Performing bank switching operations

The VESA BIOS does not provide graphics primitives. Furthermore, not even pixel setting and reading operations are included in the standard. Due to this design the software overhead is kept at a minimum. The actual implementation of the functions are left to the chipset manufacturer, who also has the option of furnishing the BIOS in ROM, or as a TSR.

Of the functions provided by the VESA BIOS the bank switching operation is the most crucial in regards to display system performance. This is because bank switching is usually included in read and write loops and, therefore, in the program's critical path of execution. To provide the best possible performance the VESA BIOS allows access to the bank switching function directly, by means of a far call to the chipset manufacturer's own entry point to the service routine. This approach simplifies and accelerates access to the actual bank switching code. The result is that display routines that use VESA BIOS functions can perform bank switching operations almost as efficiently as routines that access the SuperVGA hardware directly.

8.2.1 VESA BIOS Services

The VESA BIOS is an extension of VGA BIOS video services located at interrupt 10H. Access to the VESA BIOS is by means of service number 79 (4FH). The subfunction refers to the specific VESA BIOS service. Eight VESA BIOS services have been implemented to date. These are shown in Table 8.2.

Table 8.2 VESA BIOS Sub-services to BIOS INT 10H

SUB-SERVICE	DESCRIPTION
00H	Return SuperVGA information
01H	Return SuperVGA mode information
02H	Set SuperVGA mode
03H	Return current video mode
04H	Save/restore SuperVGA video state
05H	Switch banks
06H	Set/get logical scan line length
07H	Set/get display start

The following code fragment is a general template for accessing the VESA
BIOS sub-services:

```
MOV       AH,79          ; VESA BIOS service number
MOV       AL,?           ; AL holds subservice number
  .                      ; Other registers are loaded
  .                      ; with the values required by
  .                      ; the subservice
INT       10H
```

All VESA BIOS functions return the same error codes: AL = 79 (4FH) if the
function is supported, AH = 0 if the call was successful.

Subservice 0 — System Information

VESA BIOS sub-service number 0 provides general VESA information. The
caller furnishes a pointer to a 256-bytes data buffer which is filled by the VESA
service. The following code fragment shows the set of variables and the register
setup for this service.

```
DATA      SEGMENT
;********************|
;    parameter block |
;********************|
VESA_BUFFER      DB      '      '  ; 'VESA' signature
VESA_VERSION     DW      ?         ; Version number
OEM_PTR_OFF      DW      ?         ; OEM string offset pointer
OEM_PTR_SEG      DW      ?         ; OEM string segment pointer
CAPABILITIES     DD      ?         ; Adapter capabilities
                                   ; (first implemented in VESA
                                   ; BIOS version 1.2)
MODES_PTR_OFF    DW      ?         ; Pointer to modes list, offset
MODES_PTR_SEG    DW      ?         ; Segment for idem
MEM_BLOCKS       DW      ?         ; Count of 64K memory blocks
                                   ; (first implemented in VESA
                                   ; BIOS version 1.1)
```

```
                     DB        242 DUP (?) ; Remainder of block
;
DATA    ENDS
;
;
CODE    SEGMENT
          .

          .

          .


; Call VESA BIOS sub-service number 0 to obtain SuperVGA
; information
; Passed by caller:
;          DS:DI = pointer to 256-byte data buffer
; Returned by service:
;          AX = 004FH if no error
;          Data stored in the caller's buffer
;
;********************|
;   setup registers  |
;********************|
; Initialize entry registers
        LEA      DI,VESA_BUFFER ; Start of data buffer
; VESA BIOS sub-service number 0 uses ES as a segment base
        PUSH     ES              ; Caller's ES
        PUSH     DS              ; CAller's DS
        POP      ES              ; to ES
;********************|
; get VESA information |
;********************|
        MOV      AH,79           ; VESA BIOS service number
        MOV      AL,0            ; This subservice
        INT      10H             ; BIOS video service
; At this point AX must hold 004FH if the call executed
        CMP      AX,004FH        ; Returned code
        JE       OK_VESA_0       ; Go if valid value
;********************|
;     ERROR exit      |
;********************|
; The programmer should code an error routine at this point
; to handle an invalid call to the VESA BIOS function
BAD_VESA:
          .

          .

          .

OK_VESA_0:
```

```
; Test buffer for a valid 'VESA' signature
        CMP     WORD PTR [DI],'EV'       ; First two letters
        JE      OK_VE           ; Go if matched
        JMP     BAD_VESA        ; Exit if not matched
OK_VE:
        CMP     WORD PTR [DI+2],'AS'     ; Last two letters
        JNE     BAD_VESA        ; Go if not matched
; At this point the VESA BIOS call to sub-service number 0
; was successful
            .
            .
            .

CODE    ENDS
```

The call to subservice number 0 is usually made to determine if there is a VESA BIOS available, although the subservice provides other information that could also be useful. Testing for a valid VESA BIOS is a two step process: first the code tests for the value 004FH in the AX register. This value corresponds to the standard VESA error codes mentioned at the beginning of this section. Once this first test is passed, the code makes certain that the 4-character 'VESA' signature is stored at the start of the buffer. If these tests are satisfactory, execution can continue on the assumption that a valid VESA BIOS is present and that its functions are available to the software.

The data segment of the above code fragment shows the most important items returned by sub-service number 0. The field contents are as follows:

VESA_BUFFER is the label that marks the start of the buffer. At this label the BIOS will store the word 'VESA' which serves as a string signature that identifies the BIOS.

VESA_VERSION is a two-byte field that encodes the current version of the VESA BIOS. The encoding is in fractional form, for example, the value 3131H corresponds to the ASCII digits 1,1 and represents version 1.1 of the VESA BIOS. An application can assume upward compatibility in the VESA BIOS.

OEM_PTR_OFF and OEM_PTR_SEG are two word variables that encode the offset and segment values of a far pointer to an identification string supplied by the board manufacturer. Board-specific routines would use this string to check for compatible hardware.

The CAPABILITIES label is a 4-byte field designed to hold a code that represents the general features of the SuperVGA environment. This field was not used until VESA BIOS version 1.2, released in October 22, 1991. At this time bit number 0 of this field was enabled to encode adapters with the possibility of storing extended primary color codes. In VESA BIOS version 1.2, and later, a value of 1 in bit 0 of the CAPABILITIES field indicates that the DAC registers can be programmed to hold more than 6-bit color codes. A value of 0 indicates that the DAC register is standard VGA, with 6-bits per primary color. Changing the bit width of the DAC registers is performed by calling subservice number 8, discussed later in this section.

MODES_PTR_OFF and MODES_PTR_SEG are word variables that hold the offset and segment values of a far pointer to a list of implemented SuperVGA modes. Each mode occupies one word in the list. The code 0FFFFH serves as a list terminator. An application can examine the list of modes to make certain that a specific one is available or to select the best one among possible candidates.

MEM_BLOCKS field encodes, in a word variable, the number of 64K blocks of memory installed in the adapter. Notice that this field was first implemented in VESA BIOS version 1.1.

Subservice 1 – Mode Information

VESA BIOS subservice number 1 provides information about a specific Super-VGA VESA mode. The caller furnishes a pointer to a 256-bytes data buffer, which is filled by the VESA service, as well as the number of the desired mode. The following code fragment shows a possible set of data variables and register setup for this service.

```
DATA      SEGMENT
;
;*********************|
;   first field group  |
;*********************|
VESA_INFO          DW        ?              ; Mode attributes, mapped as
                                            ; follows:
                                            ; 4 3 2 1 0 <= bits
                                            ; | | | | |__ 0 = mode not supported
                                            ; | | | |     1 = mode supported
                                            ; | | | |____ 0 = no extended mode info
                                            ; | | |       1 = extended mode info
                                            ; | | |_______0 = no output functions
                                            ; | |         1 = output functions
                                            ; | |________ 0 = monochrome mode
                                            ; |           1 = color mode
                                            ; |__________ 0 = text mode
                                            ;             1 = graphics mode
                                            ; 15..5 = RESERVED
WIN_A_ATTS         DB        ?              ; Window A attributes
WIN_B_ATTS         DB        ?              ; Window B attributes
WIN_GRAIN          DW        ?              ; Window granularity
WIN_SIZE           DW        ?              ; Window size
WIN_A_SEG          DW        ?              ; Segment address for window A
WIN_B_SEG          DW        ?              ; Segment address for window B
BANK_FUN           DD        ?              ; Far pointer to bank switch
                                            ; function
BYTES_PER_ROW      DW        ?              ; Bytes per screen row
```

```
        ;********************|
        ;   second field group  |
        ;********************|
        ; Extended mode data. Optional until VESA BIOS version 1.2
        X_RES           DW      ?       ; Horizontal resolution
        Y_RES           DW      ?       ; Vertical resolution
        X_CHAR_SIZE     DB      ?       ; Pixel width of character cell
        Y_CHAR_SIZE     DB      ?       ; Pixel height of character cell
        BIT_PLANES      DB      ?       ; Number of bit planes
        BITS_PER_PIX    DB      ?       ; Bits per pixel in this mode
        NUM_OF_BANKS    DB      ?       ; Number of video memory banks
        MEM_MODEL       DB      ?       ; Memory model, as follows:
                                        ; 00H = text mode
                                        ; 01H = CGA graphics
                                        ; 02H = Hercules graphics
                                        ; 03H = 4-plane architecture
                                        ; 04H = Packed pixel
                                        ;       architecture
                                        ; 05H = 256 color (unchained)
                                        ; The following were defined
                                        ; in VESA BIOS version 1.2:
                                        ; 06H = Direct color
                                        ; 07H = YUV color
                                        ; 08H - 0FF = not yet defined
        BANK_SIZE       DB      ?       ; Kilobytes per bank
        PLANES          DB      ?       ; Number of planes:
                                        ; 4 in 16 color modes
                                        ; 1 in 256 color modes
                        DB      1       ; Reserved for BIOS
        ;********************|
        ;   third field group   |
        ;********************|
        ; Direct color fields. Defined in VESA BIOS version 1.2
        RED_MASK        DB      ?       ; Bit size of red mask
        RED_POSITION    DB      ?       ; Red mask LSB position
        GREEN_MASK      DB      ?       ; Bit size of green mask
        GREEN_POSITION  DB      ?       ; Green mask LSB position
        BLUE_MASK       DB      ?       ; Bit size of blue mask
        BLUE_POSITION   DB      ?       ; Blue mask LSB position
        RSVD_MASK       DB      ?       ; Bit size of reserved mask
        RSVD_POSITION   DB      ?       ; Reserved mask LSB position
        DC_INFO         DB      ?       ; Attributes of direct color
                                        ; modes, as follows:
                                        ; bit 0 = color ramp
                                        ;       0 = fixed
                                        ;       1 = programmable
```

```
                                        ; bit 1 = Reserved field bits
                                        ;          0 = not usable
                                        ;          1 = usable
                        DB        216 DUP (?) ; Remainder of block
DATA      ENDS
;
CODE      SEGMENT
              .

              .

              .
;*********************|
;  get VESA mode info |
;*********************|
; Passed by caller:
; CX = mode number, as follows:
; GRAPHICS         number           resolution          colors
;                  100H             640-by-400            256
;                  101H             640-by-480            256
;                  102H             800-by-600             16
;                  103H             800-by-600            256
;                  104H             1024-by-768            16
;                  105H             1024-by-768           256
;                  106H             1280-by-1224           16
;                  107H             1280-by-1224          256
; TEXT             108H              80-by-60
;                  109H             132-by-25
;                  10AH             132-by-43
;                  10BH             132-by-50
;                  10CH             132-by-60
;          DS:DI = pointer to 256-byte data buffer
; Returned by service:
;          AX = 004FH if no error
;          Data stored in the caller's buffer
;*********************|
;    register setup   |
;*********************|
; CX to hold requested mode number
; DS:SI -> information block supplied by service
; Initialize entry registers
        LEA       DI,VESA_INFO      ; Start of data buffer
        MOV       CX,105H           ; Mode requested
; VESA BIOS sub-service number 1 uses ES as a segment base
        PUSH      ES                ; Caller's ES
        PUSH      DS                ; Caller's DS
        POP       ES                ; to ES
;*********************|
```

```
; get VESA information  |
;**********************|
        MOV     AH,79           ; VESA BIOS service number
        MOV     AL,1            ; This subservice
        INT     10H             ; BIOS video service
; At this point AX must hold 004FH if the call executed
        CMP     AX,004FH        ; Returned code
        JE      OK_MODE         ; Go if valid value
;**********************|
;       ERROR exit     |
;**********************|
; The programmer should code an error routine at this point
; to handle the case of an invalid VESA BIOS call
        .
        .
        .

OK_MODE:
; At this point the VESA BIOS call to subservice number 1
; was successful. However, the code cannot assume that the
; mode requested is implemented in the system
        .
        .
        .

CODE    ENDS
```

The call to subservice number 1 is usually made to determine if the desired mode is available in the hardware and, if so, to obtain certain fundamental parameters required by the program. If the call is successful, the code can examine the data at offset 0 in the data buffer in order to determine the mode's fundamental attributes. These mode attributes are shown in Figure 8.4.

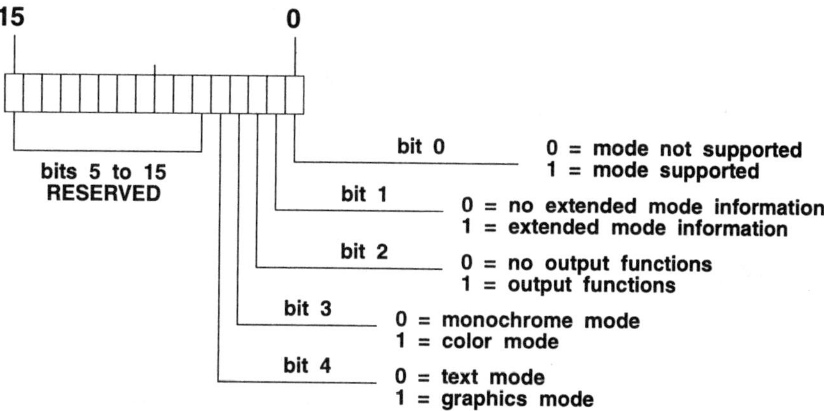

Figure 8.4 *VESA Mode Attribute Bitmap*

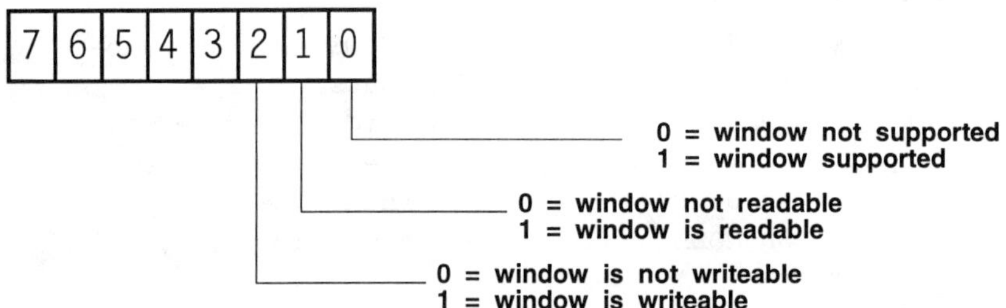

Figure 8.5 *Window Attributes Bitmap*

The data segment of the above code fragment show the items returned by subservice number 1. The data items are divided into three field groups. The contents of the variables in the first field group are as follows:

WIN_A_ATTS and WIN_B_ATTS are two bytes that encode the attributes of the two possible memory banks, or windows. Figure 8.5 is a bitmap of the window attribute bytes.

The code can inspect the window attribute bits to determine the window types used in the system. (See Figure 8.3.)

The WIN_GRAIN word specifies the granularity of each window. The granularity unit is one kilobyte. The value can be used to determine the minimum video memory boundary for the window.

The WIN_SIZE word specifies the size of the windows in kilobytes. This value can be used in tailoring bank switching operations to specific hardware configurations. (See Section 8.3.1.)

The word labeled WIN_A_SEG holds the segment base address for window A and the word labeled WIN_B_SEG the base address for window B. The base address in graphics modes is usually A000H, however, the code should not take this for granted.

The doubleword labeled BANK_FUN holds a far pointer to the bank shifting function in the BIOS. An application can shift memory banks using VESA BIOS sub-service number 5, described later in this section, or by means of a direct call to the service routine located at the address stored in this variable. The call can be coded with the instruction:

```
CALL      DWORD PTR BANK_FUN
```

BYTES_PER_ROW is a word variable that encodes the number of bytes in each screen logical pixel row. Notice that this value can be larger than the number of pixels in a physical scan line.

The variables in the second field group are of optional nature. Bit number 1 of the mode attribute bitmap (see Figure 8.4) can be read to determine if this part of the data block is available. The contents of the various fields in the second group are described in the data segment of the preceding code fragment.

The direct color fields from the third field group. These fields were first implemented in VESA BIOS version 1.2 to support SuperVGA systems with color capabilities that extended beyond the 256 color modes. The contents of the various fields in the third group are described in the data segment of the preceding code fragment. Because, to date, very few SuperVGA adapters support the direct color modes, their programming is not considered in this book.

Subservice 2 – Set Video Mode

VESA BIOS subservice number 2 is used to initialize a video mode supported by the adapter. The VESA mode number is passed to the subservice in the BX register. The high-order bit, which is sometimes called the *clear memory flag*, is set to request that video memory not be cleared. The following code fragment shows a call to this VESA BIOS service.

```
;*********************|
;    set video mode   |
;*********************|
; Select mode 105H using VESA BIOS subservice number 2
        MOV     BX,105H             ; Mode number and high bit = 0
                                    ; to request clear video
        MOV     AH,79               ; VESA BIOS service number
        MOV     AL,2                ; This subservice
        INT     10H                 ; BIOS video service
; Test for valid returned value
        CMP     AX,004FH            ; Status for no error
        JE      MODE_IS_SET         ; No error during mode set
;*********************|
;    ERROR exit       |
;*********************|
; The programmer should code an error routine at this point
; to handle the possibility of a mode setting error
        .
        .
        .

; At this label the mode was set satisfactorily
MODE_IS_SET:
        .
        .
        .
```

Subservice 3 – Get Video Mode

VESA BIOS subservice number 3 is used to obtain the current video mode. The VESA mode number is returned by the subservice in the BX register. The following code fragment shows a call to this VESA BIOS service.

```
;********************|
;     get video mode     |
;********************|
; VESA BIOS sub-service number 3 to obtain current video mode
        MOV     AH,79           ; VESA BIOS service number
        MOV     AL,3            ; This subservice
        INT     10H             ; BIOS video service
; Test for valid returned value
        CMP     AX,004FH        ; Status for no error
        JE      MODE_AVAILABLE  ; No error during mode set
;********************|
;     ERROR exit          |
;********************|
; The programmer should code an error routine at this point
; to handle the possibility of a mode reading error

        .

        .

        .

; At this label the mode was read satisfactorily. The BX
; register holds the mode number
MODE_AVAILABLE:

        .

        .

        .
```

Subservice 4 – Save/Restore Video State

VESA BIOS subservice number 4 is used to save and restore the state of the video system. This service, which is an extension of BIOS service number 28, is often used in a multitasking operating system to preserve the task states and by applications that manage two or more video environments. The subservice can be requested in three different modes, passed to the VESA BIOS routine in the DL register.

Mode number 0 (DL = 0) of subservice number 4 returns the size of the save/restore buffer. The 4 low bits of the CX register encode the machine state buffer to be reported. The bitmap for the various machine states is shown in Figure 8.6.

The units of buffer size returned by mode number 0, of subservice number 4, are 64-byte blocks. The block count is found in the BX register.

Mode number 1 (DL = 1), of subservice number 4, saves the machine video state requested in the CX register. (See Figure 8.6.) The caller should provide a pointer to a buffer sufficiently large to hold the requested state data. The size of the buffer can be dynamically determined by means of a call using mode number 0, described above. The pointer to the buffer is passed in ES:BX.

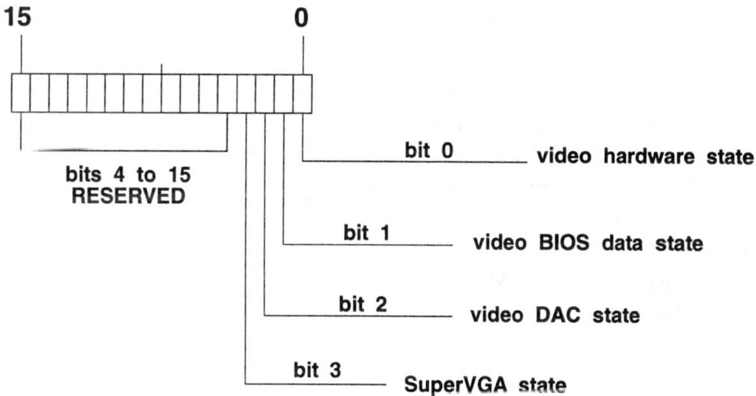

Figure 8.6 *VESA BIOS Machine State Bit Map*

Mode number 2 (DL = 2), of subservice number 4, restores the machine video state requested in the CX register (see Figure 8.6). The caller should provide a pointer to the buffer that holds data obtained by means of a call using mode number 1. (See Figure 8.6.)

Subservice 5 – Switch Bank

VESA BIOS subservice number 5 is used to switch memory banks in those modes that require it. Software should call subservice number 1 to determine the size and address of the banks before calling this function. Two modes of this sub-service are implemented: one to switch to a desired bank and another one to request the number of the currently selected bank.

Mode number 0 (BH = 0) is the switch bank command. The BL register is used by the caller to encode window A (value = 0) or window B (value = 1). The bank number is passed in the DX register. The following code fragment shows the necessary processing:

```
; VESA BIOS subservice number 5 register setup
        MOV     BX,0                    ; Select bank in window A
                                        ; and bank switch function
; BH = 0 to select bank
; BL = 0 to select window A
; DX = bank number
        MOV     AX,4F05H                ; Service and subservice
        INT     10H
        .

        .

        .
```

Mode number 1 of subservice (BH = 0) is used to obtain the number of the memory bank currently selected. The BL register is used by the caller to encode window A (value = 0) or window B (value = 1). The bank number is reported in the DX register.

Earlier in this section we mentioned that an application can also access the bank switching function in the BIOS by means of a far call to the service routine. The address of the service routine is placed in a far pointer variable by the successful execution of subservice number 1. For the far call operation the register setup for BH, BL, and DX is the same as for using subservice 5. However, in the far call version AH and AL need not be loaded, no meaningful information is returned, and AX and DX are destroyed.

Subservice 6 – Set/Get Logical Scan Line

VESA BIOS subservice number 6 is used to set or read the length of the logical scan line. Observe that the logical scan line can be wider than the physical scan line supported by the video hardware. This subservice was first implemented in VESA BIOS version 1.1. For this reason it is not available in the BIOS functions of earlier adapters.

Subservice 7 – Set/Get Display Start

VESA BIOS subservice number 7 is used to set or read from the logical page data the pixel to be displayed in the top-left screen corner. The subservice is useful to applications that use a logical screen that is larger than the physical display in order to facilitate panning and screen scrolling effects. As is the case with subservice number 6, this subservice was first implemented in VESA BIOS version 1.1. For this reason it is not available in the BIOS functions of many adapters.

Subservice 8 – Set/Get DAC Palette Control

VESA BIOS subservice number 8 was designed to facilitate programming of SuperVGA systems with more than 6-bit fields in the primary color registers of the DAC. The subservice contains two modes. Mode number 0 (BL = 0) is used to set a DAC color register width. The desired width value, in bits, is passed by the caller in the BH register. Mode number 1 (BL = 1) is used to obtain the current bit width for each primary color. The bit width is returned in the BH registers. The standard bit width for VGA systems is 6.

This subservice was first implemented in version 1.2 of the VESA BIOS, released in October 22, 1991. Therefore, it is not available in adapters with earlier versions of the VESA BIOS. Another feature introduced in VESA BIOS version 1.2 is the use of bit 0 of the CAPABILITIES field (see subservice 0 earlier in this section) to encode the presence of DAC registers capable of storing color encodings of more than 6 bits. Applications that propose to use subservice 8 should first test the low-order bit of the CAPABILITIES field to determine if the feature is implemented in the hardware.

8.3 Programming the SuperVGA System

Programming a particular SuperVGA chipset requires obtaining specific technical data from the manufacturer. The resulting code has little, if any, portability to other systems. This approach is used in coding hardware-specific drivers that take full advantage of the capabilities of the system. An alternative method that insures greater portability of the code at a small price in performance is the use of the VESA BIOS services described starting at Section 8.2.

It is theoretically possible to design a general-purpose graphics routine that operates in every SuperVGA chipset and display mode. However, this universality can only be achieved at a substantial price in performance, an element that is usually critical to graphics software. For this reason, the design and coding of mode-specific graphics routines is generally considered a more efficient approach. By using VESA BIOS functions it is possible to design mode-specific routines that are compatible with most SuperVGA systems that support the particular mode.

In the examples that follow we have used VESA BIOS mode number 105H with a resolution of 1024-by-768 pixels in 256 colors. We have selected this mode because it is compatible with modes used in 8514/A and XGA systems, and also because it is widely available in fully-equipped SuperVGA adapters. The reader should be able to readily convert these routines to other SuperVGA graphics modes.

8.3.1 Address Calculations

Address calculations in a SuperVGA mode depend on the screen dimensions and the location of the video buffer in the system's memory space. In a mode-specific routine the number of pixels per row can be entered as a numeric value. In modes that require more than one memory bank the bank size must also enter into the address calculations. Most SuperVGA adapters use a bank size of 64K, which can be hard-coded in the address calculation routine. On the other hand, it is possible to use a memory variable that stores the number of pixels per row and the bank size parameters in order to design address calculation routines that will work in more than one mode. In the following code fragment we have assumed that the SuperVGA is in VESA mode 105H, with 1024 pixels per scan line and that the bank size is 64K. The display routines assume that the base address of the video buffer is A000H.

```
; Calculate pixel address from the following coordinates:
;       CX = x coordinate of pixel
;       DX = y coordinate of pixel
; Code assumes:
;       1. SVGA is in a 1024 by 768 pixel mode in 256 colors
;            (mode number 105H)
;       2. Bank size is 64K
; Get address in SVGA memory space
```

```
        CLC                              ; Clear carry flag
        PUSH    AX                       ; Save color value
        MOV     AX,1024                  ; Pixels per scan line
        MUL     DX                       ; DX holds line count of address
        ADD     AX,CX                    ; Add pixels in current line
        ADC     DX,0                     ; Answer in DX:AX
                                         ; DL = bank, AX = offset
        MOV     BX,AX                    ; Offset to BX
          .

          .
```

At this point BX holds the pixel offset and DX the bank number. Note that the pixel offset is the offset within the selected bank, and not the offset from the start of the screen as is often the case in VGA routines.

8.3.2 Bank Switching Operations

In a SuperVGA adapter set to VESA mode number 105H (resolution of 1024-by-768 pixels in 256 colors) the number of video memory banks depends on the bank size. With a typical bank size of 64K the entire video memory space requires 12 memory banks, since:

$$\frac{1024 \times 768}{65536} = 12$$

In order to update the entire video screen the software has to perform 12 bank switches. This would be the case in performing a clear screen operation. Furthermore, many relatively small-sized screen objects cross one or more bank boundaries. In fact, in VESA SuperVGA mode 105H any graphics object or window that exceeds 64 pixels in height will necessarily overflow one bank.

For these reasons bank switching operations should be optimized to perform their function as quickly as possible. The ideal solution would be to embed the hardware bank switching code within the address calculation routine. This is the method adopted for the XGA pixels display routine listed in Section 7.3.1. However, XGA software does not have to contend with variations in hardware. We have seen that in the SuperVGA environment to hard-code the bank switching operation would almost certainly make the routine not portable to other devices. An alternative solution is to perform bank switching by means of VESA BIOS service number 5, described in Section 8.2.1. The following code fragment shows the code for bank switching using the VESA BIOS service.

```
;*********************|
;     change banks    |
;*********************|
; Select video bank using VESA BIOS subservice number 5
; VESA BIOS subservice number 5 register setup
```

```
; BH = 0 to select bank
; BL = 0 to select window A
; DX = bank number
        MOV     BX,0            ; Select bank in window A
        MOV     AX,4F05H        ; Service and subservice
        INT     10H

        .

        .

        .
```

An alternative option that would improve performance of the bank switching operation is by means of a far call to the service routine, as mentioned in Section 8.2.1. The following code fragment shows bank switching using the far call method. The code assumes that the address of the service routine is stored in a doubleword variable named BANK_FUN. This address can be obtained by means of VESA BIOS subservice number 1 (get mode information) discussed in Section 8.2.1.

```
;********************|
;    change banks    |
;  by far call method |
;********************|
; Select video bank by means of a far call to the bank switching
; routine provided by the chipset manufacturer
; Code assumes that the far address of the service routine is
; stored in a doubleword variable named BANK_FUN
; Register setup for far call method
; BH = 0 to select bank
; BL = 0 to select window A
; DX = bank number
        MOV     BX,0                    ; Select bank in window A
        PUSH    AX                      ; Preserve caller's context
        PUSH    DX
        CALL    DWORD PTR BANK_FUN
        POP     DX                      ; Restore context
        POP     AX

        .

        .

        .
```

Observe that to use the far call method the doubleword variable that holds the address of the service routine must be reachable at the time of the call. Therefore, if the variable is in another segment, a segment override byte is required.

8.3.3 Setting and Reading a Pixel

Once the pixel address has been determined and the hardware has been switched to the corresponding video memory bank, setting the pixel is a simple write operation. For example, in VESA mode number 105H, once the address calculation routine in Section 8.3.1 and the bank switching routine in Section 8.3.2 have executed, the pixel can be set by means of the instruction:

```
MOV      BYTE PTR ES:[BX],AL
```

The code assumes that ES holds the base address of the video buffer, BX the offset within the bank, and AL the 8-bit color code. Note that since VESA mode number 105H is not a planar mode, no previous read operation is necessary to enable the latching mechanism. (See Section 3.1.1.)

Reading a pixel in a SuperVGA mode is usually based on the same address and bank switching operations as those required for setting a pixel. The actual read instruction is in the form:

```
MOV      AL,BYTE PTR ES:[BX]
```

The SVGA_PIX_105 procedure in the SVGA module of the GRAPHSOL library performs a pixel write operation while in SuperVGA mode number 105H. The procedure named SVGA_READ_105 can be used to read a screen pixel in this same mode.

8.3.4 VGA Code Compatibility

The SuperVGA enhanced graphics mode presents three basic differences in relation to VGA modes: multiple banks, nonplanar architecture, and greater resolution. Once these factors are taken into account by the SuperVGA specific graphics read and write routines, many VGA calculations can be used directly in SuperVGA graphics. In the following section we describe the use, from SuperVGA modes, of several VGA routines in the VGA modules of the GRAPHSOL library. These include the VGA routines developed in Chapter 3 to access the LUT registers in the DAC, since most SuperVGA systems use the same color look-up table and DAC as VGA.

8.4 Using the SuperVGA Library

The GRAPHSOL library furnished in the book's diskette includes the module named SVGA which contains SuperVGA graphics routines. Many of these procedures were designed as mode-specific in order to optimize performance. The procedures in the SVGA module serve to initialize the SuperVGA system, to establish the presence of a VESA SuperVGA BIOS, to select a VESA mode number 105H, and to set and read individual screen pixels while in mode 105H.

In addition to the routines in the SVGA library, SuperVGA programs use several procedures in the VGA modules of GRAPHSOL.LIB. The use of the VGA procedures by a SuperVGA system requires a previous call to the SET_DEVICE routine in the VGA3 module. For SuperVGA systems this call is made with the AL register holding the ASCII character "S." The call sets a device-specific display switch to the VESA SuperVGA pixel display routine in the SVGA module. By enabling the SuperVGA display routine (named SVGA_PIX_105) the code makes possible the use of the geometrical procedures in the VGA3 module named BRESENHAM, LINE_BY_SLOPE, DIS-PLAY_LINE, CIRCLE, ELLIPSE, PARABOLA, and HYPERBOLA. Also the use of the text display procedures in the VGA2 module named FINE_TEXT, FINE_TEXTHP, and MULTITEXT, as well as the corresponding text display support routines FONT_TO_RAM and READ_HPFONT. Information regarding the VGA text display and geometrical routines can be found in Chapters 4 and 5 as well as in the source files VGA2.ASM and VGA3.ASM contained in the book's software.

Since most SuperVGA systems use the VGA LUT and DAC registers in the same architecture as VGA mode number 19, a SuperVGA program can use the color register procedures for VGA mode number 19 that appear in the VGA1 module of the GRAPHSOL library. These procedures are named TWO_BIT_IRGB, GRAY_256, SUM_TO_GRAY, SAVE_DAC, and RE-STORE_DAC. The source file and program named SVGADEMO furnished in the diskette demonstrates the use of the SuperVGA library services in the SVGA module and the use of the compatible VGA services in the VGA modules of GRAPHSOL.LIB.

8.4.1 Procedures in the SVGA.ASM Module

SVGA_MODE

Call VESA BIOS subservice number 0 to obtain SuperVGA and VESA information and subservice number 1 to obtain mode-specific information.

Receives:

```
1. word integer of VESA SuperVGA graphics mode number, as
   follows:
                   number        resolution        colors
   GRAPHICS        100H          640-by-400          256
   MODES           101H          640-by-480          256
                   102H          800-by-600           16
                   103H          800-by-600          256
                   104H          1024-by-768          16
                   105H          1024-by-768         256
                   106H          1280-by-1224         16
                   107H          1280-by-1224        256
   TEXT            108H          80-by-60
   MODES           109H          132-by-25
```

```
                     10AH        132-by-43
                     10BH        132-by-50
                     10CH        132-by-60
    DIRECT COLOR     10DH        300-by-200              32K
    MODES            10EH        320-by-200              64K
                     10FH        320-by-200            16.8Mb
                     110H        640-by-480              32K
                     111H        640-by-480              64K
                     112H        640-by-480            16.8Mb
                     113H        800-by-600              32K
                     114H        800-by-600              64K
                     115H        800-by-600            16.8Mb
                     116H        1024-by-768             32K
                     117H        1024-by-768             64K
                     118H        1024-by-768           16.8Mb
                     119H        1280-by-1024            32K
                     11AH        1280-by-1024            64K
                     11BH        1280-by-1024          16.8Mb
```

Returns:

1. carry clear if no error, then ES:SI —> VESA_BUFFER, formatted as follows:

```
VESA_BUFFER      DB      '      '   ; VESA signature
VESA_VERSION     DW      ?         ; Version number
OEM_PTR_OFF      DW      ?         ; OEM string offset pointer
OEM_PTR_SEG      DW      ?         ; OEM string segment pointer
CAPABILITIES     DD      ?         ; System capabilities
MODES_PTR_OFF    DW      ?         ; Pointer to modes list, offset
MODES_PTR_SEG    DW      ?         ; Segment for idem
MEM_BLOCKS       DW      ?         ; Count of 64K memory blocks
                                   ; (Only in June 2, 1990
revision)
                 DB      242 DUP (0H)


        ES:DI —> VESA_INFO, formatted as follows:
VESA_INFO        DW      ?         ; Mode attribute bits
                                   ; 4 3 2 1 0 <= bits
                                   ; | | | | |__ 0 = mode not supported
                                   ; | | | |     1 = mode supported
                                   ; | | | |____ 0 = no extended mode info
                                   ; | | |       1 = extended mode info
                                   ; | | |______ 0 = no output functions
                                   ; | |         1 = output functions
                                   ; | |________ 0 = monochrome mode
                                   ; |           1 = color mode
                                   ; |__________ 0 = text mode
                                   ;             1 = graphics mode
```

```
                                  ; 15..5 = RESERVED
WIN_A_ATTS         DB       ?     ; Window A attributes
WIN_B_ATTS         DB       ?     ; Window B attributes
WIN_GRAIN          DW       ?     ; Window granularity
WIN_SIZE           DW       ?     ; Window size
WIN_A_SEG          DW       ?     ; Segment address for window A
WIN_B_SEG          DW       ?     ; Segment address for window B
WIN_PTR            DD       ?     ; Far pointer to window function
BYTES_PER_ROW      DW       ?     ; Bytes per screen row


; Extended mode data. Optional until version 1.2
X_RES              DW       ?     ; Horizontal resolution
Y_RES              DW       ?     ; Vertical resolution
X_CHAR_SIZE        DB       ?     ; Pixel width of character cell
Y_CHAR_SIZE        DB       ?     ; Pixel height of character cell
BIT_PLANES         DB       ?     ; Number of bit planes
BITS_PER_PIX       DB       ?     ; Bits per pixel in this mode
NUM_OF_BANKS       DB       ?     ; Number of video memory banks
MEM_MODEL          DB       ?     ; Memory model
BANK_SIZE          DB       ?     ; Kb per bank
                   DW       0     ; Padding
; Direct color fields. Defined in VESA BIOS version 1.2
RED_MASK           DB       ?     ; Bit size of red mask
RED_POSITION       DB       ?     ; Red mask LSB position
GREEN_MASK         DB       ?     ; Bit size of green mask
GREEN_POSITION     DB       ?     ; Green mask LSB position
BLUE_MASK          DB       ?     ; Bit size of blue mask
BLUE_POSITION      DB       ?     ; Blue mask LSB position
RSVD_MASK          DB       ?     ; Bit size of reserved mask
RSVD_POSITION      DB       ?     ; Reserved mask LSB position
DC_INFO            DB       ?     ; Attributes of direct color
                                  ; modes, as follows:
                                  ; bit 0 = color ramp
                                  ;         0 = fixed
                                  ;         1 = programmable
                                  ; bit 1 = Reserved field bits
                                  ;         0 = not usable
                                  ;         1 = usable
                   DB  216 DUP (?) ; Remainder of block
```

2. Carry set if error

VESA_105

Set SuperVGA to VESA mode number 105H with a resolution of 1024-by-768 pixels in 256 colors.

Receives:
   Nothing
Assumes:
   That the data variables in the buffers VESA_BUFFER and VESA_INFO
   have been filled by a previous call to the VESA_MODE procedure
Returns:
   Carry clear if mode was set
   Carry set if error

SVGA_PIX_105

Write a screen pixel accessing SVGA memory directly and using a far call to
the bank switching routine.
   Receives:
      1. word variable of x pixel coordinate
      2. word variable of y pixel coordinate
      3. byte variable of 8-bit color code
   Assumes:
      1. SVGA in VESA mode 105H (1024-by-768 pixels in 256 colors)
      2. Size of video bank is 64K
      3. ES holds base address of video buffer (A000H)
   Returns:
      Nothing
   Action:
      Pixel is set

SVGA_CLS_105

Clear video memory while in VESA mode number 105H.
   Receives:
      1. byte integer of 8-bit color code
   Assumes:
      1. SVGA in VESA mode 105H (1024-by-768 pixels in 256 colors)
      2. Size of video bank is 64K
      3. ES holds base address of video buffer (A000H)
   Returns:
      Nothing
   Action:
      Screen is initialized to requested color code

SVGA_READ_105

Read a screen pixel accessing SVGA memory directly and using a far call to the
bank switching routine.
   Receives:
      1. word variable of x pixel coordinate
      2. word variable of y pixel coordinate
   Assumes:

1. SVGA in VESA mode 105H (1024-by-768 pixels in 256 colors)
2. Size of video bank is 64K
3. ES holds base address of video buffer (A000H)

Returns:

1. byte integer of pixel color

Action:

Pixel is read

9

Animation

Chapter Summary

This chapter describes the principles and programming techniques of image animation in IBM microcomputers as well as mouse programming by means of the Microsoft mouse interface. The discussions include image mapping, panning and geometrical transformations, as well as imagining techniques by looping, and by system timer and vertical retrace interrupts.

9.0 Computer Graphics Animation

Computer graphics animation is usually defined as the simulation of lifelike qualities by digital manipulations of a computer-generated image. The concept is somewhat limiting since it excludes analog operations and assumes that the only objects which can be computer animated are images on the CRT. However, in the microcomputer environment animation is mostly about manipulating screen images so as to mimic life. This is often performed by moving images on the screen, but color and shapes can also be changed to create a lifelike illusion.

Computer graphics animation can take place in a real- or a delayed-time frame. For example, a computer program can generate and store a series of consecutive images that simulate the movement of an object. The stored images can be recorded on storage devices, such as a video tape, and later played back at a faster rate than they were generated. In this case we can say that the computer animation took place in a delayed-time frame; the animated action was not visible until the images were played back on a television set. On the other hand, a computer program can simulate a ping-pong game on the screen. In this case, the animation takes place in a real-time frame. Graphics animation in the microcomputer environment is, for the most part, image animation in real-time. For this reason in the present chapter we emphasize real-time operations. Delayed-frame is also known as frame-by-frame animation.

Animated screen images can be classified according to the user's interaction with the graphics object. When the object is directly controlled by the user of the software we speak of interactive animation. Screen object that are animated independently of the user's action often move by means of a machine-generated time-pulse. In this sense we speak of time-pulse animation. The mouse is an input device closely related to interactive animation. For this reason, we have incorporated mouse programming into the present chapter. Although not all mouse programming operations are related to animated screen objects, we have, for practical reasons, included all phases of mouse programming in the present treatment. Time-pulse animation is also discussed in some detail.

9.0.1 Physiology of Animation

The image of an object created by the human eye can persists in the brain for a brief period of time after the object no longer exists in the real world. This physiological phenomena is called *visual retention*. Although the biological mechanisms of retention are not fully understood, we do know that it involves the chemistry of the retina and the structure of cells and neurons in the eye. First cinematography, and more recently television, have taken advantage of visual retention to create the illusion of continuous movement. This is done by consecutively flashing still images at a faster rate than the period of visual retention. This technique, by which a new image replaces the old one before the period of retention has expired, creates in our minds the illusion of a smoothly moving object.

It has been determined experimentally that the critical image update rate for smooth animation is from 22 to 30 images per second. Modern day moving picture films are recorded and displayed at a rate of 24 images per second. Although the threshold for smooth animation varies with individuals, it is generally estimated at a rate of approximately 18 images per second. This means that if the consecutive images are projected at a rate slower than this threshold, the average individual is able to perceive a certain jerkiness. However, If the flashing rate exceeds the threshold, our brains merge the images together with no perception of the individual flashes. This threshold rate can be called the *critical jerkiness frequency*.

9.0.2 Microcomputer Animation

Animated graphics systems, such as the ones used in many electronic video games, are based on vector refresh technology. In these systems the movement of the electron beam is limited to the objects that must be redrawn during a refresh cycle. Therefore, vector refresh displays are more efficient in animating small objects than raster scan systems in which the entire screen area must be scanned by the electron gun or guns during each cycle.

IBM microcomputer graphics use raster scan technology. Animation on a raster scan computer is based on creating an illusion of movement by displaying successive images. The graphics object is typically stored in a dedicated buffer which is imaged on the CRT by the video hardware. The name *frame buffer animation* has often been used in this context. In VGA systems the frame buffer is the video memory itself. In XGA systems, in addition to video memory, there is a second, smaller, frame buffer dedicated to storing the sprite image. Image changes can be made by altering the contents of video memory or by changing the screen position at which the frame buffer is displayed.

Image size and critical jerkiness frequency are usually the limiting factors in frame buffer animation. For example, assume a VGA video system in mode number 18 (640-by-480 pixels in 16 colors). If to produce smooth animation the system must redraw the screen at a rate of 20 images per second, then the changes in the frame buffer must be performed in less than 1/20s. Furthermore, consider that to animate a screen object its image must be erased from the current position before it is redrawn at a new position, otherwise the animation would leave a track of objects on the video display. Therefore, the buffer update sequence is, in reality, a sequence of redraw, erase, redraw operations, which means that the critical jerkiness frequency is the time elapsed from redraw to redraw cycle. Consequently, the allotted time for the redraw-erase cycle becomes 1/48th of a second.

Although the above example is a worse-case scenario, it does show the constraints in which animation must be performed in a raster scan system. In IBM microcomputers, in particular, graphics animation is a battle against time: the time in which the frame buffer must be updated before the entire screen is redrawn by the video hardware. Hence, the animation programmer must resort to every known trick and stratagem in order to squeeze the maximum performance while updating the frame buffer. But, in many cases, even the most efficient and imaginative programming is not able to overcome the system's limitations and the animated image is bumpy and coarse.

9.0.3 Software Support for Animation Routines

In previous chapters we provided software support mainly in the form of library routines which can be called by a graphics program. But most animation routines have extremely critical performance constraints. This determines that animation software be customized and optimized for a particular program design. Furthermore, animated programs are often designed with these hardware limitations in mind. To provide animation routines in the form of library procedures would introduce, in the first place, an unnecessary call-and-return overhead over on-line code. In addition, the procedures would have to be adaptable to the many varying circumstances of animated programs and, at the same time, optimized for maximum performance. Code that is simultaneously flexible and efficient is a programming contradiction.

For these reasons we have opted to provided code support for the animation techniques discussed in this chapter in the form of coding templates, rather than as library routines. The reader can use these templates to avoid having to recode the routine manipulations in the various animation techniques.

However, we have left blank lines in the templates (marked by ellipses) to indicate where the programmer must supply the customized code.

The microdisk furnished with this book contains a VGA animated program named MATCH. The reader should consult the README file included in the MATCH directory before executing the program. The source files for the MATCH program demonstrate interactive and time-pulse animation in a VGA system.

9.1 Interactive Animation

Interactive animation refers to screen objects that are moved at will by the user. Typically the animated screen object is controlled by means of an input device, such as a mouse, puck, or graphics tablet. (See Section 1.1.2.) In the present section we discuss programming the mouse device as a means for animating an interactive screen object. Other interactive input devices are specialty tools used mostly in CAD software, therefore they are outside the scope of this book.

9.1.1 Programming the Mouse

The IBM BIOS, as documented in the IBM Personal System/2 and Personal Computer BIOS Interface Technical Reference (see bibliography), describes a pointing device interface associated with service number 194 of INT 15H. However, there are several difficulties associated with this service. In the first place, the IBM documentation dealing with this mouse service is not sufficient for programming the device. Another consideration is that the services are not compatible with different mouse hardware. Then there is the problem that various non-IBM versions of the BIOS do not include this service. Finally, the service is not recognized in the DOS mode of OS/2.

If the BIOS mouse services of INT 15H were operational and compatible with standard mouse hardware, a program could use these functions much the same way as it uses the video, printer or the communications services in the BIOS. However, due to the difficulties mentioned in the preceding paragraph, most applications must find alternative ways of controlling mouse operation. But all alternative solutions have the disadvantage of requiring an installed mouse driver. To an application this leaves three alternatives: (1) the software must assume that the user has previously installed and loaded a compatible mouse driver, (2) the software must provide an installation routine that loads the driver, or (3) the code must include a low-level driver for the mouse device.

9.1.2 The Microsoft Mouse Interface

The mouse driver software that has achieved more general acceptance is the one by Microsoft Corporation. The Microsoft mouse control software is installed as a system driver or as a TSR program. The system version is usually stored in a disk file with the extension .SYS and the TSR version in a file with the extension .COM. The Microsoft mouse interface services are documented in the book *Microsoft Mouse Programmer's Reference*, published by Microsoft Press (see Bibliography).

Most manufacturers of mouse devices provide drivers that are compatible with the one by Microsoft. Therefore, the use of the Microsoft mouse interface is not limited to mouse devices manufactured by this company, but extends to all Microsoft-compatible hardware and software. The installation command for the mouse driver is usually included in the CONFIG.SYS or AUTOEXEC.BAT files. The Microsoft mouse interface attaches itself to software interrupt 33H and provides a set of 36 sub-services. These mouse sub-services are accessible by means of an INT 33H instruction.

9.1.3 Checking Mouse Software Installation

We have mentioned that applications that use the mouse device must adopt one of three alternatives regarding the support software: assume that the driver was installed by the user, load a driver program, or provide the low-level services within its code. By far, most applications adopt the first option, that is, assume that the user has previously loaded the mouse driver software. Although the more refined programs that use a mouse device include an installation utility that selects the appropriate driver and creates or modifies a batch file in order to insure that the mouse driver is resident at the time of program execution.

In any case, the first operation usually performed by an application that plans to use the mouse control services in interrupt 33H is to test the successful installation of the driver program. Since the driver is vectored to interrupt 33H, this test consists simply of checking that the corresponding slot in the vector table is not a null value (0000:0000H) or an IRET operation code. Either one of these alternatives indicates that no mouse driver is presently available. The following coding template shows the required processing.

```
; Template file name: MOUSE1.TPL
; Code to check if mouse driver software is installed in the
; interrupt 33H vector. The check is performed by reading the
; interrupt 33H vector using MS-DOS service number 53,
; of INT 21H
        MOV     AH,53           ; MS_DOS service request
        MOV     AL,33H          ; Desired interrupt number
        INT     21H             ; MS-DOS service
; ES:BX holds address of interrupt handler, if installed
        MOV     AX,ES           ; Segment to AX
        OR      AX,BX           ; OR with offset
        JNZ     OK_INT33        ; Go if not zero
; Test for an IRET opcode in the vector
        CMP     BYTE PTR ES:[BX],0CFH   ; CFH is IRET opcode
        JNE     OK_INT33        ; Go if not IRET
```

```
; At this point the program should provide an error handler
; to exit execution or to load a mouse driver
        .
        .
        .
; Execution continues at this label if a valid address was found
; in the interrupt 33H vector
OK_INT33:
        .
        .
        .
```

9.1.4 Subservices of Interrupt 33H

The Microsoft mouse interface was designed to provide control of the mouse
device from high- and low-level languages. VGA alphanumeric programs can
use the Microsoft mouse software by selecting one of two available text cursors.
In the alpha modes the mouse driver manages the text cursor on a coarse grid
of screen columns and rows, according to the active display mode. VGA
programs that execute in graphics modes must provide their own cursor
bitmap, which is installed by means of an interrupt 33H subservice. However,
since the graphics cursor operated by the driver is limited to a size of 16-by-16
pixels, many graphics programs create and manage their own cursor. In this
case the driver services are used to detect mouse movements, but the actual
cursor operation and display are handled directly by the application. This is
also the case of XGA programs that use the sprite functions to manage a mouse
cursor image

   In addition to mouse cursor management and display, the subservices of
interrupt 33H include functions to set the mouse sensitivity and rate, to read
button press information, to select video pages, and to initialize and install
interrupt handlers that take control when the mouse is moved or when the
mouse buttons are operated. However, some of the services in the interrupt
33H drivers re-program the video hardware in ways that can conflict with an
application. For this reason, we have limited our discussion to those mouse
services that are not directly related to the video environment. These services
can be used from any VGA, XGA, or SuperVGA graphics modes without
interference. However, in this case, it is the application's responsibility to
perform all video updates.

Subservice 0 – Initialize Mouse

Subservice number 0 of interrupt 33H is used to reset the mouse device and to
obtain its status. An application usually calls this service to certify that the
mouse driver is resident and to initialize the device parameters. The following
coding template shows a call to this subservice.

```
; Template file name: MOUSE2.TPL
; Initialize mouse by calling subservice 0 of interrupt 33H
        MOV     AX,0                    ; Reset mouse hardware and
                                        ; software
        INT     33H                     ; Mouse interrupt
        CMP     AX,0                    ; Test for error during reset
        JNZ     OK_RESET                ; No problem
; At this point the program should provide an error routine to
; handle an invalid initialization call
            .

            .

            .

; Execution continues at this label if the mouse was initialized
OK_RESET:
            .

            .

            .
```

Subservice 5 – Check Button Press Status

Programs that do not use interrupts can check mouse button press status by calling subservice number 5 of the Microsoft mouse interface. The call is typically located in a polling loop. The calling program passes the button code in the BX register; the value of 0 corresponds to the left mouse button and a value of 1 to the right button. The call returns the button status in the AX register; bit 0 is mapped to the left mouse button and bit 1 to the right mouse button. A value of 1 indicates that the corresponding button is down. The BX register returns the number of button presses that have occurred since this call was last made or since a driver software reset (see subservice 0 earlier in this section). The CX and DX registers hold the x and y cursor coordinates of the screen position where the last press occurred. The following coding template shows a call to this subservice.

```
; Template file name: MOUSE3.TPL
;****************************************************************
;                     button action handler
;****************************************************************
; The following routine calls service 5 of interrupt 33H to
; detect mouse press action on the mouse device
; If the right button was pressed execution is directed to the
; label RIGHT_BUT, if the left button was pressed execution is
; directed to the label LEFT_BUT
;*******************|
;   check left button   |
;*******************|
        MOV     AX,5                    ; Service request to read
```

```
                                         ; mouse button status
        MOV     BX,0                     ; First test left button
        INT     33H                      ; Mouse interrupt
; Number of button presses is returned in the BX register
        CMP     BX,0                     ; Test for no presses
        JE      TEST_RIGHT_BUT  ; Not pressed. Test right button
; Code at this point should take the program action
; corresponding to one or more presses of the left mouse button

        .
        .
        .

; Execution should be allowed to fall through to the right
; button test routine
;*********************|
;  check right button |
;*********************|
TEST_RIGHT_BUT:
        MOV     AX,5                     ; Service request to read
                                         ; mouse button status
        MOV     BX,1                     ; Test right button
        INT     33H                      ; Mouse interrupt
; Number of button presses is returned in the BX register
        CMP     BX,0                     ; Test for no presses
        JE      END_BUTTON_RTN  ; Not pressed. End of routine
; Code at this point should take the program action
; corresponding to one or more presses of the right mouse button

        .
        .
        .

; Button press status processing ends at this label
END_BUTTON_RTN:
        .
        .
        .
```

Subservice 11 – Read Motion Counters

The actual movement of the mouse-controlled icon is dependent on the state of
two counters maintained by the mouse interface software. The Microsoft mouse
interface at interrupt 33H stores the motion parameters in 1/200-in units called
mickeys. The changes in the motion counters represent values from the last
time the function was called. Subservice 11, of interrupt 33H, returns the
values stored in the horizontal and vertical motion counters. The horizontal
motion count is returned in the CX register and the vertical count in the DX
register. The values are signed integers in 2's complement form. A negative
value in the horizontal motion counter indicates mouse movement to the left,

while a negative value in the vertical motion counter indicates a movement in the upward direction. Both the vertical and the horizontal counters are automatically reset by the service routine.

We mentioned that the detection of mouse action can be by a polling loop or by interrupts. Polling loops are often used in reading the motion counters so as to keep interrupt processing times to a minimum, specially considering that the Microsoft mouse interface does not allow the installation of more than one service routine. The processing inside a polling loop or a service routine takes place in similar fashion. The following coding template shows the structure of a basic mouse movement handler.

```
; Template file name: MOUSE4.TPL
;*************************************************************
;                     mouse movement handler
;*************************************************************
;
; The following routine calls service 11 of interrupt 33H to
; detect horizontal or vertical movement of the mouse device
; If the movement is along the x axis (horizontal) execution is
; directed to the label H_MOVE, if the movement is along the y
; axis, execution is directed to the label Y_MOVE. If no change
; is detected in the motion counters, then execution is directed
; to the label NO_MOVE
;
;********************|
;  service No. 11 of |
;       INT 33H      |
;********************|
        MOV     AX,11           ; Service request to read
                                ; motion counters
        INT     33H             ; Mouse interrupt
; CX = Horizontal mouse movement from last call to this service
; DX = vertical mouse movement from last call
        MOV     AL,CL           ; Horizontal counter to AL
        MOV     AH,DL           ; Vertical counter to AH
        CMP     AX,0            ; If AX is 0 then no mouse
        JNE     XORY_MOVE       ; Some movement detected
        JMP     NO_MOVE         ; Go if no movement
; At this point there is vertical or horizontal mouse movement
XORY_MOVE:
        CMP     CX,0            ; Test for no horizontal
        JE      Y_MOVE          ; Go to vertical movement test
;
;********************|
;   horizontal move  |
;********************|
```

```
; Code at this point moves the mouse icon according to the
; direction and magnitude of the value in the CX register
X_MOVE:
        PUSH    DX                  ; Save vertical move counter
          .

          .

          .

        POP     DX                  ; Restore vertical counter
;
; Once the horizontal movement is executed the code should fall
; through to the vertical movement routine. This takes care of
; the possibility of simultaneous movement along both axes
;
;********************|
;     vertical move  |
;********************|
; Code at this point moves the mouse icon according to the
; direction and magnitude of the value in the DX register
Y_MOVE:

          .

          .

          .

;********************|
;     no movement     |
;********************|
; This label is the routine's exit point
NO_MOVE:

          .

          .

          .
```

Subservice 12 – Set Interrupt Routine

The user action on the mouse hardware can be monitored by polling or by
interrupt generation, as is the case with most other input devices. Polling
methods are based on querying the device status on a time lapse basis, therefore
polling routines as usually coded as part of execution loops. In the case of the
mouse hardware the polling routine can check the motion counter registers and
the button press and release status registers that are maintained by the mouse
interface software. The services to read these registers are described later in
this section.

  The second and often preferred method of monitoring user interaction with
the mouse device, particularly mouse button action, is by means of hardware
interrupts. In this technique the program enables the mouse hardware actions
that generate interrupts and installs the corresponding interrupt handlers.
Thereafter, user action on the enabled hardware sources in the mouse auto-

matically transfers control to the handler code. This frees the software from polling frequency constraints and simplifies program design and coding.

A typical application enables mouse interrupts for one or more sources of user interaction. For example, a program that uses the mouse to perform menu selection would enable an interrupt for movement of the trackball (or other motion detector mechanism) and another interrupt for the action of pressing the left mouse button. If the mouse is moved, the interrupt handler linked to trackball movement changes the screen position of the marker or icon according to the direction and magnitude of the movement. If the left mouse button is pressed, the corresponding interrupt handler executes the selected menu option.

Another frequently used programming method is to poll the mouse motion counters that store trackball movement and to detect button action by means of interrupts. This design reduces execution time inside the interrupt handler, which can be an important consideration in time-critical applications. The MATCH demonstration program furnished in the book's microdisk uses a polling routine to move the mouse icon and an interrupt handler to detect button action.

In the mouse interface software, the hardware conditions that can be programmed to generate an interrupt are related to an integer value called the *call mask*. Figure 9.1 shows the call mask bitmap in the Microsoft mouse interface software. To enable a mouse interrupt condition the software sets the corresponding bit in the call mask. To disable a condition the call mask bit is cleared.

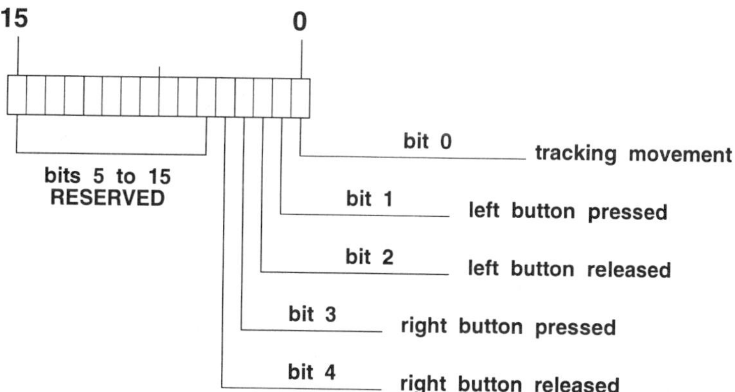

Figure 9.1 *Mouse Interrupt Call Mask*

Subservice number 12 of the mouse interface at interrupt 33H provides a means for installing an interrupt handler and for selecting the action or actions that generate the interrupt. The following coding template shows the necessary processing for enabling mouse interrupts on the right and left button pressed.

```
; Template file name: MOUSE5.TPL
; Select left mouse button pressed and right mouse button
; pressed as interrupt conditions and set address of service
; routine by means of mouse sub-service number 12, interrupt 33H
;
; The code assumes that the interrupt handler is located in the
; program's code segment, at the offset of the label named
; MOUSE_ACTION
;
        CLI                             ; Interrupts off
        PUSH    ES                      ; Save video buffer segment
        PUSH    CS                      ; Program's segment
        POP     ES                      ; to ES
        MOV     AX,12                   ; Mouse service number 12
; Interrupt mask bitmap:
; 15 ——————— 5 4 3 2 1 0
;  |— these bits unused —-| | | | | |___ Tracking movement
;                          | | | |______ Left button pressed
;                          | | |________ Left button released
;                          | |__________ Right button pressed
;                          |____________ Right button released
        MOV     CH,0                    ; Unused bits
        MOV     CL,00001010B            ; Interrupt on left button and
                                        ; right button pressed
        MOV     DX,OFFSET CS:MOUSE_ACTION ; Address of the
                                        ; service routine
        INT     33H                     ; Mouse interrupt
        POP     ES                      ; Restore segment
        STI                             ; Interrupts on

        .
        .
        .
```

When the user's interrupt service routine receives control the mouse interface software passes a condition code in the AL register that matches the call mask bitmap. (See Figure 9.1.) In this manner the user's handler can determine which of the unmasked conditions actually generated the interrupt. An interrupt condition bit is set when the corresponding condition originated the interrupt. For example, if the conditions that originate the interrupt are the left or right mouse buttons pressed (as enabled by the previous coding template), then the program can test the state of bit number 1 to determine if the interrupt was caused by the left mouse button. If not, the code can assume that it was caused by the user pressing the right mouse button, since only these two conditions are active. (See Figure 9.1.)

A characteristic of service number 12 or the Microsoft mouse interface is that only one interrupt handler can be installed. If two consecutive calls are made to this service, even if the call mask settings enable different bits, the address in the latest call replaces the previous one. Therefore, it is not possible to install more than one service routine by means of this service. On the other hand, service number 24 allows the installation of more than one service routine, each one linked to a different interrupt cause. However, this service operates only when the Shift, Ctrl, or Alt keys are held down while the mouse action is performed. In addition, in several non-Microsoft versions of the mouse interface software the service does not perform as documented. For these reasons it is not considered in this book.

9.2 Image Animation

In IBM microcomputers video animation usually consists of successively displaying images that vary in composition or in screen location according to a specific pattern of change. Notice that the concept of a *pattern of change* does not imply that this pattern be known beforehand to the software. For example, the image changes can be determined by user interaction or by the occurrence of random events. In this respect we can speak of the animation of object with predictable or unpredictable movements. The direction of movement of a mouse icon, for example, cannot be normally predicted by the software, therefore it falls in the second category. On the other hand, a graphics program could animate a screen object that moves in a predictable path across the screen. It is also possible for the movement of a screen object to contain both a predictable and an unpredictable element. For example, a mouse-controlled icon can be allowed to move inside a certain screen window, or the image of a planet that moves diagonally across the screen can exhibit random rotation on its own axis.

The combinations and variations of the predictable and unpredictable elements in the movement of screen objects can be quite complex. For example, the following screen image in an animated game could depend on screen objects with programmed movement, with random movement, and controlled by user interaction. The one common element to all three animated movements is the concept of a pattern of change, which means that the subsequent images of animated objects are somehow related to previous ones. The elements of this relationship are usually location, gradation (color hue), and object shape. In other words, to produce a realistically animated movement of a screen object the software must control the pattern of change. This usually implies restricting the transformations of location, gradation, and shape from one screen image of the object to the next one.

Many of the complexities of the theory and practice of computer image animation are beyond the scope of this book. In the bibliography we have listed some useful theoretical references in the field of computer graphics. However, computer animation in IBM microcomputers is much more limited than in dedicated systems. The processing power of CPU and video hardware impose very restrictive limits on the number and size of objects that can be smoothly animated in this environment. The following discussion is also limited by these hardware limits.

9.2.1 Image Mapping and Panning

Image animation in raster scan systems is often based on manipulating a stored image map. This map can be located in a mechanical or optical device, in video memory, in ROM, or in the application's memory space. In previous chapters we have manipulated image maps contained in disk files, in ROM, in RAM, and in video memory. The storage location of the image map is often less important than its format. Bitmap formats and conventions are the subject of Chapter 10. Processing speed is usually an important consideration in image animation. Therefore the storage location for image maps is usually limited to the video memory and the applications's RAM space. The terms video buffer and image buffer are often used in this context.

Video and Image Buffers

While the video buffer is a physical device the concept of an image buffer is a logical one. Graphics systems use the concept of a *virtual graphics device*, which assumes an imaginary display of fictitious characteristics. Frequently, the attributes of the virtual machine exceed those of the physical one. Therefore, the capacity of the image buffer can exceed that of the video buffer. For example, a VGA system is equipped with a video buffer suitable for holding an image of 640-by-480 pixels in 16 colors. Yet a program running in the VGA environment may support an image buffer capable of storing 2000-by-1200 pixels in 512 colors.

We have made use of this concept in developing the calculation routines in the VGA libraries furnished with this book. In this manner the storage areas for screen coordinate points (named X_BUFFER and Y_BUFFER) in the VGA2 module are capable of storing 2048 values for each coordinate axis. This considerably exceeds the best available resolution in VGA systems, which is of 640 by 480 pixels. However, this additional storage space makes possible the use of the geometrical calculation routines in XGA and SuperVGA modes that have greater screen resolution (1024-by-768 pixels) than the VGA. As far as the VGA calculation routines are concerned the limits of the video system are not those of the physical device (VGA, XGA, or SuperVGA) but those of an image buffer with a storage space for 2048-by-2048 pixels.

Viewport and Windows

The viewport is defined as the display area used for graphic operations. In IBM microcomputer graphics the entire display must be set for a chosen graphics or alphanumeric mode. Therefore, the viewport is the entire display surface. In other words, the dimensions of the graphic viewport coincide with the those of the physical video display. A window is an area of the display surface, usually rectangular in shape. However, there is no reason for excluding windows of other shapes. In fact, circular and elliptical windows are visually pleasant and would serve to break the geometrical monotony of squares and rectangles.

A rectangular display window is usually defined by the coordinates of its start and end points. For example, on a 640-by-480 pixel display, a window filling the upper left quarter would have start coordinates (0,0) and end coordinates (320,240). Windows can also be defined descriptively; for example, we sometimes speak of the graphic window, the text window, and the menu window.

Panning

Image buffers, viewport, and windows are often used in producing a form of image animation called *panning*. In panning an image appears to move by changing the rectangular region of the image buffer that is mapped to the viewport or window. The elements of panning animation are shown in Figure 9.2.

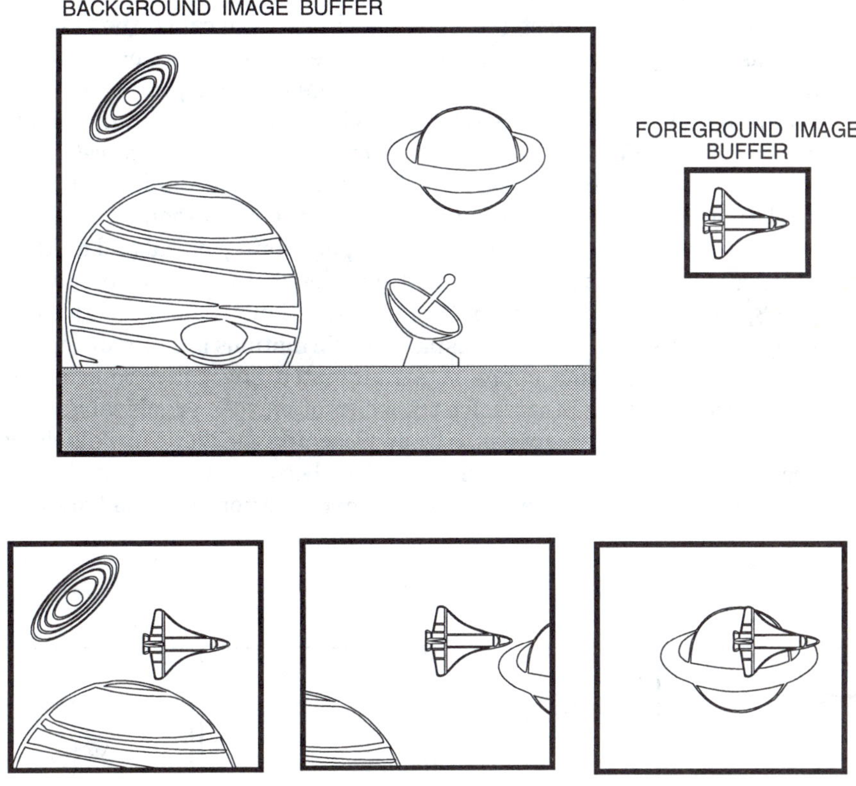

Figure 9.2 *Elements in Panning Animation*

In Figure 9.2 we can see that the viewport or window is smaller than the background image buffer. Therefore, the display routine can show only a portion of the background image buffer at one time. A smooth panning effect can be produced on the video display by progressively changing the portion of the image buffer that is mapped to the viewport. An additional enhancement can be added in the form of a separate foreground screen object (in Figure 9.2 this object is a space shuttle). The foreground object is stored in its own image buffer (labeled the foreground image buffer in Figure 9.2). The panning effect can be further enhanced by changing the portion of the background image buffer mapped to the viewport, while the foreground object (in this example the shuttle image), remains in a fixed position. The resulting panning animation simulates the shuttle moving in space.

9.2.2 Geometrical Transformations

Graphical systems employ elaborate schemes for encoding image data. The purpose of these data structures is to facilitate image manipulation by hardware and software. The organization of graphical data is based, first, on identifying the fundamental image elements, such as lines, curves, arcs, polygons, and bitmaps. These primitive elements are stored in a logical structure called the *display file*. In turn, this display is composed of one or more modeling elements placed in structural levels sometimes called image files, image segments, and image descriptors. The design of graphical data storage devices and the manipulation of this data is a specialized field outside the scope of this book. The interested reader should consult a book on theoretical computer graphics (see Bibliography).

The subject of graphical data structures is related to animation by the fact that it is possible to transform a graphical image by performing logical and mathematical operations on the data structure that encodes it. In Chapter 5, starting in Section 5.3, we discussed geometrical transformations that are performed by manipulating image data. The most usual transformations are mirrowing, translation, rotation, scaling, and clipping. An animated effect can be achieved by performing and displaying progressive transformations of a graphical image. For example, a screen object can appear to be approaching the viewer by displaying a sequence of scaled images in which the object becomes progressively larger. Figure 9.3 shows how rotation and scaling transformations are used to simulate this effect.

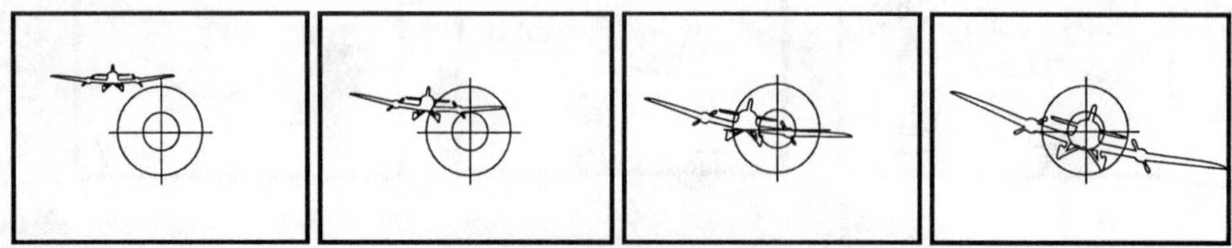

Figure 9.3   *Animation by Scaling and Rotation*

Notice in Figure 9.3, that the simulation is enhanced by introducing a second, non-transformed object in the viewport (the reticle symbol). In any case of real-time animation by image transformation the quality of the simulation depends on the rate at which the successive images are displayed as well as on the rate of change between successive images. The faster the display rate and the slower the rate of image change, the more realistic the animation.

9.3 Imaging Techniques

We saw that computer animation often depends on the display of a series of images, called the *image set*. In some forms of animation the images themselves are progressively changed to form the image set. For example, panning animation is based on changing the portion of the image that is visible on the viewport. Other geometrical transformations can be used to generate the image set. In Figure 9.3 we see how scaling and rotation transformations are applied to a graphical object in order to simulate its approaching the viewer. In all cases, animation in real-time requires two separate programming steps: the creation of an image set and the sequential display of these images.

Many graphics and nongraphics techniques are used in the creation of an image set that follows a predefined pattern of change. We have mentioned how the image set can be generated by performing geometrical transformations on the display file. Hand-drawn or optically scanned bitmaps are also used to create the image set. Notice that the creation of the image set need not take place in real-time; it is its display that is time-critical. But whether the image set is in the form of geometrical display commands or encoded in consecutive bitmaps, the actual animation requires displaying these images consecutively, in real-time, and ideally, at a rate that is not less than the critical flicker frequency. In this section we discuss some programming methods used for displaying the animation image set in real-time.

9.3.1 Retention

We mentioned that the human visual organs retain, for a short time, the images of objects that no longer exist in the real world. This physiological phenomenon makes possible the creation of an illusion of animation by the frame-by-frame projection of a set of progressively changing images of a graphics object. We have referred to this collection of smoothly changing images as the animation image set. If the rate at which the individual images are shown on the video display is close to the critical rate of 22 images per second, then the animation appears smooth and pleasant. On the other hand, if the software cannot approximate this critical rate the user perceives a disturbing flicker and the animation appears coarse and bumpy to various degrees.

It is image retention which imposes performance requirements on real-time animated systems. If a computer animation program is to create a smooth and pleasant effect, all the manipulations and changes from image to image must be performed in less than 1/20th of a second. We mentioned that raster scan video systems, with bit-mapped image buffers such as those in IBM microcomputers, are not well suited for computer animation.

9.3.2 Interference

A raster scan display system is based on scanning each horizontal row of screen pixels with an electron beam. The pixel rows are usually scanned starting at the top-left screen corner and ending at the bottom-right corner. At the end of each pixel row, called a scan line, the electron beam is turned off while the gun is re-aimed to the start of the next scan line. When this row-by-row process reaches the bottom scan line, the beam is turned off while the gun is re-aimed to the top-left screen corner. The period of time required to re-aim the electron gun from the right-bottom of the screen to the top left corner is known as the *vertical retrace* or *screen blanking* cycle.

Some of the original graphics systems in IBM microcomputers were prone to a form of display interference called *snow*. The direct cause for the interference was performing a buffer update during a screen refresh. Programmers soon discovered that on the CGA card this could be avoided or reduced by synchronizing the buffer updates with the period of time that the electron gun was turned off during vertical retrace. EGA and VGA systems were designed to avoid this form of interference when conventional methods of buffer update are used. However, the interference problem reapears when an EGA or VGA screen image has to be updated at short time intervals, as in animation.

The result is that, in order to avoid interference, the frequent screen updates required by most animation routines must be timed with the period during which the electron gun is off. This usually means synchronizing the buffer updated with the vertical retrace cycle of the CRT controller. This requirement, which applies to EGA, VGA, XGA, and SuperVGA systems, imposes a substantial burden on programs that perform animated graphics. For example, the screen refresh period in VGA graphics modes takes place at an approximate rate of 70 times per second. Since the individual images must be updated in the buffer while the electron gun is off, this gives the software 1/70th of a second to replace the old image with the new one. How much buffer update can be performed in 1/70th of a second. is the most limimiting factor in programming smooth, real-time animation on IBM microcomputer video systems.

Notice that a screen refresh rate of approximately 1/70th of a second considerably exceeds the critical jerkiness frequency of 1/24th of a second used as the image refresh rate in motion picture technology. (See Section 9.0.1.) This difference is related to the time period required for the human eye to adjust to a light intensity change and detect flicker. We can speak of a *critical flicker frequency*, as different from the critical jerkiness frequency mentioned above. The motion picture projector contains a rotating diaphragm that blackens the screen only during the very short interval required to move the film to the next frame. This allows projection speeds to take place at the critical jerkiness rate rather than at the flicker rate. By the same token, a computer monitor must adjust the screen refresh cycle to this critical flicker frequency.

9.3.3 XOR Operations

In Section 9.0.2 we mentioned that in order to animate a screen object its image must be erased from current screen position before being redrawn at the new position. Otherwise the object's movement would leave an image track on the video display. The buffer update sequence takes the form: redraw, erase, redraw, erase, redraw, and so on. For example, in lateral translation, an object is made to appear to move across the screen, from left to right, by progressively redrawing and erasing its screen image at consecutively larger x coordinates. Notice that erasing the screen object is at least as time consuming as drawing it, since each pixel in the object must be changed to its previous state.

The are several ways of performing the redraw-erase cycle required in figure animation. The most obvious method is to save that portion of the screen image that is to be occupied by the object. The object can then be erased by redisplaying the saved image. The problem with this double pixBlt is that it requires a preliminary, and time-consuming, read operation to store the screen area that is to be occupied by the animated object. Therefore the redraw-erase cycle is performed by a video-to-RAM pixBlt (save screen), RAM-to-video pixBlt (display object), and another RAM-to-video pixBlt (restore screen).

A faster method of erasing and redrawing the screen is based on the properties of the logical exclusive or (XOR) operation. The action of the logical XOR is that a bit in the result is set if both operands contain opposite values. Consequently, XORing the same value twice restores the original contents, as in the following example:

```
                    10000001B
          XOR mask  10110011B
                    ---------
                    00110010B
          XOR mask  10110011B
                    ---------
                    10000001B
```

Notice that the resulting bitmap (10000001B) is the same as the original one. The XOR method can be used in EGA, VGA, and SuperVGA systems because the Data Rotate register of the Graphics Controller can be programmed to write data normally, or to AND, OR, or XOR, the CPU data with the one in the latches. In XGA systems, mix mode number 06H produces a logical XOR of source and destination pixels. (See Table 7.8.)

The logical XOR operation provides a convenient and fast way for consecutively drawing and erasing a screen object. Its main advantage is that it does not require a previous read operation to store the original screen contents. This results in a faster and simpler read-erase cycle. The XOR method is particularly useful when more than one animated object can coincide on the same screen position since it insures that the original screen image is always restored.

The disadvantage of the XOR method is that the resulting image depends on the current screen contents. In other words, each individual pixel in the object displayed by means of a logical XOR operation is determined both by the XORed value and by the present pixel contents. For example, the following XOR operation produces a red object (in IRGB format) on a bright white screen background:

```
                    I R G B
    background =    1 1 1 1    (bright white)
    XOR mask   =    1 0 1 1
                    ───────
    image      =    0 1 0 0    (red)
```

However, if the same XOR mask is used over a bright green background the resulting pixel is blue, as in the following example:

```
                    I R G B
    background =    1 0 1 0    (bright green)
    XOR mask   =    1 0 1 1
                    ───────
    image      =    0 0 0 1    (blue)
```

This characteristic of XOR operations, whereby an object's color changes as it moves over different backgrounds, can be an advantage or a disadvantage in graphics applications. For example, a marker symbol conventionally displayed will disappear as it moves over a background of its same color, while a marker displayed by means of a logical XOR can be designed to be visible over all possible backgrounds. On the other hand, the color of a graphics object might be such an important characteristic that any changes during display operations would be objectionable.

In conclusion, the peculiar effect of XOR operations on the object's color may not be objectionable, and even advantageous under some conditions, but in other applications it could make this technique unsuitable. More advanced video graphics systems include hardware support for animated imagery. In XGA, for example, the sprite mechanism allows for the display and movement of marker symbols or icons independently of the background. In this manner, the XGA programmer can move the sprite symbol by defining its new coordinates. The XGA hardware takes care of erasing the old marker and restoring the underlaying image.

Programming the Function Select Bits

To make possible the XOR operation the software must manipulate the function select bits of the Graphics Controller Data Rotate register. (See Section 2.2.4 and Table 2.6.) The following code fragment shows the required processing.

```
; Set the Graphics Controller function select field of the Data
; Rotate register to the XOR mode
        MOV     DX,03CEH     ; Graphic controller port address
        MOV     AL,3         ; Select Data Rotate register
        OUT     DX,AL
        INC     DX           ; 03CFH register
        MOV     AL,00011000B    ; Set bits 3 and 4 for XOR
        OUT     DX,AL
```

Many conventional graphics operations, such as pixBlt and text display functions, require that the function select bits of the data rotate register be set for normal operation. The following code fragment shows the necessary processing.

```
; Set the Graphics Controller function select field of the Data
; Rotate register to the normal mode
        MOV     DX,03CEH     ; Graphic controller port address
        MOV     AL,3         ; Select Data Rotate register
        OUT     DX,AL
        INC     DX           ; 03CFH register
        MOV     AL,00000000B    ; Reset bits 3 and 4 for normal
        OUT     DX,AL
```

The procedure named LOGICAL_MODE in the VGA1 module of the GRAPHSOL library can be used to set the function select field of the Graphics Controller Data Rotate register to any one of four possible logical modes.

9.3.4 Time-Pulse Animation

Time-pulse animation is a real-time technique by which a screen object is successively displayed and erased at a certain rate. Ideally, the redraw rate in time-pulse animation should be higher than the critical jerkiness frequency of 20 images per second. Although, in practice, the time pulse is often determined by the screen refresh rate.

Looping Techniques

The programmer has several methods of producing the timed pulse at which the animated image is updated. Which method is selected depends on the requirements of the application as well as on the characteristics of the video display hardware. The simplest method for updating the screen image of an animated object is by creating an execution loop to provide some form of timing device. But the loop must include, not only the processing operations for updating the screen image, but also one or more polling routines. In addition, the loop's execution can be interrupted by hardware devices requiring processor attention. Another factor that can affect the precision of the loop timing is processor speed and and memory access facilities of the particular machine. The result is that an animation pulse created by loop methods is difficult to estimate, leading to nonuniform or unpredictable movement of the animated object.

The System Timer

Another time-pulse source available in IBM microcomputers is the system's timer pulse. This pulse, which can be intercepted by an application, beats at the default rate of approximately 18.2 times per second. However, an application can re-program the system timer to generate a faster rate. An interrupt intercept routine can be linked to the system timer so that the program receives control at every timer beat. If it were not for interference problems, the system timer intercept would be an ideal beat generator for use in animation routines.

The following coding template installs a system timer intercept routine. The installation routine accelerates the system timer from 18.2 to 54.6 beats per second, or three times the original rate.

```
; Template file name: ANIMATE1.TPL
;*******************************************************************
;*******************************************************************
;                    timer-driven pulse generator
;*******************************************************************
;*******************************************************************
;
; Changes performed during installation:
; 1. The BIOS system timer vector is stored in a code segment
;     variable
; 1. The timer hardware is made to run 3 times faster to ensure
;     a beat that is close to the critical flicker frequency
; 3. New service routine for INT 08H is installed in the
;     program's address space
;
; Operation:
; 3. The new interrupt handler at INT 08H gains control with
;     every bear of the system timer. The program maintains a
;     beat counter in the range 0 to 2. Every third beat
;     (counter = 2) execution is passed to the original INT 08H
;     handler in the BIOS in order to preserve the
;     timer-dependant services
;
CODE     SEGMENT

START:
```

```
;****************************************************************
;              installation routine for INT 08H handler
;****************************************************************
; Operations:
;       1. Obtain vector for INT 08H and store in a CS variable
;          named OLD_VECTOR_08
;       2. Speed up system timer by a factor of 3
;       3. Set INT 08H vector to routine in this module
;****************************************************************
;
;********************|
;   save old INT 08H |
;********************|
; Uses DOS service 53 of INT 21H
        MOV     AH,53              ; Service request number
        MOV     AL,08H             ; Code of vector desired
        INT     21H
; ES -> Segment address of installed interrupt handler
; BX -> Offset address of installed interrupt handler
        MOV     SI,OFFSET CS:OLD_VECTOR_08
        MOV     CS:[SI],BX         ; Save offset of handler
        MOV     CS:[SI+2],ES       ; and segment
;********************|
;   speed up system  |
;     timer by 3     |
;********************|
; Original divisor is 65,536
; New divisor (65,536/3) = 21,845
;       CLI                        ; Interrupts off while write
                                   ; LSB then MSM
                                   ; xxxx 011x binary system
        OUT     43H,AL
        MOV     BX,21845           ; New divisor
        MOV     AL,BL
        OUT     40H,AL             ; Send LSB
        MOV     AL,BH
        OUT     40H,AL             ; Send MSB
;********************|
; set new INT 08H in |
;     vector table   |
;********************|
;
; Mask off all interrupts while changing INT 08H vector
        CLI
; Save mask in stack
```

```
        IN      AL,21H              ; Read 8259 mask register
        PUSH    AX                  ; Save in stack
        MOV     AL,0FFH             ; Mask off IRQ0 to IRQ7
        OUT     21H,AL              ; Write to 8259 mask register
; Install new interrupt vector
        MOV     AH,25H
        MOV     AL,08H              ; Interrupt code
        MOV     DX,OFFSET HEX08_INT
        INT     21H
; Restore original interrupt mask
        POP     AX                  ; Recover mask from stack
        OUT     21H,AL              ; Write to 8259 mask register
        STI                         ; Set 80x86 interrupt flag
; At this point the graphics program continues execution
        .
        .
        .

;***************************************************************
;                         exit routine
;***************************************************************
; Before the program returns control to the operating system
; it must restore the hardware to its original state. This
; requires resetting the time speed to 18.2 beats per second
; and re-installing the BIOS interrupt handler in the vector
; table
;*********************|
;   reset system timer  |
;*********************|
; Original divisor is 65,536
        CLI                         ; Interrupts off while write
                                    ; LSB then MSM
                                    ; xxxx 011x binary system
        OUT     43H,AL
        MOV     BX,65535            ; Default divisor
        MOV     AL,BL
        OUT     40H,AL              ; Send LSB
        MOV     AL,BH
        OUT     40H,AL              ; Send MSB
;*********************|
;   restore INT 0AH     |
;*********************|
        PUSH    DS                  ; Save program's DS
        MOV     SI,OFFSET CS:OLD_VECTOR_08
; Set DS:DX to original segment and offset of keyboard interrupt
        MOV     DX,CS:[SI]          ; DX -> offset
        MOV     AX,CS:[SI+2]        ; AX -> segment
```

```
            MOV     DS,AX               ; Segment to DS
            MOV     AH,25H              ; DOS service request
            MOV     AL,08H              ; Interrupt number
            INT     21H
            POP     DS
            STI                         ; Interrupts on again
; At this point the exiting program usually resets the video
; hardware to text mode and returns control to the operating
; system
                .
                .
                .

;*****************************************************************
;                       new INT 08H handler
;*****************************************************************
; The handler is designed so that a new timer tick cannot take
; place during execution. This is ensured by not sending the
; 8259 end-of-interrupt code until the routine's processing is
; complete
;*****************************************************************


HEX08_INT:
        STI                         ; Interrupts on
        PUSH    AX                  ; Save registers used by routine
        PUSH    BX
        PUSH    CX                  ; Other registers can be pushed
        PUSH    DX                  ; if necessary
        PUSH    DS
; User video image update routine is coded at this point
            .
            .
            .

; The intercept routine maintains a code segment variable named
; TIMER_COUNT which stores a system timer pulse count. This
; variable is used to return control to the system timer
; interrupt every third timer beat, thus maintaining the
; original rate of 18.2 beats per second
        DEC     CS:TIMER_COUNT
        JZ      TIME_OF_DAY         ; Exit through time_of_day
;********************|
;     direct exit    |
;********************|
        MOV     AL,20H              ; Send end-of-interrupt code
        OUT     20H,AL              ; to 8259 interrupt controller
        POP     DS                  ; Restore registers
        POP     DX
```

```
        POP     BX
        POP     AX
        IRET                            ; Return from interrupt
;
;*********************|
;   pass to original  |
;   INT 08H handler   |
;*********************|
TIME_OF_DAY:
        MOV     CS:TIMER_COUNT,2 ; Reset counter variable
        POP     DS
        POP     DX
        POP     BX
        POP     AX
        STC                             ; Continue processing
        JMP     DWORD PTR CS:OLD_VECTOR_08
        IRET
;
;*********************|
;   code segment data |
;*********************|
TIMER_COUNT     DB      2       ; Timer counter
OLD_VECTOR_08   DD      0       ; Far pointer to original INT
08H
                .
                .
                .
;
CODE    ENDS
```

Interference Problems

IBM microcomputer software that uses the system timer to produce a pulse for
animation routines encounter interference problems. At least two methods are
available to avoid or minimize display interference: to turn-off the CRT while
the buffer is being changed or to time the buffer updates with the vertical
retrace cycle of the CRT controller. Neither method is a panacea; as we have
already mentioned it is not always possible to produce smooth real-time
animation in an IBM microcomputer. Applications can try either or both
methods and select the better option. The following coding template fragment
shows the processing necessary to turn off the VGA video display system.

```
; Template file name: ANIMATE2.TPL
; Screen is turned off by setting the Clocking Mode register bit
; number 5 of the VGA Sequencer Group
        MOV     DX,03C4H        ; Sequencer group
```

```
        MOV     AL,01H          ; Clocking Mode register
        OUT     DX,AL           ; Select this register
        JMP     SHORT $+2       ; I/O delay
        INC     DX              ; To data port 3C5H
        IN      AL,DX           ; Read Clocking Mode register
        OR      AL,00100000B    ; Set bit 5, preserve others
        OUT     DX,AL           ; Write back to port
; At this point the VGA video display function is OFF
        .
        .
        .
```

The reverse process is necessary to turn on the VGA video display system.

```
; Template file name: ANIMATE3.TPL
; Screen is turned on by clearing the Clocking Mode register bit
; number 5 of the VGA Sequencer Group
        MOV     DX,03C4H        ; Sequencer group
        MOV     AL,01H          ; Clocking Mode register
        OUT     DX,AL           ; Select this register
        JMP     SHORT $ + 2     ; I/O delay
        INC     DX              ; To data port 3C5H
        IN      AL,DX           ; Read Clocking Mode register
        AND     AL,11011111B    ; Clear bit 5, preserve others
        OUT     DX,AL           ; Write back to port
; At this point the VGA video display function is ON
        .
        .
        .
```

The second method for reducing interference is to synchronize the video buffer update with the vertical retrace cycle of the CRT controller. In the following section we will see how, in some systems, we can enable an interrupt that occurs on the vertical retrace cycle. But whether the vertical retrace interrupt is available or not, it is possible to detect the start of the vertical retrace cycle in order to perform the buffer update operations while the CRT controller is turned off. The following coding template shows the processing necessary to detect the start of the vertical retrace in VGA systems.

```
; Template file name: ANIMATE4.TPL
; Test for start of the vertical retrace cycle of the CRT
; controller. Bit 3 of the Input Status Register 1 is set if a
; vertical cycle is in progress
        MOV     DX,3DAH         ; VGA Input Status register 1
VRC_CLEAR:
        IN      AL,DX           ; Read byte at port
```

```
        TEST    AL,00001000B      ; Is bit 3 set?
        JNZ     VRC_CLEAR         ; Wait until bit clear
; At this point the vertical retrace ended. Wait for it to
; restart
VRC_START:
        IN      AL,DX             ; Read byte at port
        TEST    AL,00001000B      ; Is bit 3 set?
        JZ      VRC_START         ; Wait until bit set
; At this point a vertical retrace cycle has just started
; The code can now proceed to update the video image
                .
                .
                .
```

Figure 2.7 is a bitmap of the Input Status register 0 and 1 of the VGA General Register Group. Notice that bit 7 of the Input Status register 0 can be used to detect the vertical retrace cycle only if the vertical retrace interrupt is enabled. If not, we must use bit 3 of Input Status register 1, as in the above code fragment.

9.3.5 The Vertical Retrace Interrupt

For many IBM microcomputer graphics applications the most satisfactory method for obtaining a timed pulse is by programming the CRT controller to generate an interrupt at the start of the vertical retrace cycle. The EGA, VGA, and XGA screen refresh rate, which is 70 cycles per second, is more than sufficient to produce smooth animation. In fact, the most important objection to this method is that it leaves very little time in which to perform image or data processing operations between timed pulses. Another consideration is that not all IBM and IBM-compatible video systems support a vertical retrace interrupt. For example, the IBM VGA Adapter is not documented to support the vertical retrace interrupt. The same applies to many VGA cards by third party vendors. Therefore VGA programs that use the vertical retrace interrupt may not be portable to these systems.

One advantage of using the vertical retrace interrupt as a time-pulse generator is that, since screen updates take place while the video system is turned off, interference is automatically avoided. The typical method of operation is to synchronize the screen update with the beginning of the vertical retrace cycle of the CRT controller. How much processing can be done while the CRT is off depends on the system hardware. In VGA systems this depends mainly on the type and speed of the CPU and the memory access facilities. XGA systems have their own graphics coprocessor and, for this reason, can execute considerably more processing during the vertical retrace cycle. Notice that in IBM XGA documentation the vertical retrace cycle is called the screen blanking period.

VGA Vertical Retrace Interrupt

In VGA systems the smooth animation of relatively small screen objects can be executed satisfactorily by vertical retrace synchronization. As the screen objects get larger it is more difficult to update the video buffer in the short time lapse of the vertical retrace cycle. Since so many performance factors enter into the equation it is practically impossible to give exact limits or guidelines for satisfactory animation. For example, the demonstration program, MATCH, furnished with the book's microdisk uses the vertical retrace interrupt to animate a running boar target. At the same time, the user interactively animates by mouse controls the image of a crosshair symbol. Both simultaneous animation operations used in the MATCH program tax VGA and system performance to the maximum. For this reason the program requires an IBM microcomputer equipped with a 80386 or 486 processor to perform satisfactorily. A certain bumpiness is noticeable in the MATCH animation when the program executes in a 80286 or slower machine.

It is often possible to program around the limitations of vertical retrace timing. In the first place, the image update operation can be split into two or more vertical retrace cycles. This is possible because the jerkiness frequency of 20 cycles per second is considerably less than the typical vertical retrace pulse of 70 cycles per second. However, splitting the update operations introduces programming complications, as well as an additional overhead in keeping track of which portion of the image is to be updated in each cycle. This method should be considered only if no simpler solution is available.

We mentioned that in VGA the vertical retrace cycle of the CRT controller takes place at a rate of approximately 70 times per second. In VGA systems that support the vertical retrace interrupt, software can enable it as a pulse generator and install a routine that receives control on every vertical retrace cycle. The following coding template contains the program elements necessary for the installation and operation of a vertical retrace intercept in a VGA system.

```
; Template file name: ANIMATE5.TPL
;*************************************************************
;*************************************************************
;             vertical retrace interrupt pulse generator
;                        for VGA systems
;*************************************************************
;*************************************************************
;
; Operations performed during installation:
; 1. The VGA port base address is stored in a code segment
;       variable named CRT_PORT and the default contents of the
;       Vertical Retrace End register are stored in a variable
;       named OLD_VRE
; 2. The address of the interrupt 0AH handler is saved in a
```

```
;        far pointer variable named OLD_VECTOR_0A
; 3. A new handler for interrupt 0AH is installed at the label
;    HEX0A_INT.
; 4. The IRQ2 bit is enabled in the 8259 (or equivalent)
;    interrupt controller mask register
; 5. The vertical retrace interrupt is activated
;
; Operation:
;    The new interrupt handler at INT 0AH gains control with
;    every vertical retrace cycle of the CRT controller.
;    The software can perform limited buffer update operations
;    at this time without causing video interference
;
;****************************************************************
;                    Installation routine for
;                  the vertical retrace interrupt
;****************************************************************
; The following code enables the vertical retrace interrupt on
; a VGA system and intercepts INT 0AH (IRQ2 vector)
;*********************|
;    save parameters  |
;*********************|
; System port address is saved in CS variables
        CLI                       ; Interrupts off
        MOV     AX,0H             ; Clear AX
        MOV     ES,AX             ; and ES
        MOV     DX,ES:[0463H]     ; Get CRT controller base
                                  ; address from BIOS data area
        MOV     CS:CRT_PORT,DX    ; Save address in memory
        MOV     AL,11H            ; Offset of Vertical Retrace End
                                  ; register in the CRTC
        OUT     DX,AL             ; Select this register
; Value stored in port's data register is saved in a code
; segment variable for later use by the software
        INC     DX                ; Point to Data register
        IN      AL,DX             ; Read default value in register
        JMP     SHORT $+2         ; I/O delay
        MOV     CS:OLD_VRE,AL     ; Save value in variable
;*********************|
;   save old INT 0AH  |
;*********************|
; Uses DOS service 53 of INT 21H to store the address of the
; original INT 0AH handler in a code segment variable
        MOV     AH,53             ; Service request number
        MOV     AL,0AH            ; Code of vector desired
        INT     21H
```

```
; ES -> Segment address of installed interrupt handler
; BX -> Offset address of installed interrupt handler
        MOV     SI,OFFSET CS:OLD_VECTOR_0A
        MOV     CS:[SI],BX          ; Save offset of original
                                    ; handler
        MOV     CS:[SI+2],ES        ; and segment
;*********************|
; install this INT 0AH |
;         handler      |
;*********************|
; Uses DOS service 37 of INT 21H to install the present handler
; in the vector table
        MOV     AH,37               ; Service request number
        MOV     AL,0AH              ; Interrupt code
        PUSH    DS                  ; Save data segment
        PUSH    CS
        POP     DS                  ; Set DS to CS for DOS service
        MOV     DX,OFFSET CS:HEX0A_INT
        INT     21H
        POP     DS                  ; Restore local data
;*********************|
;     enable IRQ2      |
;*********************|
; Clear bit 2 of the 8259 Mask register to enable the IRQ2 line
        CLI                         ; Make sure interrupts are off
        MOV     DX,21H              ; Port address of 8259 Mask
                                    ; register
        IN      AL,DX               ; Read byte at port
        AND     AL,11111011B        ; Mask for bit 2
        OUT     DX,AL               ; Back to 8259 port
;*********************|
;   activate vertical  |
;   retrace interrupt  |
;*********************|
        MOV     DX,CS:CRT_PORT      ; Recover CRT base address
        MOV     AL,11H              ; Offset of Vertical Retrace End
                                    ; register in the CRTC
        MOV     AH,CS:OLD_VRE       ; Default value in Vertical
                                    ; Retrace End register
        AND     AH,11001111B        ; Clear bits 4 and 5 in VRE
                                    ; Bit 4 = clear vertical
                                    ; interrupt
                                    ; Bit 5 = enable vertical
                                    ; retrace
        OUT     DX,AX               ; To port
        OR      AH,00010000B        ; Mask to set bit 4 to re-enable
```

```
        OUT     DX,AX
        STI                             ; Enable interrupts
; At this point the vertical retrace interrupt is active
; Program code to follow

        .
        .
        .

;******************************************************************
;                        exit routine
;******************************************************************
; Before the program returns control to the operating system
; it must restore the hardware to its original state. This
; requires disabling the vertical retrace interrupt and
;  restoring the original INT 0AH handler in the vector table
;*********************|
;   disable vertical  |
;      interrupts     |
;*********************|
; Code assumes that on program entry the vertical retrace
; was disabled
        MOV     DX,CS:CRT_PORT  ; Recover CRT base address
        MOV     AL,11H          ; Offset of Vertical Retrace End
                                ; register in the CRTC
        MOV     AH,CS:OLD_VRE   ; Default value in Vertical
                                ; Retrace End register
        OUT     DX,AX           ; To port
;*********************|
;   restore original  |
;   INT 0AH handler   |
;*********************|
        MOV     SI,OFFSET CS:OLD_VECTOR_0A
; Set DS:DX to original segment and offset of keyboard interrupt
        MOV     DX,CS:[SI]      ; DX -> offset
        MOV     AX,CS:[SI+2]    ; AX -> segment
        MOV     DS,AX           ; segment to DS
        MOV     AH,25H          ; DOS service request
        MOV     AL,0AH          ; IRQ2
        INT     21H
; At this point the exiting program usually resets the video
; hardware to a text mode and returns control to the operating
; system

        .
        .

;******************************************************************
;          VGA vertical retrace interrupt handler
;******************************************************************
```

```
; The following routine gains control with every vertical
; retrace interrupt (approximately 70 times per second)
; The code can now perform limited video buffer update
; operations without interference
; The vertical retrace interrupt is not re-enabled until the
; routine has concluded to avoid reentrancy
;*****************************************************************
HEX0A_INT:
        CLI                         ; Interrupts off
; Save registers
        PUSH    AX                  ; Save context at interrupt time
        PUSH    BX
        PUSH    CX
        PUSH    DX
        PUSH    ES
;*********************|
;   test for vertical |
;   retrace interrupt |
;*********************|
; Since several hardware interrupts can be located at IRQ2 the
; software must make sure that it was the vertical retrace that
; originated this action. This is done by testing bit 7 of the
; Input Status Register 0, which will be set if a vertical
; retrace interrupt has occurred
        MOV     DX,3C2H             ; Input Status Register 0
        IN      AL,DX               ; Read byte at port
        TEST    AL,10000000B        ; Is bit 7 set
        JNE     VRI_CAUSE           ; Go if vertical retrace
;*********************|
; chain to next handler|
;*********************|
; At this point the interrupt was not due to a vertical retrace
; Execution is returned to the IRQ2 handler
        POP     ES                  ; Restore context
        POP     DX
        POP     CX
        POP     BX
        POP     AX
        STC                         ; Continue processing
        JMP     DWORD PTR CS:OLD_VECTOR_0A
;*********************|
; animation operations |
;*********************|
VRI_CAUSE:
; At this point the handler contains the graphics operations
; necessary to perform the animation function
```

```
            .
            .
            .
;**********************|
; service routine exit |
;**********************|
; Enable 8259 interrupt controller to receive other interrupts
        MOV     AL,20H          ; Port address
        OUT     20H,AL          ; Send EOI code
; Re-enable vertical retrace interrupt by clearing bits 4 and 5
; of the Vertical Retrace End register and then setting bit 5
; so that the interrupt is not held active
        MOV     DX,CS:CRT_PORT  ; Recover CRT base address
        MOV     AL,11H          ; Offset of Vertical Retrace End
                                ; register in the CRTC
        MOV     AH,CS:OLD_VRE   ; Default value in VRE register
        AND     AH,11001111B    ; Clear bits 4 and 5
                                ; 4 = clear vertical interrupt
                                ; 5 = enable vertical retrace
        OUT     DX,AX           ; To port
        OR      AH,00010000B    ; Set bit 4 to reset flip-flop
        OUT     DX,AX           ; To port
;**********************|
;   restore context    |
;**********************|
; Registers used by the service routine are restored from the
; stack
        POP     ES
        POP     DX
        POP     CX
        POP     BX
        POP     AX
        STI                     ; Re-enable interrupts
        IRET
;***********************************************************************
;                       code segment data
;***********************************************************************
OLD_VECTOR_0A   DD      0       ; Pointer to original INT 0AH
                                ; interrupt
CRT_PORT        DW      0       ; Address of CRT controller
OLD_VRE         DB      0       ; Original contents of VRE
                                ; register
            .
            .
            .
```

Applications can extend the screen update time by locating the animated image as close as possible to the bottom of the video screen. In this manner the interference-free period includes not only the time lapse during which the beam is being diagonally reaimed, but also the period during which the screen lines above the image are being scanned. This technique is used in the MATCH program included in the book's microdisk.

XGA Screen Blanking Interrupt

The XGA documentation refers to the vertical retrace cycle as the screen blanking period. Two interrupts sources are related to the blanking period: the start of picture interrupt and the start of blanking interrupt. The start of picture coincides with the end of the blanking period. Both interrupts are enabled in the XGA Interrupt Enable register (offset 21x4H). Figure 9.4 shows a bit map of the XGA Interrupt Enable register.

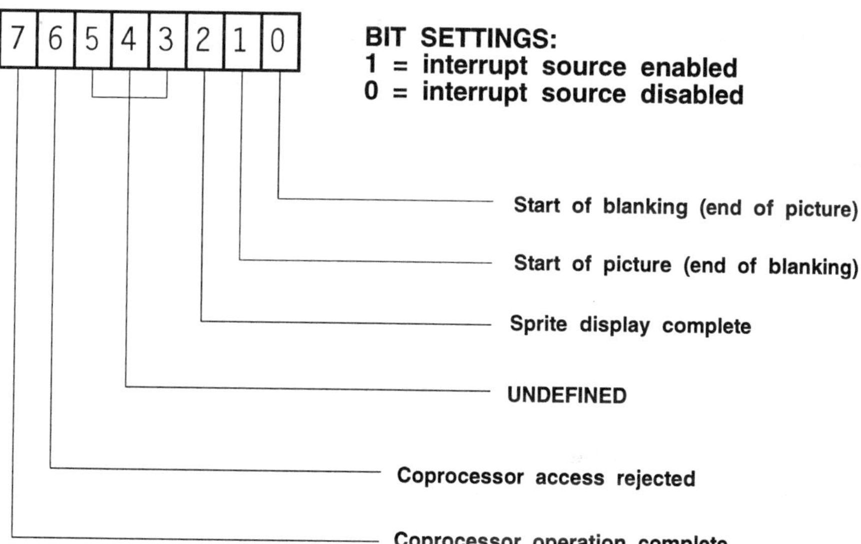

Figure 9.4 *XGA Interrupt Enable Register Bitmap*

Like the VGA interrupts, the XGA video interrupts are vectored to the IRQ2 line of the 8259/A (or compatible) interrupt controller chip, which is mapped to the 0AH vector. By testing the bits in the Interrupt Status register (at offset 21x5H) an XGA program can determine the cause of an interrupt on this line. Figure 9.5 shows a bit map of the XGA Interrupt Status register.

The XGA Interrupt Status register is also used to clear an interrupt condition. This operation is performed by the handler in order to reset the interrupt origin. The following template contains the program elements necessary for the installation and operation of a vertical retrace intercept in an XGA system.

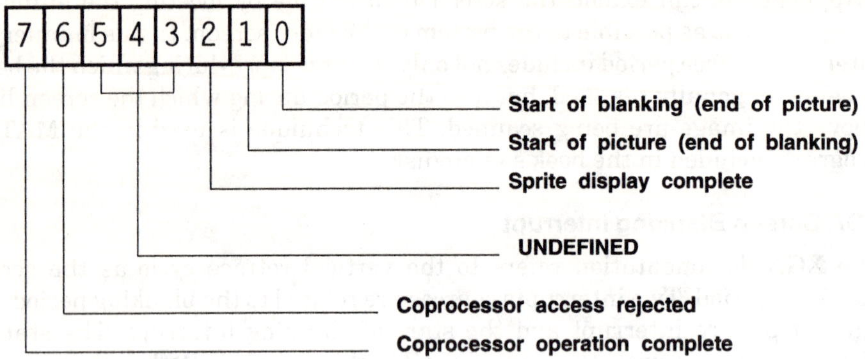

Figure 9.5   *XGA Interrupt Status Register Bitmap*

```
; Template file name: ANIMATE6.TPL
;*****************************************************************
;*****************************************************************
;            screen blanking interrupt pulse generator
;                      for XGA systems
;*****************************************************************
;*****************************************************************
;
; Operations performed during installation:
; 1. The XGA port base address is stored in a code segment
;     variable named XGA_BASE
; 2. The address of the interrupt 0AH handler is saved in a
;     far pointer variable named OLD_VECTOR_0A
; 3. A new handler for interrupt 0AH is installed at the label
;     XGA_0A_INT.
; 4. The IRQ2 bit is enabled in the 8259 (or equivalent)
;     Interrupt Controller Mask register
; 5. The XGA screen blanking interrupt is enabled
;
; Operation:
; 3. The new interrupt handler at INT 0AH gains control with
;     every vertical retrace cycle of the CRT controller.
;     The software can perform limited buffer update operations
;     at this time without causing video interference
;
```

```
;**************************************************************
;                    Installation routine for
;                  the XGA screen blanking interrupt
;**************************************************************
; The following code enables the screen blanking interrupt on
; a XGA system and intercepts INT 0AH (IRQ2 vector)
;*********************|
;       init XGA      |
;*********************|
; XGA initialization is performed by means of the services in
; the XGA1 and XGA2 modules of the GRAPHSOL library
        CALL    OPEN_AI           ; Open Adapter Interface for use
        CALL    INIT_XGA          ; Initialize XGA hardware
; The INIT_XGA procedure returns the address of the XGA register
; base in the BX register. The code stores this value in a code
; segment variable named XGA_BASE
        MOV     CS:XGA_BASE,BX ; Store in code segment variable
        MOV     AL,2              ; Select mode XGA mode number 2
                                  ; 1024-by-768 pixels in 256
                                  ; colors
        CALL    XGA_MODE          ; Mode setting procedure
;*********************|
;   save old INT 0AH  |
;*********************|
; Uses DOS service 53 of INT 21H to store the address of the
; original INT 0AH handler in a code segment variable
        MOV     AH,53             ; Service request number
        MOV     AL,0AH            ; Code of vector desired
        INT     21H
; ES -> Segment address of installed interrupt handler
; BX -> Offset address of installed interrupt handler
        MOV     SI,OFFSET CS:OLD_VECTOR_0A
        MOV     CS:[SI],BX        ; Save offset of original
        MOV     CS:[SI+2],ES      ; handler and segment
;*********************|
; install this INT 0AH |
;        handler       |
;*********************|
; Uses DOS service 37 of INT 21H to install the present handler
; in the vector table
        MOV     AH,37             ; Service request number
        MOV     AL,0AH            ; Interrupt code
        PUSH    DS                ; Save data segment
        PUSH    CS
        POP     DS                ; Set DS to CS for DOS service
        MOV     DX,OFFSET CS:XGA_0A_INT
```

```
        INT     21H
        POP     DS                  ; Restore local data
;*********************|
;    enable IRQ2      |
;*********************|
; Clear bit 2 of the 8259 Mask register to enable the IRQ2 line
        CLI                         ; Make sure interrupts are off
        MOV     DX,21H              ; Port address of 8259 Mask
                                    ; register
        IN      AL,DX               ; Read byte at port
        AND     AL,11111011B        ; Mask for bit 2
        OUT     DX,AL               ; Back to 8259 port
;*********************|
;  activate XGA screen |
;  blanking interrupt  |
;*********************|
; Reset all interrupts in the Status register
        MOV     DX,CS:XGA_BASE  ; Base address of XGA video
        ADD     DX,05H              ; Interrupt Status register
        MOV     AL,0C7H             ; All ones
        OUT     DX,AL               ; Reset all bits
; Enable the start of blanking cycle interrupt source (bit 0)
        MOV     DX,CS:XGA_BASE  ; XGA base address
        ADD     DX,04H              ; Interrupt Enable register
        IN      AL,DX               ; Read register contents
        OR      AL,00000001B        ; Make sure bit 0 is set
        OUT     DX,AL               ; Back to Interrupt Enable
                                    ; register
        STI                         ; Interrupts ON
; At this point the XGA start of blanking interrupt is active
; Program code to follow

            .

            .

            .

;***********************************************************************
;                           exit routine
;***********************************************************************
; Before the program returns control to the operating system
; it must restore the hardware to its original state. This
; requires disabling the XGA screen blanking interrupt and
; restoring the original INT 0AH handler in the vector table
;*********************|
;  disable XGA screen |
;  blanking interrupt |
;*********************|
        MOV     DX,CS:XGA_BASE  ; XGA base address
```

```
        ADD       DX,04H              ; Interrupt Enable register
        IN        AL,DX               ; Read register contents
        AND       AL,11111110B        ; Make sure bit 0 is clear
        OUT       DX,AL               ; Back to Interrupt Enable
                                      ; register
;********************|
;   restore original |
;   INT 0AH handler  |
;********************|
        MOV       SI,OFFSET CS:OLD_VECTOR_0A
; Set DS:DX to original segment and offset of keyboard interrupt
        MOV       DX,CS:[SI]          ; DX —> offset
        MOV       AX,CS:[SI+2]        ; AX —> segment
        MOV       DS,AX               ; segment to DS
        MOV       AH,25H              ; DOS service request
        MOV       AL,0AH              ; IRQ2
        INT       21H
; At this point the exiting program usually resets the video
; hardware to a text mode and returns control to the operating
; system
            .
            .
            .
;****************************************************************
;              XGA screen blanking interrupt handler
;****************************************************************
;
; The following routine gains control with every vertical
; retrace interrupt (approximately 70 times per second)
; The code can now perform limited video buffer update
; operations without interference
; In order to avoid interrupt reentrancy, the screen blanking
; interrupt is not reenabled until the routine has concluded
;
;****************************************************************
XGA_0A_INT:
        CLI                           ; Interrupts off
; Save registers
        PUSH      AX                  ; Save context at interrupt time
        PUSH      BX
        PUSH      CX
        PUSH      DX
        PUSH      ES
;********************|
;   test for screen  |
;   blanking interrupt |
```

```
;*********************|
; Since several hardware interrupts can be located at IRQ2 the
; software must make sure that it was screen blanking that
; originated this action. This can be done by testing bit 0 of
; the XGA Interrupt Status register
        MOV     DX,CS:XGA_BASE  ; XGA base address
        ADD     DX,05H          ; Interrupt Status register
        IN      AL,DX           ; Read register contents
        TEST    AL,00000001B    ; Test start of blanking bit
        JNZ     BLK_CAUSE       ; Go if bit set
;*********************|
; chain to next handler|
;   if not blanking    |
;*********************|
; At this point the interrupt was not due to an XGA screen
; blanking interrupt. Execution is returned to the IRQ2 handler
        POP     ES                      ; Restore context
        POP     DX
        POP     CX
        POP     BX
        POP     AX
        STC                             ; Continue processing
        JMP     DWORD PTR CS:OLD_VECTOR_0A
;*********************|
; animation operations |
;*********************|
BLK_CAUSE:
; At this point the handler contains the graphics operations
; necessary to perform the animation function
            .

            .

            .
;*********************|
; service routine exit |
;*********************|
; Enable 8259 interrupt controller to receive other interrupts
        MOV     AL,20H          ; Port address
        OUT     20H,AL          ; Send EOI code
; The handler must reset bit 0 of the XGA Interrupt Status
; register to clear the interrupt condition
        MOV     DX,CS:XGA_BASE  ; Display controller base
                                ; address
        ADD     DX,05H          ; Interrupt Status register
        IN      AL,DX           ; Read status
        OR      AL,00000001B    ; Set bit 0, preserve others
        OUT     DX,AL           ; Reset start of blanking
```

```
;********************|
;   restore context  |
;********************|
; Registers used by the service routine are restored from the
; stack
        POP     ES
        POP     DX
        POP     CX
        POP     BX
        POP     AX
        STI                             ; Reenable interrupts
        IRET
;*****************************************************************
;                       code segment data
;*****************************************************************
OLD_VECTOR_0A    DD      0      ; Pointer to original INT 0AH
                                ; interrupt
XGA_BASE         DW      0      ; Address of CRT controller

        .
        .
        .
```

The comparatively high performance of the XGA system makes possible the smooth animation of images much larger and elaborate than those that can be animated in VGA. Whenever possible the animation routine should use direct coprocessor programming (see Chapter 7) in order to minimize execution time. The system memory to video RAM pixBlt operation discussed in Section 7.4.3 can often be used in XGA animation.

10

Bit-Mapped Graphics

Chapter Summary

This chapter describes the various techniques and standards used in encoding computer graphics images into units of memory storage. The chapter includes a discussion of three popular image data storage formats: Compuserve's GIF, Aldus Corporation's TIFF format, and Hewlett-Packard's PCL bit-mapped fonts. It also describes the various data compression methods used in reducing the size of image data files, such as the PackBits and Lempel-Ziv-Welch (LZW) algorithms.

10.0 Image File Encoding

Bit-mapping is the graphics technique whereby a memory bit represents the attribute of a screen pixel. In previous chapters we created and manipulated bit-mapped image in an intuitive and almost primitive manner. The encodings were tailored to the specific video hardware, for example, in 16-color modes we used a 4-bit image code in IRGB format, and in 256-color modes, a double-bit format based on an IIRRGGBB encoding. In all cases the encodings we so far used have contained little more than the image's pixel-by-pixel color for a particular display system setup.

However, a graphics image can be encoded in more a complete and efficient structure than is offered by a pixel-by-pixel attribute list. A limitation of a raw pixel color list is that in most IBM graphics system the pixel attribute is not a color code in itself, but an index into a color look-up table. For example, in XGA 256-color modes the pixel value 00001100B is displayed as bright red if the LUT registers are in the default setting, but the same code corresponds to a light shade of green if the LUT is changed to the IIRRGGBB encoding (see the XGALUT program in the book's microdisk). This means that the actual pixel code is meaningless if the image encoding does not offer information about the LUT register setting. LUT register data can be furnished implicitly by designating a conventional format, such as IRGB, or explicitly, as a list of values to be loaded into the DAC registers.

The movement towards the standardization of image file encodings in IBM microcomputers originated with commercial software developers in need of methods for storing and displaying graphics images. At the present time there are over 20 different image file encodings in frequent use. It is common for a graphics application import or export service to present the user with over a dozen image file formats. Although some of these commercial encodings have gained more popularity than others, very little has been achieved in standardizing image file encodings for IBM microcomputers. In this chapter we have selected the image file formats that we believe are more useful and that have gained more widespread acceptance in the IBM microcomputer field. This selection does not imply that we endorse these particular encodings or approve of their design or operation.

10.0.1   Raw Image Data

We mentioned that the simplest possible image data encoding is a bare list of pixel attributes. This simple encoding, called the *raw image data*, is often all that is required by a graphics application. For example, the monochrome bitmap of a running boar target is encoded in the MATCH program (see book's microdisk) as raw image data. Figure 10.1 shows the bitmap and pixel list.

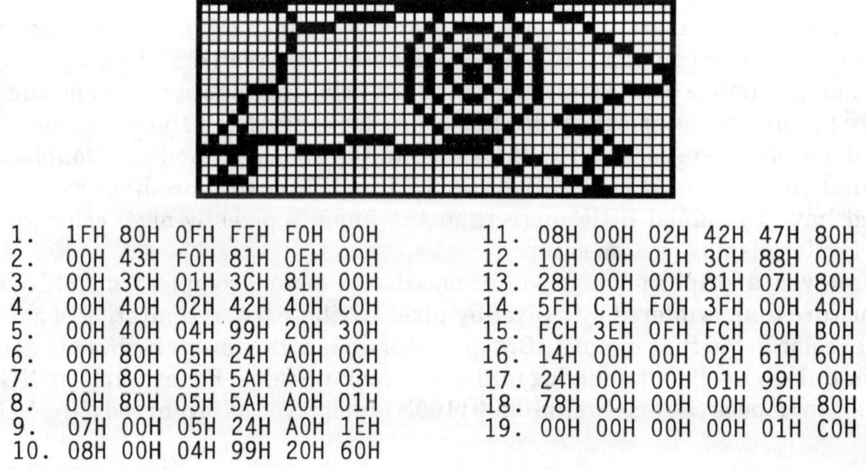

```
 1.   1FH 80H 0FH FFH F0H 00H        11.   08H 00H 02H 42H 47H 80H
 2.   00H 43H F0H 81H 0EH 00H        12.   10H 00H 01H 3CH 88H 00H
 3.   00H 3CH 01H 3CH 81H 00H        13.   28H 00H 00H 81H 07H 80H
 4.   00H 40H 02H 42H 40H C0H        14.   5FH C1H F0H 3FH 00H 40H
 5.   00H 40H 04H 99H 20H 30H        15.   FCH 3EH 0FH FCH 00H B0H
 6.   00H 80H 05H 24H A0H 0CH        16.   14H 00H 00H 02H 61H 60H
 7.   00H 80H 05H 5AH A0H 03H        17.   24H 00H 00H 01H 99H 00H
 8.   00H 80H 05H 5AH A0H 01H        18.   78H 00H 00H 00H 06H 80H
 9.   07H 00H 05H 24H A0H 1EH        19.   00H 00H 00H 00H 01H C0H
10.   08H 00H 04H 99H 20H 60H
```

Figure 10.1 *Raw Image Data for a Monochrome Bitmap*

Since the image in Figure 10.1 is displayed in monochrome, the encoding is based on a bit-per-pixel scheme; a 1-bit in the attribute list indicates that the screen pixel is set, a 0-bit indicates that it remains in the background attribute. The reader can match the first line of the encoding (1FH 80H 0FH FFH F0H 00H) with the pixels on the top image row. The first value on the list (1FII = 00011111B) corresponds to the first eight image pixels, the second value on the list (80H = 10000000B) corresponds to the next eight image pixels, and so forth to the last value on the list.

But a display routine usually requires more data than can be encoded in a pixel attribute list. For example, the procedure named MONO_MAP_18 in the VGA2 module of the GRAPHSOL library requires the x and y screen coordinates, the color attribute, and the number of pixel rows and columns in the bitmap. This data is furnished to the MONO_MAP_18 procedure in a preamble data block that precedes the pixel attribute list. The following code fragment corresponds to the image block for the left-hand running boar target used in the MATCH program (see the MATCHC.ASM module in the book's microdisk).

```
;********************|
; left-to-right boar   |
;********************|
; Block control area:                            Displacement ->
LPIG_X  DW      4              ; Present x coordinate           0
LPIG_Y  DW      440            ; y coordinate                   2
        DB      19             ; Horizontal rows in block       4
        DB      6              ; Number of bytes per row        5
; Pixel attribute list for the left-hand running boar target
        DB      01FH,080H,00FH,0FFH,0F0H,000H ; 1
        DB      000H,043H,0F0H,081H,00EH,000H ; 2
        DB      000H,03CH,001H,03CH,081H,000H ; 3
        DB      000H,040H,002H,042H,040H,0C0H ; 4
        DB      000H,040H,004H,099H,020H,030H ; 5
        DB      000H,080H,005H,024H,0A0H,00CH ; 6
        DB      000H,080H,005H,05AH,0A0H,003H ; 7
        DB      000H,080H,005H,05AH,0A0H,001H ; 8
        DB      007H,000H,005H,024H,0A0H,01EH ; 9
        DB      008H,000H,004H,099H,020H,060H ; 10
        DB      008H,000H,002H,042H,047H,080H ; 11
        DB      010H,000H,001H,03CH,088H,000H ; 12
        DB      028H,000H,000H,081H,007H,080H ; 13
        DB      05FH,0C1H,0F0H,03FH,000H,040H ; 14
        DB      0FCH,03EH,00FH,0FCH,000H,0B0H ; 15
        DB      014H,000H,000H,002H,061H,060H ; 16
        DB      024H,000H,000H,001H,099H,000H ; 17
        DB      078H,000H,000H,000H,006H,080H ; 18
        DB      000H,000H,000H,000H,001H,0C0H ; 19
        DW      0000H                                      ; padding
```

```
;
BOAR_COLOR       DB        00000100B          ; Red bit set
```

Notice that the pixel attribute list in the above code fragment corresponds to the raw data in Figure 10.1. Also that the display color is encoded in a separate variable (named BOAR_COLOR) whose address is passed to the MONO_MAP_18 display routine in the BX register. The block format in the above image is customized to store the data necessary to the MONO_MAP_18 display routine. The advantage of this method is that only the necessary data for the display manipulations is encoded with the raw pixel attribute list. This provides a compact data structure which can be used in optimizing the code. On the other hand, this customized encoding would almost certainly not be portable to any other graphics application.

The program designer must often decide whether to use a customized format, that usually includes only the data that is strictly necessary for the display routine, or to represent the image in one of the general purpose formats that are recognized by other graphics applications. The basis for this decision is usually one of image portability. A stand-alone program (such as MATCH) which has no need to communicate graphics data to other applications, can use a raw data format whenever it is convenient. On the other hand, an application that must exchange image data with other graphics programs could benefit from adopting one of the existing image data formats described later in this chapter.

10.0.2   Bitmaps in Monochrome and Color

Etymologically, the term monochrome means "of one color," however, in computer jargon, it is often interpreted as black-and-white. This equivalency is certainly untrue in bit-mapped graphics, because a monochrome bitmap can be displayed in any available color or attribute. Furthermore, it is possible to combine several monochrome bitmaps to form a multicolor image on the screen. For example, several of the color images used in the MATCH program (furnished in the book's microdisk) are composites formed by overlaying separate monochrome bitmaps. The image of the rifle in the initial MATCH screen (see color plate 6) is formed by overlaying the monochrome bitmaps shown in Figure 10.2.

The original image of the rifle used in the first screen of the MATCH program was scanned from a black-and-white catalog illustration into a bitmap editing program. The three color overlays in Figure 10.2 were created by editing the original scan. The overlays were then saved into disk based image files in the TIFF format (discussed later in this chapter). The MATCH program successively reads and displays the three monochrome bitmaps and superimposes them to form a multicolor image. Notice that the order in which the bitmaps are displayed is important, because if two overlays contain a common pixel, this pixel is shown in the attribute of the last bitmap displayed.

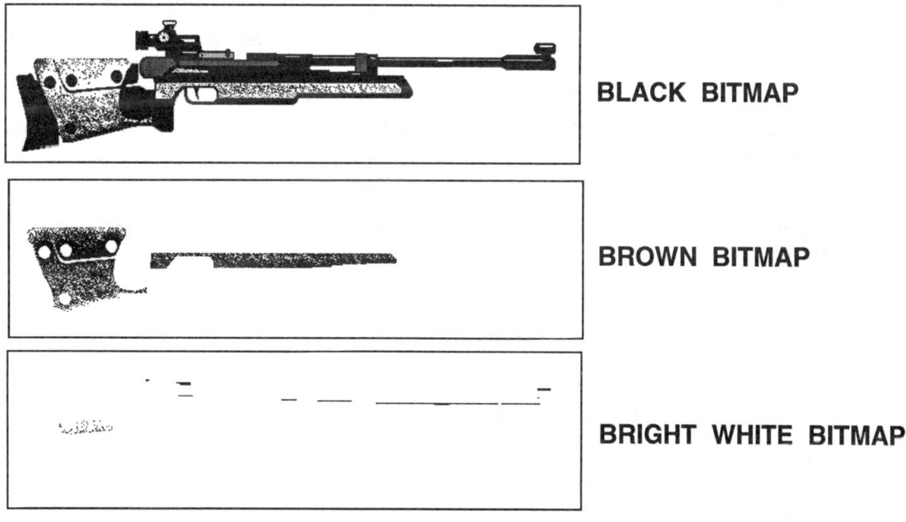

Figure 10.2 *Monochrome Overlays to Form a Color Image*

A color image can also be stored in a single bitmap in which each pixel is represented in any of the available colors. The result is a more compact image file and a faster display operation. In fact, the only reasons for using several monochrome bitmaps in the creation of a color image are convenience and limited resources. The raw pixel data format for a color image often matches the characteristics of the video system for which it is intended. In VGA, SuperVGA, and XGA systems color images are typically stored in 16 or 256 colors. We already mentioned that, in IBM microcomputers, the pixel color data is an index into a look-up table (LUT) and the actual pixel color is determined by the setting of the DAC registers.

10.0.3   Image Data Compression

Bit-mapped image data takes up considerable memory space. For example, the raw image data for a full screen, in an XGA or SuperVGA mode of 1024-by-768 pixels resolution in 256 colors, requires approximately 768K. This is three-fourth of the total memory space available in an IBM microcomputer under MS-DOS. Consequently, several data compression schemes have been devised to reduce the memory space required for storing pixel-coded images. However, image data compression is achieved at a price: the additional processing time required for packing and unpacking the image data. In microcomputer graphics, performance is usually such a critical factor that this overhead is an important consideration in adopting a compressed data format.

Many of the compression methods used for alphanumeric data are not adaptable for image data. In the first place, all of the irreversible techniques used in character data compaction cannot be used for graphics images, since image data must be restored integrally. The same applies to many semantic-dependant techniques of various degrees of effectiveness. On the other hand, some general principles of data compression are applicable to graphics and packed bits encoding schemes can be used to compress pixel color data. For example, the IRGB encoding used in VGA 16-color graphics modes can be packed into two codes per byte, saving one half the storage space required for unpacked data.

Run-Length Encoding

The principles of *run-length encoding* are particularly useful in compacting graphics data. The method is based on the suppression of repeated character codes, according to the principle that if a character is repeated three times or more, then the data can be more compactly represented in coded form. Run-length encoding is a simple and efficient graphics data compression scheme based on the assumption that image data often contains entire areas of repeated pixel values. Notice that approximately two-thirds of the bitmaps shown in Figure 10.2 consist of NULL pixels (white background color). Furthermore, even the images themselves contain substantial areas of black and of uniform shades of gray. In this case a simple compression scheme could be used to pack the data in the white, black, and gray areas so as to save considerable image storage space.

The Kermit protocol, well known in computer data transmission, uses a run-length encoding based on three data elements. The first code element indicates that a compression follows, the second character is the repetition code, and the third one represents the repetition count. The PackBits compression algorithm, which originated in the Macintosh computers, is an even more efficient run-length encoding scheme for graphics image data. The TIFF image file format discussed later in this chapter uses PackBits compression encoding.

Facsimile Compression Methods

Facsimile machines and methods (FAX) are often used in transmitting alpha-numeric characters and graphics image data over telephone lines. Several compression protocols have been devised for facsimile transmission. The International Telegraph and Telephone Consultative Committee (CCITT), based in Geneva, Switzerland, has standardized several data compression protocols for use in facsimile equipment. The TIFF convention has adapted the CCITT standards to the storage of image data in computer systems. Notice that the actual compression algorithm used in CCITT is a variation of a method known developed by David A. Huffman in the nineteen fifties. The CCITT method, which is quite efficient for monochrome scanned and dithered images, is elaborate and difficult to implement.

LZW Compression

LZW is a compression technique suited to color image data. The method is named after Abraham Lempel, Jabob Ziv, and Terry Welch. The algorithm, also known as Ziv-Lempel compression, was first published in 1977 in an article by Ziv and Lempel in the *IEEE Transactions on Information Theory*. The compression technique was refined by Welch in an article titled "A Technique for High-Performance Data Compression" that appeared in *Computer*, in 1984 (see bibliography). LZW compression is based on converting raw data into a reversible encoding in which the data repetitions are tokenized and stored in compressed form. LZW compression is used in many popular data and image compression programs, including the Compuserve GIF image data encoding format and in some versions of the TIFF standard. Notice that LZW compression has been patented by Unisys Corporation. Thereforc its commercial use requires a license from the patent holders. The following statement is inserted at the request of Unisys Corporation:

"The LZW data compression algorithm is said to be covered by U.S. Patent 4,558,302 (the "Welch Patent".) The Welch Patent is owned by Unisys Corportation. Unisys has a significant number of licensees of the patent and is comitted to licensing the Welch Patent on reasonable non-discriminatory terms and conditions. For further information, contact Unisys Welch Licensing Department, P.O. Box 500, Blue Bell, PA 19424, M/S C1SW19."

LZW algorithm is explained later in this chapter.

10.0.4 Encoders and Decoders

An encoder is a program or routine used to convert raw image data into a standard format. We speak of a GIF encoder as a program or routine used to store a graphics image in a file structured in the GIF format. A decoder program or routine performs the reverse operation, that is, it reproduces the graphics image or the raw data from the information stored in an encoded image file. In the more conventional sense, a GIF decoder displays on the screen an image file stored in the Compuserve GIF format. Therefore the fundamental tool-kit for operating with a given image data format consists of encoder and decoder code. Notice that with some compressed image formats the processing required in encoders and decoders can be quite elaborate.

10.1 The Graphics Interchange Format (GIF)

The Graphics Interchange Format (GIF) originated in the Compuserve computer information service. The first description of the GIF protocol, which appeared on the Compuserve Picture Support Forum on May 28, 1987, was identified with the code letters GIF87a, while the current version is labeled

GIF89a. GIF is the only graphics image storage format in use today that is not associated with any software company. Although the GIF standard is copyright, Compuserve grants royalty-free adoption rights to anyone wishing to use it. This means that, according to Compuserve, software developers are free to use the GIF encodings by accepting the terms of the Compuserve licensing agreement, which basically states that all changes to the standard must be made by the copyright holders and that the software utilizing GIF must acknowledge Compuserve's ownership. The agreement can be obtained form the Compuserve Graphics Technology Department or from the graphics forum files.

GIF was conceived as a compact and efficient storage and transmission format for computer imagery. The GIF87a specification supports multiple images with a maximum of 16,000-by-16,000 pixels resolutions in 256 colors. This format is quite suited to the maximum resolution available today in SuperVGA and XGA systems, although it seems that the 256-color modes will soon require expansion.

The advantages of the GIF standard are related to its being compact, powerful, portable, and, presumably, public. Also the fact that there is an extensive collection of public domain images in GIF format which can be found in the Compuserve graphics forums and in many bulletin board services. The programmer should keep in mind that images of recognizable individuals often require the person's release before the image can be legally used commercially. This is true even if the image file is publicly available.

The major disadvantage of the GIF standard is that many commercial programs do not support it. Consequently, users of popular graphics programs often discover that GIF is not included in the relatively extensive catalog of file formats which the application can import and export. This limitation can often be solved by means of a conversion utility that translates a format recognized by the particular application into a GIF encoding. Several of these format conversion utilities are available on the Compuserve graphics forums.

GIF Sources

The main sources of information about the GIF standard are the graphics forums on the Compuserve Information Service. The specifications of GIF89a are available in the file GIF89A.DOC found in library number 14 of the Compuserve Graphics Support forum. Image files in the GIF format are plentiful on the Compuserve Graphics Support libraries as well as in many BBS's. In this book's microdisk we have included several public domain image files in the GIF format. Also in the book's microdisk is a Shareware GIF file display program named Compushow.

10.1.1 The GIF File Structure

The two versions of the GIF standard at the time of this writing are labeled GIF87a and GIF89a. Version 89a is an extension of version 87a which adds several features to the original GIF protocol, namely: the display of text messages, comments, and application and graphics control data. The detailed description of the GIF protocol is found in the file GIF89A.DOC mentioned in the previous paragraph. The following description is limited to the features common to both the GIF87a and GIF89a specifications.

The GIF87a format is defined as a series of blocks and sub-blocks containing the data necessary for the storage and reproduction of a computer graphics image. A GIF data stream contains the data stored in these blocks and sub-blocks in the order defined by the GIF protocol. The first block in the data stream is the *header* and the last one is the *trailer*. Image data and other information is encoded between the header and trailer blocks. These can include a logical screen descriptor block, a global color table, as well as one or more local image descriptors, local color tables, and compressed image data. The GIF89a protocol allows graphics control and rendering blocks, plain text blocks, and an application data block. Figure 10.3 shows the elements of the GIF87a data stream.

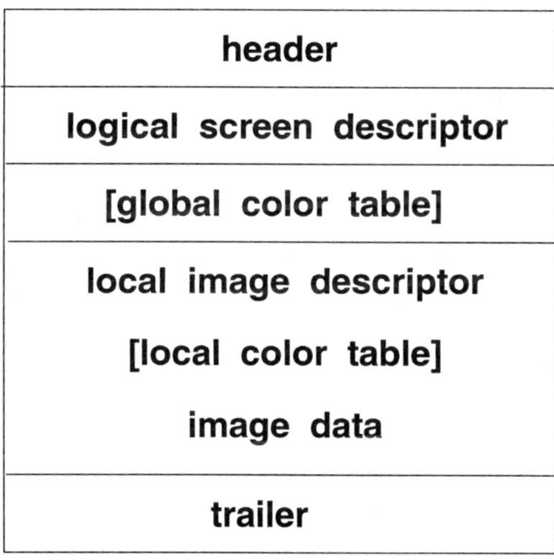

Figure 10.3 *Elements of the GIF Data Stream*

Header

The first item in the GIF data stream is the header. It consists of six ASCII characters. The first three characters, called the signature, are the letters "GIF." The following three characters encode the GIF version number. The value "87a" in this field refers to the version of the GIF protocol approved in May, 1987, while the value "89a" refers to the GIF version dated July, 1989. Figure 10.4 shows the elements of the GIF header.

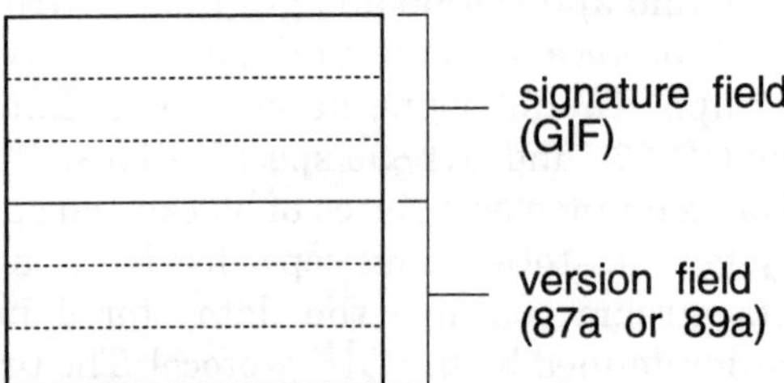

Figure 10.4 *The GIF Header*

One header must be present in each GIF data stream. A GIF encoder must initialize all six characters in the GIF header. The version number field should correspond with the earliest GIF version that defines all the blocks in the actual data stream. In other words, a GIF file that uses only the elements of the GIF87a protocol should contain the characters 87a in the version field of the GIF header, even if the file was created after the implementation of the GIF89a protocol. The GIF decoder uses the information in the header block to certify that the file is encoded in the GIF format and to determine version compatibility.

Logical Screen Descriptor

The block immediately following the header is named the *logical screen descriptor*. This block contains the information about the display device or mode compatible with the image. One logical screen descriptor block must be present in each GIF data stream. Figure 10.5 shows the elements of the logical screen descriptor block.

The fields of the GIF logical screen descriptor are formatted as follows:

1. The words at offset 0 and 2, labeled *logical screen width* and *logical screen height,* encode the pixel dimensions of the logical screen to be used by the display device. In IBM microcomputers this value usually coincides with the selected display mode.

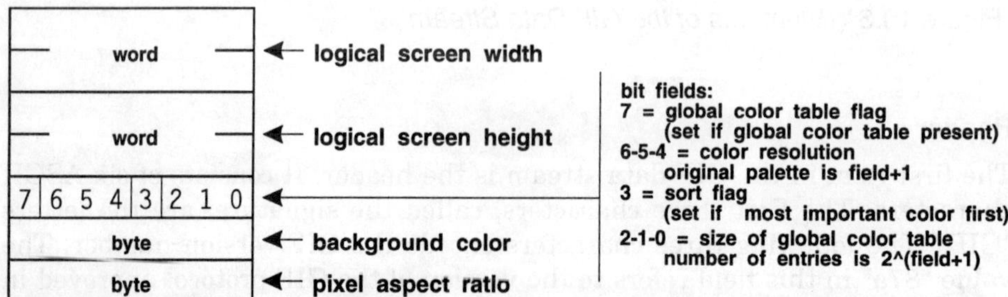

Figure 10.5 *The GIF Logical Screen Descriptor*

2. The byte at offset 4 is divided into four bit fields. Bit 7, labeled the *global color table flag*, serves to indicate if a global color table is present in the data stream that follows. The global color table is discussed later in this section. Bits 6, 5, and 4 are the *color resolution field*. This value represents the number of palette bits for the selected mode, plus one. For example, a 16-color VGA palette (4 bits encoding) would be represented by the bit value 011 (decimal 3). Bit 3, labeled the *sort flag*, is used to signal that the global color table (if present) is sorted starting with the most important colors. This information can be used by the software if the display device has fewer colors available than those used in the image. Finally, the field formed by bits 2, 1, and 0 determines the *size of the global color table* (if one is present). The value is encoded as a power of 2, diminished by 1. Therefore, to restore the original exponent it is necessary to add 1 to the value encoded in the bit field. For example, a bit value of 011 (3 decimal) corresponds to a global color table representing 2^4, or 16 colors. Notice that this value corresponds with the number of color in the global color table, not with its byte length (discussed later in this section). The maximum representable value in a 3-bit field is 7, which limits the number of colors in the global color table to 2^8, or 256 colors.

3. The field at offset 5, labeled *background color* in Figure 10.5, is used to represent the color of those pixels located outside of the defined image or images. The value is an offset into the global color table.

4. The field at offset 6, labeled the *pixel aspect ratio* in Figure 10.5, is used to compensate for non-proportional x and y dimensions of the display device. (See Section 2.0.1.) This field should be set to zero for systems with a symmetrical pixel density, such as the most used modes in VGA and XGA systems.

Global Color Table

The *global color table* is an optional GIF block used to encode a general color palette for displaying images in data streams without a local color table. The global color table serves as a default palette for the entire stream. Recall that the GIF data stream can contain multiple images. The presence of a global color table and its size is determined from the data furnished in the logical screen descriptor block (see Figure 10.5). Only one global color table can be present in the data stream. Figure 10.6 shows the structure of a global color table.

The entries in the global color table consist of values for the red, green, and blue palette registers. Each component color takes up one byte in the table, therefore, each palette color consists of three bytes in the global color table. The number of entries in the global color table can be determined by reading bits 0, 1, and 2 of the global color size field in the logical screen descriptor block. (See Figure 10.5.) The byte length of the table is three times the number of entries. The maximum number of palette colors is 256. In this case the global color table takes up 768 bytes. (See Figure 10.6.)

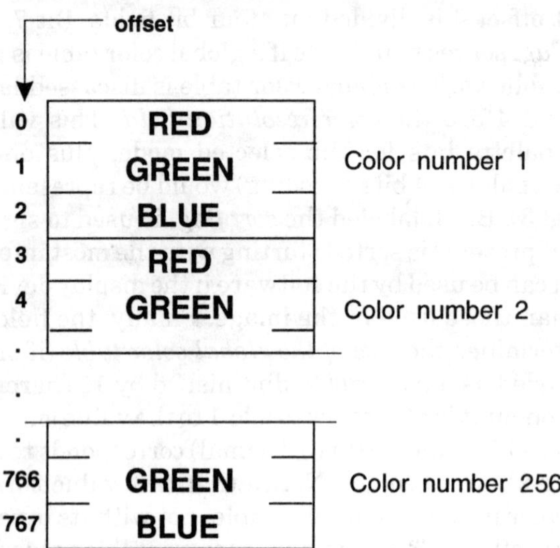

Figure 10.6   *The GIF Global Color Table*

Image Descriptor

Each image in the GIF data stream is defined by an image descriptor, an optional local color table, and one or more blocks of compressed image data. The *image descriptor* block contains the information for decoding and displaying the image. Figure 10.7 shows the elements of the image descriptor block.

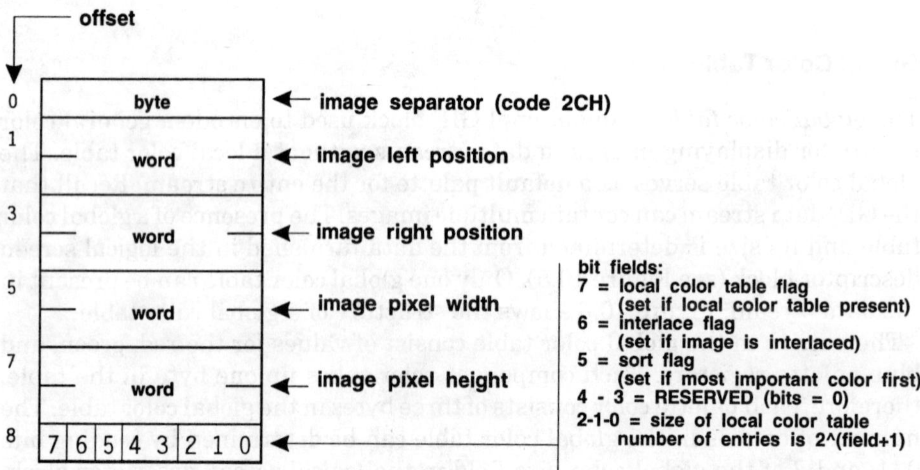

Figure 10.7   *The GIF Image Descriptor*

The fields of the GIF image descriptor are formatted as follows:

1. The byte at offset 0, labeled *image separator* in Figure 10.7, must be the code 2CH.

2. The words at offset 1 and 3, labeled *image left position* and *image right position* respectively (see Figure 10.7), cncode the screen column and row coordinates of the image's top left corner. This location is an offset within the logical screen defined in the logical screen descriptor block. (See Figure 10.5.)

3. The words at offset 5 and 7, labeled *image pixel width* and *image pixel height* respectively (see Figure 10.7), encode the size of the image, measured in screen pixels.

4. The byte at offset 8 in Figure 10.7 is divided into five bit fields. Bit 7, labeled the *local color table flag*, serves to indicate if a local color table follows the image descriptor block. If a local color table is present in the data stream it is used for displaying the image represented in the corresponding descriptor block. Bit 6, labeled *interlace flag*, encodes if the image is interlaced, that is, if its rows are not arranged in consecutive order. In IBM microcomputers interlaced images are used in some CGA and EGA display modes, but not in the proprietary VGA and XGA modes. Bit 5, labeled the *sort flag*, is used to signal that the local color table (if present) is sorted starting with the most important colors. This information can be used by the software if the display device has fewer available colors than those in the table. The field formed by bits 2, 1, and 0 determines the *size of the local color table* (if one is present). The value is encoded as a power of 2, diminished by 1. Therefore, to restore the original exponent it is necessary to add 1 to the value encoded in the bit field. For example, a bit value of 011 (3 decimal) corresponds to a global color table representing 2^4, or 16 colors. Notice that this value corresponds to the number of colors in the local color table, not with its byte length (refer to the previous discussion about the global color table).

Local Color Table

The *local color table* is an optional GIF block that encodes the color palette used in displaying the image corresponding to the preceding image descriptor block. If no local color table is furnished, the image is displayed using the values in the global color table. If neither table is present, it shall be displayed using the current setting of the DAC registers. The GIF data stream can contain multiple images, with each one having its own local color table. The structure of the local color table is identical to the one described for the global color table. (See Figure 10.6.)

Compressed Image Data

The image itself follows the local color table, if one is furnished, or the image descriptor block if the data stream does not include a local color table. The GIF standard sets no limit to the number of images contained in the data stream.

Image data is divided into sub-blocks, each sub-block can have at the most 255 bytes. The data values in the image are offsets into the current color palette. For example, if the palette is set to standard IRGB code, a pixel value of 1100B (decimal 12) corresponds to the 12th palette entry, which, in this case, encodes the LUT register settings for bright red.

Preceding the image data blocks is a byte value that holds the code size used for the LZW compression of the image data in the stream. This data item normally matches the number of bits used to encode the pixel color. For example, an image intended for VGA mode number 18, in 16 colors, has an LZW code size of 4, while an image for VGA mode number 19, in 256 colors, has an LZW code size of 8. Figure 10.8 shows the format of the GIF data blocks.

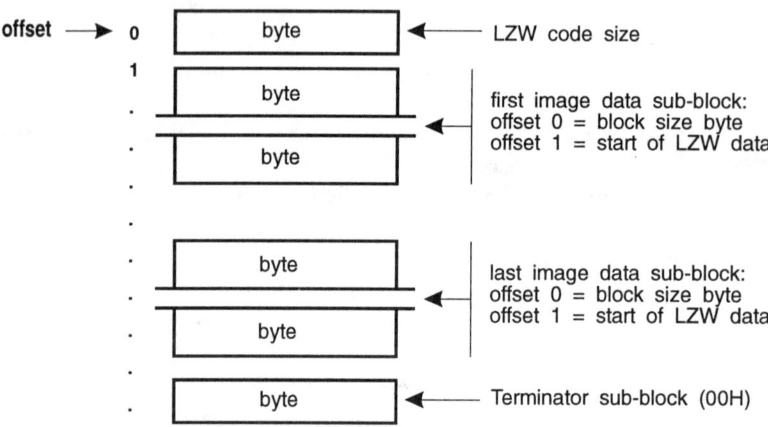

Figure 10.8   *The GIF Image Data Blocks*

The image data sub-blocks contain the image data in compressed form. The LZW compression algorithm used in the GIF protocol is discussed in Section 10.1.2. Each data sub-block starts with a block-size byte, which encodes the byte-length of the data stored in the rest of the sub-block. The count, which does not include the count byte itself, can be in the range 0 to 255. The compressed data stream ends with a sub-block with a zero byte count. (See Figure 10.8.)

Trailer

The simplest GIF block is named the *trailer*. This block consists of a single byte containing the GIF special code 3BH. Every GIF data stream must end with the trailer block. The GIF trailer is shown in Figure 10.9.

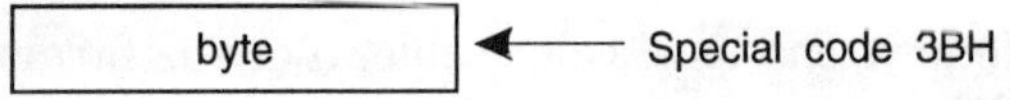

Figure 10.9   *The GIF Trailer*

GIF89a Extensions

We mentioned that GIF version 89a contains several features that are not present in version 87a. These features include the following new blocks:

1. A *graphics control extension* refers to a graphics rendering block, also a new feature introduced in version 89a. The graphics control extension contains information on displaying the rendering block. This information includes instructions about the disposing of the currently displayed image, handling the background color, action on user input, time delay during the display operation, and image transparency.

2. The *graphics rendering blocks* can be an image descriptor block, as described for GIF version 87a, or a new *plain text extension*. The plain text extension contains ASCII data to be displayed in a coarse grid of character cells determined in the block. Also in the plain text block are the foreground and background colors, the coordinates of the start position, and the text message itself.

3. The *applications extension* is an extension block in GIF version 89a that contains application-specific information. The block includes an 8-byte application identifier field intended for an ASCII string that identifies the particular piece of software. A 3-byte authentication code follows the identifier. Application data follows the authentication code field.

10.1.2 GIF Implementation of LZW Compression

One operation in creating a GIF image data file is the formatting of the various blocks according to the specifications described in the standard. (See Section 10.1.1.) This operation is quite simple and presents no programming complications. However, the image data in a GIF file must be stored in compressed form; the GIF standard offers no alternative. The compression algorithm adopted by GIF is the method originally devised by Lempel and Ziv and later improved by Welch (see Section 10.0.3). The implementation of this compression algorithm, often designated LZW (Lempel-Ziv-Welch) compression, is the most difficult programming operation in developing a GIF encoder or decoder program or routine.

LZW Concepts

The original concept of LZW compression is based on the assumption that the data to be compressed presents patterns of repetition. These repetitions can be in the form of the vowel-consonant patterns of all modern languages, in the words of a text file, or in the pixel repetition pattern of a graphics image. For this reason LZW compression has been successfully used in compressing both text and image data. Many well known compression programs found in bulletin boards, such as PAK, PKARK, PKZIP, and PKUNZIP, use LZW compression. In the graphics field LZW compression is used in GIF, TIFF, and other image file storage formats.

The programmer must consider that LZW is an algorithm, not a standard. This means that each particular implementor of a data compression scheme based on LZW feels free to adapt the algorithm to meet specific needs. In this manner LZW compression as used in the GIF standard is different from LZW compression as used in TIFF or in other data storage conventions. This in spite of the fact that the actual compression methods are quite similar in all LZW implementations. Once understood, LZW compression can be easily applied to match the requirements of any specific application.

The central idea of LZW compression is to replace repeated characters with individual symbols. In text compression this translates to encoding strings with single codes. In graphics compression the method consists of detecting repeated pixel patterns and representing them with a single value. LZW does not search the data for repetitions, but stores them as they are encountered in the data stream. The adverse consequences of this form of operation is that some significant patterns of repetition can be missed during the encoding, and that repeated patterns are often encoded more than once. The advantage of this "compress as you find them" technique is that the decoder can reconstruct the repetitions from the information in the data stream, making it unnecessary to transmit tables of patterns or other general decoding information.

The General LZW Algorithm

The LZW compression algorithm requires a basic table of codes representing each item in the data stream. For example, an alphanumeric implementation of LZW can be based on the IBM extended character set, which consists of 256 character codes. (See Table 1.2.) In this case the basic table contains 256 entries, one for each possible data code in the stream. On the other hand, an LZW implementation for pixel data in the IRGB format would require only a basic-table with 16 entries, one for each possible IRGB combination in the data stream.

The LZW compression codes start after the *basic table*. In the GIF implementation two special codes (discussed later in this section) are added at the end of the basic table. However, in the present discussion we assume that the compression codes start immediately after the basic table. For example, if the LZW implementation is based on 256 alphanumeric character codes, in the range 0 to 255, the first available compression code would be the value 256. The highest compression code in LZW is preset to the value 4095. Therefore, in this example, the compression codes would be values in the range 256-to-4095. In LZW compression, the part of the table that stores the repeated patterns is often called the *string table*.

The compression algorithm assumes that information is received in a continuous data stream and that the software has some means of detecting the end of this data stream. In our first example of LZW compression we assume, for the sake of simplicity, that the data stream consists of character bytes in the range 0-to-255. Therefore the basic table can contain codes in this range, and the string table starts at the value 256. Let us assume that the data stream consists of a series of monetary values separated by the slash symbol, as follows:

/$10.00/$22.00/$12.10/$222.00<EOI>

In the above data sample, the expression <EOI> indicates the presence of an "end of information" code in the data stream. The compression algorithm requires a scratchpad data structure which is sometimes called the *current string*. In the following description we arbitrarily designate the current string with the @ symbol. Compression takes place in the following steps:

STEP 1: Initialize the basic table with all the code combinations that can be present in the data stream. The string table codes start after the last code in the basic table.

STEP 2: Initialize the current string (scratchpad element) to a NULL string. Designate the current string as @.

STEP 3: Read character from the data stream. Designate the current character as C. If C = <EOI> then end execution.

STEP 4: Concatenate the current string (@) and the character (C) to form @+C.

STEP 5: If @+C is in the basic table or in the string table perform the following operations:

    a. @ = @+C

    b. go to STEP 3

STEP 6: If @+C is not in the basic table or in the string table perform the following operations:

    a. enter @+C in the string table

    b. send @ to the output stream

    c. @ = C

    d. go to STEP 3

The above description assumes that the data stream does not overflow the total number of allowed entries in the string-table. Later in this section we will present a working sample of GIF LZW compression that takes this possibility into account. Table 10.1 shows the LZW compression of the string listed above.

In the compression of the string in Table 10.1 notice the following interesting points:

1. On iteration number 1 the current string is initialized to a NULL string. Since the input character '/' is in the basic table, algorithm STEP 5 executes. Therefore @ = '/' at the conclusion of this iteration.

2. On iteration number 2 the current string (@) contains the initial value of '/' (previous character input). @+C becomes '/$', which is not in the basic table or the string table (the string table is empty at this time). Therefore, algorithm STEP 6 executes and '/$' is the first entry in the string-table, which is numbered 256.

Table 10.1 *LZW Compression Example*

String: /$10.00/$22.00/$12.10/$222.00<EOI>
Basic table: ASCCI codes in range 0 to 255

ITERATION NUMBER	INPUT STREAM	STRING TABLE ENTRY	OUTPUT STREAM	CURRENT STRING (@)		
				INITIAL	@+C	FINAL
1	'/'	NONE	--	NULL	'/'	'/'
2	'$'	256 = '/$'	'/'	'/'	'/$'	'$'
3	'1'	257 = '$1'	'$'	'$'	'$1'	'1'
4	'0'	258 = '10'	'1'	'1'	'10'	'0'
5	'.'	259 = '0.'	'0'	'0'	'0.'	'.'
6	'0'	260 = '.0'	'.'	'.'	'.0'	'0'
7	'0'	261 = '00'	'0'	'0'	'00'	'0'
8	'/'	262 = '0/'	'0'	'0'	'0/'	'/'
9	'$'	NONE	--	'/'	'/$'	'/$'
10	'2'	263 = '/$2'	<256>	'/$'	'/$2'	'2'
11	'2'	264 = '22'	'2'	'2'	'22'	'2'
12	'.'	265 = '2.'	'2'	'2'	'2.'	'.'
13	'0'	NONE	--	'.'	'.0'	'.0'
14	'0'	266 = '.00'	<260>	'.0'	'.00'	'0'
15	'/'	NONE	--	'0'	'0/'	'0/'
16	'$'	267 = '0/$'	<262>	'0/'	'0/$'	'$'
17	'1'	NONE	--	'$'	'$1'	'$1'
18	'2'	268 = '$12'	<257>	'$1'	'$12'	'2'
19	'.'	NONE	--	'2'	'2.'	'2.'
20	'1'	269 = '2.1'	<265>	'2.'	'2.1'	'1'
21	'0'	NONE	--	'1'	'10'	'10'
22	'/'	270 = '10/'	<258>	'10'	'10/'	'/'
23	'$'	NONE	--	'/'	'/$'	'/$
24	'2'	NONE	--	'/$'	'/$2'	'/$2'
25	'2'	271 = '/$22'	<263>	'/$2'	'/$22'	'2'
26	'2'	NONE	--	'2'	'22'	'22'
27	'.'	272 = '22.'	<264>	'22'	'22.'	'.'
28	'0'	NONE	--	'.'	'.0'	'.0'
29	'0'	NONE	--	'.0'	'.00'	'.00'
30	<EOI>	NONE	<266>			

3. On iteration number 3 the current string (@+C) contains '$1' which is not in the string table. Therefore STEP 6 executes again. In this case the '$1' is entry number 257 in the string table.

4. The iterations during which there is no entry in the string table (labeled NONE in Table 10.1) are those in which algorithm STEP 5 executes. Notice that no output takes place in this case.

5. Every iteration that produces an entry in the string table also generates output to the character stream (algorithm STEP 6). The output is the contents of the current string (@), which can be a single character or a string.

The string corresponds to an entry in the string table and is represented by its number.

6. Compression concludes when the "end of information" code is detected in the input stream. This situation takes place in iteration number 30 of Table 10.1.

Notice several important features of the LZW compression algorithm:

1. The compression codes are of variable length.

2. The decoder program is able to reproduce the string table from the input data. This table is identical to the one used by the encoder.

3. The use of variable-length codes results in greater compression efficiency than if the information were conveyed on fixed-size data packets.

4. The self-reproducing string table saves having to transmit conversion or character tables to the decoder.

The GIF Implementation

The implementation of LZW compression in the GIF protocol closely matches the original algorithm as described by Lempel, Ziv, and Welch. Two variations are introduced in the GIF implementation: a special code that serves to signal to the decoder that the string table must be cleared, and another one to signal the end of the compressed data. The code to clear the string table is often represented with the letters <CC> and the code to end the compressed data stream is identified as <EOI> (end of information).

These two special codes, <CC> and <EOI>, are added to the basic table. Since the GIF implementation is applied to graphics data, the basic table for GIF LZW compression consists of all the pixel codes used in the image, plus the "clear string table" code <CC> and the "end of information" code <EOI>. For example, in encoding a video image for VGA mode number 18, with 16 possible colors, the basic table would have the codes 0 to 15. In this case the clear code <CC> would be assigned code number 16, and the <EOI> code would be assigned number 17. Therefore, the first entry in the string table would correspond to code number 18. Since the LZW string table can extend to code number 4,095, the range in this case would be from 18-to-4,095.

LZW Code Size

We saw in Figure 10.8 that in the GIF encoding the compressed data in the first image data sub-block must be preceded with a byte that encodes the LZW code size. This value coincides with the bit-size of the elements in the basic table. In the example mentioned above, in which the image is encoded for VGA mode number 18, in 16 colors, the LZW code size is 4. By the same token, the LZW code size would be 8 for an image encoded in 256 colors.

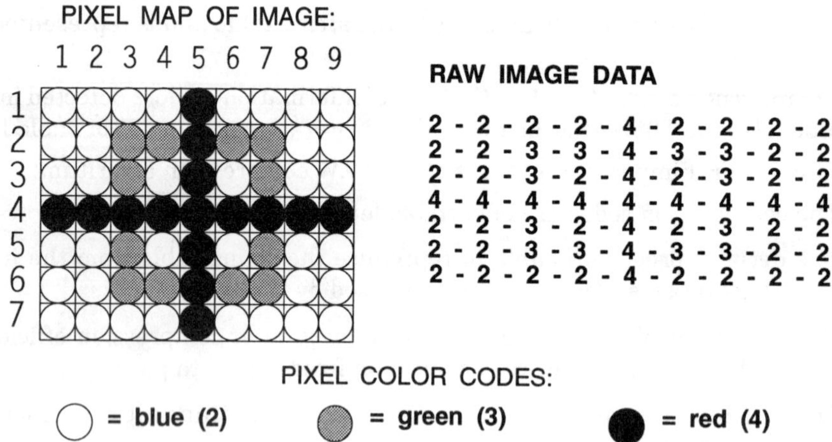

Figure 10.10   *Sample Image for GIF LZW Compression*

The GIF Image File

Perhaps the easiest way to understand the GIF encoding and its implementation of LZW compression is by an example. Figure 10.10 shows the pixel map of a simple graphics image in three colors.

The following code fragment shows the data structures necessary for encoding the image in Figure 10.10 in GIF format. In order to create a disk image of the GIF file we must first assemble the source and then strip off the object-file header appended by the assembler program. This can be easily done by means of the "write" command of a debugger program (such as Microsoft Debug or Symdeb) or of a disk file editing utility.

```
DATA      SEGMENT
;*********************|
;   GIF file header   |
;*********************|
; The 6-byte header block includes the GIF signature and version
; fields (see Figure 10.4)
      DB       'GIF87a'
;*********************|
;     logical screen  |
;       descriptor    |
;*********************|
; The logical screen descriptor block contains the information
; listed in Figure 10.5. In this example we have adopted a VGA
; resolution of 640-by-480 pixels in 8 colors
      DW       640              ; Logical screen width
      DW       480              ; Logical screen height
      DB       10100010B        ; Global flag
```

```
                              ; Global flag bitmap:
                              ; 0 0 1 1 0 0 0 0
                              ; 7 6 5 4 3 2 1 0 <= bits
                              ; | | | | | | |_|_|_ size of global color
                              ; | | | | | |         table (2 ^(field+1))
                              ; | | | | | |___ sort flag
                              ; | | | | |         1 = most important color
                              ; | | | |             first
                              ; | |_|_|_ color resolution original
                              ; |         palette is (field + 1)
                              ; |________ global color table
                              ;             1 = table present
                              ;             0 = no global table
        DB      0                 ; Background color index
                                  ; (meaningless in this case)
        DB      0                 ; Pixel aspect ration
                                  ; (symmetrical in VGA systems)
;********************|
;  global color table  |
;********************|
; The code furnishes an 8-entry global color table. Each entry
; consists of 3 bytes encoding the red, green, and blue values.
; Notice that only colors number 2, 3, and 4 are required by the
; image (see Figure 10.6)
;                     R    G    B       Color        color number
        DB      000H,000H,000H  ; Black          0
        DB      0BBH,0BBH,0BBH  ; White          1
        DB      000H,000H,0AAH  ; Blue           2
        DB      000H,0AAH,000H  ; Green          3
        DB      0AAH,000H,000H  ; Red            4
        DB      080H,080H,0AAH  ; Light blue     5
        DB      080H,0AAH,080H  ; Light green    6
        DB      0AAH,080H,080H  ; Light red      7
;********************|
;  image descriptor    |
;********************|
; This block contains the information listed in Figure 10.7
        DB      2CH               ; GIF image separator code
        DW      10                ; x coordinate for image
        DW      10                ; y coordinate
        DW      9                 ; Image width (in pixels)
        DW      7                 ; Image height (in pixels)
        DB      00000000B         ; Local flag
                      ; Local flag bitmap:
                      ; 1 0 0 0 0 0 1 0
                      ; 7 6 5 4 3 2 1 0 <= bits
```

```
;  |  |  |  |  |  |_|_|_  size of local color
;  |  |  |  |  |  |          table
;  |  |  |  |  |  |          value is 2 ^(field+1)
;  |  |  |  |  |_|________   RESERVED
;  |  |  |________ sort flag
;  |  |              1 = most important color
;  |  |                  first
;  |  |________ interlace flag
;  |              1 = image is interlaced
;  |              0 = image is not interlaced
;  |________ local color table flag
;              1 = table present
;              0 = no local table
;********************|
;      image data    |
;   (LZW compression) |
;********************|
; Follows image data compressed according to the GIF
; implementation of the LZW algorithm (see Figure 10.8)
        DB      3                       ; LZW code size
        DB      20                      ; Image size (in bytes)
        DB      028H,02AH,0B4H,03BH,083H,040H,037H,098H,0A8H,08CH
        DB      0E8H,0ADH,055H,06DH,098H,017H,04DH,08EH,0B5H,024H
        DB      0                       ; Block terminator
;********************|
;      trailer       |
;********************|
; The trailer is a single-byte block that marks the end of a GIF
; data stream. The required terminator code is 3BH (Figure 10.9)
        DB      3BH                     ; GIF terminator
DATA    ENDS
        END
```

Although only three colors are necessary for the image in Figure 10.10, we have added white and black to the palette. The monochrome colors are often added so as to allow displaying a color image in a black-and-white system. In Section 10.1.1, we mentioned that the number of colors in the GIF global and local color tables must coincide with powers of 2, therefore, 2, 4, 8, 16, 32, 64, 128, and 256 entries can be chosen for the palette. This example requires 5 colors, hence an 8-color palette is selected. Palette entry number 0 corresponds to the color black and entry number 1 to the color white. The colors corresponding to palette entries 2, 3, and 4 are shown in Figure 10.10. In actual programming we can either zero the remaining palette entries (5, 6, and 7) or set them to any given color value. However, the memory space must be reserved for the total number of palette entries. In the previous code sample, palette entries number 5, 6, and 7 have been initialized to light blue, light green, and light red respectively.

Table 10.2 *GIF LZW Compression Example*

Basic table: 0 - 7 = colors   8 = <CC>   9 = <EOI>   String table: 10 - 4095

ITERATION NUMBER	INPUT STREAM	STRING TABLE ENTRY	OUTPUT STREAM	CURRENT STRING (@) INITIAL	@+C	FINAL
1	---	NONE	8			
2	2 *	NONE	---	NULL	2	2
3	2	10 = 22	2	2	22	2
4	2	NONE	---	2	22	22
5	2	11 = 222	<10>	22	222	2
6	4	12 = 24	2	2	24	4
7	2	13 = 42	4	4	42	2
8	2	NONE	---	2	22	22
9	2	NONE	---	22	222	222
10	2	14 = 2222	<11>	222	2222	2
11	2 *	NONE	---	2	22	22
12	2	NONE	---	22	222	222
13	3	15 = 2223	<11>	222	2223	3
14	3	16 = 33	3	3	33	3
15	4	17 = 34	3	3	34	4
16	3	18 = 43	4	4	43	3
17	3	NONE	---	3	33	33
18	2	19 = 332	<16>	33	332	2
19	2	NONE	---	2	22	22
20	2 *	NONE	---	22	222	222
21	2	NONE	---	222	2222	2222
22	3	20 = 22223	<14>	2222	22223	3
23	2	21 = 32	3	3	32	2
24	4	NONE	---	2	24	24
25	2	22 = 242	<12>	24	242	2
26	3	23 = 23	2	2	23	3
27	2	NONE	---	3	32	32
28	2	24 = 322	<21>	32	322	2
29	4 *	NONE	---	2	24	24
30	4	25 = 244	<12>	24	244	4
31	4	26 = 44	4	4	44	4
32	4	NONE	---	4	44	44
33	4	27 = 444	<26>	44	444	4
34	4	NONE	---	4	44	44
35	4	NONE	---	44	444	444
36	4	28 = 4444	<27>	444	4444	4
37	4	NONE	---	4	44	44
38	2 *	29 = 442	<26>	44	442	2
39	2	NONE	---	2	22	22
40	3	30 = 223	<10>	22	223	3
41	2	NONE	---	3	32	32
42	4	31 = 324	<21>	32	324	4
43	2	NONE	---	4	42	42
44	3	32 = 423	<13>	42	423	3
44	2	NONE	---	3	32	32
45	2	NONE	---	32	322	322
46	2 *	33 = 3222	<24>	322	3222	2
47	2	NONE	---	2	22	22
48	3	NONE	---	22	223	223
49	3	34 = 2233	<30>	223	2233	3
50	4	NONE	---	3	34	34
51	3	35 = 343	<17>	34	343	3
52	3	NONE	---	3	33	33
53	2	NONE	---	33	332	332
54	2	36 = 3322	<19>	332	3322	2
55	2 *	NONE	---	2	22	22
56	2	NONE	---	22	222	222
57	2	NONE	---	222	2222	2222
58	2	37 = 22222	<14>	2222	22222	2
59	4	NONE	---	2	24	24
60	2	NONE	---	24	242	242
61	2	38 = 2422	<22>	242	2422	2
62	2	NONE	---	2	22	22
63	2	NONE	---	22	222	222
64	<EOI>	NONE	<11>			
65			9			

The image descriptor block in the previous code sample contains the x and y coordinates for image display. Notice that we have placed the image at 10 pixels from the screen's top left corner. Also that the image dimensions are 9 horizontal pixels by 7 pixel rows, as in Figure 10.10.

GIF LZW Encoding

In the previous code fragment we saw that the image data consists of the LZW code size byte, a block count byte, 20 image code bytes, and the block terminator code 00H. The process of obtaining the compressed codes is shown in Table 10.2.

Notice, in Table 10.2, that the raw data from the image in Figure 10.10 is used as an input stream for GIF LZW compression, and that the first code output to the stream is the clear string-table command <CC> which is assigned the value 8. Also that the output stream ends in the end-of-information code <EOI>, which is number 9 in this case. The rest of the output stream is generated following the LZW algorithm as described in the general example in Table 10.1.

The asterisks in Table 10.2 mark the first characters of each image row. (See Figure 10.10.) Also notice that the string-table entries in the output stream are enclosed with angle brackets to differentiate them from the basic-table entries. Table 10.3 shows the processing operations required to obtain the compressed data encoding from the output stream in Table 10.2.

Table 10.3   *GIF LZW Compression Data Processing*

STRING TABLE ENTRY	OUTPUT STREAM (FROM TABLE 10.2)		BLOCKED BINARY OUTPUT	HEXADECIMAL VALUE
	DECIMAL	BINARY		
	8	1000	00101000	28
10	2	0010		
11	10	1010	00101010	2A
12	2	0010		
13	4	0100	10110100	B4
14	11	1011		
15	11	1011	00111011	3B
16 <==	3	0011		
17	3	00011	10000011	83
18	4	00100	01000000	40
19	16	10000		
20	14	01110	00110111	37
21	3	00011	10011000	98
22	12	01100		
23	2	00010	10101000	A8
24	21	10101		
25	12	01100	10001100	8C
26	4	00100	11101000	E8
27	26	11010		
28	27	11011	10101101	AD
29	26	11010	01010101	55
30	10	01010		
31	21	10101	01101101	6D
32 <==	13	01101		
33	24	011000	10011000	98
34	30	011110	00010111	17
35	17	010001	01001101	4D
36	19	010011		
37	14	001110	10001110	8E
38	22	010110	10110101	B5
	11	001011	00100100	24
	9	001001		

We mentioned that an important characteristic of the LZW compression algorithm is the variable-length of the encoded data. In Table 10.3, we can see that the binary column of compression codes starts at four bits width, then changes to five bits, and later to six bits wide. Notice that the variable width of the output codes results from the increasing values of the string-table entry numbers, since the entries from the basic table are always limited to the initial range. In the example in Table 10.2, the first string-table entry is number 10, which is representable in 4 bits, but the last entry is number 38, which requires 6 bits.

The arrows in Table 10.3 signal the string-table entry numbers 16 and 32. The value 16 is the first one requiring a 5-bit encoding and the value 32 is the first requiring a 6-bit encoding. Therefore, as soon as table entry number 16 is generated, the representation of the output codes is increased by 1-bit. Another 1-bit increase takes place immediately after table entry number 32. The width increases take place automatically after the table entry is created (not as wider codes are required in the output stream) because the decoding software must be able to predict the code-length changes. Figure 10.11 is a flowchart of LZW compression as implemented in the GIF standard.

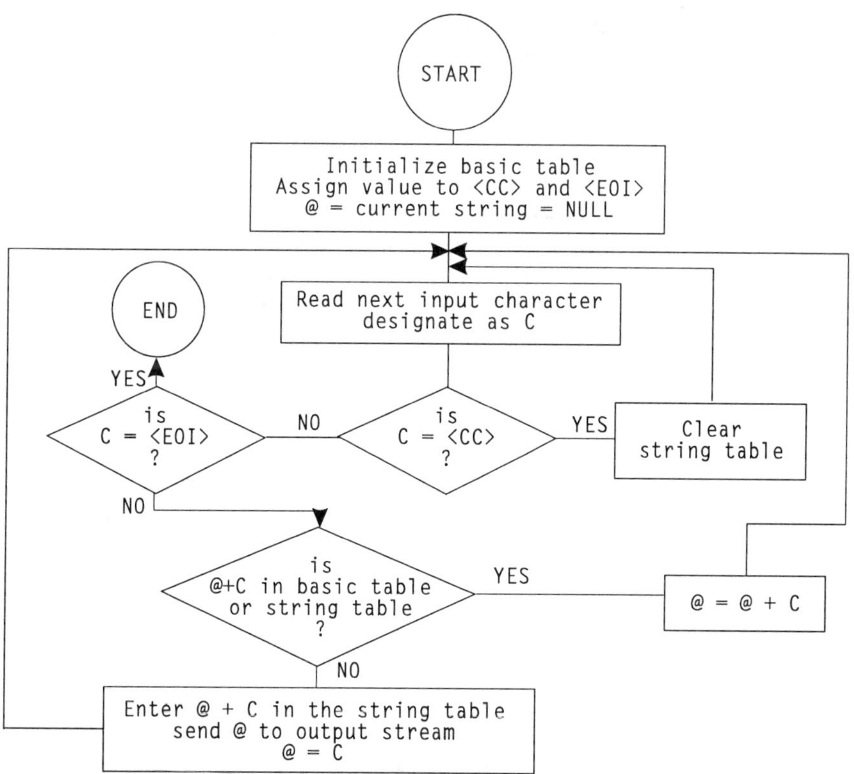

Figure 10.11 *GIF LZW Compresssion Flowchart*

GIF encoder software must block the variable-length binary output codes that result from the compression process into groups of 8-bits so that they can be stored in byte-size memory cells or transmitted through the communications lines. The blocking operation consists of packing these bits right-to-left as shown in Table 10.3. Observe that the last column of this table, labeled "hexadecimal value," coincides with the image data listed in the GIF image code fragment.

GIF LZW Decoding

GIF decoding software obtains system and image information from the standard data blocks in the file. The first operation performed by the decoder is to make certain the GIF signature is present at the start of the file and the processing software is compatible with the version field of this block. The GIF standard recommends that if the decoder encounters a version with which it is not familiar, the software should post a warning message and process the file as best it can.

As is the case with the encoder, the most elaborate operation to be performed by the decoder software is regarding the LZW compressed data. GIF LZW decompression follows the reverse process as the compression previously described. To the decoder the compression codes form the input stream. The initial bit width is calculated by adding 1 to the value in the LZW code-size field of the image block. Table 10.4 is a LZW decompression example that uses as input the compressed string generated in Table 10.1.

Table 10.4   LZW Decompression Example

ITERATION	INPUT STREAM	OLD CODE (%)	CHARACTER (C)	OUTPUT STREAM	STRING TABLE (% + C)
		Basic table: ASCCI codes in range 0-to-255			
1	'/'	—	'/'	'/'	——--
2	'$'	'/'	'$'	'$'	256 = '/$'
3	'1'	'$'	'1'	'1'	257 = '$1'
4	'0'	'1'	'0'	'0'	258 = '10'
5	'.'	'0'	'.'	'.'	259 = '0.'
6	'0'	'.'	'0'	'0'	260 = '.0'
7	'0'	'0'	'0'	'0'	261 = '00'
8	<256>	'0'	'/'	'/$'	262 = '0/'
9	'2'	<256>	'2'	'2'	263 = '/$2'
10	'2'	'2'	'2'	'2'	264 = '22'
11	<260>	'2'	'.'	'.0'	265 = '2.'
12	<262>	<260>	'0'	'0/'	266 = '.00'
13	<257>	<262>	'$'	'$1'	267 = '0/$'
14	<265>	<257>	'2'	'2.'	268 = '$12'
15	<258>	<265>	'1'	'10'	269 = '2.1'
16	<263>	<258>	'/'	'/$2'	270 = '10/'
17	<264>	<263>	'2'	'22'	271 = '/$22'
18	<266>	<264>	'.'	'.00'	272 = '22.'

The decompression algorithm, as described below uses a variable to temporarily store the previous input value. This variable is placed in the column labeled OLD CODE in Table 10.4 and designated with the % symbol. The decompression process can be described as follows:

STEP 1: Initialize the basic table with all the code combinations that can be present in the data stream. The string table codes start after the last code in the basic-table.

STEP 2: Create a variable named OLD CODE (%) to hold the previous input. Initialize % to NULL. Designate the first character of the current input value as C.

STEP 3: Read first character from the data stream. If C = <EOI> then end execution. If C = <CC> then re-initialize string table. If not, then output the first character.

STEP 4: If C is a character in the basic table perform the following operations:
    a. output C
    b. % = C
    c. create a new string table entry with the value % + C.
    d. go to STEP 4

STEP 5: If C is a compression code perform the following operations:
    a. look up compression code in string-table and output value
    b. % = C
    c. C = first character in compression string
    d. create a new string table entry with the value % + C.
    e. go to STEP 4

Notice that in performing the read-operation the software must keep track of bit boundaries in the input data. Also, note that the algorithm assumes that the first element in the input stream is a character and handles this case independently (STEP 3).

There are less iterations in LZW decompression than in compression. For example, there are 30 iterations in the compression process shown in Table 10.1 while there are only 18 in the example in Table 10.4. Notice that in the decompression process a string table entry results in each iteration after the first one. This is a consequence of the mechanics of the compression process, in which an output is generated only when an entry is made in the string table. (See Table 10.1.) Also notice that the string table that results from the decompression (Table 10.4) is identical to the one generated during compression (Table 10.1).

10.2   The Tag Image File Format (TIFF)

The tag image file format (TIFF) was developed by ALDUS Corporation with the support of several other companies, including Hewlett-Packard and Microsoft. The standard is an effort at providing a flexible file-storage format for raster images. Its origin is related to scanner hardware and software for microcomputers. The first version of TIFF was published in the Fall of 1986. The present update, designated as TIFF Revision 6.0, was released in June, 1992. TIFF is a nonproprietary standard which can be used without license or previous royalty agreement. Technical information about TIFF can be obtained from the Aldus Developer's Desk at Aldus Corporation, Seattle, Washington, or from the Aldus forum on Compuserve (GO ALDSVC).

The purpose of the TIFF standard is to provide an image storage convention with maximum flexibility and portability. TIFF is not intended for any particular computer, operating system, or application program. Consistent with this idea, the files in TIFF format have no version number or other update identification code. A typical TIFF reader searches for the data necessary to its own purposes and ignores all other information contained in the file. The format supports both the Intel and the Motorola data ordering schemes but hardware-specific features are not documented in the TIFF file. Which mode, resolution, or color range used in displaying a TIFF file is left entirely to the software.

The TIFF standard supports monochrome, grayscale, and color images of various specifications. The original TIFF documents classified the various image types into four classes. Class B was used for binary (black-and-white) images, class G for grayscale images, class P for palette color images (8 bits-per-pixel color), and class R for full-color images (24 bits-per-pixel color). A TIFF application need not provide support for all TIFF image types. For example, a VGA TIFF reader could exclude class R images since the system's maximum color range is of 8 bits-per-pixel (256 colors). By the same token, a routine or application that reads monochrome scanned images could limit its support to the class B category. The image class designations by letter codes was dropped in TIFF revision 6.0, however, the image classification into bilevel, grayscale, RGB, and palette types was preserved.

TIFF originally supported uncompressed images as well as compressed data according to several compression schemes, namely, PackBits, CCITT, and LZW. (See Section 10.0.3.) LZW compression support was dropped in TIFF version 6.0, because the compression algorithm is patented by Unysis Corporation. (See Section 10.0.3.) Notice that, in the TIFF standard, compression methods are usually associated with the particular file classes mentioned in the preceding paragraph.

10.2.1 The TIFF File Structure

The TIFF standard is an image file protocol. A file in the TIFF format is divided into three areas: the header, the image file directory, and the actual image data. These elements are described separately in the following paragraphs.

The notion of *tags* is the feature that identifies files in the TIFF format. A TIFF tag is a word integer that serves to identify the file structure that follows. For example, the tag value 103H indicates that the structure that follows contains data compression information. TIFF file processing software can search for this tag in order to determine which, if any, compression scheme was used in encoding the image data. TIFF tags are discussed in greater detail later in this section.

The TIFF Header

An image file in TIFF format must start with an 8-byte block called the header. Figure 10.12 shows the structure of the TIFF image file header.

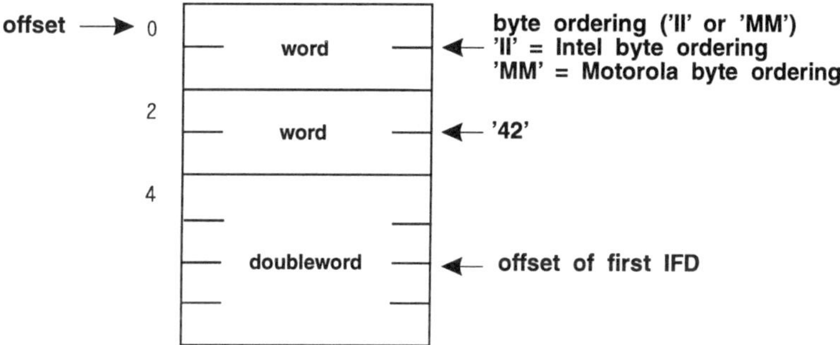

Figure 10.12 *TIFF File Header*

The word at offset 0 of the TIFF file header consists of the ASCII characters 'II' or 'MM'. The 'II' code identifies a file in the Intel byte ordering scheme, that is, word and doubleword entries appear with the least significant byte in the lowest numbered memory address. This data ordering format is sometimes known as the "little-endian" scheme. The 'MM' code identifies a file in the Motorola byte ordering order, that is, with the least significant byte of word and doubleword entries in the highest numbered memory address. This format is known as the "big-endian" scheme. The ASCII number '42' found at the word at offset 2 of the header, serves to further identify a file in TIFF format. The numbers themselves have no documented significance. The ASCII code '42' has sometimes been called the TIFF version number, although it is not described as such in the standard. The doubleword at offset 4 of the header block contains the offset, in the TIFF file, of the first image file directory (IFD).

The file header block is the only TIFF file structure that must be located at a predetermined offset from the start of the file. The remaining structures can be located anywhere in the TIFF file. TIFF file processing code reads the data in the header block to certify that the file is in TIFF format and to make decisions regarding the data ordering scheme. A sophisticated application could be capable of making adjustments in order to read data both in the Intel and in Motorola orders, while another one could require data in a specific format.

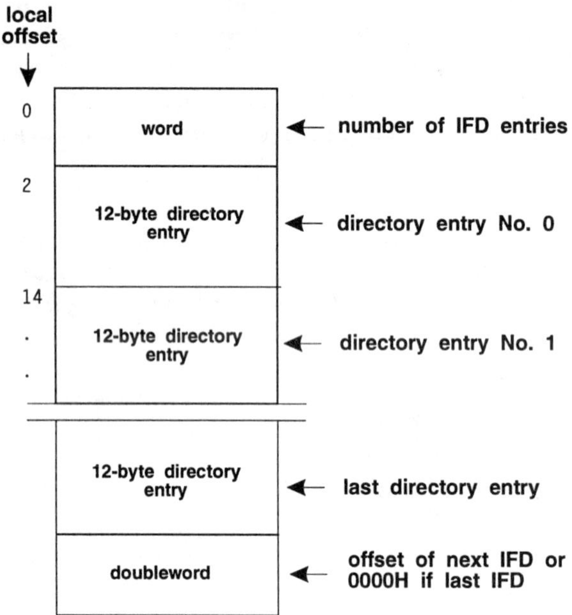

Figure 10.13   *TIFF Image File Directory (IFD)*

The TIFF Image File Directory (IFD)

Once the code determines that the file is in TIFF format and that it is encoded in a valid ordering scheme, it uses the doubleword at offset 4 of the header in order to determine the location of the first image file directory (IFD). (See Figure 10.12.) Notice that a TIFF file can contain more than one image. If so, each image in the file is associated with its own IFD. However, by far the more common situation is that a TIFF file contains a single image. This assumption is made in the code and examples for manipulating TIFF files. The structure of the IFD is shown in Figure 10.13.

Observe that the offset values in the leftmost column of Figure 10.13 (labeled "local offset") refer to offsets within the IFD block. This must be so because the IFD itself can be located anywhere within the TIFF file. The word at local offset 0 of the IFD is a count of the number of directory entries. Recall that the number of directory entries is unlimited in the TIFF standard. The last directory entry is followed by a doubleword field which contains the offset of the next IFD, if one exists. If not, this doubleword contains the value 0000H. (See Figure 10.13.) Each entry in the IFD takes up 12 bytes. The structure of each IFD entry is shown in Figure 10.14.

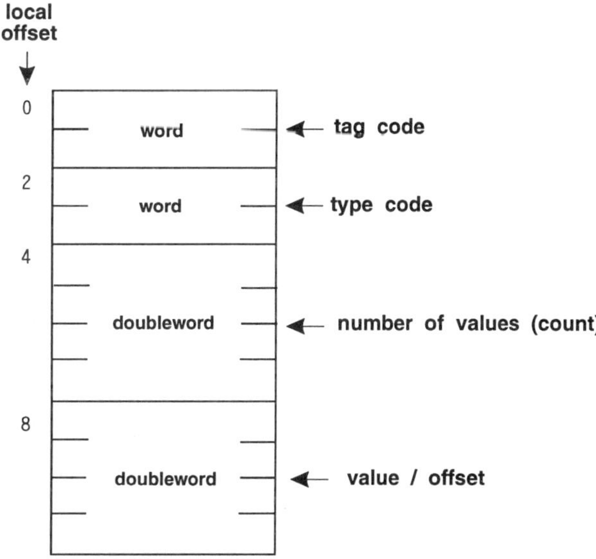

Figure 10.14   *TIFF Directory Entry*

The tag code is located at local offset 0 in the directory entry field. TIFF requires that the entry fields be sorted by increasing order of the tag codes, therefore, a lower numbered tag code always precedes a higher numbered one. This simplifies searching for a particular tag code since the search terminates when one with a higher numbered tag is encountered. The type code is located at local offset 2 within the directory entry field. Table 10.5 shows the type code values according to TIFF version 6.0. Be aware that code numbers 6 and higher were introduced in Version 6.0 and are not documented in previous versions of the standard.

The *count* field is a doubleword at offset 4 of the directory entry. This field, which was named the *length* field in previous versions of TIFF, encodes the number of data repetitions in the current directory entry. Notice that this value does not encode the number of bytes, but the number of data units. For example, if the field type code is 3 (word unit) then the count field would represent the number of data words of information that are associated with the entry.

The *value / offset* field is designated in this manner because it contains either a direct value or an offset into the TIFF file. The general rule is that if the encoded data fits into a doubleword storage (4 bytes) then the data is entered directly in the doubleword at local offset 8 of the directory entry. (See Figure 10.14.) This design saves coding space and simplifies processing. However, some TIFF tags, such as the StripOffset tag mentioned later in this section, always contain offset data in this field. The software determines if the data in the value/offset field is either a value or an offset by means of the tag, the field type code, and the data item count.

Table 10.5   *TIFF Version 6.0 Field Type Codes*

TYPE CODE	STORAGE UNIT	FIELD CONTENTS
1	byte	8-bit unsigned integer
2	ASCII character	offset of ASCII string terminated in NULL byte
3	word	16-bit unsigned integer
4	doubleword	32-bit unsigned integer
5	quadword	Rational number. The first doubleword Is the numerator of a fraction and the last doubleword the denominator
6	byte	8-bit signed integer
7	byte	Undefined. Can be used at will by the software
8	word	16-bit signed integer in 2's complement form
9	doubleword	32-bit signed integer in 2's complement form
10	quadword	Rational number. The first doubleword is the signed numerator of a fraction and the last doubleword the signed denominator
11	doubleword	Single precision floating point number in IEEE format
12	quadword	Double precision floating point number in IEEE format

If the tag contains either a value or an offset, the program must first examine the field type codes. (See Table 10.5.) In this case data corresponding to field type codes 1, 3, 4, 5, 6, 7, 8, 9, and 11, are contained in a doubleword storage unit and are therefore entered as values. (See Table 10.5.) By the same token, field types 2, 5, 10, and 12 encode an offset in the value/offset field of the directory entry. Once determined that an individual data item fits in the 4 bytes allocated to the value/offset field then the software must examine the number of values associated with the directory entry. If the total number of values exceeds the allocated space (4-bytes) then the value/offset field contains an offset. In this case the type code and the count fields are multiplied in order to determined the number of items supplied.

10.2.2   TIFF Tags for Bilevel Images

Over 50 tags have been defined in the TIFF standard, however, only a handful are used in most TIFF images. A complete description of all the TIFF tags can be found in the TIFF Revision 6.0 specification available, at no charge, from Aldus Corporation. (See Section 10.2.) The TIFF tags mentioned in the following discussion are those that would be commonly found in monochrome (bilevel in TIFF terminology) scanned images. These are also the tags decoded by the TIFFSHOW program found in the /TIFF directory of book's microdisk.

OldSubFileType (Tag Code 00FFH)

This tag, originally called the SubFileType, has been replaced by the NewSubFileType tag mentioned below, however, many older TIFF programs still use this tag. The tag provides information about the bitmap associated with the IFD. The tag can take the following values:

Value = 1 indicates that the image is in full-resolution format.

Value = 2 indicates the image data is in reduced-resolution format.

Value = 3 indicates that the image data is a single page of a multi-page image.

NewSubFileType (00FEH)

This tag, which replaces OldSubFileType, describes the kind of data in the IFD. The tag is made up of a doubleword integer with the following significant bits:

Bit 0 is set if the image is a reduced-resolution version of another image.

Bit 1 is set of the image is a single-page of a multi-page image.

Bit 2 is set if the image is a transparency mask (see the PhotometricInterpretation tag later in this section.)

ImageWidth (Tag Code 0100H)

This tag encodes the number of pixel columns in the image.

ImageLength (Tag Code 0101H)

This tag encodes the number of pixel rows in the image.

BitsPerSample (Tag Code 0102H)

This tag encodes the number of bits required to represent each pixel sample. The value of this tag is 1 for bilevel images, 4 for 16-color palette images, and 8 for 256-color palette images. In IBM video graphics systems, the number of bits per sample is usually the same as the number of bits per pixel color. Regarding images encoded in RGB format (as used in some Macintosh systems and in the XGA Direct Color mode) the number of bits per sample refers to each individual color. In this case the SamplesPerPixel tag (described below) encodes the number of pixel colors (3 colors in RGB encoding), and the BitsPerSample tag the number of bits assigned to each color. For example, if 6 bits are assigned to the red sample, 8 bits to the green, and 6 bits to the blue, the total number of bits per pixel would be 20.

Compression (Tag Code 0103H)

This tag encodes the compression scheme used in the image data. The tag can take the following values:

Value = 1 indicates that the image data in not compressed. Pixel information is packed at the byte level, as tightly as possible. Uncompressed data has the disadvantage over compressed data that it takes up more memory space. On the other hand, it has the advantage that it can be manipulated faster by the display routines.

Value = 2 indicates that image data is compressed according to CCITT Group 3 (Modified Huffman) run-length encoding.

Value = 32,773 (8005H) indicates the data is compressed according to the PackBits scheme described in detail later in this section.

PhotometricInterpretation (Tag Code 0106H)

This tag describes how to interpret the color encoding in the bitmap. The tag can take the following values:

Value = 0 is used in bilevel and grayscale images to indicate that a bit value of 0 represents the white color.

Value = 1 is used in bilevel and grayscale images to indicate that a bit value of 0 represents the black color.

Value = 2 is used to indicate an encoding in RGB format.

Value = 3 is used to indicate palette color format. In this case a ColorMap tag must be included to hold the LUT values.

Value = 4 indicates that the image is a *transparency mask* used to define an irregularly shaped region of another image.

Treshholding (Tag Code 0107H)

This tag describes the technique used for representing the gray scale in a black-and-white image. The tag can have the following values:

Value = 1 indicates that the image contains no dithering or halftoning. Bilevel images use this value.

Value = 2 indicates that the image has been dithered or halftoned.

Value = 3 indicates that a randomized process, such as the error diffusion algorithm, has been applied to the image data.

StripsOffset (Tag Code 0111H)

This tag provides the information necessary for the software to locate the image data within the TIFF file. By definition, the value in this tag is always an offset from the beginning of the TIFF file. The structure of the TIFF image data as well as the use of this tag is discussed in Section 10.2.3.

SamplesPerPixel (Tag Code 0115H)

This tag encodes the number of color components for each screen pixel. The value of this tag is 1 for bilevel, grayscale, and palette color images, and 3 for images in RGB format.

RowsPerStrip (Tag Code 0116H)

This tag determines the number of rows in each strip. Image encoding in the TIFF standard is discussed in Section 10.2.3.

StripByteCounts (Tag Code 0117H)

This tag determines the number of bytes in each strip, after compression. Image encoding in the TIFF standard is discussed in Section 10.2.3.

XResolution (Tag Code 011AH)

This tag provides information about the x-axis resolution at which the original image was created or scanned. The data is important to software that must reproduce the image exactly as it was originally produced. This is a critical factor in the reproduction of dithered images, which do not allow scaling.

YResolution (Tag Code 011BH)

This tag provides information about the y axis resolution at which the original image was created or scanned. See the text in the XResolution tab.

PlanarConfiguration (Tag Code 011CH)

This tag provides information regarding the organization of color pixel data. It is relevant only for color images in RGB format (more than 1 samples per pixel). The tag can have the following values:

Value = 1 indicates that RGB data is stored in the order of the color components, that is, in a repeating sequence of RED, GREEN, and BLUE values. This organization is called the *chunky format* in TIFF documentation.

Value = 2 indicates that RGB data is stored by bit planes. That is, the red color components are stored first, followed by the green, and then by the blue. This organization is called the *planar format* in TIFF documentation.

ResolutionUnit (Tag Code 128H)

This tag determines the unit of measurement used in the parameters contained in XResolution and YResolution tags. Many TIFF programs do not use this tag, but it is recommended by the standard. The tag can have the following values:

Value = 1 indicate no unit of resolution.

Value = 2 indicates inches.

Value = 3 indicates centimeters.

10.2.3   Locating TIFF Image Data

Although TIFF file processing software often ignores many tags and makes assumptions regarding others, one necessary manipulation in an image display operation is the locating and decoding of the image bitmap.

TIFF Image data can be located almost anywhere in the file. This is true of both uncompressed and compressed data. Furthermore, the TIFF standard allows dividing an image into several areas, called strips. The idea is to facilitate data input and output in machines limited to a 64K segment size. This is the case of Intel processors operating in MS DOS or Windows systems. The data for each individual strip is represented by a separate tag.

When the image is divided into strips, three tags participate in locating the image data: RowsPerStrip, StripOffsets, and StripByteCounts. The first operation is for the software to calculate the number of strips into which the image data is divided. This value, which is not encoded in any particular tag, can be obtained from the number of values field of the StripOffsets tag. (See Figure 10.14.) The following code fragment shows the processing necessary to determine if a TIFF image is encoded in a single strip or in multiple strips.

```
; The number of strips in the image is obtained from the length
; field of the StripOffsets tag
; Code assumes that the SI register points to the start of the
; first IFD in the TIFF file
        MOV     AX,0111H            ; Tag for strip offsets
        CALL    FIND_TAG
        JNC     OK_OFFSETS          ; Go if tag found
;*********************|
;     ERROR handler   |
;*********************|
; At this point the code should contain an error routine to
; handle the case of a TIFF file with no StripOffsets tag.
        .

        .

        .

; At this label the processing has located the StripOffsets tag.
; Image can be encoded in one or more strips. The number of
; strips is stored in the length field of the StripOffsets tag
; Unpacking and display of multistrip images requires the
; number of rows per strip and the number of bytes in each
; strip row. These parameters are not necessary if the image is
; encoded in a single strip
OK_OFFSETS:
        MOV     AX,WORD PTR [SI+4]         ; Get number of strips
        CMP     AX,1                ; Test for single strip
        JNE     MULTI_STRIP         ; Go if not a single strip
        JMP     ONE_STRIP
;*********************|
; multistrip image    |
;*********************|
MULTI_STRIP:
; Multistrip image processing routine
```

```
                .
                .
                .
;*********************|
;  single-strip image |
;*********************|
ONE_STRIP:
; Single-strip processing routine
                .
                .
                .


FIND_TAG          PROC     NEAR
; Find a specific tag code in the Image File Directory
; On entry:
;              AX = desired tag code
;              SI ==> start of Image File Directory (IFD)
; On exit:
;              Carry clear if tag code found
;              SI ==> first tag field (code)
;              Carry set code not present in IFD
TEST_TAG_CODE:
        MOV      BX,WORD PTR [SI]           ; Get tag code
        CMP      BX,0               ; Test for last IFD
        JE       END_OF_IFD         ; Go if last
        CMP      AX,BX              ; Compare with one desired
        JNE      NEXT_TAG_CODE      ; Index if not
; At this point desired tag code has been found
        CLC                         ; Tag found return code
        RET
NEXT_TAG_CODE:
        ADD      SI,12              ; Index to next tag
; Test for last tag
        JMP      TEST_TAG_CODE      ; Continue
END_OF_IFD:
        STC                         ; Tag not found
        RET
FIND_TAG          ENDP
                .
                .
                .
```

Notice that the FIND_TAG procedure in the previous code fragment provides
a convenient tool for indexing into the IFD in search of any particular tag code.
Such a procedure would be called repeatedly by a TIFF image processing
routine. The procedure named FIND_TIFF_TAG in the BITIO module of the
GRAPHSOL library performs this operation.

Locating the image data in a single-strip image consists of adding the value in the StripOffsets tag to the start of the TIFF file. In this case, the image size (in bytes) is obtained by reading the value in the ImageWidth tag (which is the number of pixels per row), dividing it by 8 to determine the number of data bytes per pixel row, and multiplying this value by the number of pixel rows stored in the ImageLength tag. The processing operations can be seen in the TIFFSHOW.ASM file in the book's microdisk.

If the image data consists of multiple strips, then each strip is handled separately by the software. In this case, the number of bytes in each strip, after compression, is obtained from the corresponding entry in the StripByteCounts tag. The display routine obtains the number of pixel rows encoded in each strip from the value stored in the RowsPerStrip tag. However, if the total number of rows, as stored in the ImageLength tag, is not an exact multiple of the RowsPerStrip value, then the last strip could contain less rows than the value in the RowsPerStrip tag. TIFF software is expected to detect and handle this special case.

10.2.4 Processing TIFF Image Data

Once the start of the TIFF image data is located within the TIFF file, the code must determine if the data is stored in compressed or uncompressed format and proceed accordingly. This information is found in the Compression tag previously mentioned. In TIFF Version 5.0 the Compression tag could hold one of six values. Value number 1 correspondes to no compression, values 2, 3, and 4 corresponded to three modes of CCITT compression, and value 5 to LZW compression, finally value 32,773 in the Compression tag indicates PackBits compression.

We mentioned that several of these compression schemes were dropped in Version 6.0 of the TIFF standard. (See Section 10.2.) In the present TIFF implementation, values 3, 4, and 5 for the Compression tag are no longer supported. Since there are substantial reasons to favor the LZW algorithm for the compression of color images (which was dropped in TIFF Version 6.0 because of patent rights considerations) we have limited the discussion on TIFF image decoding to the case of PackBits compression. Hopefully, a future TIFF version will again support LZW compression methods.

TIFF PackBits Compression

The PackBits compression algorithm was originally developed on the Macintosh computer. The MacPaint program uses a version of PackBits compression for its image files. Macintosh users have available compression and decompression utilities for files in this format. The compression scheme is simple to implement and often offers satisfactory results with monochrome and scanned images.

PackBits, as implemented in TIFF, is a byte-level, simplified run-length compression scheme. The encoding is based on the value of the first byte of each compressed data unit, often designated as the "n" byte. The decompression logic can be described in the following steps.

STEP 1: If end-of-information code then end decompression.

STEP 2; Read next source byte. Designate as n (n is an unsigned integer).

STEP 3: if n is in the range 0 to 127 (inclusive) perform the following operations:

    a. read the next n+1 bytes literally from the source file into the output stream.

    b. go to STEP 1.

STEP 4: if n is in the range 129 to 255 (inclusive) perform the following operations:

    a. negate n (n = -n).

    b. copy the next byte n+1 times to the output stream.

    c. go to STEP 1.

STEP 5: Goto STEP 1.

Notice that in the above description we assume that n is an unsigned integer. This convention, which facilitates coding in 80x86 assembly language, differs from other descriptions of the algorithm in which n is a signed value. Figure 10.15 is a flowchart of this decompression logic.

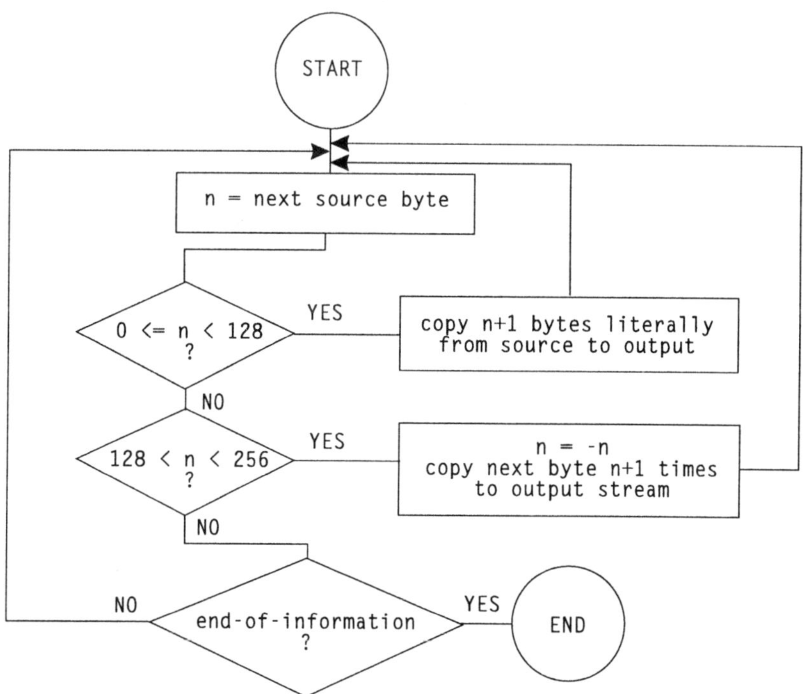

Figure 10.15 *TIFF PackBits Decompression*

Observe that in the TIFF implementation of PackBits no action is taken if n = 128. If n = 0 then 1 byte is copied literally from source to output. The maximum number of bytes in a compression run is 128. In addition, the TIFF implementation of PackBits compression adopted the following special rules:

1. Each pixel row is compressed separately. Compressed data cannot cross pixel row boundaries.

2. The number of uncompressed bytes per row is defined as the value in the ImageWidth tag, plus 7, divided by 8. If the resulting image map has an even number of bytes per row, the decompression buffer should be word-aligned.

The following code fragment shows the processing required for unpacking a TIFF file compressed as a single strip, using the PackBits method:

```
; Unpacking logic for TIFF PackBits scheme
; PackBits packages consist of 2 bytes. The first byte (n)
; encodes the following options:
;          1. if n is in the range 0 to 127 then the next n+1 bytes
;             are to be interpreted as literal values
;          2. if n is in the range -127 to -1 then the following
;             byte is repeated -n+1 times
;          3. if n = 128 then no operation is executed
; Code assumes:
;          1. SI -> start of the compressed image (1 strip)
;          2. DI -> storage buffer for decompressed image
;          3. the variable IMAGE_SIZE holds the byte size of the
;             uncompressed image. In a single strip image this
;             value is obtained by dividing ImageWidth (number
;             of pixels per row) by 8 and multiplying by
;             ImageLength
;
; Note: the routine keeps track of the number of bytes in the
;       decompressed bitmap in the variable EXP_COUNT. This
;       value is compared to the IMAGE_SIZE variable to
;       determine the end-of-information point

;*********************|
;    test value of n  |
;*********************|
TEST_N_BYTE:
        MOV       AL,[SI]           ; Get n byte
        CMP       AL,128            ; Code for NOP
        JB        LITERAL_CODE      ; Go if in the literal range
        JA        REPEAT_CODE       ; Go if in repeat range
; At this point n = 128. No operation is performed
        INC       SI                ; Skip NOP code
        JMP       NEXT_PACK_CODE    ; Continue
```

```
;*********************|
;    0 <= n < 128     |
;  (literal expansion) |
;*********************|
LITERAL_CODE:
        MOV     CL,AL           ; Counter to CL
        MOV     CH,0            ; Clear high byte of counter
        INC     CX              ; Add 1
        INC     SI              ; Skip n byte
        ADD     EXP_COUNT,CX    ; Add bytes to counter
LIT_MOVE:
        MOV     AL,[SI]         ; Get literal byte
        MOV     [DI],AL         ; Place in bitmap
        INC     DI              ; Bump pointers
        INC     SI
        LOOP    LIT_MOVE
        JMP     NEXT_PACK_CODE
;*********************|
;    128 < n < 256    |
;  (repeated expansion) |
;*********************|
REPEAT_CODE:
        NEG     AL              ; Negate to convert to 2's
                                ; complement representation
        MOV     CL,AL           ; Counter to CL
        MOV     CH,0            ; Clear high byte of counter
        INC     CX              ; Add 1
        INC     SI              ; Skip n byte
        ADD     EXP_COUNT,CX    ; Add bytes to counter
                                ; to keep track of decompressed
                                ; bytes
        MOV     AL,[SI]         ; Get byte to repeat
        INC     SI              ; Skip to next n byte
EXP_MOVE:
        MOV     [DI],AL         ; Place byte in buffer
        INC     DI              ; Bump bitmap pointer
        LOOP    EXP_MOVE
;*********************|
;     test for <EOI>  |
;*********************|
; EXP_COUNT holds the byte count in bitmap at this point
; IMAGE_SIZE holds the total bytes in the expanded bitmap
NEXT_PACK_CODE:
        MOV     AX,EXP_COUNT    ; Bytes now in bitmap
        CMP     AX,IMAGE_SIZE   ; Compare with map size
        JAE     EOI_FOUND       ; Go if at end of image
```

```
        JMP       TEST_N_BYTE
; Decompression has concluded at this label
EOI_FOUND:
        .
        .
        .
```

10.2.5   TIFF Software Samples

The book's microdisk includes several software items related to TIFF file operations. In the first place we have furnished source and executable files for a rudimentary TIFF reader program named TIFFSHOW. Notice that the code is limited to the analysis, decompression, and display of small, bilevel TIFF files. The data in the source TIFF encoding can be either uncompressed or compressed by means of the PackBits option. The code also requires that the data be located in a single strip. TIFFSHOW can be used to examine the TIFF format files (extension .TIF) that are part of the MATCH program. For this reason TIFFSHOW is included in the \MATCH directory of the book's microdisk.

In addition to the TIFFSHOW program, we have also furnished several TIFF procedures as part of the GRAPHSOL library. These procedures are located in the BITIO.ASM module. The procedure named SHOW_TIFF can be used to display a bitmap encoded in TIFF bilevel format. This procedure requires that the user pass a formatted data block, as shown in the header. The SHOW_TIFF procedures calls the procedure named LOAD_TIFF, also in the BITIO module, which decompresses and loads the encoded image. One advantage of using these library procedures is that they place the TIFF file and the image bitmap in a separate data segment, therefore freeing the caller's code from having to devote storage space to TIFF data.

10.3   The Hewlett-Packard Bit-Mapped Fonts

The LaserJet line of printers, manufactured by Hewlett-Packard Corporation, has gained considerable popularity in the microcomputer world. For use in these printers Hewlett-Packard developed a standard for encoding text characters, sometimes known as the Hewlett-Packard Printer Control Language (PCL) bitmap convention. Fonts in PCL format are widely available as disk files (soft fonts) from Hewlett-Packard and other companies. Although these fonts are primarily designed for use in laser printers that recognized the PCL printer language (discussed in Chapter 11), they can also be put to less conventional uses. For example, in the MATCH program (furnished in the book's microdisk) we have used PCL soft fonts to display text message in larger letters than those available in the VGA system (see color plate 6).

In the present section we discuss the structure and design of the PCL soft fonts. However, the PCL bitmap format is a refined and elaborate one. We believe that the information presented here is sufficient to make the PCL bitmap technology accessible to the graphics programmer. On the other hand, the design of new soft fonts in PCL bitmap format requires knowledge of typography and character graphics as well as a high degree of familiarity with the PCL encoding. Hewlett-Packard has published several technical reference manuals for their LaserJet printers which include detailed description of the PCL bitmap fonts. These titles (listed in the Bibliography) can be obtained directly from Hewlett-Packard or through one of their dealers.

Notice that PCL commercial fonts usually have a copyright notice by the font developers or vendors. The programmer should investigate the legality of the intended use before distributing or modifying the font files.

10.3.1 The PCL Character Encoding

Two technologies are commonly used for encoding text characters: bitmaps and vector graphics. We encountered vector fonts in the short stroke vector characters used in 8514/A and XGA systems.(See Section 6.1.5.) Some printers of the Hewlett-Packard LaserJet family are equipped with vector fonts supplied in the form of scalable character sets; Hewlett-Packard has adopted the scalable font technology developed by Agfa Corporation, designated as the Font Access and Interchange Format (FAIS).

Bit-mapped fonts in the PCL format are compatible with all HP PCL laser printers. In addition, several commercial programs are available to generate and edit font files in PCL format. One advantage of fixed-size bit-mapped fonts if that their display quality is often judged to be better than the one obtained from scalable fonts.

A PCL-format soft font disk file contains the following elements:

1. One *font descriptor* field that encodes the general characteristics of the font.

2. One or more *character descriptors* fields that encodes the data pertaining to each individual character as well as the character bitmap. The bitmap is the binary raster data that defines the character's shape.

3. Several command strings in PCL language.

The PCL command strings are unrelated to the font definition, although they are sometimes used to locate specific data areas within the file. These command strings are provided to facilitate programming of LaserJet printers and compatible devices, a subject discussed in detail in Chapter 11.

Font Descriptor

The first element we encounter in a font file in PCL format is a PCL language command string. The initial command in the font file is the one used to download the font descriptor field into a PCL printer. The command can be generically represented as follows:

```
1BH's???W'
```

Table 10.6 *Hexadecimal and ASCII Dump of the HP PCL Font File TR140RPN.UPS*

HEXADECIMAL DUMP

offset	0	1	2	3	4	5	6	7		8	9	A	B	C	D	E	F	ASCII DUMP
0000	1B	29	73	32	35	37	57	00	-	40	00	00	00	00	00	2B	00	.)s257W.........
0010	3C	00	3E	00	01	00	15	00	-	3C	00	E9	00	6C	00	00	00	....
0020	05	00	06	00	00	F1	04	01	-	18	00	6D	00	20	00	7F	00	....
0030	55	00	00	00	00	00	00	54	-	6D	73	52	6D	6E	20	20	20	.......TmsRmn
0040	20	20	20	20	20	20	20	00	-	BF	01	28	43	29	20	43	6F	(C) Co
0050	.	.	.															pyright Hewlett-
0060																		Packard Company,
0070																		1986. All right
0080																		s reserved. Rep
0090																		roduction, adapt
00A0																		ation or distrib
00B0																		ution of copies
00C0																		of this font is
00D0																		prohibited, exce
00E0																		pt as allowed un
00F0																.	. .	der the copyrigh
0100	74	20	6C	61	77	73	2E	20	-	1B	2A	63	33	33	45	1B	28	t laws. .*c33E.(
0110	73	35	37	57	04	00	0E	01	-	00	00	00	06	00	27	00	07	s57W............
0120	00	29	00	4C	38	7C	FE	FE	-	FE	FE	FE	FE	FE	7C	FE	7C	....
0130	7C	7C	7C	7C	7C	7C	38	7C	-	38	38	38	38	38	38	38	10	....
0140	38	10	00	00	00	00	08	7C	-	FE	FE	FE	7C	38	1B	2A	63	..............*c
0150	33	34	45	1B	28	73	34	36	-	57	04	00	0E	01	00	00	00	34E.(e46W.......

The value 1BH is the escape code that precedes all PCL commands. (See Chapter 11.) The character string 's???W' represent a generic command in which the question mark ('?') takes the place of one to three ASCII characters that encode the byte length of the descriptor field. Table 10.6 is a partial screen dump of the Hewlett-Packard font file TR140RPN.UPS

The data elements in the PCL bitmap font descriptor field are those that apply to the entire font. There are 33 data entries in the font descriptor field of PCL level 5, although software and devices often ignore many of these entries. The font descriptor field starts after the end of the download command string. In Table 10.6 the command string takes the for:

1BH)s257W

This can be seen in the first seven bytes of the dump. The ASCII characters '257' in the sample of Table 10.6 encodes the number of bytes in the font descriptor field, not including the command string. Notice, in Table 10.6, that the end of the font descriptor field coincides with the command string 1BH *c33E (see dump offset 0108H) discussed later in this section.

Font descriptor data starts at offset 0007H of the dump shown in Table 10.6. The size of the binary data section of the font descriptor is 64 bytes (40H). The remainder of the font descriptor, from the byte at offset 0048H to the end of the field, contains an optional ASCII-coded copyright message preceded by a character count (BFH). Table 10.7 shows the elements in the bitmap font descriptor field according to PCL level 5.

Table 10.7 *PCL Bitmap Font Descriptor Field*

OFFSET	STORAGE UNIT	VALUE RANGE	CONTENTS
0	word	64	Font descriptor size
2	byte	0	Descriptor format (0 = bitmap)
3	byte	0/1/2	Font type
			0 = 7 bit (96 characters)
			1 = 8 bits (192 characters)
			2 = 8 bits (256 characters)
4	byte		Style, MSB (see offset 23)
5	byte		RESERVED
6	word		Baseline distance (in PCL dots)
8	word		Cell width (in PCL dots)
10	word		Cell height (in PCL dots)
12	byte	0/1/2/3	Orientation
			0 = portrait
			1 = landscape
			2 = reverse portrait
			3 = reverse landscape
13	byte	0/1	Spacing (fixed or proportional)
			0 = fixed spacing
			1 = proportional spacing
14	word		Symbol set
16	word		Pitch (in PCL quarter-dots)
18	word		Height (in PCL quarter-dots)
20	word		x-height (in PCL quarter-dots)
22	byte		Width type (code)
23	byte		Style, LSB (see offset 4)
24	byte		Stroke weight (code)
25	byte		Typeface family, LSB
26	byte		Typeface family, MSB
27	byte		Serif style (code)
28	byte	0/1/2	Quality (code)
			0 = data processing
			1 = near letter quality
			2 = letter quality
29	byte		Placement (code)
30	byte		Underline distance (in PCL dots)
31	byte		Underline height (in PCL dots
32	word		Text height (in PCL quarter-dots)
34	word		Text width (in PCL quarter-dots)
36	word		First printable character
38	word		Last printable character
40	byte		Pitch field extension
41	byte		Height field extension
42	word		Cap height (percent of em)
44	doubleword		Font number (code)
48	15 bytes		ASCII font name
64	—		Start of optional copyright notice

Note: data is in Motorola storage format (big-endian scheme)

Data in the font descriptor field is stored according to the big-endian scheme, that is, the low-order element of word and doubleword entries are located at the highest memory location. For example, at offset 0007H of the dump of Table 10.6 is the font descriptor size word, which, in this case, has the value 00 40. If we were to load this word value into a register of a processors that follows the little-endian storage scheme (such as the ones used in IBM microcomputers) the high- and low-order elements would be inverted. In this case the code can exchange the low- and high-bytes in order to correct this situation. The processing operations can be followed in the source code for the CSETHP program furnished in the book's microdisk.

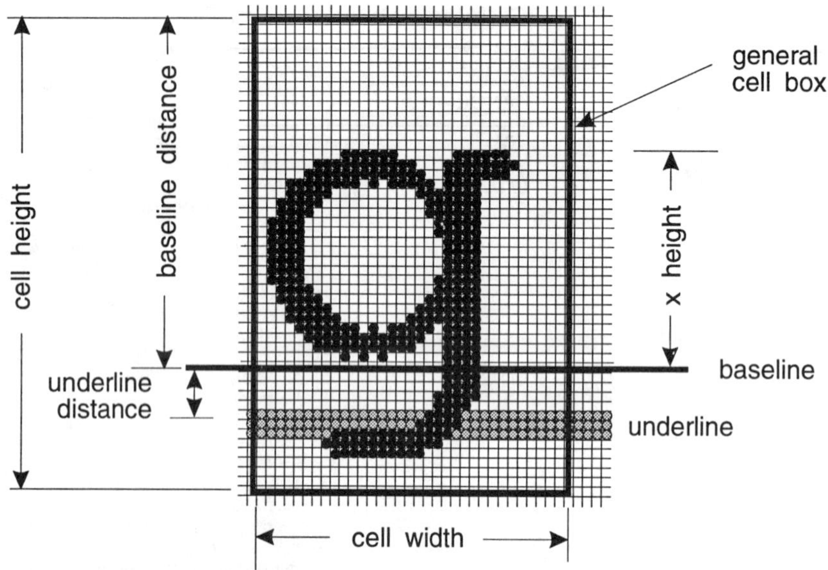

Figure 10.16   *PCL Bitmap Character Cell*

Many of the data entries in the font descriptor field would be of interest only to the font designer or graphics text specialist. Other entries contain information that would be required only in developing sophisticated text management functions, such as those expected of a typesetting or desktop publishing program. Figure 10.16 shows the fundamental information furnished by the font descriptor field.

In Figure 10.16, notice that the dimensions labeled "cell width" and "cell height" correspond to the entries at offset 6 and 8 of the font descriptor (see Table 10.7), while the "baseline distance" is found at offset 6, the "underline distance" at offset 30, and "x-height" dimension at offset 20.

Character Descriptor

The PCL format is optimized so that each bitmap takes up the minimum storage space. In this respect, the cell height and cell width parameters of Figure 10.16 refer merely to a "general cell box" that is required to enclose all the characters in the font. The character descriptor field contains the data elements that define the individual character.

Like the font descriptor field, the disk image of the character descriptor field starts with a PCL command string. In fact, in the case of individual characters two command strings are necessary: the first one, known as the *character code command*, is used to inform the device of the decimal code for the character that follows. At offset 0108H, in Table 10.6, we can see the first PCL command string, which is:

1BH 'c33E'

In this case the decimal value '33' identifies the '!' symbol, which is located at
this position in the character table. (See Table 1.2.) The second command string,
known as the *character descriptor and data command* is used to download to
the PCL device the information associated with the particular character as well
as its bitmap. At offset 010EH of the dump at Table 10.6 we can see this
command string:

1BH 's57W'

In this case the sub-string '57' encodes, in ASCII, the byte length of the data
descriptor plus its corresponding bitmap. Immediately following this PCL
command string we find a 16-byte block which is called the *character header*
area of the character descriptor field. Table 10.8 shows the data elements in
the character descriptor header.

Notice that the character header field has a total length of 16 bytes, which is
consistent with the value 14 decimal stored at offset 2 of the character descriptor header, since this last value refers to the "remaining" portion of the header
field.

Table 10.8 *PCL Bitmap Character Descriptor Header*

OFFSET	STORAGE UNIT	VALUE RANGE	CONTENTS

0	byte	4/10	Data format
			  4 = LaserJet family
			  10 = Intelifont scalable

1	byte	0/1	Continuation
			  0 = bitmap is a character block
			  1 = bitmap is a continuation of
			    another block

2	byte	14/2	Size of character descriptor header
			  14 byte for LaserJet family
			  2 for Intelifont scalable

3	byte	1/2/3/4	Bitmap class
			  1 = uncompressed bitmap
			  2 = compressed bitmap
			  3 = Intelifont scalable
			  4 = Compound contour (Intelifont)

4	byte	0/1/2/3	Orientation
			  0 = portrait
			  1 = landscape
			  2 = reverse portrait
			  3 = reverse landscape

5	byte		RESERVED
6	word		Left offset (in PCL dots)
8	word		Top offset (in PCL dots)
10	word		Character width (in PCL dots)
12	word		Character height (in PCL dots)
14	word		Delta x (in PCL quarter dots)
16	——		Start of character bitmap

The continuation entry, at offset 1 of the header block, is related to the limit of 32,767 bytes imposed by the PCL language on the character bitmap. If a character bitmap exceeds this limit it has to be divided into two or more sections. In this case the continuation entry is set to indicate that the associated bitmap (which follows this byte) is a continuation of the previous one.

The entry at offset 3 indicates the bitmap class. Most PCL character bitmaps in commercial use are in the uncompressed format (class 1). Compressed bitmaps use a run-length compression scheme. This variation, introduced in PCL level 5, is not compatible with level-4 devices, such as the LaserJet Series II and compatible printers. For this reason we will not discuss the compressed encodings any further.

The entry at offset 4 indicates the orientation of the character. The word "portrait" is used in this context in reference to a character that takes up a vertical rectangle, such as the one in Figure 10.16. By the same token, characters located in a horizontal rectangle are referred to as being of "landscape" orientation. Notice that this use of the words "portrait" and "landscape" is related to photographic terminology.

The remaining entries in the character descriptor header refer to the character's dimensions. Figure 10.17 shows the locations of these dimensions in a sample character.

Notice the two reference points along the baseline of the character in Figure 10.17. The start reference point can be thought of as the cursor position at the start of character display. The end reference point marks the cursor position once the character is displayed. The character reference points are used by software in implementing typesetting operations such as kerning and proportional spacing.

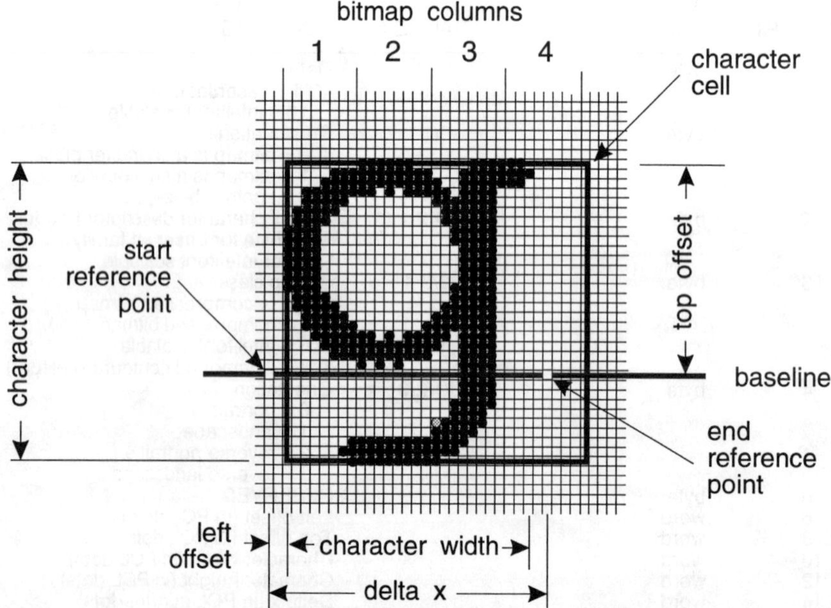

Figure 10.17 *PCL Character Dimensions*

The word entry at offset 6 in Table 10.8 indicates the character's left offset. (See Figure 10.17.) This dimension is the distance, expressed in PCL dots, from the character pattern to the start reference point. The word at offset 7 refers to the character's top offset, which is the distance from the reference points to thc top of the character pattern.

The character width entry, located at offset 10 in Table 10.8, determines the character's dot width. The dimension extends from the leftmost dot to the rightmost one. Notice that the actual bitmap often requires padding so that it can be encoded in byte-size storage units. Therefore the character width may not coincide with the width of the bitmap, as is the case in the character shown in Figure 10.17. The character height, located at offset 12 in Table 10.8, is the measurement of the number of vertical dots in the character map. (See Figure 10.17.) The delta x dimension, located at offset 14 in Table 10.8, is the distance, measured in PCL quarter dots, from the start reference point to the end reference point. (See Figure 10.17.)

The PCL Bitmap

The bitmap for each particular character starts at offset 16 of the character descriptor header. Software can obtain the bitmap dimensions from the character width and character height entries in the header. For example, in Table 10.6 we find the character width for the first character in the set at offset 011EH. The value in this case is 00 07 (7 decimal) which indicates that the character map is 7-dots wide. Since storage must be in byte units, the bitmap takes up 1 horizontal byte, in which the low-order bit is padded with zero. The bit map height is obtained from the character height dimensions at offset 120H, which stores the value 00 29 (41 decimal). Therefore we calculate that the character bitmap is 1-byte wide and 41-bytes high, which means that it occupies 41 bytes of memory space.

Notice that the first character represented in Table 10.6 corresponds with the decimal value 33. The font uses the conventional US symbol set, therefore we can refer to Table 1.2 and find that the value 33 (21H) corresponds to the exclamation point symbol. This means that the 1-by-41 bitmap mentioned in the preceding paragraph represents the exclamation point symbols in the Hewlett-Packard TmsRmn, 14-point, normal density, portrait font encoded in the file named TR140RPN.USP. Figure 10.18 shows the bitmap for the lower-case letter "q" used in the previous illustrations.

10.3.2 PCL Bitmap Support Software

The book's microdisk includes several software items related to PCL bitmap operations. The VGA2 module of the GRAPHSOL library includes two procedures which allow the screen display of a Hewlett-Packard printer font in PCL format. One procedure, named READ_HPFONT, allows loading a PCL soft font into RAM. The second procedure, named FINE_TEXTHP, allows displaying a text message using a previously loaded PCL font. The MATCH program (in the book's microdisk) uses PCL fonts to display large screen text. It is also possible to display screen text message using PCL fonts while in XGA and SuperVGA modes. In this case, it is first necessary to call the SET_DEVICE procedure in the VGA3 module in order to enable XGA or SuperVGA display operations.

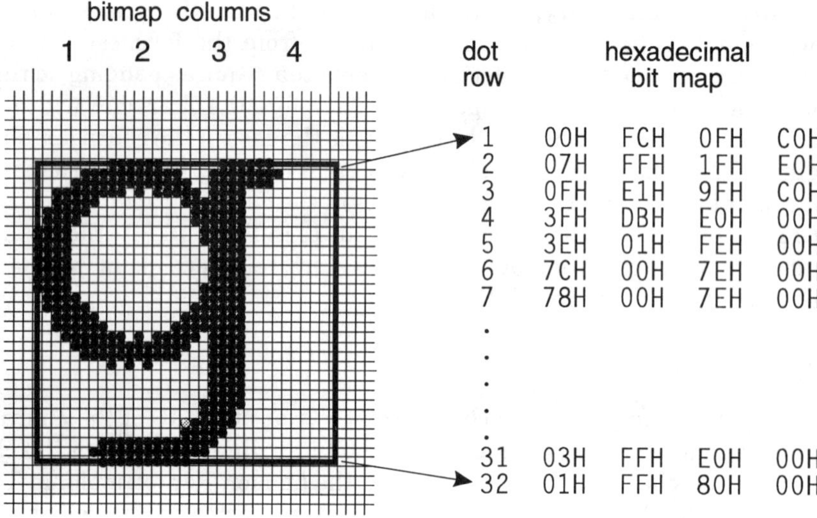

Figure 10.18 *Character Dot Drawing and Bitmap*

In addition to the library routines, the book's microdisk contains a program named CSETHP (located in the \PCL directory) which displays all the characters in a PCL disk file. The program, which uses the VGA modes in the default setting, can be easily modified to display in XGA or SuperVGA modes. The necessary editing operations are described in the source file CSETHP.ASM, also in this directory.

11

Programming Graphics
Hardcopy Devices

Chapter Summary

This chapter describes the programming of pen plotters and laser printers. Pen plotter programming is discussed in terms of the HP-GL language as implemented in the Hewlett-Packard ColorPro plotter. The discussion includes the use of scaling, plotting, labeling, and output commands, as well as the plotting of geometric curves. Laser printer programming is discussed in terms of Hewlett-Packard PCL as implemented on the LaserJet printers. A demonstration program for laser printer programming generates four color-separation negatives of a VGA graphics image.

11.0 Graphics Hardcopy Hardware

Although the video display is usually considered as the primary computer graphics output device, the video image is ephemeral. Many applications that use computer graphics technology require a more permanent copy of the generated image than the one on the CRT screen. Such is the case in computer aided design, digital typesetting, image editing, as well as in painting and drawing software. All of these programs would be of little practical use if their output were limited to the machine's CRT.

A great variety of hardcopy devices and technologies have been developed for use in the field of computer graphics. Raster-scan graphics printers, for example, range in price and complexity from a professional-grade photo-typesetter, which takes up dozens of square feet of floor space and can cost over a hundred thousand dollars, to a desktop graphics printer that costs less than five hundred. Other graphics hardcopy devices include imagesetters, laser, inkjet, and impact printers, and graphics plotters. Some low-end devices in this group were conceived mainly to provide graphics capabilities within the budget of typical home-computer users.

On the other hand, many of these high-end, specialty machines would be of interest but to a very small circle of graphics programmers. For example, the imagesetter is a device that produces photographic copy from digital data; the machine's output is typically in the form of a color slide or a print. The artwork for the cover and the color illustrations in this book were created with a drawing program on an IBM microcomputer and the resulting image files fed into an imagesetter, which generated hard-copies of the images on transparency film. Although the technology used in the imagesetter is quite sophisticated and its output is of the highest quality, in practice few programmers will ever be concerned with controlling one of these devices. Much the same could be said of programming digital typesetters and other professional-level, graphics hardcopy machines.

In this chapter we have attempted to briefly cover the graphics hardcopy machines with which the average programmer will most likely be concerned. We have excluded the devices located at both extremes of the hardcopy device list; the inexpensive at one end, and the costly, dedicated professional systems at the other one. What remains are mainly pen plotters and laser printers.

11.1 Pen Plotter Programming

The pen plotter, often simply called a "plotter," is a graphics hardcopy device that generates a drawing by means of one or more ink pens. Figure 1.3 is a photograph of a Hewlett-Packard ColorPro pen plotter. The pen plotter is a vector graphics device, that is, the plot data is input in the form of point-to-point drawing instructions. This contrasts with raster scan devices for which the graphics data is usually in bitmap form. Notice that this description refers to the principal mode of operation of each device type, since some raster scan printers have vector graphics capabilities and some pen plotters can operate on bit-mapped images.

Pen plotters are often used in the production of artistic and technical drawing in the fields of architecture, engineering, construction, and graphics art. Typical output from a pen plotter is a monochrome or color line drawing. The media on which the plot is produced is paper or film, often of comparable texture and properties as that used in traditional drafting technology. The drawing format and size for pen plotter media are also similar to those commonly used in conventional, hand-made drawings. Therefore, the use of a computer-driven pen plotter has improved the performance and quality of the conventional technical drawing and drafting without changing its character.

Presently two different plotter technologies are widely used in generating image lines. The conventional method is based on ink pens, often almost identical to those used in drafting. An alternative technology is based on the electrostatic deposit of minute ink dots. In addition to the line-generating methods, plotters have been traditionally classified according to their design into flatbed and drum types. In the flatbed plotter the drawing media is placed in a flat bed and the drawing is produced by moving the drawing pens along the machine's x and y axes. In the drum plotter the drawing media is wrapped around a circular drum which generates one of the axis movements. Larger plotters are usually of the drum type. Figure 11.1 is a photograph of a Hewlett-Packard electrostatic plotter.

Figure 11.1 *HP 7600 Series Model 355 Electrostatic Plotter*
(Photo courtesy of Hewlett-Packard Company)

Whatever technology is used to hold the drawing media or to generate the line, all plotters are considered vector devices. The drawing operation is defined as a line segment between two coordinate points. In this technology it is customary to refer to the x and y vectors as determining the two axes of the drawing media. The drawing pen, usually represented by the z-axis vector, can be lowered into contact with the surface of the paper or raised away from this surface. The actual operations are performed by movements along the x and y axes. If the axis movement is performed while the pen is in contact with the drawing surface it is a draw operation; if the movement is executed while the pen is not in contact with the surface it is a translation operation. Figure 11.2 shows the conventional representation of pen plotter axes.

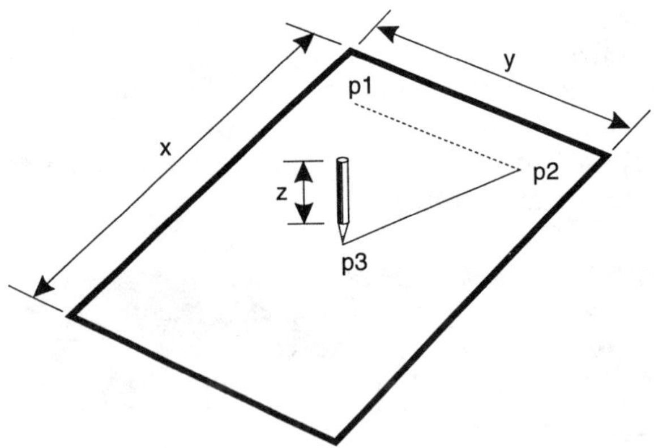

Figure 11.2 *Plotter Coordinates*

In Figure 11.2 we represented two pen movements; the first one, from point p1 to point p2 on the drawing media takes place while the pen is lifted from the surface. This movement is shown by a dotted line. The second pen movement, from point p2 to point p3 takes place while the pen is in contact with the drawing surface. In Figure 11.2 this movement is shown with a continuous line.

Plotters, as well as many industrial robots and machine tools, are driven by electric stepper motors. These are constructed with a magnetically polarized rotor and a variable polarity stator. The rotor turns in very precise angular increments by switching the polarity of the stator element. A driver program for a particular stepper motor can be coded so as to turn the rotor a certain number of steps in either the clockwise or the counterclockwise direction. If the linear motion that results from one motor gyration step is known, the design and coding of the graphics primitive routines for vector devices becomes quite similar to the plotting routines used in programming raster devices. Furthermore, the primitive routines developed in previous chapters for calculating and storing the video system coordinate points of geometric curves can serve as a model in developing graphic primitives for a vector device, as discussed later in this chapter.

Modern plotters are usually furnished with an internal command set that makes unnecessary programming the device at the hardware level. Since the hardware operations executed by a hardcopy device are considerably slower than any digital calculation performed by the driver, the use of a higher-level programming interface has, in this case, no detrimental effect on overall system performance.

11.1.1 The HP-GL Language

Hewlett-Packard Corporation has developed a vector-command plotter control language, known as Hewlett-Packard Graphics Language, or HP-GL. For the lack of a standard plotter control language, in the present chapter we will discuss plotter programming using HP-GL. Notice that the HP-GL language is not limited to pen plotters, since it has also been extended to laser printers, electrostatic plotters, and other hardcopy devices.

A plotter command in HP-GL is in the form of an ASCII string transmitted to the device. The string consists of a two-letter mnemonic code, one or more command parameters (if necessary), optional and required separators, and a terminator code. Figure 11.3 shows the syntax elements of an HP-GL command.

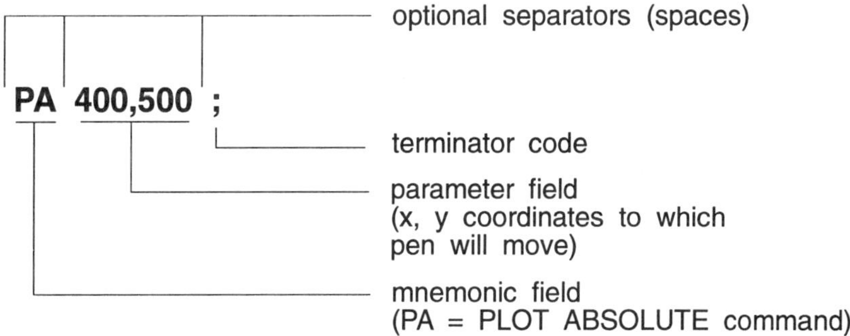

Figure 11.3 *HP-GL Command Syntax*

Notice in Figure 11.3 that the first element of the HP-GL command string is the mnemonic letters "PA" which represent the plot absolute command described later in this section. The plot absolute command includes a parameter field with the coordinates of the point to which the pen moves from its current position. In Figure 11.3 the coordinates are the value 400,500. In this case the "," symbol is a required separator that must be inserted between the two values. The command string concludes with the ";" symbol, which serves as a terminator code. The HP-GL language allows the use of spaces and other symbols as optional separators to improve the readability of the command string. In Figure 11.3 we have inserted a space at the start of the string to separate the mnemonic, the parameter field, and the terminator code.

The HP-GL language has undergone modifications with the introduction of new plotter models and hardware. For this reason it is difficult to code programs or drivers that execute correctly in any HP-GL plotter and, at the same time, take advantage of the hardware characteristics of each machine. This explains why many applications provide a separate driver for each plotter supported. The situation can be justified considering that there are more substantial variations in plotter hardware than there are in laser printers or other output devices, as can be seen by comparing the plotter in Figure 1.3 to the ones in Figure 11.1. The result is that practically every plotter uses its own implementation of HP-GL. The examples in this chapter were designed for the HP-GL implementation used by the Hewlett-Packard ColorPro plotter. Although the ColorPro uses the simplest subset of the HP-GL language, no general portability statement can be made.

Table 11.1   *HP-GL Instruction Set in ColorPro Plotter (No Cartridge)*

MNEMONIC	COMMAND DESCRIPTION
CA	Designate alternate character set
CP	Character plot
CS	Designate standard character set
DS	Digitize clear
DF	Set Default
DI	Absolute direction
DP	Digitize point
DR	Relative direction
DT	Define label terminator
IM	Input mask
IN	Initialize
IP	Input scaling points p1 and p2
IW	Input window
LB	Label (plot text string)
LT	Select line type
OA	Output actual position and pen status
OC	Output commanded position and pen status
OD	Output digitized point and pen status
OE	Output error
OF	Output factors
OH	Output hard-clip limits
OI	Output identification
OO	Output options
OP	Output scaling points p1 and p2
OS	Output status
OW	Output window
PA	Plot absolute
PD	Pen down
PR	Plot relative
PU	Pen up
RO	Rotate coordinate system
SA	Select alternate character set
SC	Scale
SI	Select character size
SL	Slant characters
SM	Enable symbol mode
SP	Select pen
SR	Set relative character size
SS	Select standard character set
TL	Set tick length
UC	User defined character
VS	Velocity select
XT	x-axis tick
YT	y-axis tick

11.1.2 HP-GL Instruction Set

We saw that the format of an HP-GL command string is a two-letter mnemonic code, an optional parameter field, optional and required separators, and a terminator code. Table 11.1 shows the basic set of HP-GL instructions for the Hewlett-Packard ColorPro plotter.

11.1.3 The ColorPro Plotter

The Hewlett-Packard ColorPro is a small, flatbed plotter equipped with an 8-pen carousel. (See Figure 1.3.) The ColorPro uses ANSI A-size (8.5-by-11 inches) media, which can be drawing paper or transparency film. The ColorPro is supplied with either an RS-232C or a HP-IB interface with the computer system. The HP-IB interface is designed for compatibility with Hewlett-Packard microcomputers, such as the HP Touchscreen, the Series 200, and HP Portable. The RS-232C interface can be used with any microcomputer equipped with a standard serial port. Dip switches in the back of the ColorPro allow selecting the Baud Rate and Parity parameters in machines equipped with the RS-232C interface option. The ColorPro can be equipped with an optional Graphics Enhancement Cartridge which adds 14 additional instructions to the instruction set listed in Table 11.1. The ColorPro plotter programming examples in the present chapter assume a machine not equipped with the Graphics Enhancement Cartridge.

We mentioned that although HP-GL is designed to offer a common programming language for plotters and other graphics hardcopy devices, each machine implements the language with specific variations to suit its characteristics and hardware. This means that a program or driver developed for the ColorPro plotter may not work correctly in another model machine, and vice versa. However, the fundamental instructions of the language are the same in every case, and converting a program or driver so that it is compatible with another model machine is not a major chore.

Information about a particular implementation of HP-GL or other programming commands can usually be obtained from the plotter manufacturer. Hewlett-Packard publishes a programming manual for each plotter model. These books can be obtained directly from the Company or through a Hewlett-Packard dealer.

Serial Port Initialization

Most plotters are connected to the computer system via the serial port (RS-232C line). There are two reasons for using the serial port for the plotter connection. First, the serial interface is fast enough for driving the device. Second, this leaves the system's parallel port available for printer output. When the plotter is connected to the serial port, the first programming operation must be initializing the port's communications protocol to match the device.

In the ColorPro plotter the communication parameters are selected by means of dip switches located at the back of the machine. The default values are as follows:

```
Baud rate = 9600
Parity = none
Stop bits = 1
Word length = 8
```

The following code fragment shows the processing necessary for intializing the ColorPro serial interface using BIOS service number 0 of Interrupt 14H.

```
; Note: This operation assumes the following setting in the
; ColorPro rear-panel switches
;                                       I      O
;                                 B1    ==>    |
;                                 B2    <==    |   Baud rate
;                                 B3    ==>    |
;                                 B4    <==    |
;
;                                 US    <==    |   Paper type 8 1/2 by 11
;
;                                 SI    ==>    |   No parity
;                                 S2    ==>    |
;*********************|
;   set communications  |
;   to ColorPro values  |
;*********************|
; Values to match ColorPro default protocol
; Bit mask: 111xxxxx ...... Baud = 9600
;           xxx00xxx ...... Parity = none
;           xxxxx0xx ...... Stop bits = 1
;           xxxxxx11 ...... Word length = 8
;           11100011
;
        MOV     AL,11100011B    ; Bit mask for ColorPro default
        MOV     AH,0            ; BIOS service request number
        MOV     DX,0            ; COM1 in all hardware types
        INT     14H             ; BIOS service request
; At this point the machine's serial communications line has
been
; set to match the default setting of the ColorPro real panel
; switches
```

The procedure named INIT_CP in the BITIO module of the GRAPHSOL library can also be used to intialize the ColorPro plotter to these default values.

Sending HP-GL Commands

ColorPro plotter programming in HP-GL consists of sending command strings to the device and receiving data from the device through the serial port (RS-232C line). The operation can be simplified by having the software store the ASCII string in its data area and the processing routine read the characters in the string and transmit them, one by one, through the serial port. The code determines the end of the string by means of the ";" symbol which serves as a terminator, or by a NULL byte appended at the end of the string. The following code fragment shows the command string in Figure 11.3 as a data segment variable:

```
PA_$        DB          'PA '
X_VAL       DB          '500  '                ; x-coordinate substring
            DB          ','                    ; Required separator
Y_VAL       DB          '500  '                ; y-coordinate substring
            DB          ';'                    ; Command terminator code
            DB          0                      ; NULL byte terminator
```

Notice that in the above code fragment the x and y coordinates are entered as named variables. This allows the code to change these parameters in the command string. We have padded the values with blanks so as to allow 5 ASCII digits for either the x or the y coordinate. This is possible because HP-GL allows the use of blank characters as optional padding, anywhere in the command string. Later in this chapter we will develop a routine to plot absolute coordinates using a command string formatted as the one listed above.

The serial port sending operation consists of transmitting the HP-GL command string through the previously initialized RS-232C port. In the following discussions we assume that the reader is familiar with serial communications programming. If this is not the case, refer to Chapter 5 of our book *Programming Solutions Handbook for IBM Microcomputer* (see Bibliography) or to another title on the subject.

Serial communications between the computer and the ColorPro plotter are based on the fact that the plotter's data-terminal-ready line (pin number 20) is wired to the computer's data-set-ready line (pin number 6). This setup can be easily obtained by means of an appropriately wired RS-232C cable, as described in the ColorPro documentation. This cable can also be purchased commercially from Hewlett-Packard or other companies. The software tests bit 5 of the modem status register to determine the plotter's DTR signal, as shown in the following code fragment:

```
; Routine to send a character (in AL) to the ColorPro plotter
; assuming a hardwired handshake, in which the plotter's DTR
; signal (pin # 20) is connected to the computer's serial port
; DSR line (pin # 6)
;
        PUSH    AX                      ; Save character to send
;
;********************|
; get serial port base |
;       address        |
;********************|
; Read base address of RS-232C port in BIOS data area
        PUSH    DS                      ; Save operation segment
```

```
              MOV       DX,0              ; BIOS data area segment
              MOV       DS,DX             ; Data segment to BIOS area
              MOV       CX,DS:0400H       ; Offset of card 1
              POP       DS                ; Restore program DS
;
; At this point CX holds the base address of the serial port
;*********************|
;  check status line  |
;*********************|
WAIT_FOR_DTR:
              MOV       DX,CX             ; RS-232C base port address
              ADD       DX,6              ; Modem status register
              IN        AL,DX             ; Read byte at status register
              JMP       SHORT $+2         ; I/O delay
              MOV       AH,AL             ; Store in AH
              DEC       DX                ; Line status register
              IN        AL,DX             ; Status
              JMP       SHORT $+2         ; I/O delay
; At this point AH holds the modem status register contents and
; AL holds the line status register
; Bit 5 of the modem status register holds the state of the
; plotter's DTR signal, as received in the computers DSR line
; Bit 5 of the line status register holds the state of the
; transmitter holding register (1 = THR is empty)
; Note: the THR must be empty before data can be sent
              AND       AX,2020H          ; Mask off all other bits
              XOR       AX,2020H          ; Test for both high
; XORing with the original mask sets the zero flag if both bits
; were set
              JNZ       WAIT_FOR_DTR      ; Repeat if not high
; At this point the plotter is ready to receive
;*********************|
;    send character   |
;*********************|
              POP       AX                ; Restore character to send
              MOV       DX,CX             ; Recover base address of port
; Transmitter holding register is at base address + 0
              OUT       DX,AL             ; Send character
              JMP       SHORT $+2         ; I/O delay
; At this point the character has been transmitted to the
; ColorPro plotter
              .

              .
              .
```

The procedure named CP_COMMAND in the BITIO module of the GRAPHSOL library can be used to send a command string to the ColorPro plotter. This procedure uses a local routine named SEND_ONE_CP that employs similar processing as the one shown in the preceding code fragment.

Receiving HP-GL Data

Computer/plotter communications work both ways; the computer sends a command string to the plotter through the serial port and the plotter returns information to the computer through this same line. Although it is possible to develop plotter software which does not listen to the data returned on the serial line, this style of programming is, at best, risky. A correctly designed plotter driver should listen to the device in order to query hardware and software options, determine the device's status, certify communications links, and diagnose possible errors.

The routine for receiving plotter data consists of a simple serial-port-read operation. In order to avoid a program hang-up if communications are faulty, it is a good idea to include in the processing some form of timed or user-activated break. The following code fragment is a procedure for receiving a ColorPro character through the serial port. The routine monitors the keyboard and breaks if the user presses any key.

```
GET_CP_CHAR      PROC      FAR
; Procedure to receive one character through the serial line
; Processing assumes that the communication parameters have
; been previously selected to match the computer and the
; ColorPro plotter
;
; On exit:
;         Carry clear if character received
;         AL = A8H if transmission error detected
;         Carry set if user aborted by pressing a key
;
; First flush keyboard buffer of old characters
         CALL     KBR_FLUSH          ; Routine in SOLUTION.LIB
;**********************|
; get serial port base |
;         address      |
;**********************|
; Get address of RS-232C card from BIOS data area
         PUSH     DS                 ; Save operation segment
         MOV      DX,0               ; BIOS data area segment
         MOV      DS,DX              ; Data segment to BIOS area
         MOV      CX,DS:0400H        ; Offset of card 1
         POP      DS                 ; Restore program DS
; Card base address is not in CX
```

```
            MOV     DX,CX           ; Serial card base address
            ADD     DX,5            ; Status register
CHK_STAT:
            IN      AL,DX           ; Character ready?
            TEST    AL,1            ; Data ready bit on status
                                    ; register
            JNZ     D_READY         ; Get data
            TEST    AL,1EH          ; Bits 1, 2, 3 and 4 are error
                                    ; bits
            JNZ     DATA_ERROR      ; Go if error bit set
; Test for key pressed
            PUSH    DX              ; Save card base address
            MOV     AH,1            ; BIOS service request number
            INT     16H             ; for keyboard status
            POP     DX              ; Restore card address
            JZ      CHK_STAT        ; No key pressed, continue
; Key was pressed during line monitoring
            STC                     ; Carry flag is return code
            RET
D_READY:
            SUB     DX,5            ; Return DX to port base address
            IN      AL,DX           ; Read character into AL
            CLC                     ; Normal exit
            RET
DATA_ERROR:
            MOV     AL,0A8H         ; A8H = error received
            CLC                     ; Normal exit
            RET
GET_CP_CHAR     ENDP
```

The procedure GET_CP_CHAR is included in the BITIO module of the
GRAPHSOL library.

Intializing the ColorPro Plotter

In programming the ColorPro plotter it is necessary to intialize the device to
its default state as well as to test that computer-plotter communications are
operating correctly. The plotter initialization command (mnemonic code IN in
Table 11.1) serves to return the device to a known condition. The IN command
cancels any command entered through the front-panel keys, raises the drawing
pen, cancels rotation, clears previous errors, and resets the p1 and p2 scaling
points (described later in this chapter) to their default values. Although the
machine is automatically initialized when turned on, it is good programming
practice to precede any new operations with the IN command. The IN command
string takes no parameters.

Software can test plotter communications by means of the output identification command (mnemonic code OI in Table 11.1). This command returns a 5-character string through the serial port. In the ColorPro plotter the correct identification string is "7440A." Other Hewlett-Packard plotters return their own identification code; for example, the model 7550 plotter returns the string "7550A." The following code fragment shows the initialization and testing commands for a ColorPro plotter. The code uses several procedures from the BITIO module of the GRAPHSOL library.

```
DATA      SEGMENT
;
; HP_GL command strings          Command action:
INIT_$    DB        'IN ;'       ; Initialize
          DB        00
ID_$      DB        'OI ;        ; Output plotter ID string
          DB        00
ID_BUF    DB        '     '      ; Buffer for plotter ID
CP_ID     DB        '7440A'      ; Correct string
             .
             .

             .
DATA      ENDS


CODE      SEGMENT
             .
             .

             .


; Set serial communications to ColorPro default values
        CALL      SERIAL_2_CP     ; Procedure in GRAPHSOL.LIB
;*********************|
;    Init and get ID  |
;*********************|
; Initialize plotter
        LEA       SI,INIT_$       ; Initialization command string
        CALL      CP_COMMAND      ; Send command to ColorPro
; Flush old characters from RS-232C Receiver Register
        CALL      FLUSH_232       ; Procedure in GRAPHSOL.LIB
; Get plotter ID string
        LEA       SI,ID_$         ; Output plotter ID command
        CALL      CP_COMMAND      ; Send command to ColorPro
; At this point the program must wait for a 5-character string
; returned by the plotter
; The ID string for the ColorPro plotter is "7440A"
; The terminator character is the carriage return code (0DH)
        LEA       DI,ID_BUF       ; Storage buffer for plotter ID
```

```
GET_IDS:
        PUSH    DI                  ; and pointer
        CALL    GET_CP_CHAR         ; RS-232C receive routine
        POP     DI                  ; Restore registers
        JC      USER_ABORT          ; User pressed a key
; At this point AL holds the character received
        CMP     AL,0DH              ; End of message
        JE      MESSAGE_RCVD        ; Received
; Character received is not CR
        MOV     [DI],AL             ; Store character in buffer
        INC     DI                  ; Bump buffer pointer
        JMP     GET_IDS             ; Continue reception
;********************|
;     user aborted   |
;********************|
USER_ABORT:
; Code at this point will handle the user abort condition
            .

            .

;********************|
;   message received |
;********************|
MESSAGE_RCVD:
; Message received must be the ColorPro ID string "7440A"
        LEA     SI,ID_BUF           ; Received string
        LEA     DI,CP_ID            ; Test string "7440A"
        MOV     CX,5                ; Test 5 characters
COMPARE_5:
        MOV     AL,[SI]             ; Get received character
        MOV     AH,[DI]             ; String character
        CMP     AL,AH               ; Compare them
        JNE     BAD_8440A           ; Go if not equal
        INC     SI                  ; Bump pointers
        INC     DI
        LOOP    COMPARE_5
; At this point the received string has compared correctly
        JMP     OK_7440A
;********************|
;  ID string error   |
;********************|
BAD_8440A:
; Code at this point will handle the possibility of an invalid
; ColorPro identification string
            .

            .

;********************|
```

```
;    ID string matched   |
;********************** |
OK_7440A:
; Processing can continue at this point assuming that a
; ColorPro plotter is connected and is communicating correctly

        .

        .

        .

CODE      ENDS
```

The program named CPDEMO in the book's microdisk contains code to exercise the ColorPro plotter routines in the BITIO module of the GRAPHSOL library.

11.1.4 The HP-GL Drawing Surface

The drawing surface is to a plotter as the CRT screen is to the video system. This drawing surface can be visualized as a two-dimensional Cartesian plane. The axes of the plotter's drawing plane are conventionally identified with the letter x (horizontal axis) and the letter y (vertical axis). Any point in the drawing surface can be designated by means of its x, y coordinates. Figure 11.4 shows the default orientation of the ColorPro coordinate system.

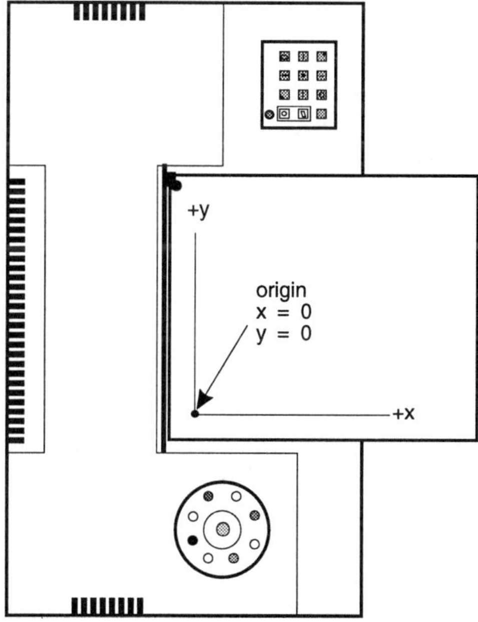

Figure 11.4 *ColorPro Default Coordinate System Orientation*

The origin of the coordinate system (see Figure 11.4) is defined as the point at which both coordinates have a zero value (0,0). By placing the origin at one of the corners of the drawing surface it is possible to restrict the x and y values to the positive range.

The HP-GL system allows two different units for expressing coordinate points. One *plotter unit* measures the smallest movement that can be performed by the plotter hardware. In the ColorPro a plotter unit is 0.00098 in., therefore there are 1016 plotter units per inch. The *user units* are determined by the programmer according to the application. Each user unit consists of a number of plotter units; for example, if the code assigns 10 plotter units per user unit, then the user unit corresponds to a plotter movement of 9.8 thousands of an inch. Notice that user units can be defined separately for each axis.

11.1.5 HP-GL Scaling Commands

The process by which the programmer assigns a number of plotter units to user units is known as *scaling*. Scaling facilitates programming by adding flexibility to the plotting system. In the ColorPro and other HP-GL plotters scaling is based on two imaginary points, designated as p1 and p2. Figure 11.5 shows the default setting of scaling points p1 and p2 on the ColorPro plotter.

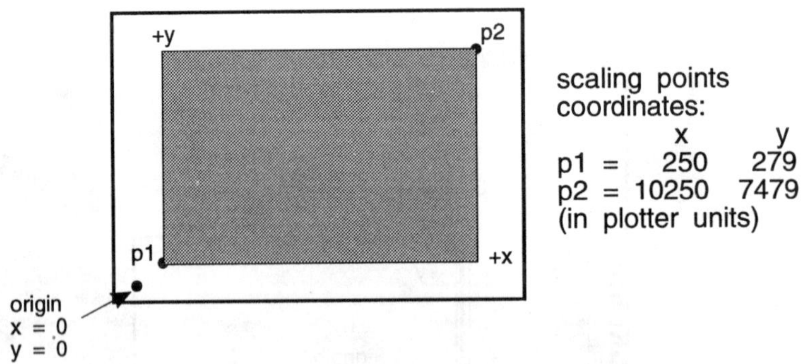

Figure 11.5   *ColorPro Default Location of Scaling Points*

Notice in Figure 11.5 that, in the default position, scaling point p1 does not coincide with the origin. In the ColorPro the default coordinates of p1 are $x_1 = 250$, $y_1 = 279$ and the default coordinates of p2 are $x_2 = 10250$, $y_2 = 7479$. This means that, in the ColorPro plotter the origin point is approximately 0.5 in. from the left border of the drawing surface and 0.375 in. from the bottom border. The IP instruction (described on the following page) allows relocating the scaling points. p1 and p2 can also be re-positioned by means of the corresponding buttons in the ColorPro control panel.

Input Scaling Points (IP) Command

The scaling points can be interpreted to define two diagonally opposite corners of a drawing rectangle, shown shaded in gray in Figure 11.5. The dimensions (in plotter units) of the default drawing rectangle are obtained by subtracting the x and the y coordinates of p1 and p2. Therefore in Figure 11.5 the x dimension is 10000 plotter units and the y dimension is 7200 plotter units. If we approximate 1 plotter unit = 0.001 in. then the default drawing rectangle is of 10-by-7.2 in. In order to simplify the arithmetic operations we will use this approximation in the all plotter unit calculations in the rest of this chapter.

By redefining points p1 and p2 the program can create a new drawing rectangle of different dimensions. For example, to create a drawing rectangle of 4.5-by-7 inches approximately centered on the 8.5-by-11 in. drawing media we proceed as follows.

1. p1, which defines the bottom-left corner of the drawing rectangle, is located 2 in. from the left border and 2 in. from the bottom border. Therefore, taking into account the location of the origin point, p1 is relocated to 1.5 in. to the right of the origin and 1.625 in. above the origin.

2. p2, which defines the top-right corner of the drawing rectangle, is located 7 in. to the right of p1 and 4.5 inches above it.

Using these values we can input the new scaling points with the command:

```
'IP 1500,1625,8500,6125 ;'
```

Figure 11.6 shows the 4.5-by-7 in. rectangle shaded in darker gray than the default drawing rectangle.

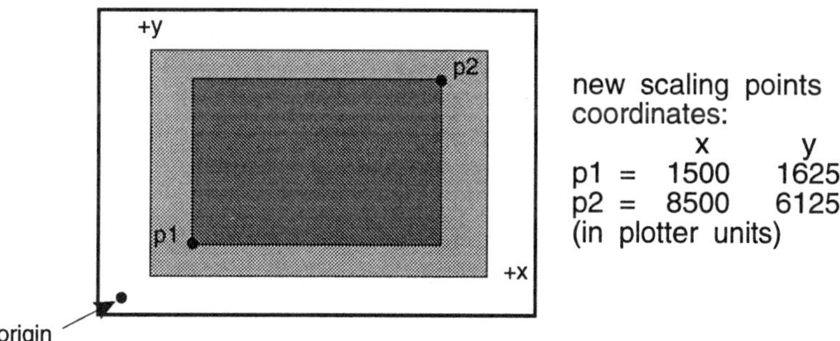

Figure 11.6   *Scaling Points Relocation for a 4.5-by-7 in. Surface*

Recall that in the above calculations (as well as in those that follow) we have used the approximation: 1 plotter unit = 0.001 in. For this reason the actual plots would not be exactly to scale.

The Scale (SC) Command

Once the new drawing surface has been defined by relocating the p1 and p2 scaling points, the program can create its own units of measurements for use within this drawing surface. The scale instruction (mnemonic code SC) is used to map the scaling points to a user-unit coordinate system. The command divides the rectangle defined by points p1 and p2 into horizontal and vertical units defined by the user. We can scale the 4.5-by-7 in. drawing surface shown in Figure 11.6 to divide its surface into more convenient units of measurement than the native plotter units. For example, to divide the 4.5-by-7 in. surface into units of 0.01 in. we use the following scale command:

```
'SC 0,700,0,420 ;'
```

Thereafter the code can address any point within the drawing rectangle using its user-units coordinates. Point p1 would be located at user-unit coordinates 0,0 and point p2 at user-unit coordinates 700,420. By the same token, the center of the drawing surface would be located at user-unit coordinates 350,210.

The input scaling points (IP) and scale (SC) commands can be jointly used to transform the plotter's coordinate system, to reduce or enlarge objects within the drawing surface, to create mirror images, and to perform other advanced functions. For example, a program can emulate the VGA video mode number 18, with 640-by-480 pixels resolution, on the plotter's drawing surface. In this case, the code can adopt user units of approximately 0.001 in. and locate the bottom-left corner of the drawing surface 1 in. to the right and above the origin. Programming operations are as follows:

1. Relocate scaling points p1 and p2 to define a drawing rectangle of 480-by -640 units of 0.001 in. In this case point p1 is located at the top-left corner of the drawing surface and p2 at the bottom-right corner, so as to reproduce the VGA coordinate system convention. If the bottom-left corner of the image is to be 1 in. (1000 plotter-units approximately) to the right and above the origin, then point p1 would be located at $x = 1000, y = 5800$, and point p2 at $x = 7400, y = 1000$, as shown in Figure 11.7.

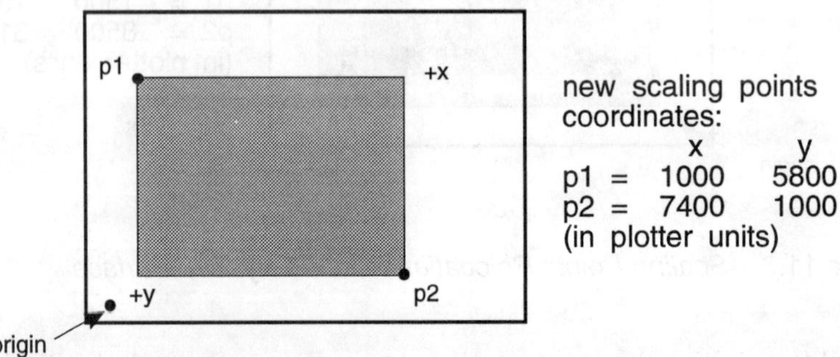

Figure 11.7 *Scaling Points Relocation for VGA Emulation*

2. Once the scaling points have been relocated, the code can define the new user-units so that the drawing surface can be addressed as if it contained 480-by-640 pixels. This can be accomplished by a scale command in which the range of x values is defined from 0 to 640 and the range of y values from 0 to 480, as in the following HP-GL command string:

```
'SC 0,640,0,480 ;'
```

For most applications that perform geometrical drawings the scale would have equal units along both axes. In this case, the scaling system is *isotropic*. On the other hand, some plotter applications could benefit from having different user-units along each axis. For example, a program to produce a chart in which monetary values (in the range 0 to 5000) are plotted along the y axis and days-of-the-year (in the range 0 to 365) are plotted along the x axis could use 5000 user-units on the y-axis and 365 user-units on the x axis. In this case, the scaling system is *anisotropic*.

11.1.6 HP-GL Plotting Commands

Plotting operations in HP-GL consists of selecting a drawing pen, raising and lowering the pen to clear or contact the drawing surface, selecting the pen speed, and moving it to different locations on the drawing surface. Recall that the present discussion refers to the HP-GL commands as implemented for the ColorPro plotter and that these commands could vary in other plotter hardware.

Select Pen (SP) Command

The ColorPro plotter is equipped with an 8-pen carrousel. The pen storage mechanisms in this carrousel are usually called *stalls*. The *pen holder* is the device that moves the pen on the drawing surface. The select pen (SP) command loads a pen from the corresponding stall in the carrousel into the pen holder or returns a pen to the stall. In the ColorPro, the pen number is a value in the range 0 to 8. A select pen (SP) command with a value of 0, or no parameter, returns the pen in the holder to its stall. If its original stall is now occupied, the pen is placed in the first vacant one. If a number in the range 1 to 8 is entered as a value in the SP command, then the corresponding pen is loaded into the pen holder. For example, the HP-GL command string

```
'SP 4;'
```

loads pen number 4 from the carrousel into the pen holder.

Pen Up (PU) and Pen Down (PD) Commands

The Pen Up (PU) command raises the pen currently in the pen holder and the pen down (PD) command lowers it into contact with the drawing surface. The PU and PD commands can also be used in plotting operations, as described below.

The Plot Absolute (PA) Command

The plot absolute (PA) command moves the pen holder to the corresponding position specified in absolute coordinates. If the pen is up at the time of the command, then the movement is a translation to a new location in the drawing surface. If the pen is down, then the command draws a straight line from the current position to the one specified in the command. The PA command can include several coordinate pairs.

For example, once the scaling points have been relocated as shown in Figure 11.7 and the scale command issued to establish a 480-by-640 points drawing grid (see Section 11.1.6), the following sequence of commands can be used to select pen number 4 and draw a rectangle along the border of the drawing surface

```
'PU ;                                    <-  pen up
'PA 0,0 ;'                               <-  move to point P1
'SP 4;'                                  <-  select pen number 4
'PD ;'                                   <-  pen down
'PA 640,0,640,480,0,480,0,0 ;' <-  draw rectangle
'PU ;'                                   <-  pen up
```

Notice, in the above example, that the plot absolute command used to draw the rectangle contains four coordinate pairs and that these are separated by commas. In this case the comma is a required separator symbol.

The plot absolute command with no parameters establishes the absolute plotting mode, which is also the plotter's default condition. Once the absolute mode is established, the pen up (PU) and pen down (PD) commands can include coordinate pairs. In this case PU and PD are interpreted as plot absolute commands. Therefore the rectangle drawing command in the previous example could have been coded as follows:

```
'PU ;                                    <-  pen up
'PA 0,0 ;'                               <-  move to point P1 and set
                                             absolute mode
'SP 4;'                                  <-  select pen number 4
'PD 640,0,640,480,0,480,0,0 ;' <-  pen down and draw
                                             rectangle in absolute
                                             mode
'PU ;'                                   <-  pen up
```

The Plot Relative (PR) Command

The plot relative (PR) command moves the pen holder to the corresponding position, specified in relative coordinates. As is the case with the plot absolute command, if the pen is up at the time of the PR command, then the movement is a translation to a new location in the drawing surface. If the pen is down, then the command draws a straight line from the current position to the one specified. The PR command can also include several coordinate pairs.

For example, the following series of instructions use the plot relative command to draw a rectangle enclosed at a distance of 10 user-units within the one drawn in the example for the PA command.

```
'PU ;                                      <- pen up
'PA 0,0 ;'                                 <- move to point p1
'SP 6;'                                    <- select pen number 6
'PD ;'                                     <- pen down
'PR 620,0,0,460,-620,0,0,-460 ;'  <- draw rectangle
'PU ;'                                     <- pen up
```

Notice, in the above example, that the plot relative command contains four coordinate pairs, separated by commas, and that these coordinates are signed values.

The plot relative command with no parameters establishes the relative plotting mode. Once the relative mode is enabled, the pen up (PU) and pen down (PD) commands can include coordinate pairs. In this case PU and PD are interpreted as plot relative commands. Therefore the rectangle drawing commands in the previous example could have been coded as follows:

```
'PU ;                                      <- pen up
'PA 0,0 ;'                                 <- move to point p1
'PR ;'                                     <- set relative mode
'SP 6;'                                    <- select pen number 6
'PD 620,0,0,460,-620,0,0,-460 ;'  <- pen down and draw
                                              rectangle in relative
                                              mode
'PU ;'                                     <- pen up
```

Velocity Select (VS) Command

The velocity select (VS) command is used to establish the plotter movement speed when the pen holder is in the down position. The ColorPro plotter movement when the pen holder is in the up position is always at 52 cm/s. The parameter for the VS command is a pen drawing speed, in cm/s. The range is 1 to 40. If the VS command is entered with no value the default pen speed is selected. The following HP-GL command string sets the pen speed at 20 cm/s.

```
'VS 20 ;'
```

Pen speed selection depends on the type of pen and on the drawing media; for example, a pen speed of 10 cm/s. is recommended for plotting on transparency film.

11.1.7 Variables in Command Strings

In the previous examples we used hard-coded plotter coordinates in the HP-GL command strings. In practical programming this technique is of limited use since frequently the plotter driver does not have access, beforehand, to the coordinate data. To overcome this limitation, the software can manipulate plotter coordinates as data variables, instead of constants. For example, once the plotter coordinate system and scaling has been set to emulate the VGA screen in 640-by-480 pixels resolution (see Section 11.5.6), the software can address the plotter surface as if it were a pixel grid. If the coordinate values are stored in machine registers, the program can convert these coordinate into ASCII and insert them in a HP-GL command string. The following code fragment shows the necessary processing operations:

```
; Routine to convert pixel coordinates for VGA mode number 18
; (640-by-480 pixels resolution) into ASCII and store these
; values in a HP-GL command string
;
DATA    SEGMENT
;*********************|
; HP-GL command string |
;(absolute coordinates)|
;*********************|
; The command string VARS_$ performs a pen down and plot
; absolute function using the coordinates in the variables
; VAR_X and VAR_Y
;
VARS_$  DB        'PD; PA '
VAR_X   DB        '    '              ; Absolute x-axis coordinate
        DB        ','                 ; variable
VAR_Y   DB        '    '              ; Absolute y-axis coordinate
        DB        '; PU;'             ; variable
        DB        00H

DATA    ENDS


CODE    SEGMENT
              .
              .
              .
; At this point:
;          CX holds x-pixel coordinate (range 0 to 639)
```

```
;            DX holds y-pixel coordinate (range 0 to 479)
; Note:
;      The plotter's coordinate system must have been
;      previously reset to emulate the VGA screen in 640 by 480
;      resolution (mode number 18)

        PUSH    AX
        PUSH    BX
        PUSH    CX
        PUSH    DX
        PUSH    DX                  ; DX is pushed twice
;
; Convert x screen coordinate to ASCII and store in command
; string
        MOV     DX,CX               ; For conversion
        LEA     DI,VAR_X            ; Pointer to x-coordinate area
                                    ; in plotter command string
        CALL    BIN_TO_ASC          ; Procedure in SOLUTION.LIB
;
; Convert y screen coordinate to ASCII and store in string
        POP     DX                  ; y coordinate from stack
        LEA     DI,VAR_Y            ; Pointer to y-coordinate area
        CALL    BIN_TO_ASC          ; Procedure in SOLUTION.LIB
;
; Execute string command
        LEA     SI,VARS_$           ; Command string
        CALL    CP_COMMAND          ; Procedure in the BITIO module
                                    ; to output a ColorPro command
                                    ; string via the serial port
; Restore context
        POP     DX
        POP     CX
        POP     BX
        POP     AX

          .

          .

          .
```

Notice that in the above code fragment, the conversion of a binary value in a machine register to an ASCII character string that can be plugged into a HP-GL command is performed by the routine named BIN_TO_ASC. This routine is part of the SOLUTION.LIB library furnished in the book's microdisk. The program named CPDEMO, also in the book's microdisk, contains a sample operation that uses string variables in an HP-GL command.

Table 11.2 *Character Sets in the Standard ColorPro Plotter*

NUMBER	CHARACTER SET NAME	ISO CODE
0	ANSI ASCII	006
1	HP 9825 HPL	-
2	French/German	-
3	Scandinavian	-
4	Spanish/Latin American	-

11.1.8 HP-GL Labeling Commands

Many plots include text messages; in HP-GL the ASCII strings that form these messages are called labels. The ColorPro plotter includes several labeling commands that facilitate plotting text messages. In the following discussion we will cover the fundamentals of the ColorPro labeling commands. A more extensive treatment can be found in the *ColorPro Programming Manual* available from Hewlett_Packard. Labeling commands for other plotters are described in their respective technical or programming manuals.

The Hewlett-Packard plotters are furnished with several character sets corresponding to different fonts, alphabets, and special characters. The standard ColorPro plotter is equipped with five character sets, as shown in Table 11.2.

In addition to the five standard character sets shown in Table 11.2, the ColorPro Graphics Enhancement cartridge has fourteen additional character sets. Other Hewlett-Packard plotters are equipped with more character sets than the ColorPro. For example, the Model 7550A plotter is furnished with 49 character sets which include fixed-space and variable-space fonts.

The printable characters in the HP-GL character sets are in the ASCII range, starting at code 32 decimal (space) to code 126 decimal. Several nonprinting characters are used as plotter control functions. The control codes recognized by the ColorPro plotter are shown in Table 11.3.

Character set number 0 in the ColorPro plotter corresponds to the characters in the IBM set, as shown in Table 1.2. Sets 1 to 4 have certain replacement characters that provide special and foreign alphabet characters. Table 11.4 shows these characters.

Table 11.3 *Control Codes Recognized by the ColorPro Plotter*

DECIMAL CODE	DESGINATION	ACTION
0	NULL	No operation
3	ETX	End lable instruction (default)
8	BS	Backspace
9	HT	Horizontal tab (1/2 backspace)
10	LF	Line feed
11	VT	Inverse line feed
13	CR	Carriage return
14	SO	Shift out (select alternate character set)
	SI	Shift in (select standard character set)

Table 11.4 *Special Characters Recognized by the ColorPro Plotter*

DECIMAL CODE	CHARACTER SET				
	0	1	2	3	4
39	'	'	BK'	'	BK'
94	^	↑	BK^	æ	BK^
95	_	BK_	BK_	BK_	BK_
96	'	BK'	BK'	'	'
123	{	π	BK"	BK"	BK~
124			|-	BK.	BK.	BK.
125	}	→	BK"	BK"	BK~
126	~	B K~	'	BK.	BK.

Note: BK = automatic backspace before character

Notice that some characters in sets 1 to 4 are preceded by a backspace code (labeled BK in Table 11.4). Therefore, to produce an accented letter, the letter code is entered first and then the code for the desired accent symbol.

The HP-GL characters are defined within a rectangular area called the *character cell*, or character plot cell. The character height, width, spacing, and position are determined by its character cell dimensions. Figure 11.8 shows the elements defined in terms of the character cell.

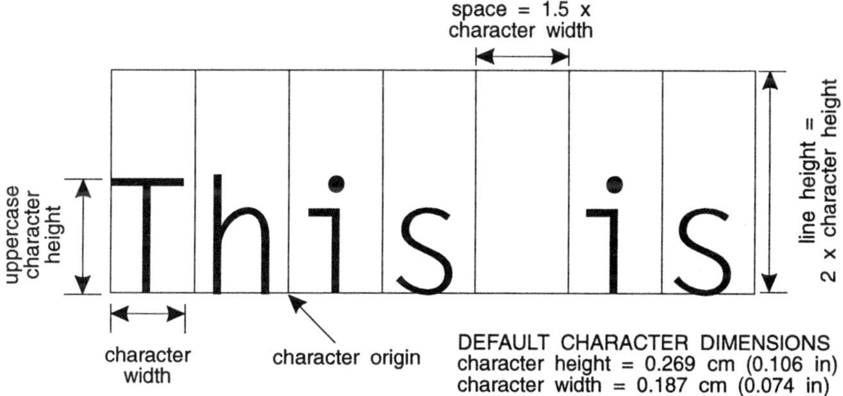

Figure 11.8 *The HP-GL Character Cell*

Notice that the spacing between character lines in a multiline text message is determined by the line height dimension in Figure 11.8, and that this value is double the character height. The width of the character cell is 1.5 times the character width, which is also the dimension of the space between characters.

Designate Standard Character Set (CS) Command

The ColorPro can perform text operations with two simultaneous character sets, named the *standard character set* and the *alternate character set*. The default setting is character set number 0, ANSI ASCII in Table 11.2, designated as both the standard and the alternate set. The software can designate any of the available character sets as the standard set using the designate standard character set (CS) command. The following is a sample HP-GL command string designating character set number 4 (Spanish/Latin American in Table 11.2) as the standard set.

```
'CS 4 ;'            <— Character set 4 designated as standard
```

Designate Alternate Character Set (CA) Command

HP-GL programs software can designate any of the available character sets as the alternate set using the designated alternate character set (CA) command. The following is a sample HP-GL command string designating character set number 1 (HP 9825 HPL in Table 11.2) as the alternate character set:

```
'CA 1 ;'            <— Character set 1 designated as alternate
```

Select Standard Character Set (SS) Command

The ColorPro select standard character set (SS) command determines that all future text commands will use the character set currently designated as the standard character set. The command requires no parameters, as in the following HP-GL command string:

```
'SS ;'              <— Enable text operations using standard
                       character set
```

Select Alternate Character Set (SA) Command

The ColorPro select alternate character set (SA) command determines that all future text commands will use the character set currently designated as the alternate character set. The command requires no parameters, as in the following HP-GL command string:

```
'SA ;'              <— Enable text operations using alternate
                       character set
```

Notice that to use a non-default character set the code must first designate this set either as the alternate or the standard set by means of the CS or CA plotter commands, then enable the set by means of an SS or SA command. For example, the following command string designates character set number 1 as the alternate set and enable text plotting operations using it:

```
'CA 1; SA ;'            <- Select and enable character set 1
```

Label (LB) Command

The label (LB) command is used to plot a text message. The message typically contains one or more ASCII characters and embedded control codes. (See Table 11.3.) In every case the message must conclude with the ETX (end label instruction) control code. The line-feed and carriage return control codes (decimal values 10 and 13 respectively) can be used to index to a new linc in a multiple text line message. The following code fragment shows an HP-GL command string plot a text message formatted as a data variable:

```
DB            'LB'
DB            'Alternate character set:'
DB            10,13
DB            '012345678 ABCDEFGH ijklmnopqrstuvwxyz{}|'
DB            03
```

Notice in the above code that the label command (LB) does not terminate with the conventional ";" symbol but with the ETX code. Also that the line feed and carriage return control codes (10 and 13 decimal) are used to index to the second text line.

Absolute Character Size (SI) Command

HP-GL characters can be scaled to any desired size. In Figure 11.8, we listed the default character dimensions for the ColorPro plotter. The absolute character size (SI) command can be used to change these default value. The command format must include two parameters: the first one expresses the new character width and the second parameter the new character height. Both dimensions are entered in centimeters (one in. = 2.54 cm). The following HP-GL command string sets the absolute character size to 0.5 and 0.75 cm respectively:

```
'SI 0.5,0.75 ;'        <- Set character size
```

Absolute Direction (DI) Command

The ColorPro, as well as other HP-GL plotters, allow positioning the text message at any desired angle relative to the plot's horizontal axis. The absolute direction (DI) command is used in HP-GL to define the new text plotting angle in terms of two values, named the *run* and the *rise*, as shown in Figure 11.9.

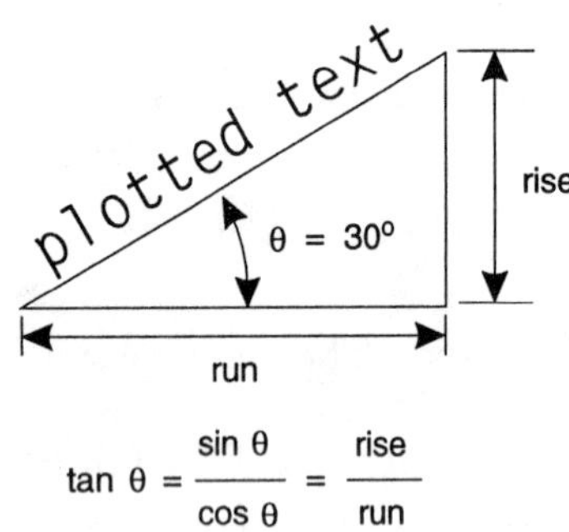

$$\tan\theta = \frac{\sin\theta}{\cos\theta} = \frac{rise}{run}$$

SINE/COSINE OF COMMON ANGLES

θ	cosine	sine
-90	0	-1
-60	0.50	-0.87
-45	0.71	-0.71
-30	0.87	-0.50
0	1	0
30	0.87	0.50
45	0.71	0.71
60	0.50	0.87
90	0	1

Figure 11.9   *Parameters for Absolute Direction (DI) Command*

Notice in Figure 11.9 that the rise/run value corresponds to the trigonometric tangent of the angle, expressed as the ratio sine/cosine. The ratios for some common angles are listed in Figure 11.9. Other inclinations can be found by obtaining the sine and cosine functions of the desired angle. The following HP-GL command string is used to set the text plotting angle to 45 degrees from the horizontal axis.

```
'DI 0.71,0.71 ;'            <— text plotting angle to 45 degrees
```

11.1.9 HP-GL Output Commands

We saw that HP-GL plotters receive commands in the form of ASCII strings transmitted through the communications lines. The HP-GL output commands are based on the plotter's capability to use the communications line to return information to the computer. The information returned by the plotter consists of identification data, error conditions, installed hardware options, and device status.

In Section 11.1.4, we discussed the processing necessary to receive plotter data through the RS-232C port. The procedure named GET_CP_CHAR allows obtaining plotter data in the ColorPro. This procedure is one of the services in the BITIO module of the GRAPHSOL library furnished in the book's microdisk.

When the ColorPro plotter is connected via the serial port, the device signals the end of its output function by means of a carriage return code (decimal 13). The software can monitor this character to determine the end of the plotter output. In the discussion that follows, we describe the most useful output commands for the ColorPro plotter. Other output commands are described in the ColorPro Programming Manual mentioned in Section 11.1.8.

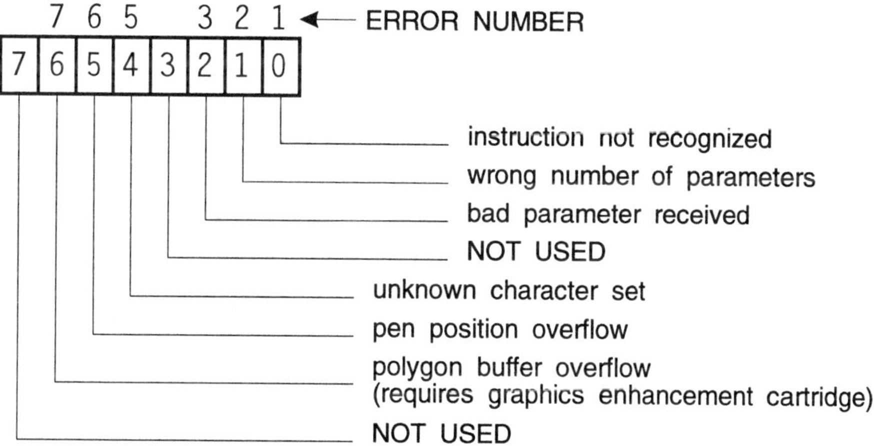

Figure 11.10 *ColorPro Error Mask Bitmap*

Input Mask (IM) Command

The input mask (IM) command is used to select which error conditions are reported by the ColorPro plotter. The error mask, also called the *E mask* in Hewlett-Packard literature, maps the error conditions to individual bits, as shown in Figure 11.10.

The default value in the E mask allows reporting of all error conditions except error number 6 (position overflow). This default mask corresponds to a value of 223 (11011111 binary). Notice that the position overflow error takes place when a positioning command attempts to move the pen holder to a location outside the plotter's range. The following HP-GL command string is used to unmask all error conditions:

```
'IM  255 ;'              <- unmask all errors (11111111B)
```

Observe that the required E mask is passed to the plotter in the form of an ASCII string.

Output Status (OS) Command

The plotter's status is encoded in an 8-bit field that contains some important settings of the ColorPro hardware and processing flags. The ColorPro status bit map is shown in Figure 11.11.

One status condition requires explanation: bit number 2 (see Figure 11.11) is used to encode the availability of a digitized point. The bit's function is related to the use of the ColorPro plotter as a digitizer; this function consists of obtaining the coordinates of points on the plotting surface by using the front panel buttons to move the pen holder to the desired locations and then pressing the ENTER key. Since the digitizing function is of very limited practical use it will not be discussed any further.

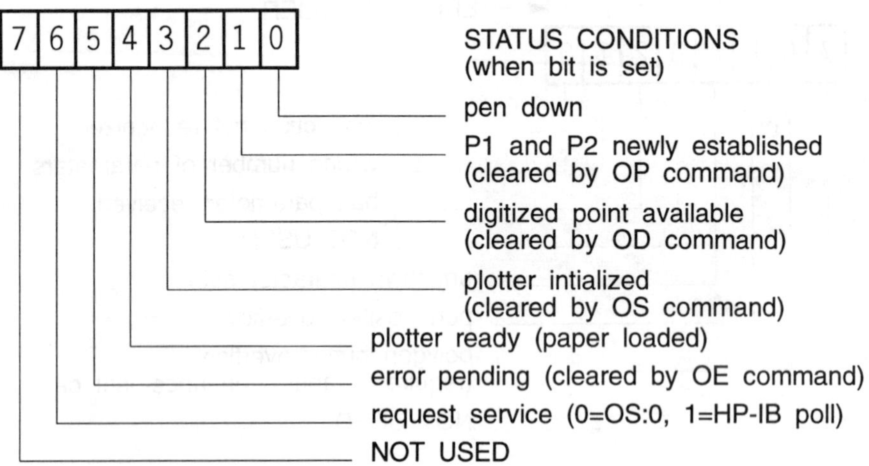

Figure 11.11 *ColorPro Status Condition Bitmap*

The status is reported as a string of three ASCII characters that represent a decimal value in the range 0 to 255. The most convenient way of testing for the various status conditions listed in Figure 11.11 is to first convert this ASCII string into a binary value in a machine register. The CP_STATUS procedure in the BITIO module of the GRAPHSOL library executes the output status command, converts the ASCII string reported by the plotter into a binary value, and returns the result in the DL register. At this point, the calling program can test any of the status bits and direct execution accordingly, as shown in the following code fragment:

```
;*********************|
;  test plotter status |
;*********************|
; The code calls the library procedure CP_STATUS to obtain the
; plotter's status conditions, then tests bit 4 to determine
; if paper is loaded
        CALL    CP_STATUS         ; Procedure in BITIO module
; At this point DX holds binary value of plotter status
        TEST    DL,00010000B      ; Test bit 4 (paper loaded)
        JNZ     OK_PAPER          ; Go if bit set
; At this point the routine should contain code to handle the
; execution if no paper has been loaded in the ColorPro plotter
        .
        .
        .
; Code at this label continues execution on the assumption that
; the ColorPro plotter is ready
OK_PAPER:
```

.
.
.

Notice that the status bits are unrelated to the error mask bitmap shown in Figure 11.10.

Output Identification (OI) Command

The output identification (OI) command returns the plotter's model number in the form of an ASCII string. The use of this command was described in Section 11.1.4 regarding the initialization of the ColorPro plotter.

Output Error (OE) Command

The output error (OE) command returns the error number of the first plotter error detected by the hardware. The data is in the form of a single ASCII digit in the range 0 to 7. The value 0 indicates that no error has occurred. Error conditions number 1, 2, 3, 5, 6, and 7 are those shown in Figure 11.10. The OE command clear bit number 5 of the status conditions (see Figure 11.11) indicates pending error conditions. If an HP-GL command contains more than one error, only the first one is reported.

Output Options (OO) Command

The output options (OO) command returns the hardware options installed in the ColorPro plotter, as shown in Figure 11.12.

The data returned by the OO instruction is in the form of eight ASCII integers, separated by commas. Each integer corresponds to the hardware options in Figure 11.12. A 1 value indicates that the option is available and a 0 value that it is not.

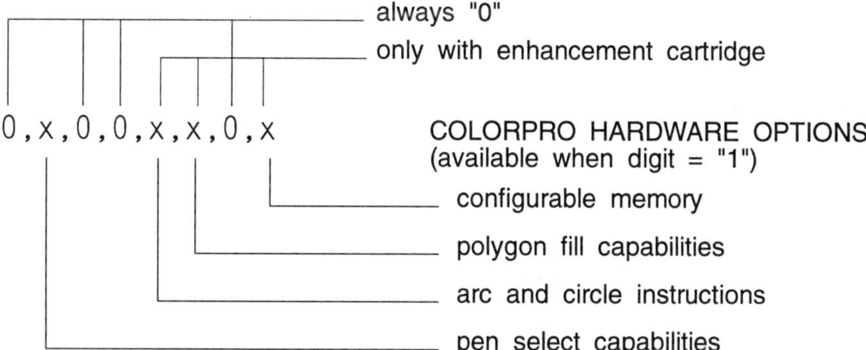

Figure 11.12 *ColorPro Hardware Options Response String*

Output Actual Position and Pen Status (OA) Command

The output actual position (OA) command outputs the coordinates of the pen holder and its up/down status. The function can be compared to the BIOS service that reports the current position of the system cursor. The service returns three parameters; the first two are the x and y pen holder coordinates, in plotter units. The coordinate values are in the form of ASCII digits, separated by commas. The third parameter, also preceded by a comma, is an ASCII 1 if the pen holder is in the down position or 0 if it is in the up position. Perhaps the most interesting use for this plotter command is in developing software that interacts with the user through the front panel keys.

11.1.10 Plotting Geometric Curves

The standard version of the ColorPro plotter has no commands for drawing conic sections or other geometric curves. However, the ColorPro is the exception rather than the rule, since most other Hewlett-Packard plotters contain geometric drawing commands. The Graphics Enhancement Cartridge for the ColorPro plotter also provides circle, arc, polygon, rectangle, area fill, pen thickness control, and other commands that can be useful in generating geometric plots.

In any case, plotter software can generate geometric curves, even if no specific command is available, by moving the pen point-to-point along the path of the desired curve. Since the finer the distance between plotted points, the smoother the curve, the ideal plotting increment is the minimum unit of pen movement. In other words, the best plot is obtained when the drawing surface is divided into a grid of plotter-unit pen increments.

In Chapter 5, we developed geometric curve plotting routines for the VGA video system. These routines use the 80x87 mathematical coprocessor, in its real or emulated version, to perform the pixel path calculations. The curve plotting routines (which can be found in the VGA3 module of the GRAPHSOL library) serve as patterns for developing geometric procedures for pen plotter software. In order to furnish a demonstration of the pen-path plotting operations we have provided a special switch in the SET_DEVICE procedure of the VGA3 module. The "P" (plotter) switch in SET_DEVICE directs output to the CP_PLOT procedure in the BITIO module, which, in turn, converts the screen coordinates to plot coordinates and outputs the data to a HP-GL command string. In this manner, a program can call the SET_DEVICE procedure with the value "P" in the AL register to enable output to the ColorPro plotter. A demonstration of these manipulations can be found in the CPDEMO program furnished in the book's microdisk.

However, the reader using the "P" switch in the SET_DEVICE procedure should consider that the geometric routines in the VGA3 module were designed for pixel operations on a video display surface. Therefore, the use of these procedures in calculating plotter coordinates is intended only as a coarse demonstration of a programming methodology. The use of these geometric plotting routines also requires setting the plotter coordinate system to emulate the VGA screen and increasing the scaling parameters to a finer grid than the VGA resolution. These manipulations can be observed in the CPDEMO program.

11.2 Laser Printer Programming

A laser printer is a hardcopy device which uses electro-photographic methods to transfer a dot image, created on a sensitive drum or belt, onto a sheet of paper. The technology is similar to that used in many popular types of copy machines. Printers using laser technology have been available since 1975, however, their popularity in the microcomputer field started in 1984 with the introduction of the first Hewlett-Packard desktop laser printer, called the *LaserJet*. Shortly thereafter, Apple Computers announced a desktop laser printer named *Laser Writer*. The Laser Writer printer came with a built-in programming language called *Postscript*, developed by Adobe Systems Incorporated. The LaserJet, on the other hand, used a programming language developed by Hewlett-Packard called *Printer Control Language* (PCL).

Postscript has been accepted as a major programming language, not only for laser printer programming, but also in several other graphics fields. Documentation about Postscript can be found in numerous published books on the Postscript language and in Postscript programming. The official source is *The Postscript Language Reference Manual, Second Edition,* published by Addison-Wesley (see Bibliography).

In the present section we provide an overview of laser printer programming in Hewlett-Packard's PCL. More detailed information about the PCL language can be found in the Technical Reference Manuals published by Hewlett-Packard for the various printers of the LaserJet line. This material, listed in the Bibliography, can be obtained directly from:

> Hewlett-Packard Company
> Boise Division
> Documentation Department M.S. 112
> P.O. Box 15
> Boise, Idaho 83707

11.2.1 Hewlett-Packard's Printer Control Language (PCL)

Hewlett-Packard's Printer Control Language (PCL) is an effort at standardizing printer character sets and control codes so as to ensure code portability. In its original conception, PCL aimed at controlling many types of printers, from base level, inexpensive devices, to the most intricate laser printers and professional typesetting machines. In reality the use of the PCL language is mostly limited to the Hewlett-Packard LaserJet line of laser printers and compatible devices.

Table 11.5   *PCL Control Codes*

| NAME | VALUE | | DESIGNATION | |
	HEX	DECIMAL	HP	ASCII
Backspace	08H	8	B_S	BS
Line feed	0AH	10	L_F	LF
Carriage return	0DH	13	C_R	CR
Form feed	0CH	12	F_F	FF
Escape	1BH	27	E_C	ESC
Horizontal tab	09H	11	H_T	HT
Shift in	0FH	15	S_I	SI
Shift out	0EH	14	S_O	SO

Five levels of the PCL language have been implemented, which are designated with the roman numerals I to V. PCL Levels IV and V are the page-oriented super-set of the language used in the Hewlett-Packard LaserJet Series II and Series III printers respectively. PCL level IV introduced the concept of page-level control and PCL V incorporates HP-GL graphics (see Section 11.1.1) into the printer language and added the use of scalable fonts in FAIS format (see Section 10.3.1). PCL levels I, II, and III are not applicable to laser printer programming.

PCL Control Codes

PCL activates printer features through the use of standard control codes and escape sequences. The PCL printer control codes can be seen in Table 11.5.

Notice in Table 11.5 that the PCL designation (labeled HP) consists of a two-letter code in which the second character is printed as a subscript. The control codes Backspace, Line-feed, Carriage return, Form-feed, and Horizontal tab correspond to printer functions available in any standard laser or nonlaser device. The Shift-out control is used to select characters from a secondary font and Shift-in to reselect the primary font. The Escape code is used to initiate an escape sequence, described later in this section.

PCL Printer Commands

Most PCL commands require more information that can be encoded in a single control code. The *escape sequence* provides structure for transmitting complex commands to a PCL device. The escape sequence begins with the ESC character (1BH) and is followed by other data. The sequence is interpreted by the printer as a single command. The PCL language uses escape sequences that consist of two or more characters. For example, the PCL command to reset the printer is

E_CE

while the generic form for the command to position the printer cursor to a certain screen row is expressed

$$E_C\&a\#R$$

Table 11.6 lists some values that have been assigned special meaning in the PCL language as well as the literal codes or symbols used in Hewlett-Packard documentation for describing them.

Table 11.6 *PCL Symbols with Special Meaning*

PCL SYMBOL	HEX VALUE OR RANGE	MEANING
E_C	1BH	Start of PCL printer command
#	23H	Represents a value field in the PCL command Characters represented must be in the range '0' to '9', may be signed + or -, and may be fractions.
X	"!" to "/"	ASCII symbol indicating a parameterized escape sequence, for example: & = Job control, cursor positioning, font orientation or pitch, and macro commands (= Symbol set selection, spacing, pitch, and typeface commands) = Soft font creation command * = Font management and graphics commands
y	"`" to "~ "	Lowercase character specifying a group control.
zi	"`" to "~ "	Lowercase character used in combining escape sequences.
Zn	"@" to "^ "	Uppercase character that specifies the value of a zi field.

A general printer command can be expressed in PCL using the symbols in Table 11.6. For example, the resolution of a LaserJet Series II or Series III printer can be 75, 100, 150, or 300 dots per inch. In its generic form, the PCL command to set the printer's resolution is

$$E_C*t\#R$$

where the # symbol represents the ASCII characters corresponding to one of the resolutions listed above. The actual command requires transmitting these characters to the printer, usually through the parallel port. On IBM microcomputers a convenient method for sending an escape sequence is to set up a data string terminated in a special character. The value 00H can be used as a string terminator since it is not used by PCL for any other purpose. The command string can be set up in a memory variable, as in the following example:

```
RES_150_DOTS      DB        1BH,'*t150R',00H
```

The following procedure can be used to send a PCL string to a LaserJet or compatible printer. The procedure receives a pointer to a PCL command string, terminated in a NULL code.

```
PCL_STRING      PROC    NEAR
; Send printer control string terminated in 00H
; On entry:
;       DS:SI -> PCL command string
;
        PUSH    BX                      ; Save operational registers
        PUSH    CX
        PUSH    DX
        PUSH    DI
;
SEND_CHAR:
        MOV     AL,[SI]         ; Get character
        CMP     AL,0            ; Test for message terminator
        JNE     NOT_END         ; Continue if not terminator
        JMP     END_PCL         ; End of message
NOT_END:
        MOV     DX,0            ; Printer port
; Test printer status and send character when printer ready
; At this point:
;       AL = character to send
;       DX = printer port (valid range is 0, 1, and 2)
;*********************|
;    initialize port  |
;*********************|
INIT_PORT:
        MOV     AH,1            ; Service request number
        INT     17H             ; Transfer to BIOS
        TEST    AH,80H          ; Test printer not busy bit
        JNZ     NOT_BUSY
        TEST    AH,1            ; Time out bit
        JNZ     STATUS_ERROR
        JMP     INIT_PORT       ; Repeat initialization and
                                ; status check

;******************|
;    error exit     |
;******************|
; Code notifies the caller of a status error by setting the
; carry flag
STATUS_ERROR:
        POP     DI              ; Restore registers
        POP     DX
        POP     CX
```

```
        POP     BX
        STC                         ; Error return code
        RET
;*****************|
;  send character |
;*****************|
NOT_BUSY:
        MOV     AH,0                ; Function request code
        INT     17H                 ; Transfer to BIOS
;*****************|
; next character  |
;*****************|
        INC     SI                  ; Bump message pointer
        JMP     SEND_CHAR
;*****************|
;  end of message |
;*****************|
END_PCL:
        POP     DI                  ; Restore registers
        POP     DX
        POP     CX
        POP     BX
        CLC                         ; No error return code
        RET
PCL_STRING      ENDP
```

The PCL_STRING procedure is also contained in the BITIO module of the
GRAPHSOL library. Table 11.7 lists some of the most frequently used PCL
commands. The list is far from complete since it does not include symbol set
selection, soft-font creation, font management, graphics, macros, and other
commands.

PCL Page

Laser printers are page-oriented devices. The software driver usually begins
by setting certain general parameters, sometimes called the *print environment*
or *job control commands*, and then proceeds to compose the printed document
page by page. In this task PCL uses the concept of a print cursor, which
represents the current print position on the page. The concept is a useful one,
since programmers can easily relate the print cursor to the flashing screen
cursor. Several PCL commands allow positioning the print cursor anywhere on
the active page. As in the screen counterpart, the next character transmitted
is printed at the current cursor position.

Table 11.7   *Frequently Used PCL Commands*

FUNCTION	UNITS/RANGE	PCL COMMAND	SAMPLE ENCODING
Reset		E$_C$E	DB 1BH,'E',00H
Number of copies	1-99	E$_C$&l#X	DB 1BH,'&l20X',00H
Eject page		E$_C$&l0H	DB 1BH,'&l0H',00H
Feed from tray		E$_C$&l1H	DB 1BH,'&l1H',00H
Manual feed		E$_C$&l2H	DB 1BH,'&l2H',00H
Envelope feed		E$_C$&l3H	DB 1BH,'&l3H',00H
Executive form		E$_C$&l1A	DB 1BH,'&l1A',00H
Letter size form		E$_C$&l2A	DB 1BH,'&l2A',00H
Legal size form		E$_C$&l3A	DB 1BH,'&l3A',00H
Top margin	No. of lines	E$_C$&l#E	DB 1BH,'&l12E',00H
Text length	No. of lines	E$_C$&l#F	DB 1BH,'&l56F',00H
Left margin	Left Column	E$_C$&l#L	DB 1BH,'&l5L',00H
Right margin	Right Column	E$_C$&l#M	DB 1BH,'&l7M',00H
Horizontal Motion Index	1/20'	E$_C$&k#H	DB 1BH,'&k6H',00H
Vertical Motion Index	1/48'	E$_C$&k#C	DB 1BH,'&k10C',00H
Lines per inch	1,2,3,4,6, 8,12,16,24, and 48	E$_C$&l#D	DB 1BH,'&l4D',00H
Set cursor, vertical	Row No.	E$_C$&a#R	DB 1BH,'&a12R',00H
	Dots	E$_C$&p#Y	DB 1BH,'&p300Y',00H
	Decipoints	E$_C$&a#V	DB 1BH,'&a720V',00H
Set cursor, horizontal	Row No.	E$_C$&a#C	DB 1BH,'&a12C',00H
	Dots	E$_C$&p#X	DB 1BH,'&p300X',00H
	Decipoints	E$_C$&a#H	DB 1BH,'&a720H',00H
Set portrait		E$_C$&l0O	DB 1BH,'&l0O',00H
Set landscape		E$_C$&l1O	DB 1BH,'&l1O',00H
Set resolution 7	5,100,150 and 300	E$_C$*t#R	DB 1BH,'*t150R',00H
Start graphics at left margin		E$_C$*r0A	DB 1BH,'*r0A',00H
at cursor position		E$_C$*r1A	DB 1BH,'*r1A',00H
Tansfer raster image	bytes per row	E$_C$*b#W	DB 1BH,'*b80W',00H
End graphics		E$_C$*rB	DB 1BH,'*rB',00H

The PCL coordinate system uses four different units of measurement: columns, rows, dots, and decipoints. The distance between columns is set by a corresponding PCL command. This distance is often called the *horizontal-motion index* (HMI). The distance between rows is set by the PCL command to change the *vertical-motion index* (VMI). Dots in the Hewlett-Packard LaserJet printers are 1/300th of an inch in diameter. Therefore, a distance of 300 dots is equal to 1 in. One typographical point is 1/72th of an inch. A decipoint, the smallest unit of cursor movement in PCL, is equivalent to one-tenth point, or

1/720th of an inch. Although the cursor can be moved in decipoint increments, the smallest printable unit in the LaserJet printers is a dot 1/300th of an inch in diameter. The printable area is the region of a page accessible to the printer. This area is called the *picture frame* in PCL Level V. The maximum printable area changes for different media and devices.

11.2.2 The COLNEG Program

The book's microdisk contains a program intended as a demonstration of PCL laser printer programming. This program, named COLNEG, reads the VGA graphics screen in mode number 18 and prints four negative images, one for the red, one for the green, one for the blue, and one for the intensity color components. The result is a set of color-separation negatives which can be used in reproducing the VGA graphics screen photographically. Figure 11.13 shows four images obtained by means of the COLNEG program.

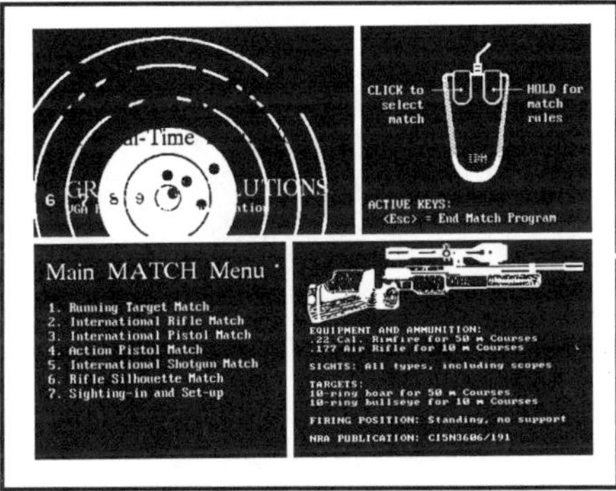

Red color separation

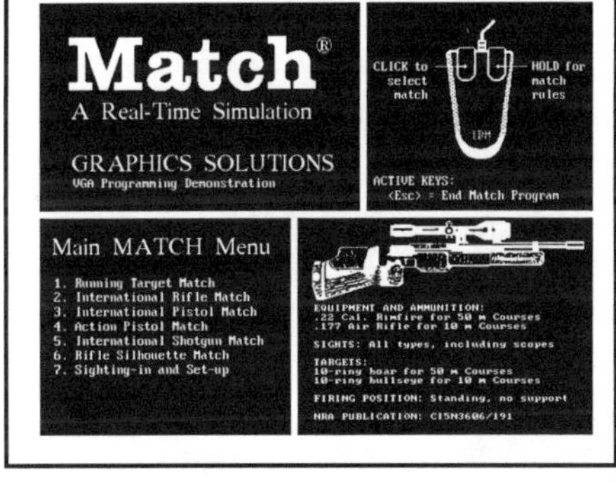

Green color separation

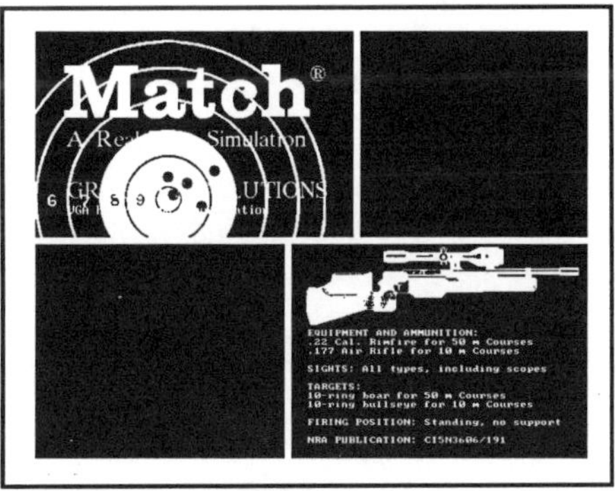

Blue color separation

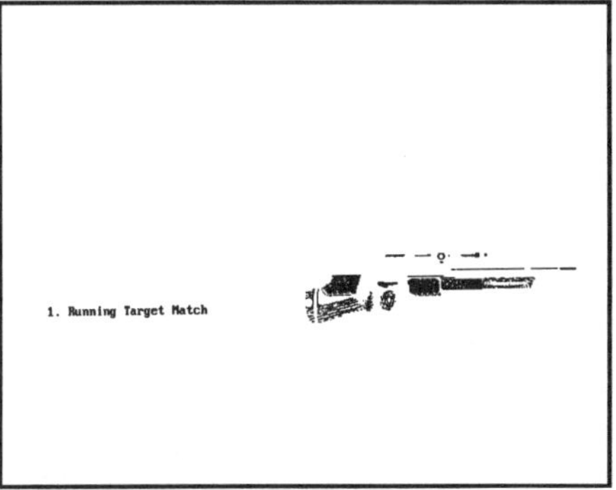

Intensity color separation

Figure 11.13   *Color Separation Negatives by the COLNEG Program*

The screen image used in the separations shown in Figure 11.13 is from the main menu screen of the MATCH program, also in the book's microdisk. However, in Figure 11.13 the printer output has been cropped and reduced. The actual separations obtained by the COLNEG program are twice as large as those in Figure 11.13. In order to facilitate registering the images for photographic reproduction, each one is printed in a separate page and include two alignment targets. Each image is marked with the letter code of the corresponding color.

Appendix A

Installing the Software

This book is furnished with a microdisk that contains graphics software related to the topics covered in the text. This software includes the following items:

1. A demo version of an animated game which simulates a shooting match. This program is furnished by courtesy of Skipanon Software Company.
2. A collection of demonstration and experimentation programs which were developed by the authors for testing the programming techniques discussed in the text.
3. A general-purpose and a graphics programming library.
4. A set of sample programs and files that demonstrate the use of the book's software from the high-level languages Quickbasic, C, and Pascal, as described in Appendix B.
5. A collection of Shareware programs and image files related to the topics covered in the book.

The software material is contained in the following files:

```
FILENAME        CONTENTS
MATCH.EXE       Self-extracting archive for a demonstration
                version of a VGA animated graphics game
DEMOS.EXE       Self-extracting archive for the demonstration
                and experimentation programs discussed in the
                text
LIBS.EXE        Self-extracting archive for the programming
                libraries SOLUTION.LIB and GRAPHSOL.LIB
INTRFACE.EXE    Self-extracting archive for the demonstration
                programs and files for using the book's software
                from the high-level languages Quickbasic, C, and
                Pascal
```

SHAREWRE.EXE	Self-extracting archive for the README file related to the Shareware programs furnished with the book, which are contained in the files CSHOW.EXE, 87EMU.EXE, XGAKIT.EXE, and IMAGES.EXE.
CHSOW.EXE	Self-extracting archive for Compuserve's image display program and support files (version 8.20a)
87EMU.EXE	Self-extracting archive for an 80x87 mathematical coprocessor emulator program by Ron Kimball (version 1.4)
XGAKIT.EXE	Self-extracting archive for the XGA Programmer's Toolkit by Bert Tyler (version 1.1)
IMAGES.EXE	Self-extracting archive for four public domain video images in Compuserve GIF format
INSTALL.BAT	Installation file for expanding the self-extracting archives (listed above) onto the user's hard disk.
README	Readme file with information regarding the book's software and last-minute notes.

Note that the executable files listed above (those with .EXE extension) are not conventional programs and cannot be run as such. Before using the software the reader must extract the compressed files from the archives by running the INSTALL program or by following other installation methods described in this appendix.

A1. Backing-up the Software

In order to protect yourself against accidental loss of data it is recommended that you make a back-up copy of the book's microdisk before attempting to install the software or to manipulate the original files in any way. This backup can be performed in MS DOS by means of a global copy command or by using the Diskcopy program. Instructions can be found in the MS DOS program manual.

A2. Installing to Hard-Disk Drive C

If your computer is equipped with a hard-disk drive designated as C:, and if you have available a minimum of 2.8 Mb of free disk space, you can quickly install the book's software by running the INSTALL batch file contained in the microdisk. This can be performed by means of the following operations:

1. Insert the microdisk supplied with the book in drive A

2. Log-on to drive A

3. Type the command: INSTALL <Enter>

The installation program expands the compressed files and creates the following directory tree on your hard-disk drive:

```
C:\MPS\
        MATCH\
        DEMOS\
        LIBS\
        INTRFACE\
        SHAREWRE\
                 CSHOW\
                 87EMU\
                 IMAGES\
                 XGAKIT\
```

Note that each of the second-level sub-directories created during the installation (\MATCH, \DEMOS, \LIBS, \INTRFACE, and \SHAREWRE) contains a README file which describes the software available in that sub-directory. Also that the main README file is copied during installation to the \MPS sub-directory.

Once the software is installed, you may release hard-disk space by copying the files in the various sub-directories onto diskettes or microdisks, then erasing the hard-disk files and sub-directories created during installation. Table A.1 shows the approximate size (in bytes after expansion) of the various sub-directories.

Table A.1 Approximate Size of Expanded Sub-Directories

SUB-DIRECTORY	APPROXIMATE SIZE (in bytes)
GPS\MATCH	378,000
GPS\DEMOS	816,000
GPS\LIBS	472,000
GPS\INTRFACE	13,000
GPS\SHAREWRE	900
GPS\SHAREWRE\CSHOW	298,000
GPS\SHAREWRE\87EMU	26,000
GPS\SHAREWRE\IMAGES	665,000
GPS\SHAREWRE\XGAKIT	67,000

A3. Installing to other Directories

The individual self-extracting archives furnished in the book's microdisk can also be expanded into hard-disk directories or sub-directories designated by the user. For example, the following sequence of operations can be used to install the book's library files, furnished in the LIBS.EXE self-extracting archive, onto the user's directory \TEMP, in drive G.

1. Insert the microdisk supplied with the book in drive A

2. Log-on to drive A

3. Type the command: LIBS G:\TEMP <Enter>

Note that this sequence assumes that the path G:\TEMP exists in the user's system.

A4. Direct Installation to Microdisks or Diskettes

It is possible, in a machine equipped with two disk drives, to install the book's software directly to microdisks or diskettes. However, because of the size of some expanded files (see Table A.1), the destination drive must be either a 1.2 Mb diskette or a 1.4 Mb microdisk. Otherwise the destination media will not be capable of storing all the expanded files and an error will be generated.

The following sequence of operations can be used to expand the files in the DEMOS.EXE self-extracting archive onto a diskette or microdisk in drive B.

1. Insert the microdisk supplied with the book in drive A

2. Insert a blank, formatted diskette or microdisk in drive B

3. Log-on to drive A

4. Type the command: DEMOS B: <Enter>

The remaining self-extracting archives can be expanded in similar fashion.

Appendix B

Using the Library Software

Two programming libraries are furnished in the book's microdisk: SOLU-TION.LIB contains general-purpose procedures coded in 80x86 and 80x87 assembly language and GRAPHSOL.LIB contains the graphics routines developed and discussed in the text. SOLUTION.LIB was developed and is described in detail in our book *Programming Solutions Handbook for IBM Microcomputers* (see Bibliography). This library is used as support for some graphics routines in GRAPHSOL.LIB. The source files for both libraries were assembled using Microsoft MASM version 6.0. The resulting object files were collected into libraries by means of the LIB.EXE library manager that is part of the MASM development package. Table B.1 lists the modules contained in GRAPHSOL.LIB.

Table B.2 is a listing in alphabetical order of the procedures and the corresponding module names.

B1. Using the GRAPHSOL Library from Assembly Language

The procedures in GRAPHSOL.LIB are designed and optimized to be used from Assembly Language code, therefore programs written in 80x86 assembler should find no difficulty in accessing and using the library services. The source files for the libraries are furnished in the book's microdisk (see Appendix A). The listing for each procedure is preceded by a header that describes the entry parameters. In some procedures the entry parameters are integer values loaded into machine registers. For example, the following code fragment is the header for the procedure named GET_OFFSET in the ALFAGRAF module.

Table B.1 *Module and Procedures in GRAPHSOL.LIB*

ALFAGRAF MODULE (Chapter 1)			
BOX_LINE_HOR	BOX_LINE_VER	CLEAR_AREA	CLEAR_SCREEN
CURSOR_OFF	DRAW_BOX	GET_CURSOR	REPEAT_HOR
REPEAT_VER	SET_CURSOR	SHADE_BOX	SHOW_BLOCK

VGA1 MODULE (Chapters 3 and 4)			
ES_TO_APA	ES_TO_VIDEO	FREEZE_DAC	GET_MODE
GRAY_256	LOGICAL_MODE	PIXEL_ADD_18	PIXEL_ADD_19
READ_PIX_18	RESTORE_DAC	SAVE_DAC	SET_MODE
SET_READ_MODE	SET_WRITE_256	SET_WRITE_MODE	SUM_TO_GRAY
THAW_DAC	TILE_ADD_18	TILE_ADD_19	TIME_VRC
TWO_BIT_IRGB	WRITE_PIX_18	WRITE_TILE_18	

VGA2 MODULE (Chapter 4)			
CLS_18	CLS_19	COARSE_TEXT	COLOR_MAP_18
COLOR_MAP_19	FINE_TEXT	FINE_TEXTHP	FONT_TO_RAM
GRAPHIC_TEXT	MONO_MAP_18	MULTI_TEXT	READ_HPFONT
TILE_FILL_18	TILE_FILL_19		

VGA3 MODULE (Chapter 5)			
BRESENHAM	CIRCLE	CLIP_OFF	CLIP_ON
DISPLAY_LINE	DO_4_QUADS	ELLIPSE	HYPERBOLA
INIT_X87	LINE_BY_SLOPE	PARABOLA	PIXEL_WRITE
QUAD_I	QUAD_II	QUAD_III	QUAD_IV
REGION_FILL	ROTATE_OFF	ROTATE_ON	SET_DEVICE

XGA1 MODULE (Chapter 7)			
AI_CLS	AI_COLOR	AI_COMMAND	AI_FONT
AI_PALETTE	AI_TEXT	CLOSE_AI	OPEN_AI

XGA2 MODULE (Chapter 7)			
COP_LINE_2	COP_RECT_2	COP_SYSVID_1	COP_SYSVID_8
INIT_COP	INIT_XGA	SPRITE_AT	SPRITE_IMAGE
SPRITE_OFF	XGA_CLS_2	XGA_MODE	XGA_PIXEL_2

SVGA MODULE (Chapter 8)			
SVGA_CLS_105	SVGA_PIX_105	SVGA_READ_105	VESA_105
VESA_MODE			

BITIO MODULE (Chapters 10 and 11)			
CP_COMMAND	CP_OUTPUT	CP_PLOT	CP_STATUS
FLUSH_232	GET_CP_CHAR	PCL_STRING	SERIAL_2_CP
SHOW_TIFF			

```
GET_OFFSET      PROC     FAR
; Set DI to the offset address in the video buffer that
; corresponds to a certain screen row and column position
;
; On entry:
;          DH = screen row (0 to 24)
;          DL = screen column (0 to 79)
;
; On exit:
;          DI -> buffer offset (row x 160) + (column x 2)
;          carry clear if no error
;          carry set if input out of range carry
```

Table B.2 *Alphabetical Listing of Procedures in GRAPHSOL.LIB*

PROCEDURE	MODULE	PROCEDURE	MODULE
AI_CLS	XGA1	AI_COLOR	XGA1
AI_COMMAND	XGA1	AI_FONT	XGA1
AI_PALETTE	XGA1	AI_TEXT	XGA1
BOX_LINE_HOR	ALFAGRAF	BOX_LINE_VER	ALFAGRAF
BRESENHAM	VGA3	CIRCLE	VGA3
CLEAR_AREA	ALFAGRAF	CLEAR_SCREEN	ALFAGRAF
CLIP_OFF	VGA3	CLIP_ON	VGA3
CLOSE_AI	XGA1	CLS_18	VGA2
CLS_19	VGA2	COARSE_TEXT	VGA2
COLOR_MAP_18	VGA2	COLOR_MAP_19	VGA2
COP_LINE_2	XGA2	COP_RECT_2	XGA2
COP_SYSVID_1	XGA2	COP_SYSVID_8	XGA2
CP_COMMAND	BITIO	CP_OUTPUT	BITIO
CP_PLOT	BITIO	CP_STATUS	BITIO
CURSOR_OFF	ALFAGRAF	DISPLAY_LINE	VGA3
DO_4_QUADS	VGA3	DRAW_BOX	ALFAGRAF
ELLIPSE	VGA3	ES_TO_APA	VGA1
ES_TO_VIDEO	VGA1	FINE_TEXT	VGA2
FINE_TEXTHP	VGA2	FLUSH_232	BITIO
FONT_TO_RAM	VGA2	FREEZE_DAC	VGA1
GET_CP_CHAR	BITIO	GET_CURSOR	ALFAGRAF
GET_MODE	VGA1	GRAPHIC_TEXT	VGA2
GRAY_256	VGA1	HYPERBOLA	VGA3
INIT_COP	XGA2	INIT_X87	VGA3
INIT_XGA	XGA2	LINE_BY_SLOPE	VGA3
LOGICAL_MODE	VGA1	MONO_MAP_18	VGA2
MULTI_TEXT	VGA2	OPEN_AI	XGA1
PARABOLA	VGA3	PCL_STRING	BITIO
PIXEL_ADD_18	VGA1	PIXEL_ADD_19	VGA1
PIXEL_WRITE	VGA3	QUAD_I	VGA3
QUAD_II	VGA3	QUAD_III	VGA3
QUAD_IV	VGA3	READ_HPFONT	VGA2
READ_PIX_18	VGA1	REGION_FILL	VGA3
REPEAT_HOR	ALFAGRAF	REPEAT_VER	ALFAGRAF
RESTORE_DAC	VGA1	ROTATE_OFF	VGA3
ROTATE_ON	VGA3	SAVE_DAC	VGA1
SERIAL_2_CP	BITIO	SET_CURSOR	ALFAGRAF
SET_DEVICE	VGA3	SET_MODE	VGA1
SET_READ_MODE	VGA1	SET_WRITE_256	VGA1
SET_WRITE_MODE	VGA1	SHADE_BOX	ALFAGRAF
SHOW_BLOCK	ALFAGRAF	SHOW_TIFF	BITIO
SPRITE_AT	XGA2	SPRITE_IMAGE	XGA2
SPRITE_OFF	XGA2	SUM_TO_GRAY	VGA1
SVGA_CLS_105	SVGA	SVGA_PIX_105	SVGA
SVGA_READ_105	SVGA	THAW_DAC	VGA1
TILE_ADD_18	VGA1	TILE_ADD_19	VGA1
TILE_FILL_18	VGA2	TILE_FILL_19	VGA2
TIME_VRC	VGA1	TWO_BIT_IRGB	VGA1
VESA_105	SVGA	VESA_MODE	SVGA
WRITE_PIX_18	VGA1	WRITE_TILE_18	VGA1
XGA_CLS_2	XGA2	XGA_MODE	XGA2
XGA_PIXEL_2	XGA2		

In this case, the calling program loads the desired integer values into DH and DL and receive a buffer offset value in the DI register. The carry flag is used to report errors to the calling program. Other procedures in the GRAPHSOL library require a pointer to a formatted data block. The following code fragment is also from the ALFAGRAF module.

```
SHOW_BLOCK        PROC     FAR
; Display a preformatted block message
; On entry:
;           DS:SI —> start of block message
; Message format:
;      Offset:              Function:
;              0 —— Display row for start of message
;              1 —— Display column for start of message
;              2 —— Attribute for block
;              3 —— Start of ASCII text message
; Embedded codes:
;              00H = End of message
;              FFH = End of row
; On exit:
;        carry clear
```

Notice that DS:SI is a pointer to a data block in the caller's memory space. The text message must be formatted as described in the procedure header. Some procedures in the library modules require no parameters at call time. In this case, the procedure header indicates it, as in the following code fragment from the ES_TO_VIDEO procedure in the ALFAGRAF module.

```
ES_TO_VIDEO       PROC     FAR
; Set ES register to the base address of the video buffer
according
; to the video mode stored in BIOS address 0040:0049
; On entry:
;        nothing
; On exit:
;        ES —> segment address of video buffer for alphanumeric
;                display
;        carry clear
```

B2. Using the GRAPHSOL Library from High-Level Languages

There is no generally accepted convention for interfacing high-level languages with assembly language, therefore the interfacing rules vary from language to language, implementation to implementation, and even version to version. For this reason, a detailed discussion of the problems and complications of interfacing high-level languages with assembler code could easily fill an entire volume. To reduce the problem to more manageable terms we provide concrete interface examples with three well known implementations of high-level languages: Microsoft QuickBasic, Microsoft/IBM C language, and Borland Turbo Pascal.

Interfacing through Header Routines

There are two common ways of interfacing assembly language procedures with high-level programs. One method is to modify the routines themselves so that they meet the interface requirements of the language in question. This solution entails editing the code of each procedure. A second alternative is to code an interface header routine that adapts the requirements of the high-level language to the assembler code.

One advantage of the interface header approach is that it allows coding the assembly language routines without taking into consideration the naming and calling conventions of any specific high-level language. However, there are also disadvantages. In the first place, since the assembly language routines are designed to receive the caller's data through the most convenient registers and pointers, it is not possible to develop a general-purpose interface header that works with all the routines. In fact, most routines require a particular, customized header that removes the parameters from the caller's stack and places them in the corresponding machine registers and buffers. A second disadvantage of the interface header method it that it adds an additional processing step, with a resulting delay in execution.

In the examples furnished in this appendix we have used both interface methods in order to provide the reader with sufficient information for using either option.

B3. Interfacing with Quickbasic

Quickbasic is an implementation of the BASIC programming language developed and marketed by Microsoft Corporation for the IBM microcomputers. The Quickbasic programming environment includes an editor and an interactive interpreter, as well as separate compiler and linker software. Most of the information necessary for interfacing Quickbasic with assembly language code is not found in the Quickbasic manuals, but in a booklet titled *Mixed-Language Programming Guide* which is included in the documentation package for Microsoft Macro Assembler 5.0 and later versions. This booklet also includes interface information for the Microsoft implementations of the C, Pascal, and Fortran languages.

Passing Quickbasic Parameters by Value

The first interface example with Quickbasic is in the form of a subroutine that passes three parameters, by value, to an assembly language procedure. The example consist of two modules. The Quickbasic module (TESTQB.BAS) can be created in the Quickbasic environment, or with an ASCII text editor. This source file is compiled in DOS using the program named BC.EXE, which is part of the Quickbasic software. The assembly language module is created using any text editor and assembled with a DOS assembler compatible with the Microsoft system, preferably with the Microsoft Macro Assembler. The assembled file is named QBCALLS.OBJ. The two files, TESTQB.OBJ and QBCALLS.OBJ, are linked using the linker program in the Quickbasic software. These source files can be found in the book's microdisk (see Appendix A).

The following is a listing for the Quickbasic module in this interface example:

```
' ** Quickbasic 4.5 demonstration program for interfacing with
' ** an assembly language module. The assembly language routine
' ** in this demo displays any number of asterisks at any screen
' ** position. The Quickbasic call passes the desired screen row
' ** and column, and the asterisk count, to the assembly
' ** language routine.
'

' ** This Quickbasic module is compiled and saved as TESTQB.BAS.
' ** The assembly language module is assembled as QBCALLS.OBJ.
' ** TESTQB.BAS is compiled using the Quickbasic DOS compiler
' ** program named BC.EXE. The resulting file, TESTQB.OBJ, is
' ** linked with the assembly language module named QBCALLS.OBJ.
' ** The final run file is named TESTQB.EXE.
'

DECLARE SUB SHOWS ALIAS "QB_SHOW_IT" (BYVAL ROW%, BYVAL COL%,
BYVAL CNT%)
'

CLS
PRINT "Test program for interfacing Quickbasic and assembly"
INPUT "Enter display row: "; ROW%
INPUT "Enter display column: "; COL%
INPUT "Enter asterisk count: "; CNT%
CALL SHOWS(ROW%, COL%, CNT%)
END
```

Note the following points in the Quickbasic module:

1. A DECLARE statement is generated automatically by Quickbasic only if there is a subroutine that was created interactively. In this case the programmer must manually enter the DECLARE statement, which should appear near the beginning of the BASIC source file.

2. The ALIAS keyword, which is part of the DECLARE statement, allows referencing a procedure in another module even if the procedure name does not meet the Quickbasic conventions. In this example, the procedure QB_SHOW_IT, which is a PUBLIC name in the assembly language module, is not a Quickbasic legal name. Also note that the aliasname QB_SHOW_IT must be enclosed in quotes.

3. Quickbasic normally passes parameters by near reference. In order to force Quickbasic to pass parameters by value, the BYVAL keyword is entered preceding each variable in the parameter list of the DECLARE statement. Passing parameters by value is the default method for Microsoft C and

Pascal. Parameters passed by value are easier to recover by the assembly language module.

4. The assembly language routine named QB_SHOW_IT appears to the Quickbasic program as a subroutine named SHOWS. Quickbasic accesses the assembly language procedure with the CALL SHOWS instruction.

The following is a listing for the assembly language module:

```
;****************************************************************
;                          QBCALLS.ASM
;****************************************************************
; Assembly language interface header routine for Quickbasic,
; starting with version 4.0
;
;
PUBLIC          QB_SHOW_IT
PUBLIC          LSHIFT
;
P_TEXT          SEGMENT WORD  PUBLIC 'CODE'
      ASSUME CS:P_TEXT
;********************************|
;  Quickbasic interface routines |
;********************************|
QB_SHOW_IT  PROC    FAR
; Quickbasic version 4.0 (and later) interface header to call the
; assembly language routine AST_DISPLAY (also in this module)
; Note: This procedure is called by the Quickbasic demo program
; named TESTQB.BAS
; On entry:
;       FROM:       TO:          FUNCTION:
;    [BP+10]     ->> DH    Screen row at which to set cursor
;    [BP+8]      ->> DL    Screen column at which to set cursor
;    [BP+6]      ->> CX    Counter for asterisks to display
; On exit:
;    Nothing
;
        PUSH    BP              ; Save caller's BP
        MOV     BP,SP           ; Set pointer to stack frame
        PUSH    AX              ; Save caller's registers so that
        PUSH    BX              ; they can be used by header
        PUSH    CX
        PUSH    DX
        MOV     AX,[BP+10]      ; Get first passed parameter to AX
        MOV     DH,AL           ; Passed value is a byte, although
                                ; storage space is word-size
```

```
            MOV     AX,[BP+8]       ; Get second parameter passed by
            MOV     DL,AL           ; call into DL
            MOV     AX,[BP+6]       ; Get third parameter passed by
            MOV     CX,AX           ; BASIC and move to CX
            CALL    AST_DISPLAY     ; Call routine to display *
            POP     DX              ; Restore registers
            POP     CX
            POP     BX
            POP     AX
            POP     BP              ; Restore base pointer register
            RET     6               ; Return and repair stack
QB_SHOW_IT  ENDP
;
;
AST_DISPLAY PROC    NEAR
; On entry:
;           DH = cursor row
;           DL = cursor column
;           CX = count of asterisks to display
; On exit:
;     Nothing
;
            PUSH    CX              ; Save counter register
            MOV     AH,2            ; Service request number
            MOV     BH,0            ; Assume display page No. 0
            INT     10H
; Display CX characters at cursor
            POP     CX              ; Restore counter from stack
            MOV     AL,'*'          ; Character to display
            MOV     AH,10           ; Service request number
            MOV     BH,0            ; Display page zero
            INT     10H
            RET
AST_DISPLAY ENDP
;
P_TEXT          ENDS
        END
```

Note the following points in the assembly language module:

1. The module contains two procedures. The procedure named QB_SHOW_IT
   is of the FAR type. This is necessary in order to make the procedure
   accessible to Quickbasic. It is declared PUBLIC so that it will be visible to
   Quickbasic. The procedure named AST_DISPLAY is of type NEAR, therefore, it is internal to the assembly language module and cannot be called
   from Quickbasic.

2. The segment declaration line is as follows:

```
P_TEXT   SEGMENT WORD      PUBLIC    'CODE'
         ASSUME   CS:P_TEXT
```

This declaration conforms to the Microsoft segment structure for the medium and large memory models, listed in Table B.3.

Table B.3 *Segment Structures in Microsoft/IBM Memory Models*

MEMORY MODEL	SEGMENT TYPE	SEGMENT NAME	ALIGN TYPE	COMBINE TYPE	CLASS NAME	GROUP
Small	CODE	_TEXT	word	PUBLIC	'CODE'	
	DATA	_DATA	word	PUBLIC	'DATA'	DGROUP
		CONST	word	PUBLIC	'CONST'	DGROUP
		_BSS	word	PUBLIC	'BSS'	DGROUP
	STACK	STACK	para	STACK	'STACK'	DGROUP
Compact	CODE	_TEXT	word	PUBLIC	'CODE'	
	DATA	_DATA	word	PUBLIC	'DATA'	DGROUP
		CONST	word	PUBLIC	'CONST'	DGROUP
		_BSS	word	PUBLIC	'BSS'	DGROUP
		FAR_DATA	para	PRIVATE	'FAR_DATA'	
		FAR_BSS	para	PRIVATE	'FAR_BSS'	
	STACK	STACK	para	STACK	'STACK'	DGROUP
Medium	CODE	xx_TEXT	word	PUBLIC	'CODE'	
	DATA	_DATA	word	PUBLIC	'DATA'	DGROUP
		CONST	word	PUBLIC	'CONST'	DGROUP
		_BSS	word	PUBLIC	'BSS'	DGROUP
	STACK	STACK	para	STACK	'STACK'	DGROUP
Large	CODE	xx_TEXT	word	PUBLIC	'CODE'	
	DATA	_DATA	word	PUBLIC	'DATA'	DGROUP
		CONST	word	PUBLIC	'CONST'	DGROUP
		_BSS	word	PUBLIC	'BSS'	DGROUP
		FAR_DATA	para	PRIVATE	'FAR_DATA'	
		FAR_BSS	para	PRIVATE	'FAR_BSS'	
	STACK	STACK	para	STACK	'STACK'	DGROUP

3. After the instruction PUSH BP executes, the entry parameters are located at stack offsets 10, 8, and 6, respectively. The first argument passed is at the highest offset in the stack. Each parameter takes up 2 bytes of stack space. The Quickbasic variables are word-size, since they were defined using the percent (%) symbol. Figure B.1 shows the stack frame at the time of the Quickbasic call.

4. The instruction MOV BP,SP sets the base pointer (BP) register to the stack top. Now BP can be used to remove the passed parameters from their respective stack offsets. This is more convenient than using SP, which does not allow indexed addressing forms. BP is sometimes called a *framepointer* when used in this manner.

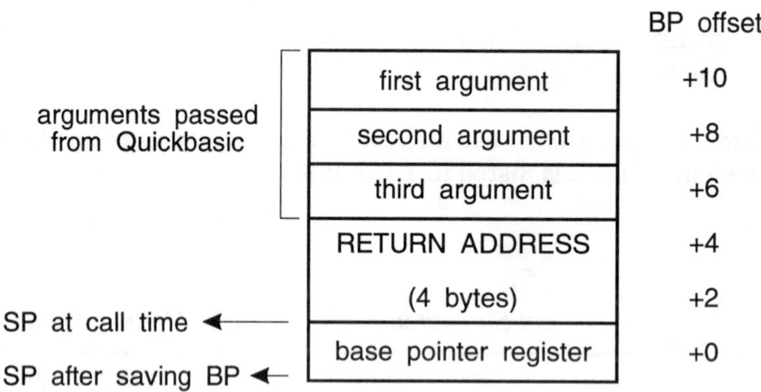

Figure B.1. *Stack Frame after Quickbasic FAR Call*

5. After the caller's general-purpose registers are saved, the interface header uses BP to remove the entry parameters from the stack and to place these parameters in the registers where the procedure AST_DISPLAY expects them. After the registers are loaded, the interface header calls the processing routine using the instruction CALL AST_DISPLAY.

6. As soon as the assembly language processing routine returns to the interface header, the code restores the machine registers from the stack (including BP) and returns to the Quickbasic module. Notice that the return instruction RET 6 also repairs the stack by adjusting to the number of word-size items passed in the call. This means that if the calling procedure had passed a single word-size item in the stack, the return instruction would be coded in the form RET 2. This same method of stack repair is used in other high-level languages (excluding C language).

Passing Quickbasic Parameters by Reference

In the previous example, we used the BYVAL operator in the DECLARE statement to override the Quickbasic default parameter passing mode, which is by near reference. In this way the assembly language procedure is able to obtain the present value of Quickbasic variables from the stack, but since the storage location of these variables is not known to the assembly code, the stored values of the variables are protected from undesirable alterations. In many cases, this interface mode is safe and useful, but occasionally it may be preferable to have the assembly language code change the value of a Quickbasic variable. Note that changing the stored value of a variable is an expedient way to pass parameters back to Quickbasic.

The following is a listing for the Quickbasic module in this interface example:

```
' ** Quickbasic 4.5 demonstration program for interfacing with
' ** an assembly language module and for passing and returning
' ** parameters by near reference.

' ** This demo program calls an assembly language procedure
' ** named LSHIFT, which shifts left the bits of a Quickbasic
' ** integer variable named TARGET% and updates the variable
' ** by writing the result to its storage address.
'
' ** This Quickbasic module is saved as TESTQB1.BAS
' ** The assembly language module is part of QBCALLS.OBJ
' ** listed in the previous interface example.
' ** TESTQB1.BAS is compiled using the Quickbasic DOS compiler
' ** named BC.EXE. The resulting file, TESTQB.OBJ, is linked
' ** with the assembly language module named QBCALLS.OBJ. The
' ** final run file is named TESTQB1.EXE.
'
DECLARE SUB LSHIFT (TARGET%)
'
CLS
INPUT "Enter the value to shift left by 1 bit: "; TARGET%
CALL LSHIFT(TARGET%)
PRINT "The shifted value of the variable is: "; TARGET%
END
```

Note the following points in the Quickbasic module:

1. The DECLARE does not need the ALIAS operator, as in the previous example, since the name of this assembly language procedure is legal in Quickbasic. Note that the programmer must manually enter the DECLARE statement, as in the previous example.

2. In this example Quickbasic passes parameters by near reference, which is its default mode. Therefore, the BYVAL operator is not used in the parameter list.

The following is a listing for the assembly language module:

```
;****************************************************************R
;                          QBCALLS1.ASM
;****************************************************************
; Assembly language interface header routine for Quickbasic,
; starting with version 4.0
;
PUBLIC  LSHIFT
```

```
P_TEXT  SEGMENT WORD     PUBLIC  'CODE'
       ASSUME  CS:P_TEXT
;*******************************|
;  Quickbasic interface routine  |
;*******************************|
LSHIFT         PROC    FAR
; Procedure to shift left the bits in an integer passed by
; Quickbasic
; Note: This procedure is called by the Quickbasic offset
; address of passed variable
; On exit:
;     [BP+6] is updated with the shifted value
;
       PUSH    BP              ; Save caller's BP
       MOV     BP,SP           ; Set pointer to stack frame
       MOV     BX,[BP+6]       ; Value passed by near reference
                               ; which is Quickbasic default mode
       MOV     AX,[BX]             ; Load AX from variable's address
       SHL     AX,1            ; Shift left AX 1 bit
       MOV     [BX],AX             ; Restore result to the variable's
                               ; address
       POP     BP              ; Restore caller's BP
       RET     2               ; Return and repair stack
LSHIFT         ENDP
;
P_TEXT         ENDS
       END
```

In addition to the points noted in relation to the previous assembly language module, note the following:

1. Since the variable TARGET% is passed by near reference, the value stored at BP+6 is the variable's offset in the data segment. In this case, the assembly language module retrieves this value using BX as a pointer. in the previous example, in which the parameters were passed as values in the stack, these parameters were loaded directly into machine registers.

2. After the instruction SHL AX,1 has operated on the passed parameter, the result is placed back in the Quickbasic variable using the same pointer to the variable's address in memory. Quickbasic can now access the new value using the variable's original name.

B4. Interfacing with Microsoft/IBM C Language

Of all high-level languages, C provides the easiest interface with assembly language routines, because a C language program calls an assembly language procedure in the same manner as it would a C language function. In the case of C language, variables, parameters, and addresses are passed to the assembly language routine on the stack. These values appear in the stack in opposite order to the program listing. A unique feature of the C language interface is that C automatically restores stack integrity. For this reason the assembly language routine can return with a simple RET or RETF instruction, and is not compelled to keep count of the parameters that were pushed on the stack by the call.

But not all implementations and versions of C follow identical interface conventions. In the Microsoft/IBM versions of C discussed in this chapter, the memory model adapted by the C language program determines the segment structure of the assembly language module. The Microsoft/IBM segment structures are listed in Table B.3. In practice this means that if the C module was compiled using the small or compact model, the assembly language procedure should be defined using the NEAR directive. However, if the C module was compiled using the medium or large models, then the assembly language procedure should be defined with the FAR directive.

The Microsoft/IBM versions of the C language have two additional and distinctive interface requirements. One is that the these implementations of C language use the SI and DI machine registers to store the values of variables defined with the "register" keyword. For this reason, the assembly language procedure must be careful to preserve these registers. These implementations also assume that the processor's direction flag (DF) is clear when C language regains control. Therefore, if there is any possibility of this flag being changed during processing, the assembly language code should contain a CLD instruction before returning. In fact, it is a safe programming practice to include this instruction in the interface model, even though it may not always be necessary.

C Language Naming Conventions

The Microsoft/IBM C language compilers automatically add an underscore character (_) in front of every public name. For example, a C language reference to a procedure named RSHIFT is compiled so as a call to the procedure _RSHIFT. In coding the assembly language module, the programmer must take this peculiarity of the C compiler into account and add the required underscore character in front of the name of every assembly language element that is to be referenced in the C language module.

This convention applies not only to functions but also to data items that are globally visible in the C module. For example, if the C language module contains a variable named ODDNUM, which was declared globally, this variable is visible to an assembly language module under the name _ODDNUM. The assembly language module can gain access to the variable by using the EXTRN statement. Accessing C language variables from assembly language modules is shown in the following example.

Passing C Parameters by Value

The interface example with Microsoft/IBM C language compilers is in the form of a C program that calls an assembly language routine. The caller passes an integer variable to the assembly language subroutine and the subroutine returns the value with all bits shifted right by one position. In addition, the assembly language routine modifies the value of a C variable named NUMB2. The example consist of two modules. The C language module (TESTC.C) is created using a standard editor and compiled using a Microsoft or IBM C language compiler. The assembly language module is created with an ASCII text editor and assembled with a DOS assembler compatible with the Microsoft system, preferably with the Microsoft Macro Assembler. The assembled file is named CCALLS.OBJ. Note that the examples refer to the Microsoft/IBM full-featured compilers, but not to the Microsoft QuickC programming environment.

The following is a listing for the C language module in this interface example.

```
/* Module name: TESTC.C */


/* C Language module to show interfacing with assembly */
/* language code. This sample assumes the use of       */
/* Microsoft/IBM C/* compilers, excluding QuickC        */


#include <stdio.h>


extern int RSHIFT(int);


/* Variables visible to the assembly module must be declared  */
/* globally in the C module.*/


int numb1, NUMB2;


main() {
     printf("Enter the variable numb1: ");
     scanf("%i", &numb1);
     printf("The shifted number is: %d\n", RSHIFT(numb1));
     printf("The variable NUMB2 has the value: %u\n", NUMB2);
}
```

Note the following points in the C language module:

1. The assembly language module is declared external to the C code with the *extern* C language keyword. The name in this declaration is not preceded with an underscore character, since it is automatically appended by the compiler.

2. Once declared external, the RSHIFT routine is called as if it were a C function.

3. The variables numb1 and NUMB2 are declared to be of *int* type. The value of numb1 is transferred by the C module to the assembly language module in the statement RSHIFT(numb1). The assembler module recovers the value of the variable numb1 from the stack. However, the assembly language module accesses the variable NUMB2 directly, using the variable's name. Note that the variable to be accessed by name is declared using capital letters. This is for compatibility with assembler programs that automatically convert names to uppercase.

The assembly language code is as follows:

```
;******************************************************************
;                         CCALLS.ASM
;******************************************************************
; C language-to-assembly language interface header routine for
; Microsoft/IBM C language compilers, excluding QuickC
;
PUBLIC          _RSHIFT
;
EXTRN _NUMB2: WORD
;
_TEXT SEGMENT word      PUBLIC   'CODE'
        ASSUME  CS:_TEXT
;
;******************************************|
;   C language interface routine  |
;******************************************|

_RSHIFT         PROC    NEAR
; Function to right-shift the bits in an integer passed by
right-shifted value returned to caller
        PUSH    BP              ; Save caller's BP
        MOV     BP,SP           ; Set pointer to stack frame
        MOV     AX,[BP+4]       ; Value passed by value
                                ; which is C language default mode
        CALL    INTERNAL_P      ; Procedure to perform shift and
                                ; to access C variable NUMB2
        CLD                     ; Clear direction flag
        POP     BP              ; Restore caller's BP
        RET                     ; Simple return. C repairs stack
_RSHIFT         ENDP
;
INTERNAL_P  PROC    NEAR
; value of arbitrary new value assigned to C variable
```

```
        SHR     AX,1            ; Shift right AX 1 bit
                                ; Return value is left in AX
        MOV     CX,12345        ; Arbitrary value to CX
        MOV     _NUMB2,CX       ; and to C variable NUMB2
        RET
;
INTERNAL_P   ENDP
_TEXT ENDS
        END
```

Note the following points of the assembly language module:

1. The procedure _RSHIFT is declared PUBLIC to make it visible to the C module at link time. An underscore character is affixed at the start of the procedure's name so that it matches the name used by the C compiler.

2. The segment structure is compatible with the Microsoft small memory model as shown in Table B.3. The memory model of the C program is determined at link time by the library selected.

3. Procedures to be linked with C programs of the small or compact model must be declared with the NEAR operator, as the one in the example. If the C program used the medium or large models, then the assembly language procedure would have been declared using the FAR operator.

4. The _RSHIFT procedure in the assembly language module serves as an interface header routine. The reader should note that this header requires modifications in order to adapt it to C programs using other memory models or with different specifications for the parameters passed and returned.

5. The structure of the stack frame at call time also depends on the adopted memory model. In this case, since the chosen model is small, the parameter passed is located at BP+4 and the return address consists of only the offset component (2 bytes). This stack frame can be seen in Figure B.2.

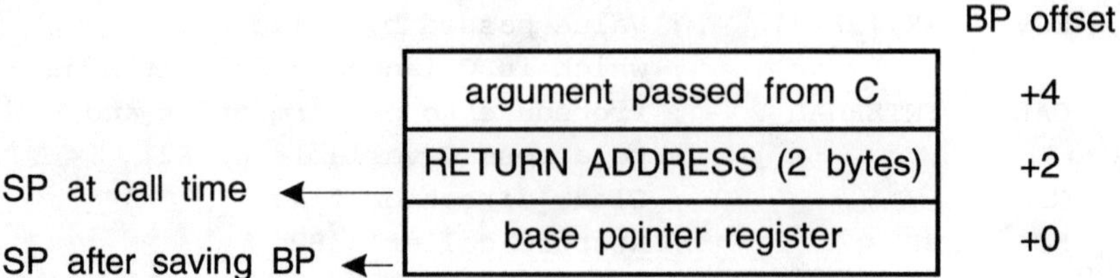

Figure B.2   *Stack Frame after C Language NEAR Call*

If the C language module conformed with the medium or large models, the stack frame would be similar to the one shown in Figure B.1.

6. The variable declared as NUMB2 and initialized as "int" in the C language module is declared as EXTRN _NUMB2: WORD in the assembly language code. The underscore character is added in the assembly module because the C compiler appends this character at the beginning of the variable name. The variable is assigned a value in the INTERNAL_P procedure.

7. The routine clears the direction flag (CLD), restores the BP register (POP BP), and returns with a simple RET instruction. Note that the processing routine in this example does not use the SI or DI registers; hence they were not preserved. However, if SI or DI is used in processing, the entry value must be saved and restored by the assembler code.

Return Values in Microsoft/IBM C Compilers

In the Microsoft/IBM implementations of C for the IBM microcomputers parameters are returned to the calling routine in the AX register (as in the previous example), or in the AX and the DX registers. Table B.4 shows the return value conventions for different data types and pointers.

Table B.4 *Microsoft/IBM C Language Returned Values*

DATA TYPE OR POINTER	REGISTER OR REGISTER PAIR
char short int unsigned char unsigned short insigned int	AX
long unsigned long	DX = high-order word AX = low-order word
struc or union float or double	AX = address value
near pointer	AX = offset value of address
far pointer	DX = segment value of address AX = offset value of address

Another way of interchanging values between the modules is to access the C variables by name (as shown in the previous example). This method requires that the assembly module use the same storage format as the C language. Since variable storage formats change in different implementations of the C language, this access technique must be adapted to each particular implementation of the language.

B5. Interfacing with Turbo Pascal

Borland Turbo Pascal allows linking of its modules with modules written in assembly language. However, the interface conventions and the required segment definitions are different from those of other Pascal compilers, including Microsoft Pascal. For this reason the interface examples in the following sections apply exclusively to Borland Turbo Pascal starting with version 5.0.

The fundamental interface rules for Turbo Pascal are as follows:

1. The assembly language procedure to be interfaced must be declared in the Pascal module using the *external* keyword.
2. The segment structure for the code and data segments in the assembler module must be as listed in Table B.5.

Table B.5 *Segment Structures in Turbo Pascal 5.0*

SEGMENT TYPE	SEGMENT NAME	ALIGN TYPE	COMBINE TYPE	CLASS NAME	GROUP
CODE	CODE	word	PUBLIC	—	—
DATA	DATA	word	PUBLIC	—	—

3. Parameters passed by Turbo Pascal are passed by value or by reference, according to the variable type and size. Integer and real variables are pushed on the stack and so are arrays of less than 4 bytes. A pointer to the variable's address is passed for values larger than 4 bytes. Byte-size variables are passed as a word, with the high-order byte undefined. Table B.6 shows the parameter passing conventions for Turbo Pascal, starting with version 5.0.

Table B.6 *Parameter Passing in Turbo Pascal*

VARIABLE TYPE	PASSED AS	PASSED BY	RETURNED IN
integer	byte word doubleword	Value	AX (AH undefined) AX DX-AX
char	byte	Value	AX (AH undefined)
boolean	byte	Value (0 or 1)	AX (AH undefined)
enumerated	byte	Value	AX (AH undefined)
real	1 to 6 bytes	Value	DX-BX-AX
8087	10 bytes	Value	8087 ST(0)
pointer	doubleword	Reference	DX:AX
string	doubleword	Reference	DX:AX
arrays/records (less than 4 bytes)	byte word doubleword	Value	AX (AH undefined) AX DX-AX
arrays/records (more than 4 bytes)	doubleword	Reference	DX:AX

4. Turbo Pascal can interface with an assembly language procedure using a NEAR or FAR call. If the procedure was declared in the interface section of a unit, it is always accessed using a FAR call. On the other hand, if the procedure is declared in the program section, Turbo Pascal assumes that it is of NEAR type. The programmer can override this assumption using the $F+ compiler directive, which forces a FAR call to all procedures and functions. This last method is the one used in the example later in this section.

5. The name of the assembly language module that contains the procedures to be accessed by Turbo Pascal must be listed using the $L compiler directive. This declaration is found in the Turbo Pascal module of the sample program in this section. The declaration is necessary since the Turbo Pascal compiler also performs linking operations. If the module data is not available at compile time, the Turbo Pascal system is not able to generate an executable file.

The following sample program includes the listing of a Turbo Pascal program and an assembly language module. The Turbo Pascal program passes the variable num1 to the assembler code, which, in turn, shifts all bits right by one position and returns the shifted value in the AX register.

```
Program AL_INTERFACE (INPUT, OUTPUT);
   {$F+}
   {$L TPCALLS}
{ Turbo Pascal 5.0 demonstration program for interfacing with
  assembly language code. This file is named TESTTP.PAS }
function R_SHIFT (num1 : integer): integer; external;
var
    num1 : integer;
 begin
     Write('Enter value: ');
     Readln (num1);
     Writeln ('The shifted value is: ',  R_SHIFT (num1));
end.
;********************************************************************
;                          TPCALLS.ASM
;********************************************************************
; Turbo Pascal to assembly language interface routine
; This code is compatible with Turbo Pascal version 5.0 and
; later.
PUBLIC   R_SHIFT
CODE  SEGMENT byte     PUBLIC
      ASSUME  CS:CODE
;*******************************|
; Turbo Pascal interface routine |
;*******************************|
```

```
R_SHIFT        PROC    FAR
; Function to right-shift the bits in an integer shifted value
; of variable
       PUSH    BP                ; Save caller's BP
       MOV     BP,SP             ; Set pointer to stack frame
       MOV     AX,[BP+6]         ; Parameter is passed by value
       SHR     AX,1              ; Shift right AX 1 bit
       POP     BP                ; Restore caller's BP
       RET     2                 ; Return and repair stack
R_SHIFT                ENDP
CODE  ENDS
       END
```

Note the following points in code:

1. The {$F+} assembler directive in the Turbo Pascal module forces all calls to be of FAR type. For this reason the assembly language procedure is declared FAR.

2. The assembly language module is assembled with the name TPCALLS.OBJ. This module name is referenced in the Turbo Pascal section using the statement {$L TPCALLS}.

3. The interfaced assembler routine is named R_SHIFT. This procedure is declared PUBLIC in the assembler module and external in the Turbo Pascal function declaration. Note that the word *procedure* has an unconventional meaning in the context of the Pascal language. To Pascal, a procedure is a function that returns no values. Or, in other words, a function is a procedure that returns a value. Therefore, in order for Turbo Pascal to receive a value from the assembler code, the assembler routine must be designated as a Turbo Pascal *function*.

4. The structure of the stack frame at call time depends on whether the interfaced procedure is of NEAR or FAR type. In this example the use of the {$F+} directive forces all procedures to be of the FAR type. Therefore, the parameter passed is located at BP+6 and the return address consists of a segment and an offset (4 bytes). This stack frame can be seen in Figure B.3.

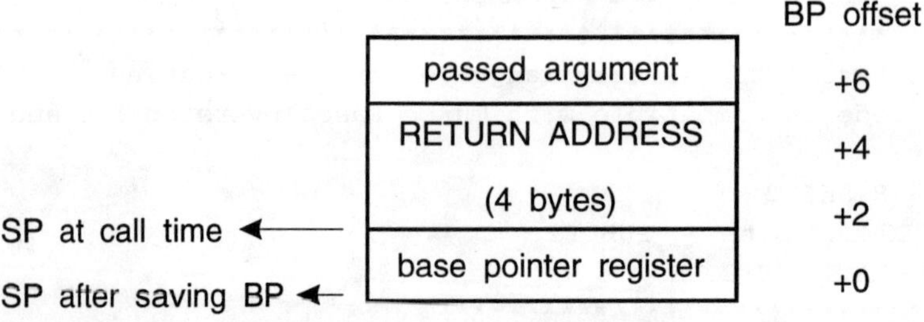

Figure B.3 *Stack Frame after Turbo Pascal FAR Call*

Appendix C

IBM BIOS Data and Video Services

Table C.1 *Video Display Data in BIOS*

LOGICAL ADDRESS	DATA SIZE	CONTENTS
0040:0049	Byte	Active display mode
0040:004A	Word	Number of display columns
0040:004C	Word	Length of video buffer (in bytes)
0040:004E	Word	Starting address in video buffer
0040:0050	Word	Cursor position in display page 1
0040:0052	Word	Cursor position in display page 2
0040:0054	Word	Cursor position in display page 3
0040:0056	Word	Cursor position in display page 4
0040:0058	Word	Cursor position in display page 5
0040:005A	Word	Cursor position in display page 6
0040:005C	Word	Cursor position in display page 7
0040:005E	Word	Cursor position in display page 8
0040:0060	Word	Cursor type
0040:0062	Byte	Number of active display page
0040:0063	Word	CRT controller base address
0040:0065	Byte	Current setting of register 3x8H
0040:0066	Byte	Current setting of register 3x9H

Table C.2. *Index to BIOS Video Functions — Interrupt 10H*

SERVICE REQUEST NUMBER	DESCRIPTION
AH = 0	Set video mode
AH = 1	Set cursor type (determine top and bottom lines)
AH = 2	Set cursor position (screen row and column)
AH = 3	Read cursor position (screen row and column)
AH = 4	Read light pen position
AH = 5	Select display page (in multipage systems)
AH = 6	Scroll text up or initialize window
AH = 7	Scroll text down or initialize window
AH = 8	Read character and attribute at cursor position
AH = 9	Write character and attribute at cursor position
AH = 10	Write character (no attribute) at cursor position
AH = 11	Set color palette in CGA, EGA, VGA, and PCjr
AH = 12	Write pixel (in graphics modes)
AH = 13	Read pixel (in graphics modes)
AH = 14	Write character at cursor using teletype style
AH = 15	Get current video mode
AH = 16	Set color palette
AH = 17	Character generator
AH = 18	Alternate function select
AH = 19	Write string (PC XT BIOS 01/10/86 and later)
AH = 26	Read/write display combination codes
AH = 27	Read functionality and state information

Table C.2 *BIOS Interrupt 10H — Video Functions*

SERVICE NUMBER (IN AH)	ON ENTRY	ON EXIT	DESCRIPTION
0	AL	Nothing	Set video mode (in AL)
1	CX	Nothing	Set cursor type

```
0  1  2  4  3  2  1  0  CL bits
|__|__|  |__|__|__|__|
               |________________ Top cursor line
               |________________ RESERVED (must be 0)

0  1  2  4  3  2  1  0  CH bits
|__|__|  |__|__|__|__|
               |________________ Bottom cursor line
               |________________ RESERVED (must be 0)
```

SERVICE NUMBER (IN AH)	ON ENTRY	ON EXIT	DESCRIPTION
2	DX-BH	Nothing	Set cursor position DH = row number (0-based) DL = column number (0-based) BH = page number (0-based)
3	BH	CX-DX	Read cursor position BH = page number (0-based)

Returns:
DH = current cursor row (0-based)
DL = current cursor column (0-based)
CH = cursor start line
CL = cursor end line

SERVICE NUMBER (IN AH)	ON ENTRY	ON EXIT	DESCRIPTION
4	Nothing	AH-CH-BX DX	Read light pen position Returns: AH = 01 if valid value in registers

CH = light pen pixel row (0 to 199)
BX = light pen pixel column (0 to 639)
DH = character row (0 to 24)
DL = character column (0 to 79)
Note: The light pen function is not available in the
PC convertible and the PS/2 line.

SERVICE NUMBER (IN AH)	ON ENTRY	ON EXIT	DESCRIPTION
5	AL	Nothing	Select display page (except PCjr) AL = page number
5	AL-BX	BX	Select diplay page in PCjr AL = page number

BL = microprocessor page register
BH = CRT page register
Returns:
BH = microprocessor page register selected
BL = CRT page register selected
Note: This function is not legal in single-page video systems.

SERVICE NUMBER (IN AH)	ON ENTRY	ON EXIT	DESCRIPTION
6	AL-BH-CX DX	Nothing	Scroll page up or initialize AL = number of lines to scroll AL = 0 to initialize window

BH = attribute for initialization
CH/CL = row/column of upper left corner of window
DH/DL = row/column of lower right corner of window

(continued)

Table C.2 *BIOS Interrupt 10H — Video Functions (Continued)*

SERVICE NUMBER (IN AH)	ON ENTRY	ON EXIT	DESCRIPTION
7	AL-BH-CX DX	Nothing	Scroll page down or initialize AL = number of lines to scroll AL = 0 to initialize window BH = attribute for initialization CH/CL = row/column of upper left corner of window DH/DL = row/column of lower right corner of window
8	BH	AX	Read character and attribute at present cursor position BH = page number (0-based) Returns: AL = character AH = attribute
9	AL-BX-CX	Nothing	Write character and attribute at current cursor position AL = character to write (in ASCII) BL = attribute (character color in graphics modes) BH = display page (0-based) CX = count of characters to repeat Note: The repeat count (in CX) is valid only for the same row. This function can be used to display text while in a graphics mode.
10	AL-BH-CX	Nothing	Write character at current cursor position (no attribute) AL = character to write (in ASCII) BH = display page (0-based) CX = count of characters to repeat Note: The repeat count (in CX) is valid only for the same row.
11	BX	Nothing	Set color palette in CGA systems (See also service number 16) BH = color ID (0 or 1) If BH = 0, set background color for 320 x 200 graphics modes or border color in alpha modes. Set foreground color in 640 x 200 graphics modes. BL must be in the range 0 to 31. BL = color value
12	AL-CX-DX	Nothing	Write pixel in graphics modes AL = pixel color requested If bit 7 of AL is set, then color is XORed with pixel contents. CX = pixel column DX = pixel row
13	CX-DX	AL	Read pixel in graphics modes CX = pixel column DX = pixel row Returns: AL = color value of pixel read

(continued)

Table C.2 *BIOS Interrupt 10H — Video Functions (Continued)*

SERVICE NUMBER (IN AH)	ON ENTRY	ON EXIT	DESCRIPTION
14	AL-BX	Nothing	Write character in teletype mode (at current cursor position)

AL = character code in ASCII
BH = display page
BL = foreground color in graphics modes
Note: Carriage return (0DH), line feed (0AH), backspace (08H), and bell (07H) codes are intepreted as commands. Line wrapping and screen scrolling are provided.

15	Nothing	AX-BH	Get current video mode Returns:

AL = active mode
AH = number of screen columns
BH = active video page (0 based)

16	AL-BL ES:DX	ES:DX	Set color palette (EGA/VGA BIOS extension)

PCjr, EGA, AND PS/2 SYSTEMS
AL = 0 to set individual palette registers
    BL = register to set BH = color value
AL = 1 to set overscan register (border color)
    BH = color value
AL = 2 to set palette and overscan registers
    ES:DX -> 17-byte table:
        bytes 0–15 = palette register values
        byte 16 = border color value
AL = 3 to toggle intensity and blinking attribute
    BL = 0 to enable intensity
    BL = 1 to enable blinking

PS/2 MICRO CHANNEL SYSTEMS
AL = 4 to 6 RESERVED
AL = 7 to read individual palette registers
    BL = register to set (range 0 to 15)
    Returns: BL = value read
AL = 8 to read overscan register (border color)
    Returns: BL = value read
AL = 9 to read all palette and overscan registers
    ES:DX -> 17-byte table:
        bytes 0–15 = palette register values
        byte 16 = border color value
AL = 16 to set individual color registers
    BX = color register to set
    DH = red value to set
    CH = green value to set
    CL = blue value to set
AL = 17 RESERVED
AL = 18 to set a block of color registers
    ES:DX -> table of color values in the sequence
    red, green, blue, red, green . . .
    BX = first color register to set
    CX = count of color registers to set

(continued)

Table C.2 *BIOS Interrupt 10H — Video Functions (Continued)*

SERVICE NUMBER (IN AH)	ON ENTRY	ON EXIT	DESCRIPTION
16	(continued)		

```
AL = 19 to set color page
BL = 0 to select paging mode
        BH = 0 selects 4 register blocks of 64 registers
        BH = 1 selects 16 register blocks of 16 registers
BL = 1 select page
        BH = page number (0 based)
        64-register block mode:
                BH = 00H selects first block of 64 registers
                01H selects second block of 64 registers
                03H selects third block of 64 registers
                04H selects fourth block of 64 registers
        16-register block mode:
                BH = block number of 16 color registers
                (range 0 to 15)
AL = 20 RESERVED
AL = 21 to read individual color registers
        BX = color register to read
        Returns:
                DH = red value read
                CH = green value read
                CL = blue value read
AL = 22 RESERVED
AL = 23 to read a block of color registers
        ES:DX -> table of values in red, green, blue sequence
        BX = first color register to read
        CX = number of color registers to read
        Returns: ES:DX pointer
```

PS/2 MICRO CHANNEL SYSTEMS
```
AL = 24 RESERVED
AL = 25 RESERVED
AL = 26 to read the color page state
        Returns:
        BL = current paging mode
        BH = current page
AL = 27 to sum color values to gray shades
        BX = first color register to sum
        CX = number of color registers to sum
```

PS/2 NON-MICRO CHANNEL SYSTEMS
```
AL = 0 to set color registers to 8 consistent colors
        BX = 0712H
AL = 1 RESERVED
AL = 2 RESERVED
AL = 3 to toggle intensity and blinking attribute
        BL = 0 to enable intensity
        BL = 1 to enable blinking
AL = 4 to 7 RESERVED
AL = 16 to set individual color registers
        BX = color register to set
        DH = red value to set
        CH = green value to set
        CL = blue value to set
```

(continued)

Table C.2 *BIOS Interrupt 10H — Video Functions (Continued)*

SERVICE NUMBER (IN AH)	ON ENTRY	ON EXIT	DESCRIPTION
16	(continued)		

AL = 17 RESERVED
AL = 18 to set a block of color registers
    ES:DX -> table of color values in the sequence
    red, green, blue, red, green, ...
    BX = first color register to set
    CX = count of color registers to set
AL = 19 RESERVED
AL = 20 RESERVED
AL = 21 to read individual color registers
    BX = color register to read
    Returns:
    DH = red value read
    CH = green value read
    CL = blue value read
AL = 22 RESERVED
AL = 23 to read a block of color registers
    ES:DX -> table of values in red, green, blue sequence
    BX = first color register to read
    CX = number of color registers to read
    Returns: ES:DX pointer
AL = 24 to 26 RESERVED
AL = 27 to sum color values to gray shades
    BX = first color register to sum
    CX = number of color registers to sum

SERVICE NUMBER (IN AH)	ON ENTRY	ON EXIT	DESCRIPTION
17	AL-BX-CX DX-ES:BP	CX-DL ES:BP	Character generator (EGA/VGA BIOS extension)

EGA SYSTEMS
AL = 0 to load user-defined character set
    ES:BP -> user character table
    CX = count of characters to store
    DX = offset of first character to load
    BL = block to load (range 0 to 3—see note)
    BH = count of bytes per character
AL = 1 to load ROM 8 x 14 character set
    BL = block to load (range 0 to 3—see note)
AL = 2 to load ROM 8 x 8 character set
    BL = block to load (range 0 to 3—see note)
AL = 3 to set block specifier in alpha modes
    Create 512-character set if more than 64K
    EGA memory

    7 6 5 4 3 2 1 0 BL bitmap

    Block number (range 0 to 3) if attribute byte bit 3 = 0
    Block number (range 0 to 3) if attribute byte bit 3 = 1
    must be 0 in EGA

Note: Each EGA character set is called a block. There is
one block for each 64K of EGA memory.

(continued)

Table C.2 *BIOS Interrupt 10H — Video Functions (Continued)*

SERVICE NUMBER (IN AH)	ON ENTRY	ON EXIT	DESCRIPTION
17	(continued)		

AL = 16 to load user-defined character set after mode reset
    ES:BP -> user character table
    CX = count of characters to store
    DX = offset of first character to load
    BL = block to load (range 0 to 3—see note)
    BH = count of bytes per character
AL = 17 to load ROM 8 x 14 character set after mode reset
    BL = block to load (range 0 to 3 —see note)
AL = 18 to load ROM 8 x 8 character set after mode reset
    BL = block to load (range 0 to 3 — see note)
AL = 32 to set vector for INT 1FH to point to user-defined
    8 x 8 character set
    ES:BP holds address of user table
AL = 33 to set vector for INT 43H to point to user-defined
    character set
    ES:BP holds address of user table
    CX = bytes per character
    BL = character rows per screen
        BL = 0 for user defined set
    DL = number of rows (if BL = 0)
        DL = 1 for 14 rows
        DL = 2 for 25 rows
        DL = 3 for 43 rows
AL = 34 to set vector for INT 43H to point to ROM table
    of 8 x 14 characters
    BL = character rows per screen (see AL = 33)
AL = 35 to set vector for INT 43H to point to ROM table
    of 8 x 8 characters
    BL = character rows per screen (see AL = 33)
AL = 36 to set vector for INT 43H to point to ROM table
    of 8 x 16 characters
    BL = character rows per screen (see AL = 33)
AL = 48 to obtain EGA register information
    BH = font pointer
        BH = 0 to obtain pointer to current INT 1FH
        BH = 1 to obtain pointer to current INT 43H
        BH = 2 to obtain pointer to ROM 8 x 14 set
        BH = 3 to obtain pointer to ROM 8 x 8 set
        BH = 4 to obtain pointer to upper half of
            ROM 8 x 8 set
        BH = 5 to obtain pointer to ROM 9 x 16
            alternate set
    Returns:
    CX = bytes per character in font
    DL = number of rows
    ES:BP -> character table

PS/2 MICRO CHANNEL SYSTEMS
AL = 0 to load user-defined character set
    ES:BP -> user character table
    CX = count of characters to store
    DX = offset of first character to load
    BL = block to load (range 0 to 3 —see note)
    BH = count of bytes per character

(continued)

Table C.2 *BIOS Interrupt 10H — VIDEO FUNCTIONS (Continued)*

SERVICE NUMBER (IN AH)	ON ENTRY	ON EXIT	DESCRIPTION
17	(continued)		

AL = 1 to load ROM 8 x 14 character set
    BL = block to load (range 0 to 7 — see note)
AL = 2 to load ROM 8 x 8 character set
    BL = block to load (range 0 to 7 — see note)
AL = 3 to set block specifier in alpha modes
    Create 256- or 512-character set

```
7  6  5  4  3  2  1  0  BL bit map
└─┘        └──┴──┴──┴──┴──── Block number (range 0 to 7)
                            if attribute byte bit 3 = 0
           └──────────────── Block number (range 0 to 7)
                            if attribute byte bit 3 = 1
 └───────────────────────── must be 0 in VGA
```

Note: Each character set is called a block. There are 8 blocks
    in VGA systems.
AL = 4 to load ROM 8 x 16 character set
    BL = block to load (range 0 to 7)
AL = 16 to load user-defined character set after mode reset
    ES:BP -> user character table
    CX = count of characters to store
    DX = offset of first character to load
    BL = block to load (range 0 to 7)
    BH = count of bytes per character
AL = 17 to load ROM 8 x 14 character set after mode reset
    BL = block to load (range 0 to 7)
AL = 18 to load ROM 8 x 8 character set after mode reset
    BL = block to load (range 0 to 7)
AL = 32 to set vector for INT 1FH to point to user-defined
    8 x 8 character set
    ES:BP holds address of user table
AL = 33 to set vector for INT 43H to point to user-defined
    character set
    ES:BP holds address of user table
    CX = bytes per character
    BL = character rows per screen
        BL = 0 for user defined set
    DL = number of rows (if BL = 0)
        DL = 1 for 14 rows
        DL = 2 for 25 rows
        DL = 3 for 43 rows
AL = 34 to set vector for INT 43H to point to ROM table
    of 8 x 14 characters
    BL = character rows per screen (see AL = 33)
AL = 35 to set vector for INT 43H to point to ROM table
    of 8 x 8 characters
BL = character rows per screen (see AL = 33)
AL = 36 to set vector for INT 43H to point to ROM table
    of 8 x 16 characters
    BL = character rows per screen (see AL = 33)

(continued)

Table C.2 *BIOS Interrupt 10H — Video Functions (Continued)*

SERVICE NUMBER (IN AH)	ON ENTRY	ON EXIT	DESCRIPTION
17	(continued)		

AL = 48 to obtain VGA register information
    BH = font pointer
    BH = 0 to obtain pointer to current INT 1FH
    BH = 1 to obtain pointer to current INT 43H
    BH = 2 to obtain pointer to ROM 8 x 14 set
    BH = 3 to obtain pointer to ROM 8 x 8 set
    BH = 4 to obtain pointer to upper half of
        ROM 8 x 8 set
    BH = 5 to obtain pointer to ROM 9 x 16 alternate set
Returns:
    CX = bytes per character in font
    DL = number of rows
    ES:BP -> character table

PS/2 NON-MICRO CHANNEL SYSTEMS
AL = 0 to load user-defined character set
    ES:BP -> user character table
    CX = count of characters to store
    DX = offset of first character to load
    BL = block to load (range 0 to 3 —see note)
    BH = 16 bytes per character (400 scan lines)
AL = 1 RESERVED
AL = 2 to load ROM 8 x 8 character set
BL = block to load (range 0 to 4 —see note)
AL = 3 to set block specifier in alpha modes
    Create 256- or 512-character set
    7   6   5   4   3   2   1   0   BL bit map

                        Block number (range 0 to 3)
                        if attribute byte bit 3 = 0
                        Block number (range 0 to 3)
                        if attribute byte bit 3 = 1
                        must be 0 in MCGA
Note: Each character set is called a block. There are
        4 blocks in an MCGA system.
AL = 4 to load ROM 8 x 16 character set
    BL = block to load (range 0 to 7)
AL = 16 to 18 RESERVED
AL = 20 RESERVED
AL = 32 to set vector for INT 1FH to point to user-defined
    8 x 8 character set
    ES:BP holds address of user table
AL = 33 to set vector for INT 43H to point to user-defined
    character set
    ES:BP holds address of user table
    CX = bytes per character
    BL = character rows per screen
        BL = 0 for user-defined set
    DL = number of rows (if BL = 0)
        DL = 1 for 14 rows
        DL = 2 for 25 rows
        DL = 3 for 43 rows
AL = 34 RESERVED

(continued)

Table C.2 *BIOS Interrupt 10H — Video Functions (Continued)*

SERVICE NUMBER (IN AH)	ON ENTRY	ON EXIT	DESCRIPTION
17	(continued)		AL = 35 to set vector for INT 43H to point to ROM table of 8 x 8 characters BL = character rows per screen (see AL = 33) AL = 36 to set vector for INT 43H to point to ROM table of 8 x 16 characters BL = character rows per screen (see AL = 33) AL = 48 to obtain MCGA Register information BH = font pointer BH = 0 to obtain pointer to current INT 1FH BH = 1 to obtain pointer to current INT 43H BH = 2 to obtain pointer to ROM 8 x 14 set BH = 3 to obtain pointer to ROM 8 x 8 set BH = 4 to obtain pointer to upper half of ROM 8 x 8 set BH = 5 to obtain pointer to ROM 9 x 16 alternate set Returns: CX = bytes per character in font DL = number of rows ES:BP -> character table
18	BX-CX	AX-BX	Alternate select

EGA AND PS/2 MICRO CHANNEL SYSTEMS
BL = 16 to return VGA/EGA information
Returns:
       BH = 0 if color mode active
       BH = 1 if monochrome mode active
       BL = 0 if 64K of video memory
       BL = 1 if 128K of video memory
       BL = 2 if 192K of video memory
       BL = 3 if 256K of video memory (VGA)
       BL = 4 to 256 RESERVED
       CH = Feature control register bit settings
       CL = Switch setting on EGA card or equivalent VGA functions
       BL = 32 to activate alternate print-screen routine

PS/2 MICRO CHANNEL SYSTEMS
BL = 48 to change the number of scan lines in an alpha mode (usually for MDA, CGA, and EGA compatibility)
AL = 0 for 200 scan lines (CGA-compatible)
AL = 1 for 350 scan lines (EGA-compatible)
AL = 2 for 400 scan lines (MDA-compatible)
BL = 49 to control default palette during mode reset
AL = 0 enables default palette during mode changes
AL = 1 disables default palette during mode changes
Returns:
       AL = 18 if function supported
       BL = 50 to disable the video function
       AL = 0 to enable
       AL = 1 to disable

(continued)

Table C.2 *BIOS Interrupt 10H — Video Functions (Continued)*

SERVICE NUMBER (IN AH)	ON ENTRY	ON EXIT	DESCRIPTION
18	(continued)		

BL = 51 to activate summing to gray shades, as follows:
    30% gray for red, 59% for green, and 11% for blue
    Gray shades are displayed at the next mode change
AL = 0 to enable summing
AL = 1 to disable summing
Returns:
    AL = 18 if function supported
    BL = 52 Enable cursor emulation by scaling cursor to
        present character height
    AL = 0 to enable cursor emulation
    AL = 1 to disable cursor emulation
Returns:
AL = 18 if function supported

PS/2 NON-MICRO CHANNEL SYSTEMS
BL = 48 RESERVED
BL = 49 to control default palette during mode reset
AL = 0 enables default palette during mode changes
AL = 1 disables default palette during mode changes
Returns:
    AL = 18 if function is supported
    BL = 50 to disable the video function
    AL = 0 to enable
    AL = 1 to disable
Returns:
    AL = 18 if function supported
    BL = 51 to activate summing to gray shades,
    as follows:
    30% gray for red, 59% for green, and 11% for blue
    Gray shades are displayed at the next mode change
    AL = 0 to enable summing
    AL = 1 to disable summing
Returns:
    AL = 18 if function supported

ALL PS/2 SYSTEMS
BL = 53 to control motherboard and external adapter video
    systems in address or port conflict
AL = 0 is initial command for external adapter OFF
AL = 1 is initial command for system board video ON
AL = 2 is to set active adapter OFF
AL = 3 is to set inactive adapter ON
ES:DX -> 128-byte switch state save area
Returns:
    AL = 18 if function is supported
    BL = 54 to blank screen
    AL = 0 to turn screen ON
    AL = 1 to turn screen OFF

(continued)

Table C.2 *BIOS Interrupt 10H — Video Functions (Continued)*

SERVICE NUMBER (IN AH)	ON ENTRY	ON EXIT	DESCRIPTION
19	AL-CX-DX BX-ES:BP	Nothing	Write string

**PC XT BIOS 01/10/86 AND LATER, AT, EGA,
PC CONVERTIBLE, AND PS/2 SYSTEMS**
AL = 0 to display characters only and cursor not moved
AL = 1 to display characters only and cursor to string end
AL = 2 to display character/attributes and cursor not moved
AL = 3 to display character/attributes and cursor to end
     of string
BL = attribute if AL = 0 or 1
BH = page number (0-based)
CX = Character count (attributes not included)
DH = start row for string display
DL = start column for string display
ES:BP -> string in memory

26	AL	AL-BX	Read and write display combination code

ALL PS/2 SYSTEMS
AL = 0 to READ display combination codes
Returns:
    AL = 26 if function is supported
    BL = display system code, as follows:
    0 = no display   1 = monochrome with 5151
    2 = CGA with 5153/4   3 = RESERVED
    4 = EGA with 5153/4   5 = EGA with 5151 (mono)
    6 = PGS with 5175 (color) 7 = PS/2 MC with mono
    8 = PS/2 MC with color   9 and 10 = RESERVED
    11 = PS/2 not MC mono   12 = PS/2 not MC color
    13 to 256 = RESERVED
    BH = Alternate display code
    AL = 1 to WRITE display code combination
    BL = display system code (see AL = 0)
    BH = alternate display code

27	BX ES:DI	BX ES:DI	Read functionality/state information

ALL PS/2 SYSTEMS
BX = implementation type
    ES:DI -> 64-byte buffer
Returns:
BX = 0 for implementation type 0
ES:DI -> 64-byte buffer formatted as follows:

Offset	Size	Contents
0	Word	Offset of static functionality table
2	Word	Segment of static functionality table
4	Byte	Active video mode
5	Word	Number of character columns
7	Word	Size of video buffer (in bytes)
9	Word	Starting address of video buffer
11 to 26	Area	8 words of cursor position (row/column format) for video pages 0 to 7
27	Byte	Cursor start line
28	Byte	Cursor end line

(continued)

Table C.2 *BIOS Interrupt 10H — Video Functions (Continued)*

SERVICE NUMBER (IN AH)	ON ENTRY	ON EXIT	DESCRIPTION
27	(continued)		

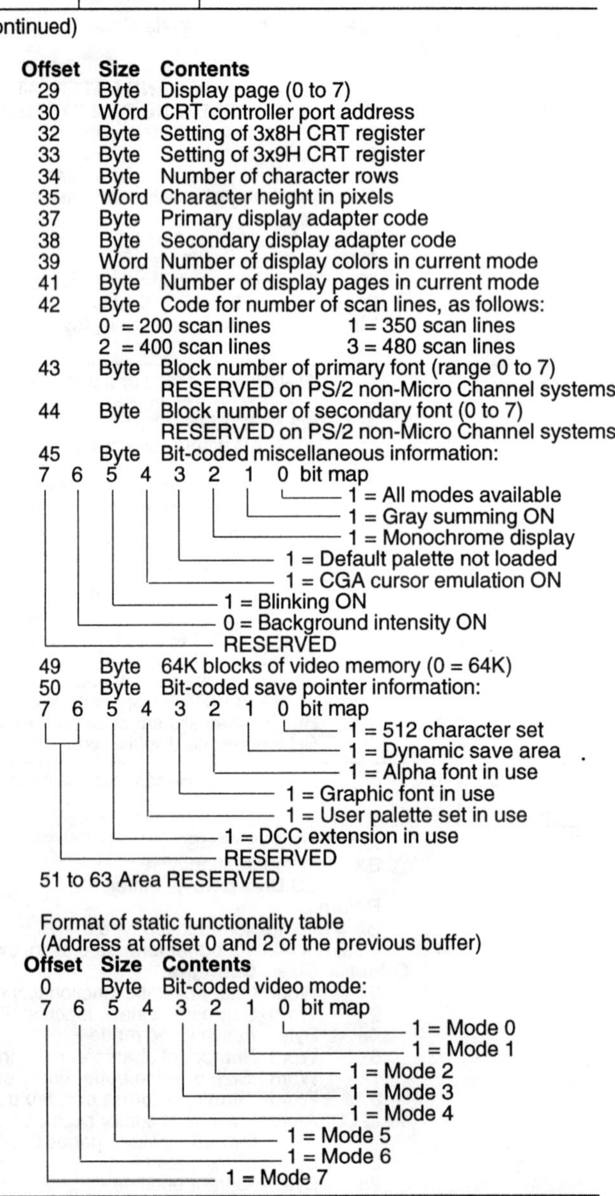

(continued)

Table C.2 *BIOS Interrupt 10H — Video Functions (Continued)*

SERVICE NUMBER (IN AH)	ON ENTRY	ON EXIT	DESCRIPTION
27	(continued)		

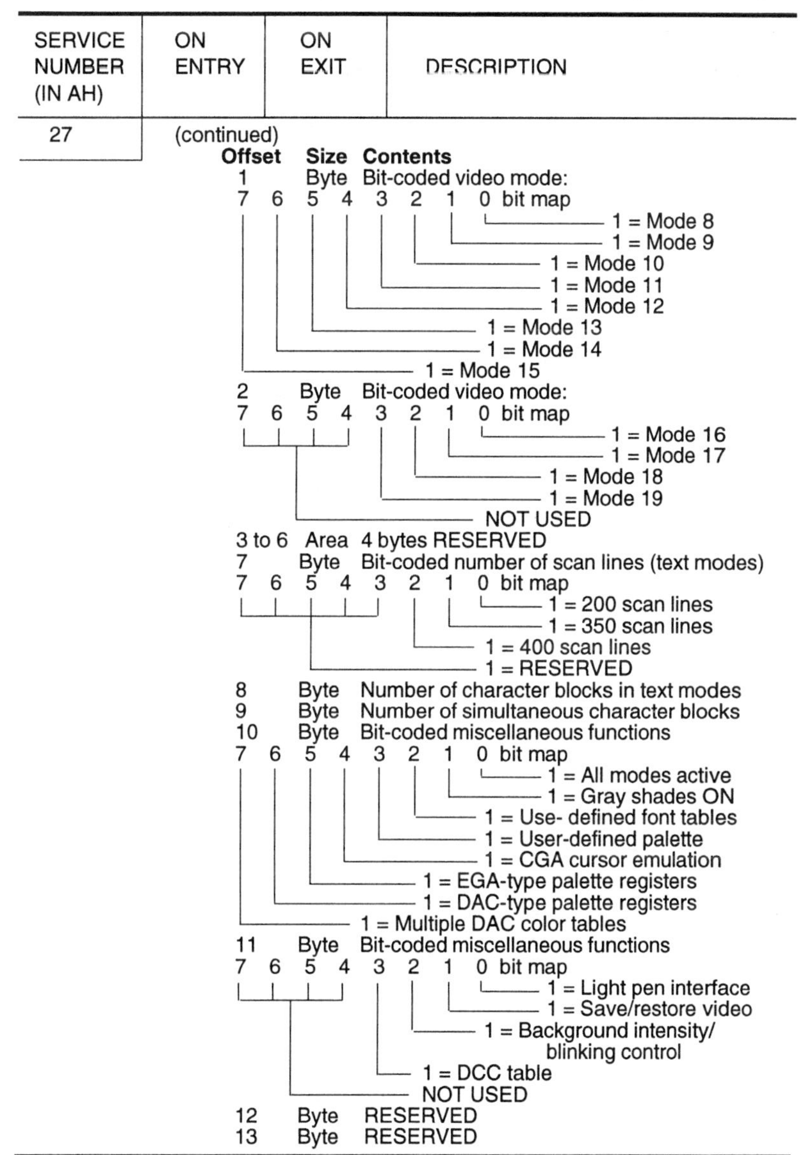

(continued)

Table C.2 *BIOS Interrupt 10H — Video Functions (Continued)*

SERVICE NUMBER (IN AH)	ON ENTRY	ON EXIT	DESCRIPTION
27	(continued)		

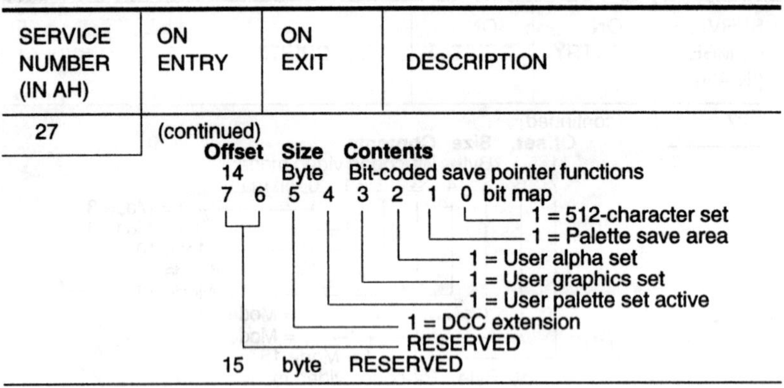

Bibliography

Books and Technical Manuals

Adobe Systems. *Postscript Language Reference Manual,* Second Edition. Reading, MA: Addison-Wesley, 1990.

Agfa. *Creating Intellifont-Compatible Fonts Using the AGFA Compugraphics FAIS Standard.* Agfa Compugraphic Division, 1990.

———Aldus Corporation. *TIFF Developer's Toolkit.* Seattle, WA: Aldus Corporation, 1990.

———Aldus Corporation. *TIFF,* Revision 5.0. Seattle, WA: Aldus Corporation, 1988.

———Aldus Corporation. *TIFF,* Revision 6.0, June 3, 1992. Seattle, WA: Aldus Corporation, 1992.

Arnheim, Rudolf. *Art and Visual Perception.* Berkeley, CA: University of California Press, 1974.

Artwick, Bruce A. *Applied Concepts in Microcomputer Graphics.*Englewood Cliffs: Prentice-Hall, 1984.

Black, Uyless. *Data Networks: Concepts, Theory, and Practice.* Englewood Cliffs: Prentice-Hall, 1989.

Buddenbrock, Wolfgang von, *The Senses.* Ann Arbor: University of Michigan Press, 1958.

Conrac Corporation. *Raster Graphics Handbook.* New York: Van Nostrand Reinholt, 1985.

Doty, David B. *Programmer's Guide to the Hercules Graphics Cards.* Reading, MA: Addison-Wesley, 1988.

Enderle, G., K. Kansy, and G. Pfaff. *Computer Graphics Programming.* Berlin: Springer, 1984.

Ferraro, Richard F. *Programmer's Guide to EGA and VGA Cards.* Reading, MA: Addison-Wesley, 1988.

Frisby, John P. *Seeing: Illusion, Brain and Mind.* Oxford: Oxford University Press, 1980.

Harrington, Steven. *Computer Graphics: A Programming Approach.* New York: McGraw-Hill, 1983.

Harris, Dennis. *Computer Graphics amd Applications.* London: Chapman and Hall Computing, 1984.

Hearn, Donald, and M. Pauline Baker. *Computer Graphics.* Englewood Cliffs: Prentice-Hall, 1986.

Hewlett-Packard. *LaserJet Series II Printer Technical Reference Manual.* Hewlett-Packard. 1987,

———*HP 7550A Graphics Plotter Interfacing and Programming Manual.* Hewlett-Packard, 1986.

———*HP ColorPro Programming Manual.* Hewlett-Packard, 1985.

———*LaserJet III Technical Reference Manual.* Hewlett-Packard, 1990.

———*A Guide to the Tag Image File Format (TIFF)* Version 5.0. Hewlett-Packard, 1990.

Hu, T. C. *Combinatorial Algorithms.* Reading, MA: Addison-Wesley, 1982.

IBM Corporation. *Technical Reference, Personal Computer.* Boca Raton: IBM, 1984.

———*Technical Reference, Personal System/2.* Boca Raton: IBM, 1987.

———*Personal System/2 and Personal Computer BIOS Interface Technical Reference.* Boca Raton:IBM, 1987.

———*Technical Reference, Options and Adapters.* Boca Raton: IBM, 1986.

———*Technical Reference, Options and Adapters: XGA Video Subsystem.* Boca Raton: IBM, 1986.

———*XGA Video Subsystem Hardware User's Guide.* Boca Raton: IBM, 1990.

———*Video Subsystem Technical Reference.* (Aproval Draft. by Nick Crenshaw.) Boca Raton, IBM, 1991.

Intel Corporation, *iAPX 86/88, 186/188 User's Manual* (Programmer's Reference.) Santa Clara: Reward Books, 1983.

———*iAPX 86/88, 186/188 User's Manual* (Programmer's Reference.) Santa Clara: Intel, 1987.

———*80286 and 80287 Programmer's Reference Manual.* Santa Clara: Intel, 1987.

———*80386 Programmer's Reference Manual.* Santa Clara: Intel, 1986.

Kepes, Gyorgy, ed. *Education of Vision.* New York: George Braziller, 1965.

Kepes, Gyorgy, ed. *Sign, Image, Symbol.* New York:George Braziller, 1966.

Kliewer, Bradley Dyck. *EGA/VGA A Programmer's Reference Guide.* New York: McGraw-Hill, 1988.

Magnenat-Thalmann, Nadia, and Daniel Thalmann. *Computer Animation, Theory and Practice.* Tokyo: Springer, 1985.

Microsoft. *Microsoft Mouse Programmer's Reference.* Redmond, WA: Microsoft Press, 1989.

Myers, Roy E. *Microcomputer Graphics.* Reading, MA: Addison-Wesley, 1982.

Pokorny, Cornel K, and Curtis F. Gerald. *Computer Graphics: The Principles Behind the Art and Science.* Irvine, CA: Franklin, Beedle & Associates, 1989.

Ralston, Anthony, and Chester L. Meek. *Encyclopedia of Computer Science.* New York: Mason and Charter, 1983

Richter, Jake, and Bud Smith. *Graphics Programming for the 8514/A.* Redwood City, CA: M & T Books, 1990.

Rimmer, Steve. *Supercharged Bitmappted Graphics.* New York: McGraw-Hill, 1992.

———*Bit-Mapped Graphics.* New York: McGraw-Hill, 1990.

———*The Graphics File Toolkit.* Reading, MA: Addison-Wesley, 1992.

Rogers, David F. *Procedural Elements for Computer Graphics.* New York: McGraw-Hill, 1985.

Salmon, Rod, and Mel Slater. *Computer Graphics, Systems & Concepts.* London: Addison-Wesley, 1987.

Sanchez, Julio, and Maria P. Canton. *Programming Solutions Handbook for IBM Microcomputers.* New York: McGraw-Hill, 1991.

——*IBM Microcomputers: A Programmer's Handbook.* New-York: McGraw-Hill, 1990.

Sanchez, Julio. *Graphics Design and Animation on the IBM Microcomputers.* Engelwood Cliffs: Prentice-Hall, 1990.

——*Logical and Mathematical Methods for IBM Microcomputers.* Boca Raton: CRC Press, 1991.

Sproull, Robert F., W. R. Sutherland, and Michael K. Ullner. *Device Independent Graphics.* New York: McGraw-Hill, 1985.

Sutty, George, and Steve Blair. *Advanced Programmer's Guide to SuperVGAs.* New York: Simon & Schuster, 1990.

VESA. *Super VGA BIOS Extension,* June 2, 1990. San Jose, CA:VESA, 1990.

VESA. *Super VGA Standard,* Version 1.2, October 22, 1991. San Jose, CA: VESA, 1991.

VESA. *XGA Extensions Standard,* Version 1.0, May 8, 1992. San Jose, CA: VESA, 1992.

Video Seven. *Video Seven VGA Programmer's Reference Manual.* Headland Technology Inc., 1991.

Wilton, Richard. *Programmer's Guide to PC & PS/2 Video Systems.* Redmond, WA: Microsoft Press, 1987.

Periodicals

Greg Williams: "A Graphics Primer," *BYTE* vol. 7, No. 11. November 1992

Mark R. Nelson: "LZW Data Compression," *Dr. Dobb's Journal.* October 1989

Welsh, T.: "A Technique for High-Performance Data Compression," *Computer.* June 1984.

Ziv, J. and Lempel, A.: "A Universal Algorithm for Sequential Data Compression," *IEEE Transactions on Information Theory.* May 1977.

Index

ABOUT THE AUTHORS

Julio Sanchez is a professor of computer science in the Montana University system. He has served as a programmer and consultant on several major microcomputer programming projects in the areas of computer graphics, industrial scheduling, linear systems analysis, and computer assisted manufacturing. He is the author and coauthor of numerous books in the field of microcomputer programming. He holds a Juris Doctor from Villanova University and a Doctorate of Mathematics from the University of Havana. He resides in Great Falls, Montana.

Maria P. Canton is president of Skipanon Software, a software development and consulting firm. She is the author of six program manuals and serves as a documentation consultant. She and Mr. Sanchez are the coauthors of *IBM Microcomputers: A Programmer's Handbook* and *Programming Solutions Handbook for IBM Microcomputers*, also published by McGraw-Hill. She resides in Great Falls, Montana.

ABOUT THE SERIES

The J. Ranade Workstation Series is McGraw-Hill's primary vehicle for providing workstation professionals with timely concepts, solutions, and applications. Jay Ranade is Series Editor in Chief for the IBM and DEC series, and Senior Advisor to the McGraw-Hill Series on Computer Communications.

Jay Ranade, Series Editor in Chief and best selling computer author, is a Senior Systems Architect and Assistant V.P. at Merrill Lynch.

DISK WARRANTY

This software is protected by boh United States copyright law and international copyright treaty provision. You must treat this software just like a book, except that you may copy it into a computer to be used and you may make archival copies of the software for the sole purpose of backing up our software and protecting your investment from loss.

By saying, "just like a book," McGraw-Hill means, for example, that this software may be used by any number of people and may be freely moved from one computer location to another, so long as there is no possiblity of its being used at one location or on one computer while it is being used at another. Just as a book cannot be read by two different people in two different places at the same time, neither can the software be used by two different people in two different places at the same time (unless, of course, McGraw-Hill's copyright is being violated).

LIMITED WARRANTY

McGraw-Hill warrants the physical diskette(s) enclosed herein to be free of defects in materials and workmanship for a period of sixty days from the purchase date. If McGraw-Hill receives written notification within the warranty period of defects in materials and workmanship, and such notification is determined by McGraw-Hill to be correct, McGraw-Hill will replace the defective diskette(s). Send requests to:

Customer Service
TAB/McGraw-Hill
13311 Monterey Avenue
Blue Ridge Summit, PA 17294-0850

The entire and exclusive liablility and remedy for breach of this Limited Warranty shall be limited to replacement of defective diskette(s) and shall not include or extend to any claim for or right to cover any other damages, including but not limited to, loss of profit, data, or use of the software, or special, incidental, or consequential damages or other similar claims, even if McGraw-Hill's liability for any damages to you or any other person ever exceed the lower of suggested list price or actual price paid for the license to use the software, regardless of any form of the claim.

McGRAW-HILL, INC. SPECIFICALLY DISCLAIMS ALL OTHER WARRANTIES, EXPRESS OR IMPLIED, INCLUDING BUT NOT LIMITED TO, ANY IMPLIED WARRANTY OF MERCHANTABLILTY OR FITNESS FOR A PARTICULAR PURPOSE. Specifically, McGraw-Hill makes no representation or warranty that the software is fit for any particular purpose and any implied warranty of merchantability is limited to the sixty-day duration of the Limited Warranty covering the physical diskette(s) only (and not the software) and is otherwise expressly and specifically disclaimed.

This limited warranty gives you specific legal rights; you may have others which may vary from state to state. Some states do not allow the exclusion of incidental or consequential damages, or the limitation on how long an implied warranty lasts, so some of the above may not apply to you.